thomson.com

changing the way the world learns

To get extra value from this book for no additional cost, go to:

http://www.thomson.com/wadsworth.html

thomson.com is the World Wide Web site for Wadsworth/ITP and is your direct source to dozens of on-line resources. *thomson.com* helps you find out about supplements, experiment with demonstration software, search for a job, and send e-mail to many of our authors. You can even preview new publications and exciting new technologies.

thomson.com: *It's where you'll find us in the future.*

From the Wadsworth Series in Mass Communication and Journalism

UPDATED EDITION

Communications Media in the Information Society

Joseph Straubhaar
BRIGHAM YOUNG UNIVERSITY

Robert LaRose
MICHIGAN STATE UNIVERSITY

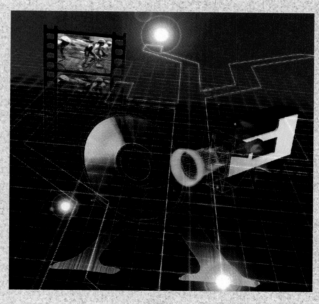

WADSWORTH PUBLISHING
COMPANY

I T P®

AN INTERNATIONAL THOMSON
PUBLISHING COMPANY

BELMONT, CA • ALBANY, NY • BONN
• BOSTON • CINCINNATI • DETROIT •
JOHANNESBURG • LONDON •
MADRID • MELBOURNE •
MEXICO CITY • NEW YORK • PARIS •
SAN FRANCISCO • SINGAPORE •
TOKYO • TORONTO • WASHINGTON

Communication & Media Studies Editor: Randall Adams

Assistant Editor: Lewis DeSimone

Editorial Assistant: Michael Gillespie

Production: Del Mar Associates

Print Buyer: Barbara Britton

Permissions Editor: Robert Kauser

Illustrations: John Odam, Janet Ashford

Photo Research: Linda L. Rill, Stuart Kenter

Cover Design: William Reuter

Cover Photography: © 1996 The Image Bank/Steven Hunt

Interior Design: John Odam

Digital Typography: John Odam Design Associates, Del Mar Associates

Separations: Digital Output

Printer: Quebecor Printing/Hawkins

Printed in the United States of America

1 2 3 4 5 6 7 8 9 10

For more information, contact Wadsworth Publishing Company, 10 Davis Drive, Belmont, California 94002, or electronically at http:/www.thomson.com/wadsworth.html

International Thomson Publishing Europe
Berkshire House 168-173
High Holborn
London, WC1V 7AA, England

International Thomson Editores
Campos Eliseos 385, Piso 7
Col. Polanco
11560 México D.F. México

Thomas Nelson Australia
102 Dodds Street
South Melbourne 3205
Victoria, Australia

International Thomson Publishing GmbH
Königswinterer Strasse 418
53227 Bonn, Germany

Nelson Canada
1120 Birchmount Road
Scarborough, Ontario
Canada M1K 5G4

International Thomson Publishing Asia
221 Henderson Road
#05-10 Henderson Building
Singapore 0315

International Thomson Publishing
 Southern Africa
Building 18, Constantia Park
240 Old Pretoria Road
Halfway House, 1685 South Africa

International Thomson Publishing Japan
Hirakawacho Kyowa Building, 3F
2-2-1 Hirakawacho
Chiyoda-ku, Tokyo 102, Japan

Library of Congress Cataloging-in-Publication Data

Straubhaar, Joseph D.
    Communications media in the information society / Joseph
Straubhaar, Robert LaRose. — Update ed.
      p. cm. — (Wadsworth series in mass communication and journalism)
    Includes bibliographical references and index.
    ISBN 0-534-52128-2
    1. Telecommunication—United States. 2. Information technology—
United States. I. La Rose, Robert. II. Title. III. Series.
HE7775.S79 1996b
384'.0973—dc 20   96-23298
                                                        CIP

 This book is printed on acid-free, recycled paper.

Preface

We wrote this book to be the first in a new generation of textbooks about mass communications. Our focus is on the kinds of communications that are mediated by technology. Our theme is that the convergence of these technologies is creating a new communications environment. Our goal is to prepare students to thrive in that environment.

The specific reason we wrote this book is that we could not find an existing introductory mass media textbook that adequately prepared our students for the real world as it stands today, much less as it will stand in five years. We saw too many students diligently studying mass media in the traditional way—only to discover after graduation that the vast majority of today's real jobs require skills and a knowledge base that their textbooks had barely touched on. They were finding jobs in innovative places—at phone companies, in corporate communications divisions, and so on—but discovering that they did not always know enough to succeed in these new environments. Their introductory textbooks had treated the telephone and computer industries only as an afterthought, usually in one chapter pasted on at the end. The books paid little or no attention to how industries that had always been disparate are now converging. As a result, students were prepared for the communications environment of the 1970s but not the one they were stepping into.

This book is meant to rectify that situation. It certainly shows where today's communications industries came from and how they got to where they are. But, more important, it also seriously assesses their trajectories into the future. It helps students understand how conventional mass media are being transformed as they converge with technologies such as the computer and telephone. It helps them rethink what we mean by *mass media*. It helps them create a vision of their future in the information society and information economy.

As educators, we owe our students nothing less. Some of our students will earn their living in the communications media and information industries. Many others will use new media as an indispensible tool in whatever work they do. All will use them as consumers. The better they understand these media and how they are evolving, the more intelligently they can decide how to think about them, what to plan for, what else to learn, what to major in, and what kinds of careers to avoid or pursue. They can begin to think about not only how the new communications media environment will affect them but how they might affect it.

No matter what careers our students go into or how often they change careers, mediated communication will only become more and more important to them. This book is designed to give them a solid grounding in the knowledge base, skills, and perspectives that will generalize across careers and help them navigate the changing workplace. It is also designed to get them—in their roles as parents and citizens of the information society—thinking about the implications of the changing communications media environment on society at large. It teaches them about conventional mass communications media plus new forms like multimedia and electronic mail.

We see these changes as a challenge not only to our students but to our field. In many colleges and universities, the new information services have been dominated by business and engineering schools, because communication programs have not moved into these new areas. At a time when communication departments should be leading the way, many have been cut back, others have been marginalized, and some have been eliminated. With cable and telephone companies merging and publishers rushing into multimedia, the new communications environment offers an extraordinary opportunity to reinvigorate and redefine our field. We must seize that opportunity. This book is meant to be a step in that direction.

Some instructors may question whether an emphasis on technology and on unfamiliar industries like telephony, computers, and information services is appropriate for an introductory course. We believe that these communications media and the technologies they utilize have become such an intrinsic part of communication that an introductory course would miss the mark without them. An appreciation of the convergence of communications media may well be the single-most important thing we can impart to our introductory students today. Even the would-be television production student is as likely to end up working for a phone company as for a TV station and should understand where that kind of company is coming from.

Our purpose is not to be cheerleaders for communication technology. In fact, we try to raise critical issues about the implications of information technologies parallel to the way we discuss the implications of mass media. However, we have seen the lights turn on behind our students' eyes when we begin a class discussion with a headline from the morning paper. They realize that the convergence of technologies we are talking about is not dry history or mere speculation but is really happening right now. Most of them already have some personal experience with it, and the rest have a strong curiosity about it. Our service course at Michigan State University, Introduction to the Information Society, attracts students from all over the campus, particularly from our business college.

We have used a draft of this book in that course and have revised it based on feedback from our students. Our editor suggested that we keep specific students in mind and write the book "just for them." The two we picked are Melissa Schwartz and Susan Hatt. When we first met Melissa, she had no interest in technology and was afraid of computers. By the end of our class, her curiosity had been piqued and she was comfortable working in our computer lab. Susan was a very talented student who wanted to be a performer in the mass media— a field to which so many are lured and so few are chosen. Although she may still want to make it as a performer, she broadened her interest over the course of the semester and ended up writing a paper on high-definition TV.

This book is geared for students like Melissa and Susan: general students in introductory-level mass media courses, especially courses with a primary emphasis on electronic media. This is the only mass media class most of them will ever take. That is precisely why it is so important to expose them to—and to demystify—communication technologies. In this book, we assume no technical sophistication on the student's part. We keep our explanations of technology simple and technical detail minimal. We also include a great deal of anecdotal material to bring the subject to life. We begin the historical treatments with the very earliest forms of each technology or medium, since these are the easiest starting points for nontechnical readers. At every turn, we have taken care to emphasize the social impacts and policy issues raised by the uses of mass media and information technologies.

The first section of the book introduces key themes that we explore in greater depth later. We feel it is important to maintain the integration of mass media and information technologies throughout. So we integrate coverage of mass media and information technology in the introductory theory, history, economics, policy, and globalization chapters.

The early chapters introduce the key issues that cut across and reflect the convergence of various media forms, their links to economic history, and the economic and policy institutions that surround them, their uses, and their implications. Mark Porat's characterization of sectors or industries in the information society provides a point of departure here. The middle chapters offer parallel treatments of the various mass media and information industries, focusing on their history and current structure, the way they are used, and the effects of that use. The final chapters offer some perspectives on the broader implications of communications media, including separate treatments of the effects of the mass media and information technologies.

Some instructors may wonder why a book on mass media gives extensive coverage to the telephone. The reason is that we believe the telephone is central to understanding the media of today and tomorrow. The telephone preceded radio and television; in fact, radio and television were in large part invented by the telephone company researchers. The infrastructure through which most new communication technologies make their connections is the telephone. Faxes are sent over telephone lines. Internet messages are sent by telephone lines. Online services such as Prodigy and America Online are conducted over telephone lines. Television shows, movies, games, custom-selected newspaper articles, interactive educational programs, and databases all will soon be coming into our living rooms via telephone lines. What cable alone could do yesterday, the telephone, too, will do tomorrow (and vice versa). In short, the telephone and cable infrastructures will serve as the central nervous system of the communications environment in which our students will soon live and work.

Similarly, we emphasize the computer industry because personal computers in one form or another are becoming the terminal at home or work through which people receive and interact with the new media and information services. Moreover, it is increasingly clear that all mediated communication will soon be created and distributed in computer readable digital form. We likewise discuss the information services area to see how the existing services, like the Internet or videotex (broadly defined) may predict new forms of mass media in the near future.

Helps Available

This book comes with a rich set of resources for the instructor. The Instructor's Manual includes all of our own class-tested overheads, visuals, graphics, and test bank. It also provides a suggested lecture outline, suggestions for class exercises and discussion topics, a carefully chosen bibliography of background readings, and a class-tested videography. It recommends publications to help anyone keep up on the latest developments.

Acknowledgments

We wish to thank the following reviewers for their thoughtful suggestions and guidance in the preparation of this book: Sandra Braman, University of Illinois–Champaign; Joseph Chuk, Kutztown University of Pennsylvania; Michael Doyle, Arkansas State; Linda Fuller, Worcester State College; Ken Hadwiger, Eastern Illinois University; Rick Houlberg, San Francisco State University; James Hoyt, University of Wisconsin–Madison; Maclym McClary, Humboldt State University; Tim Meyer, University of Wisconsin–Green Bay; Peter Pringle, University of Tennessee–Chattanooga; Humphrey Regis, University of South Florida; Marshall Rossow, Mankato State University; Gay Russell, Grossmont College; Roger Soenksen, James Madison University; and Don Tomlinson, Texas A & M University.

Contents

10 Multichannel Media 234

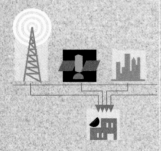

Communications Media in the Information Society

Telecommunications. The Internet. Fax machines. Multimedia. In just a few short years information technology has become part of our everyday lives—and promises to profoundly shape the future. So to learn about modern mass communication, it's no longer enough to study just the conventional media industries, such as broadcast, print, and film. Preparing for your future requires an extension of your thinking to information technologies and their convergence with mass media. *Communications Media in the Information Society, Updated Edition,* will help you do just that.

This book is designed to enable you to live and work in a dynamic information society, armed with a knowledge of the enduring issues and changing nature of our communications environment. You will find a number of features inside the book that are designed to make your learning more effective, and ultimately more valuable to you in a changing world. The following pages give you an advance look so you can get the most out of this book.

A Consistent Chapter Structure

To help you learn about specific media industries and issues common to them all, each media chapter follows a consistent format. Whether a chapter discusses a mass media or an information industry, it includes sections on the following topics:

- historical development
- technology
- content and genres
- industry structure
- audiences and users
- policy and ethical issues

As you read each media chapter, keep these topics in mind and use them to compare and contrast the different industries. Doing so will help you gain a much deeper understanding of the links among the media as well as the distinctions.

Chapter-Opening Previews and Vignettes

Each chapter in this book begins with a Preview. The Preview gives you an idea of what to expect as you read the chapter—the ideas and issues to be discussed, as well as a sense of their significance. Taking a moment to read and absorb these Previews will help you learn more from the chapter by mentally "prepping" for it.

Each chapter also starts with a thought-provoking vignette to start you thinking about life in the information society of tomorrow, and what that future might hold for you.

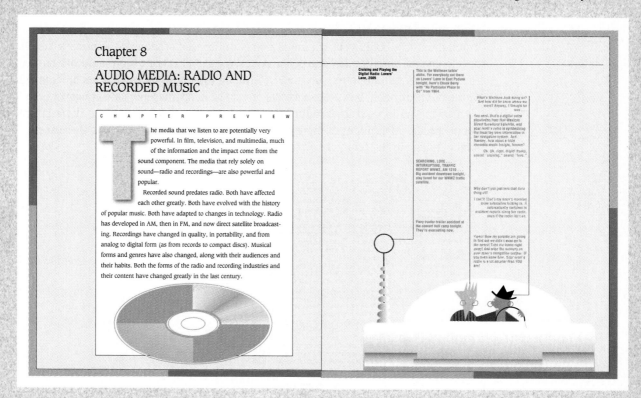

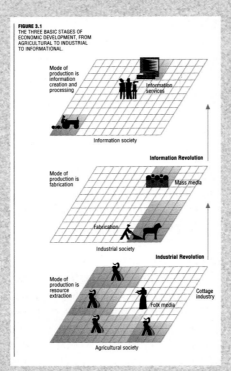

FIGURE 3.1
THE THREE BASIC STAGES OF ECONOMIC DEVELOPMENT, FROM AGRICULTURAL TO INDUSTRIAL TO INFORMATIONAL.

Mode of production is information creation and processing

Information services

Information society

Information Revolution

Mode of production is fabrication

Mass media

Fabrication

Industrial society

Industrial Revolution

Mode of production is resource extraction

Cottage industry

Folk media

Agricultural society

Visuals That Speak Volumes

The illustrations in this book do more than paint a picture of an idea. As you can see in this example, the illustrations are designed to help you visualize the links between concepts, understand a process, or grasp an abstract or complex idea. Spending a little extra time studying these illustrations will pay off in a much deeper and clearer understanding of what you are reading.

Spotlight on Key Topics

Throughout this book, you will find a number of special sections on important historical developments, timely ethical and policy issues, the globalization of communications media, economics issues, and other key topics. Although many of these subjects are addressed throughout the book, boxes such as this one on soap operas lend added dimension to the discussion and to your understanding. They give you an opportunity to think critically about specific applications of more general concepts, and to imagine how these scenarios might change in the future.

SOAP OPERAS AROUND THE WORLD

For a time around 1980, American soaps such as *Dallas* seemed to dominate world television. But as it turns out, most people prefer soap operas or serial dramas from closer to home.

In Latin America, *telenovelas* run in prime time and usually depict romance, family drama, upward mobility, and getting ahead. The archetypal *telenovela* for many was *Simplemente María*, about a Peruvian peasant girl who moves to the city, works as a maid, saves money, buys a sewing machine, and becomes a seamstress. All sewing machines in Lima sold out after that plot development.

Martial arts dramas from Hong Kong and China follow some soap opera themes—romance, love, family intrigues, and rivalries—but add a lot of martial arts action, battles, historical plots, and costumes. These are popular all over Asia. Japan makes its own versions, focused on the samurai era and featuring a similar mix of rugged heroes, beautiful heroines, and battles. These programs are also becoming popular worldwide (the author once saw one dubbed into Spanish in Los Angeles).

Indian soap operas tend to be more epic, mythological, and even religious. A recent popular soap opera retold the national Hindu religious epic *The Ramayana*, with the story of the Hindu gods. It had a powerful effect, according to critics, who saw it as perhaps reinforcing nationalist Hindu political parties and also as standardizing throughout India a previously diverse set of versions of *The Ramayana*, which has sometimes had very different characters as the main figures of good and evil.

All of these series are popular not only in their home countries but in surrounding regional television markets, which share languages and cultures. *Telenovelas* now sell to all of Latin America; Hong Kong soaps show on satellite Star TV; and Indian soaps are popular even in neighboring and rival Pakistan.

TABLE 11.1. TELEPHONE INDUSTRY MILESTONES

Year	Event
1876	Alexander Graham Bell invents the telephone
1893–1894	Bell patents expire, independent telephone companies organized
1899	American Telephone and Telegraph (AT&T) founded
1907	Theodore Vail becomes AT&T president
1910	Interstate Commerce Commission (ICC) established
1913	Kingsbury Commitment—AT&T sells Western Union, allows interconnection and ICC oversight
1915	First transcontinental telephone call
1918–1919	U.S. Post Office takes over Bell System
1934	Federal Communications Commission (FCC) established
1949	Antitrust case filed against AT&T
1951	Direct long-distance dialing
1955	Hush-a-Phone case permits connection of non-Bell equipment to public network
1956	AT&T signs Consent Decree, keeps Western Electric, promises to stick to telephone business
1962	First digital telephone call
1977	MCI's Execunet service authorized
1982	Modified Final Judgment splits local and long-distance networks
1989	FCC's price cap decision relaxes AT&T regulation
1992	Local telephone competition permitted, video dial tone authorized

Historical Milestones

Throughout *Communications Media in the Information Society,* you will learn about the history of mass media and information technology. The historical sections of each media chapter also feature "Historical Milestones." These Milestones highlight significant events, dates, and trends so you can put new developments into context.

Technology Demystified

You don't have to be a technical expert to appreciate new developments in media and information technologies. However, a basic understanding of technology can help you make sense of its impact on communication and society. The technological section of each media chapter provides you with clear, practical explanations of important concepts and terms.

Technological Milestones highlight some of the significant technological developments and dates in the history of communications media, giving you a look at where we've been and where we may be headed.

WHY YOU CAN HEAR A PIN DROP: THE BASICS OF FIBER OPTIC COMMUNICATIONS

The basic principles of fiber optic transmission are quite easy to grasp. Essentially, fiber optic systems shine a laser light into a very long glass tube. If the information we wish to transmit is in digital form, we simply turn the laser on when we want to transmit a "1" and turn it off when we want to send a "0." The light rays reflect off the sides of the tube and can be made to propagate hundreds of miles without amplification or retransmission if the glass is pure enough. At the other end of the glass tube, the light shines onto a detector that converts light to electrical current and the original sequence of digital electrical pulses is recovered. The signal can be regenerated for retransmission, switched into another circuit, or converted back into the human voice. By the way, these are not *Star Wars* lasers, but tiny solid-state devices that fit into a package about the size of your thumb and would not put out enough light to singe your eyebrows, let alone burn through the hull of a space cruiser.

The main advantages of fiber optic systems are speed and quality. Fiber optic systems can transmit data at rates of billions of bits per second, compared to a few thousand bits for today's telephone system and tens of millions of bits per second for coaxial cable systems. Since the data are transmitted as light waves instead of electrical pulses, they are immune to the electrical interference that causes static and distortion in electronic systems. That is why you literally can "hear a pin drop" over a fiber optic telephone network.

Not all fiber optic systems are digital, by the way. It is also possible to vary the intensity of the light going down the glass fiber to match the amplitude of an analog communication signal. Some cable TV systems use this approach.

Definitions in the Margins

Look in the margins for definitions of terms that may be new or challenging to you as you read. These definitions also point out terms of particular significance to your understanding the chapter material. Use these definitions before you read to enhance your comprehension of the chapter and afterward as an aid to reviewing. The definitions also appear in a glossary at the end of the book.

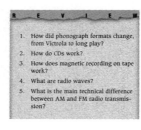

REVIEW

1. How did phonograph formats change, from Victrola to long play?
2. How do CDs work?
3. How does magnetic recording on tape work?
4. What are radio waves?
5. What is the main technical difference between AM and FM radio transmission?

offered over cable TV systems. Both digital audio broadcasting and DBS would require new receivers and antennas.

Audio is a major component of multimedia productions as well. In fact, some of the first multimedia products were enhanced sound recordings—music or voice—plus imagery and text. CD-ROM (compact disc–read only memory) stores various kinds of digital information, including sound, graphics, text, photos, images, and even video. The CD-ROM disc is played back through a computer, which interprets the digital information into coordinated sound, and images. Among the first commercial CD-ROM products were recordings of symphonies, along with the scores, commentaries, and images that might accompany the music.

FORMS AND GENRES

Even before radio, in the Victrola and phonograph era, popular music was developing out of ethnic and historical traditions and into certain formulas and genres that are still present. The roots of American popular music can be traced to several earlier **traditions**. The main ones are, arguably, English, Irish, and Scottish ballads and hymns; a variety of African vocal music, rhythm, and percussion traditions; Polish polkas; and German and Austrian waltzes. In the United States, many of these blended into various traditional strains that preceded recording and radio: black gospel, white gospel, Appalachian folk and country, Delta blues, Cajun, and Mexican border *rancheras* and *boleros*. The early hits of the phonograph era were John Philip Sousa marches and ragtime, along with pop and light songs. Jazz became popular in the 1920s and 1930s, along with show tunes taken from the new talking movies. **Blues** developed as a music popular among many African Americans but did not cross over much at that time (Dominick, 1993).

Traditions in music are genres passed along from one generation to another.

Blues is an African American musical tradition based primarily on guitar and distinctive plaintive lyrics.

Radio Genres

The most popular musical formats of the network era were big band jazz, light classical music, and movie and show tunes. Some important musical genre developments also occurred away from the main networks. For example, a network of southern stations carried the Grand Ole Opry and bluegrass music. These radio formats built on some of the main regional American music traditions, such as southern **gospel**, blues, bluegrass/old-timey **Appalachian music,** western music, western swing, and others. Although these kinds of music were not played much on national network radio, they were recorded and played on various local and regional stations, and some spread across the country. For example, the blend of Appalachian, gospel, western, and western swing that eventually became known as country and western, or country, was most popular in the rural south, southwest, and west but also followed southern migrants north as they looked for jobs in the industrial midwest and east. The blues followed African American migrants from the south to Chicago and New York, where a harder electric blues developed that greatly affected rock 'n' roll. For example, rock bands in the 1960s did versions of Chicago blues songs by Muddy Waters and Howlin' Wolf.

Gospel originated as southern Protestant religious music, with distinctive but related African American and white forms.

Appalachian music developed from English, Scottish, and Irish roots with similar instrumentation and ballad forms.

Network radio in the 1930s and 1940s also created a number of program genres besides music. Comedy series were among the early successes of radio networks. In the early 1930s, for instance, the top network show was *Amos 'n' Andy,* a comedy show imitating African

Quick Reviews

In each chapter you will find short reviews after each major section. These reviews contain a brief series of questions to test your knowledge. The questions also help you keep important points in mind and make mental connections as you read. Taking the time to run through these reviews will improve your recall and help you build a solid knowledge base as you go, rather than trying to put it all together at the end.

Chapter Summaries and Reviews

Each chapter concludes with a summary and review so you can reinforce your knowledge of the main issues. By working through the question-and-answer format on your own or with classmates, you'll gain a much better grasp of the main points.

Information services reproduce media content for multiple receivers and are produced by information service providers.

Network service providers transmit information over telecommunications networks.

transmission-reception chains. With analog media, we have entire transmission-reception systems dedicated to single functions and restricted by presentation modalities—text, sound, and image. With digitization, separate television, radio, print, and telephone networks may disappear.

Anticipating that day, we will distinguish the network from the content by using the term **information service** to denote content that serves a mass media function—that is, content reproduced for multiple receivers—and we will use **information service providers** for the institutions that produce the content and **network service providers** for those that transmit the information over telecommunication networks (LaRose, 1992). The two functions may or may not continue to reside in the same organization as we complete the transition to the information society.

SUMMARY & REVIEW

What Is the Importance of Communications Media and Information Technologies?

What is the information society?
The information society is one in which the production, processing, and distribution of information are the primary economic and social activities. In an information society, an ever-increasing amount of time is spent with communications media and using information technologies such as the telephone and the computer. More and more people are employed as information workers—people who produce, process, or distribute information as their primary work activity. The information society is a further step in the evolution of society from its former bases in agriculture and manufacturing into an information economy, in which the manipulation of information is the primary economic activity.

What do we mean when we say that mass media and information technologies are converging?
More and more communication is created and distributed in computer-readable digital form. This means that the same basic technologies can be used to transmit all forms of communication—whether in the form of text, audio, or video—and that computer technology can be used to manipulate information in so-called intelligent networks. In fact, the processes of telecommunication and computing are merging to such a degree that we can refer to them as telematic systems in which data transmission and processing are fully integrated. Thus, separate channels are no longer needed for each medium. The organizations that produce and distribute communication are also merging as

part of the convergence trend. The information superhighway is a term used to describe the low convergent media systems.

What Is the Process of Communication?

What are the components of the communication process?
All communication processes can be described in terms of a simple model in which a corporate or individual *source* encodes a *message* and transmits it through a physical *channel* to the person for whom the message is intended, the *receiver*. We call this the SMCR model. In most communication situations, feedback is also provided between the receiver and the source. The communication process takes place in the context of a culture shared by the source and the receiver.

What are the types of communication?
When the communication channel is an electronic or mechanical device—such as a radio station or a printing press—we call it *mediated* communication. Mediated communication may be *point-to-point, point-to-multipoint,* or *multipoint-to-multipoint.* Communication can be characterized according to the number of people involved. Intrapersonal communication involves one person, interpersonal communication usually includes only two people, and small-group communication encompasses less than a dozen participants. Large-group communication involves dozens or hundreds of persons, but feedback is still immediate. Mass communication involves hundreds or thousands of people, and there is no immediate feedback. Communication can also be characterized according to the setting in which

Chapter 1

THE CHANGING COMMUNICATIONS MEDIA ENVIRONMENT

C H A P T E R   P R E V I E W

n this chapter we will introduce the notion that the convergence of computers and communication technology is changing the world around us. We will examine the basic nature of the communication process and distinguish mass communication—such as television, radio, newspapers, and film—from other types of communication. Next we will see how new communication and information technologies are affecting various types of communication, particularly the mass media. Along the way, we will introduce some basic concepts that will help you begin to understand how communications media and information technologies provide a framework for an information-based society.

A Glimpse into Hell

An evening at home in Hell, Michigan, with the digital video (DeeVee) machine, 2010.

<ESPN1—ESPN2—ESPN3—Detroit Sportschannel—Pro-Am Sports System—Southeast Michigan SportsChannel—HellSports—>

Honey, quit channel surfing and switch over to Interactive Movie Classics. I want to remake <u>Gone With the Wind</u> with Bette Davis and Clint Eastwood in it.

<NFL Channel—Basketball Channel—Volleyball Channel—Swimming Channel—Water Polo Channel—Scuba Channel—Trashsport Channel—Sportrivia Channel>

<Sportnews—Sportstalk Channel—Baseball Card Auction—Sports Movie Classics—Sports Memorabilia Shopping—Sports Newsreel—Sports Music Channel—>

D-a-a-a-d, I have to watch my calculus tutorial NOW, or I'll miss the live interactive feed from Ann Arbor!

And I promised I'd video Gramma to show her my new talking sneakers!

<Golf Virtuality Game—The Bookie Channel—Interactive Mud Wrestling—Interactive Mud Wrestling—Interactive Mud Wrestling—>

That does it! Kids, remote control override with three-way screen split and lockout Dad's controller, NOW!

<Interactive Movie Classics/UM Calculus 101/Dialing 667-205-4323>

Hey! I was watching that!

ommunications media and information technologies are increasingly important components of our lives. The sheer amount of time we expend on communication makes up a significant portion of our daily activities. In terms of media consumption, the average American adult spends about four hours a day watching television, about three hours listening to the radio, and about half an hour reading the newspaper. **Information technologies**—such as advanced telephone systems and personal computers—are growing in importance. Americans spend about half an hour each day talking on the telephone and about two hours at their personal computers. When we add in the time spent attending movies, watching home videos, listening to recorded music, reading books and magazines, or engaging in face-to-face and written communications, we can see that well over half our leisure hours are spent on activities that in some way involve an information exchange.

On the job, the exchange of information is an increasingly important component of many work activities. Well over three-fourths of the economic activity in the United States now involves producing, processing, or distributing information. **Information workers** now make up the majority of the work force, and the proportion of workers engaged in information work has more than doubled in the space of a single generation (Dordick & Wang, 1993). Even in service, agricultural, and manufacturing occupations—which dominated the world of work as late as the 1970s—information technologies are an increasingly important presence. The impact of these changes is so sweeping that many observers have concluded that we now live in an **information society.**

Information technologies store, process, or transmit computer-readable information.

Information workers produce, process, or distribute information as their primary work activity.

Information society refers to a society in which exchange of information is the predominant economic and social activity.

Convergence means integration into a common technological base.

Digital means computer readable.

THE CONVERGENCE OF COMPUTERS AND COMMUNICATIONS

The transition to an information-based society is accelerating through the rapid **convergence** of communications and information technologies and the growth of integrated high-capacity networks that carry communication in computer-readable **digital** form. Already, the public long-distance telephone network is all digital, and ever-growing portions of the music and print media we consume in our homes are produced and distributed in digital form. Plans are rapidly falling into place to deliver digital audio and video entertainment to homes in the very near future. Meanwhile, the convergence process is well under way in the world of work, where large corporate networks freely mix digitized phone conversations, electronic documents, computer data, and video transmissions.

The technical convergence of computing and communications is reflected on an institutional and societal level as well (see Figure 1.1). Telephone, computer, cable television, and media firms merge in an effort to win the upper hand in the race to invent and control the future of communications. The fact that formerly distinct forms of telecommunication, such as voice telephone and cable television, can now be integrated into a single digital network means that it makes sense to forge alliances across formerly rigid industry boundaries. Meanwhile, large businesses and public institutions are reorganizing to take advantage of new ways of doing business made possible by the technological convergence.

The convergence of communications and information technologies is so important that it has emerged as a public policy issue around the world. Rich and poor countries alike recognize the significance of this development and have made it a centerpiece of their economic development strategies. Nations now vie to put advanced communications

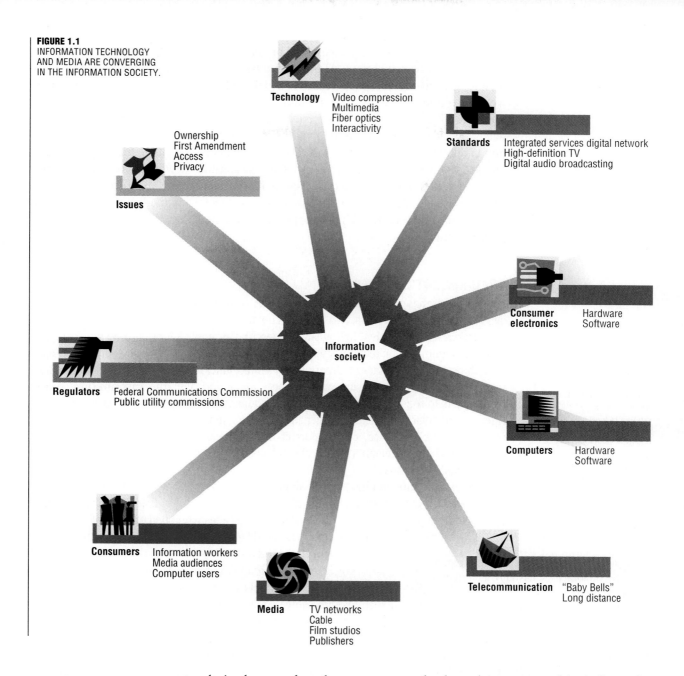

FIGURE 1.1
INFORMATION TECHNOLOGY
AND MEDIA ARE CONVERGING
IN THE INFORMATION SOCIETY.

Technology   Video compression
Multimedia
Fiber optics
Interactivity

Standards   Integrated services digital network
High-definition TV
Digital audio broadcasting

Ownership
First Amendment
Access
Privacy

Issues

**Information
society**

**Consumer
electronics**   Hardware
Software

Regulators   Federal Communications Commission
Public utility commissions

Computers   Hardware
Software

Consumers   Information workers
Media audiences
Computer users

Media   TV networks
Cable
Film studios
Publishers

Telecommunication   "Baby Bells"
Long distance

networks in place, much as they once competed to have the most powerful missiles or the biggest battleships. Although the United States was arguably the first nation to make the transition to an **information economy**, nations such as Singapore, France, and Japan have now surpassed the United States in some aspects of providing the basic facilities needed to support life in the information society.

The use and abuse of communications media and information technologies also give rise to numerous social and political issues that periodically force their way to the top of the public agenda. These issues range from the effects of violence, racism, and sexism in the media to the threats to individual privacy and personal freedoms engendered by the spread of advanced computer and telephone systems. Information technology raises mounting concerns about job security, equal opportunity, privacy, and health in the workplace and about the ever-widening gap between rich and poor. The flow of information across international boundaries and the balance of trade in information technologies and communication services are increasingly important issues of contention in relations between nations. As we shall see in later chapters, the list goes on and on. The main point is, that from a social and cultural viewpoint, as well as from a technological perspective, the convergence of information technologies and communications media is a far-reaching development. It represents a fundamental change in the fabric of life, one fraught with both opportunity and peril that merits the attention of all informed citizens.

COMMUNICATIONS MEDIA

Various terms have been used to describe the convergence of technologies we've been describing. In the late 1970s, two French scholars, Nora and Minc (1980), coined the term *telematique*—"**telematics**" in English—to describe the implications of combining computer and telecommunication technology. That term has gained some currency but seems to lose something in the translation. Others prefer "informatics," to emphasize that information networks are involved in the convergence. Metaphorically, the **information superhighway** is to the Information Age what the superhighway system was to the Industrial Age: a universal network on which all travelers may ride, whether their purpose is commerce, public service, or the pursuit of happiness. This term is often used when describing advanced telephone and cable television systems that combine voice, data, and video in a single network.

Recently, the **Internet** has become almost synonymous with the information superhighway concept. The Internet is a worldwide "network of networks" that connects computers so that they can exchange messages with one another and access files of computer data. The World Wide Web is a portion of the Internet that is rich in graphics and that allows users to navigate bewteen "pages" by selecting key words or graphic symbols. Many web pages offer audio and video as well as text and graphics and epitomize the convergence of technologies. However, it is not certain whether the web will evolve into the information superhighway or be co-opted by it.

Still, we need an umbrella term to refer to the convergence of mass media, telecommunications, and computers that does not entail coining a (potentially transient) neologism. So we will simply use **communications media.** This term encompasses not only the media that are central to conventional mass communication studies—radio, television, print, and film—but also the telephone and the computer.

One way to truly appreciate the significance of communications media today is to begin with an understanding of views of human communication and mass communications media developed in the years before their integration with computer technology. We therefore start with a brief explication of "classical" views of the communication process and various types of communication.

Telematics describes the combination of telecommunications and computers.

The information superhighway is a universal, high-speed network that will carry all forms of text, audio, computer data, and video.

Internet is a network of computer networks used by millions for E-mail and database access.

Communications media include all forms of communication mediated through mechanical or electronic channels.

R E V I E W

1. Why are mass media and information technologies increasingly important in our lives?
2. What technological development is speeding the transition to the information society?
3. Give five examples of communications media you use every day.
4. Give an example of a communications medium that is *not* also an information technology.
5. Which of the following is *not* an information worker?

   A college professor

   A computer programmer

   A newspaper editor

   A computer repair technician

THE PROCESS OF COMMUNICATION

Communication is the process of exchanging information. **Information** is, put simply, the content of communication. It may include the content of communications that are primarily social or entertaining as well as those that are more strictly "informative," such as when we ask someone for the time, when we attend a class, or when we tune in the evening news.

The process of communication can be broken down into eight components that are present in every exchange of information (Schramm, 1982):

The *source* is the originator of the communication.

The *message* is the content of the communication, the information that is to be exchanged.

An *encoder* translates the message into a form that can be communicated—often a form that is not directly interpretable by human senses.

A *channel* is the medium or transmission system used to convey the message from one place to another.

A *decoder* reverses the encoding process.

The *receiver* is the destination of the communication.

A *feedback* mechanism between the source and the receiver may be used to regulate the flow of communication.

Noise is any unwanted distortion or errors that may be introduced during the information exchange.

FIGURE 1.2
THE SMCR MODEL IS ONE WAY OF DESCRIBING THE COMMUNICATION PROCESS.

These components are diagrammed in Figure 1.2. Some examples will help to demonstrate the application of the model to a wide range of communication contexts.

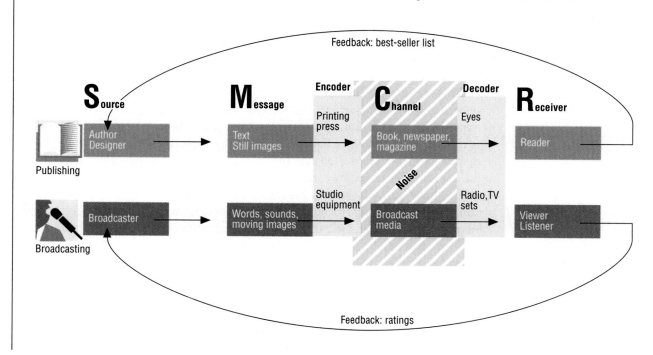

In a college lecture hall, the professor is the source and her lecture is the message. She encodes the message with her larynx, and her voice is carried in the form of pressure waves, using the air in the lecture hall as the communications "channel." The students are the receivers, and their ears are the decoders. Students provide feedback to the instructor through such actions as raising their hands with questions, shuffling their papers, or nodding off to sleep. Noise components might include misstatements by the instructor, the din of the college marching band practicing outside the window, or students who surreptitiously listen to portable stereos instead of attending to the lecture.

When you are at home watching a television program, the television network (a corporate "source") is the originator of the message, which is encoded by the microphones and television cameras in the television studio. In this case, the channel is not literally the number on the television dial to which you are tuned, but rather the entire chain of transmitters, satellite links, and cable television equipment required to convey the message to your home. Although we sometimes call a TV set a "receiver," it is really the decoder in this scheme of things, and the viewer is the receiver. Feedback from viewers is provided via television rating services and by cards, letters, and phone calls. Electronic interference with the communication channel and the distractions of barking dogs or fighting neighbors are possible noise components in this situation.

Electronic mail is a written message sent over a computer network.

A relatively new form of communication is **electronic mail**, which uses computer networks to send written messages to other users of a network. In this case, the source is the person with a message to send—say, an insightful commentary on the latest episode of *Star Trek: Deep Space 9*. The source encodes the message using word-processing and communications programs on a personal computer. The channel consists of the phone line or local computer network that links the source's personal computer to a central computer, which stores the electronic mail message in computer-readable form. The receiver decodes the message with his or her own personal computer. One interesting feature of electronic mail services is that messages can easily be addressed to groups of users as well as individuals or can be "posted" in publicly accessible files for anyone to see. Readers of the message provide feedback via return electronic mail. In this situation, common noise sources are typographical errors made by the source when inputting the message and data errors in the networks that transmit the message.

This description of the communication process, sometimes called the source-message-channel-receiver (SMCR) model, has been criticized for representing an unrealistically mechanistic approach to human communication. Others criticize this model because it tends to stress the transmission of information from the source to the receiver rather than a reciprocal exchange, placing too little emphasis on the receiver of the communication and, some think, legitimizing a power relationship between a dominant source and a submissive receiver (Downing, Mohammadi, & Sreberny-Mohammadi, 1990).

An alternate view is that the communication process is a reciprocal activity involving the joint creation of meaning. From this perspective, communication takes place in the context

Culture is a system of images and symbols shared by a group.

of **culture**. Communication involves the exchange of meaning through the use of the language and images that compose the shared culture of participants. The receiver of the communication plays an active role, filtering messages through the lens of his or her own culture and personal experience.

Both of these approaches are valid, and we will draw upon the cultural studies paradigm extensively in later chapters. We begin here with the SMCR model because it was developed in an effort to understand the communication of information in mathematical terms for purposes of computer communication, making it especially relevant to our discussion of the convergence of human and computer communication.

TYPES OF COMMUNICATION

Communication can be categorized in many ways. We will begin by classifying it according to the number of persons involved in the communication process (Williams, 1987).

Classification by Size

Size classifications include intrapersonal, interpersonal, small group, large group, and mass communication (see Table 1.1). Each mode of communication may or may not involve the use of a mechanical or electronic medium to transmit the flow of information. When such means are used, we say that the communication is *mediated*.

Intrapersonal communication is an exchange of information we have with ourselves, such as when we think over our next move in a video game or sing to ourselves in the shower. Making notes on a pad of paper is a form of mediated intrapersonal communication involving a mechanical medium. Typing a file into a computer is a form of electronic-mediated intrapersonal communication.

Interpersonal communication can include all communication exchanges in which two or more people take part, but in the annals of communication studies the term is usually reserved for situations in which just two people are communicating with each other. Having a *face-to-face* conversation over lunch and writing a letter to a friend are everyday examples. When interpersonal communication between two parties is mediated, as in a telephone conversation, the term *point-to-point* communication is sometimes used to describe it.

Group communication generally refers to situations in which three or more people communicate with one another. Not all communication that takes place in a group setting is referred to as group communication, however. When pairs of students talk to each other in a classroom before the start of a lecture, for example, they are engaged in *interpersonal* communication.

TABLE 1.1. TYPES OF COMMUNICATION

Intrapersonal	To own self • Thoughts • Personal diary
Interpersonal	Face to face • Conversation • Body language
	Point to point • Telephone call • Electronic mail
	Point to multipoint • Broadcast fax message • Electronic mail list
Small group	Face to face • Group conversations
	Point to point • Conference call
	Point to multipoint • Teleconference
Large group	• Speech • Lecture
Mass Media	Central source to individual receivers • Newspapers • Television, radio

Intrapersonal communication is with ourselves.

Interpersonal communication involves two or more people.

Group communication involves three or more people.

Small-group communication, usually involving fewer than a dozen people, is an extension of interpersonal communication beyond individuals into situations where group dynamics become important. For example, when a group of students get together to "scope out" an exam, their interaction is likely to follow one of several well-known patterns of small-group interaction as they define a study plan for the group.

Large-group communication typically involves anywhere from a dozen to several hundred participants, and the communication situation restricts active involvement to only a few of the parties. Speeches, lectures, concerts, and live theatrical performances are examples. Unlike with mass communication, large-group communication still involves immediate feedback from the receivers of the message.

COMMUNICATION CAN OCCUR AT MANY LEVELS, FROM INTRAPERSONAL TO INTERPERSONAL, TO SMALL-GROUP, TO LARGE GROUP, TO MASS COMMUNICATION.

New technologies are making mediated group communication much more common than they were a few years ago. As we will see in later chapters, teleconferencing allows groups of users at three or more locations to interact with one another via electronic means. Many teleconferences are examples of *multipoint-to-multipoint* communication, in which participants at multiple locations contribute equally to an information exchange.

Mass communication is one-to-many, with limited means for audience feedback.

Mass communication is usually defined as one-to-many or *point-to-multipoint* communication, in which a single message is communicated from a single source to hundreds or thousands of receivers, with relatively restricted opportunities for the audience to communicate back to the source. Classic examples are newspapers, radio, television, and film.

Of course, many communication situations do not fit neatly into these categories. For example, when a community activist goes door-to-door with a petition, delivering basically the same pitch at every stop, is that interpersonal communication or a type of serial large-group communication? Are talk radio shows, in which audience members provide instant communication back to the source—and even, in a sense, become the source themselves—still true mass media forms? For a high-tech example, consider personal data assistants (PDAs). They fill the functions of notepad, personal computer, and telephone, effectively combining intrapersonal and interpersonal communication in a single device.

In addition, the number of participants is not always a reliable way of classifying the type of communication. For example, some ostensively mass communication forms, such as local cable television channels, might have fewer than a dozen viewers at some times of the day, whereas some large-group events such as papal addresses and Lollapalooza festivals reach hundreds of thousands. A college lecture delivered on the last day before spring break to only six students would still be a large-group communication (because of the style of presentation), even though the audience is a small group. Thus, both the nature of the communication setting and the size of the gathering must be considered.

Other Classification Methods

There are many other ways of classifying communication, such as by the setting in which the communication takes place and by the nature of the communication process. We will now consider some of these.

Organizational communication is that which takes place in formally structured organizations, such as large corporations or public agencies. It spans the entire spectrum of communication types, from one-to-one to large-group communication. In these settings, a person's position and function within the organization are likely to affect the structure and content of his or her communication.

Organizational communication is within a formally structured organization.

Asynchronous means "not all at the same time."

Not all forms of communication involve the gathering of every participant at a particular point in time. Home video and computer games are examples of **asynchronous** mass media that present the same message to large groups of people, but the message may be received over the course of months or even years. Examples of asynchronous interpersonal communication include answering machines, voice mail, and electronic mail.

Communication can also be classified in terms of its directionality. That is, is it *one-way* communication, in which the flow of information goes exclusively from source to receiver, or *two-way*, in which both participants take an active role? Mass communication is usually thought of as being predominantly one way, with the feedback from the audience relatively restricted and slow in coming. Interpersonal communication is usually two way, with immediate feedback and active contributions from both sides.

Another way of characterizing communication is by its degree of *interactivity*. Everyone, it seems, is talking about interactive television, interactive cable, interactive telephones, interactive computer services, interactive games, interactive commercials, interactive compact discs, even interactive soda cans (with computer chips that talk to you when you pull the tab). However, it is hard to pin down just what "interactivity" means.

Sometimes, "interactive" is used as a synonym for "two way," but few of the systems developed to date are truly two way in the same way that a conversation between two people is, where the two parties not only take turns responding to each other but also modify the nature of their interaction based on preceding exchanges. Computer games that get harder as you score more points and transactional systems such as home banking systems perhaps come the closest to this sense of the word. In these cases, the course of the information exchange is continually modified depending on the reactions of the user. Perhaps the ultimate form of interactivity would be a system that would pass the so-called Turing test, named after the British mathematician and computer pioneer Alan Turing. To pass this test, an information system must be able to convince users that they are interacting with a human being rather than a machine.

At the other extreme, "interactivity" is sometimes used to describe any situation in which the content of an extensive media system is selectable and customizable by the user. On-line computer systems that let users assemble their own version of the daily newspaper from a vast library of digital information are a good example. Interactive television systems that would allow viewers to select alternate endings to soap operas or to switch between wide-angle and close-up shots while watching football games are examples of this sort of interactivity. However, textbooks with indexes and tables of contents, television sets with remote controls, and candy machines are also "interactive" in this sense, and no one seems to get very excited about their "interactivity."

We will use the term **interactive** to refer to situations where real-time feedback is collected from the receivers of a communications channel and is used by the source to continually modify the message as it is being delivered to the receiver. By this definition, on-line newspapers, interactive soap operas, and home banking systems are interactive, but TV remote controls and textbooks are not (no real-time feedback to the source). In the video game example, there is no real-time feedback to the source either, but we could consider the computer program in the game to be acting as the "Turing agent" of the person who authored the game and can still count it as interactive. What about the candy machine? The lever mechanism inside is a crude type of mechanical "programming," too, but there is no ongoing transaction that is continually modified. A truly interactive candy machine would let you select how many peanuts you want in your candy bar and would ask whether you want to wash it down with a soda (Rafaelli, 1988).

Interactive communication uses feedback to modify a message as it is presented.

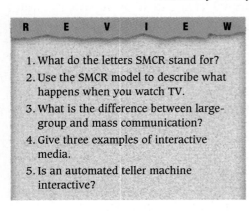

R E V I E W

1. What do the letters SMCR stand for?
2. Use the SMCR model to describe what happens when you watch TV.
3. What is the difference between large-group and mass communication?
4. Give three examples of interactive media.
5. Is an automated teller machine interactive?

NEW TECHNOLOGIES AND THE MASS MEDIA

Because much of this text deals with the mass media, we will next examine the mass communication process in greater depth. We will build on classic definitions of mass media originated some fifty years ago by Wilbur Schramm, who has been credited as the founder of mass communications studies. As we go, we will consider ways in which changes in technology have altered conceptions of the mass media, perhaps to the point where we can legitimately ask whether the mass media as Schramm and other early mass communications scholars saw them decades ago still exist. We will organize the discussion using the SMCR model we introduced previously: The *source* encodes a *message*, which is carried through a *channel*, whereupon it is decoded by a *receiver*.

Mass Media Sources

In Wilbur Schramm's heyday, mass media were produced by large, multilayered media corporations, where an elite corps of authoritative media commentators and professional producers acted as **gatekeepers**, deciding what the audience should receive, thereby serving an **agenda setting** function. The sources, recognizing their own power, were aware of themselves as shapers of public opinion and popular tastes (Schramm, 1982).

Giant media corporations are still with us today and are bigger than ever. However, new technologies have made it possible to slough away many of the middle layers of media organizations and to shrink the minimum size of mass media companies. In the case of newsletters and underground magazines ("zines") published on a desktop computer, a staff of one may be sufficient. Portable TV cameras and audio recorders have also extended audio and video production capability to a much wider array of sources. In many cases the dividing line between receivers and source is getting very weak, as occurs with call-in programs and print and computer communications media that are made up solely from user contributions. In the process, the professionalism and authoritativeness of sources is eroding, as may their ability to define culture and popular opinion.

Gatekeepers decide what will appear in the media.

Agenda setting is the ability of the media to determine what is important.

TODAY, AUDIENCES AND MEDIA SOURCES ARE OFTEN BLURRED, AS IS THE CASE WITH LIVE CALL-IN SHOWS ON RADIO AND TV.

Homogenize means to treat all audience members alike.

Narrowcasting directs media channels to specific segments of the audience.

Mass Media Messages

Formerly, mass media messages were undifferentiated and were addressed to the largest possible audiences. The underlying strategy was to **homogenize** tastes and opinions to further the goals of a mass market industrial society. This meant using the media to promote tastes in consumer products that would generalize to the widest possible groups of people so that, for example, everyone would want to buy the shiny new two-tone persimmon red and classic white 1956 Mercury advertised on *The Ed Sullivan Show*. The car manufacturer could then produce vats of persimmon red paint and tons of chrome at a time, lowering production costs and fattening profits.

One of the earliest uses of computer technology in mass media industries was for audience research, which eventually made it possible to define audiences more narrowly and to target media content—and advertising—to narrower and narrower audiences. Changes in the publishing industry—spurred in part by the advent of computer typesetting—and the development of cable television led to a proliferation of mass media outlets and the concept of **narrowcasting**—dedicating channels to specific audience subgroups, or *market segments*. At first, demographic characteristics (sex, age, and income) were used to define segments, but as specialized media channels multiplied, segmentation became more sophisticated, focusing on lifestyles and narrower and narrower leisure interests. Some print and electronic publications have gone the next step, using personal forms of address in their advertising copy, and interactive TV promoters tout their ability to customize program content to the individual viewer. Rather than homogenize tastes and cultures, the new mass media try to cater to specialized groups and even define new ones.

Mass Media Channels

Formerly, mass media channels were relatively few and were relatively universal in their coverage. Each medium required its own dedicated, purpose-built transmission or distribution system. The messages were also impermanent. If you missed the last episode of *The Fugitive*, you were out of luck.

Now the number and scope of channels have changed dramatically. Satellite transmission systems have made it possible to create channels not only for specific types of people (the idea behind narrowcasting), but also for specific types of locations, including high school homerooms, supermarket checkout lines, and doctors' offices. However, the long-term trend is away from the proliferation of dedicated, specialized media networks toward high-capacity integrated networks that will combine many channels and media forms—audio, video, text, and image—in a single network. The consolidation of the various media modalities into a single network is explained further in the following sections. One important implication is that many hybrid media forms combining text, sound, and image are likely to emerge, totally blurring the once neat distinctions among radio, television, print, cable, and telephone. Meanwhile, recording technology makes it possible to capture media presentations and replay them at the convenience of the audience members.

Mass Media Audiences

In the classical view, the audience was an undifferentiated mass, anonymous both to themselves and to the source and a passive receptacle for the mass message. The economics of the media were such that audiences of thousands or millions were needed in order for the millions of dollars needed to create and sustain mass media systems to be recovered from the widest possible base. Feedback was largely limited to reports from audience research bureaus, which took days or weeks to compile.

We have already seen that messages have been differentiated to reach narrow, highly specialized target audiences. Information technologies and a growing abundance of channels have shifted the economics to favor smaller and smaller target groups, even to the level of the individual. Advanced audience research systems enhance the richness and speed of feedback from the audience to media sources, and interactive mass media technologies hold the promise of instantaneous feedback. Perhaps more than any other change in the mass media that we have considered, this strengthening of the feedback link alters the fundamental nature of the mass communication process.

Figure 1.3 summarizes some of the changes the mass media have undergone in the course of their adaptation to the information society.

THE DIGITAL REVOLUTION

Interactive mass media are one of the many areas in which the convergence of computer and communication technologies may have a significant impact. In a sense, interactive media are nothing new. Radio talk shows, Jerry Lewis Labor Day telethons, and PBS pledge breaks are all "interactive" in the sense that we previously defined. However, the application of

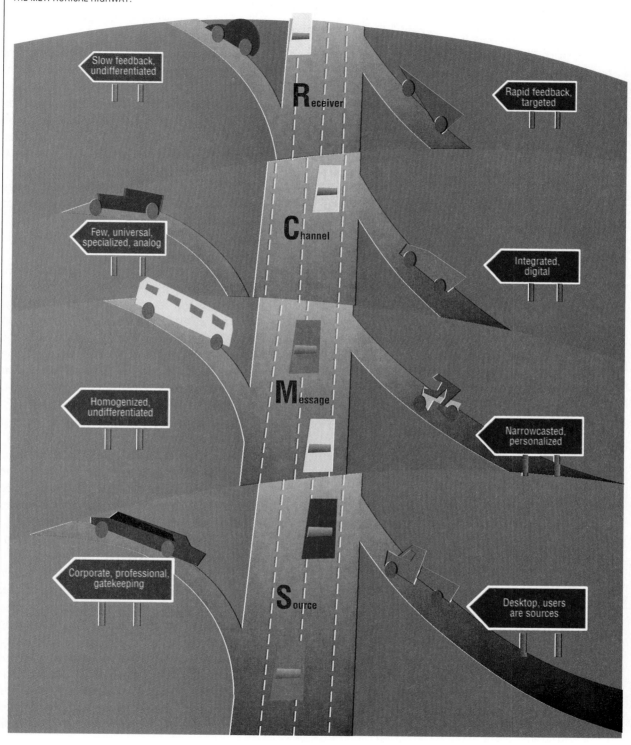

FIGURE 1.3
MASS MEDIA ARE IN A STATE OF TRANSITION ON THE INFORMATION SUPERHIGHWAY. CONVENTIONAL MASS MEDIA CHARACTERISTICS, ON THE LEFT, ARE ON THE "OFF RAMP," WHILE OTHERS, ON THE RIGHT, ARE ON THE "ON RAMP" TO THE METPHORICAL HIGHWAY.

Slow feedback, undifferentiated

Rapid feedback, targeted

Receiver

Channel

Few, universal, specialized, analog

Integrated, digital

Homogenized, undifferentiated

Message

Narrowcasted, personalized

Corporate, professional, gatekeeping

Source

Desktop, users are sources

information technologies such as the computer and advanced digital telephone systems greatly expands the scope and nature of these activities, making it possible to collate responses from much larger audiences or to tailor media presentations to individual users, for example. In this section we will examine some other trends in digital communication that can be expected to further some of the changes in the mass media.

Information technologies are used across the spectrum of types of communication. Figure 1.4 identifies some of the developments in digital technology that apply to the various types of communication we have considered. We will describe these examples in depth in later chapters. For now, they serve to illustrate how the convergence of computer and communication technologies is affecting virtually all types of human communication activities.

Analog-to-Digital Conversion

Once again, by *digital* communication we mean the conversion of sound, pictures, and text to computer-readable formats—strings of ones and zeros that carry information in encoded form (see box). Instead of all the information in the original message being retained, the data are sampled at frequent intervals and converted to computer digits. In contrast, **analog** communication relays *all* of the information present in the original message in the form of continuously varying signals that correspond to the fluctuations of sound or light energy originated by the source of communication. The human senses are all analog communication systems, as are most present-day mass media.

There are significant technical advantages to "going digital." Transmission quality is improved because the digital signals are less susceptible to electrical interference. The capacity of telecommunications systems can also be expanded if we can come up with ways to reduce the number of times we sample the original signal or the number of data bits required to encode each sample. It

DIGITAL TRANSMISSION PRIMER

To see how communications are translated into computer-readable data, we will trace the process as it takes place during the course of a typical telephone call, where the digital conversion occurs on a computer card that interfaces our telephone line with the telephone company's switch.

First, brief samples of the electrical waveform corresponding to our voice are taken. Next, the voltage level for each sample is measured. Finally, the voltage reading is "rounded off" to the nearest of 256 different possible voltage levels, and a corresponding eight-digit binary number is transmitted to indicate the approximate voltage level corresponding to each of the samples. This reduces the original analog signal to a series of "on-off" electrical pulses, in which we turn an electrical current on for a brief moment to indicate a "1" and turn it off for a "0." This process is known as *pulse code modulation*.

For example, if two lovers are talking on the phone and there is complete (if meaningful) silence on the line at the instant of one of the samples, the voltage reading is zero and the binary number corresponding to the lowest of the 256 "steps"—00000000—is sent. If the lovers begin to quarrel and start shouting at each other, the voltage reading is at the maximum and a binary number corresponding to the highest (256th) level is sent: 11111111.

Another device reverses the process at the receiving end of the line. The samples are very frequent—8000 times a second—and the reconstructed waveform is smoothed out to fill in the gaps so that the ear cannot detect them. To the couple, it seems as though they are talking to each other, but in reality they are listening to computer emulations of their voices.

By increasing the number of samples and more finely dividing the sound levels that we use, we can improve the transmission quality to the point that it meets or exceeds analog media. Since we can regenerate the digital pulses precisely, each successive copy can be a perfect copy. This feature led to the development of compact discs. In fact, compact disc music uses the same pulse code modulation process, except that the samples are more frequent and the "rounding off" process is more precise. In that case the 1's and 0's are stored on the surface of the disc in the form of tiny pits (for each 0).

Analog communication uses continuously varying signals corresponding to the light or sounds originated by the source.

is also possible to share a single communications medium among several channels simultaneously: the streams of computer bits can be intermingled in a high-capacity channel and later sorted out into their component parts at the receiver's end. Supplementary digital

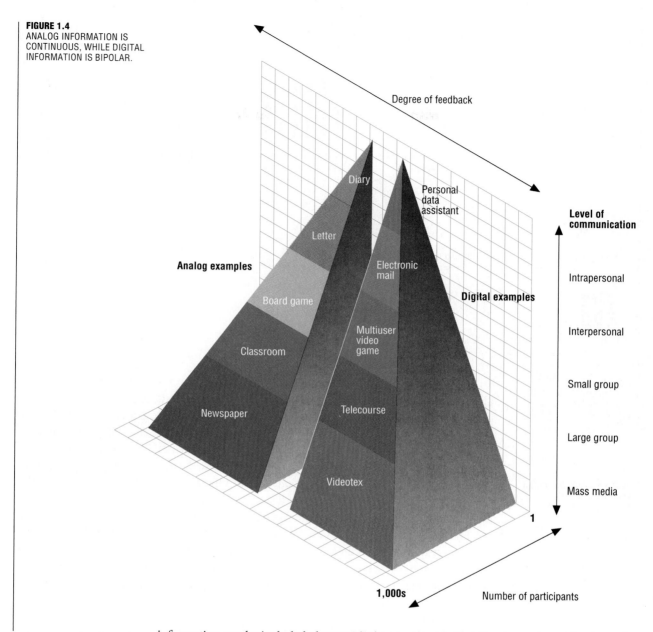

FIGURE 1.4
ANALOG INFORMATION IS
CONTINUOUS, WHILE DIGITAL
INFORMATION IS BIPOLAR.

Degree of feedback

Level of
communication

Diary

Personal
data
assistant

Letter

Analog examples

Electronic
mail

Intrapersonal

Board game

Digital examples

Multiuser
video
game

Interpersonal

Classroom

Small group

Newspaper

Telecourse

Large group

Videotex

Mass media

1

1,000s

Number of participants

Intelligent networks can sense
and respond to the content of the
information they carry.

information can be included along with the message so that the channel carrying it can be **intelligent**—that is, behave differently depending on the nature of the content carried or accept information from the end user that shapes the presentation.

The first consumer communications medium to be digitized was the telephone, beginning in the early 1960s with high-speed lines in the heart of telephone networks that were capable of carrying dozens of conversations simultaneously. Today, most telephone conversations are converted to digital form before they leave your neighborhood and are conveyed as computer data throughout the long-distance telephone networks. The next generation of telephone sets will be part of an all-digital network, with the conversion of voice to digital information—known as *analog to digital conversion*—taking place inside your telephone receiver (see Figure 1.5).

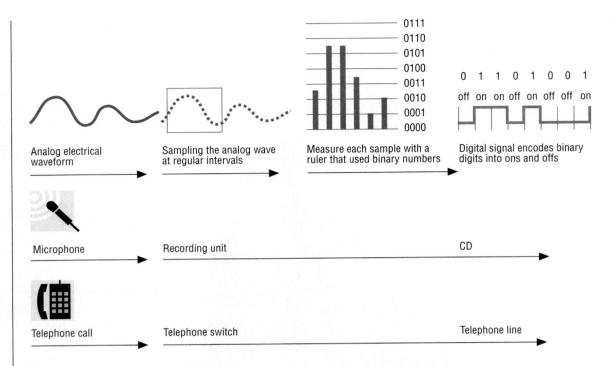

0111
0110
0101
0100
0011
0010
0001
0000

0 1 1 0 1 0 0 1

off on on off on off off on

Analog electrical
waveform

Sampling the analog wave
at regular intervals

Measure each sample with a
ruler that used binary numbers

Digital signal encodes binary
digits into ons and offs

Microphone

Recording unit

CD

Telephone call

Telephone switch

Telephone line

FIGURE 1.5
THE ANALOG-TO-DIGITAL
CONVERSION PROCESS
OCCURS IN A VARIETY OF
MEDIA.

**Videotex services deliver text
and graphics through
computer networks.**

The next phase in the evolution to digital transmission was the compact disc, which digitally encodes music in the form of microscopic pits on the surface of the disc. This method of digital encoding closely resembles that used in the telephone network, except that the number of samples is increased, and each sample is allocated more computer digits to improve sound quality. The latest tape recording media also utilize digital formats.

Of course, the introduction of personal computers into the home marks another important step in the digitization of communications media. **Videotex**—communication services that offer personal computer users access to a vast store of news and consumer information and the capability of sending electronic mail and completing electronic transactions—represents the final phase of the digitization of print media. Already most print publications are computerized throughout their production cycle. It is only in the final printing process that the information is again converted to noncomputer-readable, analog form. About a dozen daily newspapers are available electronically, often through consumer videotex services.

Digital Convergence

Broadcasting is also set for a digital revolution. The next generation of television transmitters and receivers and home video players, **high-definition television (HDTV)**, will be all-digital, as will the next generation of radio, **digital audio broadcasting (DAB)**. (We will examine these developments further in later chapters.) Thus, the media world seems about to "go digital." This transformation in turn has several important implications for the future evolution of the mass media in terms of the abundance of channels, user control, and the emergence of new multimedia forms.

**HDTV and DAB are the digital
versions of TV and radio,
respectively.**

Channel Abundance

We noted earlier that the growing number of channels is a significant change in the nature of the mass media. The advent of digital technology greatly accelerates this trend. When messages are digitally encoded it becomes possible to use **digital compression.** This means subtracting redundant information from media content—such as stationary backdrops that do not change between frames of a TV picture—or finding more efficient ways of encoding the information that is transmitted. The effect of digital compression is to allow multiple channels to be carried where only one was possible before. For example, video compression makes it possible to transmit three to five programs simultaneously on cable TV or satellite channels that now carry only a single channel.

While more programs can be crammed into existing channel space, the supply of channel space is also increasing. New **broadband media**—high-capacity transmission media capable of carrying full-motion video—are appearing. Broadcast television, home video, and cable television are familiar examples of broadband media. In contrast, audio recordings and the telephone are *narrowband media* because they are not capable of carrying moving visual information, only the audio. Computer media fill a middle ground, since they contain textual and graphic information, but they do not have the capacity, or **bandwidth,** to handle full-motion video. Broadband media thus require relatively large amounts of bandwidth to transmit their messages, while narrowband media require relatively little.

Fiber optics represent a significant step forward in broadband media. Fiber optic systems are simply those that rely on light energy rather than electricity to communicate information. Eventually fiber optic systems may be connected directly to home telecommunications terminals such as the telephone, the television set, and the radio. However, other broadband network options are being developed, including new satellites capable of broadcasting to miniature satellite antennas, improved telephone lines that can carry video signals as well as voices, and new digital broadcast services with interactive capabilities.

Future networks may also be *switched broadband networks,* which will make it possible to "call up" an extremely wide variety of channels instead of being limited to a preselected set of channels. Digitization also makes it possible to store media content in computer-readable form, enabling us to retrieve and manipulate media programs in much the same way that we access computer files on personal computers. The ultimate evolution of these developments is likely to be a system of video **on demand**—or more generally, media on demand—which will enable users to "call up" virtually any media product from anywhere in the world at any time without making a trip to the newsstand, library, or video store. Users of the Internet's World Wide Web can glimpse this future today. With the click of a computer mouse, they can switch back and forth between millions of "computer channels." These range from humble personal "home pages" that are created by individual users—the equivalent of computer-mediated résumés or personal photo scrapbooks—to grand corporate sites that have audio, video, and interactive features. Among the most sophositicated web sites are those created by mass media organizations to put themselves onto the information superhighway. The web has several navigation options. The user can select "channels" by typing in computer addresses (e.g., http://www.white.house.gov), explore with key words (e.g., "fun," "Bible studies," "higher education"), or aimlessly "surf" from place to place by activating links between pages (Bradley, 1995).

The digitization of media may make the computer the prime producer of media content. As with other industries where information technologies have been applied, this step is likely to eliminate much of the labor involved in production. Character-generated cable television channels are a familiar, if mundane, example of this capability in conventional mass media. **Desktop publishing** is another example. Individuals working at desktop computers can now turn out professional-looking print publications that might have required a staff of a dozen print specialists a decade ago. When information is digitized, it can also be readily transformed from one format to another or linked across media modalities. For example, newspaper copy prepared on a computerized word processor can easily be transferred to a videotex system, recorded on computer disc, or even spoken aloud by a computerized voice box. While computer animation is currently more expensive to create than live-action film or video and is therefore largely limited to special effects sequences in big-budget film spectaculars, it seems likely that further technical advances will eventually reverse the equation, perhaps making it possible for a single individual to "author" a completed theatrical film from a powerful media workstation.

User Control

How will the user keep up with the proliferation of channels? The digital remote controls now included with most television sets and VCRs point the way toward more sophisticated content selection methods. Videotex systems that follow a preprogrammed set of selection instructions ("First show me the weather, then the sports, then the news, and then my electronic mail") foreshadow one solution. All-digital production and transmission systems will enable us to program our receivers with highly personalized selection rules. To take one example, digital radio broadcasts will soon include a digital format code, making it possible to program radios for such functions as "heavy metal seek." Digital media will also allow us to search channels for the occurrences of specific patterns of sound or image, so that we may eventually be able to program intelligent receivers with such rules as "Clint Eastwood seek."

As telecommunications terminals grow in sophistication, it will also be easier to customize messages for individual users. Personal messages that greet users of on-line information systems are current examples. Magazine publishers are already able to personalize advertising copy by inserting the subscriber's name in the text of ads. Magazine content can also be varied according to the location and demographic characteristics of the reader—one national news magazine now boasts over 150 different weekly versions. With ever-growing channel abundance and increasingly sophisticated computer chips in the receivers, it might someday be possible to change the content of ads for specific types of households or to introduce variations in entertainment programs to tailor them to the tastes of narrowly defined audiences, or even specific individuals. *Wheel of Fortune*'s letter turner might appear in a lowcut gown in college fraternity houses but be seen in a demure "granny dress" in a minister's home.

As we have already noted, interactivity represents a further development in user control. Arcade video games and computer-based video games are perhaps the best-known examples. Dramatic shows in which plot developments are determined by viewer votes or quiz shows in which the home audience plays along are oft-cited examples of the types of video programs that could become possible with truly interactive systems.

Multimedia Convergence

Multimedia systems integrate text, audio, and video and let the user select the presentation mode.

A final implication of the digital media revolution is **multimedia** convergence. The integration of digital audio, visual, and text information into all-purpose data networks is erasing the once rigid distinctions between media systems. The conventional analog mass media—radio, television, print, and film—all used to have quite distinct production and transmission systems. But in today's world of digital media, these conventional media forms, along with new hybrid forms, will perhaps merge into a single medium—large-scale

VIRTUAL REALITY SYSTEMS LIKE THIS LET THE USER ENTER A COMPUTER-GENERATED WORLD OF HIS OR HER OWN.

Virtual reality gives users the sense that they are "inside" a computer-generated reality.

computer memory connected to a high-speed data network. *Hypermedia* is another term used to describe this development. Hypermedia allow users to control their own consumption of a media product by selecting key words or graphic symbols, allowing them to branch to multimedia "extensions" employing combinations of audio, visual, and text modalities.

The creation of media products in digital form and the resulting ease with which they may be converted from one modality to another simplifies the task of creating and presenting the extensions to the user. For example, a reader of page 18 who was especially interested in DAB systems could highlight the key word with a computer mouse and then select from such options as a demonstration videotape of a DAB receiver in use, an explanation of the DAB transmission technology, a sample of how DAB would sound in "top 40 seek mode," or an oral recitation of an encyclopedia entry on digital broadcasting. Ultimately, the evolution of interactive technology, combined with multimedia broadband transmission systems, will create media products that will be difficult to distinguish from reality, creating a sense of **virtual reality** for their users.

A final implication of media convergence is that the "media" part of the term "mass media" is fast becoming as obsolete as the first word. When we use the term "media" we are talking about the

R E V I E W

1. What fundamental changes in the SMCR model as it applies to mass media are taking place in the transition to interactive media?
2. Give some examples of digital forms of intrapersonal, interpersonal, group, and mass communication.
3. What are three advantages of "going digital"?
4. What is the significance of digital compression?
5. In what three important ways will tomorrow's digital media differ from today's analog media?

transmission-reception chains. With analog media, we have entire transmission-reception systems dedicated to single functions and restricted by presentation modalities—text, sound, and image. With digitization, separate television, radio, print, and telephone networks may disappear.

Anticipating that day, we will distinguish the network from the content by using the term **information service** to denote content that serves a mass media function—that is, content reproduced for multiple receivers—and we will use **information service providers** for the institutions that produce the content and **network service providers** for those that transmit the information over telecommunication networks (LaRose, 1992). The two functions may or may not continue to reside in the same organization as we complete the transition to the information society.

Information services reproduce media content for multiple receivers and are produced by information service providers.

Network service providers transmit information over telecommunications networks.

SUMMARY & REVIEW

What Is the Importance of Communications Media and Information Technologies?

What is the information society?
The information society is one in which the production, processing, and distribution of information are the primary economic and social activities. In an information society, an ever-increasing amount of time is spent with communications media and using information technologies such as the telephone and the computer. More and more people are employed as information workers—people who produce, process, or distribute information as their primary work activity. The information society is a further step in the evolution of society from its former bases in agriculture and manufacturing into an information economy, in which the manipulation of information is the primary economic activity.

What do we mean when we say that mass media and information technologies are converging?
More and more communication is created and distributed in computer-readable digital form. This means that the same basic technologies can be used to transmit all forms of communication—whether in the form of text, audio, or video—and that computer technology can be used to manipulate information in so-called intelligent networks. In fact, the processes of telecommunication and computing are merging to such a degree that we can refer to them as telematic systems in which data transmission and processing are fully integrated. Thus, separate channels are no longer needed for each medium. The organizations that produce and distribute communication are also merging as

part of the convergence trend. The information superhighway is a term used to describe the low convergent media systems.

What Is the Process of Communication?

What are the components of the communication process?
All communication processes can be described in terms of a simple model in which a corporate or individual *source* encodes a *message* and transmits it through a physical *channel* to the person for whom the message is intended, the *receiver*. We call this the SMCR model. In most communication situations, feedback is also provided between the receiver and the source. The communication process takes place in the context of a culture shared by the source and the receiver.

What are the types of communication?
When the communication channel is an electronic or mechanical device—such as a radio station or a printing press—we call it *mediated* communication. Mediated communication may be *point-to-point, point-to-multipoint,* or *multipoint-to-multipoint.* Communication can be characterized according to the number of people involved. Intrapersonal communication involves one person, interpersonal communication usually includes only two people, and small-group communication encompasses less than a dozen participants. Large-group communication involves dozens or hundreds of persons, but feedback is still immediate. Mass communication involves hundreds or thousands of people, and there is no immediate feedback. Communication can also be characterized according to the setting in which

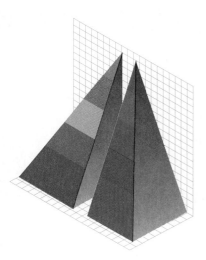

it takes place. Organizational communication happens inside a formally structured organization.

What is interactivity?
A variety of meanings have been attached to the term "interactive," ranging from the simple ability to select content from a large number of options to devices that could pass the Turing test by faithfully mimicking human interaction. The term should be reserved for communication situations in which there is a give and take between two or more parties—that is, an interaction in which all parties respond to one another and the character of their responses is contingent on their prior exchanges.

How Are New Technologies Affecting the Mass Media?

How are mass media changing in the information society?
The convergence of computer, telecommunications, and mass media systems is bringing about some fundamental changes in the way the mass communications media function. Mass media sources are becoming more numerous, and also less authoritative and professionalized. Their ability to act as gatekeepers who set the agenda for public opinion is also being diminished. Messages are customized for smaller and smaller specialized audience segments, sometimes even using personal forms of address, and are narrowcast to these segments, rather than being broadcast to a homogeneous audience. Channels are proliferating not only to reach the new audience segments but also to target specific

locations. However, the long-term trend is to integrate the many specialized channels into a single, all-purpose digital network that will provide access at the convenience of the audience. Audiences are likewise becoming smaller and less anonymous than they were formerly and have improved and more expeditious means of providing feedback to the source of the media content—and even to participate in the creation of that content.

What are the characteristics of emerging communications media systems?
The new communications media systems that are emerging are digital, as opposed to analog. Familiar mass media forms such as radio and television are evolving into new forms, such as videotex, high-definition television (HDTV), and the World Wide Web section of the Internet, that are all-digital. Technical advances such as digital compression, broadband media, and fiber optic networks will greatly increase the number of channels coming into the home. New interactive capabilities will give users a new measure of control over the channels they view and the content of those channels, including the ability to order the media presentations they wish, on demand. Digital technology also makes it possible to mix text, audio, computer graphics, and video into integrated multimedia networks to produce entire media presentations from computer workstations, as with desktop publishing.

REFERENCES

Bradley, J. C. (1995). *A quick guide to the Internet.* Belmont, CA: Wadsworth.

Dizard, W. (1990). *The coming information society.* New York: Longman.

Dordick, H., & Wang, G. (1993). *The information society: A retrospective view.* Newbury Park, CA: Sage.

Downing, J., Mohammadi, A., & Sreberny-Mohammadi, A. (1990). *Questioning the media: A critical introduction.* Newbury Park, CA: Sage.

LaRose, R. (1992). *Not your father's old mass media.* Paper presented to the International Communications Association, Miami.

Nora, S., & Minc, N. (1980). *The computerization of society.* Cambridge, MA: MIT Press.

Rafaelli, S. (1988). Interactivity: From new media to communication. In Hawkins, Pingree, & Weimann (Eds.), *Advancing communication sciences*, Vol. 16. Beverly Hills, CA: Sage.

Salvaggio, J. (1989). *The information society.* Hillsdale, NJ: Erlbaum.

Schramm, W. (1982). *Men, women, messages and media.* New York: Harper & Row.

Williams, F. (1987). *Technology and communication behavior.* Belmont, CA: Wadsworth.

Chapter 2

THEORIES OF COMMUNICATIONS MEDIA

C H A P T E R   P R E V I E W

esearchers have developed a range of ideas and theories to help explain how various kinds of communication work in our lives, their impacts, and how to use them. In this chapter we will look at theories regarding many aspects of communications media: institutional issues within media and between government and media; content or message issues; societal functions of media; media power versus audience power; individual uses of media; gratifications that media audiences and users seek; and, looking in a somewhat different direction, the patterns of diffusion of new media and information technologies.

Los Angeles, 1994

Lasswell (1960) defined communication as "who says what to whom in what channel with what effect."

Hello, Acme Media Corporation? I just watched your new show America's Funniest Pet Gladiators, and I have never seen anything so stupid, boring, insulting, and tasteless. I am calling all your sponsors, canceling my subscriptions to your company's magazines, and never buying any more of your books and CDs. (Click.)

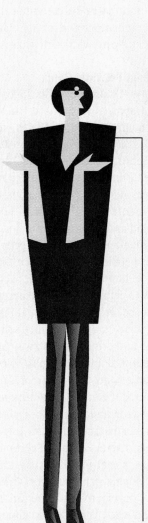

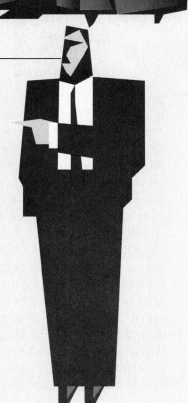

That's the fiftieth call today!. I want to know some things . . . Who wanted that show?

Well, boss, our sponsors wanted something about pets, something funny, and some violence for the 12-year-olds.

Why that idea?

We put the sponsor's target demographic and ideas through the computer, had some creative conferences, hired a director, and we had all these free home pet videos . . .

Why our best time slot?

I guess funny pet gladiators aren't ready for prime time, huh?

And our audience?

They have a short attention span. They'll forgive us.

INSTITUTIONAL MODELS OF COMMUNICATION

s we noted in Chapter 1, one of the defining characteristics of mass media is that they are fairly large institutions. The nature of these media institutions is more specifically defined by the economic context they work in, their political and social roles in society, their goals or aims, who owns them, how they are organized, how their staffs are organized and trained, and how much autonomy professionals (reporters, editors, and producers) have in creating their content.

Institutional approaches are also important to understanding telephone and computer-based media, which are even bigger than the mass media, having monopolized entire areas of service and industry, like AT&T or the Bell system used to monopolize telephony. Institutional issues in this area include the degree and kinds of competition between companies, how they are organized internally, what they see as their primary business, and what new businesses they are trying to get into (such as telephone companies wanting to offer cable TV service and vice versa). These key institutional issues determine the roles these media play for other industries and for individuals trying to use them to communicate with each other.

THE MASS MEDIA PLAY A ROLE IN ALMOST EVERY SOCIETY. HERE A QUECHUA INDIAN IN ECUADOR READS A DAILY PAPER.

Government Controls and Media Political Roles

Historian Herbert Altschull (1984) calls the media "agents of power" that represent and spread the ideas of ruling groups in almost all societies. In the United States, for example, many people see *The New York Times* and *The Wall Street Journal* as representing major economic and political power interests. Media certainly help integrate people into the basic ideologies, ideas, and consensus of their societies. Societies work more smoothly when most members share certain ideas and assumptions. Many leaders of nations, movements, and religions want to use ideas or ideologies to convince people to either accept or change things. In the United States, most people accept the idea that economic mobility and success is possible for any individual willing to go to school, work hard, and follow the main rules of society. That basic idea helps get most people to accept American rules and values and follow the laws, rather than rebel or try to change things radically. On the other hand, media often help divide people into groups by giving some access over others and by carrying content that attracts some and drives others away.

Mass media theories often focus on the media's powerful political and ideological roles. A number of scholars have tried to create categories of world media systems, which represent the underlying theories by which various nations have structured their media institutions. Most of these categorizations have reflected the polarization between nations that took place in the Cold War between the United States and the Soviet Union. For instance, the main initial work in this area, *The Four Theories of the Press*, by Siebert, Peterson, and Schramm (1956), divided media systems into authoritarian, libertarian, social responsibility, and Soviet/totalitarian. Since then, others have suggested a developmental model for **Third World** or **developing** nations. We will discuss authoritarian, developmental, libertarian, and social responsibility approaches (see Figure 2.1). Because the Soviet model has almost disappeared, we will discuss it more briefly.

Third World or **developing** countries include those in Africa, Latin America, and Asia that are less developed economically.

FIGURE 2.1
THE ROLE MEDIA PLAY IN A SOCIETY DEPENDS ON THE CONTROL OVER INFORMATION FLOWS GIVEN TO GOVERNMENT, MEDIA, INSTITUTIONS, AND AUDIENCES.

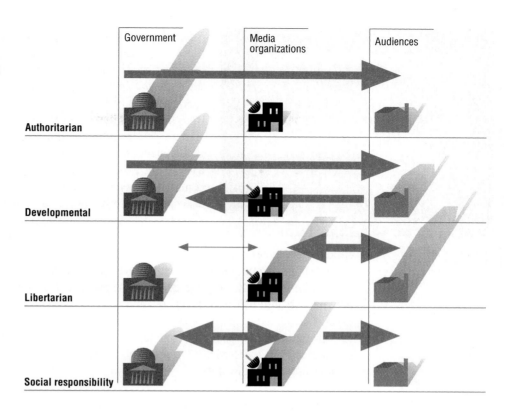

Authoritarian Model. Many governments feel entitled, even obligated, to assert authority and control over mass media. They offer several rationales for this stance. Some governments in poor and divided societies feel fragile and unable to assert much authority over their citizens if they can't control the media. Other governments are perfectly strong but see media as a threat, if not controlled, or as a potential tool that they wish to employ.

As various individuals or groups start newspapers, magazines, and later radio or television stations, many governments tend to assert at least a minimum of control. Governments often censor or prohibit things they determine to be offensive or counter to what they want to accomplish. Journalists usually fight such controls. Many people feel that media ought to be independent "watchdogs" on governments to make sure that they stay honest and nonoppressive.

From 1917 until 1992, the former Soviet Union took the authoritarian approach much further because the Communist party saw media as tools of the government in its efforts to develop the U.S.S.R.'s economy and society. The party felt that it was representing the needs and interests of the population, so no opposition or divergent views needed to be allowed. This approach differs from some other authoritarian systems in its more total form of controlling and changing society. For example, many Latin American countries have had authoritarian media controls at times, but most media remain private, and government control is often limited to censorship of news and entertainment that the government doesn't like.

Developmental Model. In a number of the developing nations of Africa, Asia, and Latin America, leaders see mass media as a strong social force that should help these nations

IN MANY NATIONS, THE GOVERNMENT OWNS THE BROADCAST MEDIA. THAT'S STILL THE CASE IN RUSSIA, FOR EXAMPLE.

develop faster or in a more planned, efficient way. This belief has led many governments to simply take over and operate electronic media themselves, to better coordinate media with their efforts to promote economic and social development.

What usually distinguishes the developmental approach from the authoritarian is that there is less overall control over content, less censorship, and a tendency to focus on media-government cooperation for development purposes. This line is a tricky one to draw, however. How much should government control or compel cooperation from media? Many nations have asked media to voluntarily cooperate with certain government programs in literacy, health, agriculture, and so on to communicate ideas to the people. How much should media be able to criticize government programs when they fail, are misguided, or are corrupt?

India is an example of a nation with a developmental media approach. While newspapers are private and fairly free, the government owns and operates radio and television to promote agriculture, health, education, and other goals. In the 1970s, Prime Minister Indira Gandhi, her Congress party, and their opponents discovered what a powerful political tool television can be. Subsequently, commercial interests, advertisers, and private film industry producers have all pressed for the commercialization of Indian television, which has reduced its developmental orientation.

Free Press/Libertarian Model. Since the eighteenth century, theorists of political democracy have emphasized that people need freedom of expression and speech to become well-informed citizens and voters. In a democracy, media inform voters about what is going on in government and elsewhere so they can become more involved. To best inform the citizens, the press must be free, uncensored, and uncontrolled if it is to provide accurate information. As governments in many countries become more democratic, they tend to reduce their control over media.

The print media in most countries tend to be run in a more libertarian manner than the electronic media. For instance, in the United States print media are closer than broadcasting media to the libertarian model because of the minimal controls on print. An emerging example of a truly libertarian system is the **Internet**, the international network of **computer conferences**, databases, and **electronic mail**, where no central authority makes decisions about content; individuals or discussion groups put on and take off whatever messages they want.

Social Responsibility Model. In the twentieth century, it is clear that free expression in and through mass media is limited by the expense and difficulty of starting a newspaper, a radio station, or a television station or obtaining access to one of the existing ones. This is particularly true in radio and television, where a finite number of available **frequencies** (the portion of the radio wave spectrum used for a specific station) requires that governments allocate them to people or groups that they somehow select as competent. In both print and electronic media, access to mass media has been effectively limited to professionals, which makes it important that those professionals behave responsibly. The average citizen has essentially delegated his or her freedom of speech to professional reporters and editors.

The British Broadcasting Corporation is a classic example of operating on a social

Internet is a network of computer networks used by millions for E-mail and database access.

Computer conferences are written communications via computer networks in which a group discussion takes place.

Electronic mail is a written message sent over a computer network.

Frequencies are positions on the radio wave spectrum used for broadcasting, mobile telephones, and other transmissions.

responsibility model. It is financed by license fees to avoid both government and advertiser control. It is a nonprofit corporation overseen by a commission that sets policy for how it should meet its public service responsibilities. Directors and programmers are guided by a strong internal ethic of responsibility to society, although critics also accuse it of being elitist and out of touch with a diverse British society.

Ownership and Control of Communications Media

The theories we have been discussing focus primarily on the twin issues of ownership (government versus private) and control. Although many countries do not allow media to be owned and controlled by private individuals or companies, the United States has a strong tradition of private ownership. The organization of American mass media into efficient industries has certainly helped them create a great number of films, recordings, television programs, books, newspapers, and magazines throughout this century. These media industries create "cultural products" using many of the same techniques used for other industrial products, such as dog food or soap. But even though Hollywood producers talk more about "product" than about art or culture, a physical product like soap and a cultural product like soap opera are not really comparable, as soap opera becomes a part of our *culture*, the ideas by which we conduct our lives and through which we communicate with each other. In short, the structure of media industries affects the content of our culture.

Ownership patterns also affect the use and content of information technologies and services (see Figure 2.2). These patterns include **monopoly**, in which one company dominates an industry; **oligopoly**, in which a few companies dominate; and **competition**, in which companies compete to provide services. Ownership-pattern theories, discussed by Eli Noam (1983) and others, are based largely in ideas of economic and technological efficiency, but some theorists, such as Vincent Mosco (1989), suggest that we should also think strongly about how such ownership patterns affect services, particularly to poor or needy people. Furthermore, given the increasing convergence between mass media and information technologies, increasing overlap and conglomeration are occurring in the ownership of the media and information industries, raising new questions about monopoly, control, and access to media and information services. These issues are crucial to regulating these industries and are discussed in greater detail in Chapter 5.

Some theorists, such as Herbert Schiller (1976), believe that we can predict much about what media will say if we know who the owners are. These theorists tend to focus on the **political economy** of media—the overlap or fit between economic and political power

Monopoly occurs when one company dominates or controls an industry.

Oligopoly occurs when only a few companies dominate an industry.

Competition refers to the existence of several companies competing for dominance in an industry.

Political economy is the overlap or fit between economic and political power and control structures.

FIGURE 2.2
MEDIA OWNERSHIP PATTERNS REFLECT THE NUMBER OF COMPETING MEDIA AND HOW THEY DIVIDE THE MARKET.

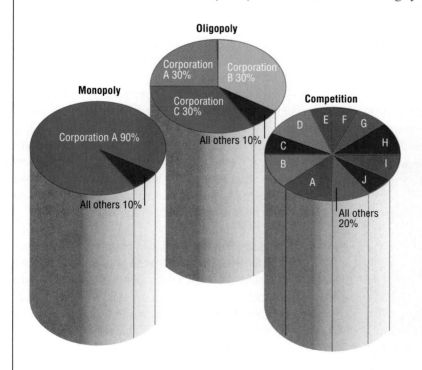

structures—and the ways that powerful or dominant economic interests tend to determine media content. In this view, the dominant political and economic groups in a society, usually those that own the major companies, tend to want to create an underlying consensus, or **hegemony**, of **ideology** favoring the system that serves their continued domination.

Other theorists believe that we cannot see major differences in media content directly attributable to the interests or styles of the owners. Even some Marxist scholars, such as the Italian Antonio Gramsci (1971), feel that owners of media compete with others to form and create media content. In this view, any hegemony, or consensus of opinion, reflected in media is the source of conflict or struggle between groups. For instance, in the United States a considerable struggle over mass media coverage has occurred between those who see cutting forests as an economic necessity and those who want to keep the forests uncut to preserve animal and bird species. The loggers want to create a hegemony of opinion that favors unrestricted economic growth, while the environmentalists want the hegemony to favor preservation of environment over economic factors.

All the groups involved in such a dispute want to create mass media coverage favorable to their position in order to influence **public opinion**, the major trends in the opinions held by members of the general public. Public opinion is important in the United States and other democracies because it ultimately influences how people vote and how the government acts on issues. For instance, both Congress and the president pay attention to surveys of what the public thinks about the issue of logging versus forest preservation, because these opinions may affect how people vote in the next election.

Deciding and Influencing Media Content

One of the main theories about how media influence public opinion is that the mass media help set the agenda for the people who watch, read, or listen to them, as well as for public and governmental discussions. According to this **agenda-setting** approach, what people talk about or see as issues depends in large part on what the media cover as news or even as entertainment. News programs, talk shows, and even sitcoms or dramas can put things on the agenda for public discussion. For example, the live coverage, news coverage, and talk shows about the 1991 Supreme Court confirmation hearings of Clarence Thomas not only raised the issue of whether he had sexually harassed Anita Hill but caused a lot of discussion of the larger issue of sexual harassment of women in the workplace. Although difficult to prove, some studies indicated that the issues raised in those hearings influenced how some women voted in the 1992 congressional and presidential elections. If that's the case, agenda setting does give political power to media, and the goals and intentions of media decision makers become an important aspect of the political system.

Media Professionals and Organizations. Another source of influence on media content has to do with how the professionals in those institutions see their own roles and agendas. Media professionals, such as reporters, editors, talent scouts, record producers, and film directors, make constant, crucial decisions every day that shape the content of the media we receive. Interestingly, both conservative and liberal critics of the U.S. mass media tend to accuse reporters and editors of having a bias toward the other position or group. For example, conservative

Hegemony is a society's underlying consensus of ideological assumptions.

Ideology is an uncritically held set of beliefs about fundamental values.

Public opinion is the views held by large numbers of people on specific politics and political issues.

Agenda setting is the ability of the media to determine what is important.

ACCORDING TO THE AGENDA-SETTING APPROACH, THE IMPORTANCE OF ISSUES SUCH AS SEXUAL HARASSMENT CAN BE RAISED BY MEDIA COVERAGE OF STORIES LIKE THE ANITA HILL TESTIMONY AGAINST SUPREME COURT NOMINEE CLARENCE THOMAS.

critics say that most reporters are Democrats, that Hollywood films tend to make military and businesspeople look bad, and that record companies issue too many recordings that are obscene or that are otherwise inappropriate for young music fans.

Gatekeeping. Another theoretical approach to influence mass media content, developed by David White (1949) and others (Shoemaker, 1991), is looking at who makes decisions about what to put into news stories or entertainment scripts. The person who decides whether to put a fact or idea in or leave it out is called a **gatekeeper**—someone who can either open or close the gate on a story, a plot idea, or a song. Reporters are gatekeepers in that they decide whether or not to report an event and how to report it if they do. Editors are gatekeepers when they decide whether to run the story or not.

A related theory, offered by David Altheide (1974) and Todd Gitlin (1983), examines how reporters or writers **frame** a story—that is, writers decide what to include within the view or frame of a story, documentary, or drama and what to leave out, much like a painter chooses what to put in the frame of his or her painting. Out of a wide range of possible ideas, facts, and points of view, the professionals in a medium decide what to include, what conceptual framework to put it in, what context to include, and how to interpret the facts.

Outside Influences on the Mass Media's Agenda. Media people do not act alone when they decide what to cover or include in their news, talk, and entertainment programs. A number of studies by scholars such as Oscar Gandy (1982) have shown that the government plays a role in setting the media's agenda, particularly in news about foreign policy. The media tend to focus on those countries and those issues that the president is talking about, visiting, negotiating with, or fighting.

Besides government, many other groups help set the agenda for media coverage. They try to call media attention to issues they care about and get the media to help them make particular points about those issues. Foundations commission studies hoping that the results make media headlines. Nongovernmental organizations, including environmental groups such as the World Wildlife Fund or the Audubon Society, issue public statements intended to influence public opinion by getting into the media. Extreme examples of groups trying to gain the attention of mass media are terrorist groups who hijack airplanes or plant bombs

Gatekeepers decide what will appear in the media.

Frame refers to what a writer chooses to include within the view or frame of a story, documentary, or drama and what conceptual framework to use.

ACTIVIST GROUPS AND ORGANIZATIONS TRY TO INFLUENCE MEDIA AND THE PUBLIC BY STAGING "MEDIA EVENTS," SUCH AS THIS ANTIABORTION GROUP'S PRESS CONFERENCE IN BUFFALO, NEW YORK.

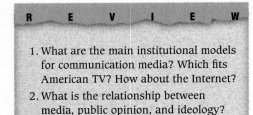

R E V I E W

1. What are the main institutional models for communication media? Which fits American TV? How about the Internet?
2. What is the relationship between media, public opinion, and ideology?
3. What are gatekeepers and the agenda setters? What is the difference?

to call attention to themselves or the grievances of the groups they represent.

A last key issue in influences on media content is how media professionals are trained and developed (McQuail, 1987). In their professional socialization, what values and ideas are encouraged? Do they develop a sense of social responsibility? Should media programmers weigh each potentially profitable, popular project in terms of whether it will be good or bad for society? Should record producers think about the social consequences of issuing songs with lyrics that refer to killing policemen? Or should they say that the artists have a right to say what they want and the public has the right to choose whether to listen?

CONTENT ISSUES

Looking at the content of electronic media is what most of us do regularly as audiences and consumers. However, studying and understanding that content is much more difficult and controversial. Some people have tried to be scientific about studying content. They've looked at how often certain kinds of actions take place or how often certain themes occur in various media. Researchers have examined depictions of such things as sex roles, teenage sexuality, driving behavior, race, and violence. Counting and quantitatively analyzing certain aspects of mass media can be useful. The easiest approach is simply to count certain kinds of specific acts, events, or roles for people. It is fairly easy to count acts of violence, drunk driving, sexual harassment, and other negative behaviors that people are concerned about showing on media. It is somewhat more complex to quantify the kinds of roles in which people are shown. For instance, it is one thing to count the times that women are shown as homemakers rather than executives, but it is another to say whether women are being shown negatively or positively in those roles.

Another limit to this type of content analysis is that we don't know whether any given member of the audience would intepret things the same way the researchers do. To avoid this problem, researchers often count only the clearest, most obviously agreed-on things, such as how many women newscasters there are and how many women are cited as authorities in news stories.

In the debate over violence on television, critics such as Action for Children's Television cite statistics on how many acts of violence occur in different kinds of programs. Knowing that a child sees thousands of acts of violence on the screen has led some American lawmakers to propose controls over violence in television content. However, industry spokespersons, such as movie industry spokesman Jack Valenti, have argued that most media violence is not realistic or harmful. They say that sheer counting of violent acts is not adequate; we must distinguish between types of violence in film and television content.

Some theorists, such as Horace Newcombe (1992) andRobert Allen (1992), feel that this kind of content analysis is not particularly useful and instead have looked at electronic media as a new kind of literature and applied traditions of literary criticism. This approach tends

Genres are types or formats of media content.

to focus on **genres,** or types or formats, of content, such as horror, mystery, and science fiction. Traditional literary theories and criticism have focused on analysis of stories, kinds of stories, and the ideas, background and intentions of the author/producer. Within this tradition, media analysts look at styles of writing or production, storytelling conventions, themes, and characterizations. With film and television, critics also look at visual images, cuts, pacing, sound, music, editing techniques, and special effects. These create a narrative, or story, that can be looked at as a whole or broken down into parts.

Analysts such as Ellen Seiter (1992) and Arthur Berger (1992a, 1992b) look at both verbal and visual symbols in media, often called **semiotics**. In semiotic analysis, the parts of media messages or productions, such as words, sounds, and images, can be interpreted individually as **signs**, or symbols. These signs can carry separate messages, as when a musical theme announces that the hero of the film is about to appear, or can modify other images, as when an actor's face is lit from below to appear more frightening. The sign has two components, a concept or the thing signified, and a sound-image or signifier.

A media program, article, or performance can be thought of as a **text**. Berger (1992b) gives the example of a *Star Trek* episode as a text, which is a system of signs. The meaning of the episode (or of a magazine article or other text) comes from the signs and the narrative system that ties them together.

Two separate aspects of signs are important: how they are **encoded** and how they are **decoded**. The encoding is by the author or producer of the content, who has certain intentions about how he or she wants the audience or receiver to interpret a particular sign. For example, romantic music in an old movie is probably supposed to convey genuine passion and romantic tension. Receivers decode signs in their own way, in their own context, relying on their own previous experience. Thus, if the audience for the old movie is modern teenagers, with their own set of music interests and exposure, they may interpret the soundtrack as corny and funny, not romantic.

Genres in Electronic Media

In books, radio, film, and television, content is usually described in terms of genres, or formats. Many kinds of formulas or genres are found in the electronic media. Viewers have become used to looking through television program schedules or movie listings for things like soap operas, action adventures, detective shows, and situation comedies. These kinds of formulas rise and fall over time. Television in the 1950s and 1960s had more westerns, like *Bonanza* or *Rawhide,* than in the 1970s or 1980s. Standup comedy was popular on television in the 1950s, faded for a while, and returned in the 1990s, especially on cable TV channels like HBO.

Analyzing these formulas or genres and how they change is one of the best ways to understand how American culture changes along with television. Chapters 7 (on print media), 8 (on audio and radio), and 9 (on film and television) explore in detail the development of specific genres in those media.

In another view, genres are conventions or formulas that evolve out of the interaction between the producers (the producer, director, writers, actors, technicians) and the audience over time (Allen, 1992). Since before written history, first oral poetry, stories, and music, then novels, films, recorded music, radio, and television have been developing specific types of genres or formulas for increasingly different kinds of audiences. For example, the centuries-old form or idea of the novel in literature has been broken down into a number of genres, including murder mysteries, spy stories, thrillers, science fiction, horror, and gothic romances, which are all still novels but very different genres. Most genre novels are now labeled specifically on their spines or covers so that would-be readers know that they are getting science fiction as opposed to gothic romance.

In the silent film era, there were historical pictures, action adventures, mysteries, horror films, comedies, westerns, and spy stories. Sound added musicals and concert films and

Semiotics is the science of signs, of how meaning is generated in media "texts."

Signs are the carriers of meaning in media "texts."

Texts are media contents and events, such as films, television programs, magazine articles, or performances.

Encoding is the creation of a text containing certain signs and meanings.

Decoding is the reading of the text by the audience or reader.

diversified the kinds of comedies that could be made. In radio, still other genres developed, such as soap operas, traditional operas, variety shows, programs devoted to specific kinds of music, situation comedies, quiz shows, game shows, talent contests, and others. Many of those genres, along with their writers, directors, musicians, and stars, moved to television when the new medium developed in the 1940s and 1950s.

Genres in Information Services

We are also beginning to see genres develop in information services as well. For instance, certain kinds of video and computer games are developing into categories. Some games involve fighting and obstacles; some are Dungeons and Dragons–style adventures in mazes; others simulate airplane flight or aerial combat; still others have the players solve mysteries. Some of these games are becoming prominent enough in popular culture that they cross over into film and television. For example, the geography and detective computer game *Where in the World is Carmen Sandiego?* became a PBS television quiz show for children and teenagers, while the video game *Super Mario Brothers* served as the basis for both a TV series and a movie.

SOCIETAL FUNCTIONS OF MEDIA AND INFORMATION SERVICES

Mass media content has important functions for us as a society and as individuals. The functions of media content link messages and audiences. For any society to exist, a number of communication functions have to be carried out. We have to keep track of what is going on around us—what researchers call surveillance. We have to put observations and ideas together, correlate them, and interpret what they mean. We have to transmit values from one generation or group to another, so we know how to get along with each other. We also need and want to be entertained and amused.

The following discussion of social functions of mass media is based on theories developed by Charles Wright (1974) and other media sociologists.

Surveillance

If you were to keep a detailed diary of all the specific pieces of information that you need and seek out over the course of a day, you would be staggered by the complexity and diversity of the information that you take in. Certain mass media specialize in providing information to help people with their surveillance of the environment, including newspapers, news magazines, national and local TV news broadcasts, CNN, Headline News, The Weather Channel, and C-Span.

Some information surveillance functions have moved to newer, more interactive media. Most of the functions of new computer-based interactive technologies are for information exchange or retrieval and could replace mass media for much of our surveillance of the environment.

Interpretation

Information is not of much use to us until it is processed, interpreted, and correlated with what we already know. We have to decide how the information might be useful or discard it. Does it fit with what we know? Does it contradict or add something new? How important is the new information compared to what we already thought we knew? While we do much of this analysis for ourselves, aided by the groups we belong to, the media also help provide much of the interpretation and meaning we associate with information.

Mass media and information services are both important in the interpretive function. Mass media offer content that lends itself to guiding interpretation—television documentaries tell us why a situation or crisis developed, soap operas tell us what families, professions, and lifestyles are supposed to look like. However, information technologies permit people with narrower common interests to discuss and share them, reinforcing world views and values. For example, people call like-minded people on the telephone to help interpret what they saw on television.

Value Transmission/Socialization

One of the most important functions of human culture is to enable us to pass on ideas, values, techniques, and knowledge from one generation to another. Anthropologists observe that as soon as human beings had language, they were using it to pass on ideas and ways of doing things to our children. People memorized complex legal codes, long genealogies, myths, ways of navigating the ocean, and ways of calculating mathematics, and they passed this information on to successors and children. Writing helped make this process much more sophisticated, as more complex and detailed things could be written down and passed along. Other media have likewise added new layers of knowledge and images that can be passed down to subsequent generations.

Mass media have changed the process of value transmission and socialization. When human cultures were exclusively oral or verbal, individuals learned things primarily from their parents or relatives, or from local teachers, priests, storytellers, and others who lived near them and were probably very much like them. As a result, villages quite near each other could have fairly different dialects, mythologies, foods, marriage customs, and so on. Today media have assumed many of the traditional roles of storyteller, teacher, and even parents (see Figure 2.3). With mass media, people all over a nation—or in the case of some particular books, films, songs, or shows, all over the world—are hearing some of the same stories, ideas, and values. For instance, many experts think that American movies were important in the early 1900s in helping a diverse mass of immigrants and their children learn what they were supposed to do to be an American. Before movies, many of those people would probably have kept longer to their old ways from their home countries.

Nearly all media are involved in the function of value transmission. News media stories reflect

FIGURE 2.3
CHILDREN USE TELEVISION TO HELP LEARN AND INTERPRET THE KINDS OF ROLES PEOPLE ARE SUPPOSED TO PERFORM, BUT THEY DO NOT THINK ALL TELEVISION PORTRAYALS ARE VERY REALISTIC. THIS GRAPH SHOWS HOW REALISTICALLY SIXTH GRADERS AND TENTH GRADERS IN A 1989 STUDY THOUGHT TELEVISION PORTRAYED JOBS (DOCTORS, POLICE, LAWYERS), FAMILIES (MOTHERS, FATHERS, BROTHERS, SISTERS), AND PEOPLE (MEN, WOMEN, CHILDREN, OLD PEOPLE, WHITES, BLACKS). IN THE SURVEY, A RATING OF 1 MEANT THAT THE CHILD AGREED A LOT THAT THE PORTRAYAL WAS REALISTIC, WHILE 4 MEANT THAT HE OR SHE DISAGREED A LOT. OVERALL, YOUNGER CHILDREN AGREED WITH TELEVISION PORTRAYALS MORE THAN DID OLDER CHILDREN, ESPECIALLY WITH PORTRAYALS OF FAMILIES AND PEOPLE IN GENERAL. SUCH ROLES PORTRAYED ON TV ARE ONE MEANS OF SOCIALIZATION FOR CHILDREN.

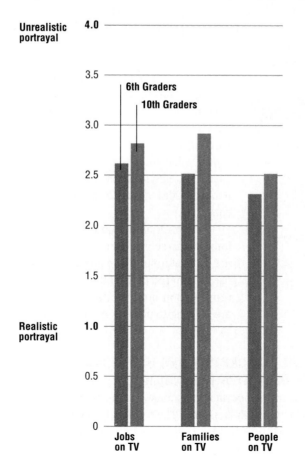

certain values, and media editorials often explicitly express the values or attitudes of the owner or editorial writer. Entertainment-oriented media may be even more important in the values-transmission function, since they are the storytellers of modern societies. Many of the arguments about values in America in the 1990s revolve around what is being portrayed in mass media. Do some kinds of movies make men think that violence against women is all right or at least compellingly interesting? Do some television talk shows promote sexual values that many people disagree with? As mass media become more targeted, narrowcast, and differentiated, we might wonder whether the values that are transmitted by narrowly targeted channels might be equally fragmented and differentiated. If one person watches only PBS and another only MTV, what common values are being transmitted?

Entertainment

Perhaps the most common daily function of mass media is to entertain. Most media space and most audience time is spent on entertainment. Many of the shared experiences of most Americans involve media entertainment: major films, popular songs, and network television programs. For generations now, for example, much of the group identity of young people has been built around the kind of music they like.

Most of the time that Americans spend on mass media is used for entertainment. With the exception of the magazine-style information program *60 Minutes* on CBS, the top ten programs on network television have been predominantly entertainment programs. Americans spend enormous amounts of time and money on going to feature films, listening to music, renting videos, and watching television action and comedy programs. One of the reasons American media program producers and schedulers put so much emphasis on entertainment is that "it's what the audience wants."

Ever since the telephone came along, some interactive media have also been used as much for entertainment as for business or professional purposes. In the 1990s, much discussion has been devoted to making cable TV more interactive and making telephone-based services more entertaining. While some of the interactivity will be used to obtain information and services, such as banking from home, industry experts agree that the real economic payoff will come if highly popular forms of interactive entertainment, based on television and computers, can be developed, such as more realistic video games and interactive novels where you can play a character.

It seems that the contents of both mass media and interactive information services serve many of the same social functions. Both are used for information or surveillance of the environment, and both are used to interpret that information. Mass media have dominated value transmission and entertainment functions, but information services are starting to become more important in these areas.

R E V I E W

1. What kinds of content have been most controversial in television?
2. What are signs or symbols in media content? List some examples.
3. What are genres, and how do they develop?
4. How have television genres changed since the 1950s?
5. Who encodes the messages in a television program or a newspaper story? Who decodes them?

INDIVIDUAL RECEPTION AND USE OF MASS MEDIA AND INFORMATION TECHNOLOGY

One of the most important questions we can ask about mass media is, just how powerful are the media over their audience? The parallel question that we must focus on here is just how

active or **passive** the audience is toward the media messages they receive. The experts don't agree. Some think the media are more powerful, others think audiences are more powerful. We will look at some of the main arguments.

Media Power Versus Audience Power

Much of the original research about media audiences before and after World War II concerned whether the extensive **propaganda** on radio and film that various nations used during the war had affected the audiences. Some experts, like Adorno and Horkheimer (1972), saw powerful media as an explanation for some of the violent and brutal acts that had happened during the war. Today many experts believe that media tend to be powerful while audiences are vulnerable and passive (Schiller, 1976). They see media as powerful carriers of ideology that tend to impose the interests and ideas of governments, economic interests, and other ruling groups on those they govern and rule. Others argue that the audience is in fact not passive in the face of powerful media.

A popular notion in current cultural studies is that media and audiences are both powerful and that it is the *interaction* of media and audiences that creates meaning and shapes our culture. Thus, neither the media nor the audience impose meanings over the other.

Audiences and Meaning

One interesting view of the audience reception process builds on the idea of **reading**. Media producers, writers, and directors create *texts* (which include radio, music, television, and film as well as written texts) that audiences *read* (which includes watching and listening). Creators of media content *do* usually put in messages that they intend the audience to get. They probably have a **preferred reading** that they would like the audience to take out of the text. However, the audience won't necessarily accept or even perceive that preferred reading. The audience might reject it, **negotiate** some compromise interpretation between what they think and what the text is saying, or **contest** what the text says with some alternative interpretation, thus actively resisting what the media are trying to tell them (Morley, 1992).

For example, during the confirmation hearings of Clarence Thomas for the U.S. Supreme Court in 1991, a number of people watched and read the testimony of Anita Hill that Thomas had sexually harassed her. Those people apparently "read" the messages in various different ways, in accordance with their own backgrounds, preoccupations, and interests. According to polls and media coverage, a number of women were outraged about the continuing prevalence of sexual harassment and became much more active in politics in 1991–1992. A number of black viewers felt that both Hill and Thomas, as African Americans, were being unfairly depicted and highlighted. A number of corporate executives decided that sexual harassment in the workplace was a potentially explosive issue for their own companies and created corporate behavior codes to reduce or deal with it. And all over the United States, many people argued about just how real a threat sexual harassment in the workplace really is, and what should be done about it.

Gratifications That Media Audiences and Information Users Seek

According to the uses and gratifications approach, people are active and selective in media use. They anticipate which media and which media contents will be more useful or gratifying for their specific needs or purposes. They then seek out and attend to those particular media.

Active audiences are selective in use of media, interpret media messages in their own way, and are not necessarily affected by media contents.

Passive audiences are not selective, readily accept media messages, and are easily, almost automatically affected by them.

Propaganda is media content aimed to persuade people to accept an idea or ideology.

Reading is the overall process by which audiences receive, interpret, and make sense of media content and events.

Preferred reading is the interpretation that the producer of some media content or text intends the audience to get.

Negotiated reading occurs when the audience makes their own interpretation of media content, accepting some of the producer's ideas but not others.

Contested reading occurs when the audience rejects the producer's preferred reading.

People's media use evolves as they discover which media gratify their needs and which nonmedia experiences may be more gratifying, as new media and information service options arise and as their own needs change over time.

One thing that keeps some media relatively "massive" is that many people read or tune in to them for similar purposes. Most people approach mass media for a common set of uses (and gratifications). These uses include cognition (things they wish to learn), diversion (entertainment and relaxation), and social utility. We will look at each.

Cognition. Cognition is usually associated with learning information or news. It is associated with the surveillance function of media. This function usually breaks down further into two more specific uses: to keep up on current events, and to learn about longer-term trends and things in general. The media therefore provide both headlines/top stories and long-run trends/general information.

Both mass media and information services meet cognitive needs for information. Newspapers, radio, and television news now compete with computer- and telephone-based information sources.

Diversion. Many people think of media primarily as a diversion from other, less pleasurable activities. They need relief from routine or boredom, distraction by things different from life as usual, stimulation with new or different ideas or events, escape from daily life stresses and challenges, and release of pent-up emotions. Much of the diversion function of media is associated with entertainment.

Television and films tend to be the main entertainment media for diversion. Their combinations of sound, images, and motion are more stimulating to multiple senses than many other media can provide. But other media can also be relaxing, escapist, and stress relieving. Some people relax best by reading or listening to music, not watching a film or television. Some people relax to Bach, others to heavy metal. Information technologies can provide these same gratifications. Thus, some people relax by talking on the telephone, some by playing video games.

Some of the new interactive media seem to be developing content very similar to that of mass media and meet with similar uses. For instance, people who like science fiction books or films also seem to gravitate toward science fiction scenarios in video games or interactive word-based computer games, such as Adventure or Zork.

Social Utility. People sometimes use media to meet or supplement social needs, such as the need to feel contact with other people, to be integrated into society. Mass media give many people occasions and conversational material for social interaction. Just as people used to get together and talk about the folks who lived down the street, we now get together with others who live miles away from us and gossip about soap opera stars or baseball players whom we watch on television. Some isolated people even tend to substitute media use for social interaction. Older people find that television fills time that was once spent with families. Many people even feel attached to media figures as if they knew them personally. One of our students once joked that she saw more of Madonna (through the media) than she did of her own grandmother.

People also use new interactive media to continue or even extend social contacts. Individuals have been using the telephone for many

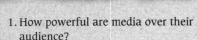

REVIEW

1. How powerful are media over their audience?
2. What makes an audience active or passive?
3. What are the main kinds of "readings" that audiences might make of media?
4. What are the main uses and gratifications of media?

```
From: AIGAHV@aol.com
To: johnodomacts.com
Date: Mon, 26 Sep 94 17:25:41 EDT
Subject: Got your message

Hi John.
Got your message on sunday.

I saw Bonnie on Friday at the AIGA President's Council meeting. She looked
great.

I went to the overpriced and under attended AIGA National Business
Conference: Strategies for Change, or How You Might Be Able to Avoid a
Nervous Breakdown in the Age of Digit, or How to Avoid Going Broke While You
Muts.

Like most of these events, there were highs and lows. All-in-all very
provocative. The personal relationships remain my primary source of
inspiration and insight.
```

E-MAIL NOW SERVES A SOCIAL FUNCTION THAT WAS ONCE FILLED ONLY BY THE TELEPHONE, LETTER WRITING, AND FACE-TO-FACE CONVERSATION.

Diffusion is the process whereby innovations spread in a social system.

Innovation is a new idea, technology, or way of doing things.

years to maintain social contacts with family and friends. Telephones enable both periodic contact with people who are very distant and frequent contact with people who are close by—business colleagues, family members, and others. Electronic mail has opened up whole new avenues of social interaction. Many users of electronic mail are developing extensive networks of contacts and friends whom they may never meet and whose voices and faces they have never heard or seen; they interact only over electronic networks, exchanging notes and letters.

DIFFUSION OF MEDIA AND INFORMATION TECHNOLOGIES

Media and information technologies are useful only when they are accepted by individuals and organizations. Research on the diffusion of innovations has discovered some predictable patterns about who starts using a new technology or idea, when, and why. In the most general sense, **diffusion** is a process by which an **innovation** (a new way of doing things) is communicated through certain channels (both mass media and interpersonal) over time (usually years) among the members of a social system (whether a corporation or the entire United States). This approach has proved to be one of the most useful in describing how new media and information technologies get accepted and used.

For example, researcher Everett Rogers (1986) observed that VCRs diffused very quickly in the United States, going from 1 percent of American households in 1980 to 20 percent in 1985 to 70 percent in 1993. Prices declined rapidly, from $2,200 in 1975 to $300 in 1985 to under $200 in 1993, which made VCRs more accessible. Recording of programs was easy, attractive, and legal. The availability of prerecorded tapes for rental or purchase also grew rapidly, from 14,000 in 1985 to over 100,000 in 1993.

People learned about VCRs from news magazines, television, television guides, newspapers, and, after the early 1980s, from friends. Most people found both recording programs for later playback and playing recorded tapes of movies to be satisfying supplements to regular television watching. The simultaneous diffusion of subscriptions to cable TV also reinforced VCR usage, since there was now more material to record off the cable. As people observed more and more of their friends with VCRs, almost everyone wanted one.

Criteria for Technology Diffusion

How well an innovation diffuses depends on what kind of new idea or technology it is. Some basic questions apply to virtually all new ideas: What is the *relative advantage* of the new idea compared to existing ways of doing things? What is the *compatibility* of the new idea with existing ways of doing things? How *complex* is the new technology or idea—how difficult is it to learn? How easy is it to *try out* the new way before committing a lot of time or money to it? Can people *observe* some other similar situations where others are already successfully using this new way of doing things?

On all these counts, VCRs scored very highly, and therefore they spread rapidly. The VCR offered a clear expansion of viewing options, was compatible with both television hardware and movie/TV "software" or content, was similar in concept to older tape-recorder technology, and was easy to use (except perhaps for timed delayed recording). And by the mid-1980s most people had a chance to watch family and friends using them.

Certain prior conditions can affect diffusion of innovations. One is the amount of previous practice or experience people have had with similar technologies. For example, among the first people to use portable cellular telephones in their cars were those who had already used mobile radios to talk to other drivers or to people in their companies. Another condition is what felt needs or problems need to be solved. Cellular telephones were also first sold to traveling salespeople who needed to confirm appointments and do business while driving around. A third prior condition is people willing to be innovative. Even among traveling salespeople, some are more inclined to try out new gadgets than others. Finally, the norms of the social system play a role. Mobile phones went from being associated with blue-collar delivery truck drivers to being chic for executives and salespeople.

Some kinds of ideas and technologies can be adopted by individuals, others have to be adopted by organizations. For example, many individual businesspeople decided on their own to buy personal computers for writing letters and making business plans. However, when these same individuals want to use their computers to send electronic mail to each other, they either have to be in large companies with central computers that can switch messages to other people, or as independent businesspeople they have to buy E-mail services from companies like America Online or Prodigy. E-mail also works best when companies encourage most of their employees to use it, so that people know that they can reach most people that way.

The extent of diffusion also depends on the kind of social system or organization into which an innovation is being introduced. Is there sufficient money or other resources available to try out new ideas without risking the success or failure of the whole organization? Does the existing pattern of communication and behavior favor change or oppose it? These factors can ease or thwart the adoption of an idea or technology.

Stages of Diffusion

Diffusion of new communication technology goes through certain stages (see Figure 2.4). The potential adopters of the new technology or idea:

FIGURE 2.4
SOME PEOPLE ADOPT NEW IDEAS EARLIER THAN OTHERS. THE MAJORITY OF PEOPLE TEND TO ADOPT ONLY AFTER INNOVATORS AND EARLY ADOPTERS HAVE TRIED SOMETHING OUT.

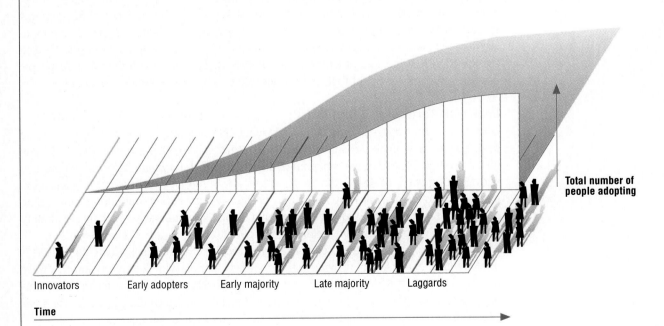

Innovators   Early adopters   Early majority   Late majority   Laggards

Total number of people adopting

Time

1. Gain knowledge about the new idea.

2. Get persuaded to try it.

3. Make a decision to try it.

4. Implement or try out that decision.

5. Confirm, reject, or modify their use of the idea.

People do not adopt new ideas at the same rates. Those who first figure out how to use a new technology or idea to accomplish something are called *innovators*. People who follow up on innovative ideas through specialized media such as trade journals or interpersonal contacts are called *early adopters*. Those who perceive a trend relatively early and decide to go with it are called the *early majority*. Those who wait to see what most people are going to do are called the *late majority*. Those who wait until the very end have been called, somewhat pejoratively, *laggards*.

New interactive communication technologies tend to diffuse in characteristic ways (Williams, 1987). First, a certain minimum number, or **critical mass**, of adopters and users of a new technology are necessary for it to be useful enough for most people to go along with. Second, the issue is often not acquiring the technology but rather how much people are actually using it. Third, because both computers and telecommunications technologies are relatively flexible tools, they tend to be used in new, unanticipated ways. Everett Rogers (1986) calls this **reinvention**. For instance, in the late 1970s and early 1980s, many offices introduced word processing via centralized computers with terminals that sat on a secretary's desk, creating an electronic extension of the old-fashioned secretarial typing pool. However, many typists wanted more flexibility, and many professionals began to use their own personal computers to do first drafts of documents. Both of these trends led to reinventing word processing into something very different from what the innovators had originally pushed.

Critical mass is the minimum number of users required for a collectively used technology to be useful and to take off.

Reinvention is the process in which users of a technology or idea create new ways to use it beyond those initially anticipated.

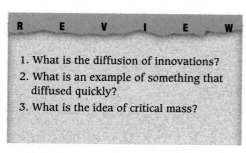

R E V I E W

1. What is the diffusion of innovations?
2. What is an example of something that diffused quickly?
3. What is the idea of critical mass?

SUMMARY & REVIEW

What Are the Main Institutional Models of Communication Media?

What are the main theories of mass media?
Mass media theories combine the economic organization of media and the overall political philosophy of media in different societies. The models include the authoritarian, in which government controls the media; developmental, in which media are supposed to cooperate with government; free press/libertarian, in which media are as free as possible; and social responsibility, which emphasizes media and media professionals behaving responsibly.

What are the main ownership patterns for media?
Media can be structured as monopolies, where one company dominates the industry; as oligopolies, where a few companies dominate; or in competition, where a number of companies or institutions vie for dominance.

Who sets the agenda for the media?
Governments, economic interests, political interest groups, and others try to create an agenda for what the media cover and what interpretation media give to their coverage. Underlying the day-to-day specific agendas is a set of assumptions about what is good for society that form the hegemony, or consensus of opinion. Media also help to set the agenda

for government and for society at large, so the battle to control media can be quite important.

Who acts as the decision maker or gatekeeper to decide what gets in the media?
Within the media themselves, a variety of media professionals make decisions at different levels to decide what goes into or stays out of newspapers, radio and television news, situation comedies, talk shows, and so on. Part of what affects gatekeeping is how media professionals are trained to act, what they consider to be news-worthy, what they consider tasteful, and what they think the audience wants.

What Are the Main Content Issues in Media Theory?

Is it better to look at media content by classifying and counting things, or by looking at symbols?
Certain kinds of observing and counting media contents can be useful. For instance, if we are worried about the effects of media violence, it is useful to know how much violence is actually shown on television. On the other hand, it is also useful to know what deeper meanings or implications media symbols have.

What is semiotics, and what are signs?
Semiotics is a systematic way of looking at media content, to examine the symbols and signs contained in it. The signs in media include visual images, music, camera angles, words, and so on that communicate something of symbolic value to the audience. The producer creates or encodes a meaning into the sign, but the audience may decode or interpret a different meaning.

What are genres in media?
In media content, formulas, or genres, evolve over time. These formulas are things like soap operas, mystery novels, and action cartoons.

They represent an agreement between producer and audience on what kinds of stories ought to be told and how, on how a music video ought to look, or on how a talk show host ought to act.

What Are the Social Functions of Communications Media?

What functions do different kinds of media content serve for society?
Among the functions of both mass and information media are surveillance, keeping track of one's world or environment; interpretation, making sense of information we learn; value transmission, passing values on from one generation to the next; and entertainment.

How Do Individuals Receive and Use Communication Media?

How powerful are media over their audience?
Some experts see media as very powerful and audiences as passive or easily influenced. However, most studies tend to show that audiences read the "texts" of media in a fairly active way. Nevertheless, the balance of power between media and audiences in forming meanings and influencing behavior is hotly debated.

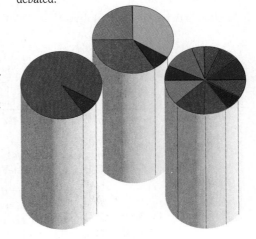

What are the main kinds of "readings" that audiences might make of media?
Some audience members might accept the "preferred" meaning or the reading that the writer or producer intended them to get out of the text. Others might use their own experiences and ideas to negotiate their own meaning out of their reading of the material. Others might contest or even oppose the meaning that the original creator intended.

Why do people use particular media?
Similar to the functions they serve for society at large, media and information technologies serve certain functions for individuals, including cognition (learning new things), diversion (entertainment), and social utility (substituting for real interactions with people). People also seek out particular media contents for specific uses and get specific gratifications from them.

How Do Media and Information Technologies Diffuse?

How do new information technologies spread in a society?
New technologies, ideas, and ways of doing things diffuse among members of society in predictable ways. There are patterns to when and how people decide to use something new. They look for relative advantage, compatibility, low complexity, and the ability to observe the idea in use or try it out themselves. Some people are innovators, some are early adopters, and some are laggards.

What is different about diffusion of innovations in organizations?
When organizations adopt information technologies, it is the result of a collective decision, rather than a series of individual ones. There also has to be a critical mass of users for things such as electronic mail before most will want to use it.

REFERENCES

Adorno, T., & Horkheimer, M. (1972). The culture industry: Englightenment as mass deception. In *The Dialectics of Enlightenment.* New York: Herder and Herder.

Allen, R. C. (1992). *Channels of discourse, reassembled.* Chapel Hill: University of North Carolina Press.

Altheide, D. (1974). *Creating reality.* Beverly Hills: Sage.

Altshull, H. (1984). *Agents of power.* New York: Longman.

Berger, A. A. (1992a). *Media analysis techniques.* Newbury Park, CA: Sage.

Berger, A. A. (1992b). *Popular culture genres.* Newbury Park, CA: Sage.

Gandy, O. H. (1982). *Beyond agenda setting: Information subsidies and public policy.* Norwood, NJ: Ablex.

Gitlin, T. (1983). *Inside prime time.* New York: Pantheon Books.

Gramsci, A. (1971). *Selections from the prison notebooks.* New York: International Publishers.

McQuail, D. (1987). *Mass communications theory—An introduction* (2nd ed.). Beverly Hills: Sage.

Morley, D. (1992). *Television, audiences and cultural studies.* New York: Routledge.

Mosco, V. (1989). *The pay-per society: Computers and communication in the information age.* Norwood, NJ: Ablex.

Newcombe, H. (1992). *Television: A critical view.* New York: Oxford University Press.

Noam, E. (1983). *Telecommunications regulation today and tomorrow.* New York: Law and Business.

Rogers, E. (1986). *Communication technology—The new media in society.* New York: Free Press.

Schiller, H. I. (1976). *Communication and cultural domination.* Armonk, NY: Sharpe.

Seiter, E. (1992). Semiotics, structuralism, and television. In R. C. Allen (Ed.), *Channels of discourse, reassembled.* Chapel Hill: University of North Carolina Press.

Shoemaker, P. (1991). *Gatekeeping.* Newbury Park, CA: Sage.

Siebert, F. S., Peterson, T., & Schramm, W. (1956). *Four theories of the press.* Urbana: University of Illinois Press.

White, D. N. (1949). The gate-keeper: A case study in the selection of news. *Journalism Quarterly, 27.*

Wright, C. R. (1974). Functional analysis and mass communications revisited. In J. G. Blumler & E. Katz (Eds.), *The uses of mass communications.* Beverly Hills: Sage.

Chapter 3

THE EVOLUTION OF THE INFORMATION SOCIETY

C H A P T E R P R E V I E W

n this chapter, we will put the information society into historical context. We will look at the stages of agricultural, industrial, and information society to understand how media technologies and industries both depend on and revolutionize the economy, society, politics, culture, and even religion. In earlier times, writing, printing, and radio led to changes probably as profound as those currently under way.

Back to the Future—Technology Revolutions Then and Now

Leicestershire, England, 1779

Ned Lud smashed two textile weaving frames belonging to his employer. He was afraid the new technology might put him out of work.

England, 1811–1816

People calling themselves Luddites smashed new labor-saving textile machinery, protesting against the reduced wages and increased unemployment they thought the new technology was bringing. They also disliked technologies that let some people work at home, since home workers often worked for less.

Detroit, Michigan, 2010

Hello, DeeVee. Anything for me today?

There is a data entry job from your old office at Gigantic Motors. One hundred purchase-record scans to verify and enter.

What does it pay?

Twenty dollars for the 100 of them.

How long does a job like that take me?

Analyzing your last job, it will take you four hours.

That's not too good. I could almost do better at Taco Duke, but I guess I'll take it.

Downloading the scans. They're in window one. Do you still want the "Days of Our Lives" channel in window two?

Sure. Can you look up the address of the nearest branch of the New Luddite Party for me? Something's gotta change here.

Aspen, Colorado, 2010

Good morning, DeeVee. What's my schedule today?

You have a work session on the Fragel account at 9 A.M. with Jan in Santa Barbara and Fred in Denver. Then a videoconference to present the project to the Fragel people in New York at 11 A.M. Then virtual lunch with your wife in Taipei. Then you scheduled time to do your taxes, with your on-line accountant.

(Groan) Well, at least I get to look at the mountains in between. Give me a five-minute warning before Jan and Fred. I'd like to watch the Idaho Fly Fishing Channel until then.

ne of the main questions in history is, which factors lead to which changes? Many experts conclude that in the development of communications media, new technologies change everything else. This approach could be called **technological determinism**. Over thirty years ago, Marshall McLuhan forcefully argued just how important, even revolutionary, first print (*The Gutenberg Galaxy*, 1962) and later broadcasting (*Understanding Media*, 1965) had been. He suggested that these two innovations had completely changed society, although other experts have proposed that media were just one piece in a larger puzzle. Some theorists have revived McLuhan's technological determinism to analyze the apparently revolutionary impact of current technology and the convergence of mass media and information media; but these, too, take place in a larger context.

Technological determinism is the idea that technological change tends to determine all other economic and social changes.

Industrialization of culture is changing both high (classical) culture and folk culture into a mass culture.

What we often think of as "technologies," such as "television," are in reality complex arrangements of technology, economics, policy, and social forces. In fact, the contexts of technology are often more important than the hardware itself. In this chapter we are going to look primarily at how economic, political, and social forces shaped or even determined the development of current and new communications media.

We also examine the implications of the industrialization of media and the changes that may go beyond mass industrialization. Some critics have charged that this process has also led to the **industrialization of culture,** changing both high (classical) culture and folk culture. Other critics have suggested that, largely because of continuing media and information technology changes, society is fragmenting into a postmodern collection of local and group views and identities.

ECONOMIC, HISTORICAL, AND POLITICAL STAGES OF DEVELOPMENT

Communications media have gone through several stages of development. The evolution of these media has depended a great deal on developments in the economies and societies around them. We could not have had mass media, for instance, before the Industrial Revolution made mass production and dissemination of books, newspapers, radio, and television possible.

Some researchers, such as Daniel Bell (1973) and Wilson Dizard (1990), write that the more developed societies have gone or are going through three stages: (1) agricultural society, (2) industrial society, and (3) information society.

Stages of development reflect changes in society that link technology, economics, politics, culture, and media together.

Identifying such **stages of development** is a way of deliberately simplifying and joining complex issues so that technological, economic, social, political, cultural, and media changes are linked. This approach can be useful, but it requires some skepticism. Some of the popular books, such as John Naisbitt's *Megatrends* (1984) and Alvin Toffler's *The Third Wave* (1980), describe stages of growth and directions of change that are probably too neat and clear. History tends to be too complex to easily yield to such straightforward analysis. For example, growth stages based on the history of the United States or Europe do not necessarily apply well to Eastern Europe or to Third World countries. Because these nations are usually not very industrialized and many are stuck in roles in the world economy that may never permit them to become very industrialized, these stages are unlikely to apply to them.

Stages are not exclusive—they frequently coexist. Most societies today have a mix of agricultural, industrial, and informational components in their economies. For example, U.S. agriculture is still very successful precisely because it has changed with industrial and information inputs and techniques. Despite the fact that less than 3 percent of its work force is in agriculture, the United States is one of the world's major food exporters.

Economic Stages

The fundamental basis of most stages of growth is economic. Economic stages are measured by several key indicators, including the key sector of the economy involved, the dominant mode of production, and the fields in which most people are employed. The **key sector of economy** is the most important factor in driving the whole economy to growth. For thousands of years that key sector was agriculture. More recently, from the late 1700s in some countries, the key sector of the economy has been industry. Since the 1960s or 1970s, the key sector of the U.S. economy has been information. For example, media and information are rapidly overtaking aerospace technology as the main U.S. export.

Mode of production refers to the major ways that work is done and money is made. In most early societies and in less developed economies, the main mode is the extraction of food, supplies, and goods directly from nature, such as with agriculture and mining. After 1850, America shifted into a second mode of production: fabrication or manufacturing. By the 1950s, much of the U.S. economy was already devoted to creating information.

Where most people are employed and what kinds of skills they need is a third indicator of economic stage. Before 1850 most Americans worked in agriculture or other extractive occupations, such as lumbering, hunting, trapping, and mining. In the mid-1800s an increasing number of Americans shifted into more specialized jobs in industry. In the late 1800s, thousands of people became steelworkers in Pittsburgh and Gary, Indiana; thousands more moved to work in the automobile industries in Detroit and Flint. By 1970 almost half (48 percent) of the U.S. work force primarily created, manipulated, or sold information.

The three basic stages of economic development are summarized in Figure 3.1.

Key sector of economy is the main sector driving overall economic growth.

Mode of production refers to the ways that work is done, money is made, and people are employed.

FIGURE 3.1
THE THREE BASIC STAGES OF ECONOMIC DEVELOPMENT, FROM AGRICULTURAL TO INDUSTRIAL TO INFORMATIONAL.

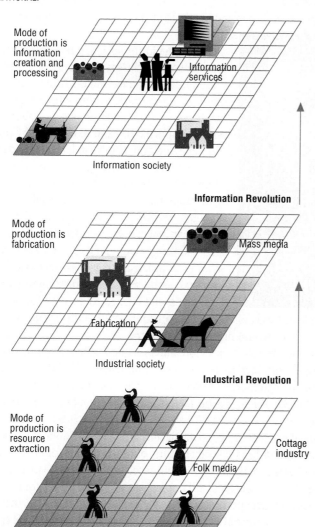

Mode of production is information creation and processing

Information services

Information society

Information Revolution

Mode of production is fabrication

Mass media

Fabrication

Industrial society

Industrial Revolution

Mode of production is resource extraction

Cottage industry

Folk media

Agricultural society

Preagricultural Societies

In preagricultural societies, most people live as hunters and gatherers. This minimal division of labor makes it relatively easy to pass on or communicate the kinds of knowledge and skills that most members of the group need, directly from person to person. Such groups are usually preliterate. However, many do have elaborate myths, genealogies, and laws or rules, which are passed along orally from generation to generation. For this reason, these are often known as **oral cultures**, with oral traditions. Many subgroups within industrialized or information societies continue to rely on oral traditions and oral communication. Many cities have illiterate dwellers who must rely on descriptions from friends instead of street signs.

Oral cultures are those that communicate primarily on the basis of spoken language.

Social stratification is the division of society into unequal groups or classes of people by wealth, education, and occupation.

Agricultural Economies

In agricultural economies most people work in farming or in extracting other resources from their environment. As these kinds of societies become more settled, they also begin to develop more specialized roles: craftspeople, warriors, priests, judges, and political leaders, and they pay more attention to communication (in the forms of storytelling, poetry, and myth).

AGRICULTURAL SOCIETIES ARE CHARACTERIZED BY PRIMARILY ORAL COMMUNICATION AND BY LESS SPECIALIZATION THAN IN INDUSTRIAL SOCIETIES.

As agricultural societies become more complex, **social stratification** occurs: people become more differentiated and less equal. More people belong to specific, nonfarming professions, becoming priests, soldiers, royal advisers and representatives, doctors, skilled craftspeople, and teachers. Few people have the time and opportunity to learn to read or write. In fact, reading and writing were specialized occupations in feudal times. A few people, often associated with religious orders, had the specialized functions of keeping records, writing and reading correspondence, and keeping and copying religious or scholarly books. In Europe most of the nobility could not read until at least the 1400s, so most communications were oral. Special couriers carefully memorized messages and carried them between leaders. Such communication was slow. News of the fall of Constantinople to the Turks in 1453 took a month to get to Venice and two months to get to Rome.

Increasing specialization requires that more and more people be able to read and write to function in their occupations. Merchants, bankers, and leaders of crafts organizations all needed to learn to read as commerce between countries and regions increased in Europe throughout the late Middle Ages. Eventually, many skills could be learned best from schooling and reading.

A largely agricultural era lasted up to the eighteenth century in most of the currently industrialized nations. In nations colonized to provide raw materials such as cotton, sugar, gold, silver, and tobacco, agriculture dominated much longer. Most colonies were intended to be sources of raw materials and markets for finished goods for the colonizing nations. Unwillingness to accept that role was part of what led to the American Revolution in 1776. An agricultural economy is still dominant in much of the recently decolonized Third World, which strongly affects the kinds of communication systems that these countries have.

PRINTING, LITERACY, AND THE PROTESTANT REFORMATION

One of the results of the religious changes building in the 1400s and 1500s was a desire by a much broader population to be able to read the Bible for themselves. This was a major point of the Protestant Reformation that began in the early 1500s. What caused what, however, is complicated, as the possibility of more cheaply reproducing the Bible for a larger audience through printing may itself have been one of the causes of the Protestant Reformation.

This example shows that the time has to be right for an invention—the economic and social contexts have to be ready to support it. But it also shows that technology can help precipitate changes that might otherwise take much longer or perhaps even go in other directions.

In this case, it seems that the new technology of mass printing helped a religious change take place in the early 1500s, whereas similar reform or change movements earlier in the Middle Ages had not had the same success. Although some were fairly large, they ultimately were stamped out by the medieval church.

AN EARLY PRINT SHOP.

Preindustrial Media

Even before the advent of printing, books were a mass medium, albeit a limited one. Several things kept books and literacy from expanding prior to the 1400s. First, before the invention of movable type and mechanical printing presses, reproducing books was very difficult. Second, a number of those in power did not particularly want the masses to be able to read. Third, the economic need for a widely literate work force had not become apparent. Only in the 1400s did more kinds of people in trades and other nonagricultural work begin to want to go to school and get information from books. Fourth, since readership prior to this time had been limited to a specialized elite, the kinds of books produced were for them (Burke, 1991).

INDUSTRIALIZATION AND MEDIA

The Gutenberg Bible first appeared in 1455, the result of Johannes Gutenberg's invention of movable metal type and mechanical printing in 1450. In Europe, explosive demand led to millions of books being printed by 1500. Prices declined dramatically. Technology continued to enable economic and social exploitation of the new medium. As printing processes became more economical, the kinds of books that could be produced for new audiences also increased.

REVIEW

1. What are the main stages of economic development?
2. What was communication like before industrial development?
3. What was the impact of printing on society?
4. What aspects of social class affect people's use of media?
5. What do we mean by mass production, mass consumption, mass media, and mass society?

Printing, Mass Media, and Society

When more books began to become available in the 1500s, the impact was profound. Literacy and reading began to change the way people thought and acted. Anthropologists have documented powerful differences between completely oral societies and literate ones (Goody and Watt, 1991). Literate cultures rely less on memory to preserve cultures and techniques, and they rely less on epic stories, myths, and images to transmit ideas from one generation to the next. These functions have been taken over by written stories, textbooks, religious writings, and (today) recorded music, television, and films. These media tend to become standardized across larger regions of time and space, with less local variation.

Public opinion is the view held by large numbers of people on specific political issues.

With literacy, the idea of **public opinion** began to take shape. People also began to think that public opinion could be molded by mass media. Political leaders as early as Oliver Cromwell in England in the 1640s used the press along with political parties and rallies to gain public support for their rule.

Urbanization, Media, and Society

Industries tended to concentrate around urban centers for convenience and ease of transportation, access to workers, access to markets, and so on. Thus, throughout the 1800s and early 1900s, large groups of people migrated from agricultural work in the countryside to industrial jobs in the cities. Urban life brought increasing numbers of people within reach of mass media. Simultaneously, people were eager to gain information that would help them get ahead in their lives.

Literacy usually refers to the number of people in a society who are able to read.

Literacy rises in industrial societies. To do their jobs, get around a city, understand product labels, and so on, urban workers need schooling to learn to read. Schooling tends to become universal among the urban population in most industrialized countries. Schools, training centers, and universities concentrate in urban areas. This has been the case in modern industrialized societies, and it is also happening in less developed countries—although many countries have worked hard to get at least elementary schools in the countryside. At the other extreme, the United States has some kind of institution of higher education, such as a community college, accessible to nearly all the population.

WITH INDUSTRIALIZATION CAME URBAN CENTERS. SHOWN HERE IS A PAINTING OF THE RIVER ROUGE PLANT OF THE FORD MOTOR COMPANY.
(Charles Sheeler, *River Rouge Plant*, 1932, oil on canvas 20 × 24¹/₈ in. [50.8 × 61.3 cm.]. collection of Whitney Museum of American Art, purchase, 32.43.)

As industrial jobs brought people to cities, politics became urban-centered and in many countries became more democratic. Some experts, such as Daniel Lerner (1958) who has written about development in the Middle East, link industrial work, urbanization, literacy, and media use into a pattern that leads to greater democracy in the long run. A number of poorer, developing countries have tried to use this model as a road map for economic and political development, but the results have been mixed.

What is the role of literacy and culture in creating an industrially based society? Some theorists, particularly in the 1800s, saw **culture as a process of refinement.** The English school of thought, led by Matthew Arnold, held that culture is knowing the best that has been thought in the world. This approach entailed paying most attention to the classic, high culture that had developed in Europe. This focus would help educate, cultivate, and civilize people moving from the countryside into the cities. Implicit in this view was the idea that media exist to educate, not entertain.

In the 1800s, American thinkers such as Ralph Waldo Emerson contested the idea that the purpose of culture and mass media was to improve the audience by focusing on European high culture. Emerson wanted to look more at the culture that was building in the United States itself and to focus on the future, not the past. Walt Whitman similarly thought of culture as the authentic expression of the "grand common stock" (of American people) that taps the "measureless wealth of latent power and capacity" of the people. These thinkers saw culture as popular, reflecting what the people liked for entertainment and pleasure.

The Birth of Industrial Media

As the Industrial Revolution picked up speed, industrially based mass media such as books and newspapers appeared and proliferated. As the demand for print media by the masses increased, media tended to become cheaper. Most countries saw the rise of large urban daily newspapers and an increase in book publishing. However, both illiteracy and lack of money continued to limit reading. Many people could not afford a newspaper or read well enough to really enjoy it.

Thus we see that **social class** is often strongly connected to media use. Industrialization sometimes increases social stratification. Although many poor people get ahead by taking industrial jobs, the relative gaps between rich and poor have widened in many developing countries.

In the United States, most people live at a level well above poverty, but a significant number still are poor. In most Third World countries, the middle class is much smaller and the gaps between rich and poor much wider.

Social class encompasses several factors, including income, education, family status, and profession or kind of job. For media, we can talk about social class in general, but it is useful to separate it into two components that Pierre Bourdieu (1984) has called economic capital and cultural capital.

Economic capital essentially is a person's personal wealth. Economic capital tends to determine what kinds of media someone can have access to. For instance, in 1850 only some people could afford newspapers, while in the 1990s only some people can afford computers to use for electronic mail.

Cultural capital is based on education, family background, and other sorts of learning. Those sources provide a kind of intellectual capital that people use in understanding things. Cultural capital tends to determine what kinds of things people like, can use, and can understand. For instance, in 1900 many new immigrants to the United States could not read

Culture as a process of refinement puts a normative or value judgment on culture, suggesting it should be used to improve people.

Social class refers to social groups divided by occupation, economic status, education, and family status.

Economic capital is a person's personal or family wealth.

Cultural capital is based on a person's education, family background, and other sorts of learning.

or understand the English-language press because they had not yet been schooled in English. In the 1990s, many people cannot use computers very well because they do not have the necessary skills, even if they have been through high school.

Film, Radio, and Popular Media

In the early 1900s, many people in the United States had neither the economic capital nor the cultural capital to gain access to or to use print media. Other media stepped in to fill this gap. In particular, film was an important American mass medium, particularly for recently arrived immigrants concentrated in the urban areas where film first developed, along with such other commercial amusements as penny arcades and dance halls.

In the 1920s, radio was also becoming a popular medium. Radio was particularly important because it reached much more easily beyond cities to the rural population. Although the United States was changing from a primarily rural society by the 1920s, the rural population was still significant. Whereas newspapers, books, and movies remained primarily urban, radio traveled across the countryside. Radio began to showcase rural cultures, by playing Appalachian, gospel, and country music and airing programs like the Grand Ole Opry from Nashville, which by the 1930s was commercializing and widely distributing what had been a traditional rural music form. This form of entertainment spoke both to rural residents and to those who had recently moved to the cities.

ADVERTISING IS CRUCIAL TO THE DEVELOPMENT OF A MASS SOCIETY.

Mass distribution uses industrial technologies like railroads to distribute media to a broader mass audience.

Mass market is a large group of consumers brought together by media, urbanization, and industrialization.

Industrial Media, Advertising, and Mass Markets

The history of advertising fits closely with the growth of the mass media in the United States. Advertising is an intrinsic part of the American industrial economy— the industrial economy functions by selling mass-produced goods to masses of purchasers or consumers. Advertising has proved to be efficient at informing consumers of new products and helping create consumer demand for those products. Economists such as John Kenneth Galbraith (1976) see advertising as crucial to creating and managing consumer demand in the U.S. economy.

As soon as industrial technology permitted mass production, businesses began to think about **mass distribution** and sales, using other new technologies, such as railroads and postal services. Mass sales of goods represented an outlet for the enormous productive capacity that modern industries were creating in Europe and the United States around the turn of the century. Industry leaders began to realize they needed an intensive selling effort to move the goods they were producing off their assembly lines and into people's homes.

Industrialization, urbanization, and communication were coming together to create a potential **mass market** of consumers. This idea of mass consumption required something of a change in thinking. In much of the United States, popular traditions, emerging from hard pioneer experience and religious teachings of self-denial and frugality, led people to conserve money rather than spend it on consumer goods. Religious and philosophical leaders had tended to preach that people, particularly poor people, should restrain their worldly desires. Practically speaking, most people before 1900 had relatively little excess cash to spend, so this philosophy fit with their habits and traditions.

But a new ethic of **consumption** began to emerge. When industry realized it needed advertising and marketing to sell its goods, marketing became a legitimate part of business, a major department of all corporations. Advertising grew as an industry and began to shovel money into the existing media, so that by 1920, two-thirds of newspaper and magazine revenues were coming from advertising (Leiss, Kline, and Jhally, 1990).

Consumption refers to a social ethic which values the purchase and possession of goods above most other competing values.

SELLING CONSUMPTION WITH THE SOAP OPERA

In the 1920s, U.S. soap companies wanted to increase the sale of mass-produced soaps to American households in new areas: rural, working class, and urban. They knew that the main purchasers of soap for households were women. So the soap companies themselves developed a new form of drama for radio networks. Colgate-Palmolive and other companies produced the shows themselves in some cases and gave them to radio stations along with their advertisements. This worked so well on radio that one of the same shows, *The Guiding Light*, moved over to television when that new medium developed.

Both radio and television soap operas were so successful in the United States that those soap companies that also sold soap in Latin America began to produce them there, first for radio, called *radionovelas*, and later for television, called *telenovelas*. These shows had a similar impact overseas in creating, or at least helping direct, consumer demand for products such as soap.

In both the United States and Latin America, the effect went beyond just selling soap to housewives. The soap opera, and related serial fiction on radio and television, helped promote the whole idea of buying mass-produced products from stores. In 1974, for example, a Brazilian television critic noted that the defining moment of a major *telenovela,* running in prime time to a huge audience, came when the leading man asked if his wife would like a refrigerator and she dissolved in tears of happiness. The critic saw it as an example of the creation of a middle-class consumer ideal in a country where most people had been sharply divided between rich and poor.

In Brazil, as in the United States, critics and scholars are divided about whether raising such consumer aspirations is good, leading to material progress, or bad, leading more often to frustration and the acceptance of otherwise unfavorable changes in industrial society. The former is called "the revolution of rising expectations," but critics see the latter, a "revolution of rising frustrations," instead. This is a critical issue in Third World nations where most of the population are poor.

Marketers told people that their individual desires to have more material things, to consume more goods were not only acceptable but desirable. The new goal became greater individual satisfaction in material things and making such consumption available to everyone. This was a new vision of an abundant society, in which all who worked hard might participate. This vision spread first in the United States, widely heralded up through the 1950s as the world's premier consumer society. However, ripples from this new vision of society spread to Europe, to East Asia, and by the 1950s and 1960s, to many of the developing countries.

Mass marketing became more apparent with the advent of department stores that permitted people to browse, roam, and dream about products without necessarily buying. To some degree visual display and promotion of the goods replaced direct interaction with a salesperson. These stores also began to use display windows that tried to dramatically present their goods to passersby and lure them into the stores. The first of these large department stores was the Bon Marché in Paris in 1852. The Paris Exhibition of 1900 and other successful world's fairs and exhibitions were also visual showcases for new industrial technologies and the new mass consumer products that they were creating.

Another step forward in mass marketing in the United States came with the first large consumer catalogs, such as the Sears & Roebuck catalog, which appeared in the late 1800s. These mail-order companies were able to take advantage of new postal and shipping services, as well as industrial developments.

Examples of advertising can be found back hundreds of years, especially in outdoor signs, but advertising has become a much more common and crucial form of support for media in the last 100 years. In the 1800s and early 1900s, advertisers painted signs on the sides of barns touting products such as chewing tobacco. Advertising also began to appear more prominently in newspapers, magazines, and, as of 1923, on radio.

Advertising has become particularly important to newspapers over time. For example, in 1880 newspapers devoted only 25 percent of their space to advertisements, whereas in 1990, 60 to 70 percent of space went to ads. By 1920 two-thirds of magazine and newspaper revenues came from advertising. Similarly, by the mid-1920s radio in the United States had come to be defined as a largely commercial, advertising-supported medium primarily devoted to entertainment to attract the maximum audience for the advertisers. In radio the share of time devoted to advertising declined in the 1950s when radio networks declined, then recovered in the 1980s as radio audiences grew, along with advertiser interest in them. Some radio ads were aimed at a general audience, while others targeted specific audiences as radio formats, particularly at FM stations, began to target specific narrower audience segments. Television has dominated the placement of ads since the 1950s. As the mass market for goods in the United States and other countries has grown, the importance of television for advertisers has grown as well.

Mass Production and Cultural Industries

The industrial combination of technology and economics introduced the **mass production of culture** for a broad audience. "Culture" had been the preserve of an educated and wealthy elite; only they could afford it, only they could read it. Mass production of cultural products such as books, newspapers, magazines, records, CDs, movies, radios, and so on changed all that by greatly lowering the costs and increasing the accessibility of these items.

From Ralph Waldo Emerson in the 1800s to now, many experts have celebrated this, the rise of a more **popular culture**—a culture with books, songs, movies, and so on familiar to and accessible to the populace. However, other experts lament the massification of culture and think that it has been compromised, commercialized, trivialized, and watered down (Adorno, 1991). Much of this debate follows from the earlier nineteenth-century debate about whether culture, specifically things such as books and music, should try to educate and uplift, bringing new ideas from high culture to the masses, or whether culture and the mass media should reflect the values of the general audience and try to entertain it.

This debate about culture and its role in our lives became more intense as the mass media industrialized and reached ever further into society, creating truly **mass audiences** (see Figure 3.2). From the beginning of industrial society in Europe, many observers were worried about how industrial society was turning people into unhappy, alienated, and easily manipulated masses. In the 1930s film *Modern Times*, Charlie Chaplin is a factory worker literally caught up in the industrial gears of the modern factory he works in, a symbol of how people were caught up by the industrialization of modern society. Just as industry was standardizing and

Mass production of culture uses the techniques of industry to create media products cheaply enough for most people to afford.

Popular culture is a culture with books, songs, movies, and so on familiar to and accessible to the general public.

Mass audiences are those that include a large proportion of the public.

CHARLIE CHAPLIN EXPERIENCES THE PITFALLS OF THE INDUSTRIAL AGE IN THE FILM *MODERN TIMES*.

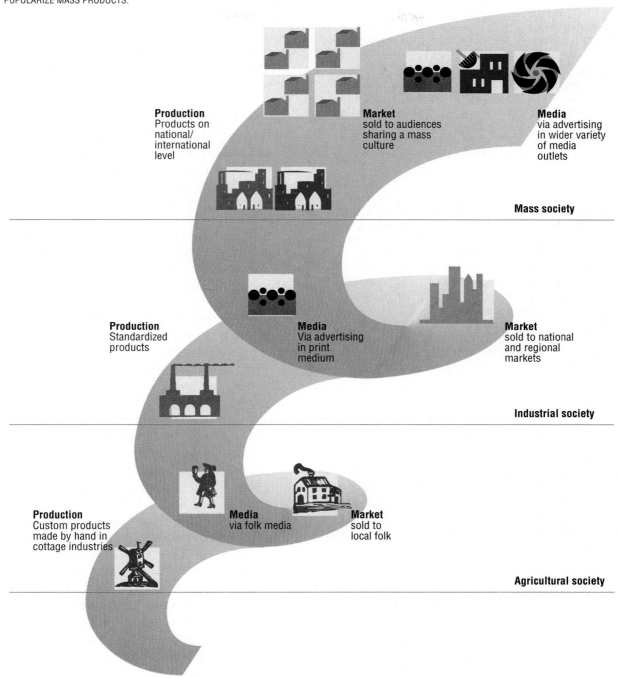

FIGURE 3.2
THE TRANSITION FROM FOLK
CULTURE TO MASS SOCIETY
WAS MARKED BY CONTINUING
EXPANSION OF MARKETS AND
PRODUCTION FACILITIES,
WHILE MEDIA EVOLVED TO
POPULARIZE MASS PRODUCTS.

Production
Products on
national/
international
level

Market
sold to audiences
sharing a mass
culture

Media
via advertising
in wider variety
of media
outlets

Mass society

Production
Standardized
products

Media
Via advertising
in print
medium

Market
sold to national
and regional
markets

Industrial society

Production
Custom products
made by hand in
cottage industries

Media
via folk media

Market
sold to
local folk

Agricultural society

MASS CULTURE, MASS MAN?

Some critics of mass culture feared that industrialized society and industrialized media had created a mass man, capable of being manipulated by propaganda. The pioneering journalist and thinker Walter Lippmann (1961) observed that media were helping to create widely held public opinions and to build up stereotypes in the audience about the world and other people.

A group of refugee German scholars, referred to as the Frankfurt School of Sociology, had moved to the United States to escape Nazi Germany in the 1930s. They were shocked at how the German people could be led to commit the aggression of World War II and, worse yet, the atrocities of the Holocaust, where over 6 million Jews and millions of gypsies, political prisoners, homosexuals, mentally deficient people, and Russian and Polish prisoners of war were killed by orders of Nazi German leaders but mostly at the hands of fairly ordinary German soldiers and policemen. Looking for explanations for how German people had been able to do these things, they looked at the manipulation of the German public as a mass audience subjected to propaganda, both by the German government and by private German mass media as well. Following this line of thought, their interests broadened to examine how other societies' mass cultures and mass audiences are manipulated, not just by governments like the Nazis but also by cultural industries oriented to making money out of mass culture, like those in the United States (Adorno, 1991).

Mass society reflects industrial mass production in which people consume the same industrialized products and culture.

mass producing products, critics feared that industrial or modern society was standardizing and massifying the culture and ideas that people lived by.

Some feared the diminishment of *high culture*, the European culture expressed in the arts of painting, classical music, opera, ballet, sculpture, and architecture, which had come to be considered "classic" in Europe and the United States. Critics such as Theodore Adorno (1991) feared that this culture would be replaced by mass-produced cultural goods of less quality or less value. If people were easily gratified by soap operas, would they ever be enticed to watch a regular classical opera? A parallel fear was that local folk cultures, music, dances, and arts would also be driven out by mass-produced cultural products. Would people still play their own traditional music for themselves if they could listen to well-produced jazz or rock played by professional musicians?

This preoccupation with the mass audience and **mass society** shaped thinking about the high point of industrial-era mass media. At a time in the United States, and many other countries, when most people watched a few television networks, listened to a fairly standard hit parade of top 40 songs, and read *Reader's Digest* and its *Condensed Books*, there seemed to be a real massification of culture. If almost everyone watched, read, and listened to the output of a few key cultural industries, perhaps people *were* mass men and women living in a mass society. This thinking particularly characterized the 1950s in the United States, the era of the organization man, suburbs, and families like those on *Leave It to Beaver*, *Ozzie and Harriet*, and *Father Knows Best*.

This perspective clashed strongly, however, with what researchers were learning about how people actually behaved, particularly with the media. Beginning in the 1940s, researchers began to realize that people were active and selective in their use of media and were often unalike. Their use of media depended on many factors, such as how old they were, whether they were male or female, how much money they had, and how educated they were.

The media also began to reflect these varying tastes and backgrounds and to target subgroups, or segments, of the mass audience, recognizing that these groups preferred more specialized or segmented media content. In retrospect, it seems that the idea of mass culture blinded many observers to the real differences that existed and continued to emerge between people and media's effect on them. As an editorial in the British media review *InterMedia* commented, "There never was a mass audience, only ways of seeing people as masses."

Information Technology in the Industrial Era

Although we have been concentrating here on mass media, which emerged in the industrial era, the interactive media of telegraphy and telephony were also essential elements of the Industrial Age itself. Before these electronic media developed, written communications had to be physically transported from one place to another by whatever means were quickest. The early American West had the Pony Express, whose riders carried mail by horseback from one station to another, where another rider would go on, passing on the mail like the baton in a relay race. But while heroic and dramatic, the Pony Express was not nearly as fast as the same messages being transmitted electronically, and it was easily replaced by the telegraph.

With these technologies we moved from a solely physical **infrastructure** of communication that depended on the speed of horses, ships, runners, and railroads to one that relied on electronic transmission—first over wires, then, years later, over radio waves as well. In fact, the railroad and the telegraph powerfully reinforced and complemented each other, as transportation and communication technologies often do. The telegraph permitted the railroads to coordinate and function better.

As parts of the infrastructure, telegraphy and telephony were called **common carriers**—that is, they carried whatever message someone else wanted to send (and could afford to pay for). This term built on the earlier idea of common carriers in transportation, such as rail lines that carried any legal goods. Telegraphy and telephony were to carry other people's messages in a neutral way, not creating content themselves but rather transmitting what other people created.

The telegraph, which first began to function in 1836, had a dramatic effect on trade, commerce, politics, and even the print media. Historian Daniel Czitrom (1982) called the telegraph "lightning lines" for the speed with which it moved and for its transforming affect, like lightning striking. The role of the basic communications infrastructure—of things like the telegraph, telephone, telex, and now the computer—is to allow both media and other kinds of business and institutions to function more effectively. With the advent of these technologies, business messages and news stories alike could be sent over much further distances much faster, changing the way both mass media and business in general structured themselves and operated.

The telegraph provided a new information infrastructure for business, in particular. Firms that had been localized could consider expanding to new parts of the country, since they could now keep closer control of remote business branches. Many companies found that with barriers of space and time reduced, they could operate much more widely than previously. The size of firms often grew, and they were able to coordinate and control much larger operations. Diverse regional markets became more standardized across the United States. For example, where regional prices had varied they now tended to become more uniform.

Like the telegraph, telephony developed first in the most industrialized societies. Telephones spread rapidly in the United States in the late 1800s, well before most other countries. Under Theodore Vail, the Bell Telephone companies sought to control most of the U.S. business, including all long-distance connections, but also sought to ensure virtually **universal service** to all American households. The pursuit of universal service was slower in Western Europe and Japan, where telephones didn't proliferate until the World War II era.

Infrastructure refers to the services and facilities that enable people to do work or other kinds of activities.

Common carriers are transportation or telecommunication companies that carry others' goods or messages.

THE TELEGRAPH WAS THE FIRST ELECTRONIC COMMUNICATIONS MEDIUM.

Universal service is the provision of telephony or other services to all or almost all households.

R E V I E W

1. What effects did increasing literacy and use of print media have on society?
2. What are economic and cultural capital? How do they affect access to and use of media?
3. What effect did advertising have on the development of media?
4. What are the pluses and minuses of promoting consumption of goods by advertising?
5. What are mass culture, folk culture, and high culture?

THE INFORMATION SOCIETY

Daniel Bell (1973), Alvin Toffler (1980), and others think that the United States and a few other countries have moved from being industrial economies and societies to becoming information economies and societies. Jorge Schement (1987) and others feel that the United States is still essentially an industrial society but one that increasingly uses industrial techniques to "manufacture" information and offer industrialized, high-information-content services. A related view is that Americans are now using information technologies and information "products" in more of the things they do. In this view, although the U.S. economy still has strong components of agriculture, industry, and services, all three are now changed by use of information technologies. Farmers, industrialists, and service providers all work differently because they use information as a major component of their work.

Postindustrial Society

In Daniel Bell's book *The Coming of Post-Industrial Society* (1973), he focused on how the American, Japanese, and other advanced economies are shifting from production of goods to services and information processing. Other people since Bell have focused more specifically on the central role of information as compared to other services—where wealth and economic activity are created, what grows most, and where most people are employed.

As Figure 3.3 shows, almost half of the U.S. work force is involved in information creation, handling, or use. In 1980, only 3 percent of American workers were in agriculture, slightly over 20 percent worked in industry, and about 30 percent worked in providing services, while the rest (47 percent) worked directly with information. Figure 3.3 builds on Marc Porat's (1977) study of the U.S. economy in the 1970s, which separated various jobs into categories and provided the first detailed estimate of how many people worked primarily with information, even though they might be working for a bank or an automobile manufacturer. **Information jobs** include all those primarily involved in producing, processing, or distributing information: secretaries, most managers, researchers, educators, insurance people, accountants, and banking/financial people, as well as journalists, media producers, computer workers, engineers in information areas, designers, and so on. These jobs are growing, while others decline. For example, the United States now has more people working in education than in agriculture.

Information jobs include all those involved primarily in producing, processing, or distributing information.

The distinction between service jobs and information jobs is an important one. *Service jobs* are frequently less well paid than industrial labor positions. The stereotype of service jobs as janitorial or fast-food is not completely inaccurate, although many high-paying jobs also exist in service areas. *Information jobs* tend to be better paid, even when they are within manufacturing or service companies. In *The Work of Nations* (1991), Robert Reich, secretary of commerce under President Bill Clinton, notes the job trends in the 1980s. Income has shifted toward jobs that involve creation or high-level manipulation of information,

FIGURE 3.3
CHANGES IN THE U.S. WORK FORCE, 1900–1990, SHOWING THE MOVEMENT OF THE UNITED STATES TOWARD BECOMING ON INFORMATION ECONOMY DOMINATED BY INFORMATION WORKERS (ADAPTED FROM DIZARD, 1989).

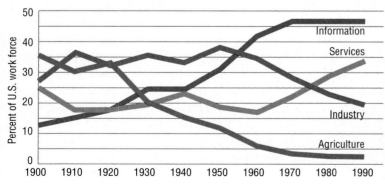

which Reich calls *symbolic analysts*: they include computer programmers, engineers, financial analysts, higher-level managers, educators, and lawyers. More traditional jobs in industry or services tend to pay less. However, Reich also notes that the information sector contains many low-paying "routine production" jobs, such as data entry.

Trends are similar in Canada, Japan, and other advanced industrial nations that are also becoming information societies, although the U.S. work force has become the most heavily concentrated in information jobs. Many traditional manufacturing industries have moved to other countries. Nations such as South Korea have become industrial powers, while some low-priced goods that they used to make have shifted to still other countries. For instance, some of the low-wage manufacturing that Korea used to do has shifted to other Asian nations. Countries such as Singapore are now heavily involved in information work (Dordick & Wang, 1993).

The Information Economy

The information economy has two key aspects. First is the growing importance of the *information sector* itself, as a source of jobs and as a generator of economic growth. Second

WHAT HAPPENED TO THE AMERICAN INDUSTRIAL ECONOMY?

American industry is changing with the overall world economy. Both individual institutions and nations are becoming increasingly specialized. The world division of labor is changing. The United States has been gaining strength in information-oriented industries such as media, computer software and hardware, telecommunications, research and development, and higher education, while declining somewhat in some kinds of manufacturing, such as steel and (until recently) automobiles. Robert Reich (1991) argues that there is no truly separate American economy anymore, that American workers and businesses both compete in global markets for labor, information, and goods. In this kind of global economy, he argues, people prosper when they can add more value to a product or service than can someone else in another country. Knowledge is the key resource, rather than natural resources.

Nations and companies are increasingly interdependent. A number of American companies, such as Coca-Cola, Paramount Studios, Citibank, and General Motors, have been global in scope for decades. Now more and more American companies are going global and competing with multinational corporations from a larger number of countries. What permits a number of these companies to act globally is the changing information infrastructure based in telecommunications and computers. Furthermore, many of the jobs that these companies keep in the United States are information oriented: management, design, research, information coordination, and telecommunications.

Most Americans need to prepare for work that will principally involve creation, manipulation, analysis, and communication of information. Even farmers and industrial manufacturing workers will probably need to be able to use computers and other information tools. Companies such as Hewlett-Packard now prefer to hire college graduates with good communication skills to assemble or manufacture computers and printers, since they need to be able to use computers in the assembly process and have to be able to work in teams, at a variety of tasks. As more and more kinds of industries and services require use of information and information technology, the educational needs for the workplace continue to grow. Virtually all information jobs require at least high school education, and many require at least some college.

COMPUTERS HAVE ENTERED ALMOST EVERY AREA OF WORK LIFE.

is the importance of the **information infrastructure** for the rest of the economy, as a focus for jobs in other industries and as a contributor to productivity in banking, manufacturing, and other areas.

The information sector can be divided into two parts: a **primary information sector**, which produces, processes, and sells information goods and services, and a **secondary information sector**, in which many companies that don't sell information still produce, process, and distribute information for their own internal use (see Figure 3.4).

Porat (1977) divided the primary information sector into five categories:

1. *Markets for information*—knowledge production and information, such as mass media and some educational institutions.

2. *Information in markets*—information management, advertising, and risk management (insurance, finance, brokerages).

3. *Information infrastructure*—information processing, including printing, data processing, telecommunications, and information goods manufacturing industries, such as paper, ink, television sets, and computers.

4. *Wholesale and retail trade in information goods*—bookstores, computer stores, and theaters.

5. *Support facilities for information activities*—buildings used by information industries, office furnishings, and so on.

The secondary information sector consists of information services consumed within firms to boost their productivity in noninformation businesses. For example, General Motors acquired an entire information company, EDS (Electronic Data Services), primarily to improve its internal (secondary) information services. These kinds of information activities include management, research, accounting, marketing, inventory control, and internal communications.

In 1974 the primary information sector represented 29 percent of the U.S. economy's Gross National Product (or overall economic activity), while the secondary information sector represented 25 percent. Overall, the information sector in 1974 represented 54 percent of the U.S. economy's GNP. That proportion grew rapidly in the 1970s and 1980s to reach 75 percent in 1988.

Primary information activities often began during the industrial and mass media era, including most of the business information services, most of the media, and many of the knowledge sales. However, these information activities have become increasingly dominant in the economy of the United States and other "postindustrial" nations.

Information in Markets. Many businesses have long had "information" as their principal product. Banking, insurance, accounting, design, and other service "products" are essentially information: financial transfers, reports, evaluations, and so on. Such firms have risen with the industrial economy but may be surpassing it in importance for the United States and industrialized countries like it. American banking, insurance, and accounting firms are relatively more competitive in the world economy than are American steel, textile, and consumer electronics producers.

Traditional primary information businesses, such as banks, are also exceptionally heavy users of the secondary information or infrastructure companies of telecommunications and

FIGURE 3.4
THE INFORMATION ECONOMY HAS
CREATED A PRIMARY SECTOR, WHICH
CREATES AND SELLS INFORMATION, AND
A SECONDARY SECTOR, WHICH
PROCESSES INFORMATION WHILE
PRODUCING NONINFORMATION
PRODUCTS.

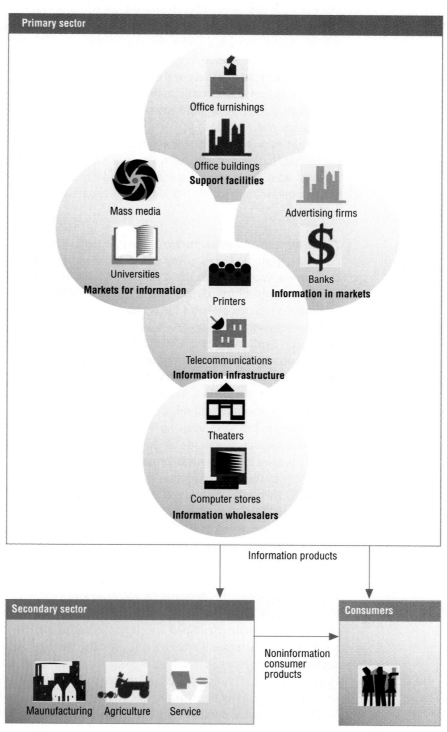

Primary sector

Office furnishings

Office buildings
Support facilities

Mass media

Advertising firms

Universities
Markets for information

Printers

Banks
Information in markets

Telecommunications
Information infrastructure

Theaters

Computer stores
Information wholesalers

Information products

Secondary sector

Maunufacturing   Agriculture   Service

Noninformation
consumer
products

Consumers

computers. New primary information businesses are also being created to take advantage of information technologies such as database firms, which offer everything from detailed information on overseas stock markets to instant access for law firms to cases from a variety of courts, kept on electronic file.

Markets for Information. The mass media—books, magazines, newspapers, films, music, and television—grew tremendously in the Industrial Age but are also changing and growing in the Information Age. In fact, for many people the increasing importance of media helps define an information society and economy. The number of media companies is increasing, as is their output and its value in the economy. In 1993 media products were the number two American export to other countries, after aerospace products (airplanes, satellites, helicopters, and rockets).

Certain knowledge industries, including education, patent licensing, and specialized publishing, have developed with the industrial society but are radically expanded and changed with the information society. In addition, several knowledge industries are new with the information society, such as access to databases and on-line computer information services.

The Information Infrastructure. The information infrastructure is crucial for everything else that happens in the economy and society. Economically, the information infrastructure can be thought of as *overhead* that must add value to other productive activities in services, industry, or agriculture. General Motors is only indirectly in the information business, but information technology helps the company make and then sell cars more efficiently.

The information infrastructure is also big business. It represented 21 percent of the U.S. GNP in the 1967 and grew fairly rapidly in the 1970s and 1980s. Increasingly, all aspects of the economy depend on information technology. Much of the management activity of business has always been concerned with gathering, creating, manipulating, and interpreting information on product research and design, manufacturing productivity, personnel, advertising, marketing, and sales. Computers and telecommunications can help industry by improving productivity, such as by automation, computer-assisted design, computer-integrated manufacturing, and electronic data interchange. Information technology can also help businesses by improving internal communication, improving access to information by employees and customers, and perhaps even extending the company's own network to the customer. This technology becomes a key competitive factor for all sectors of business in domestic and foreign markets.

The information infrastructure is thus important not only as a tool for businesses but also as a growing sector of the economy itself. The information infrastructure consists of several kinds of companies. There are local and regional telephone companies such as Ameritech and Pacific Bell and national or international companies such as AT&T and MCI, which provide the basic transmission of a variety of services, including telephony, electronic mail, data flow between computers, and video or "television." Cable television companies now plan to compete in this area. There are also enhanced service companies, which use computers and other tools to provide more specialized services for companies, such as a complete electronic mail system instead of just the basic transmission of electronic mail. Finally, there are the computer manufacturers themselves, which provide the equipment but would like to provide finished services as well.

The information infrastructure has expanded greatly. There are computers in over

R E V I E W

1. What are the main economic characteristics of information society?
2. What is the primary information sector?
3. What is the secondary information sector?
4. What is information in markets?
5. What are markets for information?
6. What is the role of the information infrastructure?

30 percent of homes and over two-thirds of schools. They are nearly universal in offices. The telephone system has been the basic network for most services (although special data telecommunications companies, cable television companies, and others are competing with telephone companies in this area). The telecommunications network for larger businesses was upgraded in the 1980s, as business computers were linked via various networks and data communication services. Although there has been continual investment in, and expansion of, the information infrastructure for business, trial projects and debate continue over how best to upgrade the base of residential service from plain old telephone service to some new combination of telephone, data, and probably television services.

CRITICAL VIEWS OF THE INFORMATION SOCIETY

A number of people are critical of the idea of the information society and what that idea represents. They question whether there is anything really that different about the information society and whether any differences that do exist are changes for the positive or the negative.

While some see the information society as an improved social milieu in which income is better distributed and more people have access to more information, others, such as Herb Schiller (1986), wonder whether the information society is just information-oriented capitalism, with all the current ills of capitalism and maybe some new ones. Will social class relations be different? What roles and what pay will there be for different kinds of workers, managers, and professionals? What kind of work force will there be? While some futurists have seen information technology as a liberating force, is this liberating promise of technology just propaganda?

Perhaps what is developing is just an information-oriented form of industrialization that treats **information as a commodity** rather than a public resource. Schiller notes that information that used to be relatively accessible for free from public libraries or government documents has actually been made more expensive after being put on computer-based systems, which are often privately owned and commercially operated for a profit. Does that limit and stratify who gets access to what kinds of information? Vincent Mosco (1989) observes that we are moving toward a **"pay-per" society** (like pay-per-view films and events on cable television), in which many things will be available on-line, based in computer systems, but will be available only to those who can pay.

Schiller also wonders whether information technologies will be used for control. Who will use the efficiencies of information technology, and to whose benefit? Because military funds have been used to develop much of the information technology, critics fear control by the military industrial complex. Who will shape the eventual uses of information technology? Will that also be military planners and funders? Some critics, including Schiller, also fear control by corporations. Since corporations have the best current access to and use of information technology, they may well use that technology to extend their control over the economies of the information society and particularly their control over workers. For instance, computer technologies permit supervisors to monitor how many keystrokes a typist makes per minute or how many calls a telephone operator or salesperson makes per hour. While that monitoring helps management, it seems intrusive to workers.

Information as a commodity refers to the idea of buying and selling information rather than seeing it as a free resource.

Pay-per society is one in which people pay to use information resources that are currently available free at libraries or from other sources.

One of the ways that information functions as a means of control is via the concept of the **information society as an ideology**, or slogan. Most critics see this idea as generally framed in positive ways, in which new information technologies solve problems and make life and society better. "Information society" thus serves as a slogan to gain acceptance for economic and other changes.

Postmodern Society?

If we think of industrial society as modern, is information society postmodern? First, what do we mean by "modern"? Many theorists think of modern society as beginning with the opening up of arts, architecture, and medicine during the Enlightenment, after the late 1600s. **Modernity** was a way of seeing the world. Key aspects of modern thinking included seeing reason as a source of progress and seeing science as having universal explanations for things. Modernity in both thought and economy was characterized by innovation, dynamism, and seeing change as positive. Modernity is also defined in terms of increasingly modern institutions, such as democratic or bureaucratic governments, large companies, and banks. Some of these things came into being before the Industrial Revolution. Still, when most of us think of modern society, we think of life after the Industrial Age began to spread in the 1800s. We usually think of modernity in terms of industrialization, the growth of science and technology, urbanization, and the evolution of mass media and culture.

SOME PRODUCTS IN OUR POSTMODERN SOCIETY ARE TRULY GLOBAL. COCA-COLA, FOR EXAMPLE, CAN BE FOUND IN SUCH REMOTE SPOTS AS PAPUA-NEW GUINEA.

Some experts see recent changes simply as an intensification of our current industrial society, what Schiller might call information-oriented industrialization or information-oriented capitalism. One view of postmodernism is as a higher stage of capitalism, in which information becomes the main commodity, and capitalism achieves a greater penetration of the world, reaching into smaller, poorer, and more out-of-the way places. In this view, information and media work with other companies to push increased global integration within a world capitalist economy. For instance, as commercial media reach into more societies, bringing both global and local advertising, potentially everyone in the world becomes aware of Coca-Cola, Nike shoes, and Kodak film. That may affect both their consumer desires and their culture. In fact, the growth of consumer culture is a key aspect of postmodernism for some, such as Mike Featherstone (1991).

Others writers, including French scholar Jean Baudrillard (1988), argue that what is taking place is a break with modernity, both in modes of thinking and in economic and political institutions. In art, culture, and society, there is a new era of postmodernism, defined in part by changes from modernism to postmodernism. For instance, Baudrillard thinks that we have moved from an era of economic determinism (economic phenomena determining others) to a time of **cultural determinism**, such that messages carried by communications technologies can impose new meanings, different from or even opposed to what was originally intended. Similarly, some experts say that we have moved from an era of supposedly universal laws and truths based in rational science to one in which local, particular, subjective understandings are more important or subjectively more valid.

The postmodern view is that there is no universal truth, that what you think depends on your own experience, which depends on what groups you belong to, what media you pay

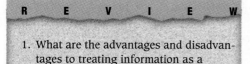

R E V I E W

1. What are the advantages and disadvantages to treating information as a commodity, buying and selling it?
2. What are some employment issues in the information society?
3. What new issues does the information society raise regarding who has control over whom?
4. What is modern? What do we mean by postmodern?
5. Do new information technologies lead to cultural fragmentation?

attention to, what your family taught you, and so on. This view fits with the idea that developments in the information society encourage **cultural fragmentation**, in which many different groups or even individuals customize their own information and cultural experience so that people share less and cultures do fragment. According to another French thinker, Jean Lyotard (1984), the new media and information technologies permit many new forms of expression, creating new forms of knowledge and new social formations. Because many kinds of groups can express their own ideas through proliferating media and information technology channels, society becomes more focused on specific groups and views and less concerned with general trends.

SUMMARY & REVIEW

How Have Society and Media Gone Through Developmental Stages?

What are the main stages of societal development?
Although stages of societal and economic development overlap and coexist, the development of economy and media can be divided into three stages: agricultural, industrial, and informational.

What are the key economic sectors, and where are most people employed in the three stages?
The key sectors are those that drive the rest of the economy: first agriculture, then manufacturing industry, now information. Most people are employed in these sectors.

What was communication like before industrial development?
Most people were not literate, and reproduction of books was done by hand. Most communication was oral, so news and information traveled slowly.

What Did Industrialization Do to Media?

When was mechanized printing developed?
The development of the printing press by Gutenberg in 1455 in Germany combined with the beginnings of a broader Industrial Revolution to produce far-reaching effects.

How did industrialized printing change society?
Books and other print materials became much cheaper and more widely available. As more people became literate, informing them and being concerned about public opinion became more of an issue. How to use the perceived power of media became an issue to politicians and social reformers.

Did people's social class become an issue in media use?
Society became more stratified into classes with the Industrial Revolution. People's social class affected their use of media in at least two ways: Economic capital limited or gave access to media, while cultural capital affected media choices, tastes, and understandings.

What do we mean by mass production, mass consumption, mass media, and mass society?
Industrial tools and processes made it possible to mass produce media, along with steel and soap. People consumed the same mass media, homogenizing to some degree their information and culture. That began to produce a society that was more standardized or massified.

What effect did advertising have on the development of media?
Advertising became the main economic support for media in many countries, particularly the United States. Advertising built on the mass

market of consumers for goods that came with industrialization, but it also pushed people toward becoming consumers.

What Is the Information Society?

What are the main economic characteristics of the information society?
Information is the main economic activity, the key sector that drives the economy, the main source of employment, and an increasingly major component in the productivity of other sectors of the economy, such as agriculture and manufacturing.

What is the primary information sector?
It is that part of the economy that directly produces and sells information. It includes direct markets for information such as mass media, information sold to be used in other markets such as insurance or advertising, the information infrastructure, wholesale and retail trade in information goods, and support facilities for information activities.

What is the secondary information sector?
It is information and information services produced and consumed within noninformation firms to boost their productivity. These activities in manufacturing and agriculture include management, research, accounting, secretarial and clerical work, marketing, inventory control, and internal communications.

What is the role of the information infrastructure?
The information infrastructure increasingly provides tools for all aspects of the economy. Consisting of computers, telecommunications, and other media, it must add value to what others do with it. It is an increasingly large sector of the economy.

What Are Some Critical Views of the Information Society?

What are the advantages and disadvantages of treating information as a commodity, buying and selling it?
In commercial media, cultural and information products have long been commodities to be sold. Getting commercial industries more involved in new forms of information will

probably bring in more money to develop them, and they will probably develop faster. The problem is that if currently free forms of access to media, such as libraries and government publications, are commercialized, some people with less economic capital or without ties to some institution that provides access will probably be cut off from access to some information that they can currently get.

What new issues does the information society raise regarding who has control over whom?
Information technology permits more direct monitoring and control in the workplace, such as tracking the number of phone calls or keystrokes made by a receptionist or data-entry worker. It is much easier for managers to control larger sections of company processes, centralizing decision making. It is also easier to gather data on people who purchase and use products so that direct marketing and sales can be targeted to them.

What is modern? What do we mean by postmodern?
Modernity is a complex idea, but for our purposes, it is a way of seeing the world as rational and controllable and seeing change as positive. Postmodernity implies that this way of seeing the world is no longer accurate or perhaps desirable. It tends to see rational attempts at explaining and controlling the world as misleading and counterproductive. It sees meaning as relative and localized. This happens in part because technologies permit people to have highly selective use of information and culture, making up their own very personalized views of the world.

Do new information technologies lead to cultural fragmentation?
It seems that new segmented or narrowcast technologies permit different groups and individuals to customize their own information and cultural experience so that people share less of a common culture. That seems to fragment some of the broad cultural values and images that people used to share across nations. This kind of idea replaces the view of the United States as a melting pot with a view of it as a tossed salad, in which the different elements may or may not complement each other and get along.

REFERENCES

Adorno, T. W. (1991). *The culture industry.* New York: Routledge.

Baudrillard, J. (1988). *America.* New York: Verso.

Bell, D. (1973). *The coming of post-industrial society.* New York: Basic Books.

Bourdieu, P. (1984). *Distinction: A social critique of the judgment of taste.* Cambridge, MA: Harvard University Press.

Burke, J. (1991) Communication in the Middle Ages. In Crowley & Heyers (Eds.), *Communication in history.* New York: Longman.

Czitrom, D. (1982). *Media and the American mind: From Morse to McLuhan.* Chapel Hill: University of North Carolina Press.

Dizard, W. (1989). *The coming information society.* New York: Longman.

Dordick, H., & Wang, G. (1993). *The information society: A retrospective view.* Newbury Park, CA: Sage.

Featherstone, M. (1991). *Consumer culture and postmodernism.* Newbury Park, CA: Sage.

Galbraith, J. K. (1976). *The affluent society* (3rd ed.). Boston: Houghton Mifflin.

Goody, J., & Watt, J. The consequences of literacy. In Crowley & Heyers (Eds.), *Communication in History.* New York: Longman.

Leiss, W., Kline, S., & Jhally, S. (1990). *Social communication and advertising.* New York: Routledge.

Lerner, D. (1958). *The passing of traditional society.* Glencoe, IL: Free Press.

Lippmann, W. (1961). *Public opinion.* New York: Harcourt.

Lyotard, J. F. (1984). *The postmodern condition: A report on knowledge.* Minneapolis: University of Minnesota Press.

McLuhan, M. (1962). *The Gutenberg galaxy: The making of typographic man.* New York: New American Library.

McLuhan, M. (1965). *Understanding media.* New York: New American Library.

Mosco, V. (1989). *The pay-per society.* Norwood, NJ: Ablex.

Naisbitt, J. (1984). *Megatrends.* New York: Warner Books.

Porat, M. (1977). *The information economy: Development and measurement.* Washington, D.C.: U.S. Government Printing Office.

Reich, R. (1991). *The work of nations.* New York: Knopf.

Schement, J. (1987). *Competing visions, complex realities: Social aspects of the information society.* Norwood, NJ: Ablex.

Schiller, H. (1986). *Information and the crisis economy.* New York: Oxford University Press.

Solomon, W. S., & McChesney, R. W. (1993). *Ruthless criticism: New perspectives in U.S. communication history.* Minneapolis: University of Minnesota Press.

Toffler, A. (1980). *The third wave.* New York: Morrow.

Chapter 4

ECONOMIC ISSUES IN COMMUNICATIONS MEDIA

Understanding the economics of communications media is crucial to understanding their structure and content. Both mass media and information technologies are shaped by economics as much as by technology. Economics means more than money and finance, although we will look closely at how media are financed and paid for. Economics also involves the ownership and structure of industries, which affects how they operate and what contents they produce.

First, we are going to look at the economics of industrialized mass media and information technologies, particularly their ownership, content, and structure. Second, we are going to look at some of the economic bases of communications media: advertising, direct sales, subscriptions, and syndication. We will also look at some of the unique economics of regulated industries, such as telecommunications, where cross-subsidy of services is a key issue.

**Paying the Monthly Media Bill,
2015**

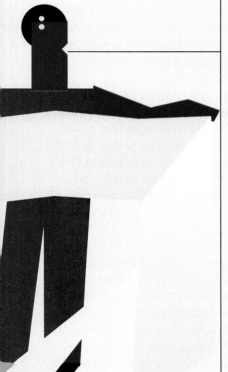

Brenda, will you and the kids come here? We've gotta talk about this monthly DeeVee bill.

Okay, what's the big problem?

Look here. Somebody spent $50 for twenty-five old episodes of *Star Trek: The Next to Last Generation.*

That was me, Dad. I really like it. It's way more interesting than virtual roller hockey and all that new stuff.

Fine. But did you have to pay for it? Why not just accept a few ads instead?

Have you ever looked at the ads they target at my demographic? It's all zit cream and thrash paddles. Booooring.

How about this? Sixty-seven hours logged on the Flash Psychomatic fan hotline, total $33.50.

But, Dad, that's my favorite group and all my friends hang out there and talk and trade holophotos and stuff. And I hate those stupid ads on the bottom of the screen so I always turn 'em off.

And how about you, Larry? Look at all these net searches for football scores. Why don't you just read the newsfax?

But I can run the searches for just the games I want, on screen, while I'm watching a game. I hate having to scan through the stupid fax and look away from the screen.

So why don't you accept a few ads to pay for them? I know, I know— the ads eat up screen space. But you could schedule a few full-screen ads after the game . . . they don't care as long as you watch them sometime and take the recall quiz.

Looks like we're stuck. Remember good old "free TV"?

Yeah, I remember. Everybody really paid for it by watching all the ads, with no choice. Remember that?

MEDIA ECONOMICS AND OWNERSHIP

everal general economic factors, including ownership structures, economies of scale, distribution costs, and technology costs, affect communications media. However, media are very different from many other kinds of economic sectors. In the United States and other market economies, communications media create and sell two kinds of products. First, they sell media or information service content to audiences or consumers. The newer, more interactive communications media make this direct sale of culture and information products particularly important. However, communications media also "sell" their audiences to advertisers, who wish to sell things to those audiences. Communications media, particularly in the mass media, compete with each other to attract those audiences and sell access to them.

Ownership structures and control of mass media are among the most controversial policy issues facing many societies, including the United States. So we will examine ownership both here as an aspect of media economics and, more extensively, in Chapter 5 as a principal issue in media policy. Thus, while some authors look at political economy as one unified subject, we are splitting political and economic aspects for separate coverage.

A number of critics of the mass media assume that owners are extremely powerful in determining the structure and performance, or content, of communications media (Bagdikian, 1993). Some critics go so far as to say that if you know who owns a newspaper or radio station or cable network, ultimately you know what the paper or station or network is going to say. In current debate, some critics fear that certain kinds of owners, such as cable TV operating companies, might be more inclined to control the contents of an interactive telecommunications system than would, say, a telephone company, which is accustomed to acting as a common carrier of all messages.

Ownership structures are patterns of who owns media industries and how concentrated and integrated that ownership is.

Private Ownership

Ownership of media by private individuals or corporations varies among media and among countries. Private ownership is traditional in print media in the United States, Europe, and most developing countries. The costs of starting a publishing house, broadcast station, or newspaper—**entry costs**—have usually been low enough for print media that a variety of individuals and companies have been willing to enter the publishing business. Whether they succeed and continue depends on the wealth of the market they enter, their own resources for reaching and attracting an audience, and their ability to sustain the new publication with content that continues to hold and build an audience (Compaigne, 1982).

Entry costs are the costs of starting up a media company: technology, distribution, personnel, and raw material.

Private initiative and ownership is less dominant in broadcast media in much of the world. Since the radio spectrum is a very limited resource, governments are almost inevitably involved in licensing broadcasters, which gives governments more control. American radio and television stations have been predominantly private since 1920, after the U.S. Navy turned stations back to private hands. Only PBS radio and television stations, and a few independent university or community nonprofit stations, are not privately owned. However, in much of the world privately owned, for-profit broadcasting has been the exception rather than the rule. Governments have often owned and controlled broadcasting. They typically feel that both radio and television are too powerful in politics and society to be controlled by private interests. Furthermore, entry costs to establish broadcasting have usually been higher than those for starting print, although this situation is changing. In many countries, governments were the only entities with the capital to start broadcasting stations in the 1940s and 1950s, although in the 1980s and 1990s production and transmission costs have fallen (Head, 1985).

Public Ownership

Public ownership refers to ownership by nonprofit groups or by government bodies.

License fees are annual fees or fees on the sales of radio or television receivers to pay for public broadcasting.

Historically in Western Europe and other industrialized democracies, such as Japan, Australia, New Zealand, and Canada, **public ownership** has been seen as preferable to either private or governmental ownership, particularly in broadcasting. These countries have also tended to see broadcasting as too powerful to be controlled by private interests, but they have also been afraid of government control. The result has been a series of efforts to find some economic formula in which either a public corporation or some other nonprivate, nongovernmental body owns broadcast media. The main obstacle has been finding means of financing that are neither privately controlled advertising nor government-controlled subsidies. In several countries, including Japan and Great Britain, the most successful means has been assessing annual **license fees**, or fees on the sales of radio or television receivers, to pay for public broadcasting (Browne, 1989).

The PTT Model: Public Ownership of Telecommunications

Regulated monopoly is a company without competitors regulated by government to prevent abuse of its position.

PTT is a national government-owned post, telephone, and telegraph monopoly, which usually runs telecommunications.

The structure of the telecommunications industry in the United States started as a Bell monopoly, followed by a series of competing local private telephone systems. Most were bought up or forced out by AT&T, which became a private, **regulated monopoly.** Since 1984 the deregulated monopoly has been gradually broken down by competing private companies. However, both private telecommunications companies and competition between them have been something of an anomaly in the international context. Throughout most of the world, telecommunications has historically been a state-run monopoly rather than a privately owned enterprise that operates with government oversight. Typically, telecommunications is part of a national post, telephone, and telegraph (**PTT**) ministry, and telecommunications workers are government employees, just as postal workers are in the United States. State ownership extends not only to the provision of basic telephone service but also to the production of telephone equipment and, in some cases, to information services as well. This model was seen as valuable for extending universal telephone service to all, since governments could enforce cross-subsidy from lucrative business services to less self-sufficient services to residences and rural areas. Many countries with PTTs are now beginning to move away from this model, either by selling off their telecommunications company to private investors (as in Great Britain and New Zealand) or by opening up certain aspects of telecommunications to competition (as in Japan) (Snow, 1986).

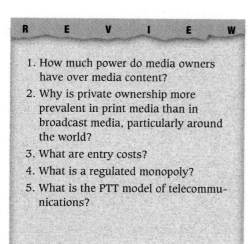

R E V I E W

1. How much power do media owners have over media content?
2. Why is private ownership more prevalent in print media than in broadcast media, particularly around the world?
3. What are entry costs?
4. What is a regulated monopoly?
5. What is the PTT model of telecommunications?

MEDIA AND ECONOMIES OF SCALE

Economies of scale refer to reduced per-unit costs when large numbers of copies are manufactured.

One of the key things that manufacturing culture and information "products" does is to increase **economies of scale**. This idea is essentially that the more copies of something you manufacture, the cheaper each copy becomes, making for lower unit costs. Cheaper copies can reach far more people, creating a much broader audience. This is especially true in mass media or cultural industries, where most of the cost and effort of producing the work goes into making the very first copy. Examples are the master print of a film, the printing plates of a newspaper or book, the master recording of a song, computer software, and on-line databases (Picard, 1989).

The **first-copy costs** require virtually all the investment in writing, directing, voicing, singing, acting, graphics, special effects, production crews, data gathering, and programming. It often costs relatively little more to produce 2 million copies than 200,000 (this is particularly true of electronic rather than print media). Although selling 2 million copies of something requires considerable investment in marketing and advertising, most of the expense of a mass media product or information service remains in its original creation.

The logic of mass production based on economies of scale has tended to make culture and information industries and producers try to reach as broad an audience as possible. Producers want to spread production costs across a broad audience. Those producing culture to make a profit can sell a larger number of copies for less money and still make a profit. A public or noncommercial medium can also afford to produce more copies and give them away or to broadcast without commercials, if the copies or broadcasts cost less.

Using a large industry to obtain economies of scale has several advantages specific to mass media and, more recently, to computer and information industries. Making many copies of the work of a few artists or journalists or programmers may make the best use of national talent and permits the best productions to be distributed to a wide audience. Of course, this presumes that nearly all members of the audience are interested in the same "best" content, an assumption that is being challenged. Furthermore, some of the best talent may be excluded by the rules and dynamics of the system. Some experts welcome the increasing growth of more specialized or segmented media as opening new opportunities for talent beyond those given by the mass media.

ECONOMIES OF SCALE ARE PARTICULARLY IMPORTANT IN COMMUNICATIONS MEDIA. WHILE IT TAKES LOTS OF MONEY TO CREATE THE FIRST MANUSCRIPT OR RECORDING, MAKING COPIES IS RELATIVELY CHEAP. PRODUCERS WANT TO SPREAD PRODUCTION COSTS ACROSS AS BROAD AN AUDIENCE AS POSSIBLE. THE MORE EXPENSIVE IT IS TO CREATE THE ORIGINAL, AS WITH BLOCKBUSTER BEST-SELLING NOVELS, THE LARGER THE MASS AUDIENCE REQUIRED TO MAKE A PROFIT.

When publishers began producing books, newspapers, and magazines in mass quantities in the 1800s, an explosion occurred in the size of the reading public. Today economies of scale have increased to the point where certain kinds of products become almost universal in the population, at least in the major industrialized nations. To understand how this happened we can apply the idea of diffusion of innovations from Chapter 2 and what we learned about social class, media access, and media choice in Chapter 3. When printed books were new, limited in range, and very expensive, lack of economic capital held back quite a few people from buying them. That was compounded by illiteracy, lack of interest, and other manifestations of a lack of cultural capital. However, printing and reading became a cyclical process that reinforced itself. As more people had sufficient money and interest to buy books, book production benefited from an economy of scale and became cheaper, which permitted even more people to buy books. And as the number of readers grew, the advantages of reading became more obvious to those who had not been "early adopters." So more people found the economic and cultural capital to begin to read.

The first peak of economies of scale in production of print media came with newspapers and books between 1830 and 1910. Newspapers were cheaply produced (the "penny press") and sold to a mass public as the dominant mass medium. Similarly, economies of scale in the recorded music industry came in the early 1900s, when music was recorded via cylinders or records and distributed directly to the public, popularizing and diffusing the idea of listening to music. After 1927, radio networks connected by telephone lines accentuated that diffusion of music listening. Similar economies of scale occurred in the film industry, when copies could be made of one expensive movie and distributed to many theaters.

Economic Logic of Networks and Centralized Production

Radio and television **networks** are the best current examples of media economies of scale. Many radio stations formed networks from the 1920s to the 1950s to share programming. When television networks rose in the late 1940s, radio networks declined. Both created national audiences that facilitated national advertising by simulcasting the same program to the largest possible audience. This advertising took advantage of emerging national markets for goods and helped consolidate those national markets. National economies of scale for various media quickly became an international economy of scale in film, music, and, after the late 1950s, television (Noam, 1985).

In film, music, and television, very large economies of production scale have been crucial because the creation of large-budget program formats or genres requires a mass audience. These media formats include feature films, television action/adventure series, and television network newscasts. In these media, production costs are still high in the 1990s and still require mass audiences to pay back the budgets required to produce them. Fortunately for the current media industries, these forms of information and entertainment are also still widely popular, with relatively "mass" audiences. These media forms and their audiences also match up with the intended audiences for some mass product advertisements.

Mass Distribution

The technology and economics of **mass distribution** have also been key in creating mass media. Economies of scale depend not only on increasingly efficient industrial production techniques but also on industrialized technologies for distributing mass-produced media products to their audiences. New technological forms of distribution can revolutionize existing media, while new means of delivering culture or information, music or news, can radically extend a medium's reach.

Railroads and other transportation industries have been very important to mass distribution. In Great Britain, the railroads helped popularize reading by making distribution of books to smaller towns cheaper and easier. Railroads also promoted low-cost books for a working-class public at bookstalls in train stations.

Point-to-point communications technologies have been crucial for mass media development as well. Development of the telegraph in the early 1800s led to a revolution in the distribution of news. Correspondents could "wire" stories quickly to their newspapers. The Associated Press "wire service" developed during the war with Mexico in 1845, when newspapers banded together to pool correspondents to cover the war and spread the news among a much broader group of U.S. newspapers.

More recently, the best examples of revolutionary distribution technologies have been the wires, microwave towers, and satellites that led to the proliferation of radio and television networks. The use of telephone wires permitted radio stations to form networks and share centrally produced programs, usually from New York or Los Angeles. Higher-capacity cable network distribution enabled the formation of the first television networks. Later, commu-

> Networks are groups of broadcast stations that share most of their programming.

> Mass distribution uses industrialized technologies for distributing mass-produced media products to their audiences.

nications satellites allowed networks to communicate with their affiliated stations more easily but also facilitated the takeoff of cable networks, such as HBO, and superstations, such as WTBS, enabling them to send their programming to cable television systems all over the United States and create national cable channels, such as CNN and MTV (Baldwin & McEvoy, 1988).

New Technologies of Production

Multimedia systems integrate text, audio, and video and let the user select the presentation mode.

The discovery and development of new technologies of production have engendered new forms of media, such as the emergence of computer-based **multimedia.** New technologies can also radically change existing media, as with the digitization of television, which permits greater use of computer technology with television production. Such developments can change existing industries or lead to the integration of previously separate industries, as with the current wave of joint ventures among cable, telephone, and computer companies.

New production technologies can change the logic of economies of scale. For example, radio networks initially depended on networking live broadcasts. Before the introduction and mass production of high-quality, inexpensive recording technology, music and other programming was broadcast live. The costs of live programming for radio were so high that stations had to form networks to share talent across a large group of stations. When record production technology became much better in the late 1940s, radio stations were able to program their own music to reach more specific local audiences with records, tapes, and, later, CDs. This evolution coincided with the rise of more specialized radio formats aimed at more specific and more localized audiences, in reaction to changes in both music genres and audience tastes. It also coincided with the decline of radio networks in competition with television. These developments reinforced each other and encouraged some stations' management to focus on new national formats and others to refocus on local or regional music traditions. When satellite technology for networks became cheaper in the 1980s and 1990s, smaller-scale radio networks could grow again, **narrowcasting** to similar, often very specific tastes and audiences across the United States (Eastman, 1993).

Narrowcasting directs media channels to specific audience segments.

Reductions in Technology Costs

In many cases, both as technology improves and as industrial techniques for efficiently using technology also improve, the costs of creating, reproducing, and distributing mass media all go down. A current example is television. The cost of production equipment, such as cameras, lights, microphones, sound mixers, switchers, special-effects generators, and animation, has dropped radically as a result of digitization, miniaturization, and more efficient manufacturing. A single desktop computer-based system in 1994 offers video switching and special effects for less than a twentieth of the cost in the 1980s.

Engineers and designers are also working on simpler techniques for doing production, so that semiprofessional and even amateur groups can create decent-looking productions. These productions don't necessarily substitute for network programs. However, in some cases, such as locally produced news programming, such technology has reduced the need for centralized network production to achieve economies of scale. Such changes permit local broadcasters, cable stations, and perhaps even community groups, religious organizations, local production companies, and businesses to do their own production at reasonable quality.

R E V I E W

1. What are economies of scale?
2. Why is the first copy of a mass media production the most expensive?
3. Why do economies of scale lead to mass audience media?
4. How have changes in technology costs affected media production? Media distribution?

Sales refers to media products themselves being sold as goods.

Subscriptions permit media to be sold on a regular basis over time for a standard fee.

Usage charges are direct charges to customers for the amount of media time, access, or content used.

Advertising is media selling audience access to those who wish to pay to put their sales message before the audience.

ECONOMIC BASES OF COMMUNICATIONS MEDIA

Changes in scale of production, technology costs, and distribution costs affect all industries. Now we need to look at some distinct aspects of the way that media have developed as industries. Media can be supported by several kinds of economic processes or economic bases: direct **sales** or **subscriptions** (where media products themselves are sold as goods), **usage charges** (where use of information or services is sold by the amount or time of access to the information), **advertising** (where media sell access to audiences), or grants and subsidies by institutions, such as governments or churches, that want to support certain kinds of media (see Figure 4.1).

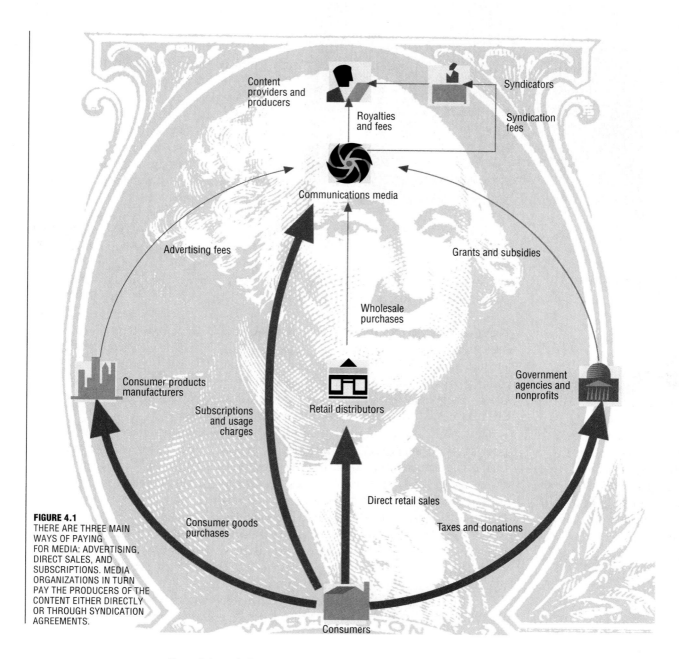

FIGURE 4.1
THERE ARE THREE MAIN WAYS OF PAYING FOR MEDIA: ADVERTISING, DIRECT SALES, AND SUBSCRIPTIONS. MEDIA ORGANIZATIONS IN TURN PAY THE PRODUCERS OF THE CONTENT EITHER DIRECTLY OR THROUGH SYNDICATION AGREEMENTS.

Information Services Economics

One of the big questions about the burgeoning information society is what it will cost, who will pay, and whether the companies and governments involved will make or lose money (Salvaggio, 1989). People are already paying more for a remarkable number of services: basic telephone service, long distance, 900 "chat" lines, mobile or cellular telephones, faxes, electronic mail services, on-line searches at libraries, ATM (automatic teller machine) usage, photocopying, basic cable, cable pay services, cable pay-per-view, video rentals, movie admissions, magazine subscriptions, and newspaper subscriptions.

Direct sales of media hardware, software, and services are straight from producers or retailers to audiences or users.

SOME SUBSCRIPTION INFORMATION SERVICES, SUCH AS PRODIGY, CARRY ADS ON THE LOWER PART OF THE SCREEN TO DIVERSIFY THEIR ECONOMIC BASE.

In the economics of information services, **direct sales** of hardware, software, and services are far more central than in mass media, where consumers pay for advertising-supported media indirectly, by buying advertised products. As mass media services, such as television, are increasingly integrated with information hardware and services, such as electronic mail and home banking, the direct sale of "media" contents, such as cable pay-per-view, may also increase in importance (Mosco, 1989). However, some information services—Prodigy, for example—also fill part of the screen with advertising to diversify their economic base.

It is still not clear whether the traditional forces of market supply and demand can pay for all desirable information services. Users do not fully pay for all current services, such as telephony. Some services, including basic telephone service, are considered so necessary that both regulators and the companies supplying services have come up with solutions in which some users are subsidized by government or other users, so that all may have access.

Sales and Subscriptions. Direct sale to consumers of a cultural or informational product, such as a book, video game, or CD, is in many ways the simplest means of paying for the production of cultural or information works. Direct sales to consumers can take a variety of forms. Books are usually sold directly from publishers as well as through stores. Sale of books, pamphlets, newspapers, newsletters, and magazines by organizations such as churches has been another important channel for direct sales.

Since mail-order operations developed in the nineteenth century, they have been a major channel for selling cultural and information products. Services that sold books by mail through subscription, such as the Book-of-the-Month Club, promoted the reading of books by a much wider public. Today **direct-mail** sales and even direct-mail advertising are still increasing rapidly in the United States.

Direct mail refers to direct targeting of customers with mailed catalogs, advertising, or other materials.

Sales of computer hardware have been another important part of the information economy. The biggest current market is for business use, although a huge potential market remains for home use. In 1992 only about 30 percent of American homes had personal computers and software. Computers diffuse and sell because of software that permits people to use them for a wide variety of purposes.

While homes are just beginning to acquire computers and sophisticated telecommunications, these technologies are almost universal in business. Within office or business settings, personal computers have diffused to use software for spreadsheets, word processing, databases, sales contacts, mailing lists, communications, and desktop publishing.

So far the main home uses of personal computers have been for word processing and for playing computer versions of video games. Educational and informational games sales are increasing. Using computers for communications is starting to spread from work to home. Increasing numbers of people are adding modems to connect their computers to others over telephone lines, to exchange electronic mail, socialize on "chat" lines, or play interactive games. Companies selling access to the Internet for these purposes were growing rapidly after 1993.

Newspapers, magazines, recordings, cable TV, and books also generate revenues by subscriptions, payment to receive a product on a continuing basis over a long term. Subscriptions to general interest magazines such as *The Saturday Evening Post*, *Harper's*, *Reader's Digest*, and other national magazines did a great deal to increase reading by the American public in the early 1900s. Both sales and subscriptions are important to such media as newspapers and magazines.

Information services can also be sold via subscriptions, both to home and to business users, usually on a monthly basis. Such information services include those aimed at home users, such as Prodigy and CompuServe, and those aimed at legal, scientific, or business institutions, such as Lexis/Nexus, which is widely used by law firms to access legal databases to supplement what is in their own law libraries.

Usage Charges. Another base of economic support for mass media has been admission fees to performances of music, theater, dance, or poetry. Live music performance is still an important source of revenues and complements sales of music on record and the playing of music on radio or music videos on television. Movies are obviously supported by admission fees as well. Group audience viewing is efficient when a technology is too expensive for people to have in their homes. In the early days of television, TV owners complained about their "television neighbors"—people who only came over to watch TV since they had no set of their own.

Today most information services are paid for by a usage fee. The main market for information services has been for basic telephone service and modest add-ons, such as fax machines, computers plus modems, and voice mail. Residential telephone customers nearly all pay a regional Bell operating company (RBOC) such as Ameritech or US West for local service. However, alternative local service is offered by cable television companies and other companies in an increasing number of areas. In addition, residential customers pay separately to companies such as AT&T, MCI, or Sprint for long-distance services or to companies like Cellular One for services such as cellular telephones. Business users often operate on a similar base, although many choose other options, such as leasing dedicated phone lines between locations or having their own international office systems connected to their regular phone lines.

Information Services Sales

Information services reproduce media content for multiple receivers and are produced by information service providers.

Beyond basic services, the main markets for **information services** such as data communications between computers, teleconferencing, and electronic mail have been businesses. New information services for businesses will probably include financial, news, and travel services.

However, the market for information services to homes is also beginning to increase, going beyond basic telephone service and cable television, both of which are beginning to carry new communications media services as well. Burgeoning new services to individuals or homes include more sophisticated telephone service, the picture or video phone, electronic mail, news services, home banking, home shopping, interactive games, home security, and mobile telephony.

Pay-per usage is a direct charge to customers for each use of various kinds of information, entertainment, and games.

Pay-per usage for various kinds of information, entertainment, and games is also increasing. Monthly subscriptions are often supplemented by charges for access to certain kinds of information or for usage beyond that which comes with the subscription. For instance, a service such as CompuServe gives users a certain number of hours of E-mail, database access, and so on for a basic monthly fee. After that, more hours of usage cost extra, as does access to some specific services, such as Lexis/Nexus. One of the problems for home sales of information services is that many people are not used to paying access charges for home computer information. They are also not used to paying for extra usage of services that have previously been "free," such as television. Both users and critics fear that pay-per usage will make some currently available information more expensive and less accessible to poorer people (Schiller, 1986; Mosco, 1989).

Syndication is rental or licensing of media products by their producers to other media companies for broadcast, distribution, or exhibition.

As home cable television services come to resemble or even include information services, they have the same problem of getting their customers used to pay-per usage. Cable companies are offering interactive video games over new-generation cable systems. In light of past failures, they have to work out easier means of delivering and "buying" such services, as well as selling the idea to their customers. Earlier experiences with interactive information technologies, such as videotex and two-way cable, are not reassuring—several countries had to scale back ambitious offerings when consumers did not respond.

BRITISH CUSTOMERS REJECT VIDEOTEX AND TWO-WAY CABLE TV

In 1979, the British telephone company, British Telecom, decided to try to get consumers to use more telephone time by offering interactive information services on the world's first commercial videotex service, Prestel. Videotex combined a simple computer screen to show text and graphics with a keyboard or keypad to enter or request information. People could request information on entertainment, news stories, home shopping, and so on. However, Prestel attracted few residential users—the equipment cost too much, and the information offered was not attractive enough to justify the costs. So British Telecom closed off consumer access in 1991. The service still succeeds with some business users.

The British government tried to introduce interactive information services for consumers again in the 1980s with cable TV. When offering cable licenses, the government encouraged two-way systems that could offer interactive services. However, those systems cost more to build, so subscription and use prices had to be higher. Consequently, fewer of the homes served by those cable systems subscribed. Most prior systems used simpler one-way cable systems and did not offer information services.

Syndication. Sometimes media producers own their own means of distribution, sale, or exhibition. American television stations and networks produce some of their own programs, primarily news programs, talk shows, and soap operas (Gitlin, 1985). In some other countries, television networks produce most of their own programming. In the United States, larger newspapers tend to produce most of their own copy, whereas smaller ones depend more on wire services, syndicated columns, and other outside sources.

Some media producers primarily sell their productions to other media companies for broadcast, sale, distribution, or exhibition. **Syndication**, the rental or licensing of media content to other media, is an important means of support for the creators and producers of news, feature columns, comic strips, films, television, and music. For instance, most television programs that run on American television networks are produced by film studios or indepen-

SYNDICATED PROGRAMMING SUCH AS *STAR TREK: DEEP SPACE NINE*, SHOWN HERE, IS BECOMING MORE POPULAR AND PROFITABLE.

First-run or **original syndication** is licensing programs directly for nonnetwork time, independent stations, and cable networks.

Copyright or **royalty fee** is a payment legally required for use of another person's intellectual property.

dent film and television production companies. After their first run on a network, these programs are often sold as reruns in syndication. Increasingly, other programs are created directly for licensing to nonnetwork time, independent stations, and cable networks, which is called **first-run** or **original syndication**. Many local television stations, both independents and network affiliates, increasingly use syndicated programs, sometimes because they think these shows will gain better audiences than network programs, sometimes because the stations make more money when they don't have to share advertising revenues with the network. The most popular original syndication television shows include *Wheel of Fortune*, *Jeopardy*, *Star Trek: Deep Space Nine*, and numerous talk shows (Eastman, 1993).

A number of syndicated services are available for radio, as well. Some stations buy their entire programming canned on tape or on computerized CD systems from syndicated programming services. Other stations, either owned by a single group or subscribers to the group's programming, now buy and simulcast programs such as Howard Stern's talk show, produced by Infinity, that runs on their stations and others. These groups become almost like new but smaller and more focused networks. Some stations subscribe to single talk shows, such as Rush Limbaugh's, or to news services, such as AP audio news.

Copyrights and Royalty Fees. Media and information products are increasingly used and reused by a variety of communications media outlets. Images, music, video, film clips, photographs, and graphics are often used in different ways by several kinds of media. For example, a photograph by a news photographer may be used by newspapers and newsmagazines via a photograph syndication service, and later in subsequent books on the subject. The newspapers will pay the photographer by paying the syndication service, and book publishers will almost certainly pay a **copyright** or **royalty fee** to the photographer for use of the photo. These fees are the photographer's compensation for his or her work in finding the right subject and situation and taking the photo (Zelezny, 1993).

There are a variety of ways for compensating copyright holders for use of a communications media product. In music, for instance, the person who holds the copyright to a song is supposed to be compensated every time the song is performed or recorded or every time a recording of it is broadcast. Compensating recording artists for direct sales of recordings is usually based on either a flat fee for the recording or a share of the sales. Because it is more difficult to determine how often songs are played on the radio or performed in public, music artist associations such as BMI and ASCAP estimate how often songs are played, collect fees from radio stations and performance venues, and pay the artists some appropriate share. This system is clumsy, however, and many songwriters are not happy with it.

Whereas today's artists try to make sure that they hold a clear copyright to their work, in the earlier days of the recording, film, and television industries, artists often accepted a flat fee and gave copyrights to the producer or studio. If a work made a great deal of money, the creators did not necessarily benefit accordingly. Now artists tend to bargain to keep the copyright or to get an agreed-upon share of earnings.

New technologies for copying and distributing images and sounds are making compen-

General Motors

"Finding out what the customer wants is easy. Doing something about it, that's the hard part."

Liz Wetzel, a member of the Cadillac Design Team at General Motors, spends a fair amount of time listening to customers react to her ideas. This is not always fun. Human nature being what it is, most people instinctively want to discount views that don't square with their own. Sometimes responding to customer input means scrapping a beloved notion. It can mean a costly retooling or a delay in production. So be it. These days at General Motors, the customer isn't just somebody with an opinion. The customer is a colleague with a whole lot of clout.

ADVERTISERS LIKE GENERAL MOTORS TARGET SPECIFIC AUDIENCES SUCH AS WOMEN THROUGH THEIR CHOICE OF ADVERTISING MEDIA, AS IN THIS MAGAZINE AD.

Target audience is a narrow, specifically defined audience that an advertiser or communications medium wants to reach.

sation to both artists and producers difficult. Photocopying of books can deprive the writer and publisher of any compensation, although publishers are now trying to force photocopy companies to obtain copyright clearances. The transfer of images and sounds into digital form on computers permits almost unlimited copying and manipulation of those items by other people. Efforts are being made to create new rules for how to enforce copyright in such instances and how to compensate the creators of sounds or images that are digitally copied or altered.

Advertising: The Main Support for American Media

The main economic base for many American media, including most television and radio stations, is advertising. In addition, it provides an important partial base for other media, such as newspapers and magazines, that also depend on newsstand sales and yearly or monthly subscriptions. As we have noted, advertising functions by selling access to the audience to the advertiser. Advertisers pay a price to place ads on radio, on television, and in newspapers and magazines hoping to persuade those who use those media to purchase their products.

Advertisers select media depending on whom they want to reach, what kind of message or information they want to communicate, and the costs involved. These decisions have an enormous effect on the media, allowing some to flourish while others die out. Often advertisers want to sell products that might potentially interest everyone in a general audience. Or they may want to use a general audience medium if it has a high impact on a particular group they want to reach. Such advertising tends to support the more traditional mass media that reach broad general audiences, such national network television, major metropolitan newspapers, and major national magazines.

Given the high cost of general audience media, especially prime-time network programs, advertisers are increasingly turning to media that reach a narrower, more specifically defined **target audience**. This type of advertising tends to support segmented media such as local television programs, cable TV networks, FM radio stations, and magazines that appeal to specific target groups (Head & Sterling, 1993).

Advertisers are also interested in newer, highly segmented or even interactive media. For example, if television becomes essentially supplied on demand, audiences or users could pay per view to watch what they select or request. They could also agree to watch some advertising to "pay" for the programming instead. (For years, broadcasters have talked about regular commercial radio and television as being "free," since the advertisers pick up the costs to get their ads to the audience.) Advertisers could also try to make the ads more entertaining or informative so that people interested in a certain type of product will choose to look at the ads for some combination of information and entertainment.

In the United States, one reason people support PBS is to avoid having to sit through advertisements on their preferred programming. Avoidance of commercials is also a major motive for many people to subscribe to pay-TV channels on cable television. This practice has reinforced the concept of paying directly for what you want to see on television, which runs counter to the television networks' emphasis that their programming is "free" to the audience because it is paid for by advertisers. Direct payment is becoming a more common way of buying desired programs, as **pay-per-view** slowly increases. New technologies for selecting and receiving individual video programs over interactive networks seem likely to make direct selection and payment for television programming increasingly prevalent, so pay-per-view programming is likely to become more important in the economics of the information society.

Pay-per-view cable is a subscription to a specific program with a separate fee just to receive that one show.

Public or Government Support for Media

Although advertising supports nearly all American mass media, some important media are supported by public contributions, by public foundations or universities, or directly by local, state, or federal governments. These kinds of public or government supports for mass media are much more common in other countries. In Europe, for example, television and radio were both primarily or exclusively public and noncommercial for a number of years, although recently advertising has become much more important.

Most Americans tend to be somewhat suspicious of government-supported media. They feel that economic control leads to political control. As the old saying goes, "He who pays the piper calls the tune." In the United States, most people tend to think that private, advertising-supported media will be more independent. However, critical studies of American commercial or advertising-supported mass media have shown that they often reflect the interests of their advertisers and in fact tend to reflect the general nature of what the government in power wants said (Altschul, 1984).

Some governments are concerned that advertising represents a source of control over media by the large corporations that supply most of the advertising investment. If funding the media gives control over media content, then many governments want to be the ones doing both the funding and the controlling. Outside the United States, the tradition in a number of countries has been to entrust governments with things essential to the public good, including broadcasting, rather than trusting private enterprises to pursue the public good.

Governments have other reasons for economically supporting mass media. In some poor countries, no one else has the capital to start expensive mass media such as newspapers, radio, or television. Before advertising develops along with a consumer market, advertiser-supported media may not be a viable option. Even in the United States there are certain kinds of media, such as public television, that governments consider desirable but that advertisers may not be willing to support. This is why the Public Broadcasting Service (PBS) and public radio stations still tend to get quite a bit of their funding from local, state, or federal governments, even though government expenditures for the media are declining (Avery, 1993).

Another major source of funding for public, noncommercial media has been subscriber support. For example, PBS depends increasingly on local contributors, as the federal government's share of PBS and its affiliated stations has declined steadily since the 1970s. Thus, PBS stations appeal directly to their audiences for annual contributions. In Great Britain and Japan, mandatory annual license fees are paid for by all television and radio set owners to support the BBC (British Broadcasting Corporation) and the NHK (Nipon Hoso Kyokai), respectively.

Educational institutions and foundations also often support public media. Many large universities are homes to the local PBS radio and television affiliates. Nonprofit foundations own or support some public stations; an example is the Pacifica Group stations in California. Major charitable foundations, such as the Ford Foundation, support specific programs on public stations—*Sesame Street*, for example. At least in the United States, businesses also sometimes support public media. It is almost necessary now for a major PBS production project to attract a major corporate sponsor. This practice also brings up the question of control through funding. Since corporations are unlikely to sponsor programs that are critical of them, even indirectly, are critical programs going to be left unmade? Who would fund a hard-hitting exposé of corporate pollution of the environment, for example?

Basic Telecommunications Services and Cross-Subsidy

Universal service is reaching all members of the population with service, usually referring to telephones.

IT IS EXPENSIVE TO BRING TELEPHONE SERVICE TO RURAL CUSTOMERS, SO THE COST HAS BEEN SUBSIDIZED BY SPREADING IT AMONG ALL CUSTOMERS.

Until 1996, many residential users of basic telephone service did not pay the full cost of reaching and serving their homes. From the early 1900s until the 1990s, basic telephone service has been promised to all Americans, a concept referred to as **universal service.** This service provides access to emergency services and basic information access to government, shopping, and business for remote and rural dwellings and for urban poor who might not have been able to pay for the actual costs of getting telephone service to their homes. The Telecommunications Act of 1996 adds:

> Consumers in all regions of the Nation, including low-income consumers and those in rural, insular, and high-cost areas, should have access to telecommunications and information services, including interexchange services and advanced telecommunications and information services, that are reasonably comparable to those services provided in urban areas and that are available at rates that are reasonably comparable to rates charged for similar services in urban areas . . . Elementary and secondary schools and classrooms, health care providers, and libraries should have access to advance telecommnications services.

> Rather that specifying what new services beyond basic telephony should be universal, the 1996 Act creates a Federal-State Joint Board for identifying those services that are essential to education, public health, or public safety; have, through the operation of market choices by customers, been subscribed to by a substantial majority of residential customers; are being deployed in public tellecommnications networks by telecommunications carriers; and are consistent with the public interest, convenience, and necessity.

Price averaging mixes the costs for areas expensive to serve, such as remote or rural areas, with costs for service to denser, cheaper urban areas.

Cross-subsidy applies revenues from a profitable area to support a less profitable one.

Providing universal service to poor and rural people has required telephone companies to subsidize the costs with revenues from more profitable services. One mechanism used was **price averaging,** in which the costs of serving expensive rural areas were averaged with the costs of servicing denser urban areas. Similarly, **cross-subsidies** have been made from profitable services, such as business and long distance, to less profitable local services, such as to poor areas.

This approach worked best when monopoly telephone companies, such as AT&T prior to 1984, or regional Bell companies, such as U.S. West in 1984–1996, could transfer revenues internally to average or cross-subsidize prices. The 1996 Telecomm Act established a subsidy pool to which all interstate telecommunications carriers must contribute and from which the FCC will supervise distribution to carriers to pay subsidy costs for universal service. States are allowed to specify extra services and create subsidy mechanisms to support them.

The original construction of telephone service in some rural areas was also subsidized by the Federal Rural Electrification Administration. Other federal and state government agencies have also subsidized certain kinds of telecommunications services, such as emergency services. Public libraries, universities, government offices, and other agencies have also paid for, provided, or subsidized various kinds of information services. If telephone companies cannot subsidize rural and low-income households, governments may be asked to. Another alternative currently being discussed is to require all those offering local telecommunications services to contribute toward a pool of money that would be used to subsidize those who cannot afford to pay the full costs of service.

Economic Logic of Segmentation in "Mass" Media

The economics of the "mass" media are changing in ways that permit and even encourage them to be less "massive." Technological changes, industry changes, and receptivity by audiences and advertisers are all encouraging media to narrowcast or segment—to focus on smaller, more specific audiences with more specialized programs or contents (Owen & Wildman, 1992).

One factor leading to segmentation is financial. Many new media or new media channels can increasingly count on lower unit costs as a result of cheaper inputs. In sound recording, television, journalism, maybe even film, there is now more competing talent—people to write, act, sing, direct, create effects, and animate. As we noted earlier, basic production costs for print, television, and music have also dropped significantly due to cheaper technologies of production. Those media that use electronic transmission also have more channels to choose from and lower transmission costs.

Another factor in segmentation is that audiences are gravitating toward more specific information and entertainment media. With more program genres on more different outlets, these genres are developing audiences whose naturally specialized interests are being reflected. The new specialized media also permit more producers to pursue their own interests.

Another major factor is advertiser interest in targeting specific groups. The increasing numbers of new media and new media outlets and channels permit advertisers to target more specific groups more cheaply. Advertisers are also simply following the audiences who are moving toward more specialized or narrowcast media.

Away from the Logic of General Audiences and Networks

The current market structure reflects coexistence between mass media and "narrowcast," segmented media. The audiences of broadcast networks are in slow decline, but space clearly exists for a fourth network, like Fox, if it targets a more specific group, as Fox has done with a younger, more urban audience. Network programming is still popular and networks are still

R E V I E W

1. What are media sales and subscriptions?
2. What kinds of media are paid for by sales? By subscriptions?
3. Are information media more likely to be paid for by sales or advertising?
4. What are direct sales and direct mail?
5. What are usage charges? What kinds of media use them?
6. What is syndication?
7. What is original syndication versus "reruns"?
8. What is a copyright? How do media creators use it to get paid for their work?
9. How does advertising work? Who is paying for what?
10. What is universal service?
11. What is a cross-subsidy? Why is it used to obtain universal service?
12. What is segmentation?
13. How do information technologies reinforce segmentation?

profitable, but some program forms are moving away from network television to cable networks, syndication sales, or independent stations.

On the other hand, new technologies are also giving rise to new kinds of networks. Small radio "networks" based on small groups of stations and syndicated programs are reemerging as a force in radio, almost forty years after the decline of the original radio networks in the mid-1950s. These groups tend to be more specific and segmented, however, not the broad general audience networks of old.

Information technologies permit almost complete segmentation in information services. Going by current models, such as the international computer network Internet, users tend to select a highly individualized set of services to subscribe to or browse through. Some music and video services are going the same way—toward a selection of what the user or audience member wants, when he or she wants it. Information technology will be critical in keeping track of who watches or reads what and when, for purposes of billing and of targeting advertising.

SUMMARY & REVIEW

What Are the Basic Economies and Ownership of Mass Media?

Why are the economics and ownership of media important?
The economics of communications media has a great deal to do with the diversity and nature of their content, their availability and accessibility to people, and their role in society. Ownership structures consist of the patterns of who owns media industries and how concentrated and integrated that ownership is.

How much power do media owners have over media content?
Some people think that the ownership of media matters little and that major decisions are usually made by professional staff. However, a number of critics of the mass media assume that owners are very powerful in determining the structure and performance, or content, of communications media. Some critics go so far as to say that if you know who owns a newspaper or a station or a cable network, you know essentially what that paper or station or network is going to say.

What are entry costs?
Entry costs are the costs of starting up a media company—technology, distribution, personnel, and raw material. Technology costs come both in the production of media and information products and in their distribution to users. Distribution costs are the costs of getting media and information products from producers to consumers or users. High entry costs can pose barriers to would-be competitors and reinforce narrow or concentrated patterns of ownership.

What is the PTT model of telecommunications?
A PTT is a national government-owned post, telephone, and telegraph monopoly. In this model, government ministries or government-controlled companies usually run telecommunications. This model was common in most countries outside the United States until very recently.

Why Are Economies of Scale So Important in Communications Media?

What are economies of scale?
Economies of scale occur when you manufacture so many copies of something that you can make each of those copies more cheaply. Cheaper copies can reach far more people, creating a broader audience.

Why is the first copy of a mass media production the most expensive?

First-copy costs in mass media require virtually all the investment in the production of the work. These costs include writing, directing, voicing, singing, acting, graphics, special effects, production crews, data gathering, and programming. Examples are the master print of a film, the printing plates of a newspaper or book, and the master recording of a song.

Why do economies of scale lead to mass audience media?

Producers want to spread production cost across a broad audience. In film, music, and television, large economies of production scale have been crucial because the creation of large-budget program formats or genres requires a mass audience.

What Are the Economic Bases of Communications Media?

What are media sales and subscriptions?

Media sales refers to media products themselves being sold as goods. Subscriptions permit media to be sold on a regular basis over time for a standard fee. Direct sale to consumers of copies of a cultural or informational product, such as a book, video game, or CD, is in many ways the simplest means of paying for their production.

What kinds of media are paid for by sales? by subscriptions?

Consumers pay for advertising-supported media indirectly, by buying advertised products. Media paid for by direct sales include basic telephone service, long distance, 900 "chat" lines, telephones, faxes, electronic mail services, on-line searches at libraries, photocopying, basic cable, cable pay services, cable pay-per-view, video rentals, and movie admissions. On-line information services as well as newspapers, magazines, music recordings, cable TV, and books are sold by subscriptions.

What is direct sale and direct mail?

Direct sales of media hardware, software, and services are straight from producers or retailers to audiences or users. Direct mail refers to direct targeting of customers with mailed catalogs, advertising, or other materials.

What are usage charges? What kinds of media use them?

Usage fees are direct charges to customers for access to or use of media, information, or services that directly depend on the amount of time, access, or content used. Admissions for movies, concerts, and so on are a kind of usage fee. Most information services are paid by subscription or a usage fee. Until recently, the main market for information services has been basic telephone service and modest add-ons, such as faxes, and voice mail.

What is syndication?

Some media producers primarily sell what they produce to other media companies for broadcast, distribution, or exhibition. Syndication or rental or licensing of media content to other media is an important means of support for the creators and producers of news, feature columns, comic strips, films, television, and music.

What is original syndication versus "reruns"?

Increasingly, television programs and some other media are created directly for licensing to nonnetwork time, independent stations, and cable networks, which is called first-run or original syndication. Many local television stations increasingly use first-run or original syndication programs to gain better audiences than network programs or to make more money when they don't have to share advertising revenues with the network.

What is a copyright? How do media creators use it to get paid for their work?

A copyright is a legal protection granted to the creator of a legal or artistic work by the government. If a copyright is registered, any use of that work requires permission of the copyright holder, who may deny permission or charge for permission to use it, which is called a royalty fee. Royalty fees are often the creator's compensation for his or her work, unless they sell the copyright.

How does advertising work? Who is paying for what?

The main economic base of many American media is advertising. Advertising functions by selling access to the audience to the advertiser. Advertisers pay a price to place ads on radio, on television, or in newspapers or magazines hoping to persuade those who use these media to purchase their products.

Which media attract general versus highly targeted advertising?

Advertisers who want to sell things that might potentially interest everyone in a general audience will use a general audience medium such as network television. Advertisers who want to reach a narrower, more specifically defined target audience use more narrowcast or segmented media, such as cable TV networks.

What is segmentation?

Technological changes, industry changes, and receptivity by audiences and advertisers are all encouraging media to narrowcast or segment—that is, focus on smaller, more specific audiences with more specialized programs or contents.

How do information technologies reinforce segmentation?

Many new segmented media channels increasingly count on the lower unit costs that result from cheaper inputs: more competing talent and lower production costs. Those media that use electronic transmission also have more channels to choose from and lower transmission costs.

REFERENCES

Altschul, J. (1984). *Agents of power*. New York: Longman.

Avery, R. (1993). *Public service broadcasting in a multichannel environment*. New York: Longman.

Bagdikian, B. (1993). *The media monopoly* (4th ed.). Boston: Beacon Press.

Baldwin, T., & McEvoy, S. (1988). *Cable communication* (2nd ed.). Englewood Cliffs, NJ: Prentice Hall.

Browne, D. (1989). *Comparing broadcast systems*. Ames: Iowa State University Press.

Compaigne, B. M. (1982). *Who owns the media? Concentration of ownership in the mass communication industry*. New York: Crown.

Eastman, S. T. (1993). *Broadcast/cable programming*. Belmont, CA: Wadsworth.

Gitlin, T. (1985). *Inside prime time*. New York: Pantheon.

Head, S. (1985). *World broadcasting systems*. Belmont, CA: Wadsworth.

Head, S., & Sterling, C. (1993). *Broadcasting in America* (5th ed.). Boston: Houghton Mifflin.

Mosco, V. (1989). *The pay-per society*. Norwood, NJ: Ablex.

Noam, E. (1985). *Video media competition*. New York: Columbia University Press.

Owen, B. M., & Wildman, S. (1992). *Video economics*. Cambridge, MA: Harvard University Press.

Picard, R. G. (1989). *Media economics: Concepts and issues*. Newbury Park, CA: Sage.

Salvaggio, J. (1989). *The information society: Economic, social and structural issues*. Hillsdale, NJ: Erlbaum.

Schiller, H. (1986). *Information and the crisis economy*. New York: Oxford University Press.

Snow, M. (1986). *Marketplace for telecommunications: Regulation and deregulation in industrialized democracies*. New York: Longman.

Zelezny, J. D. (1993). *Communications law*. Belmont, CA: Wadsworth.

Chapter 5

COMMUNICATIONS MEDIA POLICY AND ETHICS

C H A P T E R   P R E V I E W

n this chapter, we concentrate on public policy and ethics. *Public policy* involves a collective action of the whole society or its representatives, which requires a good deal of public discussion and the creation of some kind of consensus over what to do. Policy focuses on both content and structure of media. For example, sex and violence in the media have been discussed for decades. New discussions arise over pornography on the Internet. Cable TV, telephone companies, satellite companies, and broadcasters have been increasingly anxious to compete directly with each other, across industry lines that regulators had held separate. The 1996 Telecommunications Act addressed these and other issues, but its restrictions on Internet pornography have already been challenged in court on the basis of the First Amdendment, and other changes will take actions by both federal and state regulators to implement.

Washington, D.C., 2010

This hearing of the Senate Committee on Commerce will now come to order! Will the witness please introduce himself?

My name is Red Wormer, and I don't think I need any further introduction.

(Chuckle) I'm sure we all know that Mr. Wormer here is chairman of Wormer Communications, owner of 90 percent of the cable systems in the country and over 500 channels on the information superhighway.

Five hundred thirty-two, to be exact, including the one that shows this meeting and the ones that carry your campaign commercials. And don't forget that I also provide phone service to your private officers.

(Belly laugh) Now, Mr. Wormer, it's not true that you're trying to monopolize the telecommunications industry, is it?

No, sir. And I am not trying to destroy family values either.

But what about that Family Fistfight Classics channel?

Well, I believe in our First Amendment right to watch mayhem. Besides, lots of families have fights. We're just reflectin' society by showing their home videos and giving prizes for the best ones.

Of course you are! But we are also a little concerned that you have taken over the ten biggest banks.

Well, they fell behind on their payments to my Home Banking Network. What else could I do?

Perfectly understandable! Perfectly! Will you promise not to do it again?

I promise not to take over the ten biggest banks again.

And the family fistfights?

O.K., no bleeding before 8 P.M. AND I'll overlook how much the IRS owes my banking network, for now.

Wonderful! Generous! Thank you so much. Meeting adjourned.

he importance of media in public and private life leads to constant concerns about what the media are doing and how to control them. **Policy** refers to government and public consideration of how to structure and regulate certain activities, such as those of the media, so that they contribute to the public good. Private groups, such as churches, industry trade groups, minority groups, and public interest groups, also monitor media performance and lobby the media to change various practices or kinds of content. **Ethics** refer to how professional communicators should behave in situations where their activities may have negative effects on others. **Self-regulation** pertains to communication industry codes and practices of monitoring and controlling the media's performance. All of these apply to difficult situations in which those inside and outside the media have to consider how to minimize their negative impact and increase their benefits for society.

Individual communicators are constantly making ethical decisions beyond what is specifically covered by policy or law. Ethical issues include what kinds of topics to cover, how to respect the privacy of people, and how to protect the confidentiality of sources. Communicators must also be aware of pertinent laws, such as those governing defamation and copyright.

If you plan to be a communications media professional, you might well have to address several kinds of ethical issues. Imagine what you might do in the following situations:

- You are a student reporter for a campus newspaper. One of your professors is on a confidential committee investigating possible financial abuses by the director of athletics. The professor has "leaked" some incriminating information to you, which you can't corroborate, on condition that you won't identify the source. Do you print the information? What do you say about your source?

- You are a student reporter for a radio station. Someone gives you some evidence from electronic mail indicating that a popular professor may be sexually harassing a graduate student. Do you read the mail? Do you write a story on it? Do you mention the professor's name? Do you indicate your source?

- You are an aspiring young disk jockey for a local radio station. A record company offers you a block of tickets to a popular, sold-out concert if you will listen to some new recordings from their label, hoping you will play them. Do you accept? Their representative also hints that if you are interested in drugs, those are available. What do you say?

- You are a manager of a telemarketing operation to raise money for your university. You discover that you can use your computerized telephone system to monitor the number of calls per hour your telemarketing agents are making. Do you use that information to make them work harder? Do you fire those who seem to be making fewer calls?

THE POLICYMAKING PROCESS

Government policy is usually made by politicians elected to Congress or state legislatures, lawyers and judges appointed to various courts, and economists and social scientists appointed to regulatory agencies in the government. Corporations also make policy through

Policy is government or public consideration of how to structure and regulate media so that they contribute to the public good.

Ethics are moral rules or rules of conduct that guide one's actions in specific situations.

Self-regulation refers to industry codes and practices of monitoring the industry's own performance.

their own decisions, such as how much advertising to carry, how much sexual content to show, what kinds of services to offer and how much to charge. Researchers and journalists often help set the agenda for regulation by bringing issues to the attention of government or corporate policymakers.

Federal Regulation and Policymaking

All three branches of the federal government play an active role in communications regulation (see Figure 5.1). The executive branch contains the Federal Communications Commission (FCC) and a unit in the Commerce Department called the National Telecommu-

FIGURE 5.1
WHILE THE FCC IS THE MAIN REGULATOR OF ELECTRONIC MEDIA AND TELECOMMUNICATIONS IN THE UNITED STATES, OTHER FEDERAL AGENCIES, SUCH AS THE JUSTICE AND COMMERCE DEPARTMENTS, AS WELL AS CONGRESS AND THE JUDICIAL SYSTEM, ARE ALSO HEAVILY INVOLVED. THIS EXAMPLE FOCUSES ON REGULATION OF THE BROADCASTING MEDIA.

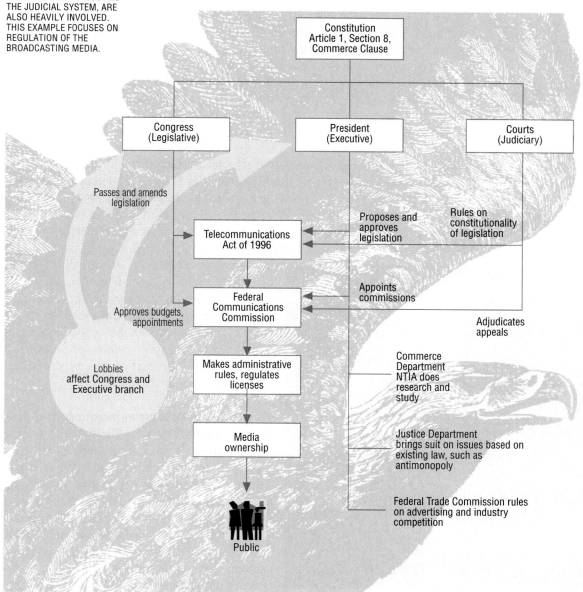

nications and Information Administration (NTIA). Because actions of the FCC are taken to federal district courts under the Communications Act of 1934, these courts are often the key media-related element in the judicial branch. Congress can also directly enact laws that affect the communications industry, although it has often been less involved than the regulatory agencies and courts.

The Federal Communications Commission. The lead federal agency is the Federal Communications Commission, or FCC. The FCC regulates broadcasting and telecommunications. Final decisions are made by a group of five commissioners nominated by the president. The FCC also has a staff divided into several bureaus. The FCC Mass Media Bureau oversees licensing and operation of broadcast stations. It also enforces the regulations inposed on cable TV by Congress in the 1992 Cable Regulation Act. The Policy and Rules Division handles studies and proceedings to produce new rules. For example, this division had to make many new rules to implement the 1996 Telecommunications Act provisions concerning ownership, frequency assignment, and competition. The Enforcement Division handles complaints, enforces compliance with rules, and interprets rules.

The FCC's Common Carrier Bureau has primary responsibility for the telecommunications industry. The FCC used to regulate AT&T's prices, or tariffs, when AT&T was a monopoly. With the 1996 Telecommunications Act, the FCC has shifted toward overseeing competition among carriers, market entry rules, universal service requirements, interconnection, and cooperation requirements. The FCC will share jurisdiction over antitrust and monopoly issues with the Justice Department and over local telecommunications carriers, such as the regional Bell operating companies (RBOCs), or Baby Bells, with their respective state public utitlity commissions (PUCs). In some cases, such as establishing definitions and procedures for universal service, the FCC will work together with PUCs in joint boards.

The FCC's Common Carrier Bureau also monitors customer service standards and overall trends in the cost of telecommunications services. Through its rule-making process, the FCC has a great deal of influence on the nature and terms of the services that all the carriers offer. Before 1996, FCC rulings allowed competing local phone companies to interconnect with local exchange carriers. Later rulings implemented the 1996 Telecommunications Act to establish conditions for much wider competition, while trying to ensure reasonable costs and standards of service to users.

The National Telecommunications and Information Administration. The National Telecommiunications and Information Administration (NTIA) was established in its current form in 1978. Its role is to act in an advisory capacity on overall telecommunications policy in the United States. It also administers some small development grants that were drastically scaled back in 1995, as part of a Congressional attempt to reduce the role of the Commerce Department. In recent years the NTIA has played a role in representing the United States in international bodies

THE NTIA IS TRYING TO GET U.S. TELECOMMUNICATIONS COMPANIES INTO COUNTRIES SUCH AS JAPAN WHERE THERE IS AN IMBALANCE IN TRADE.

Frequency allocations are parts of the radio frequency spectrum authorized for a particular purpose.

Multilateral trade negotiations are between a number of countries at the same time, usually within an international organization.

that decide issues, such as international telecommunications trade policies and communication **frequency allocations.** The NTIA and FCC often compete to represent U.S. policy in such arenas.

In recent years NTIA negotiators have focused on opening foreign markets to competition from U.S. telecommunications equipment manufacturers in an effort to reduce the imbalance in international trade. It has also been active in **multilateral trade negotiations,** such as the North American Free Trade Agreement (NAFTA) and the General Agreement on Trade and Tariffs (GATT). Another small federal agency, the Special Trade Representative, is also sometimes involved in foreign trade issues in communications media.

The Federal Trade Commission. The Federal Trade Commission (FTC) is the regulatory agency charged with domestic trade policy. It is responsible for monitoring trade practices, such as advertising. For example, it has held hearings on advertising practices aimed at children. It also investigates companies' **restraints of trade.** For example, in 1989 it began an investigation of possible **anticompetitive practices** in computer operating systems and programs by Microsoft, Inc.; the investigation was picked up by the Justice Department in 1994.

Restraint of trade refers to practices by a company that limit other companies' ability to enter or compete in trade.

Anticompetitive practices are those that unfairly use market power or statements to damage potential competitors.

The Justice Department. The Justice Department also has an important role to play in the regulation of the telecommunications industry. Charged with the enforcement of the Sherman Antitrust Act, the Justice Department initiated the suit that eventually led to the breakup of AT&T. From 1984 to 1996, the Justice Department had less involvement in telecommunications regulation, but with the 1996 Telecommunications Act it will share jurisdication on monopoly issues with the FCC and will monitor competitiveness in important sectors of the overall communications industry, such as monopoly practices in the computer industry.

The Courts. The judicial branch has a key role of interpreting aspects of the U.S. Constitution relevant to communications media. It also interprets laws made by Congress and rules made by the FCC and other federal agencies to see whether they fit within or violate the Constitution. The Supreme Court and federal district courts are both important in decisions concerning freedom of speech issues based on the First Amendment, **privacy** issues based on several amendments, and monopoly issues based in the Sherman Antitrust Act. The Third District Court of the District of Columbia had a preeminent role in the telephone and telecommunications area. It was in this court that the Justice Department originally filed the antitrust case against AT&T that eventually led to the modified final judgment (MFJ) that broke up the Bell system. Justice Harold Greene enforced the MFJ from his bench in the Third District Court until 1996, when Congress wrote new laws to regulate the telecommunications industry. In 1996 federal courts had already received a combined challenge by a number of interest groups to the constitutionality of the limits placed on Internet pornography in the 1996 Telecommunications Act.

Privacy is the right to keep certain information or activities out of the scrutiny of media, government, or private observers.

Congress. It is the U.S. Congress that ultimately writes the telecommunications laws of the land. It passed the Sherman Antitrust Act in 1890. The FCC was established through the Communications Act of 1934. After years of debate, Congress replaced the Communications Act only in 1996, to promote more competition within and across industries, to allow increased concentration of ownership, to regulate violent and indecent content, to continue to ensure universal service, and to lower costs.

Many congressional committees can and do become involved in communications issues. The main congressional committees are the House Telecommunications Subcommittee; the House Energy and Commerce Committee; the House Committee on the Judiciary; the House Committee on Science, Space, and Technology; the Senate Committee on Commerce, Science, and Transportation; and the Senate Judiciary Committee.

State Regulation

Natural monopoly is a business or service area that inherently lends itself to domination by a single firm.

Public utilities are closely regulated government or private companies, usually monopolies, that provide public services.

Deregulation refers to decreasing government oversight in the anticipation that competition will minimize abuses of power.

For many years, telecommunications seemed like a textbook case of a **natural monopoly,** a business that lends itself to domination by a single firm in each service area because of the costs of supplying the service. According to the rate of return regulatory model, telephone companies were protected monopolies in their service areas but had to submit to rate regulation by state-level public utility commissions to prevent the abuse of their monopoly power. To curb monopoly pricing, telephone companies were limited to a fixed percentage profit, calculated against the base of the capital investment represented in the telephone network infrastructure. This meant that proposed telephone rate increases were subject to close scrutiny at the hands of state **public utility** regulators, who were charged primarily with promoting the widest possible availability of telephone service at the lowest possible cost. State regulators will now become involved in a broader set of issues as the phone companies they regulate, such as Bell Atlantic, enter into cable TV, and as cable TV companies and others try to offer local telephone services, which the states have regulated.

In the 1980s–1990s, the rise of potential competitors such as cable television and a shift in political philosophy have pointed away from government control of telecommunications wherever possible. A number of states have followed this approach for local telephone service, drastically reducing the levels of regulatory oversight. A few states have gone much further, essentially **deregulating** telecommunications entirely by removing most of the restrictions on the nature and scope of activities that such companies engage in.

EDWARD O. FRITTS (RIGHT), PRESIDENT AND CEO OF THE NATIONAL ASSOCIATION OF BROADCASTERS, A POWERFUL LOBBYING GROUP, IS SHOWN HERE SHAKING HANDS WITH REPRESENTATIVE MARKEY OF THE HOUSE TELECOMMUNICATIONS SUBCOMMITTEE.

Lobbies

In media regulation, lobbies have several functions. The most obvious is to affect proposed legislation in the executive branch and in the Congress. However, a wide variety of interested parties also lobby the media directly to affect the public discussion of proposed legislation and, more broadly, to affect other kinds of media content as well.

Many groups have an interest in lobbying to affect the outcome of legislation in Congress. When an industry trade group such as the National Association of Broadcasters lobbies on its own behalf, it might be referred to as a "special-interest group," which carries a pejorative connotation. Groups that do not seem to have a direct financial interest at stake are often referred to as "public interest groups," since they are pursuing a social or political goal. For instance, Native American groups have lobbied Hollywood studios to affect how "Indians" are portrayed in films and on television.

Baby Bells are the local telephone companies created by the breakup of AT&T in 1984.

AT&T has perhaps the most potent lobbying force of any major corporation and can seemingly block any legislation that is not in its interests. The **Baby Bells** also constitute a potent lobby, and their interests are no longer aligned with those of AT&T. However, other groups, such as the National Association of Broadcasters and the National Cable Television Association, have also emerged as potent lobbies. Increasingly, telecommunications policy issues cut across industry boundaries, so that the powerful lobbies of the publishing and motion picture industries also get involved.

On the public interest lobby side, the American Association of Retired Persons lobbies to preserve universal, low-cost "lifeline" local telephone service for older Americans. The Electronic Frontier Foundation is pressing to make sure that any new "data superhighway" maintains open access to all service providers, and it opposed the Communications Decency Act, which created criminal penalites for "indecency" on the Internet and was passed with the 1996 reform bill. These competing special-interest agendas made it difficult to pass the 1996 Telecommunications Act.

On the mass media side, public interest groups press for restrictions on television violence, which are resisted strenuously by the National Association of Broadcasters (NAB) and the Motion Picture Association of America (MPAA), whose members produce most television programming. Despite this opposition, however, the 1996 reform bill required a television ratings system linked to a "V-chip" in new television sets that can be set to screen out certain content coded for violence or sex.

The Fifth Estate: The Media in the Policy Process

The mass media act as lobbyists for their own interests, either directly in their own channels or through associations such as the NAB and MPAA. However, media also have a much broader role as the forum in which much policy debate takes place. Both government and interest groups lobby Congress by trying to get their ideas into the media. They hope to use the media to set the agenda for public debate and affect public opinion. The news media pursue the goal of reporting such controversies and issues objectively, but they sometimes have a position or agenda of their own. For example, in the last several decades, much debate among both conservatives and liberals has centered on whether the news media tend to have a generally liberal or generally conservative bias and whether they might be biased against specific groups, such as business or the military.

Standards Bodies

In the United States, telecommunications standards are set in a variety of ways. Some are set nationally, either by the FCC itself or by committees sponsored by the FCC. Some standards are created by industry associations or research groups and are subsequently ratified by the U.S. government. Sometimes the FCC forces industry to create a working group to resolve a conflict over standards, such as the National Television Standards Committee (NTSC) that set the current U.S. television standard in 1941, or the recent working group instructed to find a new digital high-definition television (HDTV) standard.

International Regulation

Perhaps more than in any other industry, international regulatory bodies have influenced standards in the telecommunications field. The International Telecommunications Union (ITU), first formed in 1865 to standardize telegraph traffic between countries, is the oldest international body in the world. Now an affiliated agency of the United Nations, the ITU continues to play an important role in the development of telecommunications technology worldwide.

The ITU standards process involves negotiation and ratification of technical approaches to providing telephone services. Representatives from equipment manufacturers, telecommunications carriers, and national regulatory bodies confer within committees to define the standards, which are then ratified at quadrennial international congresses.

Another important process under ITU control is the allocation of radio spectrum frequency bands. Allocation issues are decided at the World Administrative Radio Congress (WARC), held every four years, and at regional conferences held in each of the ITU regions every two years. It is the WARC that decides, for example, which frequencies will be available for cellular radio service in various countries, which frequencies will be reserved for satellite communication, and how far apart the satellites can be. The regional conferences then deal with communications issues that crop up between neighboring countries.

At the end of 1992 the ITU held a special conference to reorganize itself for the Information Age, particularly to recognize the growing convergence between broadcast and telecommunications media. Accordingly, the formerly separate committees for telecommunications and radio were merged. The new structure has a single directorate that handles radio frequency spectrum allocation issues across both telecommunications and broadcasting. Another directorate is concerned with the use of telecommunications in fostering economic development, a key issue for developing nations.

R E V I E W

1. What are the distinctions between policy, law, and ethics?
2. What are the main institutions in the media policymaking process?
3. What is public utility regulation?
4. What is a lobby group? What are the main ones in communications media issues?
5. How are media and telecommunications standards set?
6. What is the International Telecommunications Union and what are its main functions?

KEY COMMUNICATIONS POLICIES

Policy issues that affect media run a wide gamut from First Amendment issues to copyright to ownership and control.

The First Amendment

Censorship is control over media content by those in higher authority in a society.

Libel is harmful or untruthful criticism by media which damages someone.

In many times and places, governments have directly pursued **censorship** and control of media. Sometimes governments simply want to censor criticism of themselves; sometimes they decide to seize control of media to use them as tools in their own plans for development of a society. At a lower level of control, many governments have tried to restrain or control certain kinds of media content they consider harmful. Many nations have rules about saying things intended to help overthrow or subvert the government. Most nations have some kind of law about **libel** or slander—printing or saying unjust or untruthful things that defame someone. Some nations give people who have been criticized a right of reply. Many nations also control programming for children, usually limiting advertising, violence, or sexual content (Rivers & Schramm, 1980).

The idea of exercising moral judgment and control on content is older than the idea of freedom of speech. Strong historical traditions of censorship and control lasted well into the mass media era. Printing, books, and newspapers were born under censorship by both religious and political authorities. Religious leaders in the 1400s through the 1700s felt that unrestrained print media would eventually lead people away from a religious, morally guided life. Today many feel that the media have had a considerable role in providing secular, nonreligious sources of information and values, thereby diminishing the centrality of religion in people's lives. Newspapers and books also expose people to ideas that challenge governments, as when early newspapers criticized rulers and books began to criticize key ideas, such as the divine right of kings to rule, and proposed other ideas, such as democratically electing political leaders. These ideas helped lead to great political changes in many countries from the 1700s to the present.

Current issues about media content also lead to proposals for controls on specific types of content. Since the 1950s people have worried about the effects of film and televised violence on children. In 1995 people began to worry about children's access to pornography over the Internet. In 1996 Congress passed a law restricting "indecent" programming on the Internet and requiring a *V-chip* to permit television viewers to block out programs rated to have sex or violence. Film and television industry leaders reluctantly promised to create a ratings system by 1997.

Freedom of speech is the right to speak what one wishes free of government or other restraints.

Marketplace of ideas is the concept that, with free speech, the best ideas will win in competition with others.

Free press is the extension of freedom of speech to media.

MANY GOVERNMENTS FEAR CRITICISM FROM THE PRESS, SO THEY CONTROL OR CENSOR IT. A CARTOON CRITICIZING GOVERNMENT OR A LEADER LIKE THIS WOULD NOT BE ALLOWED TO RUN IN MANY COUNTRIES.

Development of the First Amendment—Freedom of Speech and Press. In the early days of printing in Europe, both church and civil authorities gave licenses to certain guilds or companies to print books but also set controls over what could be printed. As people began to be more concerned about the importance of **freedom of speech** for developing more open societies, such control by licensing came under increasingly severe criticism from writers and philosophers. For example, in 1644 the writer and poet John Milton wrote a critique of such censorship, called *Areopagitica*, proclaiming the need for religious free speech.

Along with economic ideas about the value of a marketplace competition for goods, the idea developed of a **marketplace of ideas** in which different voices could compete for attention. In political terms, John Stuart Mill, Edmund Burke, and other early advocates of democracy promoted the idea of an active, informed citizenry. They pointed to the need for a **free press** to assist in the free circulation of ideas (Altschul, 1984).

Strong protection of freedom of speech and press developed during the American Revolution against British colonial rule in 1775–1783. Independent newspapers and pamphlets were a major force in stirring up the

REPRINTED BY PERMISSION: TRIBUNE MEDIA SERVICES, CARTOON BY MIKE PETERS.

American colonists to resist British rule. We remember Benjamin Franklin for publishing pro-independence newspapers and Thomas Paine for writing pamphlets, such as "Common Sense," that were widely read. A free press was so important to the American Revolution that it was firmly enshrined in the Declaration of Independence and in the **First Amendment** to the U.S. Constitution. The First Amendment says

> Congress shall make no law respecting an establishment of religion, or prohibiting the free exercise thereof, or abridging the freedom of speech, or of the press; or the right of the people peaceably to assemble, and to petition the Government for a redress of grievances.

The 1934 Communications Act applies these protections to broadcasting:

> Nothing in this Act shall be understood or construed to give the Commission the power of censorship over the radio communications or signals transmitted by any radio station, and no regulation or condition shall be promulgated or fixed by the Commission which shall interfere with the right of free speech by means of radio communication.

Protection of speech is very strong in the United States compared to most other countries. The legal and journalistic thinking in the United States has tended to see controls on any kind of content as a direct threat to overall freedom of the press. To ensure essential freedoms of political, religious, and other speech, must people be free to say virtually anything? Many other societies have been more willing to place some kinds of controls on freedom of speech and freedom to express ideas and images in the media. Compared to many other societies, the United States has taken a strong position for extreme liberty. This approach has placed the main responsibility for control over media content on industry self-regulation and individual communicators' sense of ethics.

Limits on the First Amendment. Some kinds of speech are not protected by the First Amendment: defamation, obscenity, plagiarism, invasion of privacy, and inciting insurrection. These are key issue areas for government policy and judicial proceedings and for the ethical decisions of professionals in their day-to-day work in communications media.

Defamation (libel and slander) refers to printing or saying untrue things about private citizens that might damage their reputations. Laws against defamation protect the welfare and dignity of citizens. U.S. legal policy balances libel concerns against the watchdog role of the press, which is to expose corruption or incompetence by officials or public figures. In ethics, journalists often have to decide how far to pursue a story and whether certain kinds of stories about individuals or certain treatment of individuals is ethical. For instance, should the names of crime victims be published (Meyer, 1987)?

The mid-twentieth century saw a sharp decline in the limits placed on **indecency,** which is usually defined as depiction or description of sex or excretion in the media or arts. This was seen as progress for freedom of speech. However, since the 1970s there has been increasing concern about obscenity again, especially with indecency on broadcast media, because of their uniquely wide availability. In the 1990s this concern also arose regarding the Internet.

A new challenge arrived with interactive computer networks. The Telecommunications Act of 1996 created a more inclusive definition of objectionable materials under the term "indecency" and imposes criminal penalties for transmitting indecent materials over computer networks in a manner that may allow viewing by children. This provision was promptly challenged in court by the American Civil Liberties Union, the Electronic Frontier Foundation, and other groups that might be held responsible under the 1996 act, such as America Online. The challenge was based on grounds that the Internet deserves First

Amendment protections as broad as those enjoyed by print rather than the more limited protection given broadcasting.

The argument is that broadcasting is more intrusive into the home than print media and that it is more likely to be received by children than print media are. One of the recent tendencies has been to limit indecency during hours when children are likely to be listening and to create "safe havens" for absolutely free speech later at night, from midnight to 6 A.M. Many question whether some of the more controversial broadcasters, such as Howard Stern, go too far and whether they and their sponsors should not exercise more self-restraint.

A new challenge is coming with access to indecent materials over interactive computer networks. Professionals in both broadcasting and information services will have new kinds of ethical choices to make about what kinds of materials to place or permit on interactive services. Schools and other institutions are already facing ethical choices about whether to restrict their students' access to sex-oriented discussion groups on the Internet, for example.

One major response to criticism about indecency, advertising content, and violence on radio and television has been a series of proposals for industry self-regulation. By taking on self-regulation, the industry accepts social responsibility for content and moves to avoid government regulation. The National Association of Broadcasters (NAB) has created a code about advertising, although it is noncompulsory because the Justice Department feared that it might restrain trade. In 1993 the television industry proposed voluntary standards about labeling violent programming, but critics felt that simple labeling was not effective. However, voluntary reliance on industry ethics and self-regulation may be the only option that does not violate freedom of speech.

Intellectual Property and Copyrights

Intellectual property rights and the more specific area of copyrights present several policy and ethical problems. Through the protection of patents, copyrights, trademarks, and other kinds of intellectual property, **copyright** law tries to make sure that people who create an intellectual product receive the economic benefit from selling, leasing, renting, or licensing their invention, song, play, book, movie, software program, or other work. The premise of this law is that if people do not benefit from their own intellectual or artistic creations, others will not be motivated to create. This issue becomes particularly important as we move toward an information economy in which most people's livelihoods will depend directly on creating, buying, and selling information.

Copyright is a legal privilege to use, sell, or license intellectual property, such as a book or film.

Policymakers must devise both legal and policy means to help protect intellectual property as technology and society change. For example, many new technologies, from tape recorders, photocopiers, and VCRs to computers and electronic mail, make it easier for people to copy books, articles, photographs, music, videos, and programs without paying anything to the creators or to those who have bought the distribution rights. One solution has been to make unauthorized copying a crime. Another has been to make copying more difficult. Policymakers have also issued appeals to personal ethics—asking people not to defraud creators by not paying for use of their creations.

Information, software, and entertainment products are among America's main exports to the rest of the world. The effort to ensure that no one copies these products without paying for their use is particularly difficult in international markets, where various countries have differing rules about protecting such intellectual property. Some countries permit practices that the United States considers to be illegal copying or piracy. In international trade negotiations, such as the General Agreement on Trade and Tariffs, the United States has been trying to obtain better protection of intellectual property, since that is now so critical to the health of the U.S. economy.

OWNERSHIP, CONTROL, AND COMPETITION

Ownership and control of mass media are among the most controversial policy issues in many societies, including the United States. Media-content issues underlie many debates about how much to regulate media ownership and financing, especially advertising, and how to do it.

Ownership and Diversity

Diversity of ownership implies that media owners are of diverse ethnic backgrounds and gender.

Diversity of content implies a variety of ideas, cultural traditions, and values in media.

One policy issue is whether **diversity of ownership** is linked to **diversity of content.** At several points, policymakers have thought that ensuring diversity of ownership might help diversify content. Specifically, U.S. policy gave preference to minority applicants for broadcast station licenses in the hope that minority owners would better serve their communities. Studies have shown that African American station owners have a slight tendency to carry more programming oriented to that community, but the results have been less dramatic than the policymakers hoped.

Concentration of Ownership

Barriers to entry include the expenses of setting up a new media business that may make it difficult for all but a few to enter.

Oligopolies occur when a few firms dominate an industry.

The relative scarcity of frequencies already dictates that some people can broadcast while others cannot. Other **barriers to entry** have also led to regulation of media. Even in print media, for example, the amount of capital or investment required to begin a major newspaper or magazine has created a barrier to entry that keeps many potentially interested people and companies out. The economics of large-scale cultural industries tends to create **oligopolies,** a kind of business competition restricted to a few companies. Therefore, these few media companies have had much greater impact and influence on society than would a larger, less concentrated group (Bagdikian, 1993).

Because this media oligopoly has concentrated power in relatively few hands, a number of governments have carefully watched and regulated these companies. While most societies want freedom of speech, a few individuals or corporations usually control the ability to reach a mass audience. Many have felt that this situation requires those few owners and professional employees involved in media to be especially careful and responsible. This led to the theory of social responsibility. A more recent tendency, evident in the 1996 Telecommunications Act, is to encourage more competition between companies that had been monopolies or oligopolies within such areas as cable TV, television, and telephony, separated by previous regulations.

Vertical integration is concentrating ownership by acquiring companies that are related businesses, such as program producton and distribution.

The concentration of ownership among relatively few individuals or groups raises several issues. One is the issue of monopoly or oligopoly, just discussed. Another is what economists call the issue of **vertical integration.** This situation occurs when a company owns nearly all aspects of a single industry. For example, the federal government once prohibited the major television networks from producing most of their own programming and from reselling the programs they buy to other companies for use as reruns. This was to prevent

A TALE OF TWO VIDEOTEX SYSTEMS

The judicial interpretations by Judge Harold Greene, who oversaw the 1984 court-mandated breakup of AT&T, specifically kept the new regional Bell Operating Companies from offering information services. He was afraid that if they offered services like videotex (computer graphics and informaton over telephone lines), smaller companies would not be able to enter the market. As it happened, most smaller companies, such as newspapers, that tried to offer mass audience videotex failed. A few companies, including CompuServe and Prodigy, gradually built up videotex-like information services aimed at a narrower audience of people who already had home computers and modems, but these served a much smaller audience than was originally envisioned for videotex.

In contrast, France decided to have its government-owned telephone company, France Telecom, offer videotex on a system called Minitel. Unlike either the United States or Great Britain, France massively subsidized the development of videotex so that terminals could be given free to over 5 million households, and certain simple uses, such as the electronic telephone book, were offered free. In fact, the electronic telephone book was mandatory—if you received a free terminal, you did not get a printed phone book. Simple electronic mail was also low cost and easy.

On that base of beginning users and potential customers, other companies offered more sophisticated, pay-per-access services, using the Minitel system. A number of successful services developed. France's concern was the opposite of the United States': they thought that subsidized development by the government monopoly would be necessary to make videotex attractive and affordable to a mass audience, which initially did not know what to make of videotex and was not inclined to pay much for it. In this instance, France's approach seems to have been more successful in developing services for a broader group of users than in the United States or the United Kingdom.

them from using their positions as distribution networks to vertically integrate and dominate other aspects of the television industry (Compaigne, 1982). The policy goal has been to diversify production sources so that a number of companies compete with each other to come up with programs for the networks, thereby producing pluralism and diversity of content. This policy has probably succeeded in funding a number of kinds of production houses, but the networks have complained that such rules, known as the Financial Interest and Syndication (or Fin-Syn) Rules, have weakened them too much, particularly in their competition with cable TV. These rules were relaxed in 1992 to permit television networks to own the syndication rights to more of the programs that they broadcast or create. The 1996 Telecommunications Act largely deregulates vertical integration, permitting integration of movie studios, broadcast networks, cable providers, and cable channels, for example.

Another form of concentration is **horizontal integration,** in which a company owns many outlets of the same kind of medium. Previous policies had set the maximum number of radio or television stations that a single company, particularly one of the networks, should be allowed to own at twelve. The 1996 act eliminates the limit and raises the national television coverage limit from 25 percent of homes to 35 percent. For radio, there are no national limits, and local ownership caps increase with market size from a total of five stations in a market with fourteen or fewer commercial stations to eight stations among forty-five or more stations.

Another ownership question has to do with **cross-ownership:** Should a company be allowed to own various kinds of media? Traditionally, U.S. regulators did not allow a single person or company to own radio, television, and newspaper media—and, more recently, cable TV and telephony—in the same area or market. Such cross-ownership was usually seen as potentially increasing a company's power over content and limiting diversity. The 1996 Telecommunications Act largely deregulates cross-ownership rules, except ownership of both local television stations and cable televisions systems.

Horizontal integration is concentating ownership by acquiring companies that are all in the same business, such as radio stations or local cable distribution.

Cross-ownership is owning various kinds of media, usually in the same geographic locale.

There has seemed to be no need to create policy about who owns newspapers. However, competition between newspapers is part of what seems to make government or public regulation unnecessary. If two competing newspapers in a city, such as Detroit's *Free Press* and *News*, decided to merge and issue combined editions, government bodies, courts, and public interest groups might get involved to see that some degree of diversity of point of view and even some degree of competition remains to benefit readers and voters in the area.

The Sherman Antitrust Act and Monopoly

One of the earliest regulatory traditions that still affects current developments in the information society is the extent to which monopolies or oligopolies are permitted in certain industries. In the U.S. economy in the last half of the 1800s, various companies in the oil, banking, and railroad industries formed what were called "trusts," which were either monopolies (a single company controlled an industry) or oligopolies (a few companies dominated an industry or a market). Monopoly permitted companies to charge higher prices than would prevail if they had competition. Within oligopolies, potential competitors sometimes agreed to "fix" prices above what they would be with real competition. Monopolists could also force suppliers and business partners to lower prices for parts and materials, since they were the only market for such suppliers. In addition, they used unfair tactics to drive out or keep out would-be competitors. For example, in its early growth days, the Bell telephone system would offer telephone service below cost to drive out a competing telephone company in a local market or would force the local company to give the Bell system part ownership of their company in order to get connected to long-distance service for local customers.

Concentration of ownership in mass media is an issue related to preservation of diversity, which in turn is ultimately related to the freedoms of speech and press protected by the First Amendment. The issue of monopoly in telecommunications has been more related to constitutional prohibitions against restraint of trade. These rules were originally intended to keep states from restraining trade with other states. However, they were stated in such general terms that no one is permitted to restrain anyone else from engaging in business or trade.

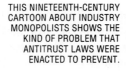

THIS NINETEENTH-CENTURY CARTOON ABOUT INDUSTRY MONOPOLISTS SHOWS THE KIND OF PROBLEM THAT ANTITRUST LAWS WERE ENACTED TO PREVENT.

After widespread realization that monopolistic business practices were hurting public interests, legal and public opinion turned against monopoly and oligopoly. Congress passed the **Sherman Antitrust Act of 1890.** Since then, U.S. courts, charged with enforcing the antitrust laws, and the U.S. Department of Commerce, charged with prohibiting restraint of trade, have both been suspicious of any monopoly.

Nevertheless, in certain kinds of industries it seemed that competition did not make much sense. Economists and technologists argued that in industries such as electric power, water, telephony, and cable television, there is a natural monopoly. They argued that it does not make sense to have competing wires, switches, and so on reaching all customers—that the investment to provide service is so heavy that it only makes sense for one company to enter such a business, and it would only be profitable without competition. This view was accepted for a series of industries—telephony, water, and power—which were called public utilities. The utility companies were given monopolies in return for accepting close regulation by government to make sure that they did not abuse their monopoly (Dizard, 1993).

The FCC became the regulator of the telephone public utility, along with state public utility commissions. It established price regulation to ensure that AT&T did not abuse its monopoly by charging telephone users too much. The FCC was also supposed to oversee the structure of the telecommunications industry itself to make sure that other abuses of monopoly did not take place.

One problem with the FCC and other regulatory bodies is that they may end up more closely attuned to the interests of the industry than to the interests of the public. Critics say that regulators are often effectively *captured* by the industry they regulate—referred to as **capture theory.**

The public utility era of telecommunications began to change as more companies wanted to get into the business and compete. Competition increased as technology became cheaper, tending to eliminate the "natural monopoly" arguments that had kept potential competitors away. The costs and barriers to entry into technology-based business became lower. Competition with AT&T was increasingly allowed by the FCC. This, coupled with continuing concern with monopoly by the Justice Department, led to the breakup of AT&T.

Universal Service

In the early 1900s the Bell telephone system had made universal service its own goal. Now both telephone operators and regulators are beginning to wonder whether plain old telephone service is enough or whether telephone companies should be required to make advanced digital services universal. Many assume that cable television is virtually universal, but fewer than two-thirds of American households have it. Does that raise questions about whether everyone has equal access to information? This question gains new significance when certain events, such as sporting events or full coverage of the national political party conventions, are shown only by cable television.

A similar issue is equitable access. Are some people getting less than fair access to information technologies and services? The question can be applied to both mass media (such as cable television) and new information technologies. In a group of students taking a college class, some will have had access to computers in high school and some won't. Of those who did, some will have actually been able to learn how to use computers to find information and some won't. Does that give those students an unfair advantage when a term paper assignment is given and they can more easily and quickly find the required information by using library computers? Until recently, access to basic education, basic

Sherman Antitrust Act of 1890 is the main U.S. law against monopolies or agreements to restrain or limit trade.

Capture theory suggests that regulators are often effectively captured by the interests of the industry they regulate.

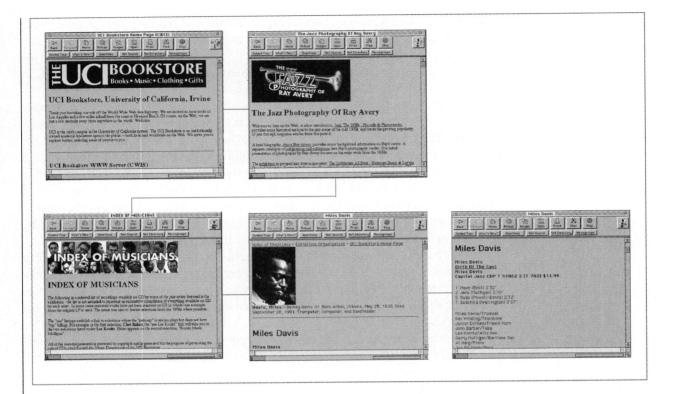

Internet is a network of computer networks used by millions for electronic mail and database access.

telephone service, and broadcast radio and television was considered the minimum for fair access to information required for social and work life. Should that minimum access be increased? To what level?

The **Internet** is a good example of the goal of using media and information technologies to extend access to education and health services to more people. For those who have access to the Internet (via an electronic mail address from a university, company, or private access provider, like CompuServe or Prodigy), a remarkable amount of educational, health, scientific, and even entertainment material is available. Again, however, the question comes up of what is equitable or "basic"—should all people have access to the Internet?

Up to now, basic telephone service has provided access to the emergency services and government agencies, while public education and libraries have provided most people with at least some access to "free" written information. All these basic functions—emergency services, general information, library information, and even education—seem likely to be transformed by information technology. Interactive information services based in telecommunications and computers will probably provide a new infrastructure for many of these services. People may get emergency information, research papers, and college course readings on-line over a computer network that can be accessed from home.

For instance, with the National Information Infrastructure (NII) proposed by the Clinton/Gore administration in 1993:

> People could live almost anywhere they wanted, without forgoing opportunities for useful and fulfilling employment, by "telecommuting" to their offices through an electronic highway.

The best schools, teachers, and courses would be available to all students, without regard to geography, distance, resources, or disability.

Services that improve America's health care system and respond to other important social needs could be available on-line, without waiting in line, when and where you need them.

How will this be provided? Will everyone have access?

Frequency Allocation and Regulation

One of the main reasons for regulation of broadcasting is the need to allocate frequencies for radio and for television among competing companies and groups that would like to be able to broadcast on them. Much of government regulation in the United States and elsewhere is justified by the scarcity of frequencies for broadcasting and some related resources, such as satellite orbits, cellular telephones, and new mobile services.

The growing crowd of radio stations in the United States in the early 1920s soon required some government authority to allocate frequencies—that is, to figure out who was going to broadcast on which channel (see Figure 5.2). Regulators drew up increasingly formal procedures as the number of groups wanting to broadcast on AM radio quickly exceeded the number of frequencies available. The Commerce Department under Herbert Hoover initially undertook the task in 1924. In 1927 the Radio Act established the Federal Radio Commission to give more direct attention to the issue. The much more comprehensive Communications Act of 1934 established the Federal Communications Commission. These bodies began to calculate how close stations could be to each other and still use the same or neighboring frequencies. Other kinds of technical regulation of frequency, station power, and antenna height also followed (Head & Sterling, 1994).

Because government regulators were now essentially deciding who got to broadcast, they also had to decide rules for allocating and renewing **licenses.** The FCC had to somehow choose the best applicant out of those who usually applied for any new frequency. Furthermore, the FCC had to ascertain whether to permit those who already had licenses to keep them or whether someone else might do a better job of serving the public interest. The FCC developed complex procedures for choosing among applicants and deciding whether to renew licenses.

In allocating licenses, the FCC had several content objectives in mind. The main criterion was the **"public interest,"** but that term was left for the FCC to define. In practice, the FCC tried to promote **localism** by giving stations to a variety of sizes of cities. The FCC later promoted diversity by giving preferential access to minority owners. After the initial rush of AM licenses in the 1920s and 1930s, the FCC began to reserve some licenses in FM and television specifically for stations that emphasized education and culture.

After 1980 the Reagan administration appointees to the FCC decided that there was not really a scarcity of frequencies or stations in either radio (given the proliferation of FM stations) or television, particularly since almost 60 percent of U.S. homes had

License is a permission to operate a service on a specific radio frequency.

Public interst is usually defined for broadcasting in terms of the variety or diversity of programming and the amount of news and public affairs programs carried.

Localism refers to giving broadcast stations to all possible local areas and encouraging them to serve local interests.

FIGURE 5.2
THERE ARE ONLY SO MANY FREQUENCIES AVAILABLE. REGULATORY AGENCIES DESIGNATE CERTAIN RANGES OF FREQUENCIES TO VARIOUS PURPOSES AND ALLOCATE SPECIFIC FREQUENCIES TO SPECIFIC USERS WITHIN EACH RANGE.

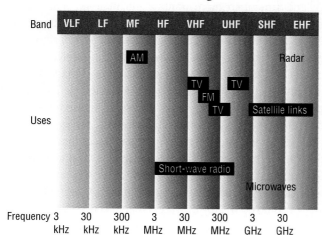

AS TELEVISION TECHNOLOGY HAS EVOLVED, NEW SETS OF STANDARDS HAVE BEEN REQUIRED TO GUIDE MANUFACTURERS. THIS IS PARTICULARLY EVIDENT IN THE PROCESS OF BRINGING HIGH-DEFINITION TV (THE JAPANESE VERSION SHOWN HERE) INTO COMMERCIAL USE.

Scarcity argument is that careful government regulation was required to allocate and oversee use of a limited number of frequencies.

multichannel cable TV to supplement or replace broadcast television stations. Therefore the **scarcity argument** for regulation was diminished. Furthermore, the Reagan-era FCC did not think that the FCC had done a particularly good job of picking license applicants and instead proposed doing so by lottery—picking applicants at random or by auction, "selling" frequencies to the highest bidder, which is increasingly used.

Technical Regulation

Although issues of ownership and content are more dramatic, the main regulatory function of governments is often more technical. Newspapers can function without any technical regulation, but the situation is different for electronic media. Someone has to design the basic equipment standards for how a television image will be broadcast and received. Someone has to establish basic technical standards so that manufacturers, broadcasters, and audiences will know which channel to tune to in order to find a particular station. Someone has to establish which station will use which channel, to avoid interference between stations. Since 1934 this task has also fallen to the FCC. The FCC works with private companies and engineering-oriented standards organizations to work out the actual details.

Agreement on basic technological standards is important for media and information technology growth and diffusion. Standards have to be set before businesses know when to mass manufacture a new technology. That is sometimes difficult. When a technology continues to improve and evolve, when do we say that the moment is right to set standards and make one for everyone to buy? In personal computers, for example, the standards keep

1. What kinds of links might exist between forms of ownership and issues of media content?
2. What contributes to concentration of ownership?
3. What are vertical and horizontal integration of ownership?
4. What is the Sherman Antitrust Act?
5. What makes for a natural monopoly in media or telecommunications?
6. What is the capture theory of regulation?
7. Why does the relative scarcity of radio spectrum frequencies require government regulation?
8. Why are technical standards important for media and telecommunications development?

evolving as technology changes. That is possible because people buy their own computer equipment and do not have to have strict compatibility with everyone else. It was more difficult in television, where we needed a single standard to permit sets, transmitters, and antennas to be completely compatible.

Standards for television have been an important example. Inventors in several countries, particularly the United States and Great Britain, raced to define the basic technical standards for television, the number of lines on the screen, the number of frames per second, and the frequencies to be used for image and sound. The FCC had asked the U.S. manufacturing industries to reach a compromise on television standards. In 1941 a committee called the National Television Systems Committee (NTSC) recommended the standards that are still in effect.

Many critics think that the United States settled on standards too early and as a result suffered with low resolution and visual quality in television for fifty years. The United States has now set a new set of standards, Advanced Television (ATV). Again the government pushed a series of manufacturers to reach a compromise. This time the standards are based on digital technology to permit greater integration with computers and other digital devices.

COMMUNICATIONS MEDIA ETHICS

We need to distinguish policy, law, and regulation, which are public or collective decisions, from ethics, which guide one's personal and professional decisions. Individuals are guided by their awareness of public or corporate policy goals. They are also guided and constrained by legal requirements and prohibitions on their actions. However, ethics are crucial because individual communicators are constantly making ethical decisions, beyond what is specifically covered by policy or law (Christians, Rotzoll, & Fackler, 1991).

We can characterize the main communications media ethics issues as revolving around **accuracy** or truthfulness, **fairness** and responsibility of treatment, and privacy for media subjects and people in information services.

Most of these ethics areas have related laws, such as libel and defamation laws related to accuracy, privacy laws about those covered in media, and intellectual property laws such as copyright. Here, however, we consider the ethical dimensions.

Accuracy of information refers to making sure that media or information content is truthful, correct, and not deceptive.

Fairness refers to responsibility in selecting and treating topics and sources.

General Considerations in Individual Ethics

Ethics are moral rules or rules of conduct that guide one's actions in specific situations. While there are ethical guidelines specific to communications media, many decisions are based on people's underlying religious, philosophical, and cultural ideas and on general rules that guide conduct in a variety of areas. Some of the classic principles that people have used in ethical decisions include Aristotle's golden mean, Kant's categorical imperative, situation ethics, and Mill's principle of utility.

Aristotle's golden mean holds that "moral virtue is appropriate location between two extremes." Moderation and balance are the key points. This principle leads to media emphases on giving balanced points of view or including various points of view to provide

Aristotle's golden mean holds that "moral virtue is appropriate location between two extremes."

balance. Or media organizations making decisions may balance the interests of getting a good story against the public interest in not releasing details that might actually harm public interests. For example, news media covering natural disasters may voluntarily omit details that might panic the public and create harm.

Kant's categorical imperative says we should act according to rules that we would like to see universally applied.

Situation ethics holds that moral ideas and judgments must be made relative to the situation at hand.

Mill's principle of utility holds that we should "seek the greatest happiness for the greatest number."

Immanuel **Kant's categorical imperative** holds that you should "act on that maxim which you will [wish] to become a universal law." That is, act according to rules that you would like to see universally applied. The idea is that what is good for one person or situation should be good for all, but it also stresses that individuals act according to their own conscience. For example, reporters who would like all other reporters to avoid deception about news sources should avoid such deception themselves.

Situation ethics is a more recent idea that conflicts with Kant's categorical imperative and similar universal principles. According to this approach, moral ideas must be made relative to the situation at hand. It also trusts individuals but stresses their intuitive sense of what is right; it thus allows specific rules to be broken if the overall purpose is good. For instance, using classified government documents without permission for a news story might be considered acceptable, even though principles and law may both be violated, if revealing the story will aid the public interest.

John Stuart **Mill's principle of utility** holds that we should "seek the greatest happiness for the greatest number." Mill was concerned about what would bring the greatest good for society, which he defined as benefiting the largest number of people. People who consider themselves utilitarians look at the consequences of possible actions, look at potential benefits and harms, determine which action would benefit or harm the largest number, and choose that. As with situation ethics, a reporter could conclude that publishing classified documents would benefit more people than it would harm.

Accuracy of Information

The question of accuracy comes up both in mass media and in new information services. What rules should exist about ensuring the accuracy of information in either a news story or a database? Do we need different rules or ethical principles for the two?

In news media, prevailing journalistic ethics about the accuracy of information are quite strict. Journalists are not to fabricate evidence, make up quotes, create hypothetical individuals to focus stories around, or create or manipulate misleading photographs. In a famous example in 1980 a *Washington Post* reporter, Janet Cooke, fabricated a story about an eight-year-old heroin addict named Jimmy. She was fired, but the story shook journalistic credibility. More recently, in 1993 NBC News staged footage of a GM pickup truck exploding on collision with another vehicle. *National Geographic* was heavily criticized for an even smaller distortion when it used computer image-manipulation techniques to move one Egyptian pyramid closer to another to make a more compact cover illustration. As the ability to digitally alter photos becomes better known, people may become less trustful of the accuracy of visual images.

THE ABILITY TO ALTER PHOTOS DIGITALLY (AS SHOWN IN THIS ONE) RAISES QUESTIONS ABOUT THE ACCURACY OF NEWS PHOTOS AS WELL AS TEXT INFORMATION.

The accuracy of computer databases and information services based on them is also becoming a critical issue in the information society. Many people already suffer because erroneous information has made it into credit information files. When such people apply for a credit card or loan, they may be refused because someone with a similar name or social security number has not made credit card or loan payments. The need for greater accuracy in information services will require both individual ethics decisions and probably legal or policy decisions as well.

Fairness or Responsibility

Fairness or social responsibility issues include the selection of topics and issues to cover. Journalists and editors make constant choices about what to cover, as do writers, television and film directors, even programmers and information service designers and operators. Media people can advance certain companies, people, and causes over others by the decisions they make on whom and what to cover. Ethical issues include favoritism, partisanship, and possibly corruption, bribery, or accepting favors. Should people advance the cause of someone they know or a cause they agree with? For example, if you accept a trip to see a company's new product, will you feel obliged to write about it or write favorably about it?

A key ethical treatment issue for news reporters and writers is the need to protect the **confidentiality** of their sources. Reporters frequently use as sources people who might be indicted for criminal activity. If a reporter is doing a story on the drug trade, she will end up talking to drug dealers. Because the knowledge the reporter gains from her sources could help convict them, law enforcement officials are sometimes drawn to try to get evidence from reporters. However, this is one ethical issue on which there is fairly widespread agreement among reporters. The reporter has promised either implicitly or explicitly to keep secret the identity and any of the details that could incriminate the person. Partially that is because an agreement has been made; but it is also because reporters could not get information from sources in the future if they could not give a credible promise of confidentiality (Meyer, 1987).

Related to confidentiality and protection of sources is the question of **source attribution**—how to cite sources without revealing their identity. The reporter wants to reveal as much as possible about the competence and position of his or her source, which will bolster the credibility of the quote or the information attributed to the source, and thus the whole story. On the other hand, many sources will talk only if they cannot be identified from what is said about them in the story. That becomes harder when the source is a well-known public figure who wants to **"leak"** an idea or a possible policy that he or she is not ready to be quoted about yet. Presidential advisers are constantly leaking ideas about what the president might do about a certain problem; they have become a means of trying out tentative ideas—trial balloons—without having to commit themselves to the idea as official policy.

Several fairly complex methods for describing the general position of a source have been developed, indicating enough of the source's expertise to lend credibility to the story while not revealing enough to enable the person to be identified. One of the more famous examples, during the 1972 Watergate investigations that led to the resignation of President Richard Nixon, was a "highly placed official," perhaps a "cabinet-level source," who leaked incriminating details under the code name of Deep Throat. Thousands of people tried to figure out who Deep Throat really was, but no one ever succeeded, because the source would not give information so specific that it could identify him and the reporters refused to give clues to his identity.

Privacy

A more complex ethical dilemma for reporters is respecting the privacy both of potential sources and of people who are objects of news investigations and reports. Source privacy is largely covered under confidentiality of sources. However, many reporters are less concerned about the privacy of those that they are covering. In fact, they have a natural desire

Confidentiality usually refers to protecting the identity of news sources.

Source attribution refers to methods used to cite sources without revealing their identity.

Leaks refer to the release of confidential information by officials, often policy ideas or facts they do not wish to be quoted about.

CRIME VICTIMS, YOUNG CRIMINALS, AND PRIVACY

The most delicate situations that raise privacy concerns involve naming crime victims and juveniles (those under 18) who commit crimes. Almost all reporters have agreed that victims of crime, particularly violent crimes such as assaults and rapes, deserve to be protected from identification. They are not responsible for their situation, but being identified as the victim of a crime, particularly rape, can still damage a person's reputation. The crime victim is usually suffering already; added publicity might make it worse.

Those who perpetrate crimes seem to have a less obvious right to remain anonymous. However, much of the coverage of a crime story comes before the person charged with the crime is actually judged guilty or innocent. Should someone accused of a crime not be identified until actually convicted? Otherwise, their reputation is probably damaged even if they are found innocent, although again that may not seem logical or fair. News media usually do identify those who have been accused of a crime. In fact, media frequently discuss cases and names so much that juries have to be isolated from exposure to media in order to render a fair verdict on the basis of the legally admissible evidence in the courtroom.

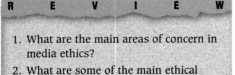

What if those charged with or even convicted of a crime are not yet legally adults—shouldn't their names be protected, maybe giving them a chance to change their ways before adulthood? Most media have followed that rule, but some now say that many children and adolescents are career criminals before adulthood and should be exposed to public scrutiny in the same way as adults.

PRIVACY ON THE INFORMATION SUPER-HIGHWAY: TONYA HARDING'S E-MAIL

Leading up to the 1993 Winter Olympics, American figure skater Tonya Harding received intense media scrutiny. She was being investigated for her possible involvement in an assault intended to disable her main U.S. rival, Nancy Kerrigan. The scandal attracted more press attention than the rest of the Olympics, and reporters were looking hard for new stories. Athletes were issued temporary electronic mail passwords to send and receive messages at the Olympic Village in Norway. Several reporters read Harding's E-mail password via a camera and used it to get access to her electronic communications. These reporters were accused of a serious ethical lapse in violating Harding's privacy, even though nobody suggested applying Norwegian privacy laws to them. One defended himself by saying that it was not that different from trying to read (upside down) the memos sitting on a source's desk while sitting in front of it. He implied, all reporters look for and use material to which they have not specifically been granted access. This episode dramatizes the fact that privacy rights have not been clarified well in either law or journalistic ethics.

to expose and describe the topic of the story. As with sources, it adds legitimacy to a story to provide greater detail about the people involved.

Privacy comes up in a new way in interactive media. Two-way media, such as telephone conversations, electronic mail, home shopping, database access, and information requests, offer a chance to collect a great deal of information about people. Some of that information has economic value, such as what people buy and what they prefer to read or watch, that could help advertisers and direct-mail marketers reach them better. This kind of information is routinely collected, collated or cross-referenced, and sold, although consumer and privacy rights groups are pushing for a clearer set of rules giving more power to individuals to control such information about themselves. The current laws primarily control how government can access and use such computer database information, but most of the ambiguous legal issues and individual ethical decisions are made by companies, communications professionals, and others in the private sphere (Schiller, 1986).

Some computer-based information might provide input to news

REVIEW

1. What are the main areas of concern in media ethics?
2. What are some of the main ethical principles that people apply to media ethics situations?
3. What are a reporter's ethical responsibilities to his or her sources?
4. What rights to privacy do those covered by the news media have?

stories or media productions. Celebrity gossip reporters could certainly learn a lot by listening to media stars' phone conversations or reading their mail. So as new media develop, are their contents to be considered private, even from reporters? The contents of mail and telephone conversations are now legally protected. Electronic mail, teleconferences, and other new media are now protected under the Electronic Communications Privacy Act of 1987 but may require more clarification.

Should there be rules about how information can be combined, both for government officials, such as drug enforcement agents, and for private interests, such as credit report agencies? Putting credit card, magazine subscription, mail-order purchase, and other seemingly straightforward information in a database can provide a detailed profile of someone, especially when various databases are combined. Those working in this industry will have a number of ongoing ethical decisions to make about when and how to protect the privacy of those whose information they handle and sell (Consumer Privacy Act of 1974).

SUMMARY & REVIEW

What Is the Policymaking Process?

What are the distinctions between policy, law, and ethics?
Policy is government and public consideration of how to structure and regulate media so that they contribute to the public good. Public policy involves a collective action of the whole society or its representatives. Laws passed by Congress and enforced by the courts cover some but not all of the policy and ethical issues in media. Ethics guide communicators in how to behave in situations where their activities may have negative impact on others.

What are the main institutions in the media policymaking process?
The main institutions in the executive branch are the FCC, which regulates most aspects of communication, the NTIA, which covers some aspects of policy research and international policy, and the FTC, which monitors trade and business practices. The Congress passes laws about communication. The Justice Department and the court system, particularly the federal district courts, enforce and interpret the existing laws.

What is a lobby group? What are the main ones in communications media issues?
Lobbies are interest or business groups that try to influence policy—lawmaking or enforcement. Some of the main business lobbies are AT&T, the Baby Bells, other telecommunications companies, the large equipment manufac-

turers, the National Association of Broadcasters, the National Cable Television Association, and the Motion Picture Association of America.

How do media and telecommunications standards get set?
Companies often develop standards for their own equipment and compete to set the industry-wide standard. Industry committees sometimes set collective standards, often when spurred or required by government bodies, like the FCC. Internationally, most standards are set or endorsed by the International Telecommunications Union (ITU). The ITU allocates frequencies and satellite orbits to countries for their use. It also sets standards for international telecommunications, which usually pushes most countries to adopt those same standards.

What is the primary law regulating electronic media?
The 1934 Communications Act established the FCC, regulated broadcasting by regulating scarce frequencies, and regulated the monopolies of AT&T and, later, the regional Baby Bells. The 1996 Telecommunications Act encouraged competition between industries such as cable TV and telephony. It deregulated rules on how many stations a group could own and rules on cross-ownership of broadcasting, cable TV, telephone companies, movie studios, and other major actors. It deregulated telephony ownership structures, areas of activity, and prices but tried to maintain universal service. The act also proposed restrictions on

Internet pornography and mandated television content ratings linked to a "V-chip" that could be programmed to block selected signals.

What Are the Main Policies Regarding Media Content?

What is the relationship between the marketplace of ideas and freedom of speech?
The marketplace of ideas is the concept that, with free speech, the best ideas will win in competition with others. The concept of a free press is the extension of freedom of speech to media.

What is the First Amendment?
The First Amendment to the U.S. Constitution says, "Congress shall make no law respecting an establishment of religion, or prohibiting the free exercise thereof, or abridging the freedom of speech, or of the press . . ." The kinds of speech not protected by the First Amendment are libel, defamation, indecency, plagiarism, invasion of privacy, and inciting insurrection.

What is libel?
Libel is harmful or untruthful written information that damages someone's reputation or good name. To be legally proven, the person or organization accused of libel must be shown to have known the information was false or that its use was intended to damage the reputation of the person being covered.

What Policy Issues Are Involved in Media Ownership, Control, and Competition?

What kinds of links might exist between forms of ownership and issues of media content?
Some owners may try to influence content to promote their own ideas and interests. If owners are too much alike, they may not produce diverse contents, whereas a greater diversity of ownership may produce more diverse content.

What makes for a natural monopoly in media or telecommunications?
An industry is considered a natural monopoly when competition would not be economically feasible, whether because of technology or other costs. This is particularly true when the infrastructure for supplying the service is extensive and costly, such as with sewers, power, or, until recently, telecommunications.

What is the capture theory of regulation?
Capture theory implies that regulators are often effectively captured by the interests of the industry they regulate. They become dependent on the industry for information, they sometimes work in it before or after government service, and they frequently come to identify with industry players and their goals.

Why does the relative scarcity of radio spectrum frequencies require government regulation?
The fact that there are far fewer frequencies than there are people wanting to use them, both for broadcasting and for two-way services such as cellular telephony, requires that someone or some agency track who is using what and allocate frequencies in such a way that radio spectrum users and broadcasters do not interfere with each other. Since the scarcity of frequencies requires that some people be given frequencies and others not, rules by governments for allocating and renewing licenses were necessary.

What Are Media Ethics?

What are the main areas of concern in media ethics?
The main communications media ethics issues are accuracy or truthfulness, fairness and responsibility of treatment, privacy for media subjects and people in information services, and respect for intellectual property or ideas of others.

What are some of the main general ethical principles that people apply to media ethics situations?
Some are absolute standards. Kant's categorical imperative directs us to act according to rules that we would like to see universally applied.

Some principles make judgments more relative to situations. With situation ethics, for example, moral ideas and judgments must be made relative to the situation at hand. According to Aristotle's golden mean, "moral virtue is appropriate location between two extremes." Mill's principle of utility states that we should "seek the greatest happiness for the greatest number."

What are a reporter's ethical responsibilities to his or her sources?
Reporters are usually concerned about protecting their sources, but they also need to refer to them as explicitly as possible to increase the credibility of what they write. Confidentiality of sources is crucial to reporters, both to protect the sources and to gain and keep access to them.

REFERENCES

Altschul, J. (1984). *Agents of power*. New York: Longman.

Bagdikian, B. (1993). *The media monopoly* (4th ed.). Boston: Beacon Press.

Bittner, J. R. (1982). *Broadcast law and regulation*. Englewood Cliffs, NJ: Prentice-Hall.

Christians, C., Rotzoll, K., & Fackler, M. (1991). *Media ethics*. New York: Longman.

Compaigne, B. M. (1982). *Who owns the media? Concentration of ownership in the mass communication industry*. New York: Crown.

Dizard, W. (1993). *The coming information age*. New York: Longman.

Head, S., & Sterling, C. (1994). *Broadcasting in America* (4th ed.). Boston: Houghton Mifflin.

Meyer, P. (1987). *Ethical journalism*. New York: Longman.

Mosco, V. (1989). *The pay-per society*. Norwood, NJ: Ablex.

Rivers, W., & Schramm, W. (1980). *Responsibility in mass communication*. New York: Harper & Row.

Schiller, H. (1986). *Information and the crisis economy*. New York: Oxford University Press.

Zuckman, H., & Gaynes, M. (1983). *Mass communications law* (2nd ed.). St. Paul, MN: West Publishing.

Chapter 6

GLOBALIZATION OF COMMUNICATIONS MEDIA

C H A P T E R   P R E V I E W

n this chapter we examine the globalization of the information society, which is rapidly changing communications media in the United States and elsewhere. We will look at three main levels of globalization.

First, we need to compare how broadcasting, cable and satellite television, telephony, and information services have developed differently in various countries. Ownership, goals, types of content or programming, and numbers of channels all vary greatly.

Second, we will examine the flow of media and information between countries. The United States has tended to dominate the sale and flow of film, music, television, news, and information or data. However, increasing numbers of international producers are challenging the United States in their own national markets, in regional markets such as Spanish Latin America or Chinese-speaking Asia, and sometimes in the global market.

Third, we will examine the globalization of ownership and operations of communications media, including multinational empires by media barons such as Rupert Murdoch and globally operated channels such as CNN and MTV. We will also look at the increasingly globalized telecommunications business.

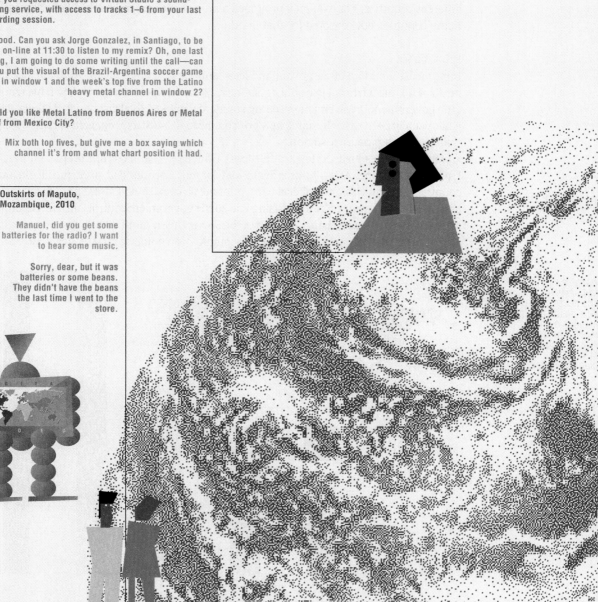

Los Angeles, 2010

Que pasa, DeeVee?

Good morning, Maria. Would you like to review your morning schedule?

Sure. Can you scroll current Latin American and Asian media stock prices in a window while we talk?

O.K. At 10 A.M. you have a conference call, with audio translation and subtitles for your charts, to Mimi Chang in Hong Kong and Gordon Banks in New York. At 11 A.M., you requested access to Virtual Studio's sound-mixing service, with access to tracks 1–6 from your last recording session.

Good. Can you ask Jorge Gonzalez, in Santiago, to be on-line at 11:30 to listen to my remix? Oh, one last thing, I am going to do some writing until the call—can you put the visual of the Brazil-Argentina soccer game in window 1 and the week's top five from the Latino heavy metal channel in window 2?

Would you like Metal Latino from Buenos Aires or Metal Sur/f from Mexico City?

Mix both top fives, but give me a box saying which channel it's from and what chart position it had.

Outskirts of Maputo, Mozambique, 2010

Manuel, did you get some batteries for the radio? I want to hear some music.

Sorry, dear, but it was batteries or some beans. They didn't have the beans the last time I went to the store.

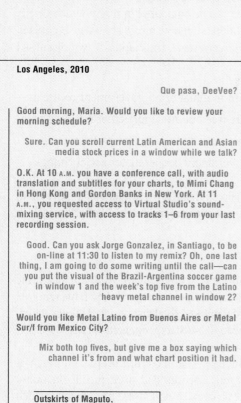

COMPARISONS OF COMMUNICATIONS MEDIA SYSTEMS

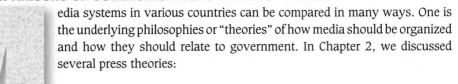

edia systems in various countries can be compared in many ways. One is the underlying philosophies or "theories" of how media should be organized and how they should relate to government. In Chapter 2, we discussed several press theories:

- Libertarian—media operate with minimal or no government controls
- Social responsibility—media are free but are regulated or self-regulated
- Authoritarian—government exercises a variety of controls on media
- Developmental—media and government cooperate for social change

These theories of the press can help explain how various media develop in different countries. For example, print media are encouraged to be critical of politicians in many countries but censored for that in others.

Print Media

Print media are more often private and less controlled by government than are electronic media. Print media do not use public resources, like radio spectrums, and they have required little government involvement in setting standards, unlike broadcast or wired media. Thus, it has usually been easier to start a new print publication, such as a magazine or a newspaper, than to start a broadcast station.

Most countries inclined toward freedom of the press—in most of Europe and much of Latin America and Asia—have private and largely uncontrolled print media. In many countries government and political party print media coexist with "free" print media, which are often heavily swayed by advertising and subtle government controls. In a few countries, such as Cuba or Russia when it was part of the Soviet Union (until 1991), governments have seen print media as a useful tool that they ought to own and control exclusively.

FIGURE 6.1
NEWSPAPER CIRCULATION AND ACCESS ARE UNEVEN AND UNEQUAL IN DIFFERENT REGIONS OF THE WORLD, MOSTLY DEPENDING ON WEALTH AND ECONOMIC RESOURCES.
(SOURCE: UNESCO)

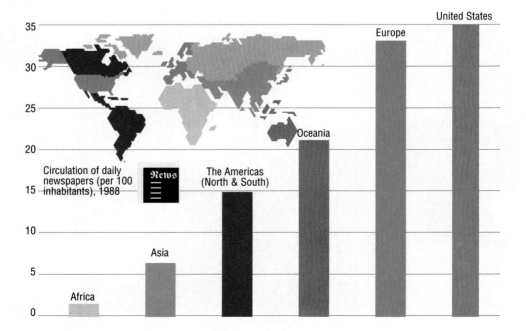

Circulation of daily newspapers (per 100 inhabitants), 1988

People's access to and use of print media are seriously limited by both education and economics in a number of the poorer parts of the **developing countries** of Asia, Latin America, the Middle East, and Africa. In many countries literacy is limited, and even people who can read may not be able to afford newspapers or magazines. While in most European countries the circulation of daily newspapers is about 33 for every 100 people, it is fewer than 2 for every 100 in Africa (see Figure 6.1).

Broadcast Media

Because print media are limited in many countries, broadcast media take on increased importance. In the poorest countries, radio is the main mass medium. However, in Africa and South Asia, many people do not even get access to radio, either because the signal doesn't reach them or they can't afford a receiver.

In contrast, most people, even among the poor, in Latin America and East Asia (Taiwan, Hong Kong, and so on) have television. Brazilians sometimes say they live in the "land of television." In the more affluent parts of these countries, increasing numbers in the middle class and up have VCRs and cable besides basic TV (see Figure 6.2).

Compared to print media, radio and television broadcasting is far more divided between public, government, and private ownership in other countries. Because broadcasters use the relatively scarce frequencies available in the radio spectrum, few channels are available and few people or groups can be involved. Nearly all governments get involved in planning who gets to use what frequencies or parts of the radio spectrum, which also tends to lead them to get involved in controlling content. Broadcasts are assumed to have greater impact on people than print media, which leads many governments to control them more. Many governments see broadcasting as having such potential for either education or political propaganda that they get more directly involved in operating radio and television.

Even when broadcast stations are privately owned, many governments use licenses to reward political allies. In 1985–1987, Brazilian President José Sarney gave over 100 radio and television licenses to congress members to get a fifth year added to his presidential

FIGURE 6.2
VCRS ARE DIFFUSING RAPIDLY INTO MANY COUNTRIES. THE EARLIEST AND FASTEST DIFFUSION WAS INTO SAUDI ARABIA, WHEN MANY PEOPLE HAD BOTH WEALTH AND A DESIRE TO CIRCUMVENT GOVERNMENT AND RELIGIOUSLY CONTROLLED TELEVISION.

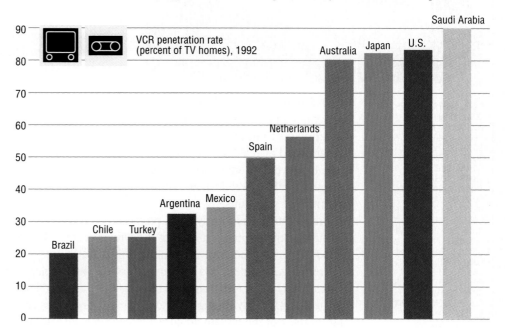

IN CHINA, WATCHING TV IS OFTEN STILL A COMMUNAL EVENT BECAUSE OF THE SCARCITY OF SETS.

mandate. Previous Brazilian military governments had given licenses to three friendly business groups to form politically supportive television networks.

In Africa, Asia, and, until recently, Eastern Europe, governments often have owned and operated broadcasting systems in order to control radio and TV. Leaders in these countries want broadcasting to help solve major health, education, and economic problems. Their stated intention has usually been to use electronic media as powerful tools to better develop their societies, but controlling politics is often part of their agenda as well. For example, in the 1970s India began experimenting with television via satellite to promote education and development of agriculture in the countryside. Then Prime Minister Indira Gandhi discovered that control over television also gave her a valuable tool for politics, which led her to continue and expand television broadcasting in that country.

Public corporations in broadcasting are nonprofit companies financed by government or license fees.

In many countries, such as most of western Europe, broadcasting has been conducted by either governments or nonprofit **public corporations.** Their goal has been to use broadcasting to promote education and culture. An example is the BBC (British Broadcasting Corporation) in Great Britain. To a large degree, the public broadcasters in Europe and Japan have succeeded in creating much more educational, informational, and cultural programming than broadcasters in the United States. The U.S. Public Broadcasting System uses a good deal of British material and increasingly coproduces programs with international public television channels. However, in some countries, such as France in the 1960s and 1970s and Italy until recently, public broadcasters sometimes let political parties control their news and information programs.

FIDEL CASTRO, SUPERSTAR! SINCE 1959 CASTRO HAS USED ALL MEDIA, BUT PARTICULARLY TELEVISION, TO MOBILIZE PEOPLE IN SUPPORT OF HIMSELF, THE COMMUNIST PARTY, AND THEIR PROGRAM TO DEVELOP THE CUBAN ECONOMY AND SOCIETY. CASTRO IS A CHARISMATIC SPEAKER, CONSIDERED BY MANY THE GREATEST ORATOR IN THE SPANISH LANGUAGE, AND HE OFTEN SPEAKS ON TELEVISION FOR HOURS. IN 1994 CASTRO'S PERSONAL POPULARITY STILL DREW SUPPORT FOR HIS GOVERNMENT, DESPITE SEVERE DOWNTURNS IN THE CUBAN ECONOMY.

Broadcasting has mostly been private in North, Central, and South America, largely because of the strong influence of the United States. Government controls over private broadcasters have been minimal in the United States. They have been stronger in Canada, where the government has tried to control the importation of programs from the United States. Many Latin American governments have asserted fairly strong control over private broadcasters, mostly through economic pressures such as control of government advertising. In most of the private broadcasting systems, entertainment programming has dominated, although some fairly effective radio education programs, run by both governments and the Catholic Church, have aired in Latin America.

There is a tendency in European, Asian, and other countries to increase private broadcasting and reduce government ownership. Many individuals and companies would like to own broadcast stations. They often come from print publishing, such as Silvio Berlusconi in Italy, who now controls the three major private networks and used them to become president of Italy in 1994. Publics often push for more broadcast choices, while advertisers, both foreign and local, push to be able to put advertising on stations. Some public broadcasters are feeling budget pressures, which also tends to increase advertising. British study commissions have even considered putting ads on the BBC, which has been the prototype of a public station supported by audience **license fees** to maintain independence from both government and advertisers. In Britain and Japan, everyone who owns a radio or a television set is obligated to pay an annual license fee. That fee goes directly to the public broadcasters (BBC in Britain and NHK in Japan), who use it to finance program production and development.

License fees are annual fees or fees on the sales of radio or television receivers to pay for public broadcasting.

Cable and Satellite TV

While cable TV has been familiar to most Americans, Canadians, and some Europeans for years, it is now expanding in many other countries of the world. On the other hand, **direct satellite broadcasting** (DSB), which Japanese and British audiences have had available for several years, is new to most Americans. DSB is also growing quickly in many other countries, often spanning borders of neighboring countries.

Direct satellite broadcasting is a television or radio satellite service that is marketed directly to home receivers.

In the 1970s and 1980s many governments in Europe and Japan saw cable TV as the potential infrastructure for interactive information services, a sort of early, cable-based version of the information superhighway. Government planners thought they could encourage two-way information services to build on the delivery of increased numbers of television channels. However, experiments with cable-based interactive or two-way systems in Japan, France, and Germany were not widely successful—audiences did not find the new services compellingly useful or attractive. Potential customers for two-way cable systems in the United Kingdom often did not subscribe because the cost of the interactive technology was too high, and many were actually satisfied with the available four broadcast channels plus a VCR.

By the 1990s, cable systems and private satellite TV channels to feed them were growing fast in Europe, Latin America, and Asia. As in the 1970s and 1980s in the United States, however, the new cable systems mostly just delivered a one-way expansion of new video channels, not two-way information services. U.S. cable channels expanded into this new market: CNN, MTV, HBO, ESPN, TNT, Nickelodeon, the Cartoon Network, Discovery, Disney, and others began to sell their existing channels in these countries or even began to translate and adapt their U.S. channels to the languages and cultures of the new audiences.

A number of channels and DSB services have been started with a more specific language or regional target. A number of European channels have been started that focus on news, music, sports, films, children's, and other targeted programming. One of the new satellite television services in Asia, Star TV, has American (MTV, film), European (BBC, news) and Chinese-language channels, which have been the most popular with Chinese audiences in Taiwan and China.

Satellite TV and cable television are beginning to expand in the less-developed countries of Asia, Latin America, and the Middle East. Again, channels exported from industrialized nations (CNN, BBC, MTV, and so on) are popular, but several nations (Brazil, Hong Kong, Mexico, Egypt, Saudi Arabia) are developing their own satellite television channels. The Mexican and Saudi channels are also aimed at regional markets in Spanish and Arabic. Figure 6.3 shows the mixture of American, Japanese, and Chinese channels on a cable system in Taiwan.

Telephony

Telephony has also developed unequally in various countries. While the United States., Japan, and a few other countries have over 50 telephones per 100 people and are speeding toward the construction of "information superhighways" built on the telephone infrastructure, some African and South Asian nations have less than 1 telephone per 100 people (see Figure 6.4).

Until recently, most telephone systems have been operated by postal, telephone, and telegraph administrations (PTTs), owned and operated by governments. Governments tended to see telephones as an essential infrastructure for their social and economic

FIGURE 6.3
THIS IS THE CHANNEL LINE-UP FOR THE BEI-YI CABLE NETWORK, ONE OF THE LARGEST IN TAIPEI, CAPITAL OF TAIWAN. IT FEATURES THREE AMERICAN CHANNELS, EIGHT CHANNELS FROM JAPAN, TWO FROM MAINLAND CHINA, TWO FROM HONG KONG, A NUMBER WITH PROGRAMS FROM VARIOUS COUNTRIES, AND TEN HOMEMADE CABLE CHANNELS PLUS THREE TELEVISION STATIONS FROM TAIWAN.

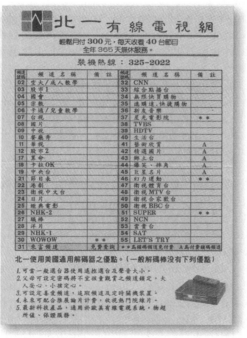

CH. NAME OR TYPE
02 ADULT EDUCATION
03 STOCK MARKET
04 CONGRESS NEWS
05 RELIGIOUS
06 CARTOON/KIDS EDUCATION (JAPAN, U.S., NATIONAL)
07 TTV (NATIONAL TV NETWORK)
08 NATIONAL MOVIES
09 CTV (NATIONAL TV NETWORK)
10 RESTAURANT SHOW (NATIONAL VARIETY)
11 CTS (NATIONAL TV NETWORK)
12 STOCK MARKET
17 FORTUNE TELLING
18 KARAOKE SING-ALONG (VARIOUS COUNTRIES)
19 CHINESE CENTRAL TV (MAINLAND CHINA)
21 PROGRAM GUIDE

22 TV SERIES AND DRAMAS (HONG KONG)
23 STAR TV CHINESE CHANNEL (VARIOUS CHINESE-SPEAKING COUNTRIES)
24 JAPANESE MOVIES
25 CLASSIC MOVIES (VARIOUS COUNTRIES)
26 NHK-2 (JAPANESE PUBLIC TV)
27 BASEBALL (TAIWAN AND U.S.)
28 WESTERN MOVIES (PRIMARILY U.S.)
29 NHK-1 (JAPANESE PUBLIC TV)
30 WOWOW (JAPANESE COMMERCIAL TV)
31 LAI-FU CHANNEL (TAIWAN SPORTS)
32 CNN (U.S.)
33 PAY-PER-VIEW
34 SHOPPING (LOCAL)
35 SHOPPING (LOCAL)
36 MUSIC (VARIOUS COUNTRIES)
37 STAR LIGHT THEATER , STAR TV MOVIES (VARIOUS COUNTRIES)
38 TVBS (STAR TV—HONG KONG)
39 HIGH DEFINITION TV (NHK—JAPAN)
40 LIFE CHANNEL—DOCUMENTARIES
41 ART—PORNO FILMS (VARIOUS COUNTRIES)
42 NATIONAL MOVIES (PAY CHANNEL)
43 GRASSROOTS (NATIONAL VARIETY)
44 COMEDY AND SUMO WRESTLING (JAPAN)
45 SUPERSTAR MOVIES (VARIOUS COUNTRIES)
46 DISCOVERY CHANNEL (U.S.)
47 STAR TV SPORTS (VARIOUS COUNTRIES)
48 ASIAN MTV/STAR TV (VARIOUS COUNTRIES, MOSTLY ASIAN)
49 STAR TV FAMILY CHANNEL (VARIOUS COUNTRIES)
50 BBC NEWS—STAR TV
51 SUPER CHANNEL (VARIOUS COUNTRIES)
52 NCN (JAPANESE NEWS)
53 YUN-KON TV (MAINLAND CHINA)
54 JAPANESE INFORMATION CHANNEL
55 LET'S TRY (JAPANESE INFORMATION AND VARIETY)

NOTE: CHANNELS 41–45 ARE PAY TV.

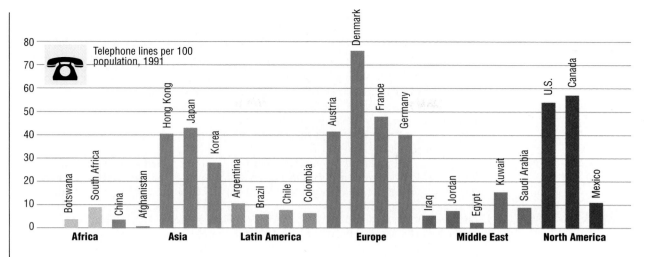

Telephone lines per 100 population, 1991

| Africa | Asia | Latin America | Europe | Middle East | North America |

Africa: Botswana, South Africa, China, Afghanistan
Asia: Hong Kong, Japan, Korea
Latin America: Argentina, Brazil, Chile, Colombia
Europe: Austria, Denmark, France, Germany
Middle East: Iraq, Jordan, Egypt, Kuwait, Saudi Arabia
North America: U.S., Canada, Mexico

FIGURE 6.4
TELEPHONES AND TELEPHONE LINES ARE UNEQUALLY DIVIDED AMONG COUNTRIES, WHICH KEEPS MUCH OF THE WORLD'S POPULATION FROM USING NOT ONLY TELEPHONES BUT ALSO ELECTRONIC MAIL, FAXES, AND OTHER BUSINESS SERVICES THAT USE TELEPHONE LINES.
SOURCE: INTERNATIONAL TELECOMMUNICATIONS UNION REGIONAL REPORTS.

Liberalization in telecommunications policy refers to opening up monopoly services to competition.

development. In many countries, governments have also been more willing to invest in telephones even when the services, such as those to rural areas, are not profitable.

More recently, though, a number of governments have decided to privatize, or sell off their phone companies to private operators. The reasons are usually financial, to reduce debt or gain new resources to expand the phone or information systems. Other reasons for privatization can include slimming down the size of government and making the telephone operation more efficient by cutting inefficiencies from overgrown bureaucratic PTTs. This reduces corruption and keeps governments from raking off telephone revenues to other operations. Some countries keep the phone company within the government but still open up some of the newer services, such as cellular telephony, data services, and electronic mail, to competition, a process called **liberalization.**

Computers and Software Services

The production of computers has been limited to a few countries in North America, Europe, and East Asia. The efforts of less industrialized countries, such as Brazil or India, to develop computer industries have often been frustrating and expensive. The use of computers is also

IN COUNTRIES SUCH AS ARGENTINA, WHERE LINES ARE LIMITED, PUBLIC PAY PHONES BECOME VERY IMPORTANT.

still highly concentrated in the most industrialized countries, because of the high cost of hardware and software and the unequal distribution of income that makes relatively few able to afford computers.

However, many countries feel that they need to obtain the advantages to be had from using computers to create and use information. The purchase and use of computers has been spreading worldwide, but unequally. In some countries, only some bureaucrats and a few of the wealthiest professionals and businesses can afford access to computers. In fact, many experts fear that relatively low access to computers will keep businesses and professionals in developing countries from competing in a globalized market where others have a sophisticated computer infrastructure to work with.

WHEN SELF-SUFFICIENCY BACKFIRES: COMPUTERS IN BRAZIL

Prior to 1976, Brazil depended almost entirely on IBM and other U.S. suppliers for computers. The Brazilian military, government planners, engineers, and even political left agreed that Brazil should try to become more self-sufficient. While leaving mainframes to IBM, they decided to completely close off the Brazilian market for personal and minicomputer hardware and software. They forbade importation of technology to avoid dependence on foreign technology and refused joint ventures with foreign companies to keep control national.

However, neither Brazilian companies nor the government had enough money to truly invent new technology, so many companies ended up copying American hardware, like the IBM PC or the Apple II, or software like MS-DOS or Word Perfect. U.S. companies complained that this was piracy, that it violated intellectual property rights, and the U.S. government threatened trade sanctions. Worst of all, the self-sufficiency program drove up the cost of computers in an already poor country. In 1991 the typical computer was a copy of an IBM personal computer, which cost $3,000 (versus $800 in the United States). With lower Brazilian incomes, where a university professor or lawyer might make less than $500 per month, it was almost impossible for Brazilian professionals or small businesses to use computers, which made them less productive than comparable American workers or companies.

Furthermore, they couldn't keep up technologically—the typical computer in the United States in 1991 was two generations ahead of and much faster than the Brazilian machines.

By 1992 Brazilian computer users were complaining of their inability to compete in a global economy with such computer costs. The law was changed in 1993 to still give incentives to Brazilian companies, but allow importation of technology, licensing of software, and joint ventures with foreign companies. This reduced Brazilian autonomy again, but for computer users and would-be users, the price of self-sufficiency had been too high.

Information Services

The concept of information services is relatively new to most countries. However, there is some experience with what was called videotex in Europe and Japan. As we noted in Chapter 5, videotex was a graphics and text service carried over telephone lines, which provided simple databases such as telephone numbers, electronic mail, and a variety of other information, such as entertainment listings.

Videotex succeeded best in France, where it was heavily subsidized and promoted by the government, which gave away millions of terminals and even required people to use the terminals to get telephone directory information. The French system required extensive government subsidy for about six years before it became profitable, but it introduced millions of people to the idea of information services and created the opportunity for a number of private businesses to become information providers through the government system.

STEALTH COMMERCIALS IN BRAZIL

Brazilian television provides one example of what can happen if the current tendency toward commercializing products within films and programs continues. Prime time in Brazil is dominated by homegrown *telenovelas,* descendants of soap operas that run six nights a week for about eight months; that is, they have a beginning, middle, and end, unlike American soaps. These shows are more like a blend of soap opera, costume drama, and situation comedy and are popular with all ages, men and women.

In the last few years, the main network, TV Globo, has begun slipping an increasing number of commercial messages into the plot, visuals, and dialogue of *telenovelas.* For instance, the most popular *telenovela* in 1989–1990 had two main "stealth" commercial sponsors, a major bank and the post office. Although set in a dusty rural town, many scenes took place in a gleaming chrome-decorated branch of that bank, and one of the main characters worked in an equally modern-looking branch of the post office. The opening of  the bank branch dominated most of one episode, while dialogue in another centered on how fast post office overnight mail packages were. Lesser attention was also given to soft drinks, beer, cars, and other products; for instance, the camera might just linger a bit on the label and brand name.

By 1991 such "commercials" were covering almost half of the production costs for these kinds of serials, making them very profitable. While some Brazilian critics have denounced these kinds of ads, the government has not regulated or controlled them.

Advertising

Advertising is not permitted by many of the world's media systems. Some governments fear that advertisers exercise too much control over content. For example, since 1923 the BBC in Great Britain has avoided advertising in order to keep its focus on education and information; it was felt that advertising ends up promoting entertainment to draw an audience. Some governments also fear the effects of encouraging people to want to consume advertised goods when they may not be able to afford to, sometimes called a "revolution of rising frustrations."

Broadcasting in many countries has been kept either state- or public-supported specifically to exclude advertising. Nevertheless, more and more countries are allowing advertising as a means of supporting media, as a result of pressure from advertisers, from lack of government funding, and from audience resistance to paying license fees to support public broadcasters.

Many governments place a variety of restrictions on what is permitted in advertising. In some countries, ads are limited in quantity or time, are placed in blocks, are kept off certain channels or media, or are prohibited for certain products (such as alcohol or tobacco). In some countries certain kinds of audiences, such as children, cannot be directly targeted. In other countries, ads are less controlled than in the United States, with products being overtly displayed within programs themselves (see box above).

REVIEW

1. Why is the government more likely to operate broadcasting than print media in many countries?
2. What is the purpose of public broadcasting?
3. How did cable TV develop in Europe and Japan?
4. Why did most countries have government telephone companies?
5. Why would countries privatize telephone companies?
6. Why was videotex a success earlier in France than in the United States?

MEDIA AND INFORMATION FLOWS

Media flows are sales or exchange of media products between countries or direct cross-border broadcasting to other countries.

Media flows between countries are closely related to limits on national media production. Countries clearly vary a great deal in what they tend to create or use in media content. Some limit entertainment, while others have virtually nothing else. They also vary in their abilities to produce their own content. Some countries can produce only fairly simple print media, such as newsletters, or inexpensive electronic media programming, such as radio and television news, talk, music, and variety shows. Others are able to produce serials, soap operas, sitcoms, dramas, adventures, and other kinds of programs. Some media are harder or more expensive to produce than others. Feature films are the most expensive, followed by television, newspapers, and magazines. Meanwhile, radio programs, newsletters, and pamphlets are produced all over the world in almost all regions. The difficulty of producing media at home has a great deal to do with what media contents are exported and imported across borders.

News

News has been flowing across borders in one medium or another for a long time. In Europe, runners, horsemen, ships, carrier pigeons, semaphore, and the earliest newspapers and newsletters carried news, usually political or economic, across borders. Many early newspapers and newsletters developed correspondents in other countries so that they could publish foreign news for their readers.

International news flow took a significant step forward in speed and volume with the development of news wire services in the 1840s, based on the then new technology of the telegraph. News flow across borders could be virtually instantaneous and much more extensive in coverage. Over time, four main wire services came to dominate international news flow. Reuters (based in Great Britain) evolved from a largely financial service covering the British Empire into a general international news service but always maintained a separate, strong economic news service. The Associated Press (AP) developed in 1848 as a cooperative of American newspapers and began to challenge Reuters's primacy in international news in the early to mid-twentieth century. AP also developed a strong regional base in Latin America, where it operated Spanish-language services as well. United Press International (UPI) developed as a rival commercial service in the international news market but failed financially by the 1980s and was sold to Saudi Arabian interests. Agence France Presse (AFP) was a joint government-private agency that served primarily France and its former colonies but also grew into a fourth primary international news source. Tass, the official news agency of the Soviet Union, became a fifth major agency after World War II, until the breakup of the U.S.S.R. in 1991, but it had served a more restricted set of countries, primarily those within the Soviet sphere of influence.

By the 1970s a number of critics were beginning to assert that the four major news wire services had too much control over international news flow. They felt that the reporters and editors of these wire services acted as gatekeepers, deciding what was newsworthy and what wasn't. The wire services tended to follow a fairly standard Western (American and European) definition of what was news: disasters, sensational or unusual events, political upheaval, wars or conflicts, famous personalities, and current (versus long-term) events. While this approach fit the Western ideal of the press as a critic and watchdog, it sometimes produced negative coverage and images of other countries, which in turn had significant impact. For example, U.S. tourism to the Dominican Republic dropped considerable in 1987–1988, after U.S. coverage of a riot there—the only major television news coverage of the country in several years.

Both socialist and developing-country leaders also distrusted the **agenda-setting** role of the international news agencies. These leaders felt that the agendas of the news agencies often represented Western interests much more than theirs, particularly in the context of the cold war (1948–1991), when U.S. coverage of Eastern Europe and the Soviet Union tended to be particularly critical. In return, Western news agencies and reporters feared that these countries wanted to assert political control and censorship over their reporting, which they felt followed Western norms of objectivity. Such complaints became a major issue in the 1978–1979 debate in UNESCO (the U.N. Educational, Scientific, and Cultural Organization) over the idea of a new world information order and the inequality of media flows between countries.

In the 1970s–1990s, television news flow began to steadily increase in prominence. It began with wire services, such as UPI Television News, and news film sources, such as Visnews from Great Britain, offering filmed (and later video) footage for various national television news operations to use in their newscasts, to supplement wire service coverage. Television news flow increased dramatically as CNN, the BBC, and other satellite-based news operations began to offer entire newscasts and even all-day news coverage across borders, primarily to satellite television receivers and cable television operations.

CABLE NEWS NETWORK (CNN) IS CARRIED ON TELEVISION SYSTEMS AROUND THE WORLD.

Film

Films of significant quality and interest have been produced in many countries, but in the 1990s few countries are producing many feature films. Many nations have produced only one or two feature-length films in their histories— some none at all. Furthermore, film production has slowed down or even stopped in many countries, as many have fallen into debt or suffered other economic crises. In a number of countries where film production had been heavily subsidized, governments found themselves unable to continue to support it. Some countries, including France and Spain, still continued to subsidize their film industries, leading to conflicts in trade talks with the United States, which considers such subsidies an unfair form of protection.

The United States has dominated international film production and distribution since World War I. During both World War I (1914–1918) and World War II (1939–1945), a number of the other major world film producers, including Italy, Germany, Japan, France, and Great Britain, had their industries disrupted and cut off from world trade in films. Hollywood stepped in to occupy world film markets both times.

American films have succeeded in a variety of markets around the world for several reasons. One is the enormous size of the U.S. market for movies, which permits Hollywood to recover most of the costs of films in their domestic release. No other country has a similarly large and affluent national audience or market to support so many films. Second is the heterogeneous nature of the U.S. audience, which has been made up of diverse immigrants since the beginning of the medium. American films have been made simpler and more universal to capture that large, diverse audience. Because of these elements, Hollywood has been the world's film production center, drawing money and talent from around the world and away from competing film industries abroad. Since the 1920s Hollywood has drawn actors, directors, writers, and musicians from Europe, Latin America, and Asia.

Furthermore, Hollywood studios, organized under the Motion Picture Export Association of America, have worked together to promote exports and control overseas distribution networks. They have done so with a degree of cooperation or collusion, which might ordinarily be considered anticompetitive and a violation of antitrust laws domestically but has been specifically permitted overseas by the U.S. Congress under the Webb-Pomerene Act.

Today the United States clearly dominates world film. American films filled over 70 percent of the theater seats in Europe in 1993. They were even more dominant in Latin America. In some ways, then, government protection of film industries in other countries is not surprising if they want to ensure that national film industries survive. Compared to Europe, more films are produced in Asia, primarily in Hong Kong and India (which has produced more films than the United States in some years). These countries, together with Egypt, the film center of the Arab world, do show that some film industries can be maintained, even in developing countries, if the domestic market is large or if they produce for a multicountry audience defined, and to some degree protected, by a shared language and culture.

Television

In the late 1950s, when the U.S. film studios also began to produce for television, they could use their existing distribution channels to start selling television programs worldwide with the same economic and cultural advantages that American films had enjoyed. This ability coincided with a need by many new television networks around the world to find something cheap to put on the air to fill up the hours of broadcast time.

Starting in the early 1960s, American films, sitcoms, action adventures, and cartoons flooded into many other countries. Because television production was expensive and new, not many countries had the equipment, people, or money to produce enough programming to meet their own needs. A few countries decided to limit broadcast hours to what they could fill themselves, but most responded to audience demands for more television by drawing on external sources.

A 1972 study for UNESCO found that over half of the countries studied imported over half of their TV programs, mostly entertainment and mostly from the United States. Many countries feared the

DALLAS ABROAD, OR J.R., UGLY AMERICAN

In 1983 Jack Lang, France's minister of culture, called *Dallas* "the symbol of American cultural imperialism." At one point, the popular nighttime soap opera was watched by people in over 90 countries. In some countries, like the Netherlands, over half of the population watched the show, according to Ien Ang, who wrote *Watching Dallas* (1985). In many countries, it became a national mania, with streets emptying and water consumption going down while it played. Critics worried that *Dallas* represented the worst possible example of American consumer capitalism, selfish individualism, and moral decadence. They feared that those values would affect other cultures.

It was hard to imagine what people around the world, ranging from veiled Muslim women to Japanese businessmen, made of *Dallas*. How did watching it affect their lives? In Britain, critic Stuart Hall noted, "It had repercussions on the whole culture, the involvement of the viewers became of a different order. At a certain moment you could no longer avoid talking about the popularity of *Dallas* when people started using categories from it to help interpret their own experiences." But he noted that that moment passed and *Dallas* became just another popular program (Ang, 1985).

According to several studies, *Dallas* was interpreted very differently by people in various cultures, in line with their own interests and biases. In fact, several of these studies concluded that the cultural imperialism idea was overblown, that people were not as affected by *Dallas* as had been feared. Other studies also showed that in many countries it had never been popular, as local family dramas and soap operas were more appealing to the audience (Liebes & Katz, 1989; Tracey, 1988).

SOAP OPERAS AROUND THE WORLD

For a time around 1980, American soaps such as *Dallas* seemed to dominate world television. But as it turns out, most people prefer soap operas or serial dramas from closer to home.

In Latin America, *telenovelas* run in prime time and usually depict romance, family drama, upward mobility, and getting ahead. The archetypal *telenovela* for many was *Simplemente Maria*, about a Peruvian peasant girl who moves to the city, works as a maid, saves money, buys a sewing machine, and becomes a seamstress. All sewing machines in Lima sold out after that plot development.

Martial arts dramas from Hong Kong and China follow some soap opera themes—romance, love, family intrigues, and rivalries—but add a lot of martial arts action, battles, historical plots, and costumes. These are popular all over Asia. Japan makes its own versions, focused on the samurai era and featuring a similar mix of rugged heroes, beautiful heroines, and battles. These programs are also becoming popular worldwide (the author once saw one dubbed into Spanish in Los Angeles).

Indian soap operas tend to be more epic, mythological, and even religious. A recent popular soap opera retold the national Hindu religious epic *The Ramayana*, with the story of the Hindu gods. It had a powerful effect, according to critics, who saw it as perhaps reinforcing nationalist Hindu political parties and also as standardizing throughout India a previously diverse set of versions of *The Ramayana*, which has sometimes had very different characters as the main figures of good and evil.

All of these series are popular not only in their home countries but in surrounding regional television markets, which share languages and cultures. *Telenovelas* now sell to all of Latin America; Hong Kong soaps show on satellite Star TV; and Indian soaps are popular even in neighboring and rival Pakistan.

Cultural imperialism occurs when countries dominate others through media exports, advertising, and media institution models.

cultural impact of this practice. People began to talk about **cultural imperialism,** or "wall-to-wall *Dallas*" all over the world.

A number of countries, from Great Britain to Taiwan to Canada, established quotas limiting the amount of television programming that could be imported. In 1989 the European Economic Community decided to try to compete by sponsoring a Europe-wide "Television Without Frontiers," which required member nations to carry at least 50 percent of television programming produced within Europe. Because this limit would reduce the amount of American programming sold to Europe, Hollywood and U.S. government officials protested it at trade talks but did not achieve an agreement.

Some American television exports are increasing fairly rapidly in their dollar values, and exports represent a steadily increasing share of television producers' profits. Because many shows now make more money overseas than they do in the United States, a number of American producers are beginning to shape their programs to anticipate and maximize overseas sales.

However, American television programs are also facing increased competition in a number of areas. More nations at virtually all levels of wealth are doing more of their own programming. Production technology costs are going down, groups of experienced technicians and artists have been trained in most countries, and a number of low-cost program forms or genres have been developed, including talk, variety, live music, and game shows. Some countries that have slowed their film production continue to produce quite a bit of television programming. As ratings in many countries reflect, audiences usually tend to prefer local programming when they can get it.

More countries are also competing to sell programs to others. Some, such as Brazil and Hong Kong, compete worldwide. Others, such as Mexico, Egypt, and India, dominate regional markets characterized by shared language and culture. American programs remain attractive to world audiences, especially among the better-educated, who are likely to be more cosmopolitan in their tastes and previous media exposure. Still, it seems that people more frequently look for television programming that is more **culturally proximate**— closer to their own languages, cultures, histories, and values. Figure 6.5 shows that nationally produced programs are more common than American in a variety of countries.

Major **regional TV markets** are developing in Spanish, Arabic, Chinese, Hindi, English, German, and French languages. These are called "regional" because they focus on a world region tied together by common language, culture, religion, and a history of being colonized by the same country (usually Great Britain, France, or Spain). Increasingly, though, these cultural markets extend beyond neighboring countries to follow populations that have migrated throughout a larger region or even the world. For instance, the Chinese audience is centered in China and nations near it (Hong Kong and Taiwan) but extends slightly farther to Chinese populations mixed in with others (Singapore, Malaysia) and then to Chinese speakers around the world.

Such world-spanning populations are not so much "regional" as they are defined by language and culture. They are reached and united through a variety of new technologies: video, satellite television, and cable TV. For instance, Turkish television is following Turkish guest workers into a number of western European countries by satellite. Similarly, Arabs in Europe are a major target for the MBC satellite channel out of Saudi Arabia.

It seems that languages and cultural differences (particularly cultural cues about what is funny, what is politically correct, and what is outrageous or sacrilegious) are both uniting and dividing world television audiences. For instance, the attempt to produce programming for a Europe-wide television market, promoted heavily by the European Economic Commu-

Cultural proximity is the desire of audiences to see or hear media products from their own or similar cultures.

Regional TV markets are based on language, culture, religious values, and geography.

FIGURE 6.5
WHAT IS ON IN PRIME-TIME TELEVISION IS USUALLY A REFLECTION OF WHAT IS MOST POPULAR WITH A COUNTRY'S AUDIENCE. THESE FIGURES ABOUT PRIME-TIME TELEVISION IN SEVERAL COUNTRIES SHOW NATIONALLY PRODUCED TELEVISION DOMINATING AMERICAN IMPORTS IN ALMOST ALL COUNTRIES. (SOURCE: STRAUBHAAR ET AL., 1992)

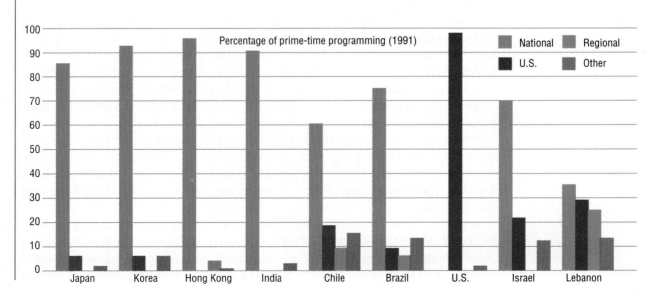

nity, is proving difficult because Europeans are divided by language and culture. French audiences, for example, prefer not to listen to either German or English, and vice versa.

Europe comprises a series of small cross-border markets. For example, there are more than 90 million German speakers in Germany, Austria, Switzerland, Luxembourg, and Lichtenstein, plus minorities in France, Belgium, Poland, and Hungary. English is widely spoken in several European countries and gives both Great Britain and Australia a unique ability to sell music, films, and television to the United States, which is difficult for most countries.

Beyond language, other aspects of culture are important in reaching audiences: jokes, slang, historical references, and mentions of current people and events are often culture- and even nation-specific. Some programs designed to average out all such differences were so bland that critics called them "Euro-pudding."

On the other hand, language and cultural cues, where they are shared across borders, can help build cross-national markets. For instance, Latin American countries used to import American situation comedies, whose jokes were not always particularly clear in translation. Now they tend to import comedy shows from each other, because the cultural proximity of Spanish-speaking Latin American nations makes slang, jokes, and references easier to understand. Even Brazilian programs, which have to be translated from Portuguese to Spanish, are funnier and more comprehensible because the languages, styles, and cultures are still more similar to those of Spanish-speaking audiences than those in U.S. programs. However, Brazilian producers have discovered that when they make very current references to politics, use too much slang, or are otherwise too topical to current Brazilian issues, their programs are harder to export to other Latin American countries or elsewhere in the world.

Music

Genres are types or formats of media content.

Many of the same dynamics found in television also apply to recorded and radio music. We are seeing the emergence of world, regional, national, and local music industries, with a wide variety of **genres** and audiences.

American, British, and some other European rock and pop music in English is currently popular throughout the world. Many of the same singers and groups can be found on the radio and in music stores from Taiwan to Russia to Argentina. In this sense there is a truly global music industry, primarily based in the United States, that speaks to a globalized youth culture, although local music remains popular in most countries, too.

Governments and policymakers in a number of other countries find this pop music globalization somewhat threatening. Because Anglo-American pop music often carries messages about sex, violence, drugs, gender roles, or racial images that clash strongly with local values around the world, many people fear its influence, particularly on the younger people most likely to listen to it. For instance, some young black people in Brazil are listening to American rap and even incorporating rap into their own music. Some of the ideas about sex (talking about "rough sex") and violence (talking about killing cops) in American rap bother older black Brazilians, who see it as alien to their own music and culture.

As with film and television, some countries have legislated rules against certain kinds of music content or require that a certain proportion of nationally produced music be played on radio stations. Some governments also subsidize national music industries to make sure that national music, or at least some of the rarer forms of it, is produced. Even the U.S. government subsidizes avant-garde, classical, and folk music, through various grants to performers and festivals.

Most often, though, music development has been left to musicians' initiative, market forces, and audience demand. To a large degree that has worked fairly well in many countries, because local and national music is often sought by the audience, who are willing to pay for it, although they also listen to and purchase global music. Music, too, is much cheaper to produce than film or television. A 1976 study, *Broadcasting in the Third World* (Katz & Wedell, 1976), estimated that music and radio production generally cost about one-tenth of television production in a variety of countries. Both music and television production costs have gone down since then because equipment costs have dropped, but it is still easier for radio and music recording markets to support a variety of musicians and types of music than equivalently numerous and diverse television productions. This is particularly true in the smallest and poorest countries. It is also true of musical subcultures that correspond to subcultures in a variety of countries, such as Turkish music among Turkish residents in Germany.

There is also a more diverse international market for the variety of music produced in most countries. Music flows across borders more easily in diverse ways than do films or television. International music trade is dominated by big companies, sometimes the same ones involved in film and television. Those companies, such as Sony, Polygram, Philips, and EMI, often play a dual role in other countries: They bring in and sell the dominant American and European pop music, but they record and sell national artists as well. That gives them something of a stake in promoting those artists, both at home and abroad, when they perceive that there might be an export market. For example, foreign firms record Jamaican reggae, Brazilian samba, and Caribbean salsa and merengue, sell them at home, and also export them to the United States. Furthermore, those international companies are more willing to risk distributing national music recordings than the equivalent television programs because musical tastes are more diverse and costs (and financial risks) are much lower. The recording industry also has a greater variety of competitors, since it is easier for small music labels in both the United States and abroad to get started, although some of them run into barriers and lack of access when they try to export to others countries.

Much of this industry development is driven by the fact that the world music market consists of diverse languages and cultures. For example, Jamaicans migrate to Great Britain and the United

THE GROWING POPULARITY OF "WORLD MUSIC" WAS EVIDENT IN THE SUCCESS OF PAUL SIMON'S *GRACELAND* ALBUM AND TOUR.

States and take their musical tastes with them. Americans visit Jamaica, hear reggae, like it, and want to be able to buy it at home. American musicians and producers visit other places, hear other musics, and incorporate them into their styles, which leads some audiences to hunt down the original influences and sources and buy them. American jazz and pop artists, including Stan Getz and Frank Sinatra, listened to and recorded with Brazilian samba musicians such as João Gilberto in the 1960s, creating American audience interest in Brazilian bossa nova. More recently, Paul Simon recorded *Graceland* with African groups such as Ladysmith Black Mambazo and introduced them to American audiences. Imported recordings also spread among networks of friends, among radio stations willing to play more unusual music, and among recording labels serving smaller, more specific or segmented music interests.

All of these factors make the global flow of music more diverse than the global flows of film and television. In particular, while few foreign films and even fewer foreign television programs ever reach the American audience, quite a bit more foreign music does. British pop music is popular in the United States, and many artists from other countries ultimately record in English to reach a broader world market. Many American audiences probably never think much about a fairly wide variety of groups from Scandinavia, Holland, or Germany as being from other countries because many of those groups record in English without noticeable accents. Even music in other languages is far more likely to achieve some popularity in the United States than is television in other languages.

> **Public diplomacy** is using media or other channels to reach and influence public opinion in other countries.
>
> **Propaganda** is media content aimed at persuading people to accept an idea or ideology.

THE CUBAN-AMERICAN RADIO WAR

One of the more fiercely fought international radio wars happened just off the Florida Keys. After Fidel Castro led the Cuban Revolution in 1959, Cuba and the United States sank into a "cold war" in which radio broadcasting of propaganda seemed to substitute for more active military hostilities following the failure of the Bay of Pigs attack on Cuba. Cuba broadcast its own programs in Spanish and English at the United States. Cuba also provided a base for Soviet radio transmitters for Radio Moscow and Radio Peace and Progress. The United States broadcast at Cuba not only its Spanish Service from the Voice of America but also Radio Swan in the 1960s and a specific anti-Castro service called Radio Marti, starting in 1984 and a television version called TV Marti, starting in 1990. Radio and TV Marti represented an escalation of the radio war by the Reagan administration, which was much more anti-Castro than its predecessors. Radio Marti was to be a very strong 50,000-watt AM signal, and the Cubans demonstrated an ability to jam it, interfering with several U.S. AM radio stations on the same frequency. TV Marti followed but never functioned well technically.

In 1995, the U.S. government was reviewing its whole strategy of international radio and television, wondering how much to change its propaganda strategy now that the cold war with the former Soviet Union seemed to be over.

International Radio Broadcasting

Direct cross-border international radio broadcasting has never been particularly important to Americans, except perhaps to amateur hobbyists in "ham" radio. The same situation is true for most countries with extensively developed radio industries, such as those in Europe and Latin America. In some other parts of the world, however, international radio has had major importance.

Most international radio has been conducted by governments over short-wave for largely political and public relations purposes—what has sometimes been called **public diplomacy,** trying to reach and influence public opinion in other countries. The main examples have been Voice of America, Radio Moscow, and Radio Havana. Some international radio has also been done for religious reasons, by Vatican Radio and several American Protestant groups, for instance, and for commercial entertainment, news, and advertising, such as Radio Monte Carlo, run in the Middle East by the French company Sofirad.

International radio has been most important during major wars. It played a significant role in the **propaganda** battles of World War II between the United Kingdom, United States, U.S.S.R., Germany, and Japan. It played a prominent role in the cold war between the United States and the Soviet Union, where the Voice of America, Radio Free Europe, Radio Moscow, and Radio Havana competed for influence in other countries.

Foreign radio is still an important source of information in areas where news media are either unavailable, like parts of Africa, or not trusted, as was the case in Eastern Europe until the breakup of the Soviet bloc. Cross-border radio from direct broadcast satellites may bring international radio back as a major issue at some time in the future, but it is eclipsed by the development of more radio options within most countries.

Information and Data Flows

Flows of film, television broadcasts, and music between countries are familiar to most of us, but there is also a rapidly increasing flow of computer-based information, graphics, and electronic mail throughout the world. For a number of years, data and information flows were largely a phenomenon of governments, banks, and large transnational corporations. More recently, all those who venture on to the Internet computer network to exchange E-mail or explore ongoing group discussions or databases are interacting with people, groups, and corporations around the globe (see Figure 6.6).

There was a long period of heavy U.S. dominance in international information flows in the 1970s and 1980s. That came in part because the United States dominated computer technology itself. In the early 1980s the United States still had well over half of the world's computers. Furthermore, **transborder data flows,** as they were originally referred to, were so expensive that they could only be afforded by large corporations and some governments.

Critics such as Herbert Schiller, in a book called *Information in the Age of the Fortune 500* (1981), began to fear that data and information flows would be a tool for increasing U.S. corporate power throughout the world, to the detriment of developing world and even

Transborder data flow is the communication of data across borders.

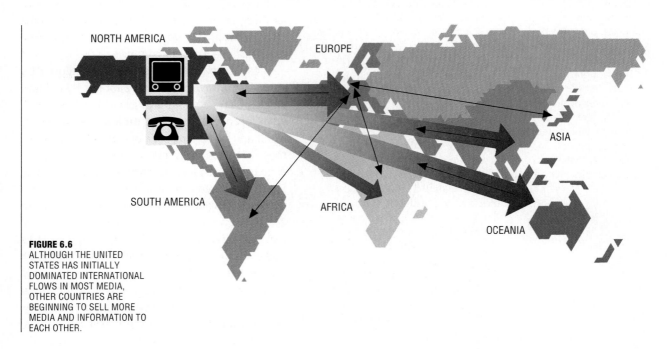

FIGURE 6.6
ALTHOUGH THE UNITED STATES HAS INITIALLY DOMINATED INTERNATIONAL FLOWS IN MOST MEDIA, OTHER COUNTRIES ARE BEGINNING TO SELL MORE MEDIA AND INFORMATION TO EACH OTHER.

Remote sensing usually refers to satellite observation using photography, infrared photography, and radar to "see" objects, vegetation, weather patterns, and so on.

European economies, political systems, and cultures. One example of how technologies permitted an increase in U.S. control came with the use of satellites to observe resources on the earth. Satellite **remote sensing** could observe the health of the Brazilian coffee crop or even locate copper deposits in Africa. Both the access to satellite signals and the computers required to interpret them were expensive, giving an advantage to corporations over poor governments.

Transborder data flows permit some corporations to centralize control over worldwide operations, sometimes causing branches to be downsized, jobs to be moved, and governments to lose tax revenues. However, other observers (Reich, 1991) have hastened to note that while such corporate centralization was indeed hastened by computer networks, as data transfers permitted low-level jobs such as data entry to be transferred to low-wage nations such as Jamaica, which became an offshore data processing center for many corporations. This situation might represent an economic opportunity for Jamaicans who get the jobs but probably a loss of jobs for some Americans who had previously done the work.

Over time, corporate data communication and information systems became cheaper, and smaller companies and a broader range of countries became involved in international information flows. U.S. dominance is no longer as pronounced, and even the corporations and governments of a number of developing countries are beginning to participate in this increasingly essential aspect of international business. However, lack of access to information communication technology, as we noted with computers, still hampers many poorer countries.

More recently, the collection of computer networks known as the Internet has begun to move computer communications beyond corporations. The Internet was originally designed as a research network, and the main users around the world have been university professors, students, researchers at think tanks, and nongovernmental organizations tied to academia. This system enabled academic researchers and students in many countries to form links with each other, get access to information, and "meet" a lot of new people. Although many people used it to communicate only with others they already knew, the Internet began to have a globalizing effect on many by making international contacts easy and inexpensive. Many individuals and groups are now joining Internet—over a million a month in 1994—so it is rapidly creating a new form of international communication flow. While most Internet traffic as of 1994 centers in the United States, people are rapidly joining from Europe, Asia, and Latin America.

R E V I E W

1. Why did American films come to dominate world film markets?
2. Why did American television also dominate world program markets?
3. What was the impact of American media products, such as *Dallas,* around the world?
4. Why might American dominance of some world television markets be slipping?
5. What are some of the main cultural differences among television programs from various countries?
6. What is cultural proximity?
7. Why do more countries produce music than television?

GLOBALIZATION OF OWNERSHIP AND OPERATION

Many kinds of media businesses and institutions are becoming more globalized in their very makeup, including their ownership and scale of operation. The trend to extend successful products, such as films, recordings, and television programs, into foreign markets sometimes leads companies to get involved in the global distribution systems. In the 1910s, investing in film distributors and **theater chains** guaranteed that the filmmakers got their films distributed. In radio and television, some companies bought into or started foreign stations or networks, sometimes to sell programming, more often just to get into a profitable business.

Theater chains are movie houses owned and operated by a single company to coordinate and control movie distribution.

In current cable and satellite television systems, similar reasons apply: a desire to guarantee program sales or to guarantee that cable program channels get carried.

Some media industries, such as the Hollywood film and TV studios represented by the Motion Picture Export Association of America, have long been global in their operation and scope, principally because they controlled a number of the companies in other countries that distributed and showed (in theaters) the films that they produced in the United States. Later, Hollywood companies also began to **coproduce** films abroad to find cheaper shooting locales and extra sources of financing. More recently, the ownership of Hollywood itself has become globalized. Sony recently bought Columbia Pictures (a major film studio), Columbia Pictures Television, and Tri-Star, a major independent production company. The resulting operation has been scrutinized by critics to see whether the kinds of films produced will now reflect Japanese rather than American sensibilities, if that is possible to detect. So far the feeling within Hollywood itself is that ownership is neutral. "It doesn't matter. The product is uniquely American, no matter who owns it," says Paul Kagan, a major entertainment industry consultant (Turner, 1993). 20th Century Fox was purchased by News Corp. of Australia, owned by Rupert Murdoch, who also acquired control of the Fox Television Network. MCA, Inc., is owned by Matsushita of Japan. The major international media conglomerates are listed in Table 6.1.

Record companies are similarly structured except that they have a more diverse set of origins and even more international ownership. Major recording companies are based in Great Britain (Thorn, EMI), the Netherlands (Philips), Germany (Bertelsmann), and Japan

> **Coproduction** indicates cooperation between film or television producers in two or more countries.

TABLE 6.1. INTERNATIONAL MEDIA CONGLOMERATES

Company	Print	TV, Films, Cable	Music	Multimedia
Bertelsmann (Germany) *Mohn family*	Gruner & Jahr Bantam Doubleday, Dell McCall's, YM, Family Circle, Fitness, Parents	RTL-Plus Canal+ (Germany) DBS service Nice Man (50%)	RCA Records BMG Music BMG Catalog Arista Killer Tracks	America Online (5%) Rocket Science BMG Interactive

Disney (Capital Cities–ABC) (U.S.)	ABC Consumer Magazines
	Diversified Pub.
	Hyperion Press
	Discover
	Miramax Books
	Disney Press
	Disney Comics
	Fort-Worth Star-Telegram
	Kansas City (MO) Star
	    Newspapers & related pubs in
	    13 states
		ABC Network
		ABC TV stations
		Disney Pictures
		Touchstone
		Hollywood Pictures
		Miramax Films
		Buena Vista TV
		Disney Television
		Touchstone TV
		ESPN (80%)
		Arts & Entertainment
		Lifetime (50%)
		Tele-Munchen
			ABC Radio Net
			ABC radio stations
			Hollywood Records
			Disney Records
			Disney Music Publishing
				Disney Software

Fininvest (Italy) *Silvio Berlusconi*	Il Giornale TV Sorisi e Canzoni Publitalia	Canale 5 Italia-1 Rete-4 LaCinq Tele-5 Reteitalia		
Gannett (U.S.)	USA Today Gannett Dailies Gannett News Service	GTG Entertainment 10 TV stations	16 radio stations	USA Today online
Hachette (France)	Elle Tele 7 Jours Jornal de Dimanche Woman's Day	Tele-Hachette Channel 1	Europe 1 (radio)	

Sources: Langdale (1991); *1996 Information Please Almanac; Multichannel News; Variety; Wired*

TABLE 6.1. *(CONTINUED)*

Company	Print	TV, Films, Cable	Music	Multimedia
News Corp. (Australia) *Rupert Murdoch*	The Times of London, The Sun, The Boston Herald, San Antonio Express, The Australian, The Daily Telegraph, The Herald Sun, South China Morn. Post, Fiji Times HarperCollins Triangle Pubs. TV Guide	Twentieth Century Fox Fox Broadcast 7 U.S. TV stations Fox Video Fox Cable Net f/x British Sky Broadcast Star TV (Hong Kong)	Twentieth Century Fox Records	Online venture with MCI Delphi
Segram (Canada) *Edgar Bronfman Jr.*	Putnam Berkley Group	MCA Universal Cinema Intl. (49%) United Intl. (33%) MCA TV USA Network	MCA Geffen Uni Distribution	Universal Interactive Interplay

Sony (Japan)		Columbia Pictures
		Tri-Star Pictures
		Sony Pictures Classics
		Columbia Tri-Star
		    Television, Home
		    Video
			Columbia Records
			Sony
			Chaos
			Epic
			Tri-Star Music
			Relativity
				Sony hardware
				TV sets, VCRs, recorders

TCI, Inc. (U.S.)
John Malone
		TCI Cable Systems
		Liberty Media
		Starz!
		Encore
		Court TV
		E!
		Home Shopping
		    Network, QVC
		Turner (15%)
		Discovery Channel
		    (49%)
			Prime Sports Radio	Sega Channel (partnership)
				Primestar DBS
				Microsoft Network
				    (investment)
				Netscape (investment)
				Western Telecom
				Sprint (partnership)

Time-Warner (U.S.)
Gerald Levin
Partial ownership by US
    West, Honshu, Toshiba
	Time, Fortune, Life, Sports
	    Illustrated, People
	Time-Life Books
	Little, Brown
	Book-of-the-Month Club
	DC Comics, Mad
	Turner Publishing
		Turner Broadcasting
		CNN, TBS, TNT
		Turner Classic Movies
		Cartoon Network
		Airport Channel
		HBO
		HBO Video
		Castle Rock
		New Line Cinema
		Savoy Pictures (3%)
		Warner Bros. Pictures
		Warner Bros. TV
		Warner Bros. Home
		    Video
		Warner Cable
		BHC Stations
			Warner Bros Records
			Atlantic Records
			WEA Intl.
			Elektra
				Pathfinder WWW site
				3DO (13%)
				Atari (25%)
				Crystal Dynamics
				Sega Channel (partnership)

Viacom (U.S.) *Sumner Redstone*	Simon & Schuster Pocket Books Free Press Macmillan Scribner's	Paramount Pictures, TV UPN Cinamerica Viacom Cable Showtime Movie Channel MTV, MTV Intl. VH1 Nickelodeon SciFi Channel Blockbuster Video TV & radio stations	Blockbuster Music Famous Music	Simon & Schuster Interactive Viacom Interactive Viacom New Media MacMillan Digital

TABLE 6.2. THE INTERNATIONAL MUSIC INDUSTRY GIANTS

Company	Home Country	Worldwide Sales (1992)
Sony	Japan	$3.5 billion
Philips/Polygram	Netherlands	$3.3 billion
Time-Warner	United States	$3.2 billion
Bertelsmann/RCA	Germany	$2.5 billion
Thorn/EMI	United Kingdom	$2.2 billion
Matsushita/MCA	Japan	$300 million

(Sony). These companies have consolidated across borders, as Table 6.2 reflects, with Philips now owning Polygram (formerly of the United Kingdom), Bertelsmann now owning RCA (formerly of the United States), and Matsushita now owning MCA (formerly of the United States). Most of these companies also have large foreign branches that often have autonomy to produce and distribute records within other markets as well as distributing American and European music. Several record companies have also been acquired by companies across borders, so that overall the firms are more global and less national in character.

Print media are becoming equally globalized. The publishing industry is highly internationalized, with book publishing houses, magazines, and newspapers frequently owned across borders. The main actors in print are Rupert Murdoch's News Corp. (Australia), Bertelsmann (Germany), Time-Warner (U.S.), and Hachette (France).

World Barons of Multimedia

Australia's Rupert Murdoch has the most diverse international empire. As of 1994 he owned much of Fox Studios, the Fox Network, British Sky Broadcasting (one of the major European direct satellite broadcasters), *TV Guide*, and HarperCollins Publishing. He also owns most of Star TV, which brings several satellite television channels as well as BBC, MTV, films, and two Chinese-language channels to most of Asia and the Middle East. His newspaper empire includes the *London Times*, *Sun*, and *News of the World*. He is expanding his satellite channels from British Sky Broadcasting, Star TV, and Fox further into Europe, Latin America, and Asia.

Ted Turner has created several television channels that are going global. His Cable News Network (CNN) has been an international operation for years. Turner's Cartoon Network and TNT are also being marketed in Europe, Latin America, and Asia.

William Gates, chairman of Microsoft Corporation, is a different kind of international communications media power. His operating systems, MS-DOS and Windows, are used in most of the world's personal computers. The software programs Microsoft sells, such as Word, Excel, and the new CD-ROM encyclopedia Encarta, are also beginning to dominate world markets.

Increasingly, multinational operation is no longer limited to the richest nations. There are also transnational media empires based in Mexico, Brazil, Hong Kong, Egypt, and elsewhere. For example, Emilio Azcarraga, Rene Anselmo, and their partners in Mexico own Televisa, whose three TV channels dominate broadcasting in Mexico. They are also involved in video distribution and cable TV in Mexico, a joint venture with TCI for Latin American cable channels, a joint venture with Fox to produce programming, the satellite television channels Univision and Galavision in the United States and Latin America, and the PanAmSat satellite system.

Telecommunications Industries: Global Providers

The infrastructure for international media and information services has also become increasingly globalized. For transoceanic transmission there are several worldwide public satellite networks, such as Intelsat, a global consortium of telephone companies that handles much the world's international telephone and data traffic, and Inmarsat, which handles much of the world's maritime and other mobile communications. There are also a number

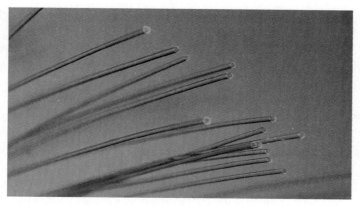

of regional satellite systems, including the Arab League's ArabSat and the European Community's Eutelsat. A few national satellite systems also exist, such as Indonesia's Palappa, that offer telephone and television transmission services to neighboring countries. Privately owned satellite systems, such as PanAmSat, are also increasing in numbers.

Satellites are being at least partially displaced by an emerging set of world and regional fiber optic networks, owned by Cable & Wireless of Great Britain, AT&T, and others. Fiber optic cables can carry the same kinds of signals carried by satellites across transoceanic distances, with greater speed and less distortion. Increasingly, for the frequently used routes between Europe, North America, and Asia, the fiber optic cables are also more cost efficient.

In another globalizing development, a number of national telecommunications networks are going international. British Telecom has bought up data services in the United States and invested heavily in long-distance giant MCI. AT&T, the Baby Bells, France Telecom, Telefonica of Spain, and others are also investing in telephone, cellular telephone, and data communications companies abroad. These companies have invested in a number of the telephone companies that have been privatized in various nations. They have also eagerly sought to supply new services, such as cellular mobile telephony, in countries where foreign investments have been allowed under newly liberalized rules.

REGULATION OF INTERNATIONAL MEDIA

International media and telecommunications systems are regulated differently than national media systems. As with most aspects of **international law,** there is no direct enforcement power, and regulation requires a consensus between nations that the proposed regulations or changes meet their various interests. Failing that, nations tend to assert their self-interest, and the larger, more powerful nations tend to get their way.

One of the few international organizations that has achieved real compromises and real changes is the International Telecommunications Union (ITU). That group faces some of the same crucial regulatory problems that individual nations must solve within their borders. Radio spectrum frequencies have to be allocated to different uses in various nations to avoid interference between users, for example. Even more important, the ITU allocates the space orbits for satellites whose **satellite footprint** areas almost automatically cover multiple countries.

Technical standards have to be established so that users of telegraph, telephone, fax, and electronic mail equipment in various countries can communicate with each other across borders. For instance, the standard for current fax machines was set by the ITU, which has enabled many manufacturers to make equipment that users around the globe may use to send and receive compatible fax messages.

International law includes treaties between countries, multicountry agreements, and rules established by international organizations.

Satellite footprint is the surface area covered by the satellite's signal.

The ITU has largely confined itself to technical issues, although the question of who gets which satellite orbits and frequencies is clearly political, too. In 1979 developing-country spokesmen, such as Mustapha Masmoudi from Tunisia, observed that the largest and most powerful 10 percent of the world's countries (particularly the United States and the former U.S.S.R.) controlled the use of 90 percent of the frequencies and orbits, which seemed an unfair domination of those resources.

The political debate over these issues was raised more directly in the United Nations Educational, Scientific and Cultural Organization (UNESCO) in the late 1970s. There was a movement among developing and Eastern European socialist countries to change aspects of the world's media system that they considered unfair or inequitable. The main points of grievance were the **unbalanced flow** of television and film entertainment from the United States and Europe to the rest of the world, a similarly unbalanced flow of news, the negative images of developing and socialist countries carried in the American and European news reports, and the inequitable division of communications resources, such as the orbits and frequencies mentioned earlier, plus computers, telephones, television and radio stations, and so on.

Debate raged in UNESCO over these issues in 1976–1979 until the United States decided to withdraw in 1983 in protest over proposed policies that it thought violated the values of the **free flow of information** and journalistic freedom. UNESCO proposed that countries create national policies to balance the flow of information. The United States feared that UNESCO's policies would give too much power to governments, which would be likely to restrict free speech and the free flow of information. Nothing much was resolved, except that some new news agencies and national media ventures were started to try to balance the unbalanced flows of news, television, film, and music between nations.

Unbalanced flow refers to an unequal flow of media or news between countries.

Free flow of information is the idea that information should flow as freely between countries as possible.

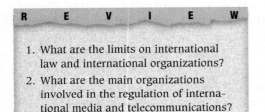

R E V I E W

1. What are the limits on international law and international organizations?
2. What are the main organizations involved in the regulation of international media and telecommunications?

ISSUES IN GLOBALIZATION OF MEDIA

Among the main issues in globalization of communications media are cultural imperialism, the free flow of information, media trade, and the effects of media on national development.

Cultural Imperialism

Perhaps the biggest international issue has been what many nations call cultural or information imperialism. Some define this primarily as the unequal flows of film, television, music, news, and information we described earlier. Unequal flow bothers many nations on various levels. First, it is seen as a cause of cultural erosion and change. So many media products flow into some countries from the United States that they fear American ideas, images, and values will replace their own. As we saw, several European critics feared that their television would become "wall-to-wall *Dallas*," with people possibly imitating some of the power-hungry and ruthless Texans it portrayed. French authorities fought to keep American words such as "drugstore" and "weekend" from creeping into common use by French people. Some poor countries in Africa saw epidemics of infant diarrhea and death when mothers gave up breast-feeding for bottle-feeding, which they had seen in European and American television programs and advertising. (The problem was caused by mixing infant formula with unsanitary water.)

One response to problems of unequal flow of media has been to increase the amount and kinds of media contents produced in the countries and regions that tend to be on the receiving end of the unequal flows. Some, such as Brazil, have pressured the national television broadcasters to produce more programming. Others, such as France, subsidize their national film industries to keep them strong. Another solution is to limit media imports. A number of countries, including those in the European Community as well as Canada and Taiwan, limit the amount of foreign television and film they import. Many countries have discovered, as we noted, that national and regional television and music production tend to increase more or less naturally because it is feasible economically and because audiences desire it.

Other critics have been more concerned about the economics underlying the flows of media. They believe that the flows of media provide models or ways of making media content that undermines national **cultural autonomy.** They believe media should be locally produced so that the content will reinforce and promote key elements of national, regional, or local cultures. Underlying the fear of commercial media, in particular, is the idea that they tend to tie countries into a global economy based on advertising and consumption, in which the poorer countries are likely to gain little and perhaps alienate those in the population who are frustrated by exposure to goods they cannot have.

Cultural autonomy refers to the goal of being mostly self-sufficient in media and cultural productions.

National sovereignty is keeping domestic forces in control over the economy, politics, culture, and so on.

Free Flow of Information Versus Cultural Sovereignty

Contrasting principles fuel the debate between free flow of information and national sovereignty. The idea of a free flow of information internationalizes the basic concept of freedom of speech, in which all people ought to be as free as possible to both send and receive information across borders. But according to the idea of **national sovereignty,** governments or other domestic forces are entitled to assert national control over natural resources, culture, politics, and so on. Both approaches are established as basic principles in the UNESCO charter and the U.N. Declaration on Human Rights.

Those who consider the current international flows of information and culture to be unequal tend to emphasize national sovereignty as a justification for a country's asserting control over media flows. The United States has opposed many such proposals in the new world information order debate. It does so in part because American commercial media interests are threatened by proposed restrictions on media sales and flows. But the United States has also opposed a number of proposed restrictions out of principle. The United States and a number of other nations believe it is important to keep as free a flow of information as possible to promote freedom of speech globally.

Free and balanced flow refers to achieving more equal flows of media via the freedom to produce and receive media.

One of the compromise proposals that emerged in 1979 in UNESCO was to promote a **free and balanced flow** by helping developing countries build up their own abilities to produce and export media and cultural products. Although this idea received little financial support, a number of developing nations succeeded in producing more media anyway.

Trade in Media

Media flow and trade issues have been raised in international or regional organizations, such as the European Community (EC). Under its "Television Without Frontiers" rules introduced in 1989, the EC promoted trade and exchange of television and film within Europe by requiring all broadcast and cable television channels to carry a minimum of 50 percent "European" films and programs, which included anything produced or coproduced by EC members. The U.S. government and Hollywood protested, since this would mean a reduction in the amount of U.S. programming that could be sold in Europe. The United States saw this as a trade policy issue, since such exports are a significant part of the American balance of trade, compensating for American purchases of Japanese VCRs, radios, and so on. European governments saw it partially as a trade issue, desiring to boost their own producers, but also a cultural policy issue in which the distinctness of European culture ought to be preserved on television and film.

The same issue has come up in the General Agreement on Trade and Tariffs (GATT), which is dedicated to lower **tariffs** on trade. In the recent round of GATT negotiations, concluded in 1993, the United States pushed hard to have new international trade rules on "audiovisual" materials (television and film) that would keep countries from protecting their own national film and television industries or setting **quotas** keeping imported films and programs out. The European Community rallied around the French, who opposed such a change—existing GATT rules permitted protection and subsidy of film industries—and succeeded in keeping audiovisual materials from being included in more liberal trade rules.

Media and National Development

The other main issue is whether media, information technologies, and telecommunications can be made to better serve national development. Part of the fear expressed in international debates is that media are primarily serving global commercial interests, not the needs of the populations of the various countries, particularly the poorer populations. Many government planners and social critics feel that most people in developing nations need media that teach them about health and how to get ahead economically, not slick American entertainment and advertising.

Many governments and international organizations, such as UNESCO, have worked hard to create models of how to use media to promote education, health, agriculture, local religious and cultural values, and so on. Some of these programs have succeeded very well, particularly radio programs based in and oriented to rural areas. Television has been less successful in these kinds of efforts, perhaps because its costs are too high, leading to centralization of programming away from local needs.

The ITU and World Bank are encouraging national governments and foreign investors to invest more funds in the expansion of developing world telephone and telecommunications systems. World Bank and other research shows that such investment in telephone system expansion contributes to economic growth.

Tariffs are taxes imposed by governments on goods imported from other countries.

Quotas are limits on imports placed by national governments, designed to keep out foreign films and programs.

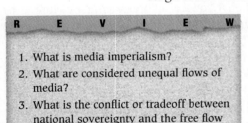

R E V I E W

1. What is media imperialism?
2. What are considered unequal flows of media?
3. What is the conflict or tradeoff between national sovereignty and the free flow of information?

SUMMARY & REVIEW

How Can Communications Media Systems Be Compared?

Why does government operate broadcasting more than print media in many countries?
Print media are easier to start and do not require frequency regulations or standards by governments. Many governments worry more about the electronic media because they reach broader mass audiences, with the potential to affect more people. Some governments see electronic media as valuable tools for either development or political control. In some of the poorest countries, governments may be among the few to have enough money to run broadcasting or telecommunications.

What is the purpose of public broadcasting setups?
Public broadcasting is oriented toward providing the public with education, culture, and information balanced with entertainment. Public broadcasting corporations are usually nonprofit companies financed by government or by license fees paid by everyone who owns a radio or television set, enabling programming to be more independent.

How did cable TV develop in Europe and Japan?
In the 1970s many of these countries tried to develop interactive or two-way cable but were not very successful because the interactive technology was too expensive and public demand turned out to be limited. Cable grew fastest in smaller countries where the national ability to produce multiple channels of television was limited. American commercial cable channels began to expand into these markets in the 1980s.

Why did most countries have government telephone companies?
Government-owned and operated PTTs (postal telephone and telegraph administrations) were the telephone companies in almost all countries. Government monopolies were seen as capable of unifying national services, investing in expansion, and extending services to those not served.

Why would countries privatize telephone companies?
Government PTTs came to be seen as inefficient, overstaffed, and incapable of generating the necessary resources for investment. Private companies, both domestic and foreign, were seen as bringing in financial resources and a more efficient approach to management.

What Are the Main Media Flows Between Countries?

Why do American films dominate world film markets?
American films were made to appeal to a large and diverse immigrant audience through a universal and entertainment-oriented style, which made its films easier to accept among diverse international audiences. The United States also benefited from the destruction or blockage of other film producers during World War I and World War II. U.S. producers developed an efficient export cartel, the Motion Picture Export Association of America (MPEAA), which owned much of the world distribution and exhibition structure.

Why did American television also rise to dominate world program markets?
After 1956 U.S. television programs were produced primarily by the MPEAA film studio companies, giving them an existing international distribution structure. American television also used many of the popular techniques and formulas of Hollywood film producers, which gave their productions much of the same universal entertainment appeal. Many other countries found American television programs were cheaper than the cost of local production and provided an easy solution to filling schedules.

What is the impact of American media products, such as Dallas, *around the world?*
American television programs, films, and music are very popular, particularly among young people. The values and ideas contained in them are often very different from those contained in other cultures. People fear that American ideas, images, and values will replace those of their own cultures. It appears that actual effects are less than was feared, since many people do not watch American programs much, and they tend to interpret them in their own way.

Why might American dominance of some world television markets be slipping?

As technology costs for television production decline and experience in producing shows increases, those in other countries are finding it easier to make their own shows. Furthermore, as other countries develop television genres or program forms that are popular at home and in nearby regions, audiences tend to prefer the local programs much of the time.

What are some of the main cultural differences among television programs from various countries?

Soap operas, variety shows, and music and talk shows tend to be more prominent in programming abroad than in the United States. Sex and nudity can vary widely among countries, as can elements considered comic. Some countries are too small to produce certain kinds of programming. Smaller countries tend to focus on these lower-cost genres.

Why do more countries produce music than television?

Recorded music is cheaper to produce than television shows. Musical preferences are often more localized within countries and to subcultures defined by age, ethnicity, religion, and so on. So there is demand for a large, diverse set of artists and recording companies.

What Leads to the Globalization Of Ownership And Operation of Communications Media?

What are the main reasons that companies buy or start media in other countries?

The trend to extend successful products into foreign markets sometimes leads companies to get involved in global distribution systems. Investing in film distributors and theater chains guarantees that the owners' films get distributed. In radio, television, cable, and satellite television systems, some companies buy into or start foreign stations or networks to sell programming, to get into a profitable business, or to guarantee that cable program channels get carried.

Which companies are the main global owners of media?

The main companies are Time-Warner (U.S.), Rupert Murdoch's News Corp. (Australia), Hachette (France), Bertelsmann (Germany), Silvio Berlusconi's Fininvest (Italy), Capital Cities–ABC (U.S.), and Gannett (U.S.).

Who Regulates International Media?

What are the limits on international law and international organizations?

International law is really just a collection of treaties between countries, multilateral agreements or treaties between groups of countries, and rules set by international organizations. The problem is that all of them rely on compliance and consensual behavior by individual governments.

What are the main organizations involved in the regulation of international media and telecommunications?

The main regulator is the ITU (International Telecommunications Union). It allocates frequencies and satellite orbits to countries and sets international standards for telecommunications. UNESCO (United Nations Educational, Scientific and Cultural Organization) has been the main forum for the new world information order debate in which a number of countries protested principally the unbalanced flows of media and news between countries.

The EC (European Community) and other European regional organizations are increasingly important in setting standards, setting rules about media production and flow, and creating regional markets for information and media industries. The GATT (General Agreement on Trade and Tariffs) has also become important in debates and rules about trade in media products and information services, which have become more central to the economy of the United States and other developed nations.

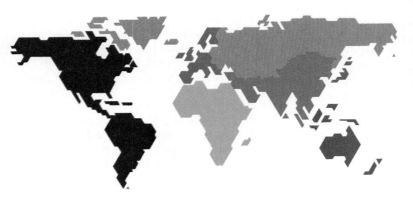

What Are the Main Issues in Globalization of Communications Media?

What is cultural imperialism?

Cultural imperialism is an unbalanced relationship in culture and media between countries. The main specific issue is unequal flows of film, news, television programs, cable channels, and music from the United States to other countries. Other aspects include the globalization of media ownership, foreign investment in national media, and the use of foreign media models.

What are considered unequal flows of media?

Unequal flows occur when one country exports substantially more to other countries than it imports. International media flows seem to become more equal as other countries produce and export more, although the United States still exports a great deal of media and information and imports relatively little. This tendency toward more balance is more notable in music and television and much less so in film or news.

What is the conflict or tradeoff between national sovereignty and the free flow of information?

The United States has promoted the free flow of information as an international extension of its national values about freedom of speech and press. The United States and many other countries feel that free flow of information will reduce conflict and increase understanding. Other countries complain that the free flow idea permits the United States to dominate international flows of media. They argue that they should have national control or sovereignty over flows of media in order to assert more balance in the flow. However, giving such power to government raises the prospects of censorship and control of information.

REFERENCES

Ang, I. (1985). *Watching* Dallas. New York: Methuen.

Katz, E., & Wedell, G. (1976). *Broadcasting in the third world.* Howard Press.

Langdale, J. V. (1991, April). *Internationalization of Australia's service industries.* Canberra: Australian Government Publishing Service.

Liebes, T., & Katz, E. (1989). *The export of meaning: Cross-cultural readings of* Dallas. New York: Oxford University Press.

Reich, R. (1991). *The work of nations.* New York: Knopf.

Schiller, H. (1981). *Information in the age of the Fortune 500.* Norwood, NJ: Ablex.

Straubhaar, et al. (1992). The emergence of a Latin American market for television programs. Paper presented at International Comunications Association Conference, Miami.

Tracey, M. (1988). Popular culture and the economics of global television. *Intermedia.*

Turner, R. (1993, March 26). Hollyworld. *Wall Street Journal Reports,* R1.

Chapter 7

PRINT MEDIA: NEWSPAPERS, BOOKS, AND MAGAZINES

C H A P T E R   P R E V I E W

he print media—newspapers, magazines, and books—are the oldest mass communications media and still among the most important. Their content forms and business institutions have distinguished histories that have raised such crucial issues as freedom of the press and intellectual property. These media are major industries that serve the information and entertainment needs of many people, even though they have been losing part of their audience and advertising to electronic media since 1927. Today, print media technologies are evolving rapidly, giving rise to the electronic publishing and information industries.

THE SUN

NUMBER 1.]   NEW YORK, TUESDAY, SEPTEMBER 3, 1833.

PUBLISHED DAILY,

Paris, Oregon (Population 15), 2010

Say, Lefty, before you shut me down for the night, you wanted to revise your newspaper subscriptions for tomorrow.

That's right. Tell me what I'm getting now.

O.K. The papers are *Idaho Daily Statesman*, *American Farm Daily*, *High Desert Tattler*, and *The Wall Street Journal*. Interests are farm equipment prices, beef prices, ranching, beef production, survivalism, local gossip, and local politics (local being Boise, Idaho, to Winnemucca, Nevada). Acceptable ads are farm equipment, light trucks, firearms, and local groceries.

Well, let's can that *Wall Street Journal*. Costs too much. And when I say local, I mean Nampa <Idaho> to Winnemucca—gettin' tired of reading about them city slickers in Boise.

Next morning:

Mornin' Lefty. I found forty items, three photos. Do you want me to print this stuff, or do you want to screen it first?

Jest print the headlines and photos for now, extra large type. My eyes are still feelin poorly. Maybe I'll look at the rest later.

If you'll accept three video farm equipment ads, they'll cover the costs of your papers. Want to see them?

Goldurn ads. Yeah, guess so. Run 'em now. Jest tell them fellers that I don't authorize resale of the information that I accepted these ads, O.K.?

They'll accept that condition, if you also accept a separate print ad, printing nonoptional.

<censored> O.K.

A BRIEF HISTORY OF PRINT COMMUNICATION

The history of the print media is a repetitive cycle of technological innovation, competition as new media forms and uses arise, increased demand for new services and abilities, changes in society wrought by media, and governmental attempts to restrict media political power.

Before printing, books were a limited medium. Literacy and reading came thousands of years before mass media. For those thousands of years, books were available only to a few among the elite. Reading was largely the job of clerks and priests. Books were copied by hand by monks who often devoted their lives to the process. The books were often beautifully illustrated as well.

In the civilizations of Greece, Egypt, China, Islam, and Rome, few people were highly educated and had access to libraries. In China and the Islamic nations, books of literature, science, and philosophy flourished among an educated few. In Europe throughout the Middle Ages, few books other than the Bible or religious or philosophical commentaries were available. This began to change by the 1300s, when universities were established to train more people as clerks, and as nobles began to take an interest in learning to read.

Early Print Media

The Gutenberg Bible first appeared in 1455, the result of the development of movable type and mechanical printing five years earlier by Johannes Gutenberg. Although many think of print media as beginning with Gutenberg, much of the early development of writing, paper, and printing took place in the Middle East and China. In A.D. 105 the Chinese began making paper from rags, but it was not until A.D. 700 that Arab traders brought this new technology to the West. Using wooden blocks to print characters had been practiced earlier during the T'ang Dynasty (A.D. 618–906), followed by the development of movable clay type in 1000 and movable metal type in 1234 in Korea. These inventions did not lead to the development of a large printing industry, however. It was not until the beginning of the Industrial Revolution that Europeans (re)discovered movable type and were able to more fully develop and exploit the printing press (Carter, 1991).

AMONG THE EARLIEST BOOKS WERE ILLUMINATED MANUSCRIPTS, CAREFULLY DONE BY HAND.

A number of the most important books that were printed in Europe came from the Hebrew Middle East (the Bible, the Torah), the Arab Middle East (books on science, math, astronomy, navigation), and Greece (classic works of science, literature, and philosophy). This gave people had access to classic ideas from books that had persisted from Greek or Roman days and from works developed elsewhere in the world. For instance, in the late 1400s Columbus learned from an Arab book on geography that he might be able to reach the East Indies, India, and Southeast Asia by sailing west across the Atlantic Ocean. People like Columbus, a son of farmers, would not have had access to such books a hundred years earlier. Clearly the European explosion of print technology and printed contents built on a much larger world context.

Gutenberg's printing press and others that followed fueled an explosion in early book printing. Almost immediately, books became much cheaper. By 1470 a French printed Bible cost one-fifth of what

TABLE 7.1. WORLD PRINT MEDIA MILESTONES

Year	Event
105	Paper invented in China
1200	First novel, *The Tale of Genji*, in Japan
1234	Movable metal type invented in Korea
1455	Gutenberg Bible appears in Germany
1470	French printed Bible at one-fifth the cost of a hand-printed one
1470	Translation/printing of Greek, Arab science classics
1500	Millions of books printed in Europe
1620	First news sheets (*corantos*) printed in Holland
1640	First daily news sheets (*diurnos*) printed in Holland, Great Britain, elsewhere

Manuscript originally meant written or copied by hand.

Chapbooks were cheaply bound books or pamphlets of poetry or prose aimed at a broader audience, much like early paperbacks.

Corantos, the ancestors of newspapers, were irregular news sheets that appeared around 1600 in Holland and England and covered foreign affairs.

Diurnos, later ancestors of newspapers, gave daily reports and tended to be more focused on domestic events.

a **manuscript** version had cost, even though the printed one was a careful, relatively expensive duplication of the hand-copied original. Printers also quickly began turning out pictorial prints, posters, and pamphlets as well. Most of these were religious and didactic—that is, explicitly aimed at teaching people or changing their ideas about religion.

Beyond the Bible and morally oriented pamphlets, new products were often more entertainment oriented and aimed at broader, less-educated groups of people. **Chapbooks** were cheaply bound books or pamphlets of either poetry or prose aimed at a broader audience, much like current small-format paperbacks. Their contents included moral tales, adventures, and strange stories. The way had been opened for a wide variety of literature to follow.

Technology facilitates and influences what is possible in media but does not define its contents. For example, book-length novels flourished with printing because mechanical reproduction allowed quantities of books to be made less expensively. However, the concepts and forms that characterize the novel began earlier. Greek poets before 1000 B.C. produced epic works. *The Tale of Genji*, recognizable as a novel by current standards, was written in Japan in the twelfth century. The antecedents of novels about daily life, romances, mysteries, and horror or terror existed well before the advent of printing. Although some story forms, or *genres*, have been around for a long time, they have still been changed by developments in technology and economics. The major events are summarized in Table 7.1.

Newspapers were first developed as irregular news sheets in Holland, Great Britain, and France to carry news about foreign events, such as the Thirty Years War in Germany and Holland (1618–1648), and commercial or economic issues. These news sheets, called **corantos,** were replaced by daily reports, or **diurnos,** that focused more on domestic events, the king, and Parliament (in Great Britain, for example) (Stephens, 1989).

Religious books, notably the Bible, prayer books, and hymnals (song books), were among the earliest books. Other nonfiction books tended to focus on moral tales and issues, but novels, poetry, and other entertainment emerged fairly early as well.

Stories that turned into novels existed in both European and non-European cultures well before the development of the printing press. In fact, epic stories that we still find in books persisted for centuries in an oral form; for example, Icelandic sagas were composed verbally,

THE EARLIEST NEWSPAPERS APPEARED IN EUROPE IN THE 1600S.

memorized, and passed on from generation to generation well before Iceland had a written language. Likewise, hand-copied written versions of those same sagas and many other stories helped preserve them until printing could extend their reach.

A key development in print media was the growth of literacy and the distribution of books in the vernacular, the everyday languages that Europeans spoke. Prior to 1100, written communication was nearly always in Latin, the language of the Catholic Church. Thus, to be literate, people had to learn a second language. By the 1200s, written versions of daily languages were more common. Books were being written in vernacular languages: Italian, French, German, English, and Swedish. In the 1300s and 1400s, literacy became commonplace among the elite, the middle class, and professionals like the sea captain Columbus. Outside this group, though, many people remained illiterate. This was true in the early 1900s for the industrialized nations, and it is still largely true today for many developing countries, where the elite and middle classes are literate and print oriented, but the masses, who are not literate, use electronic media.

Print Media in America

Print media in America began with religious books, such as the *Bay Psalm Book* in 1640, hymnals, and copies of the Bible, printed by the Puritans in Massachusetts. Soon after came newspapers in Boston, New York, and Philadelphia, reflecting the early centers of commercial, political, and intellectual activity.

The Colonial and Revolutionary Periods. The first American newspapers struggled with the question of control by local and British colonial authorities. The first U.S. newspaper, *Publick Occurrences Both Foreign and Domestick*, published in 1690 by Benjamin Harris, contained stories that scandalized both the Crown and Puritan authorities; it was shut down after one issue. The next two newspapers were started by Boston postmasters. In 1704 John Campbell started the *Boston News-Letter*, which carried a notice that it was published "by authority" of the Royal Governor. Most of the news was straightforward, if dull: news from foreign papers (often months late), notices of ship departures and arrivals (important in a port city), summaries of sermons, and legal and death notices. Campbell's replacement as postmaster also started a newspaper. These two newspapers highlighted an early and continuing connection between print media and the means of delivery, postal or otherwise (Tebbel, 1969a).

A newspaper was started in New York and a third in Boston in 1721 by James Franklin. His *New England Courant* had no "by authority" approval and was intended to be independent. Franklin was jailed and forbidden to publish without prior approval, so he made his brother, Benjamin, the new editor. Ben Franklin was very successful as a newspaper editor. He soon moved to Philadelphia and started the *Pennsylvania Gazette,* which also was successful and independent.

The question of **independence** and criticism of authority was raised openly in 1733 when Peter Zenger published a newspaper openly critical of the British governor of New York. The governor jailed Zenger for criminal libel. Despite British legal precedent to the contrary, Zenger's lawyer Andrew Hamilton argued that the truth of a published piece was a defense against libel. Appealing to the American jury to not rely on British law and precedent, Hamilton

Independence in media usually refers to freedom from governmental control, not from owners or advertisers.

THIS FAMOUS DRAWING URGING THE COLONIES TO JOIN TOGETHER IN THE REVOLUTION IS ONE OF THE FIRST "POLITICAL CARTOONS" TO APPEAR IN THE AMERICAN PRESS.

won the **libel** case, which established an important precedent or principle that true statements are not libelous.

Zenger and Franklin, among others, helped establish a **political press** that was very important in building support for the American Revolution and in establishing the role of a free press in subsequent American democracy. Newspapers proliferated before the Revolution. Most were partisan, but some tried to be neutral. Numerous key documents and ideas, including the Declaration of Independence, were published in the newspapers. in 1785, during the debates over the Constitution, James Madison, Alexander Hamilton, and John Jay first published the *Federalist Papers* in newspapers as press handouts (Altschull, 1984).

Magazines began to develop at about the same time. The first U.S. magazines were Bradford's *American Magazine* and Ben Franklin's *General Magazine,* both of which debuted in 1741. During the American Revolution, many magazines also took a more political tone. Thomas Paine edited *Pennsylvania Magazine,* which urged revolution but closed in 1776. Few magazines were popular or long-lived (Tebbel, 1969b).

Franklin also published one of the first successful nonreligious books, *Poor Richard's Almanac,* every year from 1732 to 1757. Book printers continued to print pamphlets, which were politically important to the American Revolution. Thomas Paine's *Common Sense* sold 100,000 copies in ten weeks. In 1731 Franklin started the first **subscription library** in the United States, beginning an American tradition in which lending libraries greatly helped popularize book reading. Before that reading depended on private library collections, which in turn depended on private wealth. The Library of Congress was begun with Thomas Jefferson's collection of 6,500 volumes. The high cost and difficulty of access to books also gave rise to magazines and newspapers.

The 1800s. After the American Revolution, the politicization of many newspapers and magazines continued. They took on more **partisan** leanings and were often openly involved in political campaigns. However, advertising and commercial interests began to be important as well. Frequently, political and advertising interests coincided. Benjamin Franklin was a successful publisher in large part because he was a clever writer of advertising copy.

In 1783 the first daily newspaper in the United States, the *Pennsylvania Evening Post and Daily Advertiser,* was begun. By 1800 most large cities had at least one daily, but

circulations were limited. Readers had to be literate and relatively wealthy—one issue cost as much as a pint of whiskey, around five cents.

Newspapers began to appeal to different audience groups. In 1827 the first African American newspaper, *Freedom's Journal,* was published. A number of other papers by and for African Americans were started before and after the Civil War from 1861 to 1865. The first Native American newspaper, the *Cherokee Phoenix,* began publication in 1828; the newspaper folded when the Cherokees were moved from Georgia to reservations in Oklahoma. However, the *Cherokee Advocate* started in Oklahoma and was published until 1906. As European immigration increased, many immigrants published foreign-language newspapers. By 1880 there were 800 newspapers in

TABLE 7.2. MILESTONES IN U.S. MAGAZINE DEVELOPMENT

Year Begun	Content	Magazine
1740s	Intellectual/political/general interest	Franklin's *General Magazine*
1820s	National general interest	*Saturday Evening Post, Nile's Weekly Register, Godey's Lady's Book*
1850s	National literary magazines	*Harper's Monthly, Atlantic Monthly*
Civil War (1861–1865)	Reporting, photojournalism	*Harper's Weekly*
1830s–1870s	Activism, farm magazines	*Liberator, The Nation, Tribune, The Farmer*

German, Italian, Scandinavian, Polish, and Spanish. Some of them, such as the Polish press in Chicago, reached fairly large circulations and were politically important (Sloan, Stovall, & Startt, 1993).

After the revolution, several magazines reached increasing circulations, although they were limited by literacy and cost. Aimed at the elite, *Nile's Weekly Register, North American Review,* and *Port Folio* covered weekly events, politics, and art and included reviews, travelogues, short stories, serialized fiction, and so on. By the 1820s, magazines of more general interest, such as the *Saturday Evening Post* and *Godey's Lady's Book,* began to appear. For other magazine milestones, see Table 7.2.

Newspaper printing costs decreased in the early 1800s with the invention of iron (versus wooden) presses in England and the steam-powered press in Germany. Two-sided printing by cylinders came in 1814. By 1830 a new press could print 4,000 double impressions per hour. These technological innovations permitted lower-cost papers aimed at a broader audience. At the same time, social conditions for the creation of the mass audience and mass newspapers were building. More people were learning to read via the expanding public education system, wages were increasing, more people were moving to the cities, and an urban middle class was growing. These groups created the nucleus of a mass audience.

However, many people could not read or afford newspapers. This was particularly true among the waves of immigrants who landed from 1840 on into the early 1900s. One response was to create and sell cheaper newspapers. In both the United States and Britain, the 1800s brought forth a **penny press** and cheap books called **dime novels.**

Benjamin Day launched the first low-cost daily mass newspaper, *The New York Sun,* in 1833. It sold for a penny, the first penny press. To reach that price, Day had to rely on advertising more than sales, which changed the nature of newspaper economics. This kind of mass-audience daily was one of the first media to sell a mass audience to advertisers as its main means of support. Day targeted a potential audience that could read but could not afford earlier newspapers. Day also relied on a cheaper delivery mechanism, using newsboys to sell papers in greater volume to justify the lower price. Costs decreased further in 1846 with the advent of

Penny press were daily newspapers after 1830 that sold at low costs, were aimed at a mass audience, and depended on advertising.

Dime novels were inexpensive paperback novels that aimed at a mass or at least a broad readership.

THE NEW YORK SUN WAS THE FIRST LOW-COST DAILY MASS NEWSPAPER, FIRST PUBLISHED IN 1833.

the rotary press (which placed type on a rotating cylinder). This combination of factors created the modern daily newspaper and changed the newspaper business. Audience interests and purchasing power, along with production and delivery technologies, are still crucial to how newspapers will continue to evolve (Sloan, Stovall, & Startt, 1993).

Wire services were news services that supplied a variety of newspapers, named for their use of the telegraph and its wires.

Wire services also helped newspapers lower their costs, add more general interest material, and appeal to a wider audience. In 1846, to share the costs of covering stories, several New York newspapers formed the New York Associated Press news service, which expanded with the ability to send stories over the telegraph, thus becoming "wire" services. This and other regional wire services joined to become what is now called the Associated Press (AP) in 1892. AP competed domestically with the United Press Service (UP, later UPI) of Scripps, and internationally with the British wire service Reuters and the French service Agence France Presse (AFP).

The penny press or mass-audience daily also targeted its content at a wider general audience. It set patterns that still mark newspapers' contents: sensational coverage of crime, police news, scandal, and disasters; features about prominent or sensational personalities; social events such as weddings, deaths, and parties; shipping and commercial news; stock and money prices; and advertising. The metropolitan press covered the Civil War, with great disagreement between Northern and Southern papers. Several Northern papers had a major influence on the positions and strategy of the Northern states. African American leader Frederick Douglass pushed hard for the abolition of slavery with *The North Star*. The *New York Tribune* under Horace Greeley pushed the abolition of slavery, too, whereas *The New York Times* was somewhat more neutral.

FREDERICK DOUGLASS USED *THE NORTH STAR* (MASTHEAD SHOWN BELOW) TO PUSH FOR ABOLITION OF SLAVERY.

Several magazines grew to fame during the Civil War, based on their print coverage and on their illustrations that dramatized scenes of the war. *Leslie's Illustrated Newspaper* and *Harper's Weekly* created an important new form of publication, the illustrated news weekly, predecessors to today's *Newsweek* and *Time*. War photographers exploited this new medium to create dramatic photojournalism, showing battle scenes and casualties. A number of these images by photographers such as Matthew Brady provided much of the dramatic impact in the 1992 PBS television series *The Civil War*. Along with magazines, newspapers focused on the war as news, regularly following the story as it unfolded. The use of headlines increased. So did the use of the inverted pyramid style of newswriting, in which the most important news becomes the lead sentence, then each broader, lower layer of the pyramid expands on the next most crucial aspects.

Newspapers then plunged into the post–Civil War industrial expansion. Along with other industries, newspapers saw a chance to grow and more aggressively pursued advertising and newspaper sales. **Muckraking** characterized this period, as crusading newspapers turned their attention to the "muck" of scandals and corruption in government

Muckraking is journalism that invesigates scandal, "raking up the muck" of dirty details.

and industry cartels. Although some newspapers were bought off by groups like the Tweed Ring in New York, others pursued the story. Part of *The New York Times*'s rise to prominence came with its pursuit of the Tweed Ring. This focus on investigative journalism led to an era called "The New Journalism," in which several newspapers crusaded for various causes, also building on the antislavery crusade before and during the Civil War.

Newspapers expanded westward with the American population, following the frontier into the midwest in the 1830s and farther west around the time of the Civil War. During this period, several famous writers, including Mark Twain, Steven Crane, and Ambrose Bierce, made their names as journalists. Twain followed the frontier and worked in Hannibal, Missouri, in 1847, St. Louis in 1853, Virginia City, Nevada, in 1862, and San Francisco in 1864.

Books also became a more popular medium in America in the early and mid-1800s. Access to books increased as the number of public libraries tripled between 1825 and 1850 and book prices dropped due to cheaper printing technology. Interest in reading grew with public education, an increasing literacy rate, and the advent of the penny press. Perhaps more important, however, was the popularization of book content. American novelists addressed the national experience and interests. For example, James Fenimore Cooper wrote about the frontier, while Nathaniel Hawthorne concentrated on New England. However, English authors such as Charles Dickens and Sir Walter Scott were also popular. Cooper also contributed to magazines such as *Knickerbocker,* which fed on and contributed to growing public interest in American expansion. Novels even had political effects, such as Harriet Beecher Stowe's *Uncle Tom's Cabin,* which sold 300,000 copies in its first year and did much to raise popular opposition to slavery (Davis, 1985).

HARRIET BEECHER STOWE'S *UNCLE TOM'S CABIN* WAS A BEST-SELLER IN ITS DAY AND ALSO HELPED SET THE AGENDA FOR OPPOSITION TO SLAVERY.

From 1860 to 1880, even more popular material appeared in cheaper formats. The dime novels addressed an even broader audience of middle-class and even working-class people. For instance, some 250 million Horatio Alger books were sold. In fact, "Horatio Alger story" eventually became a popular synonym for a tale of hard-working upward mobility.

Toward the end of the 1800s, newspapers and magazines began reaching even broader audiences. In 1892 the circulation of Joseph Pulitzer's *New York World* reached 374,000. In 1900 there were 1,967 English-language dailies, with a total circulation of 15 million. In the largest cities, including New York, St. Louis, and Cleveland, large-circulation papers by Pulitzer and Scripps targeted a mass audience directly with sensational stories on sex, murder, scandal, popularized science and medicine, and other human interest events. Newspapers had become the major mass medium of entertainment at the turn of the century. Scripps in the Midwest and Hearst in California started putting chains of newspapers together, some of which (the Scripps-Howard chain) still survive.

Yellow Journalism. William Randolph Hearst moved into New York by trying to hire much of Pulitzer's staff, setting off a dramatic war between Hearst's *Morning Journal* and Pulitzer's *World.* One of the chief weapons was a sensational style of journalism that came to be called "yellow journalism." This style emphasized sensational photos and story selections, large headlines, an overemphasis on personality and human interest stories, and sometimes hoaxes and fake interviews. One of the results was Hearst's spectacular coverage of the 1898 explosion of the U.S. battleship *Maine* in the Havana harbor. Many historians credit Hearst's coverage with helping to push the United States into war with Spain over Cuba and the Philippines (Sloan, Stovall, & Startt, 1993).

As newspapers grew and expanded, there were not enough qualified journalists to go around. Cheaper paper prices, faster printing technologies, such as the rotary press in 1846 and the linotype in 1890, and a more prosperous reading public accelerated the growth of this medium. Advertising flooded in, securing economic conditions for expansion. Newspapers expanded much faster than the population or even the economy as a whole. Both the technological and cost efficiency of newspaper printing increased rapidly, peaking in about 1900. By this time, the newspaper industry had grown larger than its resources—namely, advertising and circulation—could support.

After 1900, other media—motion pictures, magazines, and phonographs—began to compete with newspapers for the public's attention and money. By 1927 radio would also join the competition.

In the 1920s, newspapers began to consolidate into chains and groups. The main group owners were a number of papers. In this era, Hearst and Scripps both closed over fifteen papers each.

The Growth of Magazines. From the 1820s through the 1950s, several magazines were able to reach a broad general audience. They included general-interest magazines with features and fiction, such as the *Saturday Evening Post* from the 1820s; women's magazines, such as *Ladies Home Journal, Good Housekeeping,* and *McCall's* from the late 1800s; digests such as *Reader's Digest* from the 1920s; and pictorial newsmagazines such as *Life* and *Look* from the 1930s. By 1910, both the *Saturday Evening Post* and *Ladies Home Journal* had circulations over 1 million (Tebbel, 1969b).

Magazines had become a major mass medium by 1900. Their rise shared some of the factors that also drove mass newspapers: increased literacy, greater personal income, a growing urban population. However, magazines particularly benefited from a major change in their delivery system. The Postal Act of 1879 gave magazines special rates. This tradition continues today, providing an effective subsidy to magazine distribution, since publishers pay less than the actual cost of mailing yet the magazines are treated as full-cost "first-class" mail. (Catalogs and newsletters also use bulk mail rates and benefit from low prices.) As a result, there were 1,800 magazines in the United States in 1900, a large increase from the 260 that had existed in 1860. After the 1890s, many new kinds of magazines, such as women's magazines, investigatory magazines, digests, newsmagazines, and pictorial magazines, avowed to compete with newspapers (see Table 7.3).

In the 1920s, nationwide radio networks and magazines began to create a more nationally focused advertising market. Magazines also began to overtake newspapers as sources of investigative reporting and crusades for reform. Much of the investigative reporting known as muckraking in the early 1900s was done for maga-

THE READER'S
DIGEST

THIRTY-ONE ARTICLES EACH MONTH
FROM LEADING MAGAZINES - EACH
ARTICLE OF ENDURING VALUE AND
INTEREST, IN CONDENSED AND
COMPACT FORM

FEBRUARY 1922

THE *READER'S DIGEST* HAS GROWN SINCE 1922 TO BECOME THE MOST WIDELY READ MAGAZINE IN AMERICA.

TABLE 7.3. MAGAZINE DEVELOPMENTS AT THE TURN OF THE CENTURY

Year	Content	Name
1890s	Women's magazines	*Ladies Home Journal, Good Housekeeping, McCall's, Harper's Bazaar, Vogue, Vanity Fair*
	Investigatory/muckraking	*McClure's Magazine, Collier's*
1920s	Digests	*Reader's Digest*
	Newsmagazines	*Time, Newsweek, U.S. News*
1930s	Pictorial magazines	*Life, Look*
	Intellectual and opinion magazines	*Harper's, Atlantic, New Republic*
	Sophisticated literary magazines	*The New Yorker*

REVIEW

1. What key elements of print media developed first outside Europe?
2. What were the first topics of printed books?
3. What were the first newspapers?
4. What case established the precedent for press freedom in colonial America?
5. Who developed the political press that supported the American Revolution?
6. Why did magazines develop?
7. What was the partisan press?
8. What was the penny press? What led to it?
9. What role did sensationalism play in newspapers?
10. What was the role of the print media in the Civil War? How did the war affect the print media?
11. What was muckraking?
12. When did newspapers and magazines begin to have to compete with other mass audience media?

zines like McClure's and Collier's. They helped push for legislation such as the Pure Food and Drug Act of 1907. Newsmagazines, such as Time, and pictorial newsmagazines, such as Life, also developed in the 1920s and 1930s as mass magazines, whereas sophisticated magazines, such as The New Yorker, developed a smaller but select audience that appealed to some advertisers.

PRINT TECHNOLOGY TRENDS

Production systems for print media continue to change. High-speed printing revolutionized print media industries in the 1800s and continued to do so well into the 1900s. Fast, central printing of books, magazines, and newspapers will be very important if favorable distribution mechanisms continue to exist.

Transportation and delivery technologies have always been crucial for the development of viable print media. The growth of mass media has depended on the rest of the industrial economy and industrial technology, particularly for the means of distribution. In the past, railroads were particularly important because they could deliver large quantities of books and magazines.

Mail services grew and improved with the means of transportation. Whereas newspapers were often delivered directly in cities, and books moved in bulk along railroads and shipping lines, the mail was crucial for enabling magazines to reach a broad audience in an affordable manner. Mail service became cheaper as transportation improved and as legislation lowered mailing costs. The United States (and other industrialized countries) decided to lower and **subsidize** postal rates for magazines to facilitate the magazine industry and the audience's desire to read them. Mail also facilitated book sales and even the distribution of certain newspapers, such as The Christian Science Monitor, that are delivered by mail.

Subsidization implies transfer of funds from one source to support another activity.

Telegraph, telephones, satellites, and news services have grown up together. New technological advances continue to revolutionize the delivery of news and information, both to mass media and directly to personal or business users. In fact, bankers, political leaders, and news media have depended on the same news delivery technologies since runners, riders, sailing ships, steamships, trains, semaphore signals, and carrier pigeons provided information, even before the telegraph. The key elements in these generations of technological change have been faster delivery and higher capacity to carry more information. Sometimes speed and capacity have been a tradeoff—a carrier pigeon can only carry so much information (Smith, 1980).

Satellite delivery of copy to printers has also become commonplace. Newspaper copy, complete with layouts, can be sent by satellite from central editorial offices to remote printing plants. For example, the main national U.S. newspapers—The New York Times, The Wall Street Journal, USA Today, and The Christian Science Monitor—are printed in numerous locations for easier, cheaper, local delivery.

High-speed printing has become cheaper and more widely available in the last decade. Both local printing plants and the personal printers associated with computer printers and photocopiers are becoming faster and more sophisticated.

THE NEWSPAPER OF THE FUTURE

At research centers, various prototypes and models of the "newspaper of the future" have been created. Most of these have the following elements: a home computer, software programmed to search for the kinds of news the reader or readers at home are interested in, a telecommunications connection from the home computer to the newspaper or news service's computer, and a software system at the newspaper computer for interacting with many home computers. The home computer will probably contain software that is intelligent enough to become the reader's agent, gradually learning his or her tastes, remembering them, and acting on his or her behalf. Then every day or even more often, the home computer will contact the newspaper computer to find news items that will interest the reader. The newspaper computer then sends the stories over the line to the home computer, where they could either be printed out or read on the screen. We have already taken a few steps toward this kind of future. Today, thousands of people use existing information services such as Prodigy and America On-Line to dial up news services supplied by *The Los Angeles Times* and *The Wall Street Journal* or on-line versions of *Time* and *Newsweek*.

Desktop publishing is the composition, layout, and sometimes printing of materials using a personal computer.

Computerization has made many other changes in the print media as well (see Table 7.4). At first, computers substituted for typesetting machines by creating letters on film that was then transferred to metal printing plates. However, the layout and pasteup of a page were still done by hand. As more elements of the page were stored in the computer, more of the page layout could be done on computers as well. This process was further simplified by scanning or digitizing photographs, so they, too, could be edited and placed on the page electronically. This kind of layout and page design was made possible by new software that enabled users to set type, create headlines, put text into columns, make text wrap around photos or illustrations, and edit (or "crop") and place photos.

In the 1980s, more power and speed were packed into desktop machines. Equipment such as laser printers and scanners for digitizing photos or illustrations into computer-readable form became cheaper and more widespread. This hardware was accompanied by software such as Aldus PageMaker and QuarkXPress that enabled users to do powerful layout and page makeup on the desktop. This package of elements, known as **desktop publishing,** has done much to decentralize and even decenter the print media. Anyone can now produce local or specialized newspapers, newsletters, magazines, fanzines, flyers, posters, and "personal" family Christmas letters. However, computer hardware and software do not substitute for writing talent, visual design ability, or editorial skills.

In addition to the availability of cheap local offset printing, photocopying has enabled individuals to inexpensively produce and distribute materials created with desktop equipment. A certain minimum number of copies is required to make offset or other higher-quality

TABLE 7.4. PRINT TECHNOLOGY MILESTONES

Year	Event
105 A.D.	Rag-based paper invented in China
600s	Wooden block printing of characters in China
700	Paper brought to Europe by Arab traders
1000	Movable clay type printing invented in China
1234	Movable metal type invented in Korea
1450	Movable metal type invented in Germany by Gutenberg
1800s	Iron press invented in England; steam-powered press developed in Germany
1846	Rotary press (type on cylinder) invented in the United States
1890	Linotype press invented in the United States
1970s	Computer-based photo composition and "typesetting"
	Satellite delivery of copy to printing centers
1980s	Desktop publishing
1990s	On-line access and local publishing
	Publishing on computer media, CD-ROMs, and computer diskettes

Newsletters or gazettes were initially written by bankers or trading companies for a select group of clients who could afford to pay for specific information that interested them. Similarly, one of the earliest news services, Reuters of the United Kingdom, originally focused on supplying financial and economic news to both private clients and newspapers, then gradually grew into a broader news service that covered politics, disasters, culture, sports, and so on.

The fax machine has permitted enterprising new "print" media to be sent instantaneously to the fax machines or computers of select groups of subscribers. These new gazettes can cover any topic, from stocks to sports medicine to telecommunications equipment markets in Asia. These gazettes can be sent out daily, weekly, monthly, or irregularly.

To some degree, this is just a new, faster, perhaps even cheaper means of delivering newsletters, but it has also opened new possibilities for things that are more visual, more creatively formatted, and less regular. This is particularly the case now that the creators of such newsletters can send them directly from their computers to a regular distribution list of receivers. The computer automatically dials the list and sends the newsletter to the receiver fax over the telephone. This method also offers new possibilities for delivery in places or situations where telephone lines reach better than conventional transportation.

MOZAMBIQUE, JUST NORTH OF SOUTH AFRICA, IS THE POOREST COUNTRY ON EARTH, POOR AT INDEPENDENCE AND SUBSEQUENTLY PLAGUED BY DROUGHT AND CIVIL WAR. ITS FIRST INDEPENDENT, NONGOVERNMENT NEWSPAPER IS A FAX GAZETTE, SENT DIRECTLY TO THE FAX MACHINES OF ITS LARGELY ELITE SUBSCRIBERS; THIS METHOD IS MUCH CHEAPER THAN PRINTING AND DELIVERING THE PAPER, ALTHOUGH IT WON'T REACH THE MASSES OF THE POPULATION.

Custom publishing refers to creating customized versions of print newspapers, magazines, or books for particular audiences.

Videotex services deliver text and graphics through computer networks.

Electronic mail is a written message sent over a computer network.

printing worthwhile. Photocopies can be made for half a dozen friends, a small seminar, or a Cub Scout woodworking class.

Custom publishing have taken advantage of printing speed and the flexibility of computer-based publishing to print selected parts of books or selected chapters from a menu of possibilities. For example, publishers have fought producers of photocopied college course packets by legally prosecuting them for copyright violation and by offering to print parts of books or assemble selected chapters and articles, like photocopied course packs used to.

Personal printing of newspapers and newsletters has become a reality with the increased distribution in workplaces and homes of personal computers, software that connects computers and delivers print documents, telecommunications channels to carry the copy, and printers of adequate speed and quality. In the 1990s, newspaper printing is being localized to the personal level—using a service like Prodigy, a user can request a section of *The Los Angeles Times,* for example, and either read it on the screen or print it at home. (See the box on "The Newspaper of the Future" on page 155.)

In the 1990s, fax, E-mail, and information services are becoming alternatives for print media delivery. Currently, electronic channels can carry so much information, particularly in simple text form, that mass media have many sources to choose from for distribution. Meanwhile, many individuals, companies, and institutions are bypassing mass media by requesting the original text from **videotex services,** which is then delivered like **electronic mail.** The distinction between news services and news media may well disappear for those who use on-line information services.

R E V I E W

1. What are the main recent trends in print media production technologies?
2. What are the main recent trends in print media delivery technologies?
3. What is desktop publishing?
4. How will computers and tele-communications affect the news-paper of the future?

One other new form of publishing uses computer media, such as **CD-ROMs** or computer diskettes, to store, retrieve, and play back "printed" material, such as novels, encyclopedias, and reference works. These new computer media combine traditional print materials with audio, video, and graphics into **multimedia** publishing.

PRINT INDUSTRIES, GENRES, AND FORMS

In the following sections we discuss print industry structure and then examine some of the principal genres and forms in books, newspapers, and magazines.

CD-ROM is a compact disc computer storage medium with read-only memory.

Multimedia systems integrate text, audio, and video and let the user select the presentation mode.

Book Publishing

Books are diverse and hard to characterize in general terms. Some books are sacred, some are sensational, some are eagerly read for pleasure, some are assigned reading in college courses. Some publishers publish only books that will sell many copies, whereas others, like many university presses, publish books because they think the works are intellectually or artistically important and ought to be read. There are over 2,000 book publishers in the United States, ranging from commercial publishers to universities to religious groups, trade associations, and vanity presses that will publish anything as long as the author provides the money. While the computerized publishing technologies discussed earlier make the publication of smaller, more specialized projects possible, books continue to become more expensive to produce because marketing and other costs have increased. As a result, many publishers feel that they have to concentrate on selling more copies of fewer books.

The major categories of book forms or genres, according to the Association of American Publishers, are as follows:

Trade books. Hard or soft cover, including hard-cover fiction and most nonfiction, such as cookbooks, biographies, how-to books, and art books.

Professional books. Reference or professional education books aimed at doctors, lawyers, scientists, researchers, managers, and engineers.

Elementary, high school, and college textbooks.

Mass market paperbacks. Soft-bound books, generally smaller in format and less expensive than trade paperbacks.

Religious books. Bibles, other sacred texts, hymnals, prayer books.

Book club editions. Clubs that publish, sell, and distribute their own editions of mass market books, professional books, and other specialized books.

Mail-order publications. Books largely created by publishers to be sold by mail, usually classic novels or specialized series on subjects like cooking, Western history, wars, cars, and aviation.

Subscription reference books. Encyclopedias, atlases, dictionaries, glossaries, and thesauruses.

Audiovisual and multimedia. Videotapes, CD-ROMs, computer diskettes, slides, and audiotapes marketed primarily to schools, companies, and training groups but also to individuals, by both regular publishing houses and new multimedia publishing companies.

University presses: Scholarly or artistic books of primary appeal to scholars and libraries.

Newspaper Publishing

Many types of newspapers are published in the United States. Although the overall number of daily newspapers has been steadily declining, some of the technological trends noted earlier are increasing the numbers of certain other kinds of newspapers. There are actually more newspapers with national reach now, utilizing satellite delivery and local printing, as well as increasing numbers of local and specialized weeklies, using desktop publishing technologies (Hynds, 1980).

Dailies. Newspapers published at least five days a week are termed dailies. Their numbers have steadily declined, from a high of 2,200 in 1910 to 1,611 in 1988. Daily newspaper circulation stabilized at slightly over 63 million from 1970 to 1993, while the population grew considerably, indicating a reduction in the actual newspaper reach to households.

National Newspapers. The circulation of national newspapers has actually grown (see Table 7.5). Since the 1980s several traditional newspapers have created national editions, using satellite printing in multiple locations. *The Wall Street Journal,* with the largest circulation, is considered a specialized business paper but has a broad general readership as well. *The New York Times* has headline news, news interpretation, and media and business focuses. *The Christian Science Monitor* is delivered by mail and consequently is not headline focused but concentrates on features and news interpretation. In 1982 the Gannett Group created *USA Today* as a national newspaper. Using a graphics-oriented format, it carries shorter news items, more entertainment, more sports, and more items from various states and regions. As Table 7.5 shows, the national dailies have tended to grow slightly from 1987 to 1992, whereas most of the regional dailies have declined slightly. One regional daily, *The Los Angeles Times,* has a larger circulation than *The New York Times* but less national coverage and impact.

TABLE 7.5. CIRCULATION OF MAJOR DAILY NEWSPAPERS

	1987 Circulation	1992 Circulation
National Newspapers		
The Wall Street Journal	1,961,000	1,795,000
USA Today	1,324,000	1,418,000
The New York Times	1,022,000	1,110,000
Regional Newspapers		
The Los Angeles Times	1,113,000	1,177,000
New York Daily News	1,285,000	759,000
Washington Post	761,000	791,000
Chicago Tribune	765,000	723,000
Long Island Newsday	641,000	762,000
Detroit Free Press	649,000	598,000
San Francisco Chronicle	568,000	553,000

Large Metropolitan and Suburban Dailies. Compared with the national dailies, some of the larger metropolitan daily newspapers have shown significant declines in circulation, as many readers have shifted to national dailies, national news weeklies, national newsmagazines, or television and radio. This decline is also related to the relative decline of many large cities as centers of industry. In the last several decades, suburban areas have increasingly become industrial, business, entertainment, and commercial centers, not just bedroom communities. Many people no longer commute to a downtown, or go there to shop, to eat, or for entertainment. Consequently, suburban newspapers have risen in importance and circulation. These newspapers have grown by over half since 1985. One such paper, *Newsday,* of Long Island, New York, is now among the top ten American papers in circulation. Small-town dailies are also growing, for similar reasons, as many small towns are actually growing in economic importance. In response, many metropolitan dailies put out suburban sections and even regional editions, such as the San Fernando Valley and Orange County editions of *The Los Angeles Times.*

Weeklies. Most weeklies used to cover small-town or rural areas that were too small to support a daily. Many such newspapers still exist. With the growth of the suburbs, new residential and business areas have also started weeklies. About a third of weekly papers now cover the suburbs, and that number is growing rapidly.

Other forms of weekly are also growing. Most major cities, many medium-size cities, and some new suburban areas now have entertainment-oriented weeklies that are given away at music stores, bookstores, and other locations. These weeklies cover dining out, movies, live concerts, and local events. Some areas also have political weeklies, while others have ethnic or minority group–oriented weeklies, which focus on news and events within their particular community.

Newspaper Economics. Newspapers are having to fight harder for advertising and sales. The declining circulation of many traditional dailies, which lowers their revenues, has reinforced the wave of consolidation. Other newspapers are doing well in circulation. But all are challenged to compete for advertising. Although newspapers still lead in overall advertising revenues, their relative share has declined over the last thirty years.

In advertising, newspapers continue to have certain advantages. They can carry local supermarket ads, including coupons, as well as more extensive ads for automobiles, and electronics, for local dealers. But for other kinds of advertising, like basic advertising for national brands or for goods aimed at certain market segments, such as young adults, newspapers suffer in competition with the electronic media.

Newspaper Sections and Contents. Most newspapers contain several distinct sections that serve different audiences: national news, international news, editorial and commentary, local news, sports, economics and industry, lifestyles, entertainment, features, comics, and advertising. Newspapers vary a great deal in the sections they emphasize. National newspapers focus on international news, national news, editorials/commentaries, and eco-

TELEVISION AND MCPAPER

Newspapers have had to compete with a continually increasing number of new media. Television pulled away audiences for entertainment and news starting in the 1950s, followed by cable TV with all-news and numerous kinds of entertainment and specialty channels in the 1970s and 1980s. *USA Today,* the Gannett Group's relatively new (1982) national newspaper, seems designed to compete with television. It is more graphically oriented, with its color photos, color weather maps, and icon-oriented charts. It puts more emphasis on human interest and feature stories and generally runs much shorter stories than the other national newspapers.

Some critics have accused *USA Today* of imitating television too much, of losing what is distinctive about newspapers: greater depth, more analysis, more news, less entertainment. Some go so far as to call *USA Today* "McPaper"; that is, the newspaper equivalent of fast food, attractively packaged and seemingly tasty, but not necessarily as nourishing as some of the alternatives. Proponents say that *USA Today* uses graphics and concise stories to quickly communicate news and information essentials to a broader audience. In the near future, newspapers will also have to compete with new interactive media, based on telephones and computers.

DESPERATELY SEEKING CYBERPUNKS

New niches in audience interests continue to be perceived and developed by the magazine industry. One of the latest has been magazines that focus on new information, communication, and biological technologies, while remaining independent of or even defiant of the established industries, users, and ways of looking at these technologies and their effects. This has been termed the "cyberpunk" market, based on the science fiction subgenre begun by William Gibson's *Neuromancer* and combining computer sophistication with a punk attitude. Those in the target cyberpunk market are relatively well educated and affluent, and they buy computers, software, games, and other expensive hardware. They also buy magazines that focus on future uses of computers. So we have seen *Wired, Mondo 2000,* and other magazines aimed at this group arise and probably, by the time this book is published, fall again.

Segmentation is the trend toward audience specialization in the magazine, radio, and other industries.

Consolidation refers to a reduction in the number of media outlets and a concentration of the ownership of media among fewer owners.

nomics, with some lifestyle and entertainment news of a general nature. Metropolitan dailies usually lighten the news sections, focus more on local and regional news, and add more on lifestyles, entertainment, sports, and comics, with more localized ads for such businesses as supermarkets and auto dealers. Some newspapers go further and specialize in certain kinds of material, like localized weeklies that focus almost exclusively on local events. Some local papers also concentrate primarily on shopping and entertainment. Some daily and weekly newspapers highlight crime and other sensational stories.

Magazines: Where Does Segmentation Stop?

The trend in magazines has been toward specialization or **segmentation.** If you look closely at a large newsstand now, you will notice that while there are dozens of magazines about motorcycles, tennis, crocheting, and computers, most general-interest magazines have disappeared.

The magazine industry has both proliferated and **consolidated.** Most major magazines are published by major groups. However, the magazine industry is also one of the media areas where a new entrant or competitor can most likely break in by appealing to a new segment of the market that is not yet served by other magazines. For instance, *Rolling Stone* went quickly from being a small counterculture or "hippie" magazine in 1969 to a widely read rock music and counterculture lifestyle magazine in the 1970s. It has since become the main popular music magazine. More recently, the Ziff-Davis Group has capitalized on the rapid increase in interest in personal computers to build a very profitable magazine empire by publishing magazines like *PC Week, PC Magazine,* and *MacWeek.*

Magazines have developed into the following current general types or genres:

General interest: *People, US*

Geographic: *New York, Lansing*

Demographic: *Ladies Home Journal*

Lifestyle: *New Age, New Woman*

Newsmagazines: *Time, Newsweek*

Special interest: *Road & Track, Country Kitchens*

Trade and Professional: *Broadcasting, Multichannel News, Telephony*

Elite: *New Yorker, The New York Review of Books*

The magazine audience is interested in increasingly specialized topics. Magazines have several advantages as segmented media. For example, the number of magazines is not constrained by technical limitations, such as a limited number of radio frequencies or cable channels, so magazines can continue expanding into more specialized topics and treatments

MAGAZINES ARE BECOMING MUCH MORE SPECIALIZED, APPEALING TO NARROW SEGMENTS OF THE AUDIENCE.

until they saturate the audience. Their formats and their economic base are more flexible. A small-circulation magazine can still be profitable if those it reaches are interested enough in its contents to support it or if that audience is important to specific advertisers (Dominick, 1993).

However, the 1980s and 1990s showed that segmentation and specialization can reach insupportable extremes. Several niches or segments, such as entertainment magazines, women's magazines, health magazines, and fashion magazines, have experienced shakeouts. Audience circulation and economic support by advertisers was divided among too many magazines. Some of the less popular magazines failed as readership levels plateaued or even shrank and advertisers invested less as economic expansion slowed. Still, a number of new magazines have survived their first few years and have established stable or growing audiences, while new magazines still spring up all the time.

Newsletters, House Organs, and Micropublishing

Newsletters preceded newspapers. Medieval banks published financial and trade-oriented newsletters, which probably count as the longest-running print medium, outside of religious books and pamphlets. Newsletters tend to serve purposes and audiences that are even more specialized and segmented than magazines, because they have been even cheaper to produce. Newsletters currently cover an enormous range of interests aimed at an equally diverse audience. There are expensive business newsletters aimed at every imaginable branch of industry. There are in-house newsletters aimed at employees, union members, and supervisors. There are innumerable club and

'ZINES

One of the gray areas between magazines and newsletters is occupied by the large number of publications called fanzines or simply 'zines. These tend to be created by people who are enthusiastic about a topic, usually a hobby but sometimes something related to their work or education. Many 'zines discuss science fiction or other popular literature, movies, rock music, pop music, and other kinds of popular entertainment. 'Zines reflect the proliferation of diverse strains of popular culture and the segmentation of many people into small, distinct interest groups. 'Zines mirror groups of people whose lives or at least their spare time revolves around things as distinct as recreating the Middle Ages, reading science fiction, participating in role-playing games, collecting porcelain figures, restoring old cars, or enjoying folk music.

'Zines' creators don't usually see them as commercial ventures at first; most simply want to communicate their interests to like-minded people. However, many charge a

subscription fee to become self-supporting. A number of these then evolve into commercially successful publications. Some of them even develop higher-quality production values, using more art, more color, and higher-quality paper. At that point, they become magazines.

R E V I E W

1. What are the main trends in book publishing?
2. What are the main national daily newspapers? Why are they growing?
3. Why are major metropolitan dailies declining?
4. What are the main sections and contents of newspapers?
5. How are newspapers adapting to competition from other media?
6. What are the trends in magazines?

fan newsletters aimed at everything from those who recreate the Civil War on weekends to those who cannot believe that Elvis is really dead.

The typical newsletter format is simpler than that of a magazine: usually no pictures or illustrations, simpler type and layout, less glossy paper, no flashy cover, and no color. The line between magazines and newsletters has been blurring as technologies permit desktop publishing operations to produce increasingly sophisticated print products. Desktop computer software enables artists and designers to create sophisticated art and graphics, including color separations for quality printing, at a fraction of their former cost. Printing still separates most magazines from newsletters. Magazines tend to invest more in glossy paper, illustrations, and color, which still costs a good deal more than the paper and single-color graphics used for newsletters.

AUDIENCES FOR PRINT MEDIA

A mass audience still exists for print media, including for best-selling paperback novels and self-help books, major metropolitan and national dailies, and major general audience magazines, such as *People.* There are also many fragments of the general audience now pursuing more specific personal interests, such as sports, glamour, business, hobbies, music, and entertainment, via print media.

Among the general mass audience, approximately two-thirds of adults still read newspapers daily. The average person over age eighteen spends 175 hours per year reading newspapers (see Table 7.6), almost twice as much as the time spent with consumer magazines or books. Readers over age thirty-five read newspapers more than those age eighteen to thirty-four. Readership peaks among those age forty-five to sixty-four.

People tend to read quickly and selectively, spending less than 20 minutes on a thirty-page newspaper. That is one reason that some newspapers, such as *USA Today,* are taking a more graphic and visual approach to designing their papers—it facilitates the kind of skimming and selective reading that most readers actually do. Many readers look only at certain sections that are of particular interest to them. Many also read national, suburban, or local newspapers instead of the classic metropolitan dailies. Even among newspaper readers, most still consider television their main news source, although better-educated audiences tend to rely more on newspapers and less on television.

On the average, people now read magazines about as often as books but quite a bit less than newspapers. With over 10,000 magazines and related periodicals being published, magazine readership is quite fragmented. There are sizable subgroups, particularly among younger people, who read magazines but do not read newspapers or books. Magazine readership is highest among ages eighteen to twenty-four and thirty-five to forty-four and much lower among those over age fifty-five.

TABLE 7.6. AVERAGE HOURS SPENT USING MEDIA, 1985 AND 1990

Medium	1985	1990	Percentage Change
Television	1,530	1,470	−4
Network affiliates	985	780	−21
Independents + Fox	335	340	+2
Basic cable programs	120	260	+117
Pay cable programs	90	90	0
Radio	1,190	1,135	−5
Recorded music	185	235	+27
Newspapers	185	175	−5
Consumer magazines	110	90	−18
Consumer books	80	95	+19
Home video	15	50	+233
Movies	12	12	0
Total	3,307	3,262	+1

Sources: Veronis, Suhler & Associates; A. C. Nielsen; RADAR; Newspaper Advertising Bureau; Magazine Publishers Association; Gallup; MPAA; Television Bureau of Advertising; Leo Shapiro and Associates; Wilkovsky Gruen and Associates.

Although 49,000 book titles were published in 1992 and Americans bought 822 million adult books in 1992, the readership is uneven. Americans buy and read an average of four books a year, but that is deceptive. Many people do not read books. Others read the Bible or other religious works but few others. Many read reference books for work purposes. The United States tends to lag behind most other industrialized or information-oriented nations in books read per year.

Newspapers, books, and magazines serve an important set of communication functions for elite audiences. Political activists are served by a variety of magazines ranging from left, such as *The Nation*, to right, such as *The National Review*. Intellectual magazines, such as *The New York Review of Books,* try to set the stage and agenda for academic and political debates on various issues, often by reviewing and summarizing books that hope to help set or influence the agenda. Some government policy–oriented newspapers, such as *The New York Times*, or magazines, such as *Foreign Affairs*, pride themselves on having an influential readership and on sometimes influencing policy debates with articles.

Business audiences also meet crucial needs with magazines, trade journals, newsletters, and newspapers. Business magazines supply information for keeping up on business areas, professional development, and information about current economic trends. Some publications are fairly general, such as *The Wall Street Journal, Business Week,* and *Fortune.* Others are more specific, such as *Advertising Age* and *Broadcasting.* Some trade publications, such as *Variety,* cross the line between newspapers and magazines by having both daily and weekly editions. Most specific of all are newsletters that often serve only a few hundred readers who are willing to pay hundreds of dollars a year for the information.

Reading of print media seems to be in a slow, steady decline. Various studies show that many adults and children who are literate do not practice their reading skills enough to feel comfortable reading most print media content. Various scholars since Marshall McLuhan have speculated that many people will obtain most of the information they feel they need from audio and video media, leaving literacy essentially behind them.

R E V I E W

1. Is there still a mass audience for newspapers?
2. Who reads magazines compared to newspapers?
3. What are the trends among print media readers? How does it relate to overall literacy?

INDUSTRY ORGANIZATION

A number of trends can be seen in the ownership of both newspapers and magazines.

Newspaper Consolidation, Chains, and Shakeout

A consolidation and concentration of newspaper ownership is under way. Fewer cities have the readership or advertising base to support more than one daily. Both readers and advertisers are being drawn to suburban and local papers, to radio, television, magazines, and, increasingly, new interactive media. One result is that more and more cities are served by only one newspaper. These **local market monopolies** have political, economic, and other effects. Politically, the one newspaper is likely to reflect a single editorial line and political view, although other local media may reflect other views. Economically, the choices available to both advertisers and consumers are reduced. In addition, subscription and advertising rates may increase.

Another result of consolidation is that major newspaper group owners have steadily acquired more newspapers. These groups can share materials and reduce costs in ways that

Local market monopolies are those with only one daily newspaper.

TABLE 7.7. TEN LARGEST MAGAZINES (1994)

Magazine	Circulation	Owner
1. *Modern Maturity*	21,716,727	American Association of Retired Persons
2. *Reader's Digest*	15,126,664	Reader's Digest
3. *TV Guide*	14,037,062	Rupert Murdoch–News Corp.
4. *National Geographic*	9,203,079	National Geographic Co.
5. *Better Homes & Gardens*	7,613,661	Meredith Corp.
6. *Good Housekeeping*	5,223,935	Hearst Corp.
7. *Ladies' Home Journal*	5,048,081	Meredith Corp.
8. *Family Circle*	5,005,301	New York Times Co.
9. *Woman's Day*	4,724,500	Hachette Publications
10. *McCall's*	4,611,848	Bertelsmann Co.

Sources: *1996 Information Please Almanac; Advertising Age*

Concentration of ownership occurs when media are owned by a small number of individuals, government agencies, or corporations.

keep marginally profitable newspapers afloat. This increasing **concentration of ownership** in fewer hands threatens to reduce the diversity of opinion found in newspapers across the United States. Newspaper chains like Gannett could exercise national reach with their opinions and ideas. Newspaper owners also tend to own other media (such as radio, television, cable television systems, magazines), which also increases concentration of ownership. As the Reagan administration relaxed previous cross-ownership restrictions, this tendency accelerated in the 1980s with the overall merger mania that resulted in the consolidation and concentration of ownership in a number of industries, but particularly in the media.

Magazine Groups and Independents

Magazines have also been consolidated under the ownership of large media corporations. Many corporations, such as Time-Warner and McGraw-Hill, also have large holdings in other media as well. Table 7.7 shows the major magazines and their owners.

Magazines are distributed directly by subscription and by retailers, such as supermarkets and newsstands. Mailing and subscription operations have become a major business. Magazine subscriptions and mailing lists are highly valuable commodities to other magazines, catalogs, and direct-mail marketers. There is a brisk trade in buying and selling mailing lists, from general-interest magazines to highly specific and targeted trade journals and newsletters. Magazine wholesalers and distributors are a crucial link between publishers and retailers. Many retailers simply take what the wholesaler delivers, so the distributors have a great influence on whether a new magazine gets delivered to newsstands and thereby reaches the public.

Publishing Houses and Groups

As with other print media, a wave of consolidation has occurred among the major publishing houses, but a number of small ones still exist, and new publishing houses continually spring up, focused on new areas of interest and new audiences. There is also a trend toward some foreign acquisition of or investment in American publishing houses. The German company

DESPITE THE BURGEONING ELECTRONIC MEDIA, MAGAZINES REMAIN A MAJOR MEDIUM OF INFORMATION, WHICH RELY ON BOTH RETAIL SALES AND SUBSCRIPTIONS.

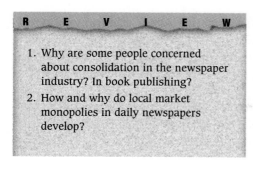
Bertelsmann bought Doubleday and Dell, the French company Hachette bought Grolier, the British Maxwell company bought Macmillan, the British Penguin company bought New American Library and Dutton, and Australian Rupert Murdoch bought Harper & Row. The major American publishing houses now include Simon & Schuster, owned by Paramount Communications; Time Publishing Group, owned by Time-Warner; Harcourt Brace & Company, owned by General Cinema Corporation; Random House, owned by the print-oriented Advance Group; and the Reader's Digest Association.

POLICY ISSUES FOR PRINT MEDIA

As we have noted, a major policy and social issue for print media is how the tendency toward consolidation and concentration of ownership in nearly all of the print industries is affecting diversity and freedom of speech. Americans have always assumed that competition among various media outlets, within media, and across media is crucial. Although not everyone really has the freedom to speak to others using the media, it has been assumed that competition will bring out relatively diverse points of view and approximate a fairly free discussion among knowledgeable people. Even before media consolidation, many people questioned the assumption that mass media reflected diverse points of view. Critics on both right and left have seen the media as too homogeneous and cautious in the ideas and points of view that they express. Consolidation and reduction of print media outlets probably worsens that problem.

Consolidation in the daily newspaper industry has been most troubling, because it leaves many medium and even large cities with only one daily newspaper, which reduces the number and diversity of voices in local debates over political issues. Newspapers, particularly major- and medium-market dailies, have also been increasingly consolidated into a number of ownership groups. That compounds the reduction in diversity brought about by the reduction in the number of daily newspapers.

Joint operation agreements occur when competing newspapers share facilities, costs, administrative structure, and advertising, while maintaining editorial independence.

Joint operation agreements are one solution to the problem of inadequate support for competing newspapers. When competing newspapers cannot survive economically, they negotiate an agreement with each other to share facilities, costs, administrative structure, and advertising, while attempting to maintain editorial independence. Only about fifty cities now have competing daily newspapers. Roughly half of those maintain two newspapers only through joint operating agreements. In Detroit, for example, the liberal *Detroit Free Press* and the more conservative *Detroit News* now have a joint operating agreement. They share facilities, although they try to keep the actual reporters and writers separate. They produce separate editions on weekdays and combined editions on weekends. In the 1992 presidential election, there were several occasions when the separate editorial pages in the combined Sunday edition endorsed different candidates with opposite editorial rationales. Still, some fear that the overall diversity of opinion between the two may well decrease.

Consolidation is also apparent in the magazine and book publishing industries, where both domestic and foreign conglomerates have been buying up magazine and book publishers. This situation raises similar issues, but they are not as severe as the increasingly typical case of one-newspaper towns. Still, most readership of both magazines and books is concentrated on the output of a few publishers.

There are also signals of growth and diversity, however. Along with the decline of competing daily metropolitan newspapers has come the rise of suburban and weekly newspapers, some of which effectively compete with the remaining city dailies. Likewise, while some magazines and publishers consolidate, new magazines and new publishing houses continue to spring up, although they tend to be small and reach far fewer people than the largest book and magazine publishers.

There is also the potential for competition and increased diversity of points of view coming from new electronic publishers and on-line sources of news and information. While electronic publishing is still finding its way among interactive electronic novels and role-playing games, on-line sources of information have been proliferating fairly quickly. However, as of 1994, access via services like CompuServe, America On-Line, and Prodigy, as well as university and corporation access to the Internet, is still limited to under 10 percent of Americans. On-line information services include computer network access to wire services, newspaper copy, or an increasing number of alternative sources, such as computer-network-based discussion groups focused on various issues and events. These services are covered further in the chapter on information services to the home.

Copyright is a legal privilege to use, sell, or license intellectual property, such as a book or a film.

Copyright issues have become crucial among print media and between print media and new electronic media. Book publishers and academic magazines both have cracked down on informal or illegal photocopying of material that has been copyrighted by publishers. Many informal newsletters and new electronic "publications" also borrow or sample images, sections of text, and headlines from newspapers, magazines, and books. As electronic distribution increases, new intellectual property rules may be required, since publishers and authors are anxious to collect royalties from such reproduction and use.

First Amendment grants freedom of interference by government with speech or expression.

First Amendment issues are also crucial. Freedom of speech and expression in print media is largely well established, but a number of community, and religious groups have objected to the contents of various print media, usually because those contents are seen as being overtly sexual or inciting violence or the sexual abuse of women or children. Since the turn of the century, most books have been exempt from overt censorship, although novels like *Lady Chatterley's Lover* went through periods of censorship in the United States. Even more recently, dozens of books have been pulled from library shelves for various reasons; for example, *Catcher in the Rye* for rough language and *The Adventures of Huckleberry Finn* for racial stereotypes and epithets. However, magazines have been far more challenged in various communities and by various legal decisions. Most stores that distribute sexually explicit magazines now separate them into a section that is off-limits to those under age eighteen. Some stores, such as convenience store chains, have gone further, blocking off the covers of such magazines from open view or removing them altogether (Altschull, 1984).

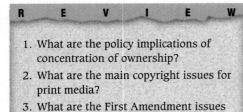

R E V I E W

1. What are the policy implications of concentration of ownership?
2. What are the main copyright issues for print media?
3. What are the First Amendment issues in print media?
4. What are the current threats to freedom of speech and of the press?

There have been fewer attempts to limit freedom of speech or press in political terms. During the 1950s, however, the anticommunist campaign of Senator Joseph McCarthy resulted in several authors being blacklisted from writing or publishing. McCarthy's main focus was Hollywood films and television, but his efforts to denounce and blacklist writers he considered communist sympathizers affected some print media as well. Most people reacted negatively to McCarthy's campaign over the long run, and modern efforts to suppress a writer or a song or a film are often referred to as "McCarthyism."

SUMMARY & REVIEW

What Are the Main Things to Be Learned from the History of the Print Media?

What key elements of the print media developed first outside Europe?
A number of essential ideas were brought to Europe; for example, using rags to make paper was imported from China. Other printing techniques developed in parallel form outside Europe but probably were not a direct influence.

What was the impact of printing in Europe?
The advent of printing greatly accelerated the growth of literacy by making books cheaper and more widely available. Education became more widespread since texts were easier to get. Printing affected religion by making the Bible widely available, politics by increasing news circulation, and economics by increasing knowledge and skills.

What established the precedents for press freedom in colonial America?
The colonial press was often critical of British governors. In a key case in 1733, Peter Zenger published a newspaper critical of the British governor of New York. Zenger was jailed for criminal libel. Despite British legal precedent to the contrary, Zenger's lawyer, Andrew Hamilton, argued that the truth of a published piece was a defense against libel.

Who developed the political press that supported the American Revolution?
Besides Zenger, James Franklin published the independent *New England Courant.* He was jailed and forbidden to publish without prior approval, so he made his brother, Benjamin Franklin, the new editor. Ben moved to Philadelphia and started the *Pennsylvania Gazette,* which was also successful and independent. Most newspapers at the time were partisan, supporting either the independence movement or the British Crown. A number of key documents and ideas were published in the newspapers, including the Declaration of Independence.

Why and how did magazines develop?
Magazines developed at about the same time as newspapers. In 1741 the first U.S. magazines were Bradford's *American Magazine* and Ben Franklin's *General Magazine.* During the American Revolution, many magazines also took a more political tone. Few magazines were popular or long-lived. They covered weekly events, politics, and art and contained reviews, travelogues, short stories, and serialized fiction; it was aimed at an educated elite. By the 1820s, magazines of more general interest, such as the *Saturday Evening Post,* began to appear. The number of magazines increased during the Civil War, and they began to serve somewhat more specific audiences. The Postal Act of 1879 made distribution cheaper.

What was the penny press? What led to it?
By 1800 most large cities had at least one daily, but circulations were limited to the literate and relatively wealthy. By 1830 new technological inventions permitted lower-cost papers aimed at a broader audience. Social conditions for the creation of the mass audience and mass newspapers were building. More people were learning to read, public education was expanding, wages were increasing, and more people were gathering in cities. Benjamin Day launched the first low-cost daily, *The New York Sun,* in 1833. It sold for a penny by relying on advertising more than sales.

The Oxford Gazette. Numb. 4.

Published by Authority.

From Thursday November 23, to Monday November 27, 1665.

What role did sensationalism play in newspapers?
The penny press targeted its content to obtain a wider general audience. It used sensational coverage of crime, police news, scandal, disasters, celebrities, features about prominent or sensational personalities, and social events such as weddings, deaths, and parties.

What was the role of print media in the Civil War? And how did the war affect the media?
Newspapers affected the issues debate that led up to the Civil War. African American leader Frederick Douglass pushed hard for the abolition of slavery with *The North Star*. The *New York Tribune* pushed for abolition as well. The newspapers covered the Civil War, with great disagreement between Northern and Southern papers. Several Northern papers had a major influence on the positions and strategy of the Northern states. Several magazines, such as *Leslie's Illustrated Newspaper* and *Harper's Weekly*, grew to fame during the Civil War, based on their print coverage and also their illustrations, which dramatized scenes of the war. Photography and illustration became prominent tools of journalism. The use of headlines increased, as did the use of the inverted pyramid style of newswriting. Circulations grew.

What was "muckraking"?
Muckraking characterized the post–Civil War period, when crusading newspapers turned their attention to scandals and corruption in government and among industry cartels.

When did newspapers and magazines peak as mass audience media?
After the Civil War, newspapers expanded much faster than the population or even the economy as a whole. Both the technological and cost efficiency of newspaper printing increased rapidly and probably peaked in about 1900, which coincided with their peak of impact as mass media. The newspaper industry had grown larger than its advertising and circulation could support. After the 1890s, many new kinds of magazines began to compete with newspapers. In addition, motion pictures and the phonograph

also began to compete harder for people's attention and money. By 1927, radio would be a competitor as well.

What Are the Main Trends in Print Technology?

What are the main recent trends or changes in print media production technologies?
From the 1970s on, computerization has done much to change print media. Computers substituted for typesetting machines, then most of the layout of a page was done on computers, particularly when photographs could be scanned or digitized, so they could be placed on the page electronically.

What are the main recent trends or changes in print media delivery technologies?
Newspapers were often delivered directly in cities, and books moved in bulk along railroads and shipping lines, but the mail was crucial for enabling magazines to reach a broad audience in an affordable manner. Mail services improved with the means of transportation. Satellite delivery of copy to printers enables national media, particularly newspapers, to use local printers. In the 1990s, electronic delivery by fax and electronic mail are becoming alternatives for print media delivery.

What is desktop publishing?
Desktop publishing is the creation of publication-quality documents using the increased power and speed of desktop computers, laser printers, and scanners that digitize photos or illustrations into computer-readable form. This has done much to decentralize and even decenter print media. People can now produce local or specialized media, but professional media also use desktop publishing for their products as well.

What Are the Current Genres and Forms of the Print Industries?

What are the main trends in book publishing?
Increasing numbers of books are being published and purchased by consumers, students, and businesses. However, books are also becoming more expensive, and the actual diversity of titles may be decreasing.

What are the main national daily newspapers? Why are they growing?
The Wall Street Journal is a specialized business paper with a broad general readership. *The New York Times* has news interpretation and media and business focuses. *The Christian Science Monitor* concentrates on features and news interpretation. *USA Today* carries shorter news items and more entertainment. They respond to a public interest in national and international news and have been able to reach national audiences at an affordable price by using new technology for satelite delivery to primary plants.

Why are major metropolitan dailies declining?
The larger metropolitan daily newspapers are losing readers to national dailies, national news weeklies, national newsmagazines, or television and radio. Their decline is also related to the relative decline of many large cities as centers of industry. Suburban newspapers, small-town dailies, and weeklies are growing.

What are the main sections and contents of newspapers?
Most newspapers contain several distinct sections that frequently serve different audiences. The national newspapers are heavy on international news, national news, editorials/commentaries, and economics, with some lifestyle and general entertainment news. Metropolitan dailies usually lighten the news sections, focus more on local and regional news, and add more on lifestyles, entertainment, sports, and comics. Some weeklies focus almost exclusively on local events, shopping, and entertainment.

What are the trends in magazines?
Magazines tend toward specialization or segmentation. General-interest magazines have declined while specialized, segmented magazines have grown in numbers and diversity.

How Are Audiences for Print Media Developing?

Is there still a mass audience for newspapers? Who reads magazines compared to newspapers?
Roughly two-thirds of all American adults still read newspapers. The average adult spends roughly twice as much time on newspapers as on books or magazines, but younger people read newspapers less and magazines more.

What are the trends among print media readers? How does it relate to overall literacy?
There seems to be an overall trend toward less reading, in part because overall functional literacy seems to be declining.

What Are the Main Trends in Print Media Industry Organization?

Is there a trend toward consolidation and concentration of ownership in print media?
The number of daily newspapers has been steadily declining since 1910, with ownership becoming more concentrated in several large chains, like Gannett or Scripps-Howard. Book publishing has also become more concentrated and internationalized. Magazine publishing has concentrated in a similar way, but more new magazine companies have continued to enter the field.

Why are some people concerned about consolidation in the newspaper industry, book publishing, and magazines?
A number of formerly competitive newspapers have formed joint operation agreements to share facilities, costs, administrative structure, and advertising, while attempting to maintain editorial independence. However, the lack of competition and the nature of the joint operation

may well reduce diversity and independence in editorial points of view. Chain ownership may similarly reduce local independence and standardize editorial and reporting approaches across the country. Concentration in book or magazine publishing might also reduce competition and diversity of their contents. publishing.

What Are the Main Policy Issues for Print Media?

What current threats are there to freedom of speech and press?

Freedom of speech and expression in print media is well established, but a number of groups object to the contents of various print media, usually because those contents are seen as overtly sexual or inciting violence or the sexual abuse of women or children. There have been fewer attempts to limit freedom of speech or press in political terms. During the 1950s, however, the anticommunist campaign of Senator Joseph McCarthy resulted in several authors being blacklisted from writing or publishing.

What are the main copyright issues for print media?

A major issue in print media is informal or illegal photocopying of material that has been copyrighted by publishers. Many newsletters and new electronic "publications" also borrow or sample images, sections of text, and headlines from newspapers, magazines, and books. Computer-based production and electronic network distribution make such copying easy. Publishers and authors are anxious to collect royalties from such reproduction and use. As electronic distribution increases, new intellectual property rules may be required.

REFERENCES

Altschull, H. (1984). *Agents of power.* New York: Longman.

Carter, T. F. (1991). "Paper and block printing—From China to Europe." In D. Crowley & P. Heyer (Eds.), *Communication in history.* New York: Longman.

Davis, K. (1985). *Two bit culture.* Boston: Houghton Mifflin.

Dominick, J. (1993). *The dynamics of mass communication* (4th ed.). New York: McGraw-Hill.

Hynds, E. (1980). *American newspapers in the 1980s.* New York: Hastings House.

Sloan, W., Stovall, J., & Startt, J. (Eds.). (1993). *Media in America: A history* (2nd ed.). Scottsdale, AZ: Publishing Horizons.

Smith, A. (1980). *Good-bye, Gutenberg.* New York: Oxford University Press.

Stephens, M. (1989). *A history of news.* New York: Penguin.

Tebbel, J. (1969a). *The compact history of the American newspaper.* New York: Hawthorne Books.

Tebbel, J. (1969b). *The American magazine: A compact history* . New York: Hawthorne Books.

Chapter 8

AUDIO MEDIA: RADIO AND RECORDED MUSIC

C H A P T E R   P R E V I E W

The media that we listen to are potentially very powerful. In film, television, and multimedia, much of the information and the impact come from the sound component. The media that rely solely on sound—radio and recordings—are also powerful and popular.

Recorded sound predates radio. Both have affected each other greatly. Both have evolved with the history of popular music. Both have adapted to changes in technology. Radio has developed in AM, then in FM, and now direct satellite broadcasting. Recordings have changed in quality, in portability, and from analog to digital form (as from records to compact discs). Musical forms and genres have also changed, along with their audiences and their habits. Both the forms of the radio and recording industries and their content have changed greatly in the last century.

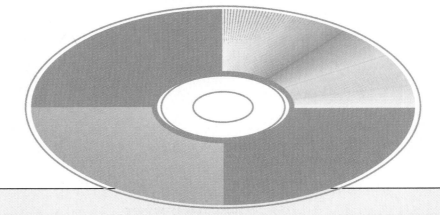

Cruising and Playing the Digital Radio: Lovers' Lane, 2009

This is the Wolfman talkin' atcha. For everybody out there on Lovers' Lane in East Podunk tonight, here's Chuck Berry with "No Particular Place to Go" from 1964.

What's Wolfman Jack doing on? And how did he know where we were? Anyway, I thought he was . . .

You nerd, that's a digital voice simulation from that Mexican Direct Broadcast Satellite, and your mom's radio is synthesizing the local tag from information in her navigation system. And, Stanley, how about a little romantic music tonight, hmmm?

Oh. Uh, right. Right! Radio, cancel "cruising," search "love."

SEARCHING, LOVE . . . INTERRUPTING, TRAFFIC REPORT WNWZ, AM 1210 . . . Big accident downtown tonight, stay tuned for our WNWZ traffic satellite.

Why don't you just turn that darn thing off!

I can't! That's my mom's morning drive subroutine kicking in. It automatically switches to accident reports along her route, even if the radio isn't on.

Fiery tractor-trailer accident at the concert hall ramp tonight. They're evacuating now.

Yipes! Now my parents are going to find out we didn't even go to the opera! Take me home right away! And wipe the memory on your mom's navigation system, IF you even know how. Your mom's radio is a lot smarter than YOU are!

A BRIEF HISTORY OF AUDIO MEDIA

uman beings have been entertaining and informing one another with sound for a long time. Well before there was a written language, people created, memorized, and performed songs and stories. There has been a lot of speculation about what might be the oldest profession, but entertaining people with songs and stories might just be it. Records and radio stand on the shoulders of a long tradition that has included shamans, village storytellers, poets, wandering minstrels, and court jesters. Even today's rock drum rhythms have their roots in sacred drumming used in ancient African religious ceremonies (Hart, 1990).

Long before sound recordings and radio, there was a substantial music industry in Europe and in the United States based on performances, written song lyrics, and printed sheet music. Popular and classical music became popular as performers traveled from village to village, taking their music with them. With the advent of printing, music traveled even more easily as **sheet music**. Some of the earliest printed materials were lyrics and musical notations. Even with many forms of recorded music are available, people still buy music written for piano or guitar and voice, so they can play the music they like at home.

Sheet music is print reproduction of song lyrics and musical notation for people to perform.

Tin Pan Alley

The music writing industry known as Tin Pan Alley originated with New York music and lyric writers who wrote sheet music for various singers and musicians to perform. For example, "She's Only a Bird in a Gilded Cage," a very popular song around 1900, was sold as sheet music to people who wanted to play it at home. Phonograph recordings were released of various renditions, as well. However, specific songs were not as closely identified with a certain singer or performer as they are now. The writer had a more central role and was more separated from the performer.

Nickelodeon is a phonograph or player piano operated by inserting a coin, originally a nickel.

Acoustic is music that is not electronically amplified.

Victrola was an early phonograph and also a specific trademark.

Various attempts were made to reproduce music for the public. Besides printing sheet music so people could play it themselves, inventors tried to create machines, such as music boxes and **nickelodeons**, that would play or reproduce music. Player pianos, for example, used a roll of paper or fabric with holes to indicate when piano keys should strike—similar in some ways to today's digital media.

The Victrola

Recorded music came some time before radio. The first **acoustic** recording technology was developed in 1877. The early **Victrola** was crude by current standards. Thomas Edison produced a prototype that played "Mary Had a Little Lamb." A cylinder wrapped in tinfoil reproduced the sound waves. In 1882, Emile Berliner created the gramophone, using disks instead of cylinders, which were harder to copy but more durable and easier to store. Edison and Berliner competed fiercely to set up a record industry (Sloan, Stovall, & Startt, 1993).

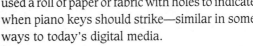

THE PHONOGRAPH, PIONEERED IN 1877 BY THOMAS EDISON, WAS ALREADY GAINING POPULARITY IN THE 1890S.

Penny arcades were commercial entertainment areas with coin-operated sound and film nickelodeons and other amusements.

The phonograph was a major breakthrough. In 1890, an entrepreneur named Lippincott started putting coin-operated phonographs in **penny arcades**. This use emphasized entertainment rather than dictation or other conceivable uses for the technology. The Victor Talking Machine Company introduced the home Victrola in 1906. People became accustomed to listening to recorded music in their homes, using a piece of furniture that supplied entertainment. The phonograph quickly became a mass medium. By the end of World War I, over 2 million players were being made and sold annually by over 200 manufacturers. Record sales soared from 23 million in 1914 to 107 million in 1919.

Recorded Music

The penny arcade and home Victrola introduced more people to new kinds of music after 1900, and helped spread music more rapidly than ever before. These developments clearly met a need for more entertainment and a wider range of musical culture. The notion of "popular music" caught on, as writers began to discover what kinds of music most appealed to a mass audience.

Ragtime is an early form of jazz most frequently played on the piano.

Patent is a written document that secures to an inventor for a number of years the exclusive right to make, use, or sell an invention.

Records moved from early pop favorites to **ragtime**, such as the music played by Scott Joplin. Jazz became popular in the Roaring Twenties. During the 1920s and 1930s, a time known as the Jazz Age, records featured show tunes taken from the new talking movies. However, the advent of radio caused the record business to slow temporarily, and almost collapse. In 1924, as radio was taking off, record and phonograph sales dropped by almost half. Later, the recording industry began to rely on radio to make people aware of artists and recordings that they could purchase.

Wireless Radio

Guglielmo Marconi helped invent radio, with **patents** in Great Britain in 1896. In the late 1890s and early 1900s, he tried to push radio into business and military use in his native Italy, but the government was not interested. Marconi was successful in England and later in the United States, where he used his business flair to dominate the early use of radio for two-way communications. Since radio was used primarily to coordinate ocean shipping between countries, Marconi's company set up a series of shore radio stations to receive and retransmit signals across the ocean or from ships at sea. His company also manufactured and operated equipment to send and receive messages. By 1913, Marconi dominated radio in Europe and the United States.

Through World War I (1914–1918), radio was seen as a two-way or point-to-point over-the-air telegraph. Radio was a business, shipping, and military medium for long-distance and mobile two-way communications. In fact, the U.S. Navy forced the radio technology to advance during World War I, by stopping patent disputes between Marconi, Reginald Fessenden, Lee De Forest, Edwin Armstrong, and other early inventors and standardizing the technologies.

RADIO AND THE SINKING OF THE *TITANIC*

The *Titanic* was a large, new, British ocean liner that struck an iceberg and sank suddenly in the North Atlantic in 1912. It sent a radio distress call, which was relayed to the Marconi radio operators in New York; they included the future director of RCA, David Sarnoff. Not only was radio crucial to the efforts to save as many passengers as possible, but it became central to reporting news about the disaster, which had riveted people on both sides of the Atlantic. Newspapers got their information from the radio, and many

people, particularly young David Sarnoff, were impressed with this new medium's news potential.

After the war, two-way radio was organized as big business. Marconi tried to buy U.S. patents to consolidate a U.S.–European communications monopoly, but the U.S. government opposed foreign control. The Navy still held temporary control over radio technology and assets and proposed to make radio a government operation—an option that was also opposed by many Americans. A negotiated settlement forced Marconi to sell its American assets to General Electric. In conjunction with AT&T and Westinghouse, GE set up a new company, Radio Corporation of America. The major corporations involved—GE, RCA, and AT&T—also set up a **patent pool** in 1920 so they could all manufacture complete radio equipment.

Patent pool was several companies sharing technologies that had been awarded government protection via a formal patent.

Broadcast Radio

During World War I, technological developments enabled radio to surpass two-way radio transmission in telegraph codes to broadcast sound, voice, and music. At first, none of the main companies involved in radio saw broadcasting to individual home receivers as a potential business.

However, inventors and hobbyists soon began broadcasting sound transmissions. First, Reginald Fessenden tried some experimental sound broadcasts in 1906, then Lee De Forest broadcast the election returns in 1916. Frank Conrad, a Westinghouse engineer, began a regular broadcast station connected to his Pittsburgh factory in 1920. His programs attracted interest and then newspaper coverage, as did other amateur broadcasters. A Pittsburgh department store decided to try to sell radios to pick up Conrad's broadcasts. Then Westinghouse realized that regular radio broadcasts could help sell radios and opened station KDKA in Pittsburgh in 1920. Unhampered by competing signals, KDKA could be heard in many parts of the United States and Canada. This encouraged people to start buying radio receivers—100,000 in 1922 and over 500,000 in 1923 (Sterling & Kittross, 1990).

It did not take long for individuals and organizations to think of other things to do with radio. Stores started radio stations just to promote their own goods. Electronics companies, such as the RCA Radio Group, started broadcast stations so there would be something on

SARNOFF AT WORK AS A RADIO OPERATOR FOR AMERICAN MARCONI IN 1912.

DAVID SARNOFF AND THE RADIO MUSIC BOX

n 1916, David Sarnoff, then commercial manager of American Marconi, wrote a prophetic memo to his boss. He proposed "a plan of development which would make radio a 'household utility' in the same sense as the piano or phonograph. The idea is to bring music into the house by wireless . . . The Receiver can be designed in the form of a simple 'Radio Music Box' and arranged for several different wavelengths, which should be changeable with the throwing of a single switch or pressing of a single button." Sarnoff's memo was ignored, but he anticipated perfectly the physical form that radio would take within ten years, and later, as head of RCA, he had a chance to help make this vision of radio and a similar vision of television a reality.

At first, Sarnoff opposed the idea of commercial radio and proposed that listeners pay a tax on new radios that would help pay for programming, not unlike the system later used by the BBC in Great Britain. Later Sarnoff made his peace with commercial radio and television and helped propel RCA's main network, NBC, into leadership for a number of years in both radio and television. Sarnoff had started as a telegraph operator for Marconi and then rose through the ranks to run RCA, through its formative years, until 1969.

the air to make people want to buy radios. Newspapers saw a news medium and schools and churches saw educational potential. To avoid frequency interference among all the broadcasters rushing into the new medium, the Commerce Department was asked to supervise radio. It issued hundreds of licenses in 1923.

Paying for Radio—The Road to Advertising

The vision of radio that determined its future came from AT&T's station WEAF. Based in part on its experience with the telephone, AT&T saw that radio could carry others' programs for a fee. This idea evolved into letting various manufacturers sponsor programs to advertise their goods, which further evolved into advertisers paying to have their ads carried on programs. WEAF broadcast the first "commercial," named for AT&T accounting practices in 1922. AT&T originally called this **toll broadcasting**, in a parallel to long-distance or "toll" telephone calls. It was also the first broadcast network, since AT&T used its phone lines to link several of its stations. Advertisers immediately responded to the opportunity, and toll broadcasting grew quickly. AT&T began to dream of having a monopoly in this new medium and created a network of stations with WEAF as flagship. However, the U.S. government and other major electronics companies opposed AT&T's having a major role in both broadcasting and telephony (Sterling & Kitross, 1990).

> **Toll broadcasting** was charging someone to carry a radio program or advertisement, parallel to long-distance or "toll" telephone calls.

The other early broadcasters were far from clear on what to do with radio or how to pay for it. For a while, RCA and the Radio Group still saw their station KJZ as a means of promoting the sale of radios. They toyed with the idea of collecting a license fee from listeners to pay for the programming and having radio manufacturers collectively pay for programming to sell radios. They did not want to see an AT&T monopoly in radio, however, and negotiations produced an agreement in 1926 in which AT&T got out of radio (to keep its telephone monopoly) and agreed to be a neutral transmission connection for other networks. This solution reinforced a policy pattern, which lasted until the 1990s, in which telephone companies were not involved in the content of communication.

ENTERTAINERS SUCH AS FRED ALLEN DOMINATED THE RADIO WAVES IN THE 1930S AND 1940S.

Advertisers were pushing hard to use radio to promote products. Radio offered them direct access to the home, coupled with an attractive leisure activity. In 1927 Edgar Felix, an advertising consultant, said, "What a glorious opportunity for the advertising man to spread his sales propaganda. Here was a countless audience, sympathetic, pleasure-seeking, enthusiastic, curious, interested, approachable in the privacy of their own homes." To increase the size of the audience for their ads, advertisers used music, comedy, and other entertainment. They steered their advertising toward entertainment programs, which pushed stations that way, too. At first, both regulators such as Herbert Hoover and the radio industry worried that audiences would reject radio if it carried too much advertising, but the audience was so eager for the new medium that they accepted the ads without much reaction (Barnouw, 1966).

The Rise of Radio Networks

> **Networks** are groups of stations that centralize the production and distribution of programming and carry most of the same programming and ads.

RCA set up its radio **network**, NBC, in 1926. After buying out AT&T's radio network in the RCA Radio Group agreement, RCA had two networks—RCA Red and RCA Blue. Competition came quickly from CBS, which had been acquired by the Paley family, owners of a cigar company who had seen the potential in advertising on radio. Both networks had their own

O&O's are stations owned and operated by corporations that also own networks.

stations, called owned-and-operated stations, or **O&O's**, but both began to attract a number of affiliated stations as well. By 1937 NBC had 111 affiliates and CBS had 105 (Sterling & Kittross, 1990).

The radio networks were put together by strong-willed leaders who saw great potential in the new medium. Both Sarnoff at RCA/NBC and William Paley at CBS were sons of Russian immigrants. Both were fascinated, even obsessed, with radio. Whereas Sarnoff started at the bottom, as a radio-telegraph operator, Paley started at the top, having seen the value of radio in advertising the cigars made by his family's company. Paley had been advertising manager at the cigar company, had experimented with radio ads in 1925–1926, and was so impressed with the results that he wanted in. He took over the struggling CBS network in 1928 and turned it around by focusing on both entertainment and news.

Economies of scale refer to reduced per-unit costs when larger numbers of copies are manufactured.

Network Programming. Networks used **economies of scale**. By producing top-quality, high-cost programs in their center or "flagship" stations and sharing the programs with their O&O stations and many affiliates, they spread the costs of production around, lowering the cost for each station. Networks also created national advertising markets by giving a national advertiser the chance to be carried simultaneously on stations that covered the entire country.

Early network radio programming was focused in large part on music (at least a quarter of the schedule), but it also included news, comedy, variety shows, soap operas, dramas, suspense, and action adventures. Many of the kinds of programming that we now associate with television, such as soap operas, adventure shows, and detective dramas, were developed on radio, although radio itself worked with genres taken from music, circus, vaudeville, serial novels, and novels. Since recording technology had not reached a point of very high fidelity, music was primarily broadcast live. Networks permitted the most popular groups and orchestras to reach the entire country. Radio brought many new kinds of music to its audiences and stimulated a demand for a variety of musical **genres,** ranging from classical to country and western. Entertainment and escape were particularly prominent during the often grim days of the Great Depression from 1929–1939 (MacDonald, 1979).

Genres are types or formats of media content, such as classical music and country and western.

Big Band Music and the World War II Generation. The most popular music in the 1930s and 1940s was the big band sound. Developed from jazz, it was the pop music of its day. Unlike jazz, big band music did not emphasize improvisation but rather popular tunes and songs. Band leaders such as Glenn Miller and Tommy Dorsey put together orchestras that introduced a number of the singers, such as Frank Sinatra, who continued to lead pop music into the 1950s. The young people who fought in World War II and worked in the factories at home thought of big band as their music in much the same way that young people today identify with different strains of rock, rap, hip-hop, or heavy metal. Musical tastes tend to fix on what people like when they are young, so a number of radio stations today now play music for the big band generation.

Frank Sinatra, Teen Heartthrob. Record sales had dipped to under 6 million in 1932 and some predicted the death of the phonograph. One event that helped revive record sales was the appearance of teen idol Frank Sinatra, the latest in a long line of idolized vocalists. Mass production had kept record prices down around a dollar, and people began asking stores for the latest Sinatra record. Not too many years later, Elvis Presley was being called the "Sinatra of the 1950s."

Network radio continued strong through World War II, which in many ways represented a peak in the importance of radio as compared to other media. Money spent on radio ads doubled from 1939 to 1945, with radio passing newspapers in 1943. Radio was the paramount information medium of the war, both domestically and internation-

WAR COVERAGE BY CORRESPONDENTS SUCH AS EDWARD R. MURROW KEPT RADIO A VITAL PART OF AMERICAN HOUSEHOLDS IN THE 1940S.

ally. Many of the networks' most famous newspeople, who subsequently started television network news, rose to prominence during the war. Internationally, the use of radio for propaganda frightened many people and began a long series of investigations into the power of mass media over their audiences.

Edward R. Murrow broadcast memorable live reports from London during World War II, dramatically covering the German bombing of London and other battlefields. His reports conveyed vivid, realistic, and often highly moving word pictures. He emerged as one of the most credible and admired newsmen in the well-respected CBS news organization. He preferred to stay in the newsroom, rather than administration, and survived the move to television better than many other radio newspeople (Whetmore, 1981).

TABLE 8.1. MILESTONES OF RECORDING AND RADIO HISTORY

Year	Milestone
1877	Edison introduces the Victrola
1882	Berliner creates the gramophone
1896–1919	Marconi pushes radio for business and the military
1906	Fessenden makes first sound broadcast
1918	2 million phonographs made
1919	117 million records sold
1920	Frank Conrad starts KDKA in Pittsburgh
1920	AT&T's WEAF starts toll broadcasting
1922	Radio fever, 600 stations go on air
1926	AT&T sells WEAF, pulls out of radio
1926	RCA starts NBC Radio Network
1927	Federal Radio Commission started
1927	CBS Radio Network assembled
1928	Advertising support becomes dominant
1934	Federal Communications Commission created
1939–1945	Murrow and others report on WW II
1947–1955	Radio networks decline against television
1960s	Rise of top 40 radio
1970s	FM stations increase, many go stereo
1970s	Format segmentation increases
1980s	Cable TV–based music audio channels

Simulcasts refer to broadcasting the same signal on several stations, such as networks, or on both AM and FM stations.

Record format in audio playback equipment refers to record standards.

The Fall of the Radio Networks

Radio networks did well through 1947, the same year that film theater attendance peaked, but as television rose in prominence, becoming the main national source of mass entertainment, network radio began to slip (see Table 8.1). The number of network affiliates dropped from 97 percent in 1947 to 50 percent in 1955, while network revenue dropped even more. Radio remained profitable, but the advertising shifted from a national to a local focus and began to rely on cheaper, more localized formats, such as music, news, and talk.

In 1933, Edwin Armstrong, an RCA engineer, developed FM radio. Armstrong had been influential in earlier developments as well, including how to best exploit that technological marvel, the vacuum tube. He perceived the new FM radio medium as having strong potential, with better sound quality and room for more stations. Although Armstrong pushed hard and RCA gave him the initial funding, RCA management, including his friend David Sarnoff, delayed FM's actual introduction. At that point, in the 1930s and 1940s, the RCA management was far more interested in developing television, which RCA saw as having more immediate profit potential. FM was introduced in 1947 but languished until the 1960s. Most of the FM operations until then consisted of **simulcasts** of the same material on AM, and FM stations were owned by the same people or groups as AM stations. FM began to develop faster after the FCC limited AM/FM simulcasting in 1963.

The Boom in Recorded Music

After World War II, several technological innovations revitalized the recording industry. In 1947, 3M introduced magnetic tape, a recording technology borrowed from Germany that improved sound fidelity, reduced costs, and made editing and multitrack recording easier. This enabled the recorded music industry to produce more artists inexpensively and with better quality. In 1948 and 1949, Columbia introduced the 33⅓ rpm long-playing record, while RCA introduced 45 rpm records. After a short battle over standards, the 33⅓ rpm LP dominated longer releases or albums, while 45 rpm "singles" dominated releases of single hit songs (Head, Sterling, & Schofield, 1994).

The fight between the 33⅓ and 45 rpm **record formats** was one of the first consumer electronics format wars, in which conflicting means of playing music or video fought for the allegiance of consumers. These two new formats both drove out the earlier 78 rpm records. By the 1970s, audiocassette tapes were also a popular means of playing recorded music, triumphing over eight-track tapes. This cartridge-tape format had been introduced in the 1960s and flourished for a few years. However, cassette tapes were smaller and offered the advantage of recording as well as playback. In most cases, the format wars resulted from rival companies creating different standards in an attempt to gain complete control over the development of the technology. If one company's standard triumphed, it dominated the initial sales, and other manufacturers would have to pay a royalty to use the technology, if it was patented.

Several industry changes also helped gear up the record industry. The new recording technology enabled small, independent labels or recording companies to develop new artists and new audiences who had not been covered or served by network radio. For example, Chess Records in Chicago carried a number of blues and rhythm and blues artists who were played only on what were called black stations.

While a number of mass entertainment forms or genres shifted from radio to television, radio itself began to look for new sources of programming, which usually meant records or tapes of recorded music. Radio also looked for more local, nonnetwork functions, including a more direct connection with the particular musical tastes of their local audience. Some of these radio stations began to connect with the new labels to create new genres of music and new musical **radio formats.** In general, radio came to depend more on the recording industry and also began to serve as a promotional device to make the public aware of new music and help the recording industry sell records. The recording industry began to concentrate on getting more airplay for its records by promoting them to radio stations.

FM Radio and Specialized Formats

As radio stations cut loose from networks and as the number of stations continued to grow, they looked for ways to attract audiences and sell those audiences to advertisers. What emerged was a tendency to narrowcast—that is, to focus on specific or **segmented** audiences with more specific formulas and formats—since the general prime-time entertainment audience was moving increasingly to television. Even the networks themselves splintered. The ABC radio network split into contemporary, informational, entertainment, and FM services in 1968. As networks declined after 1947, stations tended to produce their own records, hire their own announcers and **disk jockeys,** run their own promotions and stunts, and still try to connect with as big a piece of the local radio audience as possible (Belz, 1972).

After the late 1960s, radio industry and audience developments led to the eventual development of FM radio as a successful commercial medium. Radio continued to grow, along with the boom in pop music. AM licenses were becoming difficult and expensive to obtain, whereas licenses for FM stations were much easier to get. Specialized formats continued to succeed. Some of these formats were more linked to musical quality, such as classical, jazz, or album-oriented rock, for which FM's higher fidelity was a definite advantage. Finally, increased numbers of the audience were also interested in greater sound quality, since high-fidelity and stereo systems were becoming much more popular. The move of many FM stations into stereo broadcasting was a decisive appeal for discerning listeners (Jones, 1992).

Radio format is a programming approach, often linked to music genres, news, or talk, focused on a particular audience.

Segmentation occurs when media focus on more specific, smaller audiences with more specialized programs and formats.

Disc jockey is a radio station announcer who often emphasizes delivery and personality.

Payola occurred when record companies gave gifts or even bribes to key DJs to get their records played.

ALLAN FREED AND THE DJ ERA

Top 40 or formula radio was born in 1952–1954 and was the most popular format through the 1960s. It focused on the top-selling records, gimmicks to attract attention, and the delivery and personality of the disc jockey or DJ, who picked and announced the records. DJs became popular public figures in their own right. Alan Freed, a Cleveland DJ, was mixing R&B with Sinatra. He popularized the term *rock 'n' roll* to help get white audiences to listen to R&B and helped promote "Rock Around the Clock," by Bill Haley and the Comets, the first rock 'n' roll single to become number one on the charts. Freed and other DJs became famous.

Stations competed on the basis of their DJs. The DJs were also targeted by the record companies who wanted to promote their records. This led to abuse, known as **payola,** where record companies gave gifts or even bribes to key DJs. Some major market DJs were making up to $100,000 a year from payola; this led to a public scandal, congressional hearings, and amendments to the Communications Act. However, the DJs did help the music industry grow rapidly; in particular, they helped rock music develop into an enormous success. Rock and pop music became closely linked with the baby boomers, who had enormous numbers and purchasing power.

1. What kind of music industry existed before radio? Before the phonograph?
2. What companies dominated two-way radio? What was it used for?
3. What were the key developments that allowed for radio broadcasting?
4. How did radio broadcasting and the recording industry affect each other in their early days?
5. What were the main music genres in the 1920s and 1930s?
6. Who formed the main radio networks?
7. How did advertising come to support radio economics?
8. What kinds of programming characterized radio networks during their high point?
9. When and why did radio networks decline?
10. When did FM radio begin to increase in importance? Why?
11. How did FM radio and 1960s–1970s music genres affect each other?
12. What kinds of radio networks exist now?

Syndication is rental or licensing of media products by their producers to other media companies for broadcast or distribution.

Electromagnetic recording rearranges metallic particles in the tape according to modulated current produced by a microphone.

These developments continue to dominate the radio industry. In 1993 FM stations drew 77 percent of the audience, but other technologies, such as digital audio broadcasting and direct broadcast satellite radio, may eventually threaten this dominance. Radio in general has been passing through a financial crisis and shakeout in the last five years. In 1990 over 50 percent of all radio stations lost money, but then 1992 saw an 8 percent increase in radio earnings. Radio ads had been priced very low for years, so radio had become attractive to advertisers, particularly those pursuing a particular audience segment.

The New Network Radio Era

There are many radio ownership groups. Some of them are beginning to act as content-oriented networks again. Some large groups, like Infinity, have limited-content networks for their owned-and-operated stations, even though not all their stations have the same format. For example, all Infinity stations carry Infinity's **syndicated** Howard Stern show, plus the show is syndicated to other stations in other markets.

AUDIO TECHNOLOGY TRENDS

In the beginnings of the recording industry, the main mode was acoustic recording. Sound waves were recorded on grooves in tinfoil or wax, similar to current record technology. A needle transformed the sound wave characteristics into deformations of the circular groove in the wax or vinyl. When the record is played back, the stylus or needle vibrates in keeping with the recorded pattern. In the first phonographs, the sound was amplified mechanically through a horn, like a trumpet, not electronically as with current record, tape, or compact disc players. In electronic equipment, the stylus movements generate an electric current, which is then amplified and sent electronically to speakers, where a moving or vibrating cone turns the electric current back into sound waves.

Until 1948, the record industry was based on 78 rpm records, which had one or two songs per side. The faster speed permitted reasonable sound quality but limited the length of the material that could be recorded. The technology for playing 33⅓ rpm long-playing (LP) records, which held 23 minutes of music per side and were very durable, and 45 rpm records used better-quality needles and amplification to achieve less noisy, higher-quality sound that was referred to in the 1950s as "high fidelity."

As noted earlier, building on ideas developed by German companies during World War II, 3M introduced magnetic recording tape and tape machines. The tape passes over a recording head, an **electromagnet,** that rearranges metallic particles in the tape according to modulated current produced by a microphone (see Figure 8.1). When played back, the tape runs over another electromagnetic head, which responds to the patterns stored on the tape and generates another current that is sent to a loudspeaker. For serious audio enthusiasts, reel-to-reel tape machines based on this technology were important up to the 1970s. These machines used higher tape speeds to achieve greater sound quality. Smaller cassette tapes, developed in the 1960s, used slower speeds and smaller lengths of tape but still achieved reasonable quality. Audiocassettes are still widely used, even as 33⅓ records have declined

FIGURE 8.1.
HOW AUDIO RECORDING ON
MAGNETIC TAPE WORKS.

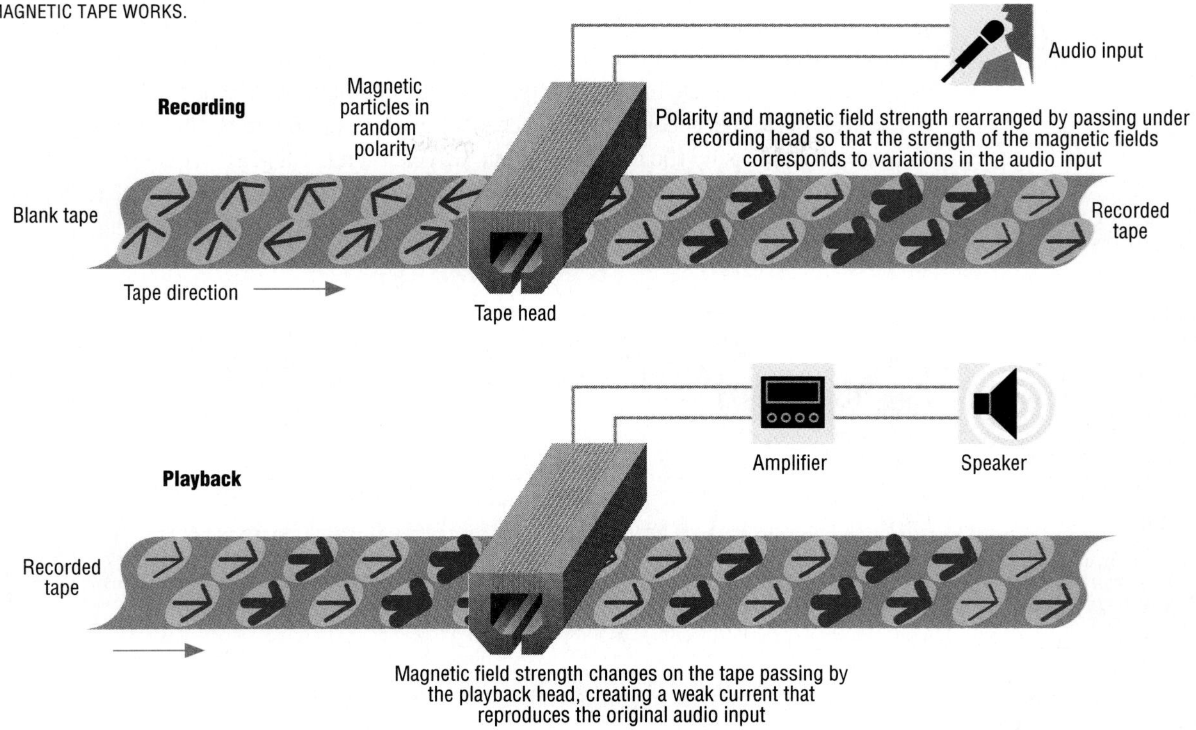

Recording

Audio input

Magnetic particles in random polarity

Polarity and magnetic field strength rearranged by passing under recording head so that the strength of the magnetic fields corresponds to variations in the audio input

Blank tape

Recorded tape

Tape direction

Tape head

Playback

Amplifier

Speaker

Recorded tape

Magnetic field strength changes on the tape passing by the playback head, creating a weak current that reproduces the original audio input

in importance. Part of their attraction is ruggedness; another is that they offer the possibility of recording sound as well as playing it back.

The next major consumer technology breakthrough was with digital formats. Compact discs (CDs) were developed as the first digital consumer format. With this technology, sound waves are sampled frequently and recorded as a series of indentations in a groove on a small disc. In playback, the indentations are read as on/off (1 or 0) codes, which the CD converts into electric pulses that are amplified and sent to speakers for reproduction into sound waves. CDs represented a considerable breakthrough in sound quality, since most noise could be eliminated via computer modification in the digital recording or rerecording process and the CD itself was a less noisy playback format. In the early 1990s, digital audio tape (DAT) was promoted as a consumer technology but succeeded primarily as a professional recording technology. Minidisks—music recordings on computer disks and other new digital tape recording methods—are still being presented to the consumer. Both technologies enable users to record digital music, an advantage over CDs.

Radio Transmission and Reception Basics

In the late 1800s, physicists such as James Clerk Maxwell (in 1872) and H. R. Hertz (in 1888) began to experiment with a new phenomenon known as **radio waves.** Like the waves that we make in the bathtub, radio waves rise and fall in regular cycles. The number of cycles that the waves complete in a set amount of time is called their **frequency** and is measured in Hertz (Hz). Radio waves have much higher frequencies than waves in a bathtub and do not require a medium, like water, to propagate. They can travel through a vacuum,

Radio waves are composed of electromagnetic energy and rise and fall in regular cycles.

Frequency is the number of cycles that waves complete in a set amount of time.

because the electromagnetic energy they use can be detected at a distance through minor perturbations in magnetic fields. In a radio system, the announcer's voice is converted to an electrical wave form by a microphone, much like a telephone mouthpiece. That signal is combined with a much higher frequency electromagnetic wave, between 535,000 and 1,705,000 cycles per second, and broadcast over an AM radio transmitter (see Figure 8.2). Your antenna picks up the electromagnetic waves, then the higher frequencies inside your radio are removed, and the announcer's voice is restored (Head, Sterling, & Schofield, 1994).

Marconi experimented with the components needed to make radio work: antennas,

FIGURE 8.2.
HOW AM RADIO BROADCASTING USES RADIO WAVES. THE ANNOUNCER'S VOICE IS CONVERTED TO AN ANALOG ELECTRICAL SIGNAL BY THE MICROPHONE. THIS ELECTRICAL SIGNAL IS THEN COMBINED WITH A POWERFUL, HIGH-FREQUENCY ELECTROMAGNETIC CARRIER SIGNAL AND TRANSMITTED TO THE HOME RECEIVER. THE RECEIVER DETECTS VARIATIONS IN THE ELECTROMAGNETIC FIELD, FILTERS OUT THE HIGHER CARRIER FREQUENCY, AND RECREATES THE ORIGINAL ELECTRICAL ANALOG SIGNAL, WHICH THE LOUDSPEAKER CONVERTS BACK TO SOUND ENERGY.

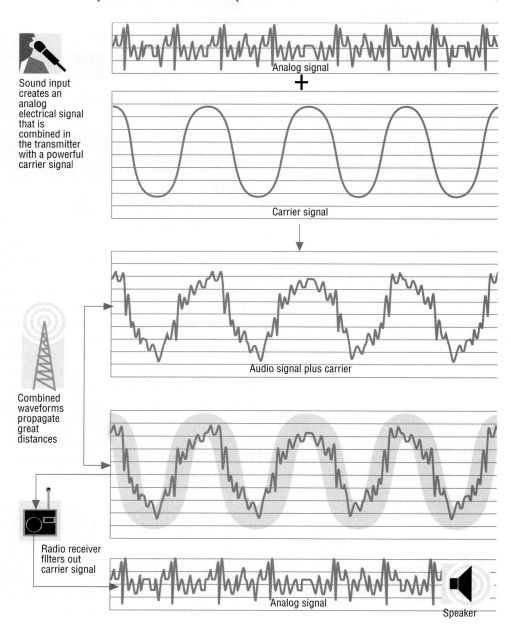

Sound input creates an analog electrical signal that is combined in the transmitter with a powerful carrier signal

Analog signal

+

Carrier signal

Audio signal plus carrier

Combined waveforms propagate great distances

Radio receiver filters out carrier signal

Analog signal

Speaker

ground systems, signal detectors, tuners, and receivers. He filed for patents in England in 1896 and in the United States in 1904. At this point, radio could only transmit in bursts of noise, not continuous waves. The kinds of transmitters used (known as spark-gap transmitters) could only turn radio energy on and off, so codes could be transmitted and received, but sound, which required the transmission of continuous waves, could not.

Building on work by Reginald Fessenden, Lee De Forest solved several problems of radio signal generation, detection, and amplification by inventing the vacuum tube, or triode, in 1906, which Edwin Armstrong improved by 1918. The **vacuum tube** permitted a weak signal to be both amplified and precisely modulated by controlling the flow of electrical charges inside a glass tube. In 1906, Fessenden made the first radio telephone "broadcast" using a telephone microphone. De Forest also adapted vacuum tubes to begin sound broadcasting in 1916. By 1922, vacuum tubes were used for tuning, amplifying, and other functions that improved radio receivers.

Radio stations used a variety of frequencies for radio broadcasting, until they were standardized by the Federal Radio Commission after 1927. The AM band was fixed at 535–1,605 KHz, then extended to 1,705 KHz in 1988. **AM** refers to **amplitude modulation**; that is, the sound information is carried in variations in the height, or amplitude, of the radio wave. In general, AM signals carry farther than FM, which travels strictly in the line of sight, so there is more potential for frequency interference among AM stations. Therefore, fewer AM licenses can be granted in the same cities. To control interference, the FCC regulates AM broadcast power, the height of antennas, and whether stations broadcast at night, when AM signals carry farther by bouncing off the ionosphere.

In 1933 Armstrong, an RCA engineer, developed **FM** or **frequency modulation** radio. In FM radio, the sound information is carried in variations in the frequency of the radio wave. The actual introduction of FM was delayed, in part due to disagreements over which section of the VHF (very high frequency) band to use for FM and which to use for television. FM was eventually moved from its pre–World War II channels in 1945 to the present 88–108 MHz, making half a million early FM receivers obsolete. FM had higher-fidelity sound characteristics than AM (e.g., a greater frequency range, cleaner sound, and less static), so stereo broadcasting was begun in FM. AM stereo is in service, but it is much less widely used.

Because FM signals can travel only in the line of sight, FM is limited in distance. However, this limitation actually means that each individual area can have more FM stations, since FM stations in neighboring cities are less likely to have overlapping signals. FM is also free of other interference problems that plague AM.

Digital audio broadcasting may be the next major breakthrough (see Table 8.2). It would actually be cheaper and a more efficient use of the radio spectrum and would offer CD-quality digital sound. Another related possibility is **DBS radio** or **RDBS** (radio direct broadcast satellite), which would bring signals directly from satellites to home receivers. (Many stations already receive programming for networks, news services, and programming services by satellite, and then rebroadcast it to homes.) The most widely developed alternative is the digital music service

Vacuum tubes can amplify and precisely modulate a weak signal by controlling the flow of electrical charges inside the tube.

AM or amplitude modification refers to the fact that the sound information is carried in the height, or amplitude, of the radio wave.

FM or frequency modulation means that the sound information is carried in variations in the frequency of the radio wave.

DBS radio or **RDBS** would bring signals directly from satellites to home receivers.

TABLE 8.2. MILESTONES OF RECORDING AND RADIO TECHNOLOGY

Year	Milestone
1872	Maxwell describes radio waves
1877	Edison introduces the "speaking phonograph"
1882	Berliner creates the gramophone
1888	Hertz transmits and receives first radio waves
1896	Marconi develops radio transmitter
1906	Fessenden makes first sound broadcast
1916	De Forest adapts vacuum tubes for receivers
1927	AM band fixed at 535–1605 KHz by FRC
1933	Armstrong develops FM radio
1947	Magnetic audiotape recorders by 3M
1948	33⅓ rpm records by Columbia
1949	45 rpm records by RCA
1956	High-fidelity and stereo push LPs
1985	Compact disc format introduced
1992	Minidisk sound recordings introduced

Car radios incorporating the new radio data system (RDS) technology will soon be here. RDS transmits a stream of computer data that can be shown on a small display built into the radio receiver and processed by the circuitry inside. With RDS, your radio will give you information about the station and its format and call letters. In the near term, you will also be able to seek channels according to music format so that future metalheads can stay tuned to pure metal from coast to coast, if they so choose. There will also be an emergency alert capability that will turn your radio on to warn you of impending danger.

RDS is just the first step in the transition to an all-digital radio broadcasting system. Spectrum has already been allocated for a satellite-based digital broadcasting service that will transmit compact disc–quality music to a satellite antenna about the size of a paper napkin. The all-digital system promises to be more immune to static and signal fading than today's radio by capitalizing on the inherent advantages of digital media. A terrestrial digital system is already on the air in Europe, but progress has been slowed in the United States by battles over spectrum allocations and the need to come up with a system that will work for both AM and FM radio.

How Is It Done?

The RDS information is packed into some of the unused space available in FM radio channels, in a manner similar to the paging and Muzak services found there today. Things get a little more tricky for AM radio, where there is no extra space available. When the transition to an all-digital system is made sometime in the late 1990s, the entire signal will go out in digital form.

Stay Tuned for Further Developments

Some of the other high-tech wizardry implied in our opening scenario is a little further down the road, but not much. There are already cellular telephones with "hands free" voice dialing, so it is not unreasonable to expect that voice tuning for radios will follow shortly. Further detail in the RDS data would allow you to conduct voice searches for music by artist, subject, or even key words in the lyrics. Car navigation systems are a reality now, and your future car is already slated to have its own onboard data network to interface all the computer gizmos. And while Wolfman Jack will surely never die, if he is not around in 2009, we should be able to recreate his rap with a good artificial intelligence program and a digital signal processor in the radio studio. Our car's own onboard voice processor could add the local tag using navigation data. Perhaps you could even make the Wolfman the computer voice for your car: "Hey, numnutz, pothole comin' atcha in this lane. I'm switchin' or you're ditchin'!"

offered over cable TV systems. Both digital audio broadcasting and DBS would require new receivers and antennas.

Audio is a major component of multimedia productions as well. In fact, some of the first multimedia products were enhanced sound recordings—music or voice—plus imagery and text. CD-ROM (compact disc–read only memory) stores various kinds of digital information, including sound, graphics, text, photos, images, and even video. The CD-ROM disc is played back through a computer, which interprets the digital information into coordinated sound, and images. Among the first commercial CD-ROM products were recordings of symphonies, along with the scores, commentaries, and images that might accompany the music.

FORMS AND GENRES

Even before radio, in the Victrola and phonograph era, popular music was developing out of ethnic and historical traditions and into certain formulas and genres that are still present. The roots of American popular music can be traced to several earlier **traditions**. The main ones are, arguably, English, Irish, and Scottish ballads and hymns; a variety of African vocal music, rhythm, and percussion traditions; Polish polkas; and German and Austrian waltzes. In the United States, many of these blended into various traditional strains that preceded recording and radio: black gospel, white gospel, Appalachian folk and country, Delta blues, Cajun, and Mexican border *rancheras* and *boleros*. The early hits of the phonograph era were John Philip Sousa marches and ragtime, along with pop and light songs. Jazz became popular in the 1920s and 1930s, along with show tunes taken from the new talking movies. **Blues** developed as a music popular among many African Americans but did not cross over much at that time (Dominick, 1993).

Traditions in music are genres passed along from one generation to another.

Blues is an African American musical tradition based primarily on guitar and distinctive plaintive lyrics.

Radio Genres

The most popular musical formats of the network era were big band jazz, light classical music, and movie and show tunes. Some important musical genre developments also occurred away from the main networks. For example, a network of southern stations carried the Grand Ole Opry and bluegrass music. These radio formats built on some of the main regional American music traditions, such as southern **gospel,** blues, bluegrass/old-timey **Appalachian music,** western music, western swing, and others. Although these kinds of music were not played much on national network radio, they were recorded and played on various local and regional stations, and some spread across the country. For example, the blend of Appalachian, gospel, western, and western swing that eventually became known as country and western, or country, was most popular in the rural south, southwest, and west but also followed southern migrants north as they looked for jobs in the industrial midwest and east. The blues followed African American migrants from the south to Chicago and New York, where a harder electric blues developed that greatly affected rock 'n' roll. For example, rock bands in the 1960s did versions of Chicago blues songs by Muddy Waters and Howlin' Wolf.

Network radio in the 1930s and 1940s also created a number of program genres besides music. Comedy series were among the early successes of radio networks. In the early 1930s, for instance, the top network show was *Amos 'n' Andy,* a comedy show imitating African

Gospel originated as southern Protestant religious music, with distinctive but related African American and white forms.

Appalachian music developed from English, Scottish, and Irish roots with similar instrumentation and ballad forms.

Americans that would be considered racist now but was very popular then with both black and white audiences.

Singers who had started with big bands, such as Frank Sinatra, recorded pop songs that appealed to a wide age group. These songs fit the form of network radio, which was still trying to appeal to a broad general audience. The formula began to fail when much of the prime-time radio entertainment audience shifted to television and stations began to leave the networks as management tried to think of ways to attract an audience.

Music Genres and Radio Formats

In the 1950s, after most stations had dropped away from radio networks, they began to target more specific audiences with particular formats, programming strategies oriented around a playlist of music and focused on a particular genre or audience. The most popular formats initially were middle-of-the-road (MOR), which continued pop elements of the old network general-audience formula; rhythm and blues (R&B), which developed from earlier blues music; and country and western (CW).

Top 40 is a radio format that plays only top single records, the top 40 on record sales charts.

Top 40. Contemporary hit radio (CHR) or **top 40** was probably invented by Todd Storz in 1949, who wondered why radio could not be more like a jukebox, playing over and over the hit songs that people really wanted to hear the most. Top 40 was the dominant radio format from the 1950s until the early 1970s. In the early 1960s, Bill Drake at KHJ in Los Angeles refined the format into playing only top single records. Casey Kasem developed a variation of playing the top 40 from *Billboard* magazine and doing popularity countdowns. He also created one of the earliest popular

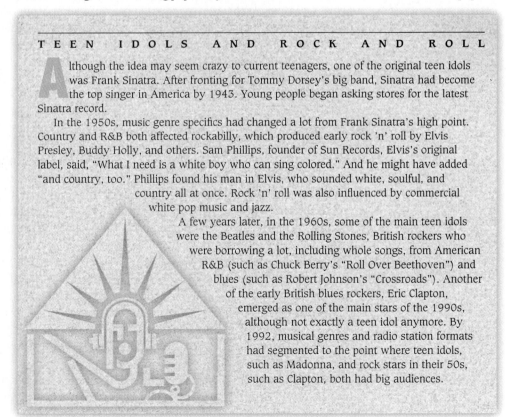

TEEN IDOLS AND ROCK AND ROLL

Although the idea may seem crazy to current teenagers, one of the original teen idols was Frank Sinatra. After fronting for Tommy Dorsey's big band, Sinatra had become the top singer in America by 1943. Young people began asking stores for the latest Sinatra record.

In the 1950s, music genre specifics had changed a lot from Frank Sinatra's high point. Country and R&B both affected rockabilly, which produced early rock 'n' roll by Elvis Presley, Buddy Holly, and others. Sam Phillips, founder of Sun Records, Elvis's original label, said, "What I need is a white boy who can sing colored." And he might have added "and country, too." Phillips found his man in Elvis, who sounded white, soulful, and country all at once. Rock 'n' roll was also influenced by commercial white pop music and jazz.

A few years later, in the 1960s, some of the main teen idols were the Beatles and the Rolling Stones, British rockers who were borrowing a lot, including whole songs, from American R&B (such as Chuck Berry's "Roll Over Beethoven") and blues (such as Robert Johnson's "Crossroads"). Another of the early British blues rockers, Eric Clapton, emerged as one of the main stars of the 1990s, although not exactly a teen idol anymore. By 1992, musical genres and radio station formats had segmented to the point where teen idols, such as Madonna, and rock stars in their 50s, such as Clapton, both had big audiences.

MOTOWN GROUPS SUCH AS THE SUPREMES DOMINATED TOP 40 RADIO IN THE 1960S.

syndicated radio programming services, American Top 40. Hundreds of stations in the United States, Europe, and Asia still carry his top 40 countdown programs to over 8 million listeners each week.

In the late 1950s and early 1960s, most of the young audience was listening to the same overall mix of rock 'n' roll, with some R&B, Motown, or soul. In the early 1960s, pop singers like Frankie Avalon mixed on top 40 with the Beach Boys (who lifted several tunes and guitar riffs from Chuck Berry), and Motown groups like The Supremes and the Temptations. Rock was still somewhat unified by top 40 stations in the middle and late 1960s, with Motown, English groups like the Beatles and Rolling Stones, and heavy rockers like Led Zeppelin and Jimmi Hendrix all being played on the same stations (Limmer, 1981).

Still, the overall impact of top 40 declined after 1970, when FM radio stations began to diversify into different rock formats, such as album-oriented rock (AOR) or oldies. In the late 1960s, the number of stations, particularly on FM, began to proliferate and seek audiences. Stations looked for ways to differentiate themselves and find more unique and loyal audiences. This fit with a musical culture that was also beginning to proliferate. Rock split a number of ways, which were reflected in different genres of music and echoed in some FM radio formats. Other music forms and genres also showed up in FM radio formats: blues, R&B, jazz, big band, gospel, classical, and country and western.

Rock grew from diverse roots and began to fragment or diversify again into a number of branches (see Figure 8.4). Some groups went further back toward their original influences and roots. Eric Clapton played blues early in his career and again in the 1990s. Some went the other way, like former blues singer Rod Stewart, who became the archetype of the pop/rock star. In the 1970s, what had been considered "rock" split into commercial or top 40, psychedelic, punk, disco, country rock, folk rock, new wave, heavy metal, techno pop, and so on. The 1980s and 1990s added blues rock, hard rock, techno, alternative, industrial, rave, reggae, rap, gangsta rap, and hip-hop. By the 1990s, literally dozens of subgenres had descended from 1960s rock, pop, and soul roots. Gradually, radio stations began to pick up combinations of these branches of music and others as formats.

Part of this proliferation was due to the continuing formation of smaller labels and radio stations that provided expression to musical subcultures. The increase in labels and stations was in turn the result of technological developments that lowered the price of recording tapes and records and of starting radio stations. Labels could and did focus on very specific kinds of music and audiences.

Proliferation of Genres and Formats. By the 1980s and 1990s, FM dominated the music-oriented radio formats. More FM licenses were available, because of their shorter geographic reach, which made it logical for a larger number of FM stations to pursue more segmented audiences with increasingly specific formats. Some of the main FM formats are as follows:

Adult contemporary—a mix of oldies and softer rock hits

Top 40 or contemporary hit radio (CHR)—mostly current hits, usually mixing pop, rock, and rap/hip-hop

Country—increasingly subdivided into traditional country, contemporary/urban country, and rock/country blends

Album-oriented rock (AOR)—album cuts (often corresponding to videos) by current groups, split into heavy metal and other branches, including a mixture of oldies for older listeners

Classic rock—1960s and 1970s rock

FIGURE 8.4.
THIS CHART SHOWS SOME OF THE ROOTS OF ROCK MUSIC AND HOW IT HAS SPLIT INTO A NUMBER OF BRANCHES OVER TIME.

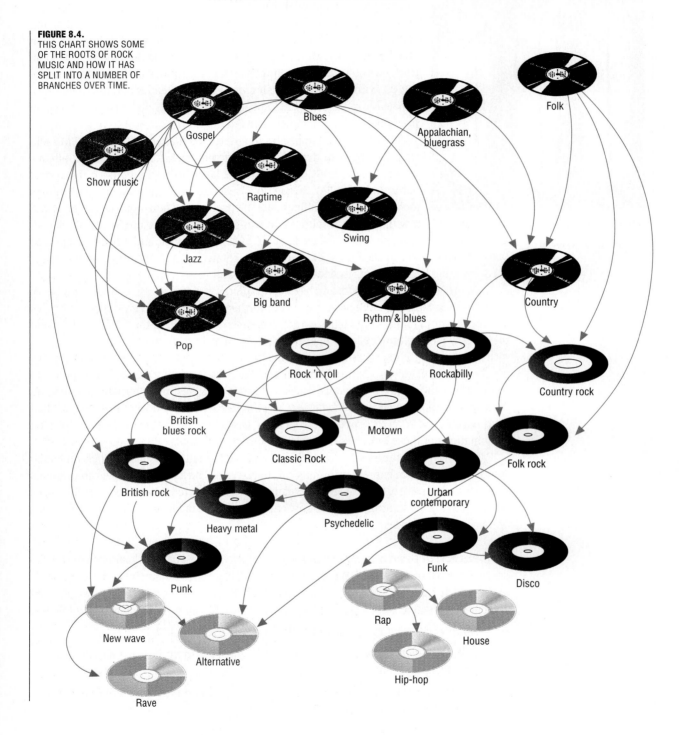

Middle-of-the road (MOR)—a mix of softer current songs and oldies; often mixed with talk forms, news, and weather, particularly on drive-time shows aimed at commuters

Oldies—1950s and early 1960s rock, pop, and R&B

Urban contemporary—African American music, rap, hip-hop, dance, house, sometimes with Hispanic sounds

Latino or Hispanic—for Spanish-speaking listeners; in larger markets, subdivided both by origin (Mexican, Cuban, Puerto Rican) and by music genres (dance music, traditional, Latin rock)

Music was not the only game on radio. As stations specialized, news, talk, weather, and sports information continued or even grew in importance. Many AM stations tend to emphasize news, talk, and sports, where music or sound quality matters less. However, a number of FM stations now feature a mixture of talk, call-ins, music, news headlines, and weather aimed at a broad audience during commuting hours (drive time). Because of AM's broader signal reach, many stations also center on smaller towns and rural areas where population is less dense and where a broad-based middle-of-the-road, country/western, or oldies format makes more sense.

R E V I E W

1. What were the main original traditions in popular music?
2. How have radio formats changed after the decline of radio networks?
3. What is top 40? How has it changed?
4. How has rock music evolved? What were its roots? How has it diverged since the 1960s?
5. How have radio formats evolved since 1970?
6. What are the top formats now on FM? On AM?

Nearly all of these formats are for commercial radio. Several noncommercial patterns have also developed on the FM stations using frequencies reserved for noncommercial alternatives. These include:

Classical music

Experimental or alternative rock and folk, mostly found on college stations

Jazz, found on both commercial and noncommercial stations

A number of stations, both AM and FM, currently run the national **PBS** morning and evening news and public affairs programs *Morning Edition* and *All Things Considered*; some stations also affiliate with the Pacifica network or others, a few do primarily local news and public affairs

PBS is the Public Broadcasting Service, which offers news and other programming to a national noncommercial radio network.

AUDIENCES FOR AUDIO MEDIA

Music audiences seem to show a steady trend toward segmentation, even fragmentation. In the 1950s, most young people listened to the same pop and rock music, although there were already separately defined audiences for rhythm and blues and country/western. In the 1960s, many young people thought of themselves as a broad cultural movement, unified in large part by rock music, but that fragmented in the 1970s.

The 1970s and 1980s saw a fragmentation of the youth audience into a variety of subcultures. Disco started with the gay subculture and turned into the main 1970s dance music. Punk rock in the 1970s started as an expression of extreme alienation from both adult culture and most existing rock music. Industrial and techno/rave music in the 1990s was sometimes linked to the technologically sophisticated descendants of punk sensibility, the cyberpunks.

TABLE 8.3. AVERAGE HOURS SPENT USING MEDIA, 1985 AND 1990

Medium	1985	1990	Percentage Change
Television	1,530	1,470	−4
Radio	1,190	1,135	−5
FM	72%	77%	+5
AM	28%	23%	−5
Recorded music	185	235	+27
Newspapers	185	175	−5
Consumer magazines	110	90	−18
Consumer books	80	95	+19
Home video	15	50	+233
Movies	12	12	0
Total	3,307	3,262	+1

Sources: Veronis, Suhler & Associates; A. C. Nielsen; RADAR; Newspaper Advertising Bureau; Magazine Publishers Association; Gallup; MPAA, Television Bureau of Advertising; Leo Shapiro and Associates; Wilkovsky Gruen and Associates.

Although their tastes may be fragmented, people still buy a lot of recordings. Listening to recordings went up from an average of 185 hours per year in 1985 to 235 in 1990, while radio listening actually declined slightly from an average of 1,190 hours per year in 1985 to 1,135 in 1990 (see Table 8.3). Spending on recordings went up roughly 10 percent per year: In 1990 people spent over $8 billion per year in the United States, $25 billion worldwide. Among other things, that makes the tastes of overseas listeners and buyers very important to record producers and distributors. Over half of Americans buy in CD format, slightly under half on cassette, and almost none on vinyl records.

Two-thirds of Americans still listen to radio at least briefly each day. The national average is about 3 hours per day. Only about 20 percent listen to radio networks; most listen to local formats, although the audiences for certain kinds of network programs, such as talk by Rush Limbaugh or Howard Stern, are growing. People listened more in their cars (25 percent) and other locations (29 percent), and less at home (45 percent) in 1990 than in 1985.

Radio formats have fragmented along with music genres. The number of stations playing the formats in Table 8.4 is a rough indication of their popularity. The formats listed in Table 8.4 have fairly distinct listening audiences. The focus on youth cultures is due to the

TABLE 8.4. RADIO FORMATS AND AUDIENCE SHARES

Format	Number of Stations	Percent of Listening Audience*	Typical Content	Target Audience Sex	Target Audience Age
News/talk	2,246	16.2	Rush Limbaugh, Howard Stern	Mostly male	25–55
Adult contemporary	1,583	15.0	Kenny G	Male/female	25–45
Country	2,386 }	12.4	The Judds }	Male/female	35–55
Contemporary country	215 }		Garth Brooks, Oak Ridge Boys }		
Top 40/contemporary hits	398	9.2	Mariah Carey, Michael Jackson	Mostly female	12–55
Urban	306	9.2	Boyz 2 Men, Dr. Dre	Male/female	18–35
Album rock	453	8.1	Arrowsmith	Male	18–25
Oldies	439	7.2	Beach Boys, Ronettes	Male/female	25–45
Spanish	318	5.2	Selena	Male/female	25–55
Classic rock	292	3.5	LedZeppelin	Mostly male	25–45
Modern/alternative rock, progressive	233	3.2	REM, Pearl Jam	Male/female	25–45
Adult standards, 60s–80s	335	3.2	U2, Eric Clapton	Male/female	25–45
Adult alternative, hot AC	136	2.4	Melissa Ethridge, Indigo Girls	Male/female	25–45
Religious	542	2.3	Amy Grant	Male/female	35–55
Classical	329	2.0	Beethoven	Male/female	35–55
Gospel	392	0.5	Mighty Gospel Tones		
Black	398	0.5	Motown	Male/female	35–55
Christian	353	0.8	Talk, music	Male/female	35–55
Nostalgia/big band	241	0.5	Benny Goodman	Male/female	55–65
Jazz	271	0.5	Thelonius Monk	Male/female	35–55
MOR (middle of road)	240	0.5	Early Beatles	Male/female	35–55
Educational	20	0.1	Formal and informal education	Male/female	35–55
Easy listening, beautiful music	146	0.5	Barry Manilow, Whitney Houston	Male/female	35–55
Remaining formats	358	0.3			

*Persons 12+ for all markets, Monday–Sunday, 6 A.M.–midnight
Sources: *Bacon's Radio Directory 1995; 1996 Information Please Almanac;* Arbitron

fact that teenagers and young adults are both the heaviest buyers of recorded music and the main listeners to music formats on radio.

INDUSTRY ORGANIZATION

There are several key aspects of the recording industry: the **talent** (the singers and groups), the recording studios and technical producers, the recording company, the distributors, and the retailers. The talent are the ever-changing crowd of groups, singers, and musicians. Also important to musicians' success are their songwriters, managers, and arrangers. They all hope to get a contract from a record company to make money.

Groups form at a local level. There are tens of thousands of aspiring local groups and singers throughout the United States. For example, the college club scene in Athens, Georgia, produced the B-52s and R.E.M., among other groups. Such acts perform locally, try to get concert or dance bookings out of town, become known, and make a recording to circulate to record companies. A number become quasi-professional as traveling acts that circulate in a state or region. A few are discovered and make it big, but most break up and the more talented musicians form new groups and move on. Talent scouts from record companies are always looking around college towns and concert circuits for new acts, but competition is fierce.

Record Companies

Recording companies get promising acts into the studio, where engineers and arrangers capture their music on tape for an album or single. Some of the main recording companies have a number of separate **labels.** Each of those labels may have a separate image and intended market. Sony Records has the Columbia and Epic labels; Time-Warner has Reprise, Elektra, and Atlantic; RCA has Arista and Ariola; Polygram has Mercury, Deutsche Grammophon, and A&M; Thorn/EMI has Capital, EMI, and Manhattan; and MCA has Motown and Geffen. Sony is Japanese, RCA is owned by the German firm Bertelsmann, Polygram is owned by the Dutch Philips, and MCA is owned by Matsushita in Japan. This ownership has raised some interesting issues about whether foreign owners will assert any kind of agenda about what kinds of musical content to pursue.

Recording companies decide which albums and songs to promote via radio, billboards, newspaper ads, and magazine ads. An important part of this promotion process for the most promising groups with national potential is making a music video for MTV, VH-1, or other music-oriented cable channels. Since MTV began in 1981, it has become a potent force in setting the agenda for which records become popular and even what gets played on radio stations. MTV was originally focused on heavy metal but has since diversified its focus with more rap, alternative, and other genres, so MTV manages to cover a number of the kinds of music played by relatively different formats on radio. MTV has 50 million subscribers and reaches the whole country—a new national network for music. It is now difficult to have a radio hit without having a music video.

The record companies distribute recordings in a variety of ways. Rack jobbers supply the recordings seen in sale racks at large retail stores like Kmart. Other kinds of distributors sell to retail music stores that specialize in recordings and related videos. Increasingly, this retail business is dominated by big chain stores, including Sam Goody, Musicland, and Tower. Record clubs such as Columbia and BMG sell CDs and cassettes directly through the mail on a large scale. These clubs are all big enough to deal directly with the record companies.

Specific recordings are also pitched via TV commercials for direct-mail ordering. Overall, spending on musical recordings has risen considerably, from an average of about $25 per person in 1985 to $41 in 1990.

Radio Stations

Radio stations vary greatly in size and complexity, but all have certain key jobs that need to be done. The manager oversees planning, audience development, ratings, and sales. The program director supervises the air sound, the playlists, DJs, and announcers. There is usually a music director who plans the **playlists.** There are usually producers for talk shows or anything more complex than simple announcing, such as talk shows or drive-time shows. Most stations have a news director, depending on the size of the news operation. Commercial stations have a sales manager and an advertising sales staff. Because almost 75 percent of radio advertising is local, the advertising sales staff is crucial for selling local advertising, as well as working with national advertisers who might want to sell **national spot ads** in the local market.

Increasingly, a number of stations use outside programming services for both music and some talk shows. Many stations buy complete packaged music services designed by outside experts who look at the prospective audience, consider the format options, and consider what has worked in other markets in similar situations. This approach has cut back the DJ's autonomy considerably since the more freewheeling days of the 1950s and 1960s, when DJs often picked their own records to play.

Most radio stations are privately owned and operated on a commercial basis, which creates a fairly broad uniformity of approach. However, radio does offer a fairly diverse set of stations. There are more noncommercial stations—university, school, city, and foundation owned—in radio than in television. Many of these have a noncommercial programming line that lets them offer more diverse cultural, entertainment, and information programs. In particular, college radio stations and PBS radio **affiliates** often offer noncommercial alternatives.

Radio stations are owned by many kinds of individuals and groups. There are so many stations in the United States that ownership is less concentrated than for newspapers or television, which are much more expensive to start up and operate. In the 1970s most of the old radio networks became simply **group owners**. The largest group owners of radio stations are CBS (19 stations), Group W (18), Capcities/ABC (21), Infinity (17), Bonneville (14), and Gannett (14). Eight of the largest ownership groups are traded on the stock exchange.

Group ownership has been facilitated by increasing FCC ceilings on ownership limits, but many stations are still locally owned and operated. The early 1980s saw a boom in financial speculation in radio and television stations, since their values had been rising rapidly. Several years of meager earnings drove most speculators/investors out, so most stations are now owned by radio groups or individuals more interested in the long-term radio business.

Some of the traditional networks still carry news and other national programming for all or most of their stations. Although most radio advertising is local, there is still interest in national ad coverage, which encourages some network-level advertising. Some large groups, such as Infinity, have limited-content networks for their own owned-and-operated stations, even though not all their stations have the same format. For example, all Infinity stations carry Infinity's syndicated Howard Stern show, plus Infinity syndicates the show to other stations in other markets. As of 1993, there were twenty to twenty-five main syndicators, such as Mediamerica, NY, which has Patrick Buchanan and Rush Limbaugh.

A variety of radio programming services are also available. Full program-service

Playlists are the categories and titles of songs picked to fit the radio station's format and target audience.

National spot advertising can be placed by national advertisers on local media, such as radio stations.

Affiliates in broadcasting are stations that contract to use the programming of and share advertising/financing with a network.

Group owners own a number of broadcast stations but do not always provide them with common programming, as a network would.

R E V I E W

1. How do singers, groups, and writers get connected with recording companies?
2. What are record labels?
3. How do records get distributed and sold?
4. How do radio station affiliates relate to networks?
5. How have radio networks developed since the 1950s?
6. What kinds of radio services are syndicated? How does that work?

companies, such as Bonneville, provide completely automated formats, such as beautiful music. Bonneville also created the disco format in the 1970s. However, this full-service automation is actually not as popular as it used to be because of the diversification and localization of formats. Locally programmed automation systems are also becoming cheaper; for example, a fully programmable system that handles up to 300 CDs, plus tape machines for commercial and announcement inserts, costs under $10,000.

Among the radio networks in the 1990s is the noncommercial PBS network. National Public Radio and American Public Radio networks supply national news, features, syndicated music, and other programs to public stations around the country. The national popularity of the main news shows, *Morning Edition* and *All Things Considered,* is very high among radio news audiences. Other, smaller networks have survived and even grown, such as the Pacifica network based in California.

POLICY AND ETHICS

The radio and recording industries are faced with a variety of policy and ethical issues.

Radio Licensing and Regulation

Radio Act of 1912 was the initial government regulation for licensing of transmitters.

Radio Act of 1927 created a Federal Radio Commission, defined the broadcast band, standardized frequency designations, and limited the number of stations operating at night, when AM signals carry farther.

The initial government regulation, the **Radio Act of 1912**, called for licensing of transmitters by the Secretary of Commerce but was not very specific in granting powers. Secretary Herbert Hoover hoped that industry self-regulation would be adequate and held a series of national radio conferences, which were not very effective. The courts questioned Hoover's right to enforce the frequency allocations he did make, so new stations started using frequencies at will, resulting in substantial frequency interference between stations.

The **Radio Act of 1927** created a Federal Radio Commission. It defined the broadcast band, standardized frequency designations, and limited the number of stations operating at night, when AM signals carry farther. The FRC and most of its rules were absorbed into the more comprehensive Federal Communications Commission (FCC), created by the Communications Act of 1934. The FCC created more systematic procedures for granting radio licenses. It had adequate power to compel compliance with its rules on transmitter power, height, and frequency use that were designed to avoid frequency interference. The FCC created rules about ownership, concentration and cross-ownership, obscenity and indecency in radio content, and the role of networks and affiliates. The Telecommunications Act of 1996 further changed a number of FCC rules about ownership, competition, and frequency allocation.

Radio Ownership and Control Rules

Concentration of ownership occurs when media are owned by a small number of individuals, government agencies, or corporations.

The overall rules about **concentration of ownership** affect radio. In the United States, previous policies limited ownership first to a maximum of five TV stations, five AM stations, and five FM stations. That was later relaxed to twelve TV stations, twelve AM stations, and twelve FM stations. The Telecommunications Act of 1996 eliminates the national limits altogether.

Until 1992, one owner could not have more than one newspaper, one AM/FM combination, or one television station per city or market. Cross-ownership of radio, television, and newspapers was deregulated in 1992, and cross-ownership with cable TV was deregulated in 1996. Under the 1996 act, local ownership caps increase with market size from a total of five stations in a market with fourteen or fewer commercial stations to eight stations among forty-five or more stations.

After people realized that few noncommercial stations had emerged from the initial scramble for AM licenses in the 1920s and 1930s, provision was made to reserve some FM frequencies for noncommercial and educational use. A certain number of frequencies are reserved in each market, typically at the lower end of the FM band. This provision has made both experimental college and independent foundation radio stations possible and laid the basis for the current national network of PBS radio news affiliates.

Networks and Program Control

Chain broadcasting refers to radio networks and their control over talent and affiliated stations.

Over time, several rules have tried to limit radio and television network control over content creation and production. In 1938 the FCC initiated hearings about **chain broadcasting** to examine the control of radio networks over talent and affiliated stations. The resulting 1941 rules gave more autonomy to radio affiliates to refuse to carry programs without fear of retaliation and put networks out of the talent-booking business.

With the decline of network radio in the United States, the question of network control became much less pressing. Although networks, programming services, news services, and syndicated programs all have some power over programming on a number of stations, the overall picture is fairly diverse.

First Amendment and Freedom of Speech Issues

Freedom of speech issues include political freedom of speech, definitions and/or protection of indecent or obscene speech.

Freedom of speech issues continue to be a focus for both radio broadcasting and the recording industry. The recording industry has traditionally been less closely scrutinized. It has been considered analogous to publishing, in that it doesn't involve use of a scarce public resource, such as the airwaves; it has a large degree of competition; and exposure to recorded music is, in principle, entirely voluntary. The industry indulged in a certain degree of self-censorship up through the 1960s. Groups that used obscene language or graphic sexual references were usually excluded from the major labels. This situation changed greatly in the late 1960s as many of the major rock groups carried by major labels began to use more graphic language and explicit themes. This use has come to be challenged by groups of parents and others concerned about exposure to songs or raps that contain violence, sexist and racist imagery, and graphic language. In 1989, Tipper Gore, wife of then Senator Albert Gore, led a group that pushed in congressional hearings for warning labels about explicit or graphic lyrics on record and CD covers. A number of record labels now place such warnings on their covers, but their effectiveness has been questioned. Some analysts think that the warnings simply attract more attention.

Radio has been more closely scrutinized as well. The FCC has maintained a series of standards restricting obscene or indecent speech. Up through the 1960s, certain words could not be used, and broadcasters were held responsible even for call-in programs to make sure that prohibited language was not used. Comic George Carlin developed a comedy routine in that era about the "Seven Dirty Words You Can't Say

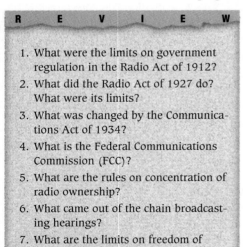

R E V I E W

1. What were the limits on government regulation in the Radio Act of 1912?
2. What did the Radio Act of 1927 do? What were its limits?
3. What was changed by the Communications Act of 1934?
4. What is the Federal Communications Commission (FCC)?
5. What are the rules on concentration of radio ownership?
6. What came out of the chain broadcasting hearings?
7. What are the limits on freedom of speech on radio broadcasts?
8. What are the limits on freedom of speech in recordings?

Indecency in terms of speech is
graphic language that pertains to
sexual or excretory functions.

on Radio." Those prohibitions were challenged in court, but the FCC has maintained a policy of restricting speech that is considered **indecent**—that is, that uses graphic language pertaining to sexual or excretory functions. The FCC prohibits such language during daytime and evening prime time but has created late-night spots that are a "safe harbor" for more explicit or indecent kinds of speech. Despite the prohibition, "shock jocks" such as Howard Stern routinely violate the rule, are fined, and consider paying the fine as the cost of doing business.

Intellectual Property in Recordings and Radio

Reuse of copyrighted music, syndicated talk shows, news wire material, and other intellectual property has been a major issue for both radio and recordings. When artists record a piece of music written by someone else, whether for direct sale as a recording or on the radio, they have to obtain permission and usually pay a **royalty,** a fee required to use the writers' intellectual property. Some well-known court cases have been fought over whether an artist used another's basic melody. This problem has been accentuated with the rise of sampling in rap music and multimedia, where artists record and reuse bits or samples of existing works. Courts are trying to decide how much has to be sampled to require getting permission and payment of royalties.

More complex yet is the **licensing** of recorded music for play over the radio. Copyright law requires payment for performance of work copyrighted by an artist, including playing a recording over the radio. Two main music-licensing groups—the American Society of Composers, Authors and Publishers (ASCAP), and Broadcast Music Incorporated (BMI)— serve as intermediaries between recording artists and radio stations. Radio stations get licenses for the music listed by the music-licensing group in return for a fee, usually 1 to 2 percent of the station's gross income. ASCAP or BMI then pay the copyright holders, according to how often each song gets played.

Royalty is a fee required to use another person's intellectual property.

Licensing is an agreement granting permission to use a copyrighted or trademarked work, usually in return for an agreed-on fee.

SUMMARY & REVIEW

What Are the Main Points in the History of Audio Media?

What kind of music industry existed before the phonograph?
Music was performed live for audiences. It was also printed as sheet music and sold for home performance. The phonograph made passive listening easier and increased the sizes of audiences for any given piece of music.

How did radio change the music industry?
It further increased the reach of a particular musical piece or performance. It also increased the size of the audience to a truly mass audience. It created national audiences for music but also permitted regional genres—like country and western, bluegrass, and blues—to evolve.

What were the key developments that led to radio broadcasting?
The development of the vacuum tube by De Forest, Fessenden, and Armstrong was crucial. It permitted continuous sound-wave transmission and reception, beyond the on/off "spark gap" transmission that had sufficed for transmission of coded messages. Other crucial developments included better microphones, amplifiers, and tuners, and more powerful transmitters.

How did radio broadcasting and the recording industry affect each other in their early days?
At first, the sales of the recording industry fell off, as people moved to purchase radios instead. Over a slightly longer period, the recording industry relied on radio to make people aware of artists and recordings that they could purchase.

What was toll broadcasting, and how did it affect advertising on radio?

Toll broadcasting was an early form of advertising developed by AT&T. People paid to have messages and advertising carried by AT&T's radio network, rather like the toll paid to carry a message over the telephone. The term "commercial," often used to describe advertising, comes from AT&T's accounting terminology.

What were the main music genres in the 1920s and 1930s?

The most popular was probably big band jazz, particularly on the national radio networks. Country, bluegrass, blues, classical, Broadway tunes, and gospel were also popular.

Who formed the main radio networks?

The main radio networks were put together by David Sarnoff at RCA/NBC and William Paley at CBS.

What kinds of programming characterized radio networks during their highpoint?

Network radio relied largely on music but carried news, comedy, variety shows, soap operas, dramas, suspense, and action adventures as well. Many of those genres moved to television after 1948.

When and why did radio networks decline?

After television coverage and audiences began to grow, around 1948, network radio began to lose much of its audience to television. Some of the entertainment types it had relied on worked better for the mass audience with a visual component on television. Radio came to rely more on music, which could be programmed locally by disc jockeys playing records.

When did FM radio begin to increase in importance? And why?

FM radio began to increase as more receivers became available in the 1960s. It also prospered as FM stereo became more widely available and as concern with music quality increased among the audience.

What kinds of radio networks exist now?

Some of the traditional networks continued, although some like ABC created more specialized subnetworks. New networks were being created by new ownership groups, such as Infinity, around popular syndicated shows, such as Howard Stern's. National Public Radio also emerged as a significant new news and public affairs network, linking most of the nation's noncommercial or public radio stations.

What Were the Main Trends in Audio Technology?

How did phonograph formats change, from Victrola to long play?

The original Victrola played music off cylinders. A needle picked up vibrations from grooves in the surface. The music was not electronically amplified. The next phonographs used flat records. The next added electronic amplification of the sound. Speeds were reduced from 78 rpm to 331/3 rpm and records were made larger so that they could play more music, longer. Finally, stereo sound was introduced.

How do compact discs work?

While phonographs reproduce analog sound from grooves in records, CDs reproduce sound digitally, from ones and zeros recorded as pits on the CD surface. In most current stereos, the digital signal is then reconverted to analog form and sent as electrical impulses to the amplifier and then to the speakers.

How does magnetic recording on tape work?

The tape passes over a recording head, an electromagnet, that rearranges metallic particles in the tape according to modulated current produced by a microphone. When playing back, the tape runs over another electromagnetic head, which responds to the patterns stored on the tape and generates another modulated current that is sent to a loudspeaker.

What are the main technical differences between AM and FM radio transmission?
AM refers to amplitude modulation. The sound information is carried in variations in the height, or amplitude, of the radio wave. FM is frequency modulation. The sound information is carried in variations in the frequency of radio wave.

In general, AM signals carry farther than FM, which travels strictly in the line of sight, so there is more potential for frequency interference among AM stations. Therefore, fewer AM licenses can be granted in the same cities. FM has higher-fidelity sound characteristics than AM (e.g., a greater frequency range, cleaner sound, and less static), so stereo broadcasting was begun in FM.

What Are the Main Forms and Genres in Radio and Recorded Music?

What were the main original traditions in popular music?
Blues is an African American musical tradition, based primarily on guitar and distinctive plaintive lyrics. Gospel originated as southern Protestant religious music, with distinctive but related African American and white forms. Appalachian music developed from English, Scotch, and Irish roots with similar instrumentation and ballad forms.

What are radio formats?
Formats are a particular radio programming strategy oriented around a playlist of music and focused on a particular genre or audience.

How have radio formats changed after the decline of radio networks?
Radio programming became decentralized as local stations pulled away from networks. Stations began to decide on their own formats, responding to local audiences and local competition from other stations. As more stations entered the market, formats tended to become more narrowly focused or segmented.

What is the top 40?
Top 40 was characterized by playing only top single records, usually the top 40 on record sales charts, which gave the format its name.

How have radio formats evolved since 1970?
Radio formats have been following the evolution of pop and rock music since 1970. They have tended to follow the segmentation or fragmentation of the music and its audience.

This trend has been accentuated by a steadily increasing number of FM stations, which have had to specialize to find audiences.

What are the top formats now on FM? On AM?
On FM, the main formats are adult contemporary, a mix of oldies and softer rock hits; album-oriented rock (AOR), album cuts (often corresponding to videos) by current groups, split into heavy metal and other branches, including a mixture of oldies for older listeners; classic rock; classical music; urban contemporary, usually focused on African American music, rap, hip-hop, dance, and house, sometimes with Hispanic sounds. Several noncommercial patterns developed on the FM stations using frequencies reserved for noncommercial alternatives: classical music; experimental or alternative rock and folk, mostly found on college stations; jazz, found on both commercial and noncommercial stations; and news and public affairs.

Some formats are prominent on both FM and AM: top 40 or contemporary hit radio; country; middle-of-the road (MOR), a mix of softer current songs and oldies; talk, news, and weather, often mixed with AOR or MOR music, particularly on drive-time shows aimed at commuters; and Latino or Hispanic, subdivided into larger markets both by origin (Mexican, Cuban, Puerto Rican) and by music genres (dance music, traditional, Latin rock).

AM stations tend to emphasize news, call-in talk shows, and talk and sports, where music or sound quality matters less. Because of AM's broader signal reach, many AM stations also center on smaller towns and rural areas, where the population is less dense and where a broad-based, middle-of-the-road, country/western, or oldies format makes more sense.

Who Are the Audiences for Audio Media?

How have rock music audiences changed since the 1960s?
They have segmented or fragmented, fracturing the rock mass audiences into smaller groups, several of which are still mass audiences.

Where do people listen to radio most?
Only about 20 percent at most listen to radio networks; most listen to local formats, although the audiences for certain kinds of network programs, such as talk by Rush Limbaugh or Howard Stern, is growing. People listened

relatively more to radio in their cars (25 percent) and other locations (29 percent) and less at home (45 percent) in 1990 than they had in 1985.

Who listens to top 40? To album-oriented rock (AOR)?
Top 40 audiences tend to be younger and more female. AOR audiences are fragmenting, but tend to reach into slightly older age groups, from teenagers into the twenties, and are more male.

What Are the Key Aspects of Recording and Radio Industry Organization?

There are several key aspects of the recording industry: the talent (the singers and groups), the recording studios and technical producers, the recording company, the distributors, and retailers.

What are record labels?
Labels of record companies are particular names for a group of recordings, which usually follow a consistent line of music. One company may own several diverse labels.

How are records distributed and sold?
Record companies decide which albums and songs to promote through radio, billboards, newspaper ads, and magazine ads. An important part of this promotion is making a music video for MTV, VH-1, or other music-oriented cable channels. The record companies distribute recordings in a variety of ways: rack jobbers, retail music stores, big chain stores, and record clubs.

How do radio station affiliates relate to networks?
Affiliates in broadcasting are stations that contract to use the programming of and share advertising and financing with a network. Networks also have owned-and-operated stations (O&Os). Group owners own a number of broadcast stations but do not usually provide them with common programming, as a network would.

What Are the Main Issues in Radio and Recording Policy and Ethics?

What were the limits on government regulation in the Radio Act of 1912?
The Radio Act of 1912 was the initial government regulation for licensing of transmitters. However, it gave no clear power to the government for allocation of frequencies and no powers adequate to limit frequency interference.

What did the Radio Act of 1927 do? What were its limits?
The Radio Act of 1927 created a Federal Radio Commission, defined the broadcast band, standardized frequency designations, and limited the number of stations operating at night, when AM signals carried farther. It still did not create an adequate enforcement body with sufficient power to obtain compliance by stations.

What was changed by the Communications Act of 1934?
The Communications Act of 1934 created a more powerful regulatory body, the Federal Communications Commission (FCC). The FCC created more systematic procedures for granting radio licenses. It had adequate power to compel compliance with its rules on transmitter power, height, and frequency use that were designed to avoid frequency interference. The FCC created rules about ownership, concentration and cross-ownership, obscenity and indecency in radio content, and the role of networks and affiliates.

What was changed by the Telecommunications Act of 1996?
The Telecommunications Act of 1996 changed a number of FCC rules about ownership, competition, and frequency allocation. It made license renewal easier, created more flexibility in what stations can do with their spectrum to create new services, and created new rules for direct broadcast services.

What are the rules on concentration of radio ownership?

The 1996 Telecommunicatons Act eliminates previous station ownership limits. For radio, there are no national limits, and local ownership caps increase with market size from a total of five stations in a market with fourteen or fewer commercial stations to eight stations among forty-five or more stations. Cross-ownership of radio, television, and newspapers was deregulated in 1992, and cross-ownership with cable TV was deregulated in 1996.

What came out of the chain broadcasting hearings?

Chain broadcasting refers to radio networks and their control over talent and over affiliated stations. After the chain broadcasting hearings, the FCC limited network control over affiliates' program selections.

What are the limits on freedom of speech and radio broadcasts?

Up through the 1960s, certain words could not be used, and broadcasters were held respon-sible. Those prohibitions were challenged in court, but the FCC has maintained a policy of restricting speech that is considered indecent and graphic language pertaining to sexual or excretory functions. The FCC prohibits such language during daytime and evening prime time but has created late-night spots that are a "safe harbor" for more explicit or indecent kinds of speech.

What are the limits on freedom of speech in recordings?

The record industry had some self-censorship up through the 1960s. Groups that used obscene language or graphic sexual references were usually excluded from the major labels. That policy changed as many of the major rock groups carried by major labels began to use more graphic language and explicit themes. Congressional hearings in 1989 pushed for warning labels about explicit or graphic lyrics on record and CD covers. A number of record labels now place such warnings on covers, but their effectiveness has been questioned.

REFERENCES

Barnouw, E. (1966). *A history of broadcasting in the United States*. New York: Oxford University Press.

Belz, C. (1972). *The story of rock*. New York: Harper & Row.

Czitrom, D. (1982). *Media and the American mind*. Chapel Hill: University of North Carolina Press.

Dominick, J. (1993). *The dynamics of mass communication* (4th ed.). New York: McGraw-Hill.

Hart, M. (1990). *Drumming at the edge of magic*. New York: HarperCollins.

Head, S., & Sterling, C. (1989). *Broadcasting in America* (6th ed.). New York: Houghton Mifflin.

Head, S., Sterling, C., & Schofield, L. (1994). *Broadcasting in America* (7th ed.). New York: Houghton Mifflin.

Jones, S. (1992). *Rock formation: Music, technology and mass communication*. Newbury Park, CA: Sage.

Lewis, T. (1991). *Empire of the air*. New York: Harper.

Limmer, J. (Ed.). (1981). *The Rolling Stone illustrated history of rock and roll*. New York: Random House.

MacDonald, J. F. (1979). *Don't touch that dial! Radio programming in American life from 1920 to 1960*. Chicago: Nelson-Hall.

Sloan, W., Stovall, J., and Startt, J. (Eds.). (1993). *Media in America: A history* (2nd ed.). Scottsdale, AZ: Publishing Horizons.

Sterling, C., and Kittross, J. (1990). *Stay tuned—A concise history of American broadcasting*. Belmont, CA: Wadsworth.

Whetmore, E. J. (1981). *The magic medium: An introduction to radio in America*. Belmont, CA: Wadsworth.

Chapter 9

VISUAL MEDIA: TELEVISION, FILM, AND HOME VIDEO

C H A P T E R   P R E V I E W

This chapter will look at several aspects of film and television. First, we will look at the historical development of the industries and the major forms or genres of programming. We will also look briefly at the development of film, television, and video technologies; their audiences; industry organization; and some major issues—ownership concentration, diversity of content and ideas, free speech, and fairness.

Bountiful, Utah, 2010

Hey kids, let's try to watch something on the DeeVee together tonight instead of everybody heading off to their own rooms.

I don't know, Dad, this doesn't usually work out so well. What do you want to watch?

How about interactive NFL football? We could each be our favorite player on the Bountiful Rattlers. I don't think there's a game tonight, but we could pick a good one from last season.

You know I don't like football. How about the MTV family–rated music video channel?

Nah, that stuff's boring. How about *America's Funniest Pet Gladiators*?

You've got to be kidding. That one was such a bomb that the network dropped it already.

How about a nice old movie, like *Sound of Music*, interactive?

Come on, Mom, we already know that you want to be Julie Andrews. I guess it's okay if I can be the German bad guy.

Only I get to play around with the audio track on my own headset. Where's the keyboard and microphone?

There is a Rattlers game tonight. Can I just put it in a screen window? I promise I'll watch *Sound of Music* between plays.

Okay, but try to sing along with me on the good parts, okay?

I have *Sound of Music* available now. Do you want to pay $2 or accept two family ads, attention mandatory? There is an extra ad required for the football window.

I guess we can live with the ads. Roll it, DeeVee.

A BRIEF HISTORY OF TV AND FILM

The early years of film were marked by experimentation with content and forms, major technological innovations, and disputes over who could use, control, and benefit from the inventions. Thomas Edison and his assistant, Thomas Dickson, invented the kinetoscope **motion picture** camera in 1888, filming 15 seconds of an assistant, Fred Ott, sneezing. By 1900, Edison found himself competing with the Biograph and Vitagraph. The first battle ended in 1909 with an agreement to pool patents under the Motion Picture Patents Company (MPPC). The MPPC collected a fee from every film and distributed it to the inventors based on the number of patents they held. Although the MPPC tried to control the new film industry, independent producers used bootleg equipment and moved their base of operations from New York to Hollywood, where a new industry grew up away from the control of the old entertainment industries based in New York. Well before 1920, the MPPC lost its control.

For a while, most films simply showed audiences what events looked like, a kind of reportage of events in motion, such as horse races. By 1903 some films were developing more of a story line and plot. *The Great Train Robbery*, made by William S. Porter in 1903, was the first **story film** or "movie" and was very popular.

In 1915, *Birth of a Nation* by D. W. Griffith made another major step forward in film form and technique. Griffith used a large screen, well-produced outdoor battle scenes, moving shots, and close-ups. It was the first **feature film** and the most popular film in the United States for over twenty years. However, the film, set during and after the Civil War, features the Ku Klux Klan as its heroes and was used by them as a recruiting film. Although the film was revolutionary in form, it was racist in content, reflecting Griffith's own prejudices.

In the silent film era, film storytelling developed considerably. Films frequently borrowed or adapted plots from novels, using the actor's expressions and gestures, as well as music and subtitles, to tell the story. Movies became longer, audiences expected the medium to tell more complex stories. Films over one and a half hours long became known as feature films (Knight, 1979).

The Studio Era, 1919–1960

Star actors and actresses became very important to movies. Fan interest in stars was a good way to draw audiences to new movies. Rudolph Valentino, Lillian Gish, and Charlie Chaplin were such attractions that their names appeared above the name of the film on the theater marquees. The importance of the star actor or actress was linked to the rise of the studio system. The major movie studios grew by developing a stable of actors, writers, and directors who worked for them on a contract basis over a period of years. The studios rose on the basis of this **star system,** using the stars' popularity to promote their movies. The actors and directors in turn had a stable environment in which to work and develop.

The main studios were United Artists (initially formed by artists like Chaplin), Paramount, MGM (Metro Goldwyn Meyer), 20th Century Fox, Warner Brothers, Universal, Columbia, and RKO. Studio ownership overlapped distribution to and exhibition at theaters. Studios wanted to make sure that their movies were booked into enough theaters to ensure a profit.

Talking pictures created a revolution. The first was *The Jazz Singer* in 1927. Acting became less overstated and stylized. The actors' voices and the use of sound effects, as well

Motion pictures are the technical means for taking a series of photographs at a constant speed to portray motion.

Story films or "movies" introduced the idea of telling a story, usually fictional, with a plot and characters.

Feature films are longer story films, usually over one and a half hours or more.

Star system was the film studios' use of stars' popularity to promote their movies.

Talkies were films with synchronized soundtracks, which emphasized dialogue, singing, and music.

as music, became important. Some actresses and actors, like Greta Garbo, made a smooth transition, but many could not. The musical classic *Singing in the Rain* partially revolves around the fictional, but representative, story of an actress who looked good in silent films but had an unappealing voice and could not make it in talking (and singing) pictures. **Talkies** required an influx of new talent, such as James Cagney, Spencer Tracy, and Fred Astaire, who came mostly from theater and Broadway. The audience liked talkies and they made more money, so by 1930 almost all films were talkies.

The Great Depression began in 1929, and movies became an important escape from a depressing economic situation. Movies emphasized their new attraction, sound, by creating a series of extravagantly produced musicals, with lavish visuals, dancing, and singing. A series of films by Ginger Rogers and Fred Astaire, starting with *Flying Down to Rio* in 1933, epitomized the elegant escapism of the new talking, singing, and dancing movies. The pure fantasy of *The Wizard of Oz* (1939) is another enduring example of brilliant 1930s escapism.

The other main genres of the 1930s were adventure serials, comedies, and crime dramas. Several comedy subgenres were created. The zany comedies of the Marx Brothers, such as *Night at the Opera* (1935), poked fun at authority. Screwball comedies, such as *It Happened One Night* (1934), featured Clark Gable, Katharine Hepburn, Cary Grant, and other big stars in elegantly set and clever but silly stories. Crime stories, such as *Little Caesar* (1930), reflected a real-life increase in organized crime that grew with the prohibition of alcohol. Suspense and mystery stories, such as Alfred Hitchcock's *The 39 Steps* (1935), created another major genre of Hollywood films.

Historical epics were another specialty. The most successful film of the 1930s was *Gone with the Wind* (1939), set in the South during the Civil War, with a melodrama-like cast of archetypal characters: the swaggering, handsome hero Rhett and the strong-willed heroine Scarlett.

In the 1940s American movies matured. They began to tell stories that were much more complex, less escapist, and frequently darker and less optimistic. The classic film of the period was *Citizen Kane* by Orson Welles in 1941, which unfolds a fictionalized account of the life of William Randolph Hearst, the newspaper baron well known for sensationalism and

excess. Like *Birth of a Nation*, *Citizen Kane* innovated in several areas. In plot, the story works backward as a reporter pieces the tale together. The film uses sound effects, echoes, and music to enhance the storytelling. In technique, Welles created dozens of new effects, including zooms, radical changes of perspective through extreme close-ups, lighting effects, the use of shadows, and unusual camera angles.

The year 1941 also saw one of the classic detective films, *The Maltese Falcon*. Directed by John Huston, it featured Humphrey Bogart, who went on to star in several other classic 1940s films, including *Casablanca* (1942). A key genre variation on these detective films was the film noir, "the dark film," which tended to be more skeptical, even cynical, and had antiheroes instead of the simpler heroes of earlier films. Classics of the genre include *Double Indemnity* (1944), *Out of the Past* (1947), and *Gun Crazy* (1952).

FILM AND TELEVISION

Theatrical films are those released for distribution in movie theaters.

The year 1946 was the peak of audience exposure and financial success for **theatrical films** in the United States. Around 90 million Americans went to the movies every week. By 1948, the film industry already had to compete with television.

In the 1920s and 1930s, television developed technologically in a series of steps, largely by independent inventors Philo Farnsworth and Allen Dumont and by a group of engineers led by Vladimir Zworykin at RCA. In 1922 Farnsworth came up with the idea of scanning an image in a series of lines, reputedly by looking at rows in the plowed fields of his native Idaho.

Zworykin invented the iconoscope tube in 1923. Both Farnsworth and Zworykin developed the essential technology for a television camera—an electronic scanning system—while Dumont had developed the essential technology for a receiver picture tube. After a long, seven-party series of patent suits, Farnsworth was compensated $1 million for his claims by RCA, while Dumont went on to manufacture television receivers. In the meantime, television was moving ahead around the world. The first British broadcast was in 1935. The first U.S. broadcast was the Harvard-Yale baseball game in 1939.

NTSC is the U.S. television standard, developed in 1941 by the National Television Systems Committee.

The final standards for television were worked out by a government-mandated compromise committee, the National Television Systems Committee **(NTSC),** which represented fifteen manufacturers. The 1941 NTSC black-and-white television standards are still in use, specifically 525 lines per frame and 30 frames per second.

World War II put television on hold in the United States. Some experimental stations stayed on the air, while hundreds of license applications were pending. Even after the end of the war in 1945, the industry was still undecided on a color standard, and investors and advertisers were uncertain. CBS's color system was mechanical, involving a wheel, whereas

ONE OF THE PIONEERS OF TELEVISION WAS VLADIMIR ZWORYKIN, SHOWN HERE WITH HIS EXPERIMENTAL TELEVISION IN THE 1930S.

RCA's was electronic. A supplementary NTSC agreement in 1952 finally set an electronic color system (Sterling & Kittross, 1994).

In the late 1940s improved cameras and AT&T coaxial cable technology for connecting stations into networks reduced some of the uncertainty, and stations started to rush onto the air in 1948. However, it looked as if the existing FCC technical standards did not allow for nearly enough stations to cover the United States or prevent signal interference, so the FCC imposed a freeze on new station applications from 1948 to 1952. The 108 stations approved before the freeze continued operation, and the number of sets in homes rose dramatically from 250,000 in 1948 to 17 million in 1952, even though many cities were not covered yet. The spread of television in America is one of the fastest and widest diffusions of an innovation in history.

VHF stands for very high frequency, most widely known for use with television in channels 2 to 13.

UHF stands for ultra high frequency, most widely known for use with television in channels 14 to 69.

The 1952 FCC rules, known as the *Sixth Report and Order*, clarified the **VHF** (very high frequency) television band (channels 2–13) and opened the **UHF** (ultra high frequency) band (channels 14–83, later reduced to 69). The VHF allocations gave no more than three to four licenses to any city, which effectively limited the number of national television networks to three until much later, when UHF and cable TV developed. At first, only VHF stations developed because it was much more economical to broadcast an adequate signal for a reasonable distance on VHF.

Three television networks grew up after 1945, based on the three radio networks—NBC, CBS, and ABC, which was split off from being NBC's second network. (The Dumont Network was a short-lived attempt to start a fourth network.) In fact, much of the programming on television came over from radio. After 1960, much programming also came from the Hollywood film studios. At first, however, the film industry fought the audience's movement to television. The early developers of network television came from radio and theater in New York. They wanted to create something new, not just reflect the style of Hollywood.

TV—FROM NEW YORK TO HOLLYWOOD

Until 1956 most television was done live from New York. Many think of the 1950s as television's "Golden Age," primarily because it concentrated more on original drama. That was partially due to the early television audience, an affluent, educated, urban group who liked live drama. Programs such as *Studio One* and *Kraft Television Theater* featured such top playwrights as Rod Serling and Gore Vidal, along with Broadway acting stars. However, by 1957 nearly all entertainment production had moved to the West Coast to take advantage of the Hollywood talent pool. Network news and soap opera production stayed in New York. The networks produced the news, and the soaps were produced either by the networks or by advertising agencies or soap company sponsors for the networks. Other programs, including sitcoms, action adventures, made-for-TV movies, and dramas, were increasingly produced by film studios or independent television producers in Los Angeles for network use.

1950S TV PRESENTATIONS, SUCH AS THE *HALLMARK HALL OF FAME,* WERE SHOT LIVE.

Television also started using Hollywood feature films. In 1961 NBC started *Saturday Night at the Movies* to use movies that were often cheaper and better made than network series. As the stock of post-1948 feature films began to run down, NBC and others began to produce "made-for-television" movies. Heavy use of movies on network television continued into the mid-1970s, when both pay channels and superstations on cable TV began to drain off much of both the supply of and the audience for movies on "television."

Radio and Television

Many of the programs that television featured came from radio. Those included westerns such as *Gunsmoke* (1955–1975), soap operas such as *The Guiding Light*, and comedies such as *The Jack Benny Show* (1950–1977). The TV variety show came in part from radio but also reached further back to **vaudeville.** Many technicians, writers, directors, actors, musicians, and singers who developed early television programming had worked earlier in radio (Whetmore, 1981).

Vaudeville was a stage show of mixed specialty acts, such as songs, dances, skits, comedy, and acrobatics.

The film industry initially fought television by not releasing any of its new movies to television. Films made after 1948 had clauses in their contracts prohibiting release to television. The film industry was closely tied to theatrical chains that showed movies, and television quickly cut into their revenues. Furthermore, the government ordered studios to get out of at least one aspect of film business: production, distribution, or exhibition. As a result, Paramount sold off its exhibition chain, which merged with ABC television. As small theaters also closed all over America in the 1950s, the film industry began to realize that if they couldn't beat television, maybe it had better join it. Disney started producing programs for television in 1954, and other studios followed. By 1961 the film boycott of television was over.

As audiences got used to television, they began to demand something different from movies. Hollywood tried big-budget, lavish spectacles, like *Ben Hur* (1959). Hollywood could also include more controversial material than TV could, such as the sex in movies like the James Bond thriller *Goldfinger* (1964). Hollywood capitalized on the youth culture with *The Graduate* (1967) and *Easy Rider* (1969). Hollywood films also began to examine social issues, such as racial prejudice, in films like *Guess Who's Coming to Dinner* (1967). By the 1960s the power of the movie studios was declining. Independent producers gained more of a role in producing movies, film studios began to spend much of their time producing series for television, and the studio system died.

Network TV

RCA dominated the technology of television, but its network, NBC, did not really dominate programming or the audience. William Paley at CBS focused on programming, paying high salaries to attract stars away from NBC. As the television networks began to develop distinct characters, CBS and NBC dominated both the ratings and the race to gain affiliated stations. In fact, ABC was rumored close to bankruptcy more than once. In 1954 only 40 of 354 stations were primarily affiliated with ABC. ABC was originally the weaker of two networks owned by NBC. The ABC radio and television networks were split off from NBC in 1941 after the FCC **chain broadcasting** hearings and rules, which limited the networks' size and power (Head, Sterling, & Schofield, 1994). (In the early days of television, many stations were affiliated with one network but carried some programs from another network.)

Chain broadcasting refers to radio networks and their control over talent and affiliated stations.

Comedy dominated television programming from 1948 to 1957. Comedy star Milton Berle, "Uncle Milty," propelled NBC popularity. Berle was the forerunner of much current comedy. He told standup jokes and wore outrageous outfits, often dressing in drag. He was the kind of new entertainment phenomenon that drove people to buy televisions. Jerry Lewis and Bob Hope followed in Berle's footsteps. Comedy combined with music on NBC to form a number of variety shows. One of the driving forces in creating new directions in programming at NBC was Sylvester "Pat" Weaver. He introduced periodic specials and magazine programs like *Today* and *Tonight*, which dominated late-night television for many years (MacDonald, 1994).

CBS also had standup comics, such as George Burns and Gracie Allen, but CBS moved in a different direction by introducing **situation comedies,** such as Jackie Gleason's *Honeymooners*, still considered a classic of the genre. Sitcoms proved to be an economical and appealing comedy format over the long run. CBS also reintroduced westerns, such as *Gunsmoke* (1955–1975). CBS addressed itself to the rural and small-town nature of much

Situation comedies feature a group of characters in a comic situation dealing with new tensions or issues each episode.

JACKIE GLEASON'S *THE HONEYMOONERS* WAS ONE OF THE PIONEER SITUATION COMEDIES.

of the television audience in the 1960s with shows like *The Andy Griffith Show* (1960–1968) and *The Beverly Hillbillies* (1962–1971).

ABC began to bridge the gap with Hollywood by ordering the first television series produced by a film studio, *Disneyland*, by the Disney studio (1954–1957, later on NBC, 1961–1971, with a different title), followed a year later by *The Mickey Mouse Club* (1955–1959), and then a studio-produced western, *Cheyenne* (1955–1963). ABC aimed many of its programs, such as the Disney shows, *American Bandstand* (1957–1987), and *Maverick* (1957–1962), at a younger audience and worked on creating a niche in sports. In the late 1950s, ABC introduced more action adventure with *77 Sunset Strip* (1958–1964), *The Rifleman* (1958–1963), and *The Untouchables* (1959–1963); these kinds of programs brought ABC into a more competitive audience position.

Television was widespread in America by 1960. That year, 65 million people watched the presidential campaign debates between John F. Kennedy and Richard Nixon, one of a series of encounters between television and politics. Those who listened to the debates on radio were more likely to think Nixon had won than those who watched on television, where Kennedy was visually appealing while Nixon had jowls and a five o'clock shadow. Television later showed Kennedy's funeral in 1963 to a shocked nation, along with the civil rights movement in the South, the Vietnam War, and the domestic protest marches against it. Color broadcasting became increasingly common by 1965, adding to television's visual impact (Barnouw, 1990).

In the 1960s and 1970s, some television variety shows (such as *The Smothers Brothers,* 1967–1975), sitcoms, and dramas began to have a more critical and social point of view. The series *M*A*S*H* (1972–1983), about a field hospital in the Korean War, was a lightly

MURROW, McCARTHY, BLACKLISTS, AND POLITICS ON TV

Television confronted an ugly political crisis early in the 1950s. In the climate of the Cold War rivalry with the Soviet Union that began in 1948, several American politicians were crusading to expel from media or government any people they thought were sympathetic to the Soviet Union or to communism, its political philosophy. This crusade led to the "blacklisting" of a number of writers and performers who were suspected of being sympathetic to left-wing causes. Those blacklisted often lost their media jobs; some even committed suicide. Senator Joseph McCarthy (Republican, Wisconsin), chair of a Senate subcommittee on investigations, staged a number of public witch hunts. *McCarthyism* became a catchphrase for politically motivated persecution. Most of the Hollywood and television managers had gone along with the blacklisting, even creating their own in-house lists.

Edward R. Murrow of CBS News had become famous for his radio news coverage during World War II from London. His fame grew after a series of controversial and pointed documentaries and subjects of his regular news show, *See It Now*. Although others had criticized McCarthy, Murrow felt strongly that the news media were not standing up to McCarthy. In 1954, on *See It Now,* he used footage of McCarthy's own press conferences to expose the excesses and damages caused by the anticommunist crusade, which had destroyed the careers and lives of many people, on the basis of little evidence.

Others corroborated that McCarthy's charges and lists were often unfounded and the Senate ended up censuring or reprimanding him. To many, these events with Murrow and McCarthy demonstrated the growing power of television news in the 1950s.

JOSEPH MCCARTHY CAMPAIGNED AGAINST COMMUNISM IN SENATE SUBCOMMITTEE INVESTIGATIONS AND AT PRESS CONFERENCES.

concealed critique of the Vietnam War. Norman Lear's *All in the Family* (1971–1983) mixed humor with satire about racial bigotry, Vietnam, and the Nixon administration (1968–1974). However, many of the most popular 1970s programs, such as *The Brady Bunch* (1969–1974), were light entertainment (MacDonald, 1994).

The 1970s also brought changes in network strategy. ABC continued to pitch toward younger people with programs like *Happy Days* (1974–1984), which held the number one position in ratings for several years. ABC also succeeded in the new miniseries format, with programs such as *Roots* (1977), about the history of an African American family brought over to America as slaves. Over 140 million Americans saw at least part of *Roots* (1977), making it one of the major television successes of the 1970s.

HOLLYWOOD RECYCLES—SON OF ANDY GRIFFITH

In the 1960s network programming, particularly situation comedies, continued to be popular, but critics and even regular viewers began to find them repetitive. The long-running *Andy Griffith Show* (1960–1968), about a rural southern sheriff, spun off *Mayberry, R.F.D.* (1968–1971). *Andy Griffith* also encouraged the *Beverly Hillbillies* (remade as a feature film in 1993), *Petticoat Junction* (1963–1970), and *Green Acres* (1969–1971). The networks ran through other similar repetitive cycles, while successful westerns, cop shows, doctor shows, spy shows, hospital shows, and lawyer/courtroom shows spawned a host of imitations. A great deal of repetition also took place in soap operas, morning and late-night talk shows, game shows, and quiz shows.

TELEVISION AND VIETNAM

The year 1968 was a dramatic one for American television and American politics. It was the year of a heated presidential campaign, in which the Vietnam War was a major issue within the Democratic party, where several dissidents, including Eugene McCarthy and Robert Kennedy, challenged the incumbent, Lyndon Johnson. Television had been covering the increasing American casualties in Vietnam, with graphic footage of the dead and wounded. In 1968 the Vietcong (South Vietnamese guerrillas) and North Vietnamese, fighting the South Vietnamese and Americans, made a desperate, intense attack in a number of cities, called the Tet Offensive. Although it was probably a military disaster for the North Vietnamese, the bloody fighting shocked American viewers who had been told they were winning the war. Large televised antiwar demonstrations in the United States also

disturbed both the public and decision makers, who were further disturbed by the 1968 assassinations of Robert F. Kennedy and Martin Luther King, Jr. Public opinion began to turn against the war and Lyndon Johnson announced that he would not continue to run for reelection; television clearly had a major role in both events.

Public Television

The current idea of public television began with the recommendations of the Carnegie Commission on Educational Television in 1967, followed by the Public Broadcasting Act of 1967. It established a funding agency, the Corporation for Public Broadcasting (CPB), followed in 1969 by the Public Broadcasting Service (PBS)—the network coordinator of public stations. Some of the major PBS stations, such as WGBH-Boston, emerged as program producers. Some programs, such as *Sesame Street* (1969–), came from Children's Television Workshop; public affairs programs by Bill Moyers and others came from WNET in New York. British programs, including *Upstairs, Downstairs* (1974–1975), were shown in the *Masterpiece Theatre* series.

Cable, Video, and Segmented TV

By the late 1970s and early 1980s, television was pressed by competition from cable TV and rented videotapes. Cable TV boomed as a source of viewing alternatives to network television, particularly after the launch of nationwide service by Home Box Office (HBO) in 1975. Videocassette recorders (VCRs) also became more widespread in American homes throughout the 1980s (see Table 9.1). People used VCRs to record and replay favorite shows off television or cable and to view movies rented from video stores. **Independent stations,** usually on UHF, began to show more old movies and reruns of hit series from syndication services. All these choices began to pull viewers away from the three networks. By the early 1990s, the networks had under 60 percent of the television viewing audience, although they continued to get most of the advertising. However, in 1993–1994, the steady erosion of the audience for the main three networks stopped.

Independent stations are those not affiliated with a network.

The response of the three main television networks was less original network programming and more concentration on a steady evening flow of the formulas or genres that get a consistent response. Research showed less program diversity in the late 1970s than in the 1950s or 1960s. Critics charged that those remaining formulas were largely centered on sex and violence. For instance, the fall 1983 network prime-time schedule included such programs as *The A-Team* (1983–1987) and *Magnum, P.I.* (1980–1988), which relied on action, violence, and sex appeal. A 1983 National Association of Broadcasters study also noted that viewers rejected network programming for too much sex and violence, too few family programs, and "sillier and more juvenile" comedies.

The networks did try some new formulas (Gitlin, 1985). They brought in evening soap operas, such as *Dallas* (1978–1991), which succeeded very well in the 1980s. They also began to target African American audiences, who tended to be somewhat more loyal network viewers, with programs such as *The Cosby Show* (1984–1992) and with increasing numbers of strong black characters in dramas like *Hill Street Blues* (1981–1987) and *Miami Vice* (1985–1989). In the 1990s, the networks were relying less on fiction, such as sitcoms and dramas, and more on talk shows and "reality" programs, such as *Rescue 911* (1991–) and *Cops* (1989–).

TABLE 9.1. TV AND FILM MILESTONES

Year	Event
1888	Edison develops motion picture camera
1900	Edison, Biograph, and Vitagraph compete
1903	*The Great Train Robbery*
1905	Nickelodeon era
1915	*Birth of a Nation* first feature film
1922	Technicolor introduced
1923	Zworykin invents iconoscope tube
1927	Farnsworth applies for TV patent
1927	*The Jazz Singer* is first "talkie"
1930	Almost all films talk
1939	*Gone with the Wind*
1941	*Citizen Kane*
1946	Peak of film box office—90 million attend weekly
1948–1952	Television takes off
1954	Disney studio makes *Disneyland* for ABC
1960	Kennedy-Nixon debates on TV
1965	Color television broadcasting increases
1968	TV coverage of Vietnam Tet Offensive
1968	MPAA movie ratings introduced
1980s	VCRs diffuse widely
1982	*E.T.* box office and video champ
1987	Fox television network debuts

1. What innovations did D. W. Griffith add to silent films?

2. What was the studio system? Which were the main studios?

3. What changed with talking pictures?

4. What were the main film genres of the 1930s and 1940s?

5. Why did the FCC freeze television licenses from 1948 to 1952?

6. What is the NTSC standard? How was it developed?

7. How did Hollywood and its films change after television?

8. When did the studio system decline?

9. How have cable and video affected television programming?

10. What enabled a fourth network, Fox, to finally succeed?

Camera tube transforms light into electrical impulses.

Scanning samples a certain number of lines per frame by the electron beam.

Picture tube fires an electron gun at dots on the inside of the TV screen, which glow with varying intensity to create an image.

Frequency bands are parts of the electromagnetic spectrum authorized for a particular purpose.

Standards rules, developed in 1952 by the FCC, created new UHF channels and clarified channel separation to avoid interference for the VHF channels.

Curiously enough, this flat time for network television was when the latest attempt to start a fourth network finally succeeded. In 1987 Rupert Murdoch started the Fox television network. One reason for its success was cable TV. Most Fox affiliates were independent UHF stations, which cable brought to a wide range of homes with perfect picture quality. Fox benefited from a network writers' strike in 1988 that resulted in more network reruns. But more important, it pursued a segmented television strategy by pursuing younger viewers with shows like *Beverly Hills 90210* (1990–), and more urban and racially diverse audiences with programs like *In Living Color* (1990–). Fox also pushed the limits of sexual innuendo and good taste with such programs as *Married . . . with Children* (1987–) and *The Simpsons* (1989–).

TELEVISION TECHNOLOGY TRENDS

The first key element required for television was the **camera tube**. It became the source of an early 1920s patent dispute between the independent inventor Philo Farnsworth and Vladimir Zworykin at RCA. Farnsworth and Zworykin had both developed the essential technology for a television camera—an electronic **scanning** system. The camera tube has to transform light into an electrical charge, which can be scanned by an electron beam. The beam causes a discharge of energy that turns the energy stored by each point of light into electrical voltage variations. The number of lines of resolution, 525 for NTSC, are the lines per frame scanned by the electron beam and later reproduced by the picture tube in the receiver.

In the 1920s, Allen Dumont had developed the essential technology for a receiver **picture tube**. The picture tube fires an electron gun at dots of a special material on the inside of the screen, which glow with varying intensity to create an image. Later color television tubes worked by firing three color guns—red, green, and blue—at the screen. The eye blends these primary colors to make various hues (Head, Sterling, & Schofield, 1994).

The television broadcast signal works a lot like AM radio, except that variations in the amplitude of light and dark values of the picture are converted to electrical voltages and placed on a high-frequency carrier wave for transmission (see Figure 9.1). Sound is added in an FM signal carried in the upper part of the television channel.

Television is transmitted in two **frequency bands**: VHF (very high frequency) and UHF (ultra high frequency). There are a maximum of twelve VHF channels: channels 2 to 13, in the frequencies 54–72, 76–88, and 174–216 MHz. (FM radio is sandwiched in between at 88 to 108 MHz.) Being lower on the frequency band, VHF requires much less power than UHF to cover a similar distance. There are currently 56 UHF channels: channels 14 to 69, in the frequencies 470–806 MHz.

The 1952 FCC television **standards rules** created new channels in the UHF band and clarified channel separation to avoid interference for the twelve VHF channels. These rules, coupled with the FCC desire to spread channels to different cities within geographic regions to emphasize localism, created a situation in which no city or market had more than four VHF channels and most had less. (This more or less determined that three commercial networks

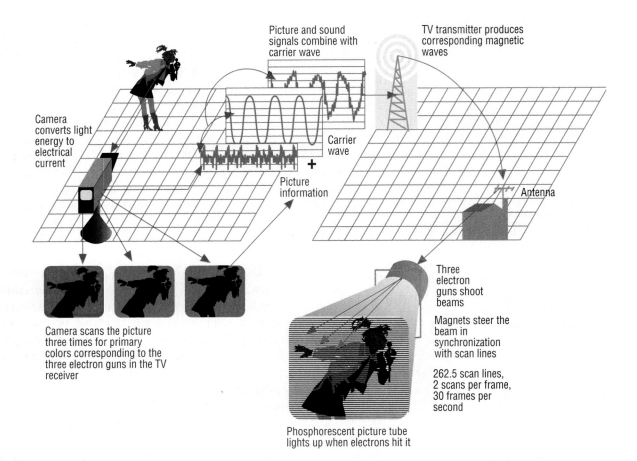

Picture and sound signals combine with carrier wave

TV transmitter produces corresponding magnetic waves

Camera converts light energy to electrical current

Carrier wave

Picture information

Antenna

Camera scans the picture three times for primary colors corresponding to the three electron guns in the TV receiver

Three electron guns shoot beams

Magnets steer the beam in synchronization with scan lines

262.5 scan lines, 2 scans per frame, 30 frames per second

Phosphorescent picture tube lights up when electrons hit it

FIGURE 9.1
A BROADCAST TELEVISION SIGNAL GOES FROM THE CAMERA THROUGH STATION/ NETWORK EDITING TO THE TRANSMITTER, THROUGH THE AIR TO AN ANTENNA, TO THE TV SET.

would evolve, since the fourth VHF frequency was for education or public channels.) The FCC also initially reserved roughly 10 percent of the channels for education purposes, mostly in the UHF band, and later reserved more.

TV Production Technology

By 1957 magnetic tape technology had improved to the point where it was useful for television. Both RCA and Ampex developed videotape recorder technology, pooled patents in 1957, and quickly sold equipment to the networks. The networks saw the advantages for production, in making editing and special effects much easier.

For videocassette recorder technology, another breakthrough was required to reduce the width of the tape required to store adequate video information. Previous technologies required huge reels of 2-inch tape. **Helical scanning** stores video frames at a slant, like cutting up tape and stacking it slantwise, enabling the length to shrink.

Helical scanning stores video frames at a slant, like cutting up tape and stacking it slantwise.

HDTV (high-definition television) uses more scanning lines or more pixels to provide a clearer and more detailed television picture.

High-Definition TV

One of the major recent television debates is over when and how to improve the original NTSC television resolution standards from 525 lines per frame to something with more lines, which would provide higher definition, a clear and more detailed television picture, usually called **HDTV** (high-definition television). The Japanese proposed a new standard in 1981 that would have 1,125 lines per screen and a more rectangular aspect, like that of a movie screen rather than the almost-square picture of the NTSC television. Their system, called MUSE, needed a wider channel than NTSC in the United States and would have outdated all existing equipment. It was also based on improved but conventional analog scanning technology.

Digital TV

In 1994 the United States rejected the Japanese HDTV proposal in favor of developing a more advanced digital TV system, which could be more easily integrated with computer equipment. That has the advantage of facilitating digital media convergence between television, computer media, multimedia, and information services that is currently being promoted in the United States. It is also a technology in which the United States has more relative advantage, based on its strength in computer research and manufacturing.

Digital technology is based on the computer processing system of converting all information into on/off signals or the "ones and zeros" of binary numbers, which are the basis of computer languages. Just as audio CD technology "samples" sound waves and turns those samples into digital information, **digital television** cameras sample pictures by cutting them up into thousands of elements (pixels) and assigning a number to each point or piece. This has several advantages: (1) it enables noise and distortion to be prevented or edited out; (2) it permits computers to manipulate images for special effects; and (3) it integrates images sampled by cameras with images, such as animation and graphics, created by computer programs.

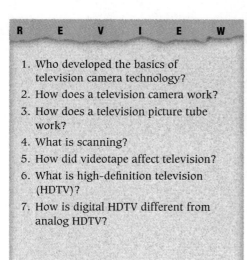

Digital television cameras sample pictures by cutting them up into thousands of elements (pixels) and assigning a binary number to each point.

R E V I E W

1. Who developed the basics of television camera technology?
2. How does a television camera work?
3. How does a television picture tube work?
4. What is scanning?
5. How did videotape affect television?
6. What is high-definition television (HDTV)?
7. How is digital HDTV different from analog HDTV?

Desktop Video

One of the results of digital video is that "television" switching, character generation, special effects, and animation can increasingly be done on desktop computers—such as the Video Toaster, on the Amiga computer—that are becoming increasingly inexpensive. Miniaturized solid-state cameras and other production components have also dropped in price, permitting more people to begin to do the kind of video productions that had required expensive studio production only a few years ago.

GENRES OF FILM AND TV

Genres are types or formats of media content.

Film formed a number of classic types or **genres** that still greatly affect film and other media. Current films, television series, made-for-TV movies, miniseries, and even new forms of video and multimedia production often follow classic film formulas. Film genres use formulas that conform to patterns that audiences expect to see. The formulas use certain kinds of narratives, images, settings, characters, plot themes, music, and effects. In a horror film, for example, people expect to see riveting and frightening images, hear creepy music, see scary characters, experience a tense plot, and see certain kinds of characters threatened. While writers and producers are always looking for new angles, they must still meet certain kinds of audience expectations.

Westerns, science fiction, mysteries, horror, and situation comedies are all forms or genres. Film critics, scholars, and fans enjoy arguing about whether a certain film is this or that genre. For instance, is *Star Wars* (1977) really science fiction, or is it a western dressed

MANY OF THE MOVIE GENRES WE ARE FAMILIAR WITH TODAY ORIGINATED IN THE SILENT ERA, INCLUDING WESTERNS, EPICS, HORROR, AND SCIENCE FICTION.

in science fiction costumes? The real point of genre categories is to better understand how the formulas work and what effect the shows have on their viewers. For instance, one of our colleagues likes to argue that you can better understand how the television series *Dallas* worked for the audience if you think of it as a western, not as a soap opera (Gitlin, 1986).

Films Set the Patterns

Silent films set down some classic genre formulas that are still followed. Because they had to rely on visuals, with little written dialogue, they were oriented toward action and lavish sets. The silent genres included:

- Westerns, such as *The Great Train Robbery* (1903)
- War movies, with battles and character conflicts, such as *Birth of a Nation* (1915)
- Romances—love stories such as *The Sheik* (1921)
- Physical comedies, with car crashes and pratfalls, such as the Keystone Cops shorts
- Gestural comedies, with reliance on facial expression and body language, such as Charlie Chaplin or Buster Keaton films
- Historical costume dramas, with fictionalized plots, such as D. W. Griffith's *Intolerance* (1916)
- Documentaries, such as *Nanook of the North* (1921)

- Newsreels that showed filmed weekly news updates
- Action/adventure, such as Douglas Fairbanks's *Thief of Bagdad* (1921)
- Melodramas, such as *The Perils of Pauline* (1914)

When "talkies" came in, new genres emphasized the advantages of the new medium, such as musicals, with singing and dancing, and more verbal comedies, with jokes as well as sight gags. Sound, dramatic visuals, and action were combined in increasingly complex formulas that often addressed concerns of the day (or at least of the decade). These new genres included:

- Crime dramas, with cops, gangsters, and violence, such as *Little Caesar* (1930)
- Screwball comedies, with glamour and light humor, such as *It Happened One Night* (1934)
- Character studies, such as *Citizen Kane* (1941)
- Detective movies, with complex heroes, such as *The Maltese Falcon* (1941)
- Youth rebellion movies, such as *The Wild One* (1954)
- Spy stories, with gadgets and action, such as the James Bond films
- Suspense, such as Alfred Hitchcock's *Vertigo* (1958)
- Romantic comedies, with varying degrees of sex, such as *Pillow Talk* (1959)
- Science fiction, such as *Forbidden Planet* (1956) or *Terminator* (1984)
- Monster movies, such as *King Kong* (1933)
- Horror movies, such as *Dracula* (1931)
- Slasher movies, such as *Friday the Thirteenth* (1980)
- Musicals, such as *South Pacific* (1958)
- Rock music movies, such as *A Hard Day's Night* (1964)
- Black audience or "blaxpoitation" movies, such as *Superfly* (1972)
- Spanish-language movies, such as *El Mariachi* (1992)

- Other foreign-language films

- Coming-of-age movies, in which teenagers discover things about themselves, such as *The Breakfast Club* (1985)

- Antiwar movies, such as *Apocalypse Now* (1979)

- Sword and sorcery movies, with magic and muscles, such as *Conan, the Barbarian* (1982)

- Disaster movies, such as *The Towering Inferno* (1974)

- Buddy movies, with pals on the road together, such as *Thelma and Louise* (1991)

Often successful movies use elements of various formulas. For instance, George Lucas's *Star Wars* movies are among the most successful films ever. They are primarily science fiction but also incorporate elements of westerns, World War II bomber and aircraft carrier movies, romantic comedies, hero quests, coming-of-age sagas, good guys versus bad guys, gunslinger movies, and samurai movies.

From Radio and Film to Television

Television was affected most in its beginnings by radio. A number of genres and even specific programs came straight from network radio programming to television in the 1950s. These genres included:

- Variety shows, such as *The Ed Sullivan Show* (1948–1971), which gave the Beatles their first U.S. television exposure

- Comedy shows dominated by a single comic, such as Red Skelton (1951–1971)

- Ensemble comedies with a group of comics, such as Sid Caesar's *Your Show of Shows* (1950–1954) or *Saturday Night Live* (1979–)

- Situation comedies, revolving around an ongoing plot, such as *The Honeymooners* (1955–1971) and *I Love Lucy* (1951–1961)

- Soap operas—daily melodramas selling soap to housewives—such as *The Guiding Light* (1952–)

- Dramas, such as *Kraft Television Theater* (1947–1958) or *The Waltons* (1972–1981)

- Western dramas, such as *Gunsmoke* (1955–1975)

- Mysteries, such as *Alfred Hitchcock Presents* (1955–1986)

- Science fiction, such as *The Twilight Zone* (1959–1987)

- Detective series, such as *Kojak* (1973–1978)

- Adventure series, such as *Adventures of Superman* (1951–1957)

- Talk shows, both morning and evening, such as *Today* (1952–) and *The Tonight Show* (1962–)

- Sports presentations

- News—many newspeople moved from radio to television

R E V I E W

1. What were some of the main silent film genres?
2. What genres came in with talking films?
3. What film genres contributed to television genres?
4. What radio programs and genres moved over to television?
5. What kinds of genres has television developed on its own?

- Public affairs programs, such as Edward R. Murrow's *See It Now*
- Documentaries

The film industry has also fed most of its movies and its formulas into television in one way or another, including:

- News—film newsreels affected TV news' visual style.
- Musicals—despite some efforts, musicals never did well on TV, with the exception of shows like *The Monkees* (1966–1968).
- Animation—cartoons, developed into series forms, from *The Flintstones* (1960–1973) to *Ren and Stimpy* (1993–)

What TV Has Created on Its Own

During the 1960s and 1970s, television made dramas and situation comedies out of the kinds of dramatic situations that people were more familiar with—courtrooms, hospitals, and police stations. Building on some roots in radio and film adventure stories, a general action adventure genre developed with a number of predictable formulas involving chases and good guy/bad guy characterizations, but subtypes focusing on cops, doctors, and lawyers also diversified into separate genres. TV's genres have included:

- Action adventure shows, usually centered on car chases and detectives—from *Dragnet* (1952–1970) to *NYPD Blue* (1993–)
- Medical programs—dramas centered on doctors, such as *Marcus Welby, M.D.* (1969–1976), or on hospitals, such as *St. Elsewhere* (1982–1988)
- Legal dramas—dramas centered on lawyers and courtrooms, such as *Perry Mason* (1957–1974) and *L.A. Law* (1986–1994)
- Prime-time soaps—dramas that used elements of melodrama (romances, rivalries), such as *Dallas* (1978–1991)
- Game shows that use visual as well as dialogue, such as *Wheel of Fortune* (1983–)
- Reality programs, which first brought real-life stories to the studio—*Queen for a Day*—but now chase it down or recreate it—*Rescue 911* (1989–)

TABLE 9.2. TV PRIME-TIME GENRES AND AUDIENCES

Genre	Number of Programs	Percentage of Average Audience
Situation comedy	43	11.9
General drama	18	9.7
Suspense/mystery	13	9.2
Feature films	6	13.2
Variety	5	9.0
Adventure	3	6.8

Source: A. C. Nielson, October 1992

Genres and Audiences

Showings of feature films tend to draw the biggest share of network television audiences, but situation comedies are the dominant program form or genre in prime time. Nielsen ratings data for October 1992 (see Table 9.2) showed the lineup between prevalence of genres in prime time and their audiences.

TABLE 9.3. AVERAGE HOURS SPENT USING MEDIA, 1985 AND 1990

Medium	1985	1990	Percentage Change
Television	1,530	1,470	−4
Network affiliates	985	780	−21
Independents+Fox	335	340	+2
Basic cable programs	120	260	+117
Pay cable programs	90	90	0
Radio	1,190	1,135	−5
Home video	15	50	+233
Movies	12	12	0
Total	3,307	3,262	+1

Sources: Veronis, Suhler & Associates; A. C. Nielsen; RADAR; Newspaper Advertising Bureau; Magazine Publishers Association; Gallup; MPAA; Television Bureau of Advertising; Leo Shapiro and Associates; Wilkovsky Gruen and Associates.

Zapping or channel surfing uses remote controls to browse briefly through a number of channels, viewing short bits of each.

AUDIENCES FOR FILM AND TELEVISION

Americans are well equipped for television. Almost all U.S. households have at least one television (98.3 percent), and almost all of those are color sets (98 percent). Around two-thirds of U.S. households have two or more television sets, more than two-thirds have remote controls (to facilitate **zapping** or **channel surfing**), and over four-fifths have video-cassette recorders. In about 64 percent of American homes, broadcast television has to compete with cable TV.

Most people still watch network television more than cable TV or independent stations. However, both cable and independents have cut into network television's share of the audience, which went from 90 percent of the prime-time audience in 1979 to around 60 percent in 1993. Although most people still watch over four hours of television per day, a decreasing amount comes from broadcast television networks or independent stations (see Table 9.3).

Television viewing in general is highest among families with children, among older people, and among women. It is lower among better-educated and higher-income viewers. Families with "basic" cable watch more total television that those with just over-the-air television, and those with pay cable watch substantially more yet. Network audiences tend to be highest compared to cable among urban, minorities, and lower income (Comstock, 1989).

Films are now viewed primarily on television, cable, or video. The average amount of time spent watching films on video has increased dramatically in the last decade. Film viewing at theaters is now most common among people in their teens and twenties.

Even before cable TV broke the audience into smaller segments, the television audience was already differentiating in terms of who watched what. In general, news is less popular than drama, suspense, mystery, sitcoms, variety shows, or feature films, especially among younger viewers and teenagers. Still, television is most people's main source of news. Sitcoms and movies appeal most to younger viewers, whereas variety and news appeal most to older viewers. Sports appeal more to men; drama and soap operas more to women.

Network television audiences tend to be older. Fox and ABC have both played to, and attracted, younger viewers, but older people subscribe to and watch cable TV less frequently than younger viewers. Women also seem slightly more likely to watch network television, although that is less the case among younger viewers.

REVIEW

1. What are the most popular prime-time television genres?
2. Is the network television audience growing or declining? Why?
3. How do network audiences differ from cable audiences?

INDUSTRY ORGANIZATION

Now that we've explored the history and genres of visual media, we'll take a closer look at how the film and TV industries are organized.

The Film Industry

Today the film industry is a high-volume mixture of big and little players. There are eight major producers: the old-time studios—Columbia, Fox, MGM, Paramount, Universal, and Warner Brothers—plus Buena Vista (Disney) and Tri-Star (Sony). They each produce fifteen to twenty-five movies per year, or about half of the roughly 400 feature films released annually by Hollywood. At the height of Hollywood's fame in 1946, the major studios produced forty to fifty movies per year. The **majors** invest an average of about $20 million per film, plus high overhead to keep the studio organizations running, so the stakes are very high and the pressure to produce big hits is enormous.

There is also an extensive, much less formal network of **independent** filmmakers. These "indies" usually produce films for much less than the majors, often a few million dollars. A classic pattern is that new filmmakers eke out a hodgepodge of financing for their first film. If that succeeds, they might get studio backing for subsequent films. For example, Michigan student filmmaker Sam Raimi borrowed money from friends to make *Evil Dead* (1983), which succeeded well enough in the horror film market to get more money for *Evil Dead II* (1987) and major studio financing for *Darkman* (1990). Likewise, Spike Lee made *She's Gotta Have It* (1986) for $200,000, but the film made $7 million, so Columbia produced his next, *School Daze* (1988). While independent filmmakers and smaller production houses have grown in power since the 1960s, accounting for about half of the movies that are distributed, they have a shaky existence, often doing only as well as their latest films.

Independent studios Carolco, which produced the *Terminator* movies, and Orion, which had *Dances with Wolves* (1990) and others, hovered on the brink of bankruptcy in 1992 until they were bought by Ted Turner.

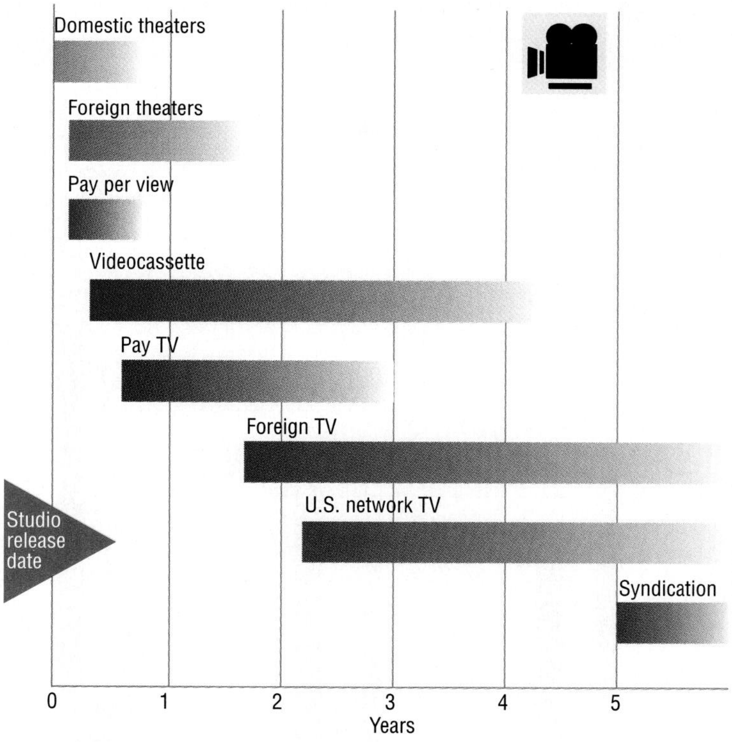

The major studios still control most film distribution, as they have since the 1920s. That gives them a stake in many of the independent films that they distribute, but it also gives them more control than independent filmmakers think is healthy.

However, there are also more options now. The archetypal distribution for a major film might be theatrical distribution, then pay cable, videocassette sales, network showings, basic cable networks, and finally, syndication (see Figure 9.2). Films are distributed to a series of **windows** or times linked to specific channels, such as theaters, video, and cable. There may be some variations on the exact order, depending on whether basic cable networks outbid a broadcast network for rights, for instance. Many films are not seen as worth the promotional costs for theatrical release and go straight to video stores and cable. A quick walk through any video rental store or channel surfing through late-night cable will

Major film producers are the larger studios that each produce fifteen to twenty-five movies per year.

Independent filmmakers ("indies") usually produce fewer films and for much less than the majors, often a few million dollars.

Windows are times in the film release sequence for showing films in theaters, on pay per view, and so on.

FIGURE 9.2
FILMS ARE NOW RELEASED IN A SERIES OF WINDOWS TO A VARIETY OF MEDIA.

unearth many teenage beach comedies and low-budget horror films that never make it to the theaters but still turn a profit in the more complex film distribution business.

The economics of the film business have changed with the rise in the importance of videocassette releases (see Figure 9.3). In 1985 box office revenues for films were $3.4 billion, compared to $2.6 billion for home video. By 1990 that difference had reversed to $3.8 billion for box office (about the same as in 1985), but $4.3 billion for home video revenues. Projected spending for 1995 was $6.9 billion for box office and $16.9 billion for home video. Home video revenues for films now exceed both box office sales and sales to television.

For years, one of the most powerful forces in the entertainment industry has been the Motion Picture Association of America (**MPAA**), along with the essentially overlapping Motion Picture Export Association of America (**MPEAA**). The MPAA, composed of the major film studios, has been a major player in American culture and politics. Its president, Jack Valenti, has been a highly effective lobbyist in Washington for years. In 1993, for example, he argued against any kind of restrictions on violence in film or television programming (since the MPAA members also produce much of American television network programming). The MPEAA has had a similar effect overseas, where they have lobbied hard for American film interests. When one of the authors lived in Brazil, for instance, the MPEAA representative was known as the "ambassador from Hollywood" and was sometimes reputed to have more clout than the regular American ambassador, since the one from Hollywood could arrange private screenings of new films for representatives and diplomats.

MPAA (Motion Picture Association of America) is a sales and lobby organization that represents the major film studios.

MPEAA (Motion Picture Export Association of America) is a sales and lobby organization that represents film studios overseas.

FIGURE 9.3
VIDEOCASSETTE RENTALS HAVE OVERTAKEN THEATRICAL BOX OFFICE TICKET SALES AS THE MAIN SOURCE OF REVENUE.

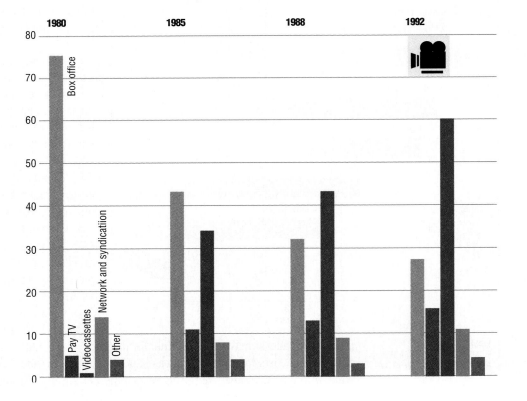

The Television Industry

The television industry is organized differently at several levels: production, distribution, and station or network broadcast or exhibition. A few television programs are produced locally. In fact, local news production increased considerably in the 1980s, from around an hour to two or more. Local news is profitable, because it is popular, it is increasingly affordable to produce (given declining equipment costs), and the advertising revenue goes to the local station—it is not shared with the network or a program syndicator (Gitlin, 1985).

Stations also show an increasing amount of **syndicated programming**. These are either reruns of programs previously aired on networks or "new" programs produced by independent production companies, usually talk shows such as *Geraldo* and *Oprah*, game shows such as *Wheel of Fortune* and *Jeopardy*, or "reality" programs like *Rescue 911*. These programs are made by various production companies, then distributed through syndicators, which are usually separate specialized companies. Stations either simply pay for the programs ("cash"), pay a reduced price plus show some advertisements or commercial spots arranged by the syndicator ("cash plus barter"), or pay nothing but give the syndicator more commercial minutes to sell to national advertisers ("barter"). Independent stations rely heavily on syndication, and network affiliates increasingly drop network programming in favor of syndicated programs that they think will draw bigger audiences.

Networks supply a great deal of programming to their **O&O's** (network owned-and-operated stations) or affiliates. The networks themselves produce news programs, sports events, some talk shows, some soap operas, documentaries, and a few series. Most entertainment programs are purchased by networks from film studio production units, such as Disney, Paramount, or Universal, or from independent producers such as Lorimar, MTM (Mary Tyler Moore) Productions, or New World TV. New rules passed by Congress on syndication in 1993 will permit networks to own or have a financial interest in more of the programs they show.

Advertisers. In 1990 television advertising revenue was $28.6 billion, which is a lot of money, even if cable TV and other "television" technologies are beginning to cut into television's advertising base. Advertising money still goes disproportionately to network television. However, cable TV advertising was growing rapidly.

The advertising money comes at three levels: national advertisers, national spot or regional advertisers, and local advertisers:

- National advertisers sell general consumption items, such as soft drinks or cars, that should reach a broad national audience. They usually buy advertising time on national television networks.

- National spot or regional advertisers usually sell things with a more regionalized or localized appeal, such as surfboards or snow tires. They usually buy spots in specific regions on both network affiliates and independent stations.

- Local advertisers, such as automobile dealers or supermarkets, sell a variety of things to local customers. They usually buy ads on local stations, either network affiliates or independents. These kinds of ads can be placed in network programming in those spots not occupied by network-arranged ads or during locally programmed news and syndicated programs.

Syndication is rental or licensing of media products by their producers to other media companies for broadcast, distribution, or exhibition.

O&O's are stations owned and operated by networks.

The Networks, the Affiliates, and the Independents. At the local level, most commercial television stations have an administrative or managerial structure, a sales force to sell local advertising, engineering or technical staff for studio and transmitter operations, a news operation, and a production staff for news and other programming. Stations also usually have contracts out for network affiliation (unless they are independent), research and ratings services, programming consultants, and legal services.

Independent stations buy most of their programming from syndication services and sell nearly all of their advertising in the local, regional, or national spot markets. So they actually need more complex programming operations than network affiliates, who take most of their programming from the networks. They also may need a larger advertising sales force, as again they do not have a network to provide national advertising. Independents are usually UHF channels, since most of the VHF channels have network affiliations. Network affiliates are more profitable, although independents have improved in the last ten years. Still, when the Fox network recruited affiliates in the late 1980s, largely out of the ranks of independent UHF stations, the stations were happy to sign up, since that improved their financial prospects and, to some degree at least, simplified their programming task. In 1995 two new networks, based at Warner Bros. and Paramount Studios, are trying to find affiliates to create national coverage.

More than 80 percent of all commercial television stations are affiliated with one of the networks: NBC, CBS, ABC, or Fox. The networks have a more complex operation than does a station. One division usually manages their owned-and-operated stations, another part deals with affiliate relations, and another handles the technical operations of network program delivery. The networks' sales staff works with national ads and advertising agencies. In programming, their staff works with producers and studios or production companies to develop entertainment programs, a news operation, and a sports program operation.

Public TV. Public television has grown into a tangle of local and regional stations linked by the PBS network. The Corporation for Public Broadcasting still has a strong role in funding, but increasingly producers depend on a mix of funding from CPB, PBS affiliate contributions, **corporate underwriting** or sponsorship, public contributions, and foreign network cosponsorship. In return for underwriting, corporations and foundations receive a short announcement that is not quite a commercial but that describes their support and what they do. At the local level, PBS stations are increasingly dependent on local institutional sponsors, such as universities, and particularly on direct viewer support, which is one reason that PBS stations always seem to be soliciting viewer membership pledges for contributions.

PBS programming tends to be developed by the larger PBS affiliate stations, such as WGBH in Boston, that initiate proposals and put together packages of support. Programming for PBS has been made more competitive by the fact that several cable TV channels, including the Discovery Channel and the Arts & Entertainment Network, now compete with PBS for audiences with somewhat similar kinds of programming: documentaries, highbrow drama, and nature programs. PBS, in turn, occasionally runs former commercial network programs, such as *The Lawrence Welk Show* and *The Avengers*, that might also be found on a cable superstation or an independent commercial station (Head, Sterling, & Schofield, 1994).

Home Video. Over two-thirds of Americans rent videotapes at least occasionally. The average household spends over $170 renting and buying videocassettes per year, over $15 billion in total. This trend has produced an enormous industry, although some people wonder whether the current video rental and sales boom will decline considerably as cable television options for viewing movies increase, in the number of film-oriented channels and in pay-per-view or movies-on-demand options.

In the production aspect of the video business, the ten largest film studios account for over two-thirds of videocassette sales. Video sales are now the most important revenue source for the film industry. In between studios and local rental shops are a group of distributors, including CBS/Fox Video, RCA/Columbia Home Pictures, Vestron, Tri-Star, Orion, and dozens of others. The retail side of video is the most complex and changeable. It is dominated by chains, such as Blockbuster Video, that have become big players, as Blockbuster's participation in the 1994 Viacom takeover of Paramount Studio shows. Many independent stores have sprung up, but most fail. Other retailers, particularly supermarkets and convenience stores, now have racks of videos for sale next to the paperback books and records.

Ownership and Control. Many television stations are owned by groups. In management, advertising sales, and equipment, station owners benefit economically from the economies of scale of multiple station ownership. In the beginning the major owners were the three networks themselves. The networks still own and operate stations in the largest U.S. markets, and these stations are a major source of revenue for the networks. Here are the situations for the four established TV networks plus two new TV networks:

- NBC is owned by General Electric, which also has interests in aerospace, financial services, appliances, home video, and TV production. It had seven TV stations and bought more in 1995, including three owned and operated stations, but sold off radio and record operations in the early 1990s.

- ABC/CapCities merged with Disney in 1995, bringing theme parks and production of movies, prime-time TV shows, and cartoons to a group that had a television network, three cable channels (including ESPN), video production, ten television stations, and twenty-one radio stations.

- CBS, Inc. was acquired by Westinghouse in 1995, which already owned Group W television and radio stations. The combined operation has fifteen television stations and thirty-nine radio stations. Group W also has satellite, sports, and international production operations.

- Fox Broadcasting Corporation is owned by Rupert Murdoch's News Corp., along with Twentienth Century Fox film and TV production studio; TV stations formerly owned by Metromedia; satellite TV channels in Europe, Asia, and Latin America; and print media in Australia, Britain, and the United States.

- UPN is a TV network started in 1993 by television station owner Chris Craft and Viacom, which had acquired Paramount movie and

R E V I E W

1. How do independent filmmakers differ from studios?
2. What is the typical current distribution cycle of a film?
3. What has been the effect of home video on the movie industry?
4. What is the Motion Picture Association of America (MPAA)? What does it do?
5. How are television stations organized?
6. What are the main differences between network affiliates and independent stations?
7. Why did many independent stations join the Fox Network?
8. What role does corporate underwriting play in PBS?
9. Where do PBS programs come from?

THE NEGROPONTE FLIP: THROW OUT YOUR TVS AND TELEPHONES, EVERYONE!

Most information we receive through the ether today—television, for example—will come through the ground by cable tomorrow. Conversely, most of what we now receive through the ground—such as telephone service—will come through the airwaves.
—Nicholas Negroponte

Who is Nicholas Negroponte, and why does he want us to throw out all of our television sets and telephones? Negroponte is the director of The Media Lab, a research laboratory at the Massachusetts Institute of Technology that is attempting to define the future direction for electronic communication. His is a very prestigious laboratory, and he made this statement in a widely read issue of *Scientific American* (1991), so his prophecy has attracted a lot of attention in industry and government circles.

His argument is essentially this: we are moving quickly toward a universal, fiber-based high-capacity network that is the logical choice to carry all of the hundreds and thousands of channels of video programming that are soon to appear. That leaves over-the-air ("through the ether") transmission available for the one type of application that wireline networks cannot handle: mobile communication. In Negroponte's world we will place all of our phone calls on wireless personal communication networks and watch all of our television over fiber-optic cables. In particular, he would like to see TV communication frequencies taken away and awarded to new mobile communication services. He finds direct broadcast television satellites to be a "perverse" misuse of scarce communications frequencies that could be much better used for mobile telephone applications.

Not all are convinced that the "Negroponte flip" is the answer. Many rural areas and developing countries are unlikely to be wired for fiber, for example. What would become of them? There are other technological solutions, too. One possibility is the so-called intelligent sunshine approach. A satellite-based network with computers on board might handle interactive video applications more efficiently and offer more universal coverage more quickly than a fiber-based solution. And who is to say that we will not want mobile broadband applications someday? At the very least we will want portable artificial reality helmets so we can project pleasing images over the decaying scrap heaps of phones and TVs that the Negroponte flip will leave in its wake!

Some also think it is unrealistic to expect that there will be such a wholesale flip-flop in communications technologies by 2010, the year Negroponte says it will all happen. History shows that new telecommunications technologies are added incrementally to existing networks at first and may take generations to fully supplant the older ones.

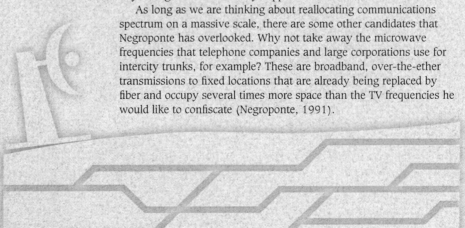

As long as we are thinking about reallocating communications spectrum on a massive scale, there are some other candidates that Negroponte has overlooked. Why not take away the microwave frequencies that telephone companies and large corporations use for intercity trunks, for example? These are broadband, over-the-ether transmissions to fixed locations that are already being replaced by fiber and occupy several times more space than the TV frequencies he would like to confiscate (Negroponte, 1991).

TV studios, Blockbuster video stores, MTV and Nickelodeon cable channels, and Simon & Schuster publishing.

- WB TV is a TV network started by Time-Warner, which owns Warner Bros. studio, Warner Music, and Home Box Office, a number of cable systems, Time Inc. magazines (including *People* and *Fortune*), and a major interest in Turner Broadcasting, which includes CNN, TNT, the Cartoon Network, and the MGM film and cartoon library.

As of 1996 most television networks were either starting or growing by acquiring film studios or other major sources of content. However, CBS/Westinghouse and NBC/General Electric were concentrating on acquiring more broadcast distribution stations.

POLICY ISSUES

The film and television industries are embroiled in a number of policy issues that have affected how they conduct business and the kinds of content they carry.

Cross-Ownership Rules

Initially, ownership groups were limited to five television , five FM , and five AM stations, to limit the power of any single group over both content and industry structure. Opponents in the 1980s argued that media are diverse because of competition, including that from cable TV, and rules were relaxed to twelve TV, twelve AM, and 12 FM stations, with a national television coverage limit of 25 percent of homes. The 1996 Telecommunications Act eliminated the limit of twelve TV stations and raised the national television coverage limit to 35 percent.

Film Ratings

After years of debate and what seemed to be an increase in the number of movies with explicit language, sex, and violence in the 1960s, the Motion Picture Association of America instituted a rating system to give people an idea of what they might encounter in a film. With some further modifications over the years, the **MPAA rating** categories are now:

MPAA ratings are a movie rating system, instituted in 1968.

G—For all ages; no sex or nudity, minimal violence

PG—Parental guidance suggested; some portions perhaps not suitable for young children, mild profanity, non-"excessive" violence, only a glimpse of nudity

PG 13—Parents strongly cautioned to give guidance to children under 13; some material may be inappropriate for young children

R—Restricted; those under 17 must be accompanied by parent or guardian; may contain very rough violence, explicit nudity, or lovemaking

NC-17—No one under 17 admitted; formerly rated X; generally reserved for films that are openly pornographic, although some serious films receive it

Many people have debated the appropriateness and utility of these ratings. Some argue that, as a form of industry self-censorship, they violate freedom of speech for filmmakers. Others argue that, as with music lyric advisories, the ratings simply excite the interest of younger viewers. Many observe that the restrictions imposed on teenagers by R and NC-17 ratings are not enforced by theaters, whose managers are aware that teens are the main moviegoers. However, many parents have expressed gratitude that the ratings do give them something to work with in guiding children's viewing.

Violence Warnings and Controls

A similar issue surfaced over the question of sex, violence, and graphic language on television. There have been debates and considerable research about the amount and effects of these elements, an issue discussed in greater detail in Chapter 17. Pressure for action built after 1993, and subsequent hearings did not produce effective industry self-regulation. The Telecommunications Act of 1996 requires that new television sets sold in the United States include a "V-chip" that enables viewers, particularly parents, to block programming, based on an electronically encoded system. The industry is required to develop a ratings system for "violence, sex and other indecent materials and to agree voluntarily to broadcast signals containing such ratings." Industry leaders agreed in a 1996 summit meeting with President Clinton to produce this ratings system.

Monopolies in Production and Distribution

With the continuing trend toward conglomeration, concentration of ownership, and **vertical** and **horizontal integration** among diverse branches of the entertainment and information industries, **monopoly** is becoming a major policy issue. A key related issue is how to promote diversity of points of view in television and film. During the 1980s, the Reagan administration policymakers at the FCC, particularly Chairman Mark Fowler and attorney Dan Brennan, argued that the increase in alternate channels created a more truly open marketplace of ideas and eliminated the problem of diversity. They argued that instead of relatively few networks dominating scarce channels, multiple channels almost automatically promoted multiple points of view. Others are less optimistic, particularly given the early 1990s trends toward cross-ownership and integration between producers, cable TV companies, and telephone companies.

Vertical integration is concentrating ownership by acquiring companies that are all in related businesses, such as program production and distribution.

Horizontal integration is concentrating ownership by acquiring companies that are all in the same business, such as televisions stations.

Monopoly is ownership or domination of an entire industry by one firm.

Right of reply gives opportunities for the expression of opposing views on broadcast stations when only one side had been aired.

Chilling effect is the idea that rules about fairness or right of reply inhibits stations from airing controversial programs.

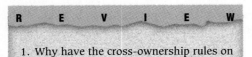

R E V I E W

1. Why have the cross-ownership rules on radio and television stations been relaxed?
2. What are the current rules?
3. Why were film ratings developed? What are their pros and cons?
4. Why are similar ratings being considered for television? What are their pros and cons?
5. Has the increasing diversity of television and cable channels increased content diversity?
6. Has channel diversity eliminated the need for regulation of content?
7. What was the Fairness Doctrine? Who supports its reinstatement and who opposes it?

Fairness Doctrine

One of the more contentious examples of Reagan administration deregulation, based on assumptions about increased options with multichannel technologies, came with the 1987 withdrawal of what had been called the Fairness Doctrine. That had put stations on notice that the FCC expected them to devote time to controversial issues of public importance *and* give opportunities for the expression of opposing views when only one side had been aired. Most attention centered on the second part, the **right of reply**. Although broadcasters were given substantial leeway in defining what was controversial and deciding what constituted equal time, the networks and individual stations still felt that the Fairness Doctrine actually had a **chilling effect**—that is, it inhibited stations from airing controversial programs. That led many conservatives, in particular, to oppose the doctrine, particularly since syndicated programs by conservative pundits such as Rush Limbaugh were among those that some stations felt reluctant to air when replies had to be allowed. A proposal in 1993 to renew the Fairness Doctrine raised this debate again, but it has not been reinstated.

SUMMARY & REVIEW

What Were the Milestones in the Development of the Visual Media?

Who invented the motion picture camera?
Thomas Edison in 1888, although others competed by 1900.

What innovations did D. W. Griffith add to silent films?
D. W. Griffith represented another major step forward in film form and technique, using a large screen, well-produced outdoor battle scenes, moving shots, and close-ups. His 1915 *Birth of a Nation* was the first feature film. However, the film, set during and after the Civil War, features the Ku Klux Klan as its heroes and has been used by them as a recruiting film.

What was the star system?
Rudolph Valentino, Lillian Gish, and Charlie Chaplin were such attractions that their names appeared above the name of the film on movie marquees. The studios rose on the basis of this star system, using the stars' popularity to promote their movies.

What was the studio system? Which were the main studios?
The studio system consisted of production companies that employed the complete set of facilities and people required to make and distribute movies. The major movie studios grew by developing a stable of actors, writers, and directors who worked for them over a period of years. They also had regular stables of musicians and technicians. The main Hollywood studios were United Artists, Paramount, MGM (Metro Goldwyn Meyer), 20th Century Fox, Warner Brothers, Universal, Columbia, and RKO.

What changed with talking pictures?
Talking pictures created a sudden change, starting with *The Jazz Singer* in 1927. Acting became less overstated and stylized. The actors' voices and the use of sound effects, as well as music, became important. Talkies required an influx of new talent, which came mostly from theater and Broadway.

What were the main film genres of the 1930s and 1940s?
In the 1930s, movies emphasized their new attraction, sound, by creating a series of extravagantly produced musicals, with dancing and singing. The other main genres of the 1930s were comedies, crime dramas, suspense, mysteries, and historical epics. The most popular film genre of the 1940s was the detective story.

When did theatrical film attendance begin to decline?
Theatrical film attendance and the revenue of studios at the box office began to decline after 1947, as television viewing made strong, steady inroads into film theater attendance.

Why did the FCC freeze television licenses from 1948 until 1952?
Television stations started to rush onto the air in 1948. However, the existing FCC technical standards did not allow for nearly enough stations to cover the United States or prevent signal interference, so the FCC imposed a freeze on new station applications from 1948 to 1952.

What is the NTSC standard? How was it developed?
The 1941 NTSC black-and-white television standards are still in use, particularly 525 lines per frame and 30 frames per second. These standards for television were worked out by a government-mandated compromise committee, the National Television Systems Committee (NTSC).

How did Hollywood and its films change after television?
The film industry initially fought television by not releasing any new movies to be shown on television. The film industry was closely tied to theatrical chains, and television quickly cut into their revenues. However, as small theaters closed all over America in the 1950s, the film industry began to realize that it couldn't beat television. Disney started producing programs for television in 1954, and other studios followed. By 1961 the film boycott of television was over.

When did the studio system decline?
By the 1960s the power of the movie studios was declining. Independent producers gained more of a role in producing movies, and film studios began to spend much of their time producing TV series.

What enabled a fourth network, Fox, to finally succeed?
In 1987, Rupert Murdoch started the Fox television network. Cable TV helped Fox, since most Fox affiliates were independent UHF stations, which cable brought to most homes with perfect picture quality. Fox also pursued a segmented television strategy by pursuing younger viewers and more urban and racially diverse audiences.

What Are the Main Trends in Video Technology?

Who developed the basics of television camera technology?
The camera tube was the source of a 1920s patent dispute between independent inventor Philo Farnsworth and Vladimir Zworykin at RCA. Farnsworth and Zworykin had both developed the essential technology for a television camera—an electronic scanning system.

How does a television camera work?
The camera tube breaks light down into scanning lines, which can be scanned by an electron beam. The beam causes a discharge of energy that turns the energy into electrical voltage variations. The lines of resolution (like 525 for NTSC) are the lines per frame scanned by the electron beam and later reproduced by the picture tube in the receiver.

How does a television picture tube work?
A picture tube, or cathode ray tube, fires an electron gun at dots on the inside of the screen; the dots glow with varying intensity to create an image.

What is scanning?
Scanning samples a certain number of lines per frame scanned by the electron beam.

What is the difference between VHF and UHF?
VHF uses the very high frequency band and UHF uses ultra high frequencies. Both require 6 MHz in channel width. There are a maximum of twelve VHF channels. Being lower on the frequency band, VHF requires much less power than UHF to cover a similar distance. There are currently fifty-six UHF channels.

What Are the Main Genres of Film and Television?

What were some of the main silent film genres?
The silent film genres included westerns, war movies, romances, physical comedies, historical costume dramas, documentaries, and fantasies.

What programming genres came to television from radio?
A number of genres and even specific programs came straight from network radio programming to television in the 1950s. Those included variety shows, comedians, ensemble comedies, situation comedies, soap operas, dramas, western dramas, mysteries, science fiction, talk shows, sports, news and public affairs, documentaries, and game shows.

What programming genres came to television from Hollywood?
The film industry has fed most of its formulas into television in one way or another: action adventure movies, westerns, detective dramas, war stories, and cartoons (developed into series forms).

What were the main television genres that evolved in the 1950s and 1960s?
Television programming from 1948 to 1957 was dominated by comedy. On NBC, comedy together with music formed a number of variety shows, periodic specials, and magazine programs. CBS innovated in a different direction by emphasizing news, introducing situation comedies, and reintroducing westerns. ABC aimed many of its programs, like the Disney shows, at a younger audience and also worked on sports and action adventure.

In the 1960s and 1970s, some television variety shows, sitcoms, and dramas began to have a more critical and social point of view.

Who Are the Audiences for Film and Television?

Who watches the most film in theaters? On VCRs?

Young people under 25 years of age watch the most films in theaters. VCR viewing is highest among those in their middle years and those with young families.

Is the network television audience growing or declining? Why?

The network audience has been declining steadily, although the decline stopped, perhaps temporarily, in 1993. Most people still watch network television more than cable TV or independent stations. However, both of the latter have cut into network television's share of the audience, which went from 90 percent of the prime-time audience in 1979 to around 60 percent in 1993. While most people still watch over four hours of television per day, a steadily decreasing amount of that comes from broadcast television networks or independent stations.

How Are the Film and Television Industries Organized?

How do independent filmmakers differ from studios?

The major film producers are the old-time studios, Columbia, Fox, MGM, Paramount, Universal, and Warner Brothers, plus Buena Vista (Disney) and Tri-Star (Sony). They produce fifteen to twenty-five movies per year. Independent filmmakers, or "indies," usually produce fewer films and for much less than the majors, often a few million dollars.

What is the typical current distribution cycle of a film?

Typical distribution for a major film might now be theatrical distribution, pay cable, videocassette sales, network exhibition, basic cable networks, and finally, syndication. There may be some variations on the exact order, depending on whether basic cable networks outbid a broadcast network for rights, for instance. Many films seen as not worth the promotional costs for theatrical release go straight to video stores and cable.

What is the Motion Picture Association of America (MPAA)? What does it do?

The MPAA is a sales and lobby organization that represents the major film studios. The MPEAA (Motion Picture Export Association of America) is a sales and lobby organization that represents film studios overseas.

How are television stations organized?

Most commercial television stations have an administrative or managerial structure, a sales force to sell local advertising, engineering or technical staff for studio and transmitter operations, a news operation, and a production staff for news and other programming. Stations also usually have contracts out for network affiliation (unless they are independent), research and ratings services, programming consultants, and legal services.

What are the main sources of programming for networks and their affiliates? For independent stations?

Networks supply a great deal of programming to their O&O's (network owned-and-operated stations) or affiliates. The networks themselves produce news shows, sports events, some talk shows, some soap operas, documentaries, and a few series. Most entertainment programs are purchased by networks from film studio production units or from independent producers. Independent stations do not affiliate with networks and buy most of their programming from syndication services, which include many of the independent producers.

Where do PBS programs come from?

PBS programming tends to be developed by the larger PBS affiliate stations, such as WGBH in Boston. They initiate proposals and put together packages of support.

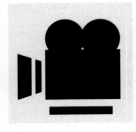

What Are the Main Policy Issues in Visual Media?

Why have the cross-ownership rules on radio and television stations been relaxed?
Initially, ownership groups were limited to five television stations and five FM and five AM radio stations. The goal was to limit the power of any single group over both content and the industry structure itself. The intent was to increase diversity of content. Opponents argued that media were diverse because of competition and that ownership rules could safely be relaxed. The limits have been steadily increased, leading to a wave of sales, price inflation, and speculation in station ownership.

What are the current rules?
The 1996 Telecommunications Act eliminated the previous limit of twelve TV stations (and twelve FM and twelve AM stations) and raised the national television coverage limit from 25 percent of homes to 35 percent.

Why were film ratings developed? What are their pros and cons?
After years of debate and what seemed to be an increase in movies with explicit language, sex, and violence in the 1960s, the MPAA instituted a ratings system to give people an idea of what they might encounter in a film.

Many parents and church groups have expressed gratitude that the ratings give them something to work with in guiding children's viewing. Some critics argue that, as a form of industry self-censorship, ratings violate freedom of speech for filmmakers. Others argue that the ratings simply draw the interest of younger viewers. The restrictions on teenagers with R and NC-17 ratings are often not enforced by theaters, as teens are the main moviegoers.

Why were television and cable ratings subsequently developed?
Pressure for action built after years of hearings did not produce effective industry self-regulation. Movie ratings were perceived as successful enough that the Telecommunications Act of 1996 requires the television industry to develop a ratings system for violence, sex, and "other indecent materials" and to broadcast signals containing those ratings. New television sets sold in the United States must include a V-chip to enable viewers to block programming based on that electronically encoded system.

Has the increasing diversity of television and cable channels increased content diversity?
During the 1980s, policymakers at the FCC argued that the increase in alternate channels created a more truly open marketplace of ideas and eliminated the problem of diversity. They argued that instead of relatively few radio or television networks dominating scarce channels, multiple channels almost automatically promote multiple points of view. Others are less optimistic, particularly given the early 1990s trends toward cross-ownership and integration between producers, cable TV companies, and telephone companies.

What was the Fairness Doctrine?
The Fairness Doctrine expected stations to devote time to controversial issues of public importance *and* give opportunities for the expression of opposing views when only one side had been aired. The Reagan administration, inclined toward deregulation and assuming that increased options with multichannel technologies eliminated the need to guarantee fairness, withdrew the doctrine in 1987.

REFERENCES

Barnouw, E. (1990). *Tube of plenty* (2nd ed.). New York: Oxford University Press.

Comstock, G. (1989). *The evolution of American television*. Newbury Park, CA: Sage.

Gitlin, T. (1985). *Inside prime time*. New York: Pantheon Books.

Gitlin, T. (1986). *Watching television*. New York: Pantheon Books.

Head, S., Sterling, C., & Schofield, L. (1994). *Broadcasting in America* (7th ed.). New York: Houghton Mifflin.

Knight, A. (1979). *The liveliest art.* New York: New American Library.

MacDonald, J. F. (1994). *One nation under television: The rise and decline of network TV.* Chicago: Nelson Hall.

Negroponte, N. (1991). Products and services for computer networks. *Scientific American 265*(3), pp. 106–113.

Sterling, C., & Kittross, J. (1990). *Stay tuned— A concise history of American broadcasting.* Belmont, CA: Wadsworth.

Chapter 10

MULTICHANNEL MEDIA

C H A P T E R   P R E V I E W

This chapter addresses mass media that deliver multiple channels of information and entertainment to the home. We will see how the cable television industry developed in rural areas and later spread to suburbs and cities, leaving a panoply of new channels in its wake. This chapter also traces the evolution of cable television technology from its humble origin as a shared television antenna system to a sophisticated interactive network that can connect the home to tomorrow's "information superhighway." New multichannel satellite, telephone, and broadcast technologies that pose a competitive challenge to cable television are also described. Finally, we will examine important issues that face the multichannel industry today, including ownership, community programming, and competition between pay TV and "free" TV.

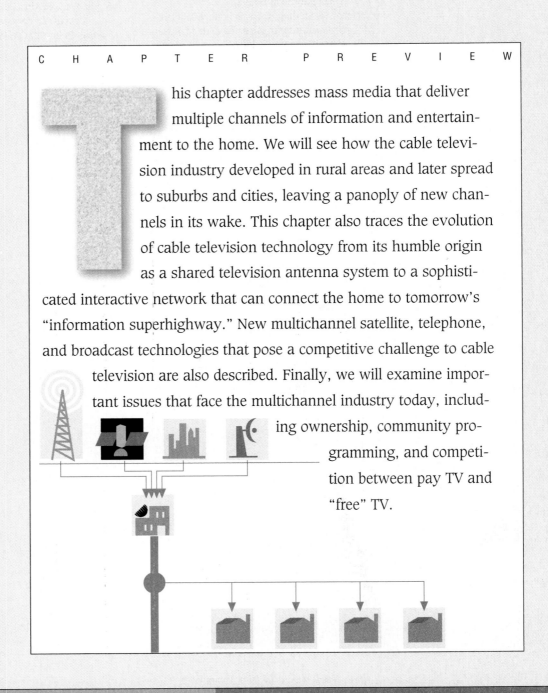

5000 Channels and Nothing On?

At last! An evening with the DeeVee all to myself!

Hiya, Mom! Whatrwegonnawatch with the kiddies tonight? Wanna see *Snow White and the Seven Dungeons!?* <Interactive Disney Classics>

Can that! Tonight I want you to impersonate that cheeky new account exec they stuck me with. He thinks he's God's gift, only I want him fawning and obedient.

Yessss, madame vice-president, sorry ma'am. What can I do for you, ma'am?

Um, let's see . . . Interactive Movie Classics, *Gone with the Wind,* with me as Scarlett O'Hara and a hunky young John Wayne in the male lead. Audition mode.

"Ta tellya thuh truth. Missy Scarlit. I don't. give uh. gol' dern."

Ugh. Try Bogart.

"I'll never forget that lasht day in Atlanta, Shcarlet, you wore gray and the Yankeesh wore blue . . ."

No, something else, romantic.

<Harlequin Channel—Jacqueline Susann Network— Boddice Ripper Classics>

DeeVee! How many times do I have to tell you— no weak females in this household!

Sorry ma'am, won't happen again, sir. <Gloria Steinem Speaks—Betty Friedan's Expert Feminist Advice System—Andrea Dworkin's Greatest Lectures>

Don't be wise, you *know* I said romantic. Can't you learn to do romantic without female submissiveness, you idiot!

You *also* said I am supposed to be "cheeky," ma'am.

Enough! Switch to the Fireplace Channel with a piano sonata in back, order me a box of chocolates from the Home Delivery Channel . . . *and* call me at the office tomorrow to remind me to transfer that macho jerk out of my division!

D I G I T A L

A BRIEF HISTORY OF THE MULTICHANNEL INDUSTRY

n the summer of 1948 the citizens of Mahanoy, Pennsylvania, were feeling left out of a new media trend that was sweeping the nation—television.* Mahanoy was situated some sixty miles from the nearest television stations in Philadelphia, and the Allegheny Mountains blocked signals from even the tallest rooftop antennas. Perhaps the unhappiest man in Mahanoy was John Walson, the local appliance dealer and an employee of the power company. He sold television sets that, unfortunately, only produced blasts of static. To demonstrate television to potential customers, he had to bring them to the top of a nearby mountain. Soon tiring of these treks, Walson connected the mountaintop antenna to his appliance shop in the valley below, stringing together eight homes along the way. To keep a forest of TV antennas from sprouting in the Alleghenies, Walson developed the concept of using one antenna to service numerous homes. At about the same time, the same idea occurred to Ed Parsons, a radio station employee in Astoria, Washington, and the cable television industry was born (see Table 10.1).

Community Antenna Television Service

Distant signals are cable channels imported from major television markets.

Cable stayed close to its rural roots for twenty years, piping television to remote areas that had no off-air reception of their own. The freeze on new television stations between 1948 and 1952 spurred cable growth in the early years. Later, cable operators expanded to small cities and towns that only received the three broadcast networks of the day—ABC, CBS, and NBC. To accomplish this, they imported **distant signals,** usually independent television stations from nearby major television markets.

TABLE 10.1. MULTICHANNEL MILESTONES

Year	Event
1948	First systems in Pennsylvania and Oregon
1948–1952	Freeze on new TV stations spurs early growth
1966	First subscription TV broadcasts
1966–1972	FCC ban on urban cable systems
1972	New FCC rules allowing urban cable
1975	HBO, WTCG go on satellite
1979–1984	Franchise wars in large cities
1984	Cable Act deregulates cable
1992	New cable law regulates cable rates, opens competition
1994	U.S. DBS systems launched

Between 1966 and 1972, cable operators were kept out of the largest television markets by FCC decree. The FCC was trying to nurture UHF stations (channels 14–69) and feared that imported distant signals would undermine independent UHF stations. In addition, if the distant signals carried the same programs as the local TV channels, their ratings might suffer. Broadcasters also felt it was unfair for cable operators to retransmit their programs at a profit without compensation.

To protect local broadcasting, government regulators intervened to "level the playing field" between cable and its competitors by restricting distant signals and duplicate programming. Without original programming, however, cable did not appeal to enough suburbanites and city dwellers to justify the expense of building cable systems in their neighborhoods. By the late 1960s, many urban residents already had access to several broadcast signals that expanded their viewing options beyond network television. Without access to large urban audiences, there was no way to justify the development of original programming for cable. Confined to rural areas and without original programming, cable stagnated.

Pay TV is the practice of charging cable customers an additional monthly fee to receive a specific channel, usually a movie or sports channel.

One solution to the programming problem was to offer movies and live sporting events on special channels. Cable subscribers were required to pay an additional monthly fee for these channels—a service that became known as **pay TV.** In the early years, local cable

*Historical accounts are drawn from Stump and Jessell (1988) and Baldwin and McVoy (1983).

BEFORE CABLE TV,
ANTENNAS FILLED THE SKIES.

Scrambling disrupts cable channels electronically so only authorized customers with descramblers can receive them.

A **superstation** is a distant signal that is distributed widely via satellite.

Basic cable includes the local channels, distant stations, and satellite signals that cable operators offer for a basic monthly fee.

Multiple system operators (MSOs) are cable companies that operate systems in two or more communities.

Local origination is cable programming created within the community by the cable operator.

Public access is cable programming created by community residents and organizations without the involvement of the cable operator.

operators picked their own movies and fed them into unused channels on their systems, using **scrambling** systems to disrupt the signals in the homes that chose not to pay the extra fee.

HBO and the Rise of the Cable Networks

In 1972 the FCC developed a new set of rules for the cable industry that paved the way for its entry into urban areas. While restricting the number of distant signals that could be carried, the new rules mandated that each new system have at least twenty channels. This created an opportunity for cable-originated programming to fill the (then) unused channels.

Home Box Office (HBO) was the first to capitalize on this opportunity. HBO began circulating videotapes to cable systems in the Northeast in the fall of 1972. In 1975 HBO created the first national cable network by beaming a championship prize fight between Joe Frazier and Muhammed Ali to a national audience via satellite. HBO followed up with a regular schedule of "first-run" movies that had not yet appeared on television. HBO proved popular, and pay television revenues lifted cable out of the doldrums.

Also in 1975 a young television station owner in Atlanta named Ted Turner put his station WTCG (later, WTBS) on satellite, extending his distant signals to a national audience. Turner thus originated the idea of a **superstation,** distributing a local television station nationally via satellite. Turner profited by selling advertising at premium rates to advertisers who wanted to reach a national audience. Since the superstation derived considerable revenue from its advertising, Turner could charge cable operators much less than HBO could. It was also in Turner's interest that his station reach the largest possible audience to increase its value to advertisers. Accordingly, cable operators included the superstation as part of the basic monthly charge for service, popularizing the term **basic cable.** WGN from Chicago and WOR (later, WWOR) from New Jersey also appeared via satellite in short order. In 1976 a new copyright law went into effect; while imposing fees on the importation of distant signals, the law at least made it possible for cable operators everywhere to include distant signals in their channel lineups. In 1980 Turner launched a second network, Cable News Network (CNN), which became a staple of cable channel lineups everywhere.

Networks that were available only on cable also began to appear. The first were the Christian Broadcasting Network (CBN, later known as The Family Channel), the Cable Satellite Public Affairs Network (C-SPAN), and the Entertainment and Sports Network (ESPN). By 1982 there were three dozen satellite networks available on cable.

Cable Comes to the City: The Franchise Wars

Now that cable had some programming of its own, it had something to offer in urban areas. Large companies that owned numerous cable systems, **multiple system operators (MSOs),** engaged in a high-stakes bidding war for the right to wire America's cities. At this time, municipal authorities typically awarded a single exclusive cable franchise after a competitive bidding process. The cities added to the franchising frenzy by setting requirements for many "extras," such as **local origination** and **public access** channels on which local residents and government bodies could show their own programs. Cities also required more and more channels and interactive capabilities. With each new round of franchising, the stakes went higher as competing cable companies offered more attractive bids. By 1985

BLACK ENTERTAINMENT TELEVISION (BET) WAS ONE OF THE FIRST NATIONAL BASIC CABLE CHANNELS. BET HAS DEVELOPED SUCH ORIGINAL PROGRAMMING AS THE MOVIE *RACE TO FREEDOM: THE UNDERGROUND RAILROAD*, FEATURING COURTNEY VANCE AND JANET BAILEY.

nearly every major city in the United States had gone through the franchising process—some more than once—and the task of building urban cable systems occupied the industry for the balance of the decade.

The Rise of Tele-Communications, Inc.

By the end of the franchising wars, a single company had assumed a preeminent role in the cable industry, Tele-Communications, Inc. (TCI). TCI got its start in 1956, supplying community antenna service to small towns in the western United States. By 1972 the company faced bankruptcy until John Malone was brought in. Under Malone, TCI won the confidence of Wall Street investors and went on an acquisition campaign that made TCI the largest cable company of all. Malone also invested in programming services, beginning with Black Entertainment Television (BET) in 1979. Over the years, TCI and its spinoff, Liberty Media, obtained financial interests in a dozen cable networks, including Ted Turner's. The other giants of today's cable industry also experienced rapid growth in the era of the franchise wars, including Continental Cablevision, Comcast Cablevision, and American Television and Communications (ATC), which would later become part of the Time-Warner conglomerate.

The Era of Deregulation: The Cable Act of 1984

The aftermath of the franchise wars prompted a political backlash from municipal officials who demanded new legislation to control cable. However, cable was coming into its own as a popular home entertainment medium, and it was time to reexamine the policy of protecting broadcasters at the expense of cable. The Cable Communications Policy Act of 1984 was a compromise between the cities and the cable industry. A key provision was to deregulate cable rates, which had previously been subject to municipal control. In return, cities could charge cable operators a 5 percent franchise fee and periodically review the performance of their franchisees. Cable operators also pledged to provide public access channels and equal

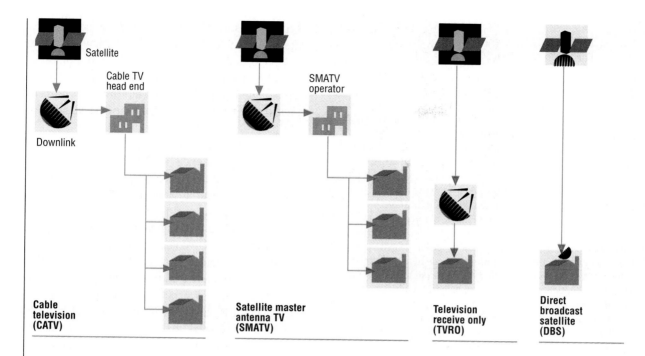

Satellite

Cable TV
head end

Downlink

Cable
television
(CATV)

SMATV
operator

Satellite master
antenna TV
(SMATV)

Television
receive only
(TVRO)

Direct
broadcast
satellite
(DBS)

FIGURE 10.1
CABLE TELEVISION, SMATV,
TVRO, AND DBS ARE VARYING
FORMS OF TELEVISION
PROGRAM DISTRIBUTION VIA
SATELLITE.

employment opportunities. Having decided to let cable live, Congress protected its new creation by prohibiting telephone companies from owning cable television systems.

Cable Meets the Competition

With rate regulation removed, cable operators increased their revenues, and the value of cable systems skyrocketed in the late 1980s. The new urban cable systems, most with fifty or more channels, opened new slots for yet more cable networks, and rate deregulation meant that cable operators could readily generate the money to pay for them. The lure of programming and profits also attracted some new competitors eager to cash in on the multichannel gold rush.

TVRO (television receive only) is a backyard satellite receiver that lets individual homes receive the same channels that are intended for cable systems.

SMATV (satellite master antenna television) is a TVRO system serving an entire apartment building or housing complex from a central satellite antenna.

DBS (direct broadcast satellite) is a satellite service that is marketed directly to home receivers.

TVRO, SMATV, and DBS: Backyard Cable. HBO's first satellite dish cost $100,000 in 1973, but a decade later a complete **television receive only (TVRO)** "dish" installation could be had for only a few thousand dollars. Anyone with the appropriate equipment could receive HBO, WTBS, MTV, and dozens of other cable channels completely free of charge. Many rural residents installed their own backyard systems. This actually benefited the industry, as it extended the audience for advertising-supported cable channels to areas that were beyond cable's reach. Soon owners of large apartment buildings and condominium complexes began installing their own dishes as well, creating **satellite master antenna television (SMATV)** systems that were, in effect, minicable systems. These systems cut both the cable operators and the cable networks out of the profits (see Figure 10.1).

Direct broadcast satellite (DBS) systems are another effort to cash in on satellite-delivered entertainment. DBS systems differ from the TVRO model in that subscribers are required to pay a fee for the programming. The signals are scrambled so only authorized subscribers can receive them. An abortive DBS service, U.S. Satellite, on the air in 1984, soon

UNDERSTANDING SATELLITES

In effect, satellites are antenna towers in the sky that retransmit television in two very long "hops," one from a satellite *uplink* station on the ground to the satellite and then back from the satellite—essentially, a microwave relay device that had been launched into earth orbit—to the *downlink* connected to the cable head end. Satellites that orbit at an altitude of 22,300 miles match the rotation speed of the earth itself and are thus called geosynchronous satellites. This means that they maintain their position in the sky so the downlink antenna can be pointed at a fixed location.

Cable networks like CNN and HBO feed their signals directly into their own satellite uplinks. Distant TV signals for superstations are boosted into space by picking them up off the air and retransmitting them through satellite uplinks to cable television operators (CATV) or satellite master antenna TV (SMATV) systems that serve individual buildings or housing complexes.

At the cable head end, the signals are converted from satellite frequencies and placed on local cable channels. Home satellite receivers can receive the same channels, and for a time in the early 1980s, thousands of homes received cable channels "free" on backyard satellite dishes called television receive only (TVRO) dishes. However, cable networks now scramble their transmissions and require home satellite viewers to pay annual fees for the descramblers. New, more powerful direct broadcast satellite (DBS) systems transmit digital programming to small rooftop antennas.

went under due to a lack of programming and consumer interest. It wouldn't be until 1995 that a new generation of DBS operators, led by DirecTV and Primestar, sucessfully reentered the U.S. market with a full range of programming options, new digital transmission technology, and easy-to-install "pizza-sized" satellite dishes.

Wireless Cable: STV and MDS. Over-the-air **"wireless"** pay TV channels actually predated HBO by several years. In 1966 a **subscription television (STV)** service began in Hartford, Connecticut, which beamed movies and sporting events to homes over a UHF television channel, originating the concept of **pay-per-view.** In 1977 the FCC began formal licensing of STV systems. Another approach to over-the-air pay TV was **multipoint distribution systems (MDS),** which used special high-frequency transmitters to reach their subscribers. STV and MDS services thrived into the 1980s in urban areas that had not been reached by cable. However, as single-channel services, they did not last long after cable came to town. Later updates of wireless cable provided for up to sixteen different channels; with the addition of digital compression technology, the choices expanded to dozens of channels. This, coupled with regulatory changes that made popular cable television networks available and that inspired telephone companies to view wireless as a speedy means of entry into the home video business, re-energized wireless cable in the 1990s.

Home Video. The spread of **videocassette recorders (VCRs)** and video stores in the 1980s also posed a potential threat to cable. It was feared that home video would wipe out the demand for pay TV channels. As it turned out, many pay cable subscribers continued their

Wireless cable delivers cable channels to homes via earth-based broadcasting systems.

STV (subscription television) is a wireless cable system that uses conventional television channels.

Pay-per-view is when cable subscribers order a specific program and pay a separate fee just to receive that one show.

MDS (multipoint distribution systems) are wireless cable systems that use high frequencies in the microwave band to transmit programs.

VCRs (videocassette recorders) are home videotape machines.

subscriptions and merely added home video to their existing entertainment options. However, the home video trend did coincide with a leveling off of pay TV subscriptions.

Cable Fights Back. Now cable moved to suppress its own competition by controlling access to cable satellite services. Cable MSOs pressured satellite networks to refuse to share their programs with competing multichannel operators and to scramble their signals to crack down on "free" reception by TVRO owners. Regulatory intervention eventually forced satellite networks to offer their programs to competing distribution systems, but by that time cable was already well established in the largest cities.

Cable also responded to the home video threat. Its answer was to create more original programming and to offer new pay-per-view services that allowed users to order movies electronically from their homes instead of having to go out to the video store.

The Regulatory Pendulum Swings

By the early 1990s, cable had become a victim of its own success. Rate deregulation resulted in rising rates and consumer complaints, while the growing dominance of a few large MSOs and industrywide efforts to keep cable programming away from competing distribution networks raised antitrust concerns. With cable networks cutting into the ratings of the broadcast networks, there was also renewed sympathy for the broadcasters' decades-old claim for compensation for the retransmission of their programs.

The Cable Act of 1992 reinstated rate regulation, required cities to open themselves to competing cable franchises, and mandated compensation to broadcasters for the right to retransmit their signals. To stimulate competition, cable networks were required to deal with competing delivery systems like MMDS and DBS, and the practice of granting exclusive cable franchises was abolished. By the time the new Cable Act went into effect, the industry was being swept into a maelstrom of change sparked by the convergence of mass media and information technologies. This led to a sweeping revision of telecommunications regulation in the Telecommunications Act of 1996. The most important implication of the reform legislation for the cable industry was that it let cable companies compete with telephone companies for local and long-distance telephone service, which had previously been forbidden. This made it possible for cable companies to bill themselves as "one stop" telecommunications providers to business and residential customers, adding a significant new source of revenue for cable operators. Moreover, local phone companies were ordered to resell their service to their competitors, including cable systems, meaning that cable could get into the phone business quickly without completely rebuilding the network. Cable rate regulation was also removed.

However, at the same time local telephone companies were allowed to enter the cable television business themselves, offering potentially potent competition for cable firms. Prohibitions against phone companies partnering with each other were eliminated, raising the specter of huge new telephone firms that would dwarf even the largest cable companies and outspend them in the race to bring the information superhighway to the homes and offices of America. The response of long-distance telephone companies such as MCI Corporation and US Sprint was to form partnerships with cable companies, with the cable operators providing local connections so that they could jointly take on the newly liberated local phone firms. In short, the Telecommunications Act of 1996 promised to start a free-for-all for new services and new customers for all sectors of the telecommunications industry, including cable.

R E V I E W

1. How did cable spread throughout the United States?
2. What laws and regulations shaped cable TV?
3. Which technologies were critical to cable's early growth?
4. What contributions did John Walson, Ted Turner, and John Malone make to the development of the cable industry?
5. What was the impact of the 1996 Telecommunications Act on cable?

TECHNOLOGY TRENDS

John Walson's first cable system in 1948 (see Table 10.2) was little more than a TV antenna with an exceptionally long cord. Another early cable operator placed TV signals on a new type of cable that telephone companies used in high-capacity phone circuits. **Coaxial cable** had a single long wire running down its axis and a second conductor that is wrapped around it like a long metal tube. This arrangement kept unwanted signals from entering the cable and also prevented the cable signals from leaking out and interfering with other communications.

Coaxial cable is the high-capacity wire used for cable television transmission.

TABLE 10.2. MULTICHANNEL TECHNOLOGY MILESTONES

Year	Event
1948	First cable systems
1949	First coaxial cable TV system
1973	First addressable system in Columbus, OH
1975	HBO first satellite transmission
1977	Qube interactive cable system
1992	Video dial tone authorized by FCC
1993	Cellular TV service authorized
1994	Full Service Network debuts
1994	DBS services launched
1994	U.S. HDTV standard set

Head ends are the origination points for local cable television systems.

Microwave is a high-capacity system that transmits information between relay towers on highly focused beams of high-frequency radio waves.

Satellites are microwave systems in which the relays are in earth orbit instead of on towers.

Converters descramble and retune cable channels so they can be received by an ordinary TV set.

Addressable converters turn themselves off and on in response to numerical computer codes that authorize reception of specific channels or programs.

Multiplying the Channels

Coaxial cable had more than enough capacity to carry the full complement of broadcast signals available in the early 1950s. As cable operators moved into urban areas, they began to look for ways to add more channels in the hopes of attracting new subscribers. The problem was where to get the channels.

One answer was to build taller antennas to draw in signals from more distant stations. Antennas at the cable **head ends** from which the signals emanated reached hundreds of feet in height so they could peer over the horizon at TV transmitters in nearby cities. However, since TV signals travel only in a straight line, the distant transmitters were eventually so far away that they fell below the horizon of even the tallest antenna. The distant signals could be brought in on coaxial cable, but there were limits to how many amplifiers a signal could pass through before it became seriously degraded. Besides, the only practical way to string the cable was on telephone or power poles, and the utility companies were not particularly helpful. They charged pole attachment fees and mounted legal challenges to keep cable TV off their poles entirely.

Another "new technology" of the 1940s, **microwave,** came to the rescue. Like coaxial cable, microwave was used in huge intercity telephone circuits and could carry video signals. Cable companies built their own microwave networks by placing a tower every thirty miles or so that could pick up the signals and repeat them to the next tower down the line. When the signals reached the head end, they were converted to regular TV channels and fed into the cable system (see Figure 10.2).

Satellite Reception

Microwave systems made it possible to import distant signals from hundreds of miles away. In its early years, HBO used microwave radio to create a regional distribution system that covered the densely settled northeastern United States. However, it would have been prohibitively expensive to extend these networks nationwide and to link each of the thousands of systems already in existence at the time. **Satellite** transmission made it possible to deliver dozens of signals to thousands of locations simultaneously.

Addressability and Interactive Cable

The popularity of pay TV presented the next technical challenge—one that would push cable down the road to the Information Age. Whenever a new subscriber wanted pay TV, the cable company had to send a truck to install a set-top **converter** device that could unscramble the picture. Pay subscribers often found that although the new channels indeed had entertaining movies, they did not have very many of them. The constant reruns and duplication between pay services led many subscribers to disconnect their pay services, but dissatisfaction with broadcast television fare kept leading them back . . . and the cable trucks kept rolling.

Some method for turning pay TV subscriptions on and off from the cable head end was needed. Unlike the telephone system, where each subscriber is connected to his or her own line, cable subscribers share the same line. To "turn off" one subscriber, the cable operator would have to turn off everyone else in the neighborhood as well. **Addressable converters** surmounted this problem by turning themselves off and on in response to numerical codes broadcast through the system. Each converter had its own unique address so the pay

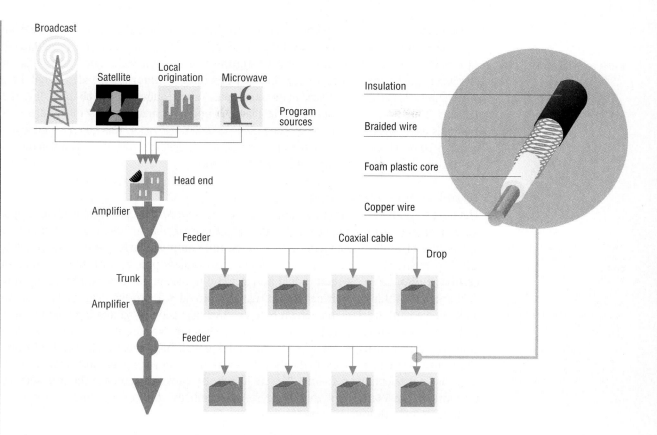

FIGURE 10.2
THE CABLE HEAD END FEEDS
BROADCAST, SATELLITE,
MICROWAVES, AND LOCAL
ORIGINATION SIGNALS INTO A
COAXIAL CABLE
DISTRIBUTION NETWORK OF
TRUNKS, FEEDERS, AND
DROPS TO INDIVIDUAL
HOMES.

Interactive cable lets cable
subscribers carry on two-way
interactions with programs and
complete transactions from their
homes.

channels could be turned on and off without sending the cable truck. Coaxial Cable Analysts introduced the first such system in Columbus, Ohio, in 1973.

The same technology also made it possible to authorize specific programs as well as entire channels. Subscribers could now order programs on a pay-per-view basis by phoning their cable systems and receiving an instant authorization through the cable system.

The next step in pay TV technology is **interactive cable.** Subscribers can order programs by pressing a button on the cable converter, which automatically records the order for billing purposes and sends the appropriate authorization code back through the system. Of course, a two-way system can also send other types of information back to the head end, including home shopping and banking transactions and even answers for TV quiz shows. This may sound simple, but it requires extensive reconstruction of cable networks, which were designed for one-way transmission only. The first interactive cable systems appeared in the late 1970s, although they did not catch on until a decade later.

Toward 500 Channels: Fiber, Digitization, and Channel Compression

Fiber optic cable systems use
light instead of electricity to
communicate.

The channel capacity of cable systems improved over the years, with the development of cable amplifiers that handled higher and higher frequencies. By the late 1980s, systems carrying over fifty channels were common, and some had over seventy channels. Coaxial cable technology was reaching its limits, though. Cable operators turned to **fiber optic cable** to transport signals from their head ends to their subscribers' neighborhoods. If extended all the way to the home TV set, fiber could theoretically expand the channel options to hundreds instead of merely dozens.

However, the coaxial cable that came into the living room was the most expensive of all to replace, and optical interfaces for individual television sets are still prohibitively expensive. Successful experiments with **digital** transmission techniques now make it possible to push coaxial cable to new limits by providing a **compressed** video signal. Five or ten channels can now be placed in the same space once required for one channel. In 1992 TCI and Time-Warner announced bold plans to upgrade their systems to hundreds of channels using the new technology. The move to digital television was given a significant boost in 1994 when the Federal Communications Commission settled on a digital standard for the new high-definition television (HDTV) service.

Toward the Full-Service Network

The next stage in the evolution of cable is to reinvent interactive cable to take advantage of the convergence of telephones, computers, and the mass media. In 1993 the FCC authorized a new type of wireless telephone service, **personal communication networks (PCNs),** which combine the low cost and convenience of cordless phones with the coverage of **cellular radio.** Cable operators could now get into the telephone business by connecting PCN antennas through their networks. This also provides a two-way capability that can make home banking and shopping and interactive television programming possible on a wide scale without completely rebuilding cable systems. Nor are the advanced services limited to residential users. Many cable companies provide high-capacity data and voice and video links to large employers in their service areas, interconnecting multiple locations with long-distance telephone networks. The cable industry calls this approach the **full-service network.** Time-Warner put the first system to embody this concept into operation in Orlando, Florida (Karpinski, 1993).

New Multichannel Competition

The advantages of digital compression also impressed some of cable's competitors. In 1994 a new generation of direct broadcast satellite (DBS) services appeared. The new DBS systems use digital channel compression to provide more programming and use more powerful satellites so the receivers need only measure one or two feet across. By late 1993 nine different DBS companies—including one owned by major cable MSOs—announced plans for DBS service (Scully, 1993).

In its continuing effort to promote competition, the FCC authorized **multichannel MDS (MMDS)** systems in 1983. These systems offer up to 33 channels using frequencies that had previously been reserved for educational television broadcasts. The MMDS industry today reaches about 400,000 subscribers in some 100 systems scattered across the United States (Brown, 1993). Now, digital compression technology offers the prospect of hundreds of channels for these systems as well, and the Cable Act of 1992 opens up access to popular cable TV channels.

Also in 1992 telephone companies won the right to provide **video dial tone** to their customers, meaning that they could offer video signals. Under the video dial tone concept, programs would have to come from a separate company. However, the restrictions against telephone companies providing their own programs were relaxed in 1992–1994 through a series of court and FCC decisions. Digital compression technology can also be applied to standard telephone lines, making it possible to carry up to six television

---

Digital means computer readable.

Digital compression reduces the number of computer bits that have to be transmitted.

Personal communication networks (PCNs) combine the low cost of cordless phones with the mobility of cellular radio.

Cellular radio is a mobile telephone service that subdivides service areas into many small cells to maximize the number of users.

Full-service networks are cable television systems that provide telephone, data transmission, and interactive television as well as conventional (one-way) cable television.

Multichannel MDS (MMDS) systems are MDS systems with more than one channel.

Video dial tone means providing the basic ability to receive and originate video calls on a telephone network.

R E V I E W

1. How are cable television pictures transmitted to the home?
2. What new technologies are emerging as competitive threats to cable TV?
3. What is the full-service network?

---

channels plus telephone and data communications and videophone service on existing telephone wiring.

In 1993 the FCC authorized another new distribution technology—**cellular television.** This system is configured like a cellular radio network with numerous transmitters broadcasting signals to "cells," each only a few miles in diameter. Cellular television has a two-way capability so transactional services as well as two-way voice and video calls are possible.

INDUSTRY STRUCTURE

On the surface, cable television appears to be a highly localized medium, a result of the practice of granting cable franchises at the municipal level. In some 13,000 individual communities, each system picks up broadcast and satellite signals and relays them to subscribers in its respective franchise area. The monthly subscription fees are used to pay cable networks for the right to carry their programming. These fees range from a few cents per subscriber per month for C-SPAN to several dollars per month for pay TV channels like HBO. The local cable operator is responsible for maintenance of the system, billing, and customer service. Many systems sell advertising slots on basic channels to advertisers in their communities. Home shopping channels pay cable operators a commission on the sales generated in their franchise areas.

TABLE 10.3. TOP TEN CABLE MSOS

Rank	Name	Subscribers
1	Tele-Communications, Inc.	13,319,000
2	Time-Warner Cable	10,058,000
3	Continental Cablevision*	3,945,000
4	Comcast Corporation	3,375,000
5	Cox Communications	3,204,000
6	Cablevision Systems	2,830,000
7	Adelphia Communications	1,635,000
8	Cablevision Industries	1,434,000
9	Jones Intercable	1,352,000
10	Viacom Cable	1,158,000

*Announced acquisition by US West, February 1996

Source: *National Cable Television Association*

Most systems are owned by cable multiple system operators, the largest of which control hundreds of systems and serve millions of subscribers across many states (see Table 10.3). The largest MSO is TCI, which covers about 22 percent of all cable subscribers. TCI and the other "Top Five"—Time-Warner, Continental, Comcast, and Cablevision Systems—account for almost 60 percent of all subscribers. Large MSOs use their market power to negotiate substantial discounts on programming fees and equipment purchases. They also set corporatewide policy on local programming and pricing and marketing strategies and often make decisions about which cable networks are carried on local systems.

Basic Cable Networks

Over 60 basic cable TV networks are now delivered via satellite. The basic networks derive their revenues from two sources: advertising revenues and **affiliate fees.** The affiliate fees are paid by cable operators, usually on a per-subscriber basis. Many basic networks also make local advertising spots available; there are about 150 cable system interconnects that link cable operators in a given metropolitan area for advertising sales. The largest cable networks—Cable News Network (CNN), ESPN, and USA Network—are found on virtually all cable systems, whereas other networks appeal to highly specialized niches. There are almost three dozen regional basic cable networks (e.g., Madison Square Garden Network, Home Sports Entertainment, SportsChannel, and New England Cable News) that distribute news or sports to specified geographic regions.

Superstations like WGN and WWOR are a special case. Third parties like United Video (WGN) and Eastern Microwave (WWOR) intercept the off-air signals and put them on satellite. The satellite carriers collect the affiliate fees from the local cable operators, while the station owners reap the benefits of advertising sales to a national audience. Some systems pick up distant signals besides the satellite-delivered superstations; often they are independent stations from nearby major television markets.

Not all basic networks carry video programming. A dozen audio services represent a wide variety of musical genres, some offering compact disc–quality digital audio. Another dozen satellite-delivered computer text services, notably X*Press, deliver computerized news and information to cable subscribers. Other text-based services specialize in program listings and news headlines. Many cable operators now interconnect their networks with the Internet.

Pay TV Networks
Home Box Office is still by far the largest pay TV network. The other leading networks are Showtime, the Disney Channel, Cinemax, The Movie Channel, and Encore. Pay TV networks generally derive their revenues from affiliate fees, although some pay sports networks carry a limited amount of advertising. With only one revenue stream, the affiliate fees are substantially higher than for basic services, sometimes reaching several dollars per month per subscriber.

Pay-Per-View Networks
Pay-per-view programming is also delivered by satellite and is financed by affiliate fees, predicated on the number of subscribers who order each pay-per-view selection. The leading pay-per-view networks are Request and Viewer's Choice; there are 10 such networks in all.

Cable Franchise Authorities
In most states, cable is regulated at the municipal or county level. New Jersey and Connecticut opted for statewide regulation. Local regulation is usually delegated to a city employee who is advised by a local cable commission. These commissions monitor the performance of their cable companies when local franchises come up for renewal.

Direct Broadcast Satellite Networks
Direct Broadcast Satellite (DBS) companies such as Primestar and DirecTV pick up satellite feeds from cable television networks, as well as originate their own programming that is not available on cable. They transmit channels on their own high-powered satellites directly to their customers, who pay subscription fees back to the DBS operator, eliminating the local cable system as the "middle person." With all-digital systems, the DBS networks have more channel capacity than cable, much of which is used for pay-per-view. Missing from DBS line-ups are local TV stations not carried on satellite.

Multichannel TV Around the World
The United States and Canada have among the most extensive cable systems in the world. Cable TV got off to a much slower start in other countries, where powerful state-run telecomunications monopolies successfully protected their positions. Where cable companies did start, they were usually limited to the wealthier neighborhoods in the largest cities. It was not until the early 1990s that countries like Great Britain, Japan, and Taiwan started to establish national cable TV networks. In much of the European Community and the Far East, direct broadcast satellite emerged as the preferred means of multichannel television distribution.

Ownership and Control
Perhaps no other segment of the communications industry has been so profoundly shaped by efforts to regulate ownership interests as cable. Its survival as an independent industry

relied on regulations that, until the early 1990s at least, prevented local telephone companies from buying cable systems or providing television services in their territories. As soon as these restrictions were relaxed, the telephone industry quickly made its move, in some cases acquiring interests in cable companies and in other instances announcing plans to build their own cable networks. Broadcast television networks and, to a lesser extent, large broadcast and publishing group owners were kept from dominating the cable industry through other ownership restrictions.

Concentration of Ownership. Protected from outside domination, cable gave birth to giants of its own. Throughout the 1980s, the largest cable companies became very aggressive in acquiring new properties. Many companies prominent in the early history of cable, including Teleprompter (and its successor, Group W), Storer Cable, and United Cable, disappeared entirely. By 1992, the fifteen largest cable MSOs controlled over half the cable subscribers in the United States and attracted the attention of Congress and antitrust regulators.

Vertical Integration. As TCI became more **horizontally integrated** by acquiring other cable MSOs, it also became more **vertically integrated** by obtaining interests in cable programming networks. TCI owned interests in the Discovery Channel and Turner Broadcasting and spun off a subsidiary, Liberty Media, which holds substantial interests in several other networks. Turner played his own vertical integration game by acquiring the MGM Studios film library and later purchasing two small Hollywood studios that could make new programs for Turner's networks. Another TCI affiliate, Tempo Enterprises, sells subscriptions to satellite services. A parallel development was the merger of Time, Inc. (owner of HBO and the second-largest MSO) with Warner (another large MSO with interests in publishing and music) into a new multimedia conglomerate, Time-Warner.

The next step in vertical integration was typified by U.S. West's investment in Time-Warner. Other cable-telco combinations include BellSouth's investments in Prime Cable and QVC Networks (owner of cable shopping channels), Nynex's investment in Viacom, and Southwestern Bell's alliance with Cox Cable. In 1994 a "megamerger" involving TCI and Bell Atlantic fell through in the wake of new cable rate regulations, but this only paved the way for new vertical alliances, such as an agreement between TCI and computer-software giant Microsoft to launch an interactive computer channel.

As transnational firms jockey for strategic position in the Information Age, they seek all of the "pieces" necessary to put multimedia telecommunications networks into the home and the workplace. The pieces include telephony, retail distribution (local cable systems and video stores), wholesale distribution (cable networks), and software production (publishers and movie studios). The final piece is the hardware to bring digital signals into the home and provide users with an interactive interface. This makes further alliances involving consumer electronics and computer firms a distinct possibility.

Horizontal integration is concentrating ownership by acquiring companies that are all in the same business.

Vertical integration is concentrating ownership by acquiring companies that are in related businesses.

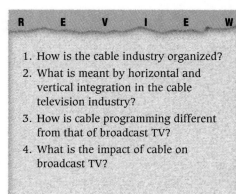

R E V I E W

1. How is the cable industry organized?
2. What is meant by horizontal and vertical integration in the cable television industry?
3. How is cable programming different from that of broadcast TV?
4. What is the impact of cable on broadcast TV?

GENRES AND FORMS IN MULTICHANNEL PROGRAMMING

Narrowcasting directs media channels to specific segments of the audience.

Perhaps cable television's most important contribution to programming is the concept of **narrowcasting,** or the creation of channels dedicated to particular interests or specialized groups of viewers. An analogy can be drawn to the magazine industry, where a wide array of magazines dedicated to special interests supplanted general-interest publications such as *Life* and *The Saturday Evening Post.* Likewise, specialized cable channels such as HBO (movies), ESPN (sports), and MTV (music) are winning more and more viewers from general-interest broadcast TV networks.

Narrowcasting probably would not have been possible without cable. For one thing, there are too few TV channel allocations available in any given area to dedicate entire channels to specific types of content. Advertising sales are predicated on reaching the widest possible audience, so it does not make sense to broadcast programs that appeal to only a small fraction of all the potential viewers. Advertising-supported basic cable networks are subject to the same advertising economics, but they also derive part of their income from subscription fees and can spread the program origination costs over thousands of cable systems, making it worthwhile to target programs to relatively small audiences.

Cable channels can also be profitable while reaching small audiences if they have an inexpensive source of programming. Although many cable channels have original programming, the staple of most networks is either "used" material (old movies or classic TV shows), free material (music videos provided by record companies), or material that is inexpensive to produce compared to prime-time entertainment programming (weather forecasts).

Genre Channels

Most cable networks represent the extension of genres of programming found on broadcast television to channel-length format. The earliest cable networks represented some of the most popular categories of programming, such as news (see the "Cable Television Channels" box on page 250). A second wave of networks went after subgenres, such as business news. As programmers grope for ideas for hundreds of channels, virtually every type of program or program segment that has ever appeared on television has its own channel. By 1995 the "news" category had expanded to channels dedicated to world news (CNN), regional news (New England Cable News), local news (News 12 Long Island), repeated-on-the-half-hour news (Headline News), weather news (The Weather Channel), entertainment news (E!), business news (CNBC), and news programs from around the world (SCOLA). Future plans call for channels devoted to talk about the news (Talk TV Network), news from Africa (World African Network), Spanish-language news (*Canal de Noticias*), and international news (CNN International).

We will call these **genre channels,** in that almost everything that appears on them is of the same genre of programming. Some other genres that have made the transition from broadcast television time slots to cable channels of their own include movies (HBO, Showtime, The Movie Channel, Disney Channel, American Movie Classics), cartoons (The Cartoon Network), sports (ESPN plus several regional sports networks such as PRISM, PASS, and MSG), religion (The Inspirational Network, VISN, ACTS), and situation comedy (Nick at Night).

ONE GENRE OF CABLE PROGRAMMING IS THE NEWS CHANNEL, AS EXEMPLIFIED BY CNBC, WHICH SPECIALIZES IN TALK AND BUSINESS NEWS.

FIRST IN BUSINESS
FIRST IN TALK

Genre channels feature programs of a certain type, such as movies or sports events.

Not all of the cable genres were imitated from commercial television. One network, the Discovery Channel, amplified the nature and history programming found on public broadcasting to channel form. The Learning Channel and Mind Extension University feature another PBS specialty, the telecourse. One of the most popular cable genres, the disk jockey format of music video channels (MTV, VH-1, Country Music Television), was copied from radio. The character-generated community bulletin boards found on cable are the descendants of local newspapers, complete with classified ads and notices of upcoming community events.

There are some relatively original cable genres, which have only distant relatives in the annals of regularly scheduled broadcast programming. Community programming is produced in the local community, often using studios provided by the cable operator. Public access programs are produced by local residents for channels dedicated to community programming. The local public affairs programs that broadcasters sometimes run in the early morning hours are the closest that off-air television comes to this style of programming. **Government access** is exemplified by the city council and local commission meetings found on many cable systems. Many local communities have their own version, with local cablecasts of town council and community board meetings. Other community organizations may also have their own channels, depending on the requirements of the local cable franchise. For example, local schools and colleges, parks and recreation departments, and fire departments sometimes have their own channels. Local origination channels are also locally produced, but by the cable operator instead of community residents. These channels often cover local high school sports and cultural events.

Home shopping channels (Home Shopping Network, QVC) hawk consumer goods and encourage viewers to phone in orders to 800 numbers. Program-length commercials were long forbidden on broadcast TV, so the shopping networks were truly cable originals. The same is true of adult channels that feature movies deemed "too sexy" for broadcast television.

Channels with Target Audiences

Another type of channel—called **demographic channels**—is built around groups of people rather than program genres. Programming is assembled from several genres to appeal to members of the target group. One of the first basic cable networks, Black Entertainment Television, is a prime example. Its programming includes sitcoms, music videos, black college sports, news, and public affairs programming for African American viewers. Women (Lifetime), children (Nickelodeon), Hispanics (Univision and Galavision), and Japanese (TV-Japan) are among other target audiences.

Other cable channels targeted to groups of people might better be described as **lifestyle channels,** since their programs are aimed at people who share a common interest or way of life, regardless of their demographic characteristics. There are channels devoted to frequent travelers (The Travel Channel), to families with children (The Family Channel), to "active adults" (The Nostalgia Channel), to families with differentially abled members (America's Disability Channel), to people who think of themselves as "country" (Nashville Network), and to others who think they are "cultured" (Arts & Entertainment).

General-Audience Channels

Other cable channels maintain a balance of programming intended to attract a broad **general audience** throughout the day. In effect, these channels translate the broadcast television

CABLE TELEVISION CHANNELS

Genre Channels

Education—The Learning Channel, Mind Extension University

Movies—American Movie Classics, Cinemax,* The Disney Channel,* Encore,* Flix,* Home Box Office,* The Movie Channel,* Showtime*

Music videos—MTV, Country Music Television, The Box, VH-1, MOR Music Television, Z Music

News—ChicagoLand Television News, Consumer News and Business Channel, Cable News Network, E! Entertainment Television, Headline News, International Channel, New England Cable News, New York 1 News, NewsChannel 8, News 12 Long Island, Orange County News Channel, Pennsylvania Cable Network, SCOLA, The Weather Channel

Government meetings—C-SPAN, C-SPAN II, The California Channel

Religious—Atlanta Interfaith, Bay Area Religious Channel, The Ecumenical Channel, EWTN, The Inspirational Network, Trinity Broadcasting Network, VISN/ACTS, Worship

Sports—Arizona Sports, Empire Sports Network, ESPN, Home Sports Entertainment, Home Team Sports,* KBL Sports Network, Madison Square Garden Network, Meadows Racing Network, Midwest Sports Channel, New England Sports Network,* Prime Sports, Prime Ticket, Prism,* Pro-Am Sports System,* SportsChannel, SportSouth, Sunshine Network

Shopping—Home Shopping Network I & II, QVC Fashion Channel, QVC Network, ValueVision

Miscellaneous genres—The Cartoon Network (Cartoons), The Sci-Fi Channel (science fiction), Comedy Central (stand-up comedy), Court-TV (courtroom coverage)

Demographic and Lifestye Channels

Women—Lifetime

Children—Nickelodeon

Families—The Family Channel

African Americans—Black Entertainment Television

Hispanics—Canal Sur,* Galavision, Telemundo, Univision

Asian Americans—TV Asia, TV-Japan

Differentially abled—America's Disability Channel

Travelers—The Travel Channel, Florida Tourism Channel

Country—The Nashville Network

Culture—Arts & Entertainment, Bravo

Active adults—Nostalgia Channel

General-Audience Channels

Superstations—KTLA, KTVT, TBS, WGN, WPIX, WSBK, WWOR

Cable originated—Fox Net, USA Network, Turner Network Television

*Pay channel
Source: *Cablevision*, September 20, 1993, pp. 42–43.

programming strategy to cable. The superstations best embody this approach, since they are TV stations in their local areas. These stations include WTBS (Channel 17 in Atlanta), WGN (Chicago's Channel 9), WWOR (Channel 9 from New Jersey), KTLA (Channel 5 from Los Angeles), and WPIX (New York's Channel 11). In addition to the usual diet of old movies and television reruns found on independent television stations everywhere, most superstations are the "home stations" of professional baseball, basketball, and hockey teams. There are also general-audience channels, such as USA Network and Turner Network Television (TNT), that are not superstations, but whose programming imitates the independent television station mix.

Trends in Multichannel Programming

Even with only a few dozen channels to fill, cable programmers are beginning to run out of program genres to make into channels. Where will they get 500 channels' worth of programs? One answer is to cater to more and more specialized genres and audience groups, such as The Sci-Fi Channel and The Golden American Network. In the music video category there is an opportunity to develop a wide range of channels that reflect various musical genres, beginning with the major strains of popular music (rap, heavy metal) and extending to more and more esoteric forms (jazz, the blues, even classical music). Movie channels have plans to "multiplex" several satellite feeds, which schedule current movies at staggered starting times, just like the multiplex movie theaters at the local shopping mall. Another approach is to dedicate channels to specific movie genres (action adventure, love stories, mystery, westerns). Dozens of the new channels will be devoted to pay-per-view programs, including live sporting events and the 30 (or 50 or 200) movie titles that are the "top renters" in home video stores.

R E V I E W

1. What is meant by narrowcasting?
2. Name four types of cable programming and give an example of each.
3. What is the difference between local origination, government access, and public access?

AUDIENCES FOR MULTICHANNEL MEDIA

Cable is in almost two-thirds of U.S. households, and all but 4 percent of American homes—mostly in remote rural areas—are passed by a cable network. Almost all (95 percent) cable households have thirty or more channels, and a third have fifty-four or more. About two-fifths of cable subscribers also subscribe to pay channels (NCTA Research and Policy Analysis Department, 1993).

Who does not have cable? Older households, especially those without children, and low-income homes are relatively unlikely to have cable. Most nonsubscribers either say that they cannot afford cable, that cable is not worth its cost, that they do not watch enough TV to justify a subscription, or that their viewing needs are met by broadcast television (LaRose & Atkin, 1988).

Viewership Patterns

Ratings for individual cable programs are minuscule by broadcast TV standards. A "hit" cable program may attract only 2 or 3 percent of all cable television households, about a tenth the audience for a "hit" prime-time broadcast television series. However, viewing accumulated across all cable channels is significant, with over two-fifths (43 percent) of all viewing in cable households accounted for by cable satellite networks. Cable homes watch over 25 percent more television overall than noncable households (Cabletelevision Advertising Bureau, 1993).

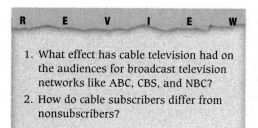

R E V I E W

1. What effect has cable television had on the audiences for broadcast television networks like ABC, CBS, and NBC?
2. How do cable subscribers differ from nonsubscribers?

Impact on Broadcasting

In recent years, cable viewing has eroded viewership of broadcast television channels. Since the early 1980s, broadcast network shares in prime time—the percentage of homes using television that are tuned to ABC, CBS, or NBC during prime evening viewing hours—has declined from seven-eighths (87 percent) to less than three-fifths (59 percent). The losses have been especially severe for some of the demographic groups that advertisers value most, including households earning over $60,000 per year and women ages 25 to 54.

ISSUES IN MULTICHANNEL MEDIA

As with other media, there are several issues challenging multichannel media.

Ownership and Competition

Even before the round of mergers, acquisitions, and alliances between cable and telephone companies in the early 1990s, there were concerns about excessive vertical and horizontal integration and the impact of competitiveness in the cable television industry. Congress and the FCC have intervened at various times in the ownership issue, at first to protect cable from being bought up by broadcasters and telephone companies and later to prevent the mature cable television industry itself from devouring newer systems, such as satellite TV and wireless cable.

The Cable Act of 1992 sought to enhance competitive balance by restricting any one cable operator to less than 20 percent of cable homes, although this provision was soon struck down in court. The new law also let stand a restriction of the Cable Act of 1984 that prevented telephone companies from owning cable systems inside their service areas. This was also prohibited by the terms of the AT&T divestiture. However, further court rulings and congressional action may yet set aside the **cross ownership** restrictions.

Why restrict ownership? Excessive horizontal integration, which might result if major MSOs kept acquiring more and more cable subscribers, can lead to anticompetitive practices. For example, TCI reportedly uses its market power as the largest cable operator to negotiate special low rates for basic and pay programming services. Other cable operators then have to pay higher rates, which they pass along to the consumer and which eventually undermine the profits of the other cable companies, in turn making them more vulnerable to further acquisitions by TCI. The networks that TCI carries on its systems are almost assured of success, while the others are severely handicapped. In one notorious case, the cable giant threatened to remove a channel from its system, dramatically lowering the value of the network, and then one of its affiliated companies turned around and bought the network at a bargain price. At some point in the future, this could give TCI and a few other multimedia giants a virtual veto power over new programming concepts.

Vertical integration—such as when cable MSOs acquire interests in movie studios, programming networks, and DBS companies as well as their core business in home distribution—also has pitfalls for the consumer, particularly when some of the businesses are regulated and others are not. There is a temptation to **"cross-subsidize"** the unregulated parts (movie studios and cable networks) with inflated rates paid by the regulated entities (local cable systems) and their customers. The addition of telephone service to the picture and the possibility of further combinations with consumer electronics firms raises issues reminiscent of the halcyon days of the AT&T monopoly, when it was accused of using its telephone equipment manufacturing division to drain profits out of its local telephone operations and of using profits from its local phone companies to subsidize competition in the long-distance market. Instead of the competition between cable and telephone companies that Congress hopes to foster, the outcome may be a single telecommunications monopoly encompassing voice, data, and

Cross ownership is owning various kinds of media, usually in the same geographic locale.

Cross subsidy applies revenues from a profitable area to a less profitable one.

BACK TO THE FUTURE WITH INTERACTIVE CABLE, AGAIN

In the 1990s interactive television has become one of the bywords that describes the convergence of computer, telephone, and mass media technologies that seems to be just around the corner. Before heading for the on-ramp to the information superhighway, it might be wise to revisit the last time interactive television was tried—and failed.

In early 1977 Warner Cable (which later became part of Time-Warner) stunned the industry by announcing plans for a two-way cable system, dubbed Qube, which would allow viewers to "talk back to their TV sets" by entering responses on hand-held keypads. The ideas that were touted back then for interactive shows are the same ones advanced today: soap operas with viewer-selectable plot twists, instant polls for community affairs programs, interactive quiz shows where the audience plays along at home. The system could also be used for home banking and shopping and, eventually, for retrieving computer information from public libraries and databases. The idea was an immediate hit with cable franchise authorities who were then in the midst of awarding lucrative urban properties to cable MSOs. The prophets of high tech waxed enthusiastic about the prospects of a "wired nation" that would bring interactive broadband services to all via cable television by the 1990s.

That future never came. Warner eventually built Qube systems in Columbus, Ohio, Pittsburgh, and Dallas but the expected consumer demand for interactive television and transactional services never materialized. By the late 1980s plans for advanced interactive services were dropped, although the two-way systems could still be used to place orders for pay-per-view programs.

Why was Qube a flop? The most fundamental problem was the failure to develop appealing services for the consumer. Interactive programs were interesting at first, but the novelty quickly wore off and the cost of developing original interactive programming was prohibitive. In the early 1980s few people were familiar enough with computer networks to make them comfortable completing shopping and financial transactions on them. Without a critical mass of users, the cost of the interactive terminals remained high, and there were insufficient numbers of subscribers across which to spread the cost of the interactive programming. By the late 1980s, companies like Warner were hard pressed to come up with the funds to build even "plain vanilla" urban systems, let alone ones with all the "bells and whistles" that interactive cable promised.

The Qube experience remains a cautionary tale for the Information Age. Despite a decade of experimentation with interactive cable and telephone-based videotex systems, no on has as yet identified a mix of services that makes them irresistible to consumers. Of course, there are many more personal computer users now than in the early 1980s, and the spread of

automated teller machines has perhaps accustomed many to the idea of letting computer systems transact their financial affairs. The integration of computer and telecommunications has also made possible some new technical solutions that may prove less costly than Qube. However, the economics of interactive program production still pose a problem, as does the willingness of the viewing public to pay for the right to "talk back to television." One thing is virtually certain: If interactive television fails again, ten years from now someone else will undoubtedly step forward to "invent" it all over again.

video communications. This could lead to higher rates, poorer service, and less diversity in the points of view presented to the consumer.

However, there are also some arguments in favor of less competition and more concentrated ownership. For example, the combination of telephone and cable companies might save the consumer money by making it possible to construct a single fiber optics–based information superhighway to the home. If telephone and cable companies compete, consumers might have to pay for two superhighway systems instead of one. As information technologies converge with mass media and assume more and more importance in the world economy, there is also a question of maintaining America's competitive position. Further vertical and horizontal integration might be desirable to create companies large enough and diversified enough to compete successfully on the world stage.

Free TV or Pay TV?

The tradition of commercial broadcasting in the United States has led to periodic protests from viewers when programs that are received "for free" over the air become available only on cable. This issue has been raised most vigorously with respect to professional sports coverage. There is not really much that lawmakers can do to manipulate the flow of programming, of course—they always run up against the First Amendment—but the pressure they bring to bear has succeeded in keeping premiere sports events like the World Series and the Superbowl on free TV, at least for now.

There is really no such thing as free TV, anyway. Consumers pay for the ads that support commercial television as part of the price of mass-market consumer goods. Since low-income households allocate a proportionately greater percentage of their incomes to such purchases, it can be argued that they bear an unfair portion of the cost of so-called free television. It can even be argued that pay TV is a more equitable arrangement than free TV, since the users of the information support it directly through their subscription fees, rather than forcing all consumers to pay in the form of higher prices for commercially advertised products.

This issue takes on some more serious implications as we travel up the "on-ramp" to the information superhighway. If cable systems become purveyors of consumer information, adult education courses, and library resources to the home, the question of what is free and what is not is much more important. If only the upper classes can afford access to these vital services, the gap between rich and poor could widen even more.

Universal service is reaching all members of the population with service.

One solution might be to expand the concept of **universal service**—the idea that everyone should have access to basic telecommunications services—to cable television. This policy has long been a central one in telephone industry regulation, where it has succeeded in bringing telephone service to all but 5 percent of American homes. One means of accomplishing this goal is to subsidize basic "lifeline service" for low-income households. Another option would be to cover the cost of advanced telecommunications service in income maintenance programs such as welfare and food stamps ("information stamps"?). But which level of service will be considered the basic entitlement? Is "dial tone" enough, or should the minimum service include access to certain types of information as well?

Community Programming

Community programming, including public access, government access, and other types of community-originated programming, is arguably one of the few original forms found on cable—and also one of the most controversial. Cable rules have long mandated that some channels be set aside for community programming, and, at the height of the franchise wars,

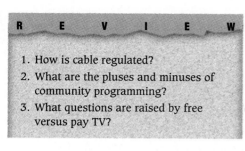

R E V I E W

1. How is cable regulated?
2. What are the pluses and minuses of community programming?
3. What questions are raised by free versus pay TV?

some cities were able to demand that large blocks of channels be dedicated to community use.

Although almost everyone would agree that giving community residents an "open camera" to express their points of view is a useful exercise in a free society, not all would agree that community television is a wise use of public resources. The cost of constructing and maintaining the extra channel capacity and origination studios is tantamount to a hidden "TV tax" for the benefit of local video stars. The programming that results from this expenditure has been something of a disappointment, usually attracting very small audiences who are dissatisfied with what little live programming they manage to find on their community channels (Atkin & LaRose, 1991), most of which show only written announcements. In some areas, sexually explicit material or offensive programs produced by "hate groups" have found their way onto community channels, sparking First Amendment controversies.

The convergence of cable, computer, and telecommunications technologies might reinvigorate the community channel concept. No one wants a channel that shows the local school lunch menu twenty-four hours a day, but a channel that could deliver a wide variety of citizen information on request could prove useful indeed. However, for this to happen the universal service question will have to be addressed. Otherwise, the cable "have nots" could become second-class citizens. For example, in Cerritos, California, where an advanced cable system was on trial, the city prohibited the use of the interactive cable systems to make reservations at the city swimming pool out of concern that lower-income residents who could not afford cable would be denied access to the facility.

SUMMARY & REVIEW

How Did the Cable Television Industry Develop?

How did cable spread throughout the United States?
Cable television started as a shared community antenna service for rural communities in 1948. It expanded into suburban areas beginning in 1972 and reached the largest cities only in the early 1980s. Today, cable is accessible to about 95 percent of all U.S. households, and over 60 percent of those homes subscribe.

What laws and regulations shaped cable TV?
Between 1966 and 1972, the FCC kept cable out of large TV markets to protect broadcasters. The Cable Act of 1984 left cable largely unregulated and kept telephone companies out of the industry through cross-ownership restrictions. The Cable Act of 1992 imposed rate regulation and paved the way for new competition.

Which technologies were critical to cable's early growth?
Coaxial cable makes it possible to transmit dozens of channels to homes in a cable franchise area. Microwave and satellite transmission made many distant signals, superstations, and other new channels available throughout the country. Scrambling systems and set-top converters restricted transmission to subscribers who paid for the appropriate level of basic and pay cable.

What is the difference between pay cable and basic cable?
Basic cable refers to the block of channels offered to all subscribers in return for their basic monthly service fee. Subscribers may also opt for additional channels for which they pay a separate monthly fee, often on a per channel basis. These are called pay channels.

What contributions did John Walson, Ted Turner, and John Malone make to the cable industry?
John Walson created the first cable television system in Mahanoy, Pennsylvania, in 1948.

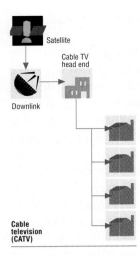

Satellite

Cable TV
head end

Downlink

Cable
television
(CATV)

Ted Turner established the first basic cable network, WTCG (later, WTBS), in 1975. John Malone is responsible for the emergence of TCI as the world's largest cable television operator.

What Are the Important Technology Trends in Multichannel Television?

How are cable television pictures transmitted to the home?
The cable operator's head end picks up transmissions from satellite, microwave, broadcast, and local studio sources. The channels are combined electronically and transmitted over a coaxial cable network to the home. A set-top converter is used to recover the channels and play them on the home television receiver. Pay TV signals may be scrambled so that only homes that pay an additional monthly fee may receive them. New addressable cable systems make it possible to electronically authorize the reception of entire pay channels or specific programs, a type of distribution called pay-per-view.

What new technologies are emerging as competitive threats to cable TV?
The Cable Act of 1992 requires that operators of new DBS, MMDS, and cellular television systems have equal access to cable programming. This should open up competition from these alternative delivery systems. Telephone companies can provide video dial tone, and advances in digital video and digital compression make them a competitive threat as well. VCRs have also had some impact on cable television.

What is the full-service network?
The full-service network is the cable TV industry's approach to the so-called information superhighway. It means offering telephone, computer, and interactive cable services as well as conventional cable television service. Thus, the full-service network is the competitive answer to the telephone companies' video dial tone offering.

What Is Unique About Cable Television?

How is the cable industry organized?
Most local cable systems are owned by multiple system operators (MSOs) and purchase their programming from the various basic, pay, and pay-per-view networks, predicated on monthly per-subscriber affiliate fees. The local systems also sell advertising on basic cable channels. Some MSOs own interests in programming services as well as in the local systems that distribute them to the public. Regulatory oversight is provided by local cable franchise authorities and the FCC.

What is meant by horizontal and vertical integration in the cable television industry?
Horizontal integration happens when large MSOs such as TCI and Time-Warner acquire interests in other cable operators who also own local distribution networks. Vertical integration happens when cable MSOs acquire interests in related businesses, such as cable programming networks. Both vertical and horizontal integration raise the potential threat of monopolistic practices that may harm the consumer.

How is cable programming different from that of broadcast TV?
Most cable channels are built around the concept of narrowcasting to specialized audiences, predicated either on a common genre of programming or on the demographic characteristics or lifestyles of their viewers. However, some general-audience cable channels emulate the broadcast TV model. Music videos and community channels are among the more novel cable programming forms to emerge.

What is the impact of cable on broadcast TV?
The proportion of viewers who tune into prime-time broadcasts from ABC, CBS, and NBC has declined dramatically in recent years. Cable households are heavy viewers of television, and over two-fifths of viewing in cable households is now devoted to channels available only on cable.

What Genres and Forms Are Offered?

Why does cable have narrowcasting instead of broadcasting?
Narrowcast channels are those devoted to special interests or audience groups, much like magazines that cater to special audiences. The large number of channels available on cable TV systems is what makes it feasible to offer channels dedicated to such specialized interests. Since cable networks derive all or part of their revenues from subscriptions, as well as from advertising sales, it is also economically

feasible to offer narrowcast channels that appeal only to relatively small audiences.

What is the difference between local origination, government access, and public access?
All three are types of programming supplied by the community in which the cable system is located. Local origination programming is produced by the cable operator, while government access is provided by local government entities, and public access programs are created by community residents or private community groups.

How do cable subscribers and nonsubscribers differ?
Almost all American homes have cable service available, but less than two-thirds subscribe. Nonsubscribers tend to have low household incomes or are older residents, often without children. Nonsubscribers also tend to have busy lives that do not allow them to watch cable, or they find that broadcast television meets their viewing needs.

What Issues Face Multichannel Media Today?

How is cable regulated?
The Cable Act of 1992 reimposed regulatory control over cable, largely reversing the Cable Act of 1984. Regulation of cable TV rates is now shared between the FCC and local franchise authorities. There is growing concern about horizontal and vertical integration in the cable industry. Telephone companies are still prohibited from owning cable systems in their service territories, but they can provide a limited form of video dial tone service, an arrangement that restricts them from owning significant interests in programming services.

What are the pluses and minuses of community programming?
Programming on public access and government access channels offers important outlets for airing diverse views in a community. However, community channels have low viewership levels, can add substantial amounts to cable rates, and sometimes contain sexually explicit material or other forms of objectionable content.

What questions are raised by free versus pay TV?
As more programming moves to cable channels and as more cable programs are offered on a pay channel or pay-per-view basis, less and less programming is available on "free" broadcast TV, raising questions about equality of access. The question takes on new importance as cable systems evolve into full-service versions of the information superhighway, leading some to call for a universal cable service concept.

REFERENCES

Atkin, D., & LaRose, R. (1991, Fall). Cable access: Market concerns amidst the marketplace of ideas. *Journalism Quarterly, 68*(3), 354–362.

Baldwin, T., & VcVoy, S. (1983). *Cable communication.* Englewood Cliffs, NJ: Prentice-Hall.

Brown, R. (1993, August 2). Wireless cable looks to expand its niche. *Broadcasting,* pp. 20–21.

Cabletelevision Advertising Bureau. (1993). *1993 cable TV facts.* New York: Cabletelevision Advertising Bureau.

Karpinski, R. (1993, November 1). Time-Warner's magic kingdom. *Telephony,* pp. 139–142.

LaRose, R., & Atkin, D. (1988, Fall). Satisfaction, demographic and media environment and predictors of cable subscription. *Journal of Broadcasting and Electronic Media, 32*(4), 403–413.

NCTA Research and Policy Analysis Department. (1993). *Twenty-first century television.* Washington, DC: National Cable Television Association.

Scully, S. (1993, August 2). The nine who would be DBS. *Broadcasting,* p. 45.

Stump, M., & Jessell, H. (1988, November 21), Cable: The first forty years. *Broadcasting,* pp. 37–49.

Chapter 11

THE TELEPHONE INDUSTRY

C H A P T E R   P R E V I E W

n this chapter we turn to the telephone, which is both one of the oldest electronic communications media and also one of the most up-to-date. We will track the evolution of the business institutions, government policies, and technologies that make the telephone system what it is today. Along the way, we will see how many of the technologies that are now revolutionizing the mass media had their origin in the public telephone system. We will also investigate the transformation of the telephone from a familiar instrument of interpersonal voice communication into a high-capacity "intelligent" network that may one day integrate voice, data, and video as well as interpersonal and mass communications.

Wow! Volume Four of Slim Whitman's Greatest Hits. Dial 1-800-W-E-Y-O-D-E-L. Gotta have it!

Hellowww Mr. Aberthnot are you calling to check on that shipment of Slim Whitman's Greatest Hits Volume Three if you remember we said we would send it out to you last Tuesday and . . .

No, I'm calling for Volume Four. Saaay, how did you know it was me and that I already ordered . . .

Oh we have Caller ID and keep a complete record of all your orders and I see that you have all of Slim's albums now and would you like to join our yodel-of-the-month club for a 30 percent discount on music in the Slim Whitman style starting with his Volume Four?

Wow! Gotta have it! Let me give you my . . .

No need just touch in your personal authorization code and the charge will show up on your next telephone bill. [CLICK.]

[RING.] Howdy, pardner. This is Slim Whitman. I'm callin' all my fans to tell them about my excitin' new exercise video, "Yodelcizin'."

Wow! Gotta have it!

A BRIEF HISTORY OF THE TELEPHONE INDUSTRY

he history of the telephone industry is a repetitive cycle of technological innovation, followed by the extension of monopoly power predicated on the technical advances, restriction by the government on the monopoly, and restructuring of the industry. It is also largely the history of American Telephone and Telegraph (AT&T) and its corporate "relatives."

The Moment of Invention

A speech teacher by the name of Alexander Graham Bell was working in his Boston laboratory one March day in 1876 when he spilled some acid on his lap and called out for his assistant. "Mr. Watson, come here, I want you," he said, and the telephone was born.* Ironically, Bell did not start out to invent the telephone at all.

Instead, he was working on the "harmonic telegraph," which would make it possible to carry multiple telegraph messages on a single wire. Another inventor, Elisha Gray, arrived at the patent office a few hours after Bell and narrowly missed his place in history. Bell's own application made no mention of a telephone, and he did not actually transmit intelligible speech until *after* the patent was granted. The description of the key operational principle was a handwritten addendum in a margin of the application, which Gray's backers later (unsuccessfully) claimed had been cribbed in after the filing. Perhaps neither Gray nor Bell really deserved the credit. Philipp Reis of Germany had invented a device that could transmit musical notes in 1860. Daniel Drawbaugh, a rustic tinkerer from Yellow Breeches Creek,

Pennsylvania, claimed he had invented the telephone in 1867 and came within one vote of winning a Supreme Court decision backing that claim. And it was Mr. Watson who invented the device that most symbolizes the telephone and the company that it spawned—the telephone bell.

The Rise of the Bell System

The Bell Telephone Company was established in 1877, and after surviving a patent challenge by the Western Union Telegraph Company—and replacing Bell himself and his in-laws with hard-nosed Yankee businessmen—it began to prosper (see Table 11.1). In 1882 the Bell System acquired Western Electric, an electrical manufacturing firm that had been cofounded by Elisha Gray, putting into place the second cornerstone of a powerful vertically integrated mo-

TABLE 11.1. TELEPHONE INDUSTRY MILESTONES

Year	Event
1876	Alexander Graham Bell invents the telephone
1893–1894	Bell patents expire, independent telephone companies organized
1899	American Telephone and Telegraph (AT&T) founded
1907	Theodore Vail becomes AT&T president
1910	Interstate Commerce Commission (ICC) established
1913	Kingsbury Commitment—AT&T sells Western Union, allows interconnection and ICC oversight
1915	First transcontinental telephone call
1918–1919	U.S. Post Office takes over Bell System
1934	Federal Communications Commission (FCC) established
1949	Antitrust case filed against AT&T
1951	Direct long-distance dialing
1955	Hush-a-Phone case permits connection of non-Bell equipment to public network
1956	AT&T signs Consent Decree, keeps Western Electric, promises to stick to telephone business
1962	First digital telephone call
1977	MCI's Execunet service authorized
1982	Modified Final Judgment splits local and long-distance networks
1996	AT&T sells its equipment business; Telecommunications Act of 1996 passes

*Historical accounts are drawn from Brooks (1976), Cole (1991), and Temin (1987).

LONG-DISTANCE LINES WERE ALREADY IN PLACE BY THE 1890S. HERE ALEXANDER GRAHAM BELL INAUGURATES THE LINE BETWEEN NEW YORK AND CHICAGO IN 1892 AS JOURNALISTS AND AT&T OFFICIALS LOOK ON.

Universal service is the provision of telephony or other services to all or almost all households.

Monopoly occurs when one company dominates or controls an industry.

Rate of return regulation allows telecommunications companies to earn only a specified fixed rate of profit based on the value of their capital investments.

nopoly. The Bell System defended its patent rights in the courts and bought out the inventors that it chose not to sue. It also pushed telephone service throughout the land by awarding franchises to local investors.

When the original patents ran out in the early 1890s, independent telephone companies sprang up around the country. Competition was cutthroat—or perhaps "cutwire," since one tactic was to cut one's competitors' wires during the night. The Bell System used its market power to undercut its competitors' rates and buy out the losers. Bell also refused to interconnect its competitors with its rapidly expanding long-distance network. It continued the battle in the courts, trying to enforce other patents it had bought, but these tactics lost their effectiveness as the sympathies of the courts swung to the new underdogs. The competition forced the company, now renamed American Telephone and Telegraph, to lower its rates and to expand rapidly while sacrificing quality of service and employee morale. By 1907 AT&T was in trouble. The Yankee aristocrats who had wrested control of the company from Bell in the 1870s were themselves ousted.

The Vail Years

The New York bankers who now controlled the company brought back Theodore Vail to manage it. Vail had previously headed Bell System operations until 1887, but resigned when the former management failed to share his expansive vision of a universal telephone company that would provide quality service to all. This principle of **universal service** became the watchword of AT&T and its regulators. Vail restored investor confidence, fostered research, reorganized management, and instilled a new devotion to customer service. He was among the first American industrialists to apply the principles of scientific management, which transformed the company into a model of efficiency.

AT&T also was a model of ruthlessness, as Vail's Wall Street ally, J. P. Morgan, cut off credit to any phone company Vail wanted to gobble up, making them easy buyout targets. Vail overreached himself by acquiring Western Union in 1910, raising for the first time—but by no means the last—the specter of a national telecommunications **monopoly** owned by AT&T. In 1910 the Mann-Elkins Act established the Interstate Commerce Commission with jurisdiction over telephone service and other interstate businesses. After being advised by the federal government that AT&T might be in violation of the Sherman Antitrust Act, Vail canceled the Western Union deal in 1913, allowed interconnection with other telephone companies, and sought government approval for further acquisitions. This agreement, the so-called Kingsbury Commitment, shaped the basic course of the American telephone industry for the next seventy years.

Concerns about monopoly power also led to state regulation. In return for the right to operate as the sole provider of telephone service in a specified service area, the telephone companies agreed to "open their books" to regulators and accept a fixed percentage of profit on their investments while extending service to the largest possible number of users. This model became known as **rate of return** regulation. This arrangement shielded telephone subscribers from the predatory pricing of an unrestrained monopoly company while assuring company stockholders a steady, if relatively modest, return on their investment.

For a time it appeared that government control might become complete, following the model of state-run phone systems in Europe. All U.S. telephone and telegraph systems were put under the control of the post office for a brief time at the end of World War I, but the rate increases that ensued provoked a public clamor for a speedy return to private ownership.

By the time Vail left office in 1919, AT&T was *the* phone company. It embarked on a long period of prosperity and wide public acceptance. Congress passed the Graham Act in 1921 to codify the Kingsbury Commitment, exempting AT&T from the Sherman Act and validating Vail's notion of a "natural monopoly"—that is, it only made economic sense to have a single phone company serving an area.

The Regulators Fight Back

In the prosperous 1920s, AT&T flirted with "new technologies" invented in its laboratories and briefly tried to dominate the industries the inventions spawned. In the early 1920s, AT&T set up its own radio network and sought to control the rest of the radio industry with two old tricks: patent enforcement and refusal of interconnection rights, this time to the telephone lines that linked national radio networks. It dominated the new talking motion picture medium by licensing sound equipment through its Western Electric subsidiary. By 1927 AT&T had demonstrated television as well. However, mindful of the threat of new government regulation, AT&T returned to Vail's game plan and gave up these interests to concentrate on telephone service.

AT&T's fortunes waned during the Great Depression when telephone subscriptions declined. AT&T's political and economic capital were depleted by continuing dividend payments to stockholders while laying off tens of thousands of employees. This did not exactly endear the company to the Roosevelt administration, and communications reform was added to the New Deal agenda.

Common carriers are transportation or telecommunications companies that carry others' goods or services.

Tariffs are the published rates that common carriers charge for their services.

The Communications Act of 1934 defined AT&T's role as a **common carrier**. That is, AT&T and other telephone companies could transport telecommunications traffic over facilities that were available on an equal basis to all paying customers, but they could not have a financial interest in the creation of the content that was carried. AT&T also had to make regular financial reports to the new Federal Communications Commission and to file the rates, or **tariffs,** they charged.

The new commission promptly launched a full-scale investigation of AT&T's ownership of Western Electric. It was virtually impossible for competing equipment manufacturers to make sales within the Bell System. Despite the fact that Western Electric equipment cost less than any other, it appeared to the investigators that the company charged more than necessary, thereby fattening local telephone rates as well as its own coffers.

World War II put this issue on the back burner, but in 1949 the Justice Department filed suit under the Sherman Antitrust Act to force the sale of Western Electric. The 1956 Consent Decree that resolved the suit kept AT&T intact, but Western Electric agreed to manufacture only the types of equipment needed for the Bell System, and AT&T agreed to confine itself to the common carrier business and to license its patents on fair terms.

Opening Cracks in the Monopoly

The 1956 Consent Decree did not fully satisfy government regulators, particularly after it came to light that some rather chummy behind-the-scenes negotiations between AT&T and government officials had transpired. AT&T's control over the equipment that could be connected to its network was the next target. AT&T claimed that complete control was essential to maintain the network's technical integrity, but this rule also conveniently preserved Western Electric's near-monopoly on customer telephone equipment. This prohibition reached ridiculous extremes in the case of the Hush-a-Phone, a simple rubber cup that attached to the telephone receiver to screen out unwanted environmental noise. It had no electronic components so there was no question of electrical interference. In 1955, after some seven years of deliberation, the FCC finally realized this point in the Hush-a-Phone Decision, although not until 1968 were the remaining equipment interconnection restrictions removed. The next blow fell on AT&T's monopoly in the long-distance business. A series of decisions by the FCC and the federal courts culminated in opening up competition for long-distance calls in 1977. This meant that Microwave Communications, Inc. (MCI) and other companies could begin to offer long-distance service to all telephone customers.

The Divestiture of AT&T

As long as the Bell System provided both local and long-distance service, there was the potential for anticompetitive behavior in the newly created long-distance market. A second antitrust case was filed in 1974, culminating in 1982 with the so-called Modified Final Judgment (MFJ). The centerpiece of the agreement, which went into effect in 1984, was the separation of local and long-distance telephone service. In return for its divestiture of the local operating companies, AT&T retained its domestic and international long-distance operations, remained active in providing business services and dedicated lines to corporate customers, and held on to Bell Labs and Western Electric. For the first time, AT&T was allowed to enter the computer manufacturing business and to sell computers and computer services. AT&T also won the right, after a seven-year waiting period, to offer information services, barred under the 1956 Consent Decree. Along with the local exchange business, AT&T also lost its identification with the "bell." That term and the familiar bell-shaped symbol became the property of the new local telephone companies. The local exchanges were parceled out to seven **Regional Bell Operating Companies (RBOCs)** (Figure 11.1).

Regional Bell Operating Companies (RBOCs) are the local telephone operating companies that were divested by AT&T in 1984.

FIGURE 11.1
THIS MAP SHOWS THE TERRITORIES OF THE REGIONAL BELL OPERATING COMPANIES.

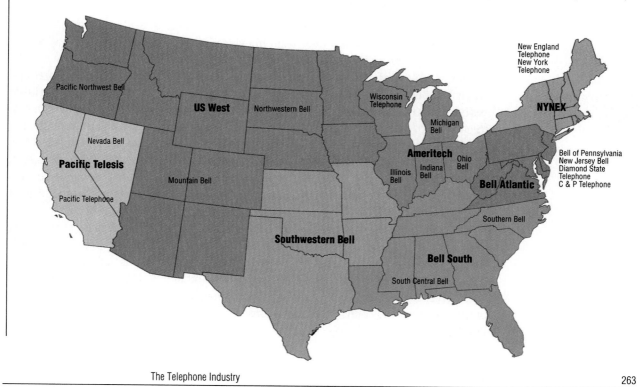

R E V I E W

1. What were the origins of AT&T?
2. How did changes in government regulation shape the telephone industry?
3. Why did the government want to break up AT&T in 1977?
4. Why did AT&T break itself up in 1996?

Price caps index telephone rates against the cost of living and replace rate of return regulation.

Competitive access providers can offer local telephone service in competition with local telephone companies, like the RBOCs.

Variable resistance transmitters create an electrical current that varies in response to the human voice.

A New Era of Competition

In the decade after divestiture, AT&T's share of the long-distance market dropped from 80 percent to about 60 percent, and the markets for residential telephone sets and for telephone transmission and switching equipment became highly competitive. Service quality improved and the cost of long-distance service decreased, although the cost of local service went up. In 1989 the Federal Communications Commission proposed an alternative to rate of return regulation. Under the new **price cap** approach, AT&T can raise its rates in proportion to changes in the cost of living, after taking into account efficiency improvements in the telecommunications industry as a whole. A number of states adopted similar plans for local telephone service, but many required that the local exchanges also open up to **competitive access providers**—companies that could offer competing local telephone service. The competitive trend intensified in 1996 with two watershed developments. The Telecommunications Act of 1996 removed the various lines of business restrictions in the telecommunications industry, including the provisions of the divestiture agreement. This meant, for example, that RBOCs could begin to offer cable TV and long-distance telephone service inside their territories, while long-distance and cable companies could break into the local telephone business. To get in fighting trim for the new era of competition, AT&T shed its unprofitable computer manufacturing business and its successful telecommunications equipment business. Thus, AT&T finally chose to do to itself what several generations of federal regulators could not force it to do: get out of the equipment manufacturing business. True to form, telecommunications firms of all stripes immediately set about forming new alliances and mergers aimed at giving them the advantage in the newly competitive markets.

TECHNOLOGY TRENDS

What was Alexander Graham Bell doing with that beaker of acid, anyway? When he called out, the air pressure waves from his voice hit a flexible membrane. A wire was attached to the membrane; as Bell shouted for help, the wire bobbed up and down in the beaker of acid, varying the electrical resistance in the circuit in response to the pressure waves in Bell's voice—this device thus incorporated the principle of the **variable resistance transmitter.** (The description of this device is what was handwritten into the margin of Bell's patent application.) The wire was connected to an electromagnet in the next room, which tugged at a flexible steel reed. In response to the varying electrical current, air pressure waves reached Watson's ears. More user-friendly substances such as carbon granules soon replaced the acid as the variable resistance element, but this basic approach to voice communication remained virtually unchanged for the next ninety years.

The earliest phones were attached to dedicated lines (there were no switches) connecting two points that were no more than a few miles apart (since there were no means to amplify the signals). Users had to shout "Hoy! Hoy!" (Bell disdained the use of "hello") into the transmitter to attract the attention of the party at the other end. The alerting problem was soon solved by Watson, who invented an electromagnetic ringing device still used today, but the distance and connectivity limitations were the subject of continuing technological development (Fagen, 1975).

Overcoming Distance—The Amplifier

One of the first inventions to emerge from AT&T's research labs was a practical **repeater amplifier.** It used an improved version of the audion tube, a 1906 invention by Lee De Forest that also paved the way for the development of radio and television. Previously, callers had to compensate for electrical noise and losses by shouting into the telephone, but no one could shout all the way from New York to San Francisco! To publicize the new invention, Bell and Watson were reunited to complete the first transcontinental call in 1915. Bell again had the honor of uttering the first words: "Hoy! Hoy! [he still refused to say "hello"] Mr. Watson? Are you there? Do you hear me?" Watson did. Long-distance amplifiers opened the world to the telephone, but not the oceans. Forty years would pass before an amplifier reliable enough to work on a transoceanic cable could be put into service, in 1956.

Untangling the Wires—Advances in Transmission Technology

Within a decade of Bell's invention, telephone poles with up to thirty cross-arms darkened the skies above the largest cities. The blizzard of 1888 knocked out telephone service in the Northeast, forcing wires to be placed underground where space was at a premium. Unfortunately, the new electrical power systems of the 1880s generated electrical interference that made it necessary to add a second wire to each circuit, doubling the volume of wire.

The search thus began for a way to put more than one telephone conversation on a pair of wires. The solution was **multiplexing.** This was essentially what Bell had set out to do with his harmonic telegraph before he got sidetracked with the telephone. The trick was to combine each telephone conversation with a high-frequency signal, called a *carrier wave,* and then transmit several calls together, each on a separate carrier frequency. This is like transmitting multiple radio programs simultaneously, each on a different channel, only telephone transmissions are confined within a wire instead of broadcast into open space. The first such **carrier system** was used in 1918.

Further advances during World War II made it possible to cram dozens, then hundreds, and eventually thousands of calls into a single circuit. The radar transmitters that detected enemy ships and planes were adapted to communications systems. **Microwave** technology entered the public network in 1948 on an intercity trunk between New York and Boston. Individual calls were multiplexed and transmitted by directional radio transmitters located atop tall buildings or towers some twenty to thirty miles apart. Using a horn-shaped antenna, each location picked up the transmissions from the last tower and retransmitted them to the next tower. Microwave also proved effective in carrying television signals between cities; the first coast-to-coast linkup was in 1951 (O'Neill, 1985).

Another technology to emerge from the battlefields was **coaxial cable,** a high-capacity wireline system. Coaxial cable was also used to connect television stations into networks and by 1949 was being used to carry TV signals to remote areas without their own service, giving birth to the cable television industry.

In 1945 science fiction writer Arthur C. Clarke recognized a revolutionary application of the new microwave technology. What if we placed the microwave transmitters in orbit around the earth so they could span the globe? Essentially, that is all **satellite** systems are. A powerful microwave transmitter, or uplink, on the ground beams the signal up to a receiver in space, which then repeats the signal down to earth stations. Another wartime innovation, the ballistic missile, made this feat possible to imagine. The first communications satellite, *Telstar I,* flew in 1962. History records the first words spoken on this occasion, too, but they were something less than momentous: "Will everybody please get off this line?" There were so many people listening in that the circuit was overloaded. During the 1970s satellite technology made major inroads on terrestrial microwave and wireline networks, especially in international long-distance routes.

TELSTAR II WAS ONE OF THE FIRST COMMUNICATIONS SATELLITES, LAUNCHED IN 1963. IT WAS BUILT BY BELL TELEPHONE LABORATORIES FOR AT&T.

Switching equipment is the other key component of the telephone system. By the end of the nineteenth century, the telephone exchange was a bustling place. Hundreds of female operators sat hunched over manual switchboards with "headsets" roughly the size and weight of a small toaster atop their heads. In those days, telephones had no dials. It was necessary to alert the operator by turning a crank on your telephone. She then inquired, "Number, please" (no other response was permitted—telephone companies had already discovered efficiency experts) and then placed an electrical plug between your line and your party's line and manually applied the ringer. Only then could you speak. Each operator could handle about 1,000 calls a day this way. Millions of telephone operators would have been needed to handle today's telephone traffic. Instead, there are far fewer than 150,000, the number employed in the 1920s before automatic switching was instituted.

In 1892 an Indiana undertaker by the name of Strowger had a serious business problem. The local switchboard operator connected bereaved parties who asked for "the undertaker" to the other funeral parlor in town. This inspired Strowger to invent an automatic telephone switch that would complete calls impartially. The Bell companies were slow to adopt the step-by-step **automatic switching** equipment, believing that requiring subscribers to dial and (in the earliest systems) ring their parties themselves was too great an imposition, but automation prevailed in the 1920s.

Automatic switching automatically connects calls without operator intervention.

The early automatic switches were close relatives of the jukebox. Mechanical arms rotated and jiggled up and down in response to the numbers dialed, touching tiny electrical contacts that were connected to subscribers' telephone sets. Unfortunately, a single call

EARLY TELEPHONE SWITCHBOARD OPERATORS COMPLETED CALLS MANUALLY UNDER CLOSE SUPERVISION AND IN DIFFICULT WORKING CONDITIONS.

completely tied up the switch, so huge banks of switches operating in parallel had to be installed. In 1938 the crossbar switch was introduced, making it possible for each piece of equipment to handle ten to twenty calls simultaneously.

Finally all local calls and, beginning in 1951, long-distance connections could be dialed directly without an operator. This prompted the introduction of area codes. By 1946 automatic switches and telephone company supervisors kept the entire Bell System running despite a nationwide telephone operator's strike (Schindler, 1982).

The Birth of Digital Communications

In the fall of 1962, an event that would eventually reshape the world of communications took place inside the AT&T central office in Skokie, Illinois. The first **digital** telephone call was made to Chicago, marking the first practical application of digital communications. What made the new system unique was the way in which the human voice was conducted through the network. Until then, telephones still worked about the same way as they had for Alexander Graham Bell: air pressure waves created by human vocal cords were converted to continuously varying electrical currents and then changed back to air pressure waves that the ear could sense as sound. We now call this process **analog** transmission. The new carrier system converted the voices to a stream of discrete digital pulses for the trip between Skokie and Chicago and then simulated the voice for the listener on the other end.

Digital Switching. Meanwhile, Bell Labs was developing ways to merge computer and telephone switching technology so the electrical paths through a telephone switch could be controlled by a program stored in computer memory instead of by the laborious motion of electromechanical components. This also meant that changes in service could simply be programmed through computer software instead of by rewiring the switch. The first telephone switch incorporating this innovation went on line in 1965. Later, switching points became semiconductor chips in the first all-**electronic switch.**

Thus, the telephone system is really a sophisticated computer network. The telephone receiver is actually a remote terminal connected to a powerful computer in the telephone company's central office. When we place a call, we submit a request to the computer for access to a data transmission path through the central office switch. If it is a long-distance call, our local office computer links with others along the way, as many as ten different ones if our call is going coast-to-coast. When we speak, a computer card in the central office samples our voice and converts the samples into brief bursts of computer digits—bit streams that mingle with those of thousands of other callers in intercity trunk lines. Those on the receiving end imagine they hear us speaking to them, but really they are listening to a re-creation of our voice reassembled from the streams of computer bits.

ISDN and the Intelligent Network. The **integrated services digital network (ISDN)** extends the digitization process all the way to the telephone itself, creating an end-to-end digital network. With ISDN we can do three things at once on a single telephone line; for example, we can call our instructor for homework help, while we share a computer screen that shows the solution to the homework problem. At the same time, our computer could be receiving an electronic mail note from a "significant other." ISDN also raises the "speed limit" on data transfers by a factor of ten or more so magazine-quality graphics can be transmitted in an instant and facsimile pages spew out as fast as the output from a copying machine—and with the same quality. (For a description of advanced telephone services, see Briere,

Digital means computer readable.

Analog transmission uses continuously varying signals corresponding to the light or sounds originated by the source.

Electronic switches replace electromechanical components with solid-state components.

Integrated services digital network (ISDN) is an end-to-end digital telephone network.

1993.) The ultimate evolution of the service will make video possible, perhaps even over the copper wires that are already attached to our phones.

ISDN also portends the arrival of the **intelligent network**, bringing with it services that can respond to and manipulate information about the call while it is in progress. What makes the network "intelligent"? Back to the earliest days of the telephone, all of the actions necessary to establish and terminate a telephone call ("signaling," in telephone jargon) passed through the same physical connection that the voices did. The intelligent network uses a separate high-speed data network for these functions. This network "checks ahead" to see if your parties are available before ringing their phones, so you no longer have to hang on the line for a minute or more while intermediate connections are established. By connecting this network to a digital display on the subscriber's telephone, we can see the numbers of calling parties. We can also intercept the calling number and link it to computer programs that can, for example, prevent calls from certain numbers from reaching us while forwarding other calls to our secret vacation hideout.

The Consumer Telephone of Tomorrow

With the advent of the intelligent network, residential telephones are taking on a new look. The advent of "feature buttons" dedicated to special service options like call forwarding and call waiting will mean that we no longer have to memorize access codes or fumble around for the instruction pamphlet. Digital displays will be added to support intelligent network services; in fact, the "phone of the future" might be *all* display screen, allowing users to dial numbers and access information services with touch-sensitive screens. Eventually, the telephone screen may also carry picturephone calls. The answering machine is also in for a makeover as advanced digital voice processing and "intelligent" features, such as personalized messages for individual callers and improved message management capabilities, are added. Eventually, the answering machine may be integrated into the telephone itself, now that digital processing eliminates the bulky analog cassette tapes.

Mobile Telephony

Mobile telephones were first used on oceangoing vessels in 1919. Experiments with land-based mobile radio date back to early police radios in the 1920s, with the first regular land mobile service starting in 1933 for public safety officials. The first public mobile telephone service went on the air in 1946. The original mobile telephone service operated from a single central antenna in each metropolitan area and had a total capacity of only forty-six simultaneous conversations. This meant that the forty-seventh caller did not receive a dial tone, which often happened. The result was years-long waiting lists for new mobile telephones and the need for numerous attempts to complete a single call.

Paging services alert miniature radio receivers with specially coded messages.

Cellular radio is a mobile telephone service that subdivides service areas into many small cells to maximize the number of users.

Paging services were introduced in 1962 to relieve some of the growing demand for mobile telecommunications. Pagers are small radio receivers that monitor a single radio channel "piggybacked" on top of a local FM radio station signal. The paging unit responds with a beeping tone or vibration whenever its identification number is transmitted; this alerts the user to call in to find out what the message is.

Pagers still did not meet the growing need for mobile communications, however, leading to the introduction of **cellular radio** in the United States in 1978. Cellular radio takes its name from the practice of dividing large service areas into clusters of small zones, or cells, each only a few miles across. Since the transmitters located in each cell are

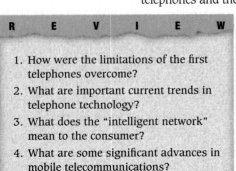

R E V I E W

1. How were the limitations of the first telephones overcome?
2. What are important current trends in telephone technology?
3. What does the "intelligent network" mean to the consumer?
4. What are some significant advances in mobile telecommunications?

relatively weak, it is possible to reuse the same communication frequencies for other users in different parts of the same city. As the user moves from one cell to the next, the call is handed off to the next antenna in the network and automatically reassigned to a new channel. If new users overwhelm the system, the original cells can be split into smaller and smaller ones.

Personal Communication Networks

Cordless telephones are slated to merge with cellular radio so the same cordless receiver that you use in the bathtub may be carried to work or school. The new **personal communication network (PCN)** technology that makes this possible is already on trial in several communities and will probably make its way into the average consumer's home by the end of the century. PCNs work a lot like cellular radio, except that the cells surrounding each transmitter are much smaller, only a few hundred yards across. This means that the transmitters can have a lower power output and hence can be made smaller, lighter, and much less expensively than cellular telephones. Some analysts believe that PCNs represent not only the future of mobile communications but also the future of the entire public network, bringing with them the possibility of having a single personal telephone that we can carry with us throughout the day.

WHY YOU CAN HEAR A PIN DROP: THE BASICS OF FIBER OPTIC COMMUNICATIONS

The basic principles of fiber optic transmission are quite easy to grasp. Essentially, fiber optic systems shine a laser light into a very long glass tube. If the information we wish to transmit is in digital form, we simply turn the laser on when we want to transmit a "1" and turn it off when we want to send a "0." The light rays reflect off the sides of the tube and can be made to propagate hundreds of miles without amplification or retransmission if the glass is pure enough. At the other end of the glass tube, the light shines onto a detector that converts light to electrical current and the original sequence of digital electrical pulses is recovered. The signal can be regenerated for retransmission, switched into another circuit, or converted back into the human voice. By the way, these are not *Star Wars* lasers, but tiny solid-state devices that fit into a package about the size of your thumb and would not put out enough light to singe your eyebrows, let alone burn through the hull of a space cruiser.

The main advantages of fiber optic systems are speed and quality. Fiber optic systems can transmit data at rates of billions of bits per second, compared to a few thousand bits for today's telephone system and tens of millions of bits per second for coaxial cable systems. Since the data are transmitted as light waves instead of electrical pulses, they are immune to the electrical interference that causes static and distortion in electronic systems. That is why you literally can "hear a pin drop" over a fiber optic telephone network.

Not all fiber optic systems are digital, by the way. It is also possible to vary the intensity of the light going down the glass fiber to match the amplitude of an analog communication signal. Some cable TV systems use this approach.

Toward the Integrated Broadband Network

The final step in the evolution of the public telephone network will be the **integration** of voice, high-speed data transmission, and video into a single network. This is referred to as a **broadband** network because of its ability to deliver services that require a broad range of communication frequencies, or bands. Broadband applications include television programming, picturephones, high-quality color graphics, and high-resolution medical images.

One of the key technologies for the broadband network is **fiber optics**. Alexander Graham Bell was granted a patent for a photophone in 1880, and the principle of optical waveguides was discovered ten years before that. However, practical application of these inventions had to await the invention of the **laser** at Bell Labs in 1958. Lasers provide a powerful beam of pure light well suited to communication by light waves. The first commercial system was installed in 1979, and within a decade fiber optics were in wide use in long-distance networks and had started to make their way into local telephone networks and corporate data communications networks. Today, one of the long-distance companies touts its all-fiber network as so good that "you can hear a pin drop." Fiber is found in transoceanic cable systems and is replacing satellite transmission along the highest-capacity international telecommunications routes.

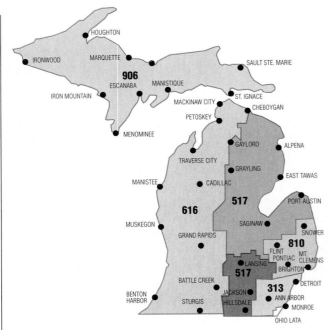

Interexchange carriers carry long-distance traffic inside the United States.

Local access and transport areas (LATAs) mark the boundaries between local and long-distance calls and are smaller than area codes.

Resellers are long-distance companies that lease their networks from other carriers and then resell telephone service to their customers.

Local exchange carriers (LECs) provide local telephone service.

INDUSTRY STRUCTURE AND ORGANIZATION

Over 100 years of technological innovation, government regulation, and industry restructuring has created a telephone industry structure that has several distinct components: *common carriers* that carry international, domestic long-distance, or local telephone traffic on wireline, satellite, or mobile communications networks; *equipment manufacturers* that produce network, transmission, and customer equipment; and *data communications services.* The recent opening of the local telephone exchange has created a new category, *competitive access providers.*

Common Carriers

Interexchange Carriers. **Interexchange carriers** (IXCs, in telephone industry jargon) have the exclusive right to carry domestic long-distance traffic. Long-distance calls include those that are made between area codes (such as between Grand Rapids, area code 616, and Detroit, area code 313) and also within area codes that cross **local access and transport area (LATA)** boundaries. These boundaries were set up at the time of the AT&T divestiture to demark local and long-distance calls. For example, the 517 area code in Michigan includes two LATAs, one serving the capital city of Lansing and one covering Saginaw (see Figure 11.2). Calls from Lansing to Saginaw are inter-LATA calls and thus can be handled by an interexchange carrier. In some states, interexchange carriers can also carry intra-LATA toll calls—calls that have toll charges but that are completed in a single LATA.

In 1992 long-distance carriers had revenues of about $58 billion (U.S. Department of Commerce, 1993). AT&T remains the dominant long-distance carrier in the United States, with about three-fifths of the market. Its two major rivals are the MCI Corporation and Sprint. Together, these three carriers account for 90 percent of the long-distance market. MCI, of course, is the grown-up version of Microwave Communications, Inc., whose lawsuit in the late 1960s first created competition in the long-distance market. Sprint has passed through the hands of a series of owners but is now a subsidiary of United Telecom, the second-largest independent telephone company.

The remaining slice of the long-distance market "pie" is divided among some 400 smaller long-distance companies, many of which are active only in specific metropolitan areas or are geared to specific niches in the market. Many smaller long-distance companies are **resellers**. They lease transmission capacity from the "big three" long-distance companies and receive substantial volume discounts. They then resell the lines they lease to their customers at usage-sensitive rates that are cheaper than those the customers can obtain, sometimes even undercutting the rates of AT&T, MCI, and Sprint. Many smaller companies operate their own switching equipment, but few own extensive transmission facilities.

Local Exchange Carriers. Local telephone service and calls that do not cross LATA boundaries are the domain of the **local exchange carriers (LECs)** (see Figure 11.3). Revenues from local exchange carriers topped $80 billion in 1992. The AT&T divestiture

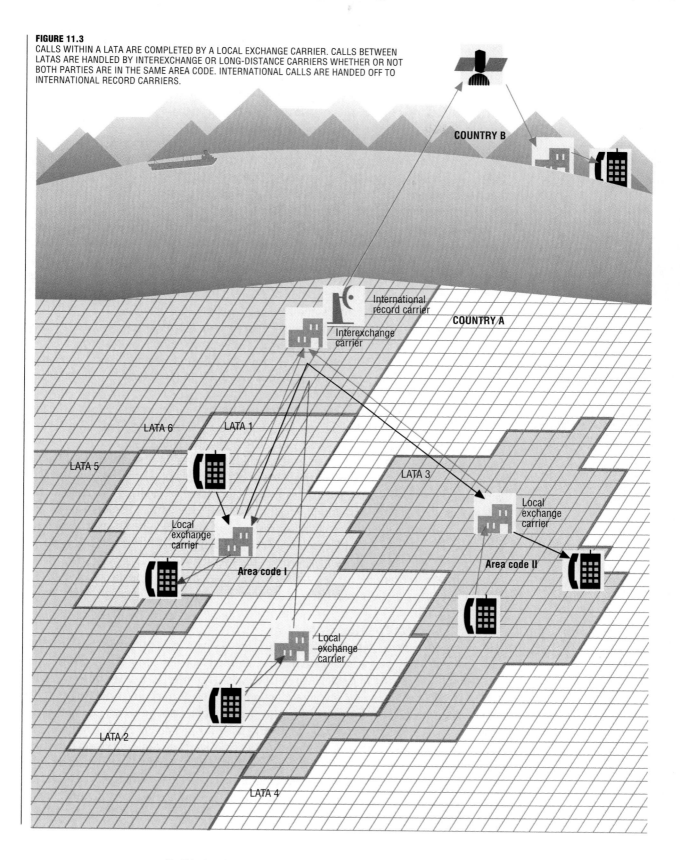

FIGURE 11.3
CALLS WITHIN A LATA ARE COMPLETED BY A LOCAL EXCHANGE CARRIER. CALLS BETWEEN LATAS ARE HANDLED BY INTEREXCHANGE OR LONG-DISTANCE CARRIERS WHETHER OR NOT BOTH PARTIES ARE IN THE SAME AREA CODE. INTERNATIONAL CALLS ARE HANDED OFF TO INTERNATIONAL RECORD CARRIERS.

COUNTRY B

International record carrier

Interexchange carrier

COUNTRY A

LATA 6   LATA 1

LATA 5

LATA 3

Local exchange carrier

Local exchange carrier

Area code I

Area code II

Local exchange carrier

LATA 2

LATA 4

organized the twenty-two Bell operating companies into seven Regional Bell Operating Companies. They provide about 80 percent of the nation's 134 million telephone lines. The RBOCs are owned by seven Regional Holding Companies (RHCs): NYNEX, Bell Atlantic, Southwestern Bell, BellSouth, Pacific Telesis, Ameritech, and US West. These RHCs are umbrella organizations for the regulated operating companies and other unregulated business ventures. At the time of divestiture, two quasi-independent companies in the old Bell System—Cincinnati Bell and Southern New England Telephone (SNETCO)—were spun off as completely independent entities. To maintain continuity with the Bell System, the identities of individual state-level companies (Michigan Bell, Illinois Bell, Ohio Bell, Indiana Bell, and Wisconsin Bell in the Ameritech region) were maintained, but they are becoming increasingly subordinated to their regional parent companies.

Although the MFJ bars the RHCs from manufacturing their own telecommunications equipment, they can create unregulated subsidiary companies that can sell telecommunications equipment manufactured by third parties and offer telecommunications consulting services to their customers. Thus, the seven RHCs have dual corporate structures, oftentimes replicated at both the state and regional levels. Each RHC also has a separate publishing company for telephone directories and a cellular telephone company. All RBOCs have a diverse mix of unregulated subsidiaries under the umbrella of the regional holding companies. These subsidiaries include cellular radio carriers that operate outside the RHC's service region (such as BellSouth cellular radio subsidiaries operating in the Ameritech region), foreign companies like the Bell Atlantic–Ameritech joint ownership of New Zealand Telecom, and real estate companies.

Independent telephone companies are LECs that are not part of the RBOCs.

About 1,300 **independent telephone companies** were never affiliated with the Bell System. The largest independents are GTE Corporation, United Telephone, Contel, and SNETCO. Only GTE rivals the RBOCs in size, although others match the size of state-level subsidiaries of the regional companies. The independents are not subject to the line-of-business restrictions that apply to the RBOCs. GTE, for example, manufactures a wide variety of telecommunications equipment and operates GEnie, a consumer videotex service, while United Telephone owns Sprint. Recently there has been a round of acquisitions and mergers among the larger independents as they jockey for position in a newly competitive environment. However, most independent telephone companies are small family businesses that serve isolated rural communities, many with fewer than a thousand subscribers. Many of these owe their existence to the Rural Electrification Act, which brought electricity to the farm in the 1930s and was extended in 1949 to finance rural telephone systems.

Competitive Access Providers

Competitive access providers (CAPs) compete with the local exchange carriers. The first CAP, the New York Teleport, was created in New York City in the early 1980s. Because of overcrowded microwave and satellite frequencies, large companies like Merrill Lynch were having difficulty transferring computer data among their Manhattan headquarters, their branch locations across the country, and their "back room" data processing centers in the New York suburbs. There was also a growing need for broadband networks to support videoconferencing and to handle satellite feeds for broadcast and cable television networks. After the AT&T divestiture, many large companies found it economical to connect their telecommunications systems directly to long-distance carriers, bypassing the local exchange carriers entirely. A rash of fires and technical problems also convinced many corporate customers that they needed a backup in case their local exchange carrier's central office failed.

The teleport was initially conceived as a satellite antenna farm located on Staten Island and connected to downtown offices via a fiber optic link. Over time, the teleports were redubbed "competitive access providers," in that they provided local access to high-capacity long-distance networks in competition with local telephone companies. Continuing changes in telephone industry regulations now make it possible for CAPs to become full-service "one-stop" providers of all local and long-distance telecommunications services. Today, Teleport Communications and Metropolitan Fiber Systems are the leading CAPs, serving about thirty of the nation's largest cities. In 1992 Teleport Communications was acquired by Cox Communications, one of the nation's largest cable television companies, perhaps paving the way for full-scale competition for local telephone service between cable television operators and telephone companies in the nation's largest cities.

Mobile Communication and Satellite Networks

Mobile communication carriers include various paging and radio telephone services, but cellular radio is the biggest, with about 10 million subscribers and annual revenues of about $7 billion. Licenses for cellular radio networks were granted in pairs for each service area, with one going to the local exchange (wireline) carrier and one allocated for a competing company. Each RHC thus has its own cellular radio subsidiary. In addition, some of them hold the **nonwireline** franchises in select metropolitan areas outside their operating regions. The largest cellular radio carrier in the United States is McCaw Cellular, which was acquired by AT&T in 1994.

The advent of personal communicaton networks is likely to radically alter the structure of the mobile telecommunications industry. This new technology, together with the newly won right of CAPs to interconnect with the local telephone exchange, makes direct

Mobile communication carriers provide paging and radio telephone services.

Nonwireline carriers are cellular radio companies that provide service in competition with the local exchange (wireline) carrier.

CELLULAR PHONES ALLOW INDIVIDUALS TO BE IN CONSTANT COMMUNICATION WITH OTHERS, WHEREVER THEY MAY GO.

competition with the Baby Bells possible, and these developments are attracting new players. AT&T's purchase of McCaw Cellular in 1994 was the opening round. MCI is working with local cable operators to establish a nationwide local telephone company. Cable companies like Tele-Communications Inc. (TCI) and Time-Warner also plan to use PCN technology for their own competing local telephone services.

Satellite carriers transmit telephone calls via satellite.

International record carriers (IRCs) carry international long-distance calls.

Satellite carriers are divided into two categories, domestic and international, and account for about $1.5 billion in annual revenues. Alascom, GTE Spacenet, GE Americom, Hughes Communications, AT&T, and Comsat are the six domestic carriers. Together, they operated thirty satellites in 1992. Most of the satellite transmissions are video, primarily the national feeds of broadcast and cable networks.

International record carriers (IRCs) are the companies responsible for carrying long-distance calls between countries. Before the AT&T divestiture every nation generally had a single international long-distance carrier, like AT&T in the United States. Now MCI and Sprint compete with AT&T for long-distance traffic, and many other countries have also instituted competition in international long distance.

INTELSAT is a consortium of 121 countries that provides international satellite service to the world via a network of nineteen satellites. It specializes in transmissions to stationary satellite receivers. INMARSAT specializes in international mobile satellite service. Comsat is the U.S. representative in both consortia. INTELSAT's competitors include Alpha Lyracom/PanAmSat, Columbia Communications, and Orion.

Interest in mobile satellite services intensified in 1992 when the World Administrative Radio Conference (WARC) authorized satellite systems that would operate in low and medium earth orbits. This means that the satellites will not stay fixed above a single area like today's communication satellites. Instead, networks of satellites will circle the globe continuously at relatively low altitudes, making it possible to use low-powered hand-held receivers. The Motorola Corporation, TRW (a U.S. aerospace firm), INTELSAT, and INMARSAT are among the entrants in this new arena.

Equipment Manufacturers

The telecommunications equipment manufacturing industry may be broken down into three major categories: network (primarily switching and carrier systems used by network operators), transmission (such as fiber, microwave, satellite, and mobile), and user equipment. The latter is commonly called **customer premise equipment** (CPE) and includes consumer telephone sets as well as the switching equipment owned by corporate users. Many telecommunications manufacturers are highly specialized, concentrating on only one or two of these categories and even filling specialized niches within the major industry segments.

Customer premise equipment (CPE) is equipment that the end user connects to the telephone network.

AT&T remains the leading U.S. manufacturer of network equipment, although since divestiture it no longer dominates this $10 billion annual market. A Canadian company, Northern Telecom, is AT&T's principal rival in the United States for central office switching equipment. Alcatel (Belgium), Siemens (Germany), Ericsson (Sweden), and NEC (Japan) are the other principal rivals in the central office switching market. This is a hotly contested business since each individual sale is worth millions of dollars, and the market is expected to explode as telephone companies around the world move to implement all-digital networks. AT&T continues to manufacture a full line of network equipment but faces competition from international companies and from a horde of domestic manufacturers that fill the many smaller niches in this market.

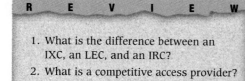

R E V I E W

1. What is the difference between an IXC, an LEC, and an IRC?
2. What is a competitive access provider?

The market for telecommunications transmission equipment, worth about $10 billion in annual sales in the United States, is highly specialized by transmission technology, although AT&T once again has a presence in many sectors of the market. AT&T, Motorola, Northern Telecom, and Ericsson are the leaders in cellular telephone equipment. Hughes Aircraft (a division of General Motors), General Electric, and a consortium of European companies called Space Systems Loral dominate the satellite market. AT&T and Siecor are the leading manufacturers of fiber optic cable.

Perhaps the most diverse segment of the telecommunications equipment industry is customer premise equipment, particularly consumer telephones. Private branch exchanges (PBXs), key systems, and facsimile sets are the other major product categories. Although AT&T still has a large slice of this $5 billion market, a host of foreign and domestic competitors have deeply fragmented it. Since divestiture, consumer electronics companies from Pacific Rim countries such as Japan, Taiwan, and Korea have made major inroads in the American consumer telephone market. AT&T, Northern Telecom, and Rolm are the major competitors in the market for PBX equipment.

TELEPHONE SERVICES

Plain old telephone service (POTS) is basic local telephone service without any extra-cost options.

Touch-tone phones have push buttons and dial with musical tones.

Unlisted numbers are not published and also may not be given out by directory assistance operators.

Unpublished numbers do not appear in the phone book but may be given out by directory assistance.

Custom calling includes call waiting, call forwarding, speed dialing, and three-way calling.

Custom local area signaling services (CLASS) are intelligent network options such as caller ID, distinctive ring, call block, redial, call trace, and selective call forwarding.

Basic telephone service has a special acronym **POTS,** short for **plain old telephone service.** The basic POTS functions—dial tone, transmission, and switching—have changed little since the 1880s. However, in recent years a number of options have been added:

- **Touch-tone** dialing allows the user to use a push-button keypad and to dial with musical tones. First introduced in 1961, touch-tone service still incurs an additional monthly charge in many states.

- **Unlisted numbers** allow users to withhold publication of their telephone numbers in directories and to prevent callers from obtaining them through directory service. In some areas, it is possible to get an **unpublished** number, which does not appear in printed directories but still may be obtained by calling directory information.

- **Custom calling services** came into being with the introduction of the first electronic telephone switches in the late 1960s. These services include *call waiting, speed dialing, three-way calling,* and *call forwarding.*

Custom local area signaling services (CLASS) represent the next phase in the evolution of custom calling services. They are part of the transition to the so-called intelligent network, which sends call information through a special network that is separate from the lines we speak on and links that information to computer programs in the switching equipment. The following services have been undergoing trials since the mid-1980s and are now being introduced throughout the country:

- *Caller ID* displays the number of the party who is trying to call on a small screen. The subscriber can see who is calling before deciding whether to answer the call. Future plans call for the display of the calling party's name as well as their number.

• *Caller ID block* allows the caller to prevent the transmission of caller identification information for a particular call. In some areas, subscribers can choose to always have their caller identification blocked.

• *Caller ID rejection* allows Caller ID subscribers to reject calls from those who block transmission of their telephone numbers.

• *Distinctive ring* lets the subscriber enter a set of priority numbers with his or her touch-tone keypad. When calls are received from these numbers, a special ringing sound lets the subscriber know that one of the priority callers is on the line.

• *Call block* is the opposite of distinctive ring: calls from the listed numbers are not allowed to ring. Instead the caller gets a recorded announcement, such as "Your party is not available at this time."

• *Redial* lets the subscriber return the last call that came in on the line, even if it was incomplete or if he or she does not know the identity of the caller.

• *Call trace* lets the user trace an abusive call. A report is made to the telephone company, which then reports it to the police. Unlike the other services listed, the user is charged by the activation rather than by the month.

• *Selective call forwarding* makes it possible to forward incoming calls to different locations depending on the originating number.

Another intelligent network service, *personal 800 numbers,* solves a long-time college student problem—paying for long-distance calls home. These numbers automatically "reverse the charges." They are also handy for home businesses that want to get calls from customers and clients. The intelligent network feature here is a simple "look-up" function that translates the 800 number to the number of the called party's telephone and keeps track of the reverse billing.

The *second number* option, sometimes also known as the "teen line," is not to be confused with installing a completely separate telephone line for a second user. Instead, this service allows one telephone line to have two numbers associated with it, each with its own distinctive ring.

The intelligent network also improves response to emergency calls, by automatically

Stock scene from the detective thrillers of the 1940s: The kidnappers call to arrange the drop for the ransom money. The detective hero muffles the receiver and says, "It's them. Quick, trace this call!" Cut to a scene of the telephone central office. Telephone technicians race in between stacks of things that look like cookie jars (actually, switching components for the old step-by-step switching systems), peer into the cookie jars, and shout "We almost have it!" Meanwhile, the detective hero is asking to speak to the victim, wants to know what size bills they want, tries to get directions to the old reservoir, anything to keep the crooks on the phone for the five minutes they need. But to no avail, the crooks seem to know exactly how much time they have, probably learned it from the last film noir detective thriller to hit the theaters. "Sorry, Sam. We traced it to somewhere on the south side, then we lost 'em."

Fast forward to the 1960s version of *Dragnet*. By now telephone switches have computer programs that route the calls, so Joe Friday needs only two minutes to catch the crooks. But the kidnappers have TVs by now, know exactly how long they have, and call from a pay phone if they have a lot to say. "Phone booth on the south side. Sorry, Joe. He was gone by the time Adam 12 got there."

Fast forward again to the 1980s. The boys and girls at *Miami Vice* have a digital display in their van and get an instant digital readout when the kidnapper calls from the hideout. Still no luck. The kidnappers have figured out how to trigger the ransom message on an answering machine at a remote location. "Sorry, Sonny, just an empty apartment with an answering machine in South Dade."

In the age of the intelligent network, old-fashioned kidnappers don't have much of a chance. The telephone switch keeps complete computerized records of all the calls to the hideout, so we can track down the crooks and their known associates at our leisure. If we can keep them on the phone for two minutes nowadays, we might even catch them with the phone in their hands. All it takes is the time for the central office technician to put down her coffee cup, tap the keys on her access terminal, and immediately call up the address of the hideout for the patrol cars. If they use a pay phone, we can sweep the entire telephone exchange looking for their voice patterns, then lock in on the call to the hideout. If we have Caller ID, we can even have a personal greeting ready for the kidnapper ("Hi, Eddie Mars, we have you now!") when he calls. In fact, everyone can be a junior G-man with the intelligent network's call trace feature. The victim's own family can activate the trace themselves from their home, saving Sam Spade's consulting fee.

It will be interesting to see how the detective movies of the 1990s will come up with new wrinkles. Ransom E-mail? Three-way conference calls with the victim? Lead the cops on a merry chase through the intelligent network with multistep call forwarding? "Launder" the calls through rural exchanges without Caller ID? Double-cross Sam Spade by forwarding the call through his office number? Better yet, make the call with a stolen cellular radio authorization code from a fast-moving car phone, combining the elements of the detective thriller and the high-speed auto chase!

Of course, there is a downside to this filmatic fantasy fun. By abusing the capabilities of the intelligent network, some future J. Edgar Hoover could keep files on everybody's known associates, check all our conversations for key words ("sex," "drugs," "rock 'n' roll"), and entrap us with computer-synthesized voices of our associates. *The President's Analyst*, a James Coburn comedy noir from 1969, warns of these dark possibilities. We could easily improve on that today. Why not just set up bogus "hotlines" and trap caller IDs from those who are calling for help with their drug problems. Better yet, we can identify potential criminals by sifting through records of the orders they place on the intelligent network for downloads of detective movie classics!

For now, legal safeguards are in place to prevent all that. The authorities have to get a piece of paper from a judge—a scene that is all too often left out of the detective shows from then and now.

looking up the address associated with the number. *Enhanced 911* also means that response times are faster, since there is no longer any delay trying to determine which water district your broken water main is hooked up to.

With a **personal telephone number,** users will have a single number for work and home—one that can follow them wherever they go throughout their lives if they so choose. Calls may be answered, blocked, or recorded based on the identity of the originating party, the time of day, and even the nature of the call, all under the control of the user. AT&T and local telephone companies are already providing numbers with 500 prefixes that offer some of these functions.

Voice mail is another new service option. Voice mail works a lot like an answering machine, only the recording device is in the telephone company's central office instead of in the user's living room. Voice mail offers some capabilities that answering machines do not, such as the ability to take a message while the line is busy and to "broadcast" voice mail messages to multiple recipients. The incorporation of intelligent network functions in voice mail systems will also make it possible to trigger personalized messages for individual callers.

USING THE TELEPHONE

Theodore Vail's vision of universal telephone service is still not quite a reality, although about 94 percent of U.S. homes now have phones. About two-fifths have answering machines and a like number have cordless phones. Intelligent network capabilities and ISDN service are available almost everywhere in the United States from long-distance carriers, but the local loop has yet to catch up. About three-fifths of telephone subscribers are now linked to the backbone of the intelligent network. Only about 1 percent of telephone lines are equipped for ISDN today, but by the mid-1990s, about half of all subscribers will have access to the service.

The Phoneless: Who Doesn't Have a Telephone?

Under the principle of universal access, everyone who wants a telephone should be able to have one. This ideal is being achieved very slowly indeed. It was not until 1946 that half the population had residential telephone service. It took almost a century for residential phone adoption to top 90 percent.

The telephone followed an itinerary of adoption not unlike that found for the home information technologies of today, such as the personal computer. A historical study of residential telephones in Palo Alto, California, found that early adopters of the telephone in 1910 tended to come from upper-income, well-educated managerial and professional classes (Fischer, 1992). The presence of adult females—whether wives, daughters, or household servants—also had an impact on telephone subscribership.

Who does not have a telephone in the Information Age? Telephone penetration among minority households is much lower than average, only about 85 percent among African American homes (Belinfante, 1989). Telephone access is a vital necessity in low-income households, a reality recognized by the public assistance system, which includes telephone service among the basic utilities covered by welfare payments. The **lifeline service** subsidizes telephone service for low-income households. However, the rise in local telephone rates since the AT&T divestiture continues to limit telephone penetration in low-income households.

Another group of the "phoneless" are rural residents. By 1940 farm phone penetration had plummeted to less than 25 percent, and many rural areas were still using ancient "crank" phones and had to share party lines with as many as sixteen homes. In 1949 Congress authorized the Rural Electrification Administration (REA) to provide low-interest loans for rural telephone cooperatives. As a result, rural telephone penetration nearly matches that in the cities, and only about 1 percent of the rural lines are still on party lines. Radio telephone systems are being installed to eliminate rural phonelessness, but a few pockets still remain, especially in the remote corners of the West.

Many other groups are phoneless by choice. Some religious sects have beliefs that prevent them from owning telephones, although most allow their use under certain circumstances. Highly orthodox Hasidic Jews are one such group. The Amish are another, allowing the use of communal telephones only for emergencies and vital business communications. Many of the communal phones have the ringers disconnected so that incoming calls cannot be detected, possibly to discourage Amish teens from using the phones for social purposes.

Outside the United States and a handful of other industrialized countries, just about *everyone* is phoneless. In some third world countries there is less than one telephone for every 100 inhabitants (AT&T International, 1988). Most of the phones are owned by businesses or by the privileged classes in the larger cities. Even in the cities, it can take twenty years or more to obtain telephone service and hours to obtain a dial tone to make a call. A running joke is that "Half the people are waiting for telephones and the other half are waiting for a dial tone."

Although they do not "count" in the various surveys of telephone ownership, the homeless are perhaps most affected by the lack of a telephone. Without access to a phone, it is extremely difficult to maintain contact with social welfare agencies to obtain benefits and health care, and it's virtually impossible to find employment. Phonelessness, joblessness, and homelessness are linked. When one homeless support group in Seattle began supplying its clients with free voice mail, it found that the average time it took for their clients to find a job dropped from several months to only a few weeks.

Telephone Behavior

As of 1986 Americans were placing over 350 billion calls each year, and about 90 percent of them were local calls (AT&T International, 1988). The average telephone user is on the phone about twenty to thirty minutes each day. Women (especially those who list their occupation as "homemaker"), minorities, and young singles are the heaviest phone users overall. Males and senior citizens over age 75 are the lightest users. Contrary to popular belief, teens are not especially heavy phone users, although there are certainly some that fit this description. However, homes with teens in them are heavy telephone users simply because they have more telephone users than other homes; this undoubtedly leads to household communications management problems (Dordick & LaRose, 1992).

What motivates telephone usage? Recalling our discussion of uses and gratifications, it appears that there are two primary motivations for telephone use. One is a utilitarian motivation—using the phone to schedule appointments, seek information, and transact business. The other is an enjoyment motivation relating to the use of the phone as an instrument for social interaction.

The most widespread local telephone service option is now touch-tone dialing, found in about two-thirds of U.S. households. Among the custom calling features now widely available, call waiting is by far the most popular and is found in about a third of U.S. homes.

About a fifth have speed dialing, but less than 10 percent subscribe to three-way calling or call forwarding. New services like voice mail and CLASS are just now finding their way into local telephone exchanges, so national penetration levels are still only a few percent. In areas where these services have been available for some time, Caller ID has proved the most popular, achieving subscription rates as high as 20 percent in some cases.

With the decrease in long-distance rates following the AT&T divestiture, long-distance calling is becoming common. The average monthly long-distance bill runs about $35 in U.S. households. International calls are still relatively infrequent, however. Only about a sixth of telephone households make an international call in six months' time. Another common option is the telephone credit card, which is used in about half of American households.

Currently, over a third of all telephone subscribers have unlisted numbers. Once regarded as the privilege of the wealthy, or a pretension for social climbers, unlisted numbers are now prevalent among many groups. Inner-city residents prefer unlisted numbers to avoid bill collectors and telemarketing scams aimed at low-income households. Residents of the largest urban markets from all walks of life are turning to unlisted numbers in hopes of avoiding bombardment from telemarketers and market research pollsters. Single females favor unlisted numbers to avoid harassing phone calls.

How do people use the telephone in the home? A 1991 study examined the purposes of calls and the relationship of callers in the United States (Dordick & LaRose, 1992). About a quarter of all calls are to chat or socialize. A fifth are to seek or give information. The exchange of news and the coordination of activities or the resolution of problems account for most of the rest. Regarding the relationships of callers, 36 percent of the calls were made to family members, 30 percent to friends, and the remainder to business or work associates. These patterns have not changed much over the years. In 1909 a telephone company manager in Seattle listened in on a sample of conversations and found that 30 percent were "purely idle gossip." If we combine the "chat" and "exchange news" categories from the 1991 survey data, we come up with 35 percent. Arrangements for social engagements accounted for 15 percent of calls then versus 14 percent now. The other categories in the 1909 study confounded the source with the purpose. A fifth were calls to stores and businesses and another 20 percent to the subscribers' workplace (Fischer, 1992). This corresponds closely to the 34 percent of calls in the 1991 study that were to persons other than family or friends.

ISSUES IN THE TELEPHONE INDUSTRY

The three main issues confronting the telephone industry are ownership and control issues, competition, and universal service.

Industry Ownership and Control

The key ownership patterns to watch in the telecommunications industry are the ventures of AT&T and its offspring, the Baby Bells. AT&T and the seven RHCs are, in a sense, at the top of the food chain—they are all publicly held, multibillion-dollar companies that are too large and in the hands of too many different investors to be readily bought up by others. Also, the telephone operating companies that contribute the bulk of their revenues would be difficult for potential corporate raiders to swallow. Any ownership changes would be subject to approval by each state-level public utility commission, which would frown on the high-rolling financial shenanigans that such deals always seem to entail.

However, in the wake of the Telecommunications Act of 1996, there is nothing to stop the Baby Bells from merging with one another. Or, they could form alliances or mergers with companies in the entertainment, cable, or computer industries—or even with long-distance carriers. Indeed, the principal thrust of the new legislation may be to create a handful of megacompanies at the turn of the century that will cut across the boundaries of today's telecommunications, computer, entertainment, and information industries. The presumption is that industry structure will remain fluid in response to the newly deregulated environment and to continuing technological change, but only time will tell if this assumption is a valid one.

The 1996 divestiture liberated AT&T from its line of business restrictions. After a "grace period" of seven years AT&T was allowed to enter the information services business, and in 1996 it began to provide Internet service. The removal of the restriction on computer manufacturing was a key part of the divestiture "deal," which AT&T quickly moved to take advantage of, perhaps to its regret. After several wasted years of trying to establish its own computer manufacturing unit, AT&T turned to the acquisition route, buying National Cash Register in 1991. In 1994 AT&T bought McCaw Cellular, America's largest cellular telephone firm, signaling a possible return to the local telephone business. In 1996 AT&T made the stunning announcement that it would leave the computer and telecommunications equipment manufacturing businesses, to focus on being a telecommunications carrier. Almost immediately, AT&T invested in a DBS company, DirecTV, giving it the potential to provide local video distribution as well as local telephone service. Under the Telecommunications Act of 1996, AT&T is also able to resell local telephone lines that it leases from RHCs, which provides another immediate route into the local telephone business. Thus, AT&T— and other long-distance companies—could rapidly reinvent itself as a full-service telecommunications provider.

Competition

Reforms in state and federal regulation, such as the institution of price cap rate regulation, coupled with the opening of the local exchange in the Telecommunications Act of 1996, are being tried as ways to stimulate competition. However, inherent in this approach is the danger that the competition will focus on big-spending corporate telecommunications users, leaving the needs of residential subscribers unmet and perhaps further raising their rates. Although competition in the long-distance market has lowered rates, local telephone rates have risen, to the detriment of poor and elderly telephone subscribers who do not make many long-distance calls (Cole, 1991). Local rates could rise anew as competitive pressures reduce the payments long-distance companies make to local phone companies to connect their calls.

Competition also raises the **cross-subsidization** issue anew. Historically, AT&T diverted revenues from long-distance operations to subsidized local telephone service through a government-mandated accounting trick that transferred some of the costs of the local network to the long-distance side of the ledger, thereby cross-subsidizing local service from long-distance revenues. In a competitive environment, there is always the potential for companies to cross-subsidize their most competitive businesses with revenues siphoned from their regulated businesses. The telephone industry also relies on a cost averaging system that forces some subscribers—city residents, for example—to pay more than the true cost of their equipment and service so others—rural residents, typically—may pay less. Competition puts pressure on telephone companies to "de-average" their rates, which could price some users out of the market.

Cross-subsidization applies revenues from a profitable area to a less profitable one.

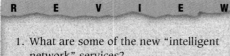

Universal Service

The prospect of greater competition in the telephone industry has the potential to undermine the principle of universal service on which the telephone system was originally founded. The transformation of the telephone from a simple instrument of interpersonal communication to an access device for the information superhighway raises serious questions about equal access to information and social inequality if universal access is not assured. Indeed, the quality and extent of universal service are growing concerns. Is universal access to POTS sufficient in the Information Age, or should all telephone users be guaranteed low-cost access to Internet as well? A related set of issues has to do with incentives telephone companies have to modernize their networks. Competition and relaxed regulation seem to be promoting network modernization, such as the upgrading of central office switches to ISDN and other advanced transmission technologies. However, the upgrades tend to happen first in exchanges serving large business users.

How will universal access be assured in an environment in which several competing companies offer local telephone service? The Telecommunications Act of 1996 pledges to maintain the concept of universal service. However, mechanisms for subsidizing universal service—such as having all telecommunications companies pay into a common fund—have yet to be determined.

SUMMARY & REVIEW

How Did the Telephone Industry Develop?

What were the origins of AT&T?
After Alexander Graham Bell invented the telephone in 1876, control of the company that would become American Telephone and Telegraph (AT&T) soon passed from his hands, first to a group of Boston businessmen and later to financial moguls in New York. The company Bell helped to found prospered into the 1890s, when its patents expired. An era of intense competition followed and AT&T's fortunes flagged until Theodore Vail assumed control, concentrating on telephone service and promising that service on a universal basis to all, a policy embodied in the so-called Kingsbury Commitment.

How did changes in government regulation shape the telephone industry?
Vail's promises in the Kingsbury Commitment were made into law by the Graham Act in 1921. Despite an abortive experiment with government control in 1918–1919, the Bell System prospered until the Great Depression of 1929. The Communications Act of 1934 was the first in a series of telecommunications policy developments aimed at restricting the AT&T monopoly. The Consent Decree of 1956 and the decision to allow competition in long-distance service in 1977 paved the way for the dismemberment of the Bell System by the modified final judgment (MFJ). The MFJ forced AT&T to divest the companies (Regional Bell Operating Companies, RBOCs) that provided local telephone service, while retaining its long-distance and manufacturing arms.

Why did the government want to break up AT&T?

AT&T effectively monopolized local and long-distance services and the manufacture of telecommunications equipment, through its subsidiary Western Electric. Since AT&T was both the biggest manufacturer of equipment and the biggest customer it was almost impossible for other equipment manufacturers to make sales in the Bell System, a type of monopolistic practice forbidden under the Sherman Antitrust Act. The introduction of competition in long-distance service further raised the specter of monopolistic practices since it might have been possible for AT&T to subsidize its long-distance operations from its local service operations, thereby giving it an unfair advantage. For these reasons, an antitrust suit was launched against AT&T that eventually resulted in the separation of the local and long-distance operations.

What Are the Important Milestones in Phone Technology?

How were the limitations of the first telephones overcome?

The first phones were very limited in their range, connectivity, and ease of use. Amplifiers and carrier systems were developed in the early twentieth century to overcome the limitations of distance and to untangle the maze of wires that darkened the skies over major cities. The capacity of telephone networks has continually improved with the succession of coaxial cable, microwave, satellite, and fiber optic transmission systems. Meanwhile, advances in switching technology gradually reduced the labor intensiveness of the telephone network and made it possible for telephone subscribers to dial numbers automatically anywhere in the world. Digital communication first came to the telephone in 1962, making possible further improvements in capacity and transmission quality.

What are important current trends in telephone technology?

The integrated services digital network (ISDN) represents a significant step in the evolution of the public telephone network to an all-digital communications medium. New features incorporated in ISDN make networks "intelligent" by giving them the ability to respond to users in new ways. ISDN also points toward the development of high-speed, integrated digital networks that will carry video and broadband data transmissions as well as voice.

What does the "intelligent network" mean to the consumer?

The intelligent network brings a wide variety of new services. Some, like Caller ID and call trace, afford the user greater control over incoming communication. Others, like automatic redial and selective call forwarding, promise greater convenience. Ultimately, many consumers will have a single personal telephone number through which it will be possible to reach them no matter where they are. However, the new technologies also bring new threats to privacy, whether at the hands of telemarketers or government agents.

What are some significant advances in mobile telecommunication?

Although mobile telephone service dates back to 1946, early systems were plagued by insufficient capacity. Paging services were originated in the early 1960s to meet some of the demand for mobile communication. In 1978 cellular radio service was introduced in the United States, expanding the capacity of mobile telephone networks by using large numbers of relatively low power transmitters so that communication channels could be reused within a particular metropolitan area. The trend continues with personal communication networks that employ still smaller transmission areas, or "cells," and make it possible for the user to carry an inexpensive and lightweight mobile phone.

What Is the Industry Structure?

What is the difference between an LEC, an IXC, and an IRC?

The companies that carry telephone calls, common carriers, may be classified according to the scope of the calls that they are permitted to carry. Local exchange carriers (LECs) can carry local calls, while interexchange carriers (IXCs) carry domestic long-distance calls and international record carriers (IRCs) carry international calls. Local access and transport areas (LATAs), established under the terms of the AT&T divestiture, distinguish local and long-distance calls. Calls that do not cross a LATA boundary are considered local calls, while those that cross a LATA boundary are long distance. LATA boundaries generally follow area codes, although some area codes are divided into more than one LATA.

What is a competitive access provider?
Competitive access providers (CAPs) are a new type of telephone carrier permitted to carry local telephone calls in competition with an established local exchange carrier. In the future, CAPs owned by cable television companies and cellular telephone companies will provide direct competition for residential as well as business users.

What Telephone Services Are Available?

What are some of the new "intelligent network" services?
Intelligent network services make it possible for the telephone network to act on information supplied by users as it processes a call. Caller ID service shows subscribers the identity of a calling party so that they can decide whether to answer a call. Other intelligent network services automate the screening process, such as by making it possible to automatically refuse calls from specific numbers (call blocking), issuing special notifications of calls from especially valued parties (priority call), or handling the forwarding of calls differently depending on the identity of the caller (selective call forwarding).

How widespread is the telephone?
In the United States, only about one household in twenty does not have a telephone. Telephone subscribership is lower among minority groups than among the general population. Lifeline service is available to subsidize basic phone service for those who cannot afford it. Certain religious sects ban the telephone. While phone use is prevalent in industrialized countries, some developing countries have fewer than one telephone for every 100 people.

How do we use the phone?
We spend between twenty and thirty minutes on the phone each day, mostly talking to family members and friends. Women, minorities, and single persons are the heaviest phone

users overall. We use the phone both for utilitarian reasons—to obtain information and to get things done—and to socialize.

Why is there a trend toward fostering more competition in the telephone industry?
Policymakers hope that competition will mean lower prices and more advanced services, faster, for the telecommunications consumer. They believe that competition is the best way to create the so-called information superhighway. They also believe that they can foster competition in a way that will shield users from some of the potential pitfalls of a purely competitive telecommunications marketplace—such as the rise of new, more powerful telecommunications monopolies and the abandonment of the universal service principle, which guarantees affordable telephone service for all.

How is telephone industry regulation evolving?
Both federal and state regulation are loosening in an effort to promote free competition in the telecommunications industry. The Telecommunications Act of 1996 gives local phone companies permission to enter the long-distance telephone and cable television businesses from which they were previously barred. Simultaneously, long-distance telephone companies and cable operators may compete for local telephone subscribers. Many state public utility commissions are also doing their part to liberalize telephone regulation and tear down barriers between industries. Legislators hope that these changes will speed construction of the information superhighway while futhering competition and preserving universal service.

REFERENCES

AT&T International. (1988). *The world's telephones*. Morristown, NJ: AT&T International.

Belinfante, A. (1989). *Telephone penetration and household and family characteristics*. Washington, DC: Common Carrier Bureau, Federal Communications Commission.

Briere, D. (1993). Communications services: An overview. In *Managing voice networks*. Delran, NJ: McGraw-Hill Information Services.

Brooks, J. (1976). *Telephone: The first hundred years*. New York: Harper & Row.

Cole, B. G. (1991). *After the breakup*. New York: Columbia University Press.

Dordick, H., & LaRose, R. (1992). *The telephone in daily life: A study of personal telephone use*. East Lansing, MI: Department of Telecommunication.

Fagen, M. D. (Ed.). (1975). *A history of engineering and science in the Bell System: The early years 1875–1925*. Murray Hill, NJ: Bell Telephone Laboratories.

Fischer, C. (1992). *America calling*. Berkeley: University of California Press.

Fleming, S., & McLaughlin, M. (1993, July 12). ADSL: The on-ramp to the information highway. *Telephony*, pp. 111–114.

McGraw-Hill, Inc. (1993). A history of telecommunications regulation. In *Managing voice networks*. Delran, NJ: McGraw-Hill Datapro Information Services Group.

O'Neill, E. F. (Ed.). (1985). *A history of engineering and science in the Bell System: Transmission technology 1925–1975*. Murray Hill, NJ: Bell Telephone Laboratories.

Schindler, G. E. (Ed.). (1982). *A history of engineering and science in the Bell System: Switching technology 1925–1975*. Murray Hill, NJ: Bell Telephone Laboratories.

Temin, P. (1987). *The fall of the Bell System*. New York: Cambridge University Press.

U.S. Department of Commerce. (1993). *U.S. industrial outlook 1993*. Washington, DC: Government Printing Office.

Chapter 12

THE COMPUTER INDUSTRY

C H A P T E R   P R E V I E W

This chapter traces the history of the computer from its early origins in the nineteenth century down to the latest developments in computer technology happening today. By following the technical evolution of the computer, we will try to demystify some of the inner workings of today's computers. We will also take a look at the current structure of the computer industry and examine how its growth has been regulated and controlled over the years. We place special emphasis on the personal computer, since it is the device that stands poised to lead the convergence of computers, telecommunications, and mass media systems today.

London, England, 1892, Scotland Yard Computer Section, 2 A.M.

Really, Watson, creeping about in the middle of the night to ferret out men who fancy peeping at women's legs!

Tut, tut, Holmes, the order to find the rascals who frequent can-can clubs comes directly from Queen Victoria herself—she wants to make examples of the most prominent scoundrels. Besides, it's been 70 years since Professor Babbage invented the difference engine, and it's time we caught up with the times, so to speak!

The next thing you know, they will want a list of men who dress up like women for musicales in exclusive London men's clubs—a list *you* would be on, my dear Watson!

Nothing of the sort! The queen is perfectly right. It's improper for ladies to show their—er—limbs in public. It's indecent!

Besides, if computers can solve crimes, what will they need *us* for?

Pish posh. The computer only does what *we* tell it. Now, tell me how *you* would solve the crime if you had a legion of dim-witted accounting clerks and an army of Bobbies at your disposal.

{GOD SAVE THE QUEEN! Enter your query.}

Very well. Make the following lists: purchasers of cheap perfume, expensive cigars, and French gloves, rank by frequency, correlate the lists and cross check with the names of gentlemen seen frequenting public waterclosets near the can-can clubs. List according to standing in British Society.

Brilliant, Holmes, the chase is afoot!

Elementary, my dear Wat . . .

Ho! Ho! Here it is, faster than you can say "My dear Wat . . ." Egad! Look at the name at the top of the list!

{GOD SAVE THE QUEEN! His Royal Highness the Prince of Wales!}

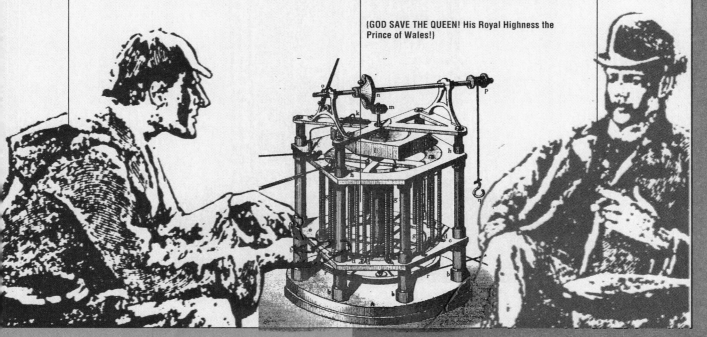

A BRIEF HISTORY OF THE COMPUTER INDUSTRY

ut for the cancellation of a research grant, the computer could have been invented in the early nineteenth century. In 1822 Charles Babbage, professor of mathematics at Cambridge University in England, created the **difference engine,** a mechanical calculator that could automatically produce mathematical tables, a tedious and error-prone manual task in those days. Babbage conceived of a large-scale, steam-driven (!) model that could perform a wide range of computational tasks. His "grantsmanship" was not equal to his mathematical genius, however, and his funding from the English government ran out in 1833. Despite the support of Lady Ada Byron, daughter of the poet laureate, the larger model was never completed. The revolving shafts and gears for the difference engine could not be manufactured with the crude industrial technology of the day.

Difference engine was an early precursor of the computer invented by Charles Babbage in England in 1822.

Moreover, no one was quite sure what the device was good for. When asked to renew the funding, British Prime Minister Benjamin Disraeli observed that the only conceivable use for it was to add up all of the money that had been squandered on the project (Evans, 1981; Wulforst, 1982).

By the 1880s manufacturing technology had improved to the point that practical mechanical calculators, including versions of Babbage's difference engine, could be produced. The new technology achieved worldwide fame in tabulating the U.S. Census of 1890. The previous census had taken several years to tabulate and was still not finished in 1887, when planning for the *next* census began. In desperation, the Census Bureau turned to a new

BABBAGE'S DIFFERENCE ENGINE WAS THE FORERUNNER OF TODAY'S COMPUTERS. IT WAS DESIGNED IN 1822 TO CREATE MATHEMATICAL TABLES.

THE VICTORIAN COMPUTER AGE: WHAT IF CHARLES BABBAGE GOT HIS GRANT?

London, England, 1875

Flying steam cars?

Scotland Yard solving cases with database searches?

Benjamin Disraeli using a word processor?

Ada Byron as the power behind the throne?

Digital multimedia lantern slide shows?

Welcome to the alternate reality of *The Difference Engine,* a science fiction novel by Bruce Sterling and William Gibson predicated on the assumption that Charles Babbage got his grant from the British government renewed and produced a working computer back in the 1830s. The plot revolves around an attempt of the French to smear Ada Byron and a cabal of neo-Luddites intent on fomenting a revolution against the Victorian Information Age. The authors offer us no insight, though, into what became of all those great works of Victorian fiction.

The mind reels at the mere thought of a word processor in the hands of a prolific author like Dickens. Perhaps Bob Cratchit would be portrayed as the victim of office automation. Scrooge would be visited by a multimedia artificial reality lantern slide projection instead of a ghost. And then there's Dickens's most famous novel of all, *A Tale of Two Databases,* the story of a French nobleman and an English gentleman who have their identities crossed by a glitch in a consumer credit database.

Arthur Conan Doyle would have to rewrite Sherlock Holmes's greatest mysteries. After all, a computer voice analysis would have quickly undone the Hound of the Baskervilles, and a few dollars slipped to a data clerk at The Yard would have produced Dr. Moriarity's home address straightaway. Would we perhaps have "The Case of the Reconstructed Data File" instead?

Would Kipling's Gunga Din be reborn as an Indian computer programmer who saves the artillery-targeting computers at the Khyber Pass from an invasion by a computer virus from Kashmir? And what about the nineteenth-century Russian novelists? With a computer, Dostoevsky might have been able to keep track of the patronymns, given names, nicknames, and diminutives of hundreds of more characters per novel. The next generation would have been so busy sorting them out that they would have no time left to start a revolution.

It is considerably less amusing to think about the computerization of Victorian social control mechanisms. All of the world's existing literary works could have been vetted for dirty words and completely republished for our century with the aid of computerized content analysis and typesetting. The government could have identified all of the dollies and rakes of London by correlating data about the purchases of cigars, brandy, and cheap perfume. Researchers could have even identified young women who checked out "dangerous" library books about science, math, and politics and referred their names to the proper authorities. It makes you wonder what life would be like under a modern government with a computer technology at its disposal to enforce Victorian norms of public morality.

tabulating machine, invented by Herman Hollerith, which reduced personal data to holes punched in paper cards. Tiny mechanical fingers "felt" the holes and closed an electrical circuit that in turn advanced a mechanical counter. This time, the final census tally was compiled in six weeks. Hollerith's invention eventually became the foundation on which the International Business Machines Corporation (IBM) was built.

Analog and digital calculators with electromechanical components appeared in a variety of military and intelligence applications in the 1930s. Many people—including the federal judge who decided a pivotal computer patent case in 1972—credit the invention of the first electronic computer to John Vincent Atanasoff. He produced working models of computer memory and data processing units at the University of Iowa in 1939, although he never assembled a complete working computer. The story goes that Atanasoff drew the inspiration for his invention from the desire to have a bourbon and soda in a southern Illinois bar. Iowa was a "dry" state back then, and he had to drive almost 200 miles for his drink, which gave him plenty of time to think about inventing the computer!

TABLE 12.1. COMPUTER INDUSTRY MILESTONES

Year	Event
1822	Babbage's difference engine
1890	Hollerith tabulating machine saves U.S. Census
1939	Electronic computer invented by Atanasoff
1943	Colossus cracks Nazi code
1946	ENIAC completed
1952	UNIVAC calls presidential election
1955	Silicon Valley founded
1956	IBM consent decree opens competition
1975	First personal computer, the Altair
1981	IBM introduces the Personal Computer

Computers at War: Colossus and ENIAC

Digital computers store and manipulate information in the form of binary code (1's and 0's).

ENIAC was the first general-purpose electronic digital computer.

More sobering inspiration came from the hostilities of World War II, which prompted the development of the first working all-electronic **digital computer,** Colossus, which the British secret service designed to crack Nazi codes. Similarly, the need to calculate detailed mathematical tables to help aim cannons and missiles led to the creation of the first full-blown, general-purpose computer, the electronic numerical integrator and calculator (**ENIAC**), at the University of Pennsylvania in 1946. Materials shortages prevented ENIAC from being finished in time to make a contribution to World War II, but Colossus had already won that war, anyway. ENIAC contributed to the cold war, though, by helping to complete calculations for the first hydrogen bomb.

After a falling out with their university over the patent rights to ENIAC, its developers, J. Presper Eckert and John Mauchly, turned to business pursuits. They also had an ugly tiff with an academic colleague, John von Neumann, whom they felt had unfairly left their names off the scientific paper that first described the computer and allowed von Neumann to claim that *he* had invented it. Eckert and Mauchly went on to create UNIVAC for the Remington Rand Corporation, an early leader in the computer industry. UNIVAC was the first successful commercial computer, and the first model was sold to the U.S. Census Bureau in 1951. Before long, however, the development of the computer became deeply intertwined with the fortunes of IBM.

The Rise of IBM

As we have seen, IBM started in the late nineteenth century as a manufacturer of electromechanical office tabulating equipment; the company took its current name in 1924. It financed one of the first digital computers, a clacking electromechanical monster known as the Mark I, in 1943. IBM's first president, Thomas Watson, Sr., commissioned the project, possibly as an expensive publicity stunt—research, advertising, and publicity all came out of the same budget in those days. Perhaps because the imperious Watson (no relation to Alexander Graham Bell's Mr. Watson, by the way) was miffed that the Mark I's inventor did not give sufficient credit to his corporate sponsor, IBM did not immediately enter the computer business after the war and did not deliver its first computer until 1953. In 1954 IBM was only the fourth-ranked computer producer, well behind computer industry pioneers Radio Corporation of America (RCA), Sperry Rand, and Bendix. That year, IBM introduced the Model 650, the first computer to utilize punch-card technology, something IBM knew quite a bit about, and its computer sales began to take off.

Over the next decade, IBM made heavy investments in research and development under Thomas Watson, Jr., who took over from his father as IBM president in the mid-1950s. IBM capitalized on its manufacturing expertise to produce a full line of peripheral equipment—printers, terminals, keypunch machines, and card sorters—that spelled enormous profits for IBM and unbeatable competition for other computer manufacturers.

By the mid-1950s, IBM threatened to dominate the entire computer industry with its fast-selling Model 650. In 1956, to resolve an antitrust suit filed by the U.S. Justice Department, the company signed a **consent decree** that required it to keep computer manufacturing and **computer services** (the processing of computer applications for its customers) in separate subsidiaries. IBM also offered its computers for sale for the first time instead of renting them,

The 1956 **consent decree** opened up competition for IBM in the computer market.

Computer services refer to the processing of computer applications and the delivery of computerized information for end users.

IN THE MID-1950S, IBM'S MODEL 650 COMPUTER WAS AN INDUSTRY STANDARD.

as it previously had insisted. This allowed leasing companies to buy computer equipment from IBM and then rent it to computer users at prices lower than IBM itself could charge. These changes opened up competition in the computer services and equipment leasing markets. The computer maintenance and punch-card businesses were also made competitive.

In April 1964 IBM introduced the Model 360, the first computer that came in a variety of sizes and that was customizable to many different applications. Software and peripheral devices that worked on any one of the versions also worked on the others and were also "backward compatible" with earlier IBM models. Before, users had to start over with entirely new software, printers, terminals, and so on whenever they switched to a larger computer or added a new application.

IBM now spread the immense costs of hardware and software development over many users, allowing IBM to undercut the competition while still garnering enormous profits. The Model 360 and its successor, the Model 370, led the company to dominance of both U.S. and international markets.

The 1956 consent decree barely slowed IBM down. In the late 1970s the Justice Department launched another antitrust case, with the goal of breaking up IBM into several companies—each with a full line of hardware, software, and computer services. Ironically, the suit was concluded in 1982, the same year that a similar action against AT&T resulted in the dismemberment of the telecommunications giant. In the IBM case, however, it was decided to keep the company intact.

Mainframe computers are large computers capable of high-speed processing for multiple simultaneous users.

Supercomputers are advanced high-speed mainframe computers.

Minicomputers are smaller than mainframes and are often dedicated to specific applications.

Personal computers are computers for individual users.

IBM's enormous success with room-sized **mainframe** computers eventually proved its undoing. It made unsuccessful or belated entries into many of the specialized computer markets that later emerged. IBM abandoned the high-performance **supercomputer** market in the 1960s, for example, and it entirely missed the **minicomputer** trend, pioneered in the early 1960s by Digital Equipment Corporation, to use low-cost, refrigerator-sized computers for specialized purposes such as manufacturing production control and scientific computing. By the time IBM came out with its own models, minicomputers were about to be made obsolete by another new product that IBM ultimately failed to capitalize on: the desktop-sized **personal computer.**

The Rise of the Personal Computer

The first personal computer, the Altair, was announced in *Popular Electronics* in its January 1975 issue. The Altair was also the first example of "vaporware"—new computer hardware that is heralded with great fanfare but that does not really exist. The first specimen was literally "lost in the mail" on the way to its photography session. An empty metal box filled in for it on the magazine cover. The "real" Altair was not very impressive; it held only enough data to store the first four lines of this paragraph. The user could not type anything with it anyway, as it had no keyboard or monitor and no word-processing software—or any type of software, for that matter. The user had to load each program into memory by toggling electrical switches on the front. About all the Altair could do was play a simple-minded game in which the user imitated the patterns of flashing lights on its control panel. Oh yes, users also had to solder the computer together themselves from raw electronic components—the Altair was only available in kit form (Freiberger & Swaine, 1984; Young, 1988).

Nonetheless, the Altair caused a sensation among electronics buffs in the computer industry who wanted their own computers to play with at home, and a mighty computer industry soon began to grow. A young computer hacker from Seattle by the name of William

APPLE PIONEERED THE PERSONAL COMPUTER IN 1977 WITH THE APPLE II, SHOWN ON THE RIGHT. ITS SUCCESSOR, THE MACINTOSH, IS SHOWN ON THE LEFT.

Gates, then a freshman at Harvard, sold the Altair's developers a computer language that would run on their machine and that made it possible to program many advanced functions. Emboldened by their success with Altair, Gates and a friend founded Microsoft Corporation, which has become the world's largest personal computer software company.

The Altair also inspired electronics enthusiasts across the country to begin building their own computers. In 1976 in a spare bedroom in Cupertino, California, college dropouts Steve Jobs and Stephen Wozniak began assembling their own **microcomputer,** which they dubbed the Apple. The second iteration of their design, the Apple II, included such amenities as a keyboard, a built-in power supply, and a color monitor (all lacking in the first version) and was an immediate success following its introduction in 1977.

The work at Xerox PARC, a research facility run by the Xerox Corporation in Palo Alto, California, also deserves mention in the history of the personal computer. Its Alto computer, developed in 1972–1974, was the first full-fledged personal computer as we think of it today. It was a personal workstation that boasted a mouse, its own advanced programming language, a "friendly" user interface, and a high-speed network connection, called Ethernet. However, the Alto was never meant to be a commercial product, and Xerox eventually fumbled its entry into the personal computer business.

Microcomputers, or personal computers, are small computers for individual users.

Floppy disk drives store computer data on a flexible ("floppy") plastic disk coated with a magnetized film.

With the inclusion of a **floppy disk drive** that stored computer-readable data on a flexible plastic disc, the Apple II added a convenient way to read computer programs. This development truly gave birth to the phenomenon of personal computing, as many software developers, working in their own spare rooms and basements, developed a wide array of computer software. In 1979 a remarkable program called VisiCalc appeared, the first "electronic spreadsheet" that made it possible for the personal computer to manipulate complex arrays of data. VisiCalc not only racked up impressive sales as a computer software package but also spurred adoption of the Apple II itself.

IBM made its entry in 1981, with its Personal Computer (PC), which was tremendously successful, soon outstripping sales of Apple and other early personal computers. However, revenues from IBM's traditional computer business soon began a long-term decline, spurred in part by the substitution of personal computers for handling what had once been mainframe applications, particularly in financial analysis and planning, for which PC-based electronic spreadsheet programs—the descendants of VisiCalc—were ideally suited.

IBM was unable to dominate personal computers as it had the mainframe market, since IBM had exclusive rights neither to the central processing chip that was the "brains" of the personal computer nor to the disk operating system (DOS) software that made the hardware perform its basic functions. The Intel Corporation, which made the chips, and Microsoft, which made the software, were free to sell their products to all comers. Microsoft developed a full line of software, such as word-processing and spreadsheet packages, that rivaled

IBM's own. Thus, it took only a matter of months to create "clones" of the IBM PC with technical specifications that matched the IBM machines and that would run all of the same software, at a much lower cost. The same feat had taken several years to accomplish in the mainframe computer business, by which time IBM had an insurmountable edge.

Meanwhile, Apple Computer began the transition from a garage brand to a multibillion-dollar corporation by maintaining control of its own destiny with a proprietary operating system and with a wealth of attractive and "user friendly" software applications, allowing it to charge premium prices for its computers. Continuing the apple motif, it called its next successful computer the Macintosh.

Apple also specialized in the development of **multimedia** computers with advanced sound and moving image display capabilities. Because Apple produced only personal computers, it could focus its attention on that market, while IBM had to worry about protecting its mainframe business. Apple eventually carved out a small, but fiercely loyal, segment of the personal computer market.

Microsoft emerged as a major force in the personal computer industry as the profits shifted from the hardware to the software end of the industry. Under the continuing guidance of William Gates, Microsoft had become a multibillion-dollar corporation by the early 1990s. Its Windows operating system outclassed IBM's own efforts to update DOS and had an easy-to-use interface not unlike Apple's own. Microsoft produced a full range of software packages that were among the leaders in virtually all of the most popular product categories. The Redmond, Washington–based company also developed multimedia and networking software products that were making companies nervous from Cupertino, California (where Apple was located), to Armonk, New York (IBM headquarters).

The personal computer phenomenon also gave new life to an area north of San Jose, California, known as Silicon Valley. The area takes its name from the primary raw material used in the manufacture of computer chips, the element silicon, more popularly known as "sand." William Shockley, one of the co-inventors of the transistor, founded one of the first Silicon Valley firms near his home in Palo Alto in 1955, where he could draw upon top scientific and engineering talent from Stanford University and the University of California at Berkeley. The area prospered greatly in the 1970s and 1980s from the production of components, peripherals, and software for the burgeoning personal computer industry.

The Rise of the Computer Network

Both IBM and Apple failed to fully capitalize on the next major computing trend, which was to link personal computers together via high-speed communication networks, called **local area networks (LANs).** It soon became apparent that large organizations could save a lot of money if the software and peripheral devices (such as printers and disk drives) that personal computers needed could be shared among multiple computers over high-speed networks. Also, some exciting new applications that could exist only in a networked environment, such as electronic mail, became popular. More and more software applications that once could run only on mainframe computers were now found on personal computers. By the early 1990s, mainframes accounted for only about half the total sales of computer equipment. Mid-range and multiuser computers—most acting as the nexus for large networks—accounted for another third, and personal computers and workstations accounted for the rest.

Multimedia systems integrate text, audio, and video and let users select the presentation mode.

Local area networks (LANs) are high-speed computer networks that link computers within a department, a building, or a campus of buildings.

R E V I E W

1. What were the contributions of Charles Babbage, Ada Byron, Herman Hollerith, John Vincent Atanasoff, John von Neumann, and Eckert and Mauchly to the early development of the computer?
2. What was the role of IBM in the development of the computer?
3. How did the personal computer come about?
4. What is behind the trend toward networks of personal computers?

Downsizing is replacing
mainframe computers with
networked personal computers.

This **downsizing** of corporate networks and the switch to network computing created a new computer industry giant, the Novell Corporation, which dominated the LAN software market by the early 1990s.

TECHNOLOGY TRENDS

The evolution of computer technology is often discussed in terms of five "generations," defined in terms of the types of components used in their basic processing and storage units. We might also identify the "zeroth" generation: computer designs such as those of Babbage, Hollerith, and the Mark I that had mechanical components for doing the data crunching.*

Computer Processor Generations

First-generation computers used
vacuum tubes in their data
processing units.

First-generation computers (circa 1944–1959) used vacuum tubes—the same kind of tubes found in antique radios—in their processing units. The first-generation computers were unique individuals, with colorful names like EDVAC, EDSAC, BINAC, ORACLE, Whirlwind, ILLIAC, JOHNNIAC (after computer pioneer John von Neumann), and even MANIAC and SILLIAC. UNIVAC was the first commercially successful computer of this generation, although the IBM Model 650 eventually outpaced it.

Babbage's difference engine used a system of toothed gears, not unlike an automobile's odometer, to perform its calculations. ENIAC, which used decimal numbers, substituted electronic tubes arranged in a circular pattern for the whirling mechanical gears. When the tenth tube in the circle was lighted, it advanced a similar electronic counter in the next circle of lights, corresponding to the next higher decimal place. ENIAC had over 17,000 electronic tubes to carry out its calculations, which made it as big as a house, weighing 30 tons and using as much electricity as a small town. Even so, its internal "clock" could only "tick" at a rate of 100,000 times per second, about twenty times slower than the average personal computer in the early 1990s.

TABLE 12.2. COMPUTER TECHNOLOGY MILESTONES	
Year	**Event**
1822	The difference engine
1939	First electronic computer
1944–1959	First-generation computers
1946	First programmable digital computer
1947	Transistors invented
1951	UNIVAC
1954	IBM Model 650
1955	FORTRAN programming language
1959–1964	Second-generation computers
1964	IBM Model 360
1964	Octopus, first local area network
1964–1972	Third-generation computers
1975	First personal computer
1972 on	Fourth-generation computers
1973	ARPANET founded
1979 on	Fifth-generation computers

Still, ENIAC was faster than the mere humans who built it. Human "clock speed" is only about 100 ticks per second. In its first public demonstration, ENIAC amazed the newspaper reporters present by multiplying 97,367 by 5,000 in two-thousandths of a second. None of those reporters could do that! Even the best mechanical tabulators of the day took several seconds to match the feat. Despite all the finicky tubes, ENIAC was capable of performing mathematical calculations in a matter of seconds that took humans hundreds of hours.

The early binary computers used electronic tubes in configurations that allowed them to perform the basic operations of binary logic—which are the essential components of all computer calculations. The De Forest vacuum tube—invented in 1906 and the same basic

*This account of computer technology relies on Evans (1981), Flamm (1988), Koff (1979), and White (1993).

FIRST-GENERATION COMPUTERS SUCH AS ENIAC, SHOWN HERE, WERE MADE WITH VACUUM TUBES, WHICH MADE THEM BOTH HUGE AND UNRELIABLE BY TODAY'S STANDARDS.

Second-generation computers used transistors for processing data.

Transistors are semiconductor devices that act like tiny electronic switches.

design used in telephone amplifiers and radio circuits—had the essential property that was required: its output could be modified based on minor changes in an electrical current fed into one of its terminals. When the tube yielded a high output level, a computer one was recorded; otherwise it was a computer zero. The tubes used in the first-generation computers presented some major problems, though. They took some time to warm up, generated lots of excess heat, burned out at unpredictable intervals, and could not be made much smaller than a Christmas tree bulb.

Second-generation computers (1959–1964) replaced the tubes with **transistors,** tiny triple-decker "sandwiches" of special materials whose ability to conduct electricity varies according to the nature of the electrical current applied to it. The transistor was invented in 1947 by three Bell Labs researchers, Bardeen, Brattain, and Shockley. Transistors had the same essential quality as the De Forest tube: the output of the device could be modified by relatively small variations in a controlling current. By arranging the transistors just so, it was possible to create electrical circuits that replicated all the binary logic functions for a computer. The transistors required no warm-up, gave off a lot less heat than the tubes did, soaked up a lot less electricity, and almost never burned out. Transistors were also much smaller than electronic tubes, and the size and weight of computers quickly shrank. The IBM 1400 models were the most successful computers of this generation. Second-generation computers still read their instructions from paper or magnetic tape and performed their tasks one program at a time.

COMPUTERS MADE WITH TRANSISTORS WERE FASTER AND MORE POWERFUL THAN FIRST-GENERATION COMPUTERS, WHILE PHYSICALLY MUCH SMALLER. HERE AN IBM 704, IN USE FROM 1955 TO 1960, IS SHOWN.

COMPUTERS AND TV IN THE 1952 PRESIDENTIAL ELECTION

An early example of the convergence of computers and the mass media took place on election night in 1952. Months earlier, CBS-Television executives made an interesting proposition to UNIVAC's manufacturer, Remington Rand. If UNIVAC would collate the election returns for CBS, the network would liberally plug Remington Rand's computers in the election night coverage. The polls were showing that the presidential race between Dwight David Eisenhower and Adlai Stevenson would be a close one, so all of America would be watching. Remington Rand's publicist had an interesting proposition, too: Why not get the computer to predict the outcome of the election before all of the votes were in?

By 9 P.M. on election night, UNIVAC had its prediction ready. Eisenhower would win by a landslide, carrying 438 electoral votes to Stevenson's 93. Total panic ensued at Remington Rand. Everyone knew from the preelection polls that the race was too close to call. UNIVAC was about to make a colossal blunder in front of one of the biggest national television audiences in history! Frantically, technicians searched for glitches in UNIVAC's program while correspondents Walter Cronkite and Charles Collingwood covered with tall tales about how slow returns were preventing UNIVAC from making a speedy prediction. Finding nothing wrong with the programs, the Remington Rand staff began to alter the formulas used to make the projections. Finally, at 10 P.M. they went on the air with a prediction that matched the "conventional wisdom," an election that was just about dead even, too close to call.

By midnight it was clear that an Eisenhower landslide indeed was in the making, and Remington Rand's research director had to eat crow on national television. The final

election tallies showed 442 electoral votes for Eisenhower—almost exactly what UNIVAC had prognosticated. CBS commentator Edward R. Murrow summed up the entire sorry episode, "The trouble with machines is people" (Wulforst, 1982).

Third-generation computers used integrated circuits.

Integrated circuits are computer "chips" with thousands of circuit elements etched onto tiny wafers of silicon.

Fourth-generation computers use very large scale integration.

Very large scale integration (VLSI) squeezes entire computers onto a single silicon chip.

In the **third-generation** computers (1964–1972), **integrated circuits,** which had thousands of electrical components on a single computer chip, served as the processing and memory components. Photographic etching processes, similar to those used to create photographic engravings, were used to carve the tiny circuits from layers of semiconductor and nonconducting materials. No longer did technicians armed with soldering irons and wire cutters place each component on a circuit board and use molten metal to hold it in place. Instead, hundreds, then thousands of components could be placed within a fingernail-sized component and reproduced by the millions. Needless to say, the size and cost of computers decreased dramatically, as did their power consumption and heating problems. Third generation machines were also the first ones able to run multiple programs at the same time. The IBM Model 360 was one of the first of its generation and also the most successful.

Fourth-generation computers (1972 to the present) use **very large scale integration (VLSI),** so that tens of thousands, even millions, of components can be squeezed onto a tiny chip. By 1971 entire computer circuits could be placed on a single chip. The Intel 4004 chip was the basis for the earliest personal computers, including the Altair, and also went into the processing units of the mainframe computers that followed. Personal computers are fourth-generation machines.

The computers of the **fifth generation** (1979 to the present) use multiple processing units capable of working simultaneously in parallel fashion on a single computing problem. So-called supercomputers such as the Cray are fifth-generation machines. Fifth-generation computers have software that can efficiently break down problems into components that can then be "parceled out" to parallel processors and later reassembled for the solutions. Some fifth-generation machines can also "program themselves," at least to a limited degree. All the prior generations of computers could execute only the exact instructions that were entered by their human operators.

Computer scientists are already looking forward to the sixth generation. There is a great deal of interest in machines that exhibit **artificial intelligence,** or the ability to mimic human problem solving and other mental abilities. Others foresee **neurocomputers** that will replicate the physiological structure of the human brain, making them capable of complex pattern recognition tasks that baffle today's computers, such as deciding not to lower a drill press because the computer "sees" the operator's hand is in the way. Computers that will be able to "learn" simple tasks without the necessity of giving them detailed instructions beforehand are also in the works. Another possibility for the future evolution of computer processing is "optical computing." Instead of using electrons to move data around in electrical circuits, we would use light moving around in strands of glass. Photons move more quickly than electrons and generate less heat, and it might take fewer components to put them through their paces.

This generational view of computer development focuses almost exclusively on the technology used in computer central processing units. It leaves out some other crucial developments in computer technology that are important to our understanding of the convergence of computer and telecommunications systems, including evolution in such key areas as software, computer interfaces, memory, and communications.

Computer Software

ENIAC had some other serious limitations besides the electronic tubes that made up its memory circuits. It used decimal arithmetic, not binary numbers. Its memory was limited to 300 numbers that had to be manually entered at the start of each run by throwing electrical switches. It had no long-term storage. The machine had to be stopped and the results of each set of calculations printed out before proceeding. Input was also a problem. ENIAC's data had to be fed in by paper tape, the first computer's only means of "communicating" with the outside world. There were no teletypes or terminals to issue commands or view the results. Worse, to reprogram the computer, such as to convert it from calculating the trajectory of an artillery shell to the design of the hydrogen bomb, it was necessary to manually reconfigure it with electrical patch cords and mechanical switches. Thus, ENIAC had no "software" as we now think of it; it could be reprogrammed only by reconfiguring its hardware.

In 1949 a British computer, the EDSAC, was the first operating computer that could store its own programs in electronic memory and that could change the operation it was performing (such as switch from multiplication to extracting square roots) without stopping the computer. EDSAC was thus the first computer to incorporate the idea for the stored program computer originated by John von Neumann; this idea is what makes the computer the adaptable tool we know it as today.

The early computer **software** was not very user friendly, to say the least. It was written exclusively in **machine language:** coded instructions, consisting entirely of 1's and 0's, that drove the binary circuits inside the computer. The next step was to develop mnemonic symbols (e.g., "A" for "Add") that served as a shorthand for long series of binary digits, known as **assembly language.** FORTRAN, released by IBM in 1955, allowed programmers to use recognizable words, such as "RUN" and "GO TO," to invoke procedures that entailed several machine operations at once. FORTRAN was thus the first **high-level language** and was especially useful for the scientific computing problems that dominated early computer applications. COBOL, the first language designed to approximate the English language, was developed by Navy commodore Grace Murray Hopper in 1959.

Multipurpose higher-level languages followed. BASIC (Beginner's All-Purpose Symbolic Instruction Code), introduced in 1965, is of particular interest since many personal computer programs and video games are based on it. It was a version of BASIC for the Altair personal computer that gave William Gates and Microsoft their start. Thus, the commands that we issue to our word-processing programs and video games are first translated into higher-level languages such as BASIC (Pascal, C, and ADA—after Ada Byron—are some others), then into lower-level languages that actually drive the computer bits and logical components inside our computers.

For many years, the ultimate "holy grail" of software development has been the creation of **natural language** programming that will allow untrained humans to issue instructions to computers in their own words. This goal still remains to be attained, and work with advanced personal computer interfaces is leading toward iconic interfaces that use pictures and symbols, rather than words, to issue commands. In computerese, these are known as **graphical user interfaces** (GUIs). Although popularized by Apple Computer, GUIs originated with Xerox's Alto computer back in the 1972–1974.

Short-Term Memory

Computers need **short-term memory** storage capabilities so that they can "remember" the results of their data processing and store their programmed instructions for ready access. For example, when a personal computer user activates a word-processing program, the computer instructions that execute the word-processing functions are loaded into short-term memory. As the user types, the document is also created in short-term memory.

A variety of electronic exotica were used to perform this function in the early days of computing. One early approach was the so-called mercury delay tube. This contraption consisted of two vibrating crystals at either end of a long tube filled with mercury. As long as the mercury kept sloshing back and forth against the vibrating crystals, a 1 was recorded; a 0 was recorded if the sloshing stopped. Each six-foot glass tube recorded only a single binary digit, and it leaked a toxic substance if it broke! How would you like to have that in your laptop?

The most common type of short-term memory in the first two generations of computers was a large matrix of tiny doughnut-shaped magnets, called magnetic cores. The rings were interlaced with wires that could change the north-south polarity of the magnetic field (one direction for a 1, the opposite for a 0). This method was devised in the late 1940s by An Wang, who went on to found Wang Computer Laboratories, which later figured in the development of both the minicomputer and the personal computer.

However, the cores could be made only so small and placed only so close together, and before long the sheer length of the wires inside the memory circuits was slowing the calculations down. Transistors and the integrated memory circuits that followed solved the problem by storing the 1's and 0's of computer data in the form of electrical voltages in solid-

Assembly language uses mnemonic symbols to simplify programming for humans.

High-level languages use words to further simplify program-ming.

Natural language programs allow untrained humans to converse with computers in their own tongue.

Graphical user interfaces (GUIs) use icons and symbols to issue commands to computers.

Short-term memory stores data and programs for immediate use in the computer.

state memory computer chips. They act something like a matrix of tiny rechargeable batteries. The processing unit charges up the battery when it wants to store a 1 at a particular memory location and discharges it when it wants a 0.

In 1967 the IBM Model 360 was the first computer to use integrated circuits in its memory unit. Henceforth, the memory capacity of the computer was limited only by the number of tiny memory circuits that could fit on an integrated circuit chip. ENIAC could store only 300 decimal numbers. The first IBM Model 360s held 256,000 binary computer words, or *bytes,* with 8 binary digits each. The first IBM personal computer equaled that. Today, mainframe computers have memories with hundreds of millions of bytes, and some personal computers sometimes hold over 10 million bytes in their temporary, or **random access memory (RAM),** units.

Long-Term Memory

Long-term memory is necessary so that computer programs and data not in use can be saved for another day. Babbage's proposed computer would have used paper for long-term memory—each set of calculations was to be printed onto a sheet of paper as it was made. The earliest electronic computers used Hollerith's punchcards or punched holes in spools of paper tape. ENIAC spewed forth data at such a high speed that the output swirled upward in twenty-foot cyclones of paper tape.

Another "new technology" of the post–World War II years, **magnetic recording,** was soon brought to bear on the long-term memory storage problem. Beginning with UNIVAC in 1951, computer data and programs were stored on multitracked magnetic tape. Computer tape systems work much like audiotape in that the information is stored in tiny globs of a magnetic material that are applied to a continuous ribbon of plastic tape. Instead of having to record and play back the full range of sound frequencies found in a musical performance, only two states of nature have to be recorded: a high frequency to indicate a 1 and a lower frequency for a 0. The early personal computers used ordinary audiocassette tapes to store data and programs. Tape drives are still found on mainframe computers today, where they

MAGNETIC TAPE PERMITTED COMPUTERS TO STORE AND PROCESS MUCH MORE INFORMATION THAN EARLIER COMPUTERS WITH PUNCH-CARD OR PAPER TAPE STORAGE.

are used primarily for long-term archival storage and also as backup systems for multiuser computer servers.

However, tape storage has one important limitation in that it is a linear medium. This means that the computer has to "fast forward" the tape to just the right point before it can "play" each piece of data or retrieve each program. Magnetic drums, first developed in 1948, had several stationary recording heads used to access several tracks on a revolving magnetic drum simultaneously.

The basic approach used in today's **hard disk drives** began to emerge in 1955, when IBM demonstrated a storage device that used a flat rotating disk and a moving arm that held the read and record heads. The data are still stored in tiny globs of magnetic material but now are on the surface of a rigid, fast-spinning surface, and the "read head" is free to move quickly back and forth across the surface to where the desired piece of data resides.

In 1973 IBM introduced a flexible vinyl disk storage system for its mainframe systems that soon became known as the **floppy disk.** In 1978 Stephen Wozniak, in one of his last contributions to Apple Computer before retiring a wealthy man, designed a small-scale disk drive system for the Apple II.

Most personal computers use another type of permanent storage that holds the basic instructions needed to start, or "boot up," the computer when it is first turned on. This is **read-only memory (ROM),** a form of permanent storage that uses solid-state circuits in which the necessary programs are permanently stored.

Computer Interface Devices

As we have seen, paper and magnetic storage media were used to "communicate" data to and from the earliest computer processing units. The keyboard input and **cathode ray tube (CRT)** output methods familiar to all personal computer users today did not become common until the 1960s. The Whirlwind computer was the first with a CRT display in 1951, while UNIVAC was the first commercially available computer to accept input from a keyboard and to produce printer output.

A computer's CRT operates much like a television tube does. An electron "gun" at the back of the tube shoots a stream of electrons at the front of the screen, lighting up globs of luminescent material on the inner surface of the screen. As in the television tube, the stream of electrons moves back and forth across the front of the screen so quickly that the moving point of light fools our eyes and gives us the sensation of a continuous image. There the similarities end, a fact which now complicates attempts to integrate computer and television media. Each frame of the computer screen is constructed from a single top-to-bottom scan of the picture tube, instead of by interlacing two scans to make one frame, as the television does. When color computer monitors were introduced, more dissimilarities cropped up from the need to limit the number of colors available and so keep to a minimum the number of data bits required to encode the color information.

Aside from the keyboard, the **mouse** is perhaps the input device most familiar to personal computer users. It originated in pioneering work at the Stanford Research Institute in the 1960s. The mouse controls the horizontal and vertical position of a pointer on the screen. It was first introduced to the general computer public in 1983 on board the Apple Lisa, forerunner to the Macintosh. Spurred by continuing efforts to make personal computers more "user friendly," a wide variety of input options are now available, including joysticks, trackballs, pressure-sensitive tablets, touch-sensitive screens, and optical scanners such as the ones found in supermarket checkout lanes.

Hard disk drives are long-term memory devices that store data inside a computer on a rigid magnetic disk.

Floppy disks store data on a felixible, removable plastic disk.

Read-only memory (ROM) stores the computer's permanent instructions in solid state memory.

Cathode ray tubes (CRTs) are the TV-like display devices on computers.

A mouse is a device used to locate objects on a computer screen and to activate program features.

FIGURE 12.1
PERSONAL COMPUTER
SYSTEMS INCLUDE THE
CENTRAL PROCESSING
UNIT (CPU), THE
MONITOR, INPUT
DEVICES (KEYBOARD
AND MOUSE), AND
DATA STORAGE (HARD
DISK AND FLOPPY
DISK).

Monitor

Expansion card to connect
to other monitors, drives,
scanners, or printers

Mother board, which
carries the CPU, to
connect and integrate
all components

Hard drive
for long-term
memory

Floppy drive
for file
exchange and
backup

Processor chip
for performing
calculations

RAM chips for
temporary
memory

Mouse for
graphic input
and menu
commands

Keyboard for text
input and
commands

The basic elements that make up a personal computer system are summarized in Figure 12.1.

Data Communications

The first wide-scale data communications application was the SAGE air defense system. Its display unit was the inspiration for the wide-screen "doomsday television" that is the backdrop for *War Games, Dr. Strangelove,* and dozens of apocalyptic movies from the cold war era. SAGE accumulated information from hundreds of remote sensors that would track waves of Soviet bombers. After the cold war ended, it turned out that the U.S.S.R. had only a handful of bombers capable of the flight to the United States back then—perhaps so few that human observers wielding binoculars and clipboards could have kept tabs on them. By that time SAGE had paid some dividends: the first light pen, for example, and major advances in magnetic disk storage, graphics displays, and computer manufacturing technology.

AT&T, which undertook the data communications aspects of the project, had to overcome a serious limitation inherent in the phone lines that were to carry the doomsday data from all over North America to SAGE's central processing unit. The easiest way to feed computers their data is to turn on a tiny electrical voltage to represent a 1 and turn the voltage off to represent a 0. This is pretty much what computers do when they are talking to themselves through their internal circuitry. Unfortunately, the telephone system filters out these kinds of electrical signals, known as pulses, after a call is established, since telephone switches use the same kind of pulse to process the numbers dialed into old-style rotary telephones. Noise in the telephone channel could also interact with the data pulse, and lightning strikes could be mistaken for legitimate data bits. This was all too chancy for a system that could end the world!

AT&T's answer was to develop the first **modem,** or MOdulator-DEModulator system. The solution is a relatively simple one: to send a 1 the modem transmits a high-frequency tone for a short amount of time. To send a 0, it sends a lower-frequency tone. At the other end of the line, the process is reversed, and a series of pulses corresponding to the 1's and 0's is reconstructed for the benefit of the computer. This simple solution does have an important limitation, though, in that the modem has to let each tone "play" for a moment before going on to the next bit, which limits the speed at which the data can be transmitted. Subsequent developments in modem technology have revolved around more and more ingenious ways to encode the data that make it possible to represent more than one data bit each time the signal changes. The "speed limit" on computer modems has doubled every few years. By 1993 modems were available that communicated data over a standard phone line at over 38,000 **bits** per second, or about three single-spaced pages of text per second.

The SAGE project was responsible for another first that inspired the first era of rapid growth in data communications: the concept of on-line **time-sharing** systems. Well into the 1960s, most computers only did batch processing. This meant that all of the programs and data were queued up on tape or in huge stacks of punch cards and fed into the computer one after another. The user had to pace back and forth while waiting for the output, a process that could take hours or even days, depending on the priority and size of the run. SAGE was the first real-time system: It was designed to immediately display the positions of the phantom bomber fleets.

Now the problem was not that the humans had to wait for the computer output but that the computer had to wait for the human input. This is an accepted state of affairs for our personal computers today, but in the 1960s computer time was still too precious for that. Time sharing allowed the computer to handle many tasks at once while waiting for the humans. Multiple users could be on-line with the computer at the same time. If the computer got started on a long problem, it took a "time out," spent a few milliseconds on another task, and then picked up again where it left off on the first job. In this way dozens and later hundreds of users could have the impression of working on their own dedicated computer.

The first civilian time-sharing systems appeared in 1962. The best known, largest, and most enduring example of a time-sharing system is American Airlines's SABRE airline reservation system, which was developed by IBM and first saw service in 1965. SABRE is what connects airline ticket counters and travel agents across the country to a central computer via modems and telephone lines, allowing central control of airline reservations and ticketing. Applications such as these inspired many other uses of time-sharing systems, such as automatic teller machines, which fostered immense growth in data communications throughout the 1970s and 1980s.

Information "Superhighways"

Outside the computer room, data communications were still very slow. By the mid-1960s, the most advanced modems were capable of sending only 1,200 bits per second, a speed that human speed-readers could still match. Large time-sharing systems were running up huge telephone bills, as each terminal needed a dedicated line all the way back to the central

Modems convert digital data to analog tones that can be transmitted over the telephone network.

Bits, short for binary digits, are the basic 1's and 0's of computer data.

Time-sharing systems share computers between multiple simultaneous users.

computer. Computer scientists began to look for ways to make data communication faster and to extend it more efficiently over wider and wider areas.

The first local area network (LAN) was the Octopus network, at the Atomic Energy Commission's Livermore Laboratory in 1964. It extended high-speed data communication to entire office buildings or campuses of buildings. Now remote terminals could enjoy the same instant communication with the central processor that the terminals in the computer room could. In the early 1970s the Xerox Corporation pioneered a type of LAN called Ethernet, which went on to become the most widely used approach to personal computer networking.

Wide area networks extend data communications beyond individual buildings or campuses.

Internet is a network of computer networks used by millions for E-mail and database access.

Packet switching is a type of data transmission that lets multiple users share the same circuit.

In 1966 experiments with a **wide area network** (WAN) dedicated to defense research and development projects began. ARPANET (Advanced Research and Projects Network), as it became known, was first operational in 1973 and was the forerunner of today's **Internet,** the "network of networks" that links researchers in academia and industry across the United States and the world. ARPANET's most important innovation was a means of transmitting data over long distances in a way that did not require dedicated connections between each and every point on the network. This approach, known as **packet switching,** divides data streams into chunks, or packets, of data and mixes the data from many different users together into a shared high-speed transmission channel, rather than dedicating a channel to each pair of users. Each chunk of data carries an address on it so that the packets can be reassembled at the receiving end.

The spread of personal computers in the 1980s spurred meteoric growth in both LANs and WANs. By the early 1990s, many corporations were beginning to retire mainframe computers from such applications as financial planning, remote job entry, transaction processing, and inquiry responses. New applications, such as word processing and electronic mail, once thought too wasteful for computing resources, became commonplace on networked personal computers.

Future Directions in Personal Computing

Networking aside, perhaps the most significant trend in the personal computer realm is *multimedia,* which entails adding voice and video processing circuits to personal computers and building software "extensions" to activate them. Here is where the convergence of mass media, computers, and telecommunications systems literally hits home. Integrated multimedia terminals may soon appear that will be usable across a wide variety of applications that we now distinguish as "television," "telephone," "radio," and "computers." **Virtual reality**

Virtual reality gives users the sense that they are "inside" a computer-generated reality.

Personal data assistants (PDAs) are pocket-sized computers.

systems take this one step further, immersing you in an environment of sound and vision that gives you the subjective impression of being in an alternate reality.

Another trend in personal computers is the so-called **personal data assistant** (PDA), a pocket-sized information device that you can carry with you through the day. The PDA will accept your handwritten scribbles and keep you in constant contact with various computer and telephone networks and monitor information services for you. It could be the nexus for all your personal communications, regardless of which medium they originate in, will automatically manage your personal affairs, and will sift through the thousands of channels of data looking for things of special interest to you.

A computer that reads your handwriting is only one of the possibili-

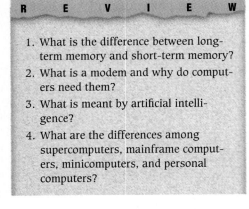

R E V I E W

1. What is the difference between long-term memory and short-term memory?

2. What is a modem and why do computers need them?

3. What is meant by artificial intelligence?

4. What are the differences among supercomputers, mainframe computers, minicomputers, and personal computers?

Voice recognition refers to the ability of computers to understand verbal commands.

ties for advanced computer interfaces. Rapid strides are also being made in **voice recognition** that will allow you to issue verbal commands to your computer. Such systems exist today but are still rather error prone and have a hard time with continuous speech, as opposed to carefully enunciated one-word commands. Some other interesting approaches to the human-computer interface are also being considered (see the box on page 306).

COMPUTER INDUSTRY STRUCTURE

Hardware manufacturers make computers.

Software publishers make the standard programs that run computers

The computer industry has two major sectors. **Hardware manufacturers** make the machines, and **software publishers** make the programs that run on the machines. Combined, the world computer hardware and software businesses comprise a $300-billion-per-year market (U.S. Department of Commerce, 1993). While some companies, such as IBM and Apple, are involved in both ends of the business, most firms prefer to specialize in either hardware or software and even to carve out very narrow specialties or niches for themselves.

Computer Hardware

Storage devices include hard and floppy disk drives.

Peripherals are computer accessories, such as printers and modems.

The hardware business breaks down into four general areas: the computers themselves (further subdivided into supercomputer, mainframe, minicomputer, workstation, and personal computer categories), computer **storage devices** (such as disk drives), computer terminals, and the **peripherals** (such as printers and modems) that go with the computers. Of course, thousands of firms are engaged in the manufacture of components and materials that go into these products, ranging from power supplies to computer cabinets to the glue used to hold the components together. Collectively, computer hardware manufacturers in the United States make up a $65-billion-per-year industry that employs about a quarter of a million people.

At the top end of the computer market are the supercomputers, which are designed to undertake the most complex forms of computing problems, such as the simulation of new designs for jet aircraft. Each unit can cost anywhere from $500,000 to $30 million. Cray

COMPUTERS READ MY MIND, CARESSED MY FLESH!

No, this is not a headline from a supermarket tabloid but rather a concise summary of some of the later developments in computer interface design. Even before voice-controlled interfaces and virtual reality helmets are fully developed, computer designers are looking forward to faster and more realistic interfaces.

Thought control for computers is not as far-fetched as it may seem. Some of the electrical activity of the brain is detectable on the surface of the skull, using the electroencephalograph, or EEG. Distinguishable components of EEG recordings are characteristic of certain brain functions, such as when one reacts to novel stimuli or gets ready to move a limb. Brain-wave control can be used to issue simple computer commands, such as moving the cursor up and down or across the screen. An operator can also produce distinctive EEG patterns by thinking about peculiar phrases, like "tangerine pillow," and get the computer to respond to the distinctive patterns. In time, trained subjects can produce the control patterns without thinking the phrase anymore.

In some respects this is nothing new. Back in the 1960s psychologists were training subjects to focus their brain waves on certain characteristic frequencies and had fun running electric trains and other electrical devices under brain-wave control (the more intense the subject's alpha waves, the faster the train went). Still, we are a long way from thinking the word "save" and having the computer save a file. Also, some of the really interesting brain functions, such as learning and pleasure and pain sensations, take place deep in the brain and cannot be readily distinguished in the EEG. Brain implants anyone?

Computers that feel and touch? That is in the realm of possibility, too. Experimental interfaces are capable of responding to the pressure of touch and of reproducing tactile sensations at the other end of the interface. Thus, we could have you place the palm of your hand on the interface and give someone a massage at the other end of the network. Run your finger in a circle, and they get tickled. Today the body glove responds with digital outputs when we move it. Tomorrow, the body glove will move around us in response to digital input.

Research, a U.S. firm, is the leading manufacturer in this category. The manufacture of mainframe computers, which are used for high-volume general-purpose business applications, is still dominated by IBM, although there are now a host of competitors from Japan and the European Community. Unisys is the sole remaining U.S. mainframe competitor.

Midrange computers, or minicomputers, have recently undergone a resurgence, finding new life at the center of large networks of personal computers. Digital Equipment Corporation (DEC), Hewlett-Packard, and IBM are the industry leaders. **Workstations** are high-performance single-user systems that put the capabilities of a mainframe or even a supercomputer on a desktop. They are used primarily in sophisticated engineering and graphics display applications. DEC, IBM, Hewlett-Packard, Sun Microsystems, and Silicon Graphics are among the leaders in this rapidly growing field.

Personal computers are also single-user machines, of course, but they have far less powerful processors than workstations do and are designed to run a wide variety of general-purpose software. Personal computers come in a variety of configurations, the most widely

Workstations place the power of a mainframe at the disposal of an individual user.

known being the desktop, laptop, and notebook varieties. IBM, Apple, and Compaq are the industry leaders, but there are over forty major international competitors in this field.

Unlike many traditional manufacturing firms, personal computer makers do not invest heavily in the fabrication of the parts that go into the machines; they instead turn to suppliers for the key components. For example, Intel Corporation and Motorola make most of the microprocessors that go into personal computers. Other companies specialize in disk drives, still others in color monitors, and so on. The manufacturers then assemble the computers from the various components. In fact, one of the major computer "manufacturers," Dell Computer, and hundreds of smaller "clone makers" from around the world do not manufacture any of their own components. They merely assemble components made by others, put their name on the outside of the box, and bear primary responsibility for marketing and customer support only. Some personal computer makers still adhere somewhat to the traditional industrial model, fabricating many of their own components. IBM and Apple are perhaps the best examples.

Another new company, 3DO, takes this even one step further. 3DO is a "virtual company" that is developing the next generation of multimedia entertainment players for the home but plans to subcontract just about everything—design, product development, assembly, marketing, and distribution—to other companies. All 3DO will provide is a concept, a name, a handful of permanent employees, and a network to coordinate the various suppliers—and perhaps a bank account to put the profits in. We will see in a later chapter that this type of arrangement is a growing trend in the Information Age that has been made possible in large part by the spread of information technology.

Consistent with the "virtual" nature of many companies in the personal computer field, they tend to form alliances with one another to help develop new products instead of engaging in the types of acquisitions and mergers that characterize Industrial Age businesses such as transportation and the mass media. For example, 3DO is an alliance of computer, telecommunications, and consumer electronics companies. Apple Computer, IBM, and Motorola worked together to create a new personal computer operating system that at last makes it easy to run Apple and IBM software on the same personal computer.

Computer Software

The software industry breaks down into three segments: companies that write customized computer programs for their clients, companies that sell prepackaged software, and companies that design computer integrated systems, such as those used to run large factories. In terms of employment, the software end of the industry is about twice as large as the hardware end, with over 400,000 employees in the United States; employment is about equally divided among these three major industry segments.

The manufacturers of prepackaged software are the ones that provide popular application programs (word processing, electronic spreadsheets, computer games) for personal computers. Currently, this is a more than $20-billion-per-year business in the United States, or about five times the size of another well-known "software" industry, motion pictures. Microsoft, the maker of Windows and DOS **operating systems** as well as Word (word processing) and Excel (electronic spreadsheet), is by far the largest software company. Lotus (maker of the Lotus 1-2-3 spreadsheet program), Borland International (Paradox database software), Novell (LAN operating systems), and Word Perfect Corporation (word processing) are other major software companies. Of course, Apple and IBM also manufacture software for the computers they make.

Operating systems are computer programs that provide basic computer functions.

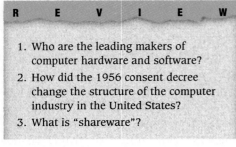

R E V I E W

1. Who are the leading makers of computer hardware and software?
2. How did the 1956 consent decree change the structure of the computer industry in the United States?
3. What is "shareware"?

Site licenses are group discounts on computer software.

Freeware and shareware are programs that may be used free of charge.

Software manufacturers resemble book publishers in some ways in that many of their sales to individual users are made through retail outlets that offer a wide selection of software titles. Much of the software that winds up in the hands of private consumers is sold bundled together with computer hardware at the time of the initial purchase. However, sales to institutional buyers, such as large corporations, account for the lion's share of software sales. Increasingly, software companies sell their software in the form of **site licenses** that allow a specified number of computer network users to access the software simultaneously, rather than buying separate copies for each member of the organization. A great deal of computer software is also distributed as **freeware** or **shareware** through computer networks. This is software for which the authors do not claim copyright protection or whose authors lack a sophisticated distribution network and who hope that users will voluntarily pay.

USING THE HOME COMPUTER

Computers first made their way into the home in the early 1970s with the advent of the first personal computers. The Apple II was the first really useful home computer with a wide array of software written for it. Today, the full range of personal computing technology developed for business users may also be found in the home, although home installations usually have fewer peripherals, have lower-cost components, and lack the network connections that corporate computers have. Some of the more common items found in home computer configurations include:

- *Personal computers,* usually Apple McIntoshes or low-cost "clones" of the IBM personal computer. Many home systems now have their own internal hard disk drives, although some still rely on floppy disk drives to load programs and input data.

- *Printers,* typically dot matrix or ink jet printers, rather than the more expensive laser printers found in corporate settings.

- *Modems* to interconnect the computer with on-line databases.

- *Game controllers,* including trackballs and joysticks that can be used to play computer games.

Fax (short for "facsimile") is a way of sending electronic images of pictures or pages of text.

CD-ROM drives hold discs that store large amounts of computer data and work like compact disc music players.

- *Fax modems,* which allow electronic documents to be sent to **fax** (facsimile) machines. Faxes can also be received on some of these devices, but this often necessitates the purchase of a separate telephone line or a special telephone line management device to be practical.

- *CD-ROM* (compact disc read-only memory) drives, which can play discs that store large quantities of text and graphics—and sometimes even video. CD-ROMs are capable of storing an entire encyclopedia and presenting interactive video programs.

- *Multimedia,* which includes a wide array of computer peripherals and internal expansion cards that make the personal computer function like an all-purpose "media box." High-fidelity stereo speakers, VCR interfaces, and video display capabilities for full-motion color video are some of the more popular—and expensive—options.

Word processing, electronic spreadsheets, communications, graphics, and database management systems are the most popular business applications for personal computers. But what is a home computer good for? That question has plagued personal computer manufacturers from the start. Until recently, many home computers gathered dust, saw most of their service as video game players, or were used for working at home.

Increasingly, access to the Internet—and especially to the fun-to-use graphical portion of it known as the World Wide Web—is the "golden application" that drives home computer purchases. In the process, the personal computer has, in a sense, been reinvented. Formerly little more than a player for video games and more prosaic work-oriented software applications, it is increasingly a means of interpersonal communication that allows users to dispatch E-mail to far-flung correspondents or to "chat" with members of new "virtual" communities that exist only inside the computer. The web is also fast becoming a substitute for conventional mass media functions, such as when it is used to check on the latest sports scores or news headlines or simply as a vehicle to "channel surf" aimlessly for hours on end. In recognition of this trend, mass media institutions have moved rapidly to colonize the web for themselves, creating eye-catching popular pages of their own.

The popularity of the web notwithstanding, the diffusion of the personal computer to the home is still in its early stages. The first personal computers reached the home in the early 1970s in the hands of computer industry professionals and electronics enthusiasts who wanted to tinker with their own computers at home. Personal computer penetration has grown slowly since that time, and about a third of all U.S. homes had personal computers in 1994.

The personal computer spread initially in better-educated, upper-income homes. Early adopters of home computers also had an interest in science and technology, tended to own other "high-tech" home information equipment, and were also likely to use a computer at work. Studies showed that many people bought a home computer without a well-defined idea of what they will use it for, other than to generally learn more about computers (Dutton,

COMPUTERS ARE BECOMING A COMMON FIXTURE IN AMERICAN HOUSEHOLDS.

Rogers, & Jun, 1987). According to a 1995 survey, 36 percent of U.S. homes have a personal computer, while 19 percent have modems and another 5 percent have the use of computers transported from the workplace.[1] However, computer ownership is by no means uniformly distributed. In a recent U.S. government survey, it was found that computer penetration among low-income rural homes is only 4.5 percent, and only about 1 percent of that group has computer modems. Among African American households in the nation's central cities, computer penetration is only 10 percent. Senior citizens are also much less likely than average to have computers or modems.[2] According to another survey (Ziegler, 1994), entertainment is what home computers are used for most often. Other common categories of usage are personal finance, schoolwork, office work, learning about computers, and education software (Caron, Giroux, & Douzou, 1989).

Another rapidly growing home computer application is Internet access. Estimates of home Internet use vary widely, ranging from a low of about 10 million[3] to a high of 24 million in 1995[4]. The disparity between the estimates has to do with varying definitions of what constitutes "Internet use"—specifically, whether electronic mail access "counts" or not—and with differences in the composition of the samples of the surveys. Usage of the Internet and the World Wide Web is examined further in the next chapter.

R E V I E W

1. What does the typical home computer configuration consist of?
2. What do home computer users do with their computers?
3. How do home computer users differ from nonusers?

COMPUTER INDUSTRY ISSUES

Among the major issues facing the computer industry today are fears of monopoly power, government intervention via some sort of industrial policy, control through government acquisition of computers, and copyright and patent issues.

Restricting Monopoly Power

In the United States, the computer industry has largely developed outside of the mantle of government regulation (see Gilchrist & Wessel, 1972). Perhaps the most significant attempts at regulatory oversight were the efforts to dismantle IBM to keep it from monopolizing the mainframe computer business. These suits were initiated by the U.S. Justice Department and pursued in federal district court. One of these efforts concluded with the signing of the 1956 consent decree by IBM, which, as we have seen, opened up competition, primarily in the computer services and equipment leasing arenas, but left the company intact. A second antitrust suit against IBM was dismissed in 1982.

With IBM's fortunes in decline, software giant Microsoft Corp. has replaced IBM as the target of antitrust regulators. The Justice Department barred Microsoft's acquisition of a maker of personal finance software to keep it from monopolizing that segment of the software industry. In 1994 Microsoft agreed to change the pricing strategy it used to promote its DOS software—forcing manufacturers to pay a fee according to the total number of computers sold—to avoid an antitrust suit. Previously, Microsoft had all but monopolized the market for operating system software with this policy, since manufacturers had to pay

---

[1] American Information User Survey at World Wide Web address http://etrg.findsvp.com/.

[2] U.S. Department of Commerce, "Falling Through the Net," at World Wide Web address http://ntiaunix2.ntia.doc.gov:70/0/newitems/urb-rur.txt.

[3] http://etrg.findsvp.com/.

[4] A. C. Nielsen Company at World Wide Web address http://www.nielsenmedia.com/whatsnew/execsum2.htm.

Microsoft's fee even if they chose to package some of their computers with another company's operating system.

Industrial Policy

Some observers are concerned that there is perhaps too little government involvement in the computer and semiconductor industries in the United States, rather than too much. Some have called for the creation of a coordinated national strategy for subsidizing research and development on new technologies such as supercomputers and HDTV that can fuel the growth of a high tech economy. Others seek special treatment for high tech firms, in the form of tax breaks for research and development or efforts to help American firms compete better in world markets. Another proposal is to invest in the "infrastructure" for information technologies, such as by creating a national "information superhighway" by building on the Internet that was originally put in place with federal funding. Collectively, these initiatives may be characterized as **industrial policy,** the idea that there should be some form of rational policy that will guide a nation's economy.

Industrial policy is a comprehensive national plan for developing certain sectors of the economy.

Industrial policy is a term that few U.S. policymakers choose to use. It implies a role for government that some find uncomfortably close to the notion of a "planned economy," an anathema in American politics. Other countries have been less reluctant to plan their future in the Information Age. In Japan, MITI, the Ministry of International Trade and Industry, deserves credit for facilitating the near-complete dominance of consumer electronics and many types of computer components enjoyed by Japanese firms. The Japanese government has made substantial investments in cooperative research-and-development projects involving industry and university researchers, including commitments to decade-long programs to push fifth-generation computers and other advanced computing technologies. The French government retains a substantial ownership interest in Thomson, its premiere electronics manufacturing firm, and has also pushed the convergence of telecommunications and computing by carefully shaping the development of its national telecommunications monopoly, France Telecom. Singapore is another nation that backs development of information industries with government support. There is also a trend toward regionalization, such as the efforts of the European Community to forge a unified approach to development in their computer, electronics, and telecommunications industries. Thus Charles Babbage was perhaps born a century too soon.

A major cooperative effort in the United States is the Microelectronics and Computer Technology Corporation, a research consortium of several leading computer and semiconductor firms. In addition, the ongoing High Performance Computing and Communications Initiative provides funding for such advanced technology projects as fifth-generation computers and the National Research and Education Network (NREN). NREN may yet prove to be the forerunner of the so-called information superhighway.

Control Through Government Acquisition

Another important method of government control of the computer industry has been through the acquisition of computers by government agencies. The history of the computer is replete with examples of breakthroughs in computer technology that responded to military requirements and the needs of various government agencies. The U.S. government is still the largest single customer for computers in the world. Since 1965 all government purchases of computer equipment have been coordinated by the General Services Administration, which sets standards and evaluates government purchasing policies. The development of the ADA high-level programming language was an effort to create a standard language across all military computer applications, for example.

One effect of government involvement has been to emphasize the development of computer technology in areas with direct military applications. However, many of these developments have found important civilian applications in later years. Yesterday's air defense system becomes today's airline reservation system and tomorrow's information superhighway. Government involvement has also tended to influence the development of technical standards that foster compatibility between computer systems.

Copyrights and Patents

Patent is a written document that secures to an inventor for a number of years the exclusive right to make, use, or sell an invention.

Copyrights is a legal privilege to use, sell, or license intellectual property.

Laws governing intellectual property—**patents** and **copyrights**—are the other primary means of control of the computer industry, although some of the patents that have *not* been awarded are perhaps as famous as the ones that have. The patent claim for the invention of the computer, made by Eckert and Mauchly for the ENIAC, was denied. The inventors waited too long to file, especially after allowing a "public use" by the government on the H-bomb project, and the credit for key aspects of their claim went to Atanasoff and von Neumann instead. AT&T gave away its patent rights to another key invention, the transistor, by choosing to freely share data about it with the scientific community. It is possible that AT&T's perpetual fear of antitrust action helped inspire its altruism.

From the software developer's perspective, patents are superior to a mere copyright in that they protect against the practice of "reverse engineering"—copying an invention that performs the same basic functions as yours but using different underlying computer instructions. Copyright offers protection only against duplicating the underlying computer instructions and the screen display and command sequences—the general "look and feel" of the software. The Lotus Development Corporation, publishers of the popular Lotus 1-2-3 spreadsheet program, won a copyright infringement case against a competitor that used many of the same command sequences in its spreadsheet product, even though the underlying computer instructions were different. However, if Lotus, or the designer of VisiCalc, which inspired all subsequent spreadsheet packages, had been able to obtain a patent, they could have had a seventeen-year monopoly on all spreadsheet software under patent law.

Until 1990 computer software was considered unpatentable on the grounds that computers merely executed mathematical calculations of formulas that were themselves the product of mental processes, rather than patentable devices. In other words, the problem was that computer programs were unpatentable thoughts, not patentable things or processes. Patent law on this point evolved rapidly in the early 1990s, including one case in which it was held that computer graphic animation was patentable. Today, software is generally regarded as patentable under U.S. law. This makes it likely that in the future, companies will attempt to control the software market through the acquisition of key patents (Glazier, 1993). There is concern that the patentability of computer software has now gone too far, to the point that it could retard the development of new applications. For example, in 1993 Compton's Encyclopedia was awarded a patent that covers virtually all forms of interactive multimedia computer applications, which could force developers—and consumers—of all such software to pay royalties to the patent holders.

R E V I E W

1. What are some important ways in which the computer industry has been regulated over the years?
2. Which countries have an industrial policy and which do not?
3. What is the difference between a copyright and a patent?

SUMMARY & REVIEW

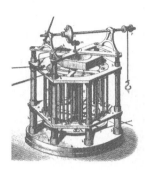

How Did the Computer Develop?

What nineteenth-century developments pointed the way to the computer?
Charles Babbage and Lady Ada Byron created plans for the difference engine, a mechanical precursor to the modern computer, in the 1820s, but they were unable to construct it with the crude manufacturing technology of the day. Herman Hollerith's electromechanical tabulating machine saved the day for the 1890 U.S. Census and was the core invention around which International Business Machines (IBM) eventually grew.

What led to the creation of the computer as we know it today?
The first electronic computer was designed, although not successfully built, by John Vincent Atanasoff in 1939. Data processing needs in World War II resulted in the construction of the first working digital computer, Colossus, and the first programmable computer, ENIAC, developed by von Neumann, Eckert, and Mauchly. The SAGE system, which produced breakthroughs in computer memory, data communications, and display technologies, was also inspired by military needs. The commercialization of the computer began with the purchase of the UNIVAC computer by the U.S. Census in 1951, but was largely driven by the success of the IBM Corporation with its Model 650 and Model 360 computers.

What are the basic types of computers and what are they used for?
Supercomputers are extremely fast computers used in research and industrial design applications that require enormous data processing capacity. Mainframe computers are used by large organizations for high-volume, general-purpose business applications. Minicomputers are medium-sized computers, often found at the center of large computer networks. Workstations are computers that make the power of a mainframe or minicomputer available to a single user. Personal computers are designed to handle the communication and computation needs of individual residential and general business users.

How did the personal computer originate?
Advances in integrated computer memory circuits made it possible to construct small-scale computers. The Altair was the first personal computer, although the Apple II was the first machine of its kind that would be recognizable to today's PC user. College dropouts Steve Jobs, Stephen Wozniak, and William Gates share the credit for key developments in personal computer hardware and software, although it was computer giant IBM that gave personal computers their initial boost into the workplace.

What Important Trends Have Occurred in Computer Technology?

What were the important developments in computer technology?
There are five generations of computer processor technology. First-generation computers used electronic tubes while second-generation computers replaced the tubes with transistors. Integrated circuits, followed by very large scale integrated circuits went into third- and fourth-generation computers, respectively. Fifth-generation supercomputers use a technique called parallel processing to speed their calculations. Advances in computer software, short-term and long-term memory, modems, local area networks, and interface devices were also critical to the development of the computer.

What are the important components of a personal computer?
The computer's central processing unit is where data are processed and calculations are carried out. Short-term memory holds the programs, or software, that run the computer and saves the results of the calculations on a temporary basis. Long-term memory, in the form of floppy or hard disks, makes it possible to save programs and information after the computer has been turned off. Computer interfaces, such as the cathode ray tube, keyboard, and mouse, let the user interact with the computer programs. A modem is a device that makes it possible to send programs and files of data between computers over telephone networks, which were originally designed to transmit the human voice, not computer data.

Where is computer technology headed?
Powerful mainframe computers continue to evolve, to the point where they may exhibit artificial intelligence that in some ways replicates human thought processes. Mainframe computer power is now available in desktop workstations. Personal computers continue to progress in speed and power to the point that some nearly match the capabilities of older workstations and minicomputers. Many now have advanced multimedia capabilities that can process audio and video as well as computer data. Virtual reality perhaps represents the ultimate in the evolution of the multimedia computer—the ability to create artificial worlds that seem real to the senses. As personal computers are linked to increasingly powerful computer networks, personal computer users are able to share software, hardware, and communications among themselves.

What Is the Nature of the Computer Industry?

What is the structure of the computer industry today?
The high end of the computer hardware industry is still dominated by a relative handful of firms, such as IBM, Digital Equipment Corporation, and Sun Microsystems. Apple, IBM, and Compaq are leading personal computer manufacturers, but they are by no means dominant, with dozens of domestic and international competitors. Microsoft is the leading manufacturer of personal computer software. Computer users may also benefit from freeware or shareware, which are low-cost computer programs in the public domain.

How do people use the personal computer?
About a third of U.S. homes have a personal computer. Minorities, women, and low-income households are unlikely to have computers available. Home computers are used only about an hour a day, on the average, primarily for work-related applications like word processing and electronic spreadsheets, although educational programs and computer games are also popular. Typical home computer configurations include a computer, printer, and game controller, although modems and CD-ROMs are increasingly common.

What important policy issues confront the computer industry?
Policymakers in many nations such as France, Japan, and Singapore try to guide the development of computer technology inside their borders to help their countries be more competitive in the worldwide information economy. In the United States this practice is called industrial policy, but is limited by political ideology and antitrust laws. Nonetheless, the government has had a significant influence on the computer industry in the past, primarily through its investments in research and development for military computer applications and through the purchasing power of government computer users. The issuance of copyrights (covering ideas) and patents (covering inventions) is another important means of guiding the development of computer technology. Recently, patent protection has been extended to computer software as well as hardware. Antitrust issues spurred the 1956 consent decree by which IBM was forced to separate its equipment manufacturing and information services businesses and open up competition in the leasing of mainframe computers, which had a major impact on the structure of the computer industry today. More recently, Microsoft Corporation settled an antitrust issue by curbing practices that made it difficult for other software firms to sell their own versions of the basic operating software found in personal computers.

REFERENCES

Caron, A. H., Giroux, L., & Douzou, S. (1989). Uses and impacts of home computers in Canada: A process of reappropriation. In J. L. Salvaggio & J. Bryant (Eds.), *Media use in the information age*. Hillsdale, NJ: Erlbaum.

Dordick, H., & LaRose, R. (1992). *The telephone in daily life*. East Lansing: Department of Telecommunication, Michigan State University.

Dutton, W. F., Rogers, E. M., & Jun, S. (1987). The diffusion and impacts of information technology in households. In P. I. Zorkoczy, *Oxford surveys in information technology* (Vol. 4). New York: Oxford University Press.

Evans, C. (1981). *The making of the micro: A history of the computer*. New York: Van Nostrand Reinhold.

Flamm, K. (1988). *Creating the computer: Government, industry and high technology*. Washington, DC: Brookings Institution.

Freiberger, P., & Swaine, M. (1984). *Fire in the valley: The making of the personal computer*. Berkeley, CA: Osborne/McGraw-Hill.

Gilchrist, B., & Wessel, M. (1972). *Government regulation of the computer industry*. New York: American Federation of Information Processing Societies.

Glazier, S. (1993). Software patents, ownership and infringement crimes: New developments. In J. G. Savage & D. Wedemeyer (Eds.), *Pacific Telecommunications Conference proceedings* (pp. 922–928). Honolulu: Pacific Telecommunications Council.

Hancock, L. (1995, February 27). The haves and the have nots. *Newsweek,* pp. 50–53.

Koff, R. M. (1979). *Home computers: A manual of possibilities*. New York: Harcourt Brace Jovanovich.

Kominski, R. (1988). *Computer use in the United States: 1984*. Washington, DC: U.S. Government Printing Office. (Current Population Reports, Series P-23, No. 155.)

U.S. Department of Commerce. (1993). *Industrial outlook*. Washington, DC: U.S. Government Printing Office.

White, R. (1993). *How computers work*. Emeryville, CA: Ziff-Davis Press.

Wulforst, H. (1982). *Breakthrough to the computer age*. New York: Scribner's.

Young, J. S. (1988). *Steve Jobs: The journey is the reward*. Glenview, IL: Scott, Foresman.

Ziegler, B. (1994, November 15). Bought for work, PCs are used for play. *Wall Street Journal*, p. B1.

Chapter 13

THE INFORMATION SERVICES INDUSTRY

C H A P T E R   P R E V I E W

This chapter focuses on the information services industry, which provides the content that is carried over telephone and computer networks. We will see how industry regulation led to the separation of information service providers, who provide entertainment and information content, from common carriers, who own and operate the networks that the information is carried on. We will trace the development of three forms of information services—audiotext, teletext, and videotex—and see how the information services industry serves as the paradigm for the emerging information superhighway.

Happy (Virtual) Birthday

Voice call coming through from Ali, sir.

Excellent! I'll take it in the study.

Happy birthday, Dad! Did you get my present?

Yes! I'm glad *someone* remembered. Where are we today?

Let me show you!

Okay. DeeVee, give me wide-screen color video. Now, what am I looking at?

This week I'm in San Francisco and you're looking at the sunset over the Golden Gate.

Spectacular! And I see you're wearing that pendant I sent you for *your* birthday.

Oh yes, it's so perfect, I wear it to all my client meetings now.

I'm glad to see you getting some wear out of it—it cost me plenty! Heard from your mother lately?

Oh, all the time. Why just yesterday she . . .

Never mind, I hear all I want to through the lawyers . . . Say, when will I get to see you?

Well, next week I'll be in Paris. I'll call you from there . . .

No, I mean *really* see you.

Oh, Dad, you know I can't . . .

Please. I'll buy the plane ticket. I'd do anything if I could just really see you, just once.

Dad, I . . . I . . . I . . . I . . . I . . . I . . . I . . . I . . . I . . . <PROGRAM INTERRUPT>

Sorry, sir, but the net just informed me that ALI the Artificial Lifelike Intelligence is not programmed for the function you have requested. Shall I reset?

(Sigh.) Okay, take it from the top.

Happy birthday, Dad! Did you get my present?

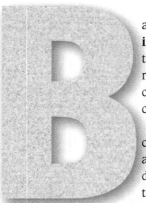

ased on our previous explorations of the mass media, the concept of an **information service provider** quite distinct from the channel or network that delivers the information may seem somewhat alien. In the newspaper, radio, television, and cable industries, the organization that owns the channel also decides what is carried on it and profits directly from that content in the form of advertising sales or subscription fees.

Among the conventional mass media, the movie industry perhaps comes closest to the information service model, with the movie studios acting as the information providers while theater chains provide the distribution channel. By law, movie studios cannot themselves own the theaters. Cable operators play a similar role in that they mainly relay content produced by others—at least in the case of the smaller cable companies, which do not themselves own interests in programming networks. However, in both the movie and cable industry examples, the owners of the distribution channels still maintain a limited degree of editorial control through their selection of the movies or cable networks that are shown. They are also able to provide and profit from their own programming if they so desire.

In contrast, the owners of telephone and computer networks generally have no say in what is carried, and they are prohibited from having a direct financial interest in the content. Information service providers pay fees to the network operators according to a published schedule, and the network must be available to all providers on an equal basis. The information providers, rather than the network owners, maintain editorial control over the content itself. This is the **common carrier** approach.

Another way of looking at information services is as mass media applications of telephone and computer networks. That is, they are services that are reproduced for multiple receivers over phone or computer networks. As conventional mass media systems merge onto the "information superhighway"—and as the boundaries between print, audio, and video media are blurred by digital technology—the information service concept is a useful one because it clearly separates the content from the electronic or mechanical channel on which it is carried.

Information service providers create or package the content for an information service.

Common carriers are transportation or telecommunications companies that carry others' goods or messages.

TABLE 13.1. INFORMATION SERVICES MILESTONES	
Year	**Event**
1850	First newspaper wire service established
1877	Telephone mass media demonstrations
1910	Mann-Elkins Act
1927	First audiotext service
1934	Communications Act
1969	ARPANET established
1974	Videotex developed by British Post Office
1976	Dial-It service introduced
1979	Prestel videotex service in Great Britain
1979	CompuServe service in U.S.
1983	French Teletel service begins
1984	AT&T divestiture
1992	Video dial tone decision
1992	Internet opened to commercial users
1993	Teletext decoders mandated for TV sets in U.S.

A BRIEF HISTORY OF INFORMATION SERVICES

The historical precursors of the information service industry predate both the telephone and the computer. In an earlier chapter, we saw how newspaper wire services such as the Associated Press originated in 1850. The relationship between the wire service and the telegraph company exemplifies the relationship between the information service provider and the network provider: The wire services maintained control over the content and profited directly from its distribution to newspapers, while the telegraph companies merely transmitted the information and charged for network usage as they would for any other user. Stock market "tickers" and "racing wires" (which telegraphed the results of horse races) are other early examples of information services. (See Table 13.1.)

The Origins of Common Carriers

The common carrier concept has roots in the transportation industry, where railroad companies and shipping lines are designated as common carriers, meaning that they are required to accept cargo on a nondiscriminatory basis from all customers who are willing to pay the published rate. The Interstate Commerce Act of 1887 applied this concept to railroad companies, and the Mann-Elkins Act of 1910 extended it to the interstate telephone service. The common carrier precept became a cornerstone for telephone regulation in the Communications Act of 1934, which separated content production from network ownership in the telecommunications industry (McGraw-Hill, 1993).

The modified final judgment that governed the divestiture of AT&T kept the information service provider/common carrier dichotomy intact by prohibiting the newly formed Regional Bell Operating Companies from providing information services, although the "new" AT&T was allowed to go into that business after a seven-year waiting period. The FCC's **video dial tone** decision in 1992 left the cross-ownership barrier substantially intact, allowing telephone companies to own only a 5 percent interest in video information service providers. As we saw previously, the information service restrictions have now been struck down in the courts, but common carriers are still reluctant to obtain interests in information services out of fear of future legislative or antitrust actions.

Somewhat similar restrictions evolved in the computer industry. The 1956 consent decree required IBM to place computer services in a separate subsidiary, independent of its computer manufacturing business.

The Origins of Audiotext

The origins of information services—in the sense of mass media applications of telephone and computer networks—can also be traced back to early demonstrations of the telephone. On February 12, 1877 Alexander Graham Bell conducted the first public demonstration of his invention in Salem, Massachusetts. His assistant, Thomas Watson, delivered a speech from Bell's laboratory in Boston to the assembled lecture audience over lines rented from a telegraph company. In later public performances, Watson sang popular songs for the appreciative audiences. The fees that Bell collected for his lectures were thus the first paid to a telephone "information service provider"—and were the first revenues that Bell realized from his invention (Brooks, 1976).

A great deal of early speculation about the telephone involved its potential as a mass medium that could convey the news events and music of the day to the home (LaRose & Atkin, 1992). Around the turn of the twentieth century there were mass-mediated telephone systems in the United States and Great Britain that offered a mixture of news and entertainment programming. The most enduring example was Telefon Hirmondo, a telephone-based news and entertainment service that was on the wire in Budapest, Hungary, for almost two decades in the years before World War I. Early telephone operators also shared the news of the day with their subscribers on an informal basis. However, the poor sound quality of telephone systems and the advent of radio broadcasting in the second decade of the twentieth century prevented the evolution of the telephone into a mass medium.

Telephone announcement services date back to 1927, but their content was limited to a few basic items (such as time and weather information) because telephone companies, as common carriers, were not allowed to charge users for them and third-party information providers were generally denied access to the public telephone network. Dial-It services, which allowed callers to receive brief recorded announcements or register "votes" in instant electronic polls, were introduced to the public in 1976 when viewers of the Ford-Carter presidential debate were asked to register their opinions about the debate. The AT&T divestiture opened the telephone network to information service providers and established the principle that the providers could receive payment for the information instead of paying for its distribution themselves. A new term, **audiotext,** was coined to describe the new audio information services that proliferated on 976 and 900 numbers in the years following divestiture.

The Origins of Videotex

Videotex grew out of early experiments with computerized information services conducted by the British Post Office in 1974 (Bouwman & Christofferson, 1992). These systems were to use home television receivers to display text and graphics, hence the "video" part of the name. The British experiments led to the world's first commercial videotex service, Prestel, in 1979. Although originally intended for the home user, Prestel attracted few residential customers and closed off consumer access in 1991.

A number of unsuccessful attempts were made in the early 1980s to establish consumer videotex services in the United States, including Viewtron, Keyfax, and Gateway. All three used telephone lines but relied on custom-built computer terminals that used the home television set as the display device. Warner Cable's Qube system used cable television as the transmission medium. By 1986 all of these services had been discontinued, owing to a variety of technical and marketing problems, notably costly and unreliable terminals and agonizingly slow graphics displays. By using TV sets as display devices, the fledgling services essentially had to compete with popular television entertainment. Another problem was the relative lack of information services, especially when the information could be obtained more cheaply through conventional "analog" sources such as the local library and the daily newspaper (Morse, 1985).

In 1979 the first successful general-interest videotex service in the United States, CompuServe, was introduced. The information is distributed to users through telephone lines and modems to personal computers or computer terminals. On of the first successful videotex systems was the French Teletel system, more commonly known by the name of the miniature computer terminals that deliver the service, the Minitel. Minitel probably succeeded where so many other early systems failed because of two factors: terminals were initially provided free of charge, and an electronic directory service was available from the start. The limited availability of paper telephone books and the initial popularity of so-called rouge services—the videotex equivalent to "adult entertainment" audiotext services—may also have had something to do with Teletel's success (Mayer, 1986).

The growing popularity of the **Internet,** and especially the World Wide Web portion of it, poses both an opportunity and a threat to commercial services such as America Online, CompuServe, and Prodigy. The (relatively) easy-to-use web gateways that these providers offer attract many of their new subscribers. On the other hand, many information service providers are abandoning exclusive distribution agreements with the commercial services to make themselves available to all Internet users directly through their own web locations, or "home pages." By moving commercial transactions onto the Internet itself (see below), the information providers will soon be able to charge

Your Road Map For The Information Superhighway— America Online®

See other side for details of your FREE trial offer from America Online!

America Online Introduces The Easiest Way To Reach The Internet!

AMERICA Online

1-800-827-6364, Ext. 4227

THE INTERNET IS A NETWORK OF MANY NETWORKS. IT IS A MODEL FOR THE INFORMATION SUPERHIGHWAY AND IS ACCESSIBLE THROUGH POPULAR CONSUMER VIDEOTEX SERVICES SUCH AS AMERICA ONLINE.

Teletext is an information service that is broadcast as part of a television signal.

users directly for information, cutting out the commercial videotex service "middle person."' Meanwhile, widely available Internet access software allows users to customize and search out their own content, potentially making the editorial function of the commercial videotex providers redundant. There are some signs that videotex services will "reinvent" themselves as Internet access providers, rather than packagers of information services.

The Origins of Teletext

Like videotex, **teletext** was first developed in Great Britain in the mid-1970s. Teletext systems are not truly interactive, in that they only allow users to select screens of data from a continuous stream of information broadcast to the television set. Decoders built into the set receive this digital information and display it on the screen at the request of the viewer. The British Ceefax system, as it is called, has flourished along with multiple competitors. Weather, news, sports, and TV program listings are the most popular features. British viewers rent their television sets rather than buy them, so the cost of the decoder can be spread across modest monthly payments instead of a one-time purchase amounting to hundreds of dollars (Greenberg, 1989). Teletext was a flop just about everywhere else it was tried. Cable television (only now becoming widely available in Britain) offers instant access to the most popular types of information updates—news, weather, and sports.

This could soon change since, beginning in 1993, the Federal Communications Commission now requires that television sets sold in the United States have a built-in decoder to display closed captions for the hearing impaired, which can also decode teletext data. Another teletext application was given a boost by the Telecommunications Act of 1996, which mandated that television receivers come equipped with a computer chip capable of receiving program content codes broadcast in teletext form. This so-called V-chip would allow parents to block programs rated V, for violent. Other codes would identify programs with sexual content or adult language.

REVIEW

1. What is the distinction between an information service provider and a common carrier?
2. What is the difference between audiotext, videotex, teletext, the Internet, and the World Wide Web?
3. What is Minitel?

TECHNOLOGY TRENDS

Audiotext and videotex services must both contend with the inherent limitations of the telephone network, which was developed as a medium for interpersonal communication rather than mass communication. In both cases, limited transmission capacity and the switched, point-to-point architecture of telephone systems pose important limitations.

Audiotext Technology

Primitive audiotext systems overcame the problem of telephone switching architecture by simply connecting multiple callers to a single telephone line that played back the recorded information in a continuous loop so that each caller broke into the middle of the message at the moment he or she placed the call. Before that, calls were connected to a live operator who read the time of day into her telephone set. Now audiotext messages are digitally recorded, and each user can hear the complete message from the beginning of the program through his or her own individual "port" on the message player.

Interactive communication uses feedback to modify a message as it is presented.

Audiotext now has an **interactive** capability, allowing users to branch to different parts of the recorded program by pressing appropriate keys on their touch-tone phones, giving it the distinction of being the first widely available interactive mass medium.

Many obviously appealing audiotext applications—such as hit song services—are prevented by the poor sound quality of the telephone system, which, while adequate for human speech transmission, filters out both low- and high-pitched sounds, making music sound unnatural. The new integrated services digital network (ISDN) service now being introduced into telephone systems around the world has the potential to overcome this limitation, raising the fidelity at least to the level of broadcast AM radio.

Videotex Graphics

For videotex services, the capacity limitations of the telephone network are reflected in the extremely limited graphic displays that are possible. As we saw in a previous chapter, computer graphics and text cannot be transmitted directly over telephone lines and instead must be converted to audible sounds using a computer modem. The rather slow data transmission speeds possible with this arrangement mean that a single full-color photograph could take as much as a few minutes to send to the user. Many videotex services transmit text files through telephone lines using ASCII (American Standard Code for Information Interchange) coding, the same code found in unformatted personal computer files. This means that images can only be constructed out of the characters that appear on the computer keyboard.

Recently, consumer videotex services found a way around the graphics limitation by storing some of the more commonly used graphic images on the user's own computer. They also use a special graphics display technique known as the North American Presentation Level Protocol System (NAPLPS), which constructs graphics from tiny icons. This yields a significant improvement over ASCII graphics but still falls far short of picture-quality magazine graphics, and it requires the user to have a full-fledged personal computer instead of a simple terminal.

Ideally, videotex systems would use the same high-quality graphics display techniques used by advanced personal computers, but these approaches require the transmission of a great deal of computer data. One answer is to adapt the techniques of digital compression, thereby reducing the amount of 1's and 0's that have to be transmitted. The other option is to speed up the transmission. New high-speed modems are now becoming affordable but

THE SHARED NETWORK: UNDERSTANDING PACKET SWITCHING

As the name implies, packet switching breaks up digital transmissions into small chunks of digits, called packets. Each packet has additional bits to indicate the network addresses of the sending and receiving parties, the sequence number of each packet, and an error-checking code. The advantage is that many simultaneous messages can share a single circuit. Using the address information and the sequence number, the message is reassembled at the other end.

An analogy can be made between packet switching and postal delivery. Imagine that you are on a Hawaiian vacation and have only a handful of postcards available as writing material. If you had to send a long letter back home—perhaps to explain the symptoms of an exotic tropical disease that will postpone your return to work—you would divide the message among several postcards and mark them "1 of 3," "2 of 3," and so on, so that your boss would be sure not to miss any of your excuses. The post office might route each of your cards differently back to the mainland. One might go via a direct flight back to your hometown, another by tramp steamer through San Diego, another via a flight through San Francisco. If one arrived out of sequence, your boss could wait for the missing one and then reassemble your message from the sequence numbers. If the tramp steamer was lost at sea, your boss could wire you to retransmit the missing "packet." You could buy an express mail package for all your postcards, ensuring that they would all arrive together, but this "dedicated circuit" would obviously be a lot more costly. In contrast, packet networks are sometimes described as being "connectionless" since they do not require a dedicated connection between any two points on a network in order for communication to take place.

The future of packet-switching technology is to increase transmission speeds by several orders of magnitude through the elimination of many of the extraneous computer bits that are used to route messages and correct for transmission errors and by relying on high-capacity fiber optic networks. Provision will also be made for prioritization of the packets so that voice and video packets that require immediate delivery will get preferential treatment to applications in which some delay can be accepted, such as videotex or electronic mail.

Packet switching breaks up long streams of computer data into packets and mixes packets from multiple users in a single communication channel.

Asynchronous transfer mode (ATM) is a standard for high-speed digital transmission of voice, text, and video.

are close to the maximum theoretical information "speed limit" of telephone lines. ISDN has the potential to increase transmission speeds several times over, leading some information service providers to lobby for more rapid deployment of this all-digital phone service. Until that happens, only users connected to high-speed local area networks will enjoy full quality videotex graphics.

Packet Switching

The architectural limitations of the telephone network are perhaps less apparent to the information service user. Here, the problem is to provide low-cost access to the centralized mainframe computers on which the information is stored. Users could simply dial up the central computer themselves on a long-distance telephone line, but this would double or triple the cost of the information to the user, since the long-distance "meter" still runs even when the user is just reading the screen and no data are actually being transmitted.

The solution is to transport the information on a special **packet-switching** network, on which each line can be shared by many users (see box). The user then simply places a local call to a "node" on this network. First developed for ARPANET in the late 1960s, the packet-switching methodology is widely used by information providers and is also the basis for communication over the Internet.

The standards for so-called "fast packet networks" that will make it possible to combine voice, data, and video have already been defined as part of the planning for worldwide ISDN. In the acronymese of the telecommunications industry, this standard is known as **ATM,** short for **asynchronous transfer mode** (McQuillian, 1993). This describes the means by which the integration of voice, data, and video telecommunications may take place in the next century. The first ATM devices became available in 1992 for use in private corporate networks, with the first public network services appearing in 1994.

Toward the Information Superhighway to the Home

Another solution to the capacity limitations of the public telephone network is to replace it with higher-speed networks. Users who access the Internet at school or at work usually connect via high-speed local area networks based on coaxial cable or fiber optic transmission media. This makes it possible to transfer computer files at rates of millions of bits per second, or roughly about a thousand times as fast as telephone lines. At these speeds, high-quality audio and graphics and even moving images can be received. This extension of high-capacity, two-way networks to the home and the workplace is essentially what the so-called "information superhighway" is all about.

The basic building blocks of a new communications infrastructure for the home are quickly falling into place (Elmer-Dewitt, 1993). To recap, it will be a broadband network capable of integrating voice, data, and video applications in a single multimedia network that will carry all types of information in a common digital format. Fiber optic cables are gradually being extended to the home by cable and telephone companies for this purpose, but coaxial cable and advanced digital telephone lines could also fill the need in the short term. Powerful computers located at the center of the network will compress and store massive digital audio and video files and provide a measure of "intelligence" that will enable new dimensions of interactivity and user control. In each city or town, one or two entities may eventually emerge as dominant "full service" telecommunications providers.

Another possiblity is that the information superhighway will gradually evolve piecemeal from the existing Internet infrastructure, rather than give birth to a fundamentally new one. In this scenario, the Internet backbone will be continually upgraded with speedier transmission technologies, such as fiber optics. A variety of options for distributing information the "last mile" from the Internet backbone to individual homes and businesses will coexist; these could include high-speed digital telephone lines, cable TV systems, satellites, and earth-bound wireless networks, perhaps even TV transmitters. Indeed, this would appear to be the vision that the U.S. Congress had in mind while opening up local telecommunications competition in the Telecommunications Act of 1996.

The exact nature of the network that will carry these services to the home depends on whether telephone or cable companies—or some other contender—emerge victorious from the race to rewire America (see box on page 326). It is also possible that hybrid systems will emerge, such as networks that use fiber optics or coaxial cable to deliver video signals "downstream" to the home and the airwaves or telephone wires to carry voice and data "upstream" back into the network.

The Home Terminals of the Future

In our homes, our TV sets, phones, radios, personal computers, CD players, slide projectors, and VCRs may be replaced by a single multimedia interface that will select, play, and interact with media presentations regardless of the sensory modalities they employ. Customizable displays will allow us to make our selections directly from on-screen program menus listing thousands of options or narrow our choices to particular genres (such as westerns only). The interface device—we really need a name for it other than "the set top box"—will also translate the compressed digital data streams from the integrated broadband network into formats that can be played through our old-fashioned analog receivers. As envisioned in Figure 13.1, the home terminal would have advanced capabilities that would allow it to work in conjunction with—or perhaps in place of—the television set, the CD player, the VCR, the home computer, the telephone, and the new multimedia interfaces.

There is a competing vision of the home receiver of the future that is more consistent with the scenario in which the information superhighway evolves from today's Internet. In that case, the home receiver might be a relatively simple affair, variously described as a "network appliance," a "stripped down" personal computer, or a "souped up" telephone. It could resemble either a laptop computer or a "feature phone" with a small display screen and keyboard added. It would be priced under $500 to promote rapid widescale adoption.

In this scenario, the receiver functions primarily to connect the user to the World Wide Web through high-speed cable television or digital telephone connections. Instead of packing its own powerful internal processing capabilities and reams of computer memory for sophisticated computer progams, it would view web pages, send E-mail, and download software modules from the Internet as needed. Little more than a keyboard with some short-term computer memory and a network interface, the network appliance may even lack a monitor, relying instead on the home TV screen as a display device.

FIGURE 13.1
THE HOME TERMINAL OF THE FUTURE MAY BE AN INTERACTIVE MULTIMEDIA RECEIVER.

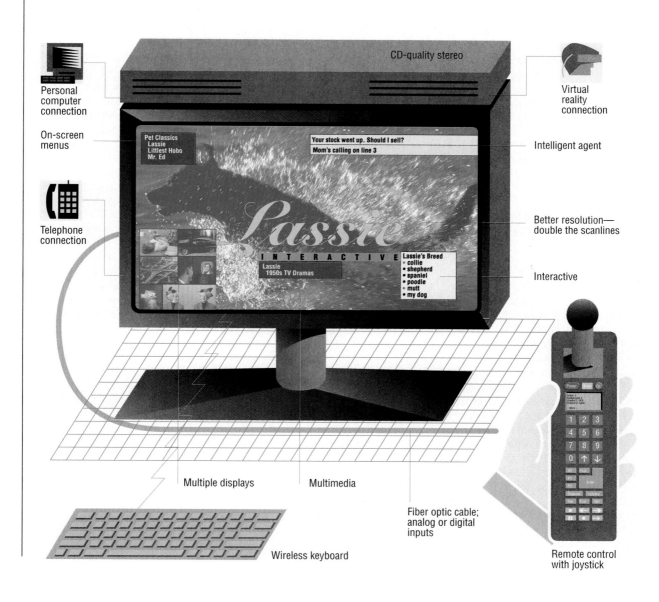

The battle of the century is going on right in your living room. It is a contest to determine whether cable companies or telephone operating companies will bring the interactive broadband network of the future to your home. To get in the ring, each contender will have to spend hundreds of billions of dollars and "bet the business" to see who wins.

Before you settle back with your popcorn to enjoy the spectacle of corporate giants fighting over you, be aware that you stand to be the big winner—or the big loser. Unless there is a knockout in the early rounds, you might get to pay for it all twice, once for the telephone company (telco) version and again for the cable version. In the bargain, you might have to throw out all your TV sets and telephones. The outcome of the fight will also do much to determine the entertainment and information services that you and your descendants will have coming into your home well into the next century. There is a lot more at stake than whether we will have 200 TV channels or 500 TV channels (all with nothing on?) in our living rooms by 2010. Some think that the choices we make now about the broadband telecommunications infrastructure of tomorrow will have a lot to do with how competitive our country will be in the future. Other countries with better infrastructures might knock us out of the ring of international economic competition.

The Contenders

The Baby Bells are the heavyweights in this contest. They have ten times the financial resources of the cable industry, and the cable companies are still paying off their debt from the last round of expansion in the 1980s and from FCC-mandated rate cuts in the 1990s. Telcos can provide video dial tone, and the rules against providing information services (like cable TV programming) and operating cable systems in their own service areas are lifting. Technically, the telcos have the advantage of operating a network that is well on track to going all-digital and all-fiber. The copper telephone wires coming into your home are their major weakness. They just cannot carry a lot of video. There are ways to squeeze VCR-quality TV signals onto those wires, and with further advances in video compression they might even be able to manage an HDTV channel. But if you are the type who wants to watch six live football games at one time or who likes to flip through thirty-six channels a minute, this is not the best option for you. To be competitive, the telcos must extend the fiber network to each home, and that could run half a trillion dollars.

The cable companies have a broadband video network and are rapidly adding fiber optic transmission technology to their networks. Their big weakness is a lack of two-way capability for telephone service and interactive video programming. They will also have to make huge investments in switching equipment. Most likely, they will adopt the personal communication network (PCN) technology so that they can get up and running quickly with a switched telephone service. Cable companies are promising 500 channels, with "something on" for everybody, but switched video services are another matter. If your vision of the broadband network is the ability to make video calls to your parents to show them how tall the grandchildren are getting, you should not be rooting for the cable companies. Regulators are letting telco competitors interconnect with the public telephone network, removing a major regulatory barrier that the cable companies faced. However, state public utility commissions still have a lot to say about this.

Opening Rounds

Both combatants have made some exploratory jabs at the competition. Southwestern Bell, for example, has acquired cable television systems in the suburbs of Washington D.C. Meanwhile, cable operators have been gobbling up so-called "competitive access providers" that are allowed to offer local telephone services on a limited basis. The nation's largest cable operator, Tele-Communications, Inc. (TCI), has announced a massive network upgrade plan that will result in extending fiber optic cabling to some 400 communities across the country by the late 1990s. It has also joined with U.S. Sprint in a plan to offer telephone services over cable TV systems.

AT&T's purchase of McCaw Cellular will get it back into the local telephone business, but it is not clear how AT&T could get a video signal into the home, except perhaps by gobbling up cable companies. Satellite technology is another possibility. Direct broadcast satellite video systems are here and satellite-based mobile telephones are just around the corner. The FCC has awarded a license to develop "cellular video" using frequencies around 28 GHz. Using a frequency reuse system not unlike that found in today's cellular radio systems, this technology would make it possible to carry voice and data transmission, video teleconferences, and hundreds of channels of video programming to the home. Electrical power utilities are a long shot, too, since they already have a fiber optic network in your neighborhood to carry monitoring and control information. And don't rule out broadcasters, either. Video compression could allow them to pack audio and text services, as well as multiple video channels, into their existing channel allocations—and the FCC has decided to give broadcasters an *extra* channel for HDTV service (Andrews, 1992, 1993).

Watching the Web

The Internet's World Wide Web gives a glimpse down the information superhighway of tomorrow (the computer addresses in the parentheses are the web addresses of illustrative material):

- *More choices.* The promise of 500 cable channels once caused a sensation, but the web has millions of "channels," ranging from elaborate sites maintained by huge corporations (e.g., General Motors' http://www.gm.com) to humble home pages created by private individuals (http://commtechlab.msu.edu/humans/larose/).

- *Entertainment on demand.* The entire web is open all the time, in (almost) every country of the world. This anticipates a general trend to "on demand" media, which can be ordered at your convenience anywhere, even pausing for trips to the refrigerator (http://pathfinder.com/@@7MW@MJLNPAMAQKif/FSN/).

- *Multimedia.* Color graphics are standard fare. You can play audio—including sportscasts or music—through speakers on your computer (http://www.realaudio.com) or make phone calls (http://www.vocaltec.com). You may view videos stored at web sites and attend videoconferences or "multicasts" of live events (http://irdu.nus.sg/videoconference/welcome.html). With virtual reality software you navigate three-dimensional "worlds" inside the computer (http://www.VRML.org).

- *Scaleable bandwidth.* Web video "windows" can be shrunk to a small corner of the computer screen, the "graininess" of the picture varied, or the smoothness of the motion adjusted to fit the transmission capacity you have—and are willing to pay for.

- *Interactive.* By activating the links between web sites, you can "surf" indefinitely. Search engines (e.g., http://www.lycos.com) help you navigate by key words (e.g., "fun") or find specific locations. You can interact with the web, even activating software applications on distant computers (http://java.sun.com).

- *On-line commerce.* Securing credit card information on the web (http://home.netscape.com/comprod/netscape_commerce.html) makes on-line commerce a reality. This foretells a future in which all banking and credit card transactions may be carried on interactive networks.

- *Personalized.* Many web sites ask you to log in, then address you by name or tailor their contents to you, adding a new personal dimension to mass communication. New wrinkles include "agent" software that looks for information on the web for you and "avatars" that let you construct images of yourself for the web (http://www.thepalace.com).

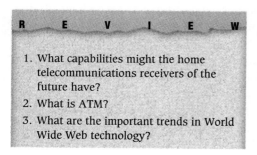

R   E   V   I   E   W

1. What capabilities might the home telecommunications receivers of the future have?
2. What is ATM?
3. What are the important trends in World Wide Web technology?

INDUSTRY STRUCTURE

The three main elements of the information services industry are the common carriers, data communications services, and the information service providers.

Common Carriers

As we indicated at the outset, common carriers are the telecommunications companies that provide the networks that deliver information services from their suppliers to their end users.

Both local (976- and 540-number) and long-distance (900- and 800-number) telephone carriers provide access to audiotext services. Videotex providers may lease circuits directly from long-distance carriers or go through intermediaries.

Data Communication Services and Value Added Networks

Value added networks (VANs) provide enhanced services on data networks, such as videotex and transactional services.

Data communication service providers are the companies that serve as the intermediaries between common carriers and information service providers. They buy telecommunications circuits in bulk from domestic and international carriers and then use these networks to provide such services as electronic mail, credit card verification, and access to on-line databases. Since these services add value to the underlying telecommunications networks, they are called **value added networks (VANs).** If they are international in scope, they are called international VANs or IVANs (no kidding!). These are usually packet-switched networks. Tymnet and Telnet are two well-known VANs, and Electronic Data Systems (EDS, a division of General Motors), General Electric, IBM, and AT&T are also active in the field. The local telephone companies were long prohibited from offering these enhanced services themselves, although these restrictions were recently struck down.

Data communication services also include companies that interconnect corporate telecommunications and data networks or provide network management services on a contractual basis. These services amount to a $10 billion yearly market in the United States (U.S. Department of Commerce, 1993).

The Internet also falls into the category of a data communication service, and although it is a very special case, it is the biggest of them all. It is run as a nonprofit, cooperative enterprise involving its users and several major regional data networks. The Internet originated as a defense-related government research project and is still partially funded by the federal government, but the government presence is slowly being withdrawn, which may mean passing more of the costs on to users.

Information Service Providers

Once again, common carriers are distinguished from information service providers in that the former may not have a financial interest in companies that create content—the information service providers. Restrictions placed on AT&T and the Baby Bells in the wake of divestiture were designed to encourage the emergence of information service providers. Two industries have burgeoned recently: companies that offer information primarily in the form of computerized text and graphics (videotex), and providers of audio information (audiotext) on 800 and 900 numbers. A small, but rapidly growing, segment of the information services industry provides information recorded on digital compact discs. Together, these industries accounted for $12 billion in sales in 1992, most in the form of business information. Because telephone networks can now carry video content as well, cable television might also be considered an information service.

The information service provider industry is highly fragmented, with thousands of videotex and audiotext providers. Major media and computer firms are active in the field. For example, Dow Jones, owner of *The Wall Street Journal*, also owns CompuServe, a leading consumer videotex service. Its rival, Prodigy, is a joint venture of IBM and Sears. Newspaper publishers and broadcasters run many of the audiotext services. The information services restriction on AT&T that was part of

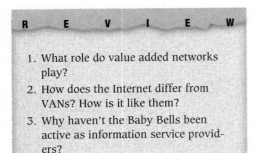

R E V I E W

1. What role do value added networks play?
2. How does the Internet differ from VANs? How is it like them?
3. Why haven't the Baby Bells been active as information service providers?

the modified final judgment that broke up AT&T has already expired, although that company has yet to make a major effort in this area. The Baby Bells have now escaped the information services restrictions that apply to them, although the video dial tone ruling severely limits how much they can own. Concern about possible congressional action to reinstate the restrictions has caused them to move slowly, however.

The reason for the immense diversity of the audiotext industry—and perhaps also the reason for the sordidness and scandal that attend it—is the extremely low entry cost for information providers. For only a few thousand dollars, you can purchase a digital tape recorder, record a program, and get access to a 900 network operated by one of the major interexchange carriers. There are even service bureaus who will rent the equipment, lowering the initial investment to a few hundred dollars. In most cases, the largest single cost is for the advertising to promote the service. Thus, just about anyone can get in the audiotext business, and with literally thousands of channels, there is little effective "policing" of the content or the content providers.

Database service providers package the products of multiple information service providers, offering users discounted rates for access to dozens of independent information providers. Dialog, Mead Data Central, and Dow Jones News/Retrieval are the industry leaders.

Database service providers package multiple information services.

Chat lines are audiotext services in which callers join together in group discussions.

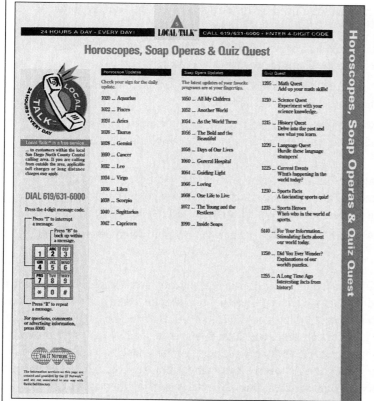

AUDIOTEXT SERVICES LIKE TO OFFER INSTANT ACCESS TO AUDIO INFORMATION . SOME OFFER THIS INFORMATION FREE OF CHARGE.

INFORMATION SERVICE FORMS AND GENRES

Both audiotext and videotex services offer a wide variety of programming.

Audiotext

More than 10,000 audiotext programs are active at any one time. Most are accessed through long-distance carriers' 900 numbers or local 976 numbers, which charge callers by the minute. Another option is to give the user a toll-free number on which to place the initial call, after which a credit card number is obtained for billing purposes. Some telephone companies have set aside special exchanges to handle specific types of services, such as adult entertainment and **chat lines,** which allow users to join in group discussions on the phone. Many areas also have advertising-supported audiotext services that are free to the user and may be found listed in the front of the local telephone book. In addition, many public and private institutions have installed free audiotext services to provide answers to commonly asked questions (*Network World,* 1992).

Until 1991 adult entertainment, or phone sex, services were the single largest category. In that year, the local telephone companies, which are responsible for audiotext billing, began to refuse billing services to phone sex operators. Most of the adult entertainment operators migrated to 800 numbers that demand bank credit card numbers before the program begins.

What is available through audiotext services? A content analysis of 900-number exchanges provides some insight into this diverse mass medium (Glascock & LaRose, 1992):

- *Adult services* that describe explicit sex acts are still to be found, but nowadays the content of most adult services is pretty tame. Adult-oriented services include "electronic personals ads," chat lines that help adult callers meet each other in group discussions (usually about sex), and lines that convey information about "mature" topics such as AIDS or drug abuse.

- *Credit services* offer information about how to obtain credit, to improve credit ratings, or even to obtain authorization for immediate cash payments, later charged to the user's telephone bill.

- *Sales promotions* provide information about products that can be obtained by recording a name and address. Other numbers give the caller names of dealers in their area that carry the product, offer them rebates on products they have purchased, or take their addresses for follow-up promotional mailings. In addition, 900 numbers are used by fund-raising organizations to obtain donations.

- *Contests* offer prizes for answering trivia questions or solving a puzzle, or they automatically enter the caller into sweepstakes drawings.

- *Information services* include such items as stock market quotations, sports scores, job announcements, and legal advice.

- *Entertainment services* (other than dial-a-porn) include chat lines, music selections, and services that are programmed like radio stations, complete with disc jockeys.

- *Children's services* include readings of children's stories, messages from children's characters, and voice mail boxes that allow young callers to record messages to media personalities and fantasy characters, including Santa Claus.

- *Instant polls* record callers' "votes" on current political and entertainment topics.

Some of the more offbeat audiotext services in recent years have included Dial-a-Zombie ("Talk to the Undead!"), Dial-a-Bakker ("Hear Jim and Tammi's side of the story!"), and Dial-an-Insult. The Confession Line lets you confess your sins to the telephone. Dial another number and you can listen to the confessions that others have made. Many such programs obviously last only a few days or weeks before their sponsors switch to a new program.

Interactive audiotext programs let users select content from audiotext menus, take part in games, or order products and services. One of the more popular interactive services is an audiotext version of the popular television game show *Jeopardy*. Home players can compete for prizes and match their wits against other callers.

The mass media use audiotext extensively to stimulate audience participation. Newspapers and broadcasters use Dial-It polls to capitalize on controversial issues ("Press 1 if you think the congressman is guilty") and to generate additional revenue by repackaging news

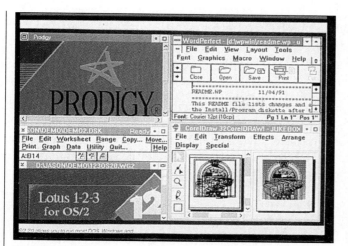

PRODIGY IS ONE OF THE LARGEST CONSUMER VIDEOTEX SERVICES.

and sports information that they already have on hand. Services are built around media personalities ("Talk to Michael Jackson!" "Hear Prince Charles talk on his cellular phone!") and popular shows ("Hear what you missed in the last episode of *Santa Barbara*!").

Consumer Videotex

Today, general-interest videotex services offer a wide variety of text-based information, transactional, and communication services. Prodigy (800-776-3449), a joint venture of IBM and Sears, was the first to pass 1 million subscribers, or about 1 percent of American homes. CompuServe (800-848-8199), now a subsidiary of Dow Jones, America On-Line (800-227-6364), and GEnie (800-638-9636) are well-established competitors, but AT&T, Apple Computer, and software giant Microsoft (in partnership with cable giant TCI) are entering the field as well (Kessler, 1992).

These services all share some standard features:

- *Electronic news services* update the leading headlines and sports scores every few minutes. A variety of specialized items not found in the daily newspaper also appear, such as financial news and stories from trade and professional magazines.

- *Consumer information* includes product reviews and consumer tips on topics ranging from kitchen recipes to pet grooming to personal finance.

- *Library information* includes such services as on-line dictionaries and encyclopedias and databases with career and college information.

- *Electronic mail* allows the user to send messages to other users.

- *Computer conferences* are available on just about any topic, from politics to computers to *Beavis and Butt-Head*—any topic, that is, that is suitable for a "family audience." These general-interest consumer systems sometimes censor material of a sexual, sexist, or racist nature.

- *Transactional services* allow users to complete electronic transactions and shop for consumer goods from the home. Home banking and travel reservation services are two popular options.

- *Computer games,* with trivia games and fantasy adventure being the standard fare, let the game-addicted compete with other users from around the country.

- *Computer software* is available, including "public domain" software that can be used without paying additional fees.

- *Gateways* are offered to other networks, most notably the Internet.

On-line services once charged a basic monthly fee plus time-sensitive usage fees that could run as high as 20 cents per minute in prime-time hours. Prodigy originated a flat-rate pricing scheme with a higher monthly fee but no usage-sensitive pricing. Most of its competitors followed suit, even though Prodigy is the only one to supplement subscriber fees with revenues from advertisers, who place ads at the bottom of each screen of information.

Videotex services now generally have additional charges for E-mail messages and have "tiered pricing" that requires an extra monthly fee or usage-sensitive charges for access to certain "premium services."

Business Videotex

Over 7,000 electronic databases in the United States cater primarily to businesses (Marcaccio, 1991). Business users spend about $10 billion a year on such services, perhaps thirty times the expenditures on consumer-oriented services such as CompuServe and Prodigy. Many users access these services through database services that provide gateways to multiple providers. Here are some of the most widely known database services:

- *DIALOG* (800-3DIALOG), the largest, has over 300 databases available. DIALOG includes many bibliographic reference services, including some in full-text form, which means that the entire text of the article, rather than just a brief citation or abstract, can be searched for key words and retrieved. Users can also instruct the service to provide automatic updates of past searches.

- *Dow Jones News/Retrieval* (609-520-4638) is geared to the serious investor, with real-time stock market quotations and a wealth of current and historical data on the performance of publicly traded companies. The service also includes the text of articles that have appeared in *The Wall Street Journal* since 1984, as well as general-interest news and sports items for the home user.

- *BRS Information Technologies* (800-345-4BRS), like DIALOG, specializes in electronic bibliographic and text databases. It carries some sources that DIALOG does not and has some specialized interest areas all its own, such as several databases devoted to AIDS research.

- *Mead Data Central* (800-227-4908) operates four services. *Lexis* is a full-text service carrying state and federal statutes and court decisions. *Nexis* features the text of stories in leading newspapers including *The New York Times* and *The Los Angeles Times*, plus stories from magazines, wire services, and industry newsletters. Medis carries medical journal articles and drug information, while Lexpat contains patents.

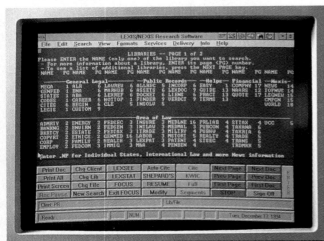

- *Wilsonline* (800-367-6770) carries electronic versions of many commonly used analog bibliographic reference tools, including *Applied Science and Technology Index*, *Business Periodicals Index*, *Education Index*, *Social Science Index*, and *The Reader's Guide to Periodical Literature*.

Bulletin Board Systems

Bulletin board systems (BBSs) are to the national videotex services what newsletters published on a desktop computer are to a national newspaper like *USA Today*. BBSs use the same basic information distribution method, in that they are typically accessed via personal computer modems over phone lines. However, the "host" computer that contains the information is usually a personal computer itself with extra disk space and some special system management software added. Much of the content is contributed by the users themselves, and many boards are operated by a single person rather than multimedia corporations. Although many BBSs charge subscription fees, most simply rely on their users to "pay" for access by contributing useful information themselves. From their inception in 1976, BBSs have been a medium of communication for personal computer hobbyists to exchange technical tips and computer programs. Today, there are over 30,000 bulletin boards in North America covering a dizzying array of topics.

What's on the Internet?

The Internet is not a videotex service but rather a network or, more precisely, a data communication service. It offers access to a wide range of information services that extend well beyond the capabilities of general-interest consumer videotex services. One way to answer the question of "what's on the Internet?" is to list some of the most frequently visited locations on the World Wide Web, the popular graphical portion of the Internet (Table 13.2). Another way to examine the various genres of content on the Internet is by listing the many functions that the Internet is capable of:

- *Electronic mail gateways.* Most E-mail users can only send mail to other members of their own organization. Internet offers connections to E-mail users around the world and to other E-mail networks, such as MCI Mail, AT&T, CompuServe, America Online, and Prodigy.

- *Electronic communities.* Internet has hundreds of electronic mailing lists (listservs) that make it possible to "broadcast" E-mail to special interest groups. Usenet is an on-line "news service" on which to post articles about topics of interest. The interests are quite varied indeed, ranging from technical computer information to current social issues to favorite TV programs.

- *Commercial database services.* The Internet can serve as a gateway to popular commercial on-line services (see previous section) and to public information sources, such as the Library of Congress catalog. Internet access saves money for

TABLE 13.2. SOME FREQUENTLY VISITED LOCATIONS ON THE WORLD WIDE WEB

Category	Examples
Business	AT&T, Microsoft, Apple, IBM, 800 number directory, *Wall Street Journal*
Government	U.S. House & Senate, White House, Library of Congress, National Science Foundation, Federal Communications Commission
Weather	National Oceanic & Atmospheric Administration, Current U.S. weather map
Education	Harvard, MIT, Michigan State University, World Lecture Hall (courses on the web)
News	*Hotwired* magazine, *Playboy* magazine, Electronic Newsstand, New York Times Fax, National Public Radio
Web resources	Cool Sites, CommerceNet (business transactions), A Guide to Cyberspace, Submit-It (publicize your site), The Internet Society
Entertainment	Sony Corporation, Paramount Pictures, Internet Underground Music Archive, Rolling Stones, *The X-Files*
Sports	ESPN, National Hockey League, Sports Scores & Updates
Reference	Job Hunt, Greenpeace, Four 11 (Internet "White Pages"), Smithsonian Institution, NASA
Travel	City Net (world city guide), The UK Guide, Subway Navigator, Switzerland, The European Home Page

Source: The Lycos 250, based on the number of web links to each site

large users since they do not incur the incremental telecommunications access fees they would otherwise pay to reach them, although subscription fees are still charged.

- *Free database services.* A variety of information from government and university sources is also available at no charge.

- *Electronic documents.* A variety of technical reports and electronic versions of published academic papers are available, either over the World Wide Web or by connecting to remote computers via a program called Telnet and then downloading them to your own computer with a file transfer protocol (FTP) program. Users can log in to computers all over the world to obtain copies of files of interest to them.

- *Software.* The Internet offers access to public domain computer software and documentation, also via Telnet and FTP and the web (such as Netscape), including copies of tools needed to use the Internet effectively.

- *Electronic libraries.* Computerized card catalogs from the Library of Congress and a large number of university research libraries all over the world can be reached through any node on the Internet.

- *Intranet.* Allows business users to exchange information with branch locations, clients, and end users, using all of the capabilities of the Internet, only limited to organization workers.

- *On-line transactions.* Internet users can "shop" on line for information and consumer products, even complete transactions *if* they are brave enough to transmit their credit card numbers over the network.

- *Chat rooms.* Internet users can engage in on-line dialog with other users from all over the world by typing messages back and forth inside private "rooms" that are sponsored at various locations on the net.

- *Self-expression.* You can make your own views on almost any topic known to the world by participating in one of the thousands of news groups or present yourself (and your vacation photos, artwork, or personal philosophy) on your own World Wide Web home page.

- *Search engines.* Many on-line indices can help you find what you are looking for on the Internet. The web has a variety of services, including Lycos, Yahoo, and InfoSeek, which let you look up specific locations or search for content with key words.

Most Internet users access the network through high-speed networks at educational institutions or their places of work (see box), but a growing number of organizations provide dial-up access to residential users as well, including major telecommunications carriers like MCI and soon the Baby Bells (see Table 13.3 on page 336).

Using Information Services

The use of audiotext is widespread, with four-fifths of all U.S. phone users reporting that they have placed an 800-number call at one time or another. Most of these calls are made to order products and to contact help lines or customer service for consumer products. About an eighth of U.S. telephone users have placed a call to a 900 or 976 number. Audiotext users

GETTING ON THE INTERNET

What is the easiest way to get on the Internet? Unfortunately, it is not all that easy no matter how you do it. If you are in school or work for a large organization, chances are that you can get a "free" connection simply by setting up a computer account with your institution. Some libraries and government agencies also provide public access. The service is free only in the sense that you, personally, will not usually be charged either for the basic service connection or for usage fees. However, your institutional sponsor is paying for the high-speed network connections and the computers, so in that sense it is not "free" at all—it is coming out of your tuition, corporate overhead, or tax dollars in the long run.

Getting an Internet account is only the first step. If you are using your own computer, you will have to invest a few hundred dollars to obtain a local area network connection if you do not already have one, complete with a computer network adapter for your personal computer. You will also need to obtain copies of the computer programs that make it possible to use the various Internet search tools and to capture and read the files once you find them. The good news is that many of these are "shareware" programs that can be obtained at little or no cost from other Internet users or via local bulletin boards or from the Internet itself, and new programs (such as Mosaic) are beginning to appear that integrate several of these functions. The bad news is that configuring a computer to run these programs can be a daunting task for the network novice.

If you do not have access to a local area network that has an Internet connection, you will have to use a phone line. Instead of a network adapter, you will have to invest in a computer modem, preferably one with a speed of at least 14,400 bits per second. You can obtain your Internet account through the providers shown in Table 13.2 or through the various consumer videotex services, but the connection will not be free, and a full array of Internet services may not be available. Telephone companies and cable operators in some areas are also beginning to offer Internet access. There will be a monthly charge and various usage-sensitive charges as well. You will need some additional software, called SLIP (Serial Line Internet Protocol) or PPP (Point-to-Point Protocol) so that you can connect your computer to the Internet "host computer" that you dial into (Littlefield, 1994). To upload and download files, you will also need file transfer software (such as Xmodem or Kermit) to send files back and forth to your local Internet host. If that host is not so local, you will also have to pay the toll call charges to connect to it.

THEN you are ready to start learning how to use the Internet and access all that "free information."

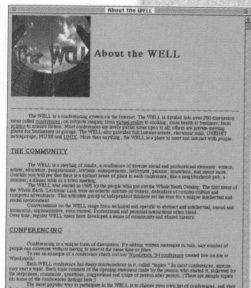

THE WORLD WIDE WEB HELPS USERS NAVIGATE THE INTERNET BY MERELY "CLICKING" ON KEY WORDS (UNDERLINED). HERE, THE "HOME PAGE" OF THE WELL, ONE OF THE BEST-KNOWN STOPS ON THE INTERNET, IS SHOWN.

tend to be younger and concentrated in the upper-middle income range. According to one estimate, some 275 million calls are placed to 900 numbers in the course of a year, with over half the calls going to entertainment and information services. Time and weather information are the most popular information categories.

The reach of consumer videotex services is limited to homes with personal computers and personal computer modems—no more than 17 million by current estimates. Seven million, or about 8 percent of U.S. homes, actually have videotex subscriptions.

How widespread is Internet usage? As we saw in the last chapter, usage estimates vary widely but appear to be on the order of 10 percent of U.S. homes by 1996. About two-thirds of Internet users are male, half are managers or professionals, and a fourth have annual

TABLE 13.3. INTERNET ACCESS PROVIDER OPTIONS

Source	Examples
Local phone companies	Ameritech, Bell Atlantic, NYNEX, U.S. West, Pacific Telesis, BellSouth, Southwestern Bell, GTE
Long-distance companies	AT&T, MCI, Sprint
Local cable companies	TCI, Time Warner, Continental Cablevision
On-line services	America Online, CompuServe, Prodigy, Microsoft Network
Internet companies	Performance Systems International (PSInet), Uunet Technologies (Uunet), Delphi, MIDnet, Cerfnet, Netcom
Satellite companies	DirecTV
Public institutions	Colleges and universities, public libraries, local public schools

Note: For local access providers near you, consult the Providers of Commercial Internet Access Directory (http://www.celestin.com/pocia) or look for a public service (freenet) provider in your area (http://lcweb.loc.gov/global/internet/freenet.html) on the World Wide Web.

REVIEW

1. What are the most common types of audiotext services?
2. What features do consumer videotex services offer?
3. What is on the Internet?
4. How extensive is videotex usage in the United States?

incomes of $80,000 or more. However, only three-fifths of Internet users access the network from home—half of U.S. adults age 16 or over access the Internet at work and another third access it at school, which means that about half of all Internet users have multiple access points. World Wide Web access is by far the most popular Internet application, attracting 77 percent of Internet users; 65 percent reported using E-mail on the Internet. Other popular Internet applications include newsgroup participation (36 percent), downloading software (31 percent), remote computing (31 percent), interactive chat (21 percent), and multimedia (19 percent). On the web, the most popular activity is browsing (90 percent of web users), followed by seeking general information or information about specific companies or products.[1]

INFORMATION SERVICE INDUSTRY ISSUES

Issues facing the information services industry include access to information, ownership and control issues, censorship, and privacy.

Equality of Access

Universal service is reaching all members of the population with a service.

In Chapters 5 and 11 we saw how the **universal service** question plagues efforts to open telecommunications networks to wider competition. The burgeoning of the Internet amplifies this issue, since it is increasingly the preferred distribution network for all types of public and citizen information. Internet access has been an elite privilege since its inception, although the privileged group has widened from a small clique of military researchers to academics at elite universities to all of those wealthy—or educated—enough to have access to a networked personal computer.

The Telecommunications Act of 1996 affirmed the goal of universal service, but how is it to be achieved? One possibility is to have all telecommunications carriers pay into a common fund to subsidize low-income users. But is telephone dial tone enough, or should Internet access be the standard? And, if so, what level of Internet access—text files only or a full range of multimedia capabilities? Another approach is to subsidize connections in public institutions, such as schools and public libraries. But public institutions in wealthy areas are usually more accessible and better prepared to integrate new technology than others, so this policy ironically risks deepening the chasm between rich and poor.

[1] A. C. Nielsen Company http://www.nielsenmedia.com/whatsnew/execsum2.htm.

Ownership and Control

In the worst case, the owners of the information superhighway could take a page out of the book of John D. Rockefeller and other Industrial Age "robber barons" by using the network as a tool to extend monopoly control. For example, they could charge discriminatory rates or refuse carriage to competing publishing, home shopping, and mass media firms, driving them into bankruptcy.

Looking at today's Internet as a paradigm, one could argue that the information service universe is too large to be ruled effectively by a few corporate entities. Recent strides in technology also seriously undermine the old **natural monopoly** imperative—that it is economically efficient to have only a single carrier providing the "last mile" connection to homes and businesses. The Telecommunications Act of 1996 signaled the beginning of a new era of virtually unbridled competition, with the tacit assumption that free competition will destroy monopolies and ultimately benefit the consumer. Only time will tell if this assumption is correct or if deregulation will lead to new monopolistic practices.

Censorship on the Internet

Just about anyone can put just about anything on the Internet—and they often do. Discussions of virtually every sexual practice imaginable—many complete with graphic pictures—are available. Hate someone? Chances are, your hate group has a forum somewhere on the Net.

The Internet poses some unique problems for anyone who might like to clean up these stains on the information superhighway. The Internet is incredibly diverse and anarchic. The number of "sources" is in the millions, and no one is really "in charge" of the network. The users of the network are also the "publishers," but they do not have to subscribe to any code of professional journalistic ethics, and in any event the authors of the most offensive forms of content have ways to "launder" the information so that it cannot be traced back to them. And how can we regulate content on an international network that encompasses societies with widely varying notions of what is obscene or violent?

These obstacles have not deterred would-be guardians of public morality, however. In 1995, a major news magazine published a study suggesting that pornography was widely available to children over the Internet. The study proved to be grossly exaggerated, but the reaction prompted tough antipornography provisions in the Telecommunications Act of 1996. The act banned the transmission of all indecent—as opposed to fully obscene—content to minors. Meanwhile, censors at leading universities barred the transmission of pornography to their (adult) students in the wake of an incident in which a male college student described his lurid fantasies about a female classmate in a graphic E-mail. Germany imposed a sweeping ban on indecent content, prohibiting all mentions of words like "breast" and "buttocks." China went further, endeavoring to set up a "firewall" around the entire country that would screen its Internet users from content deemed politically—not just morally—"indecent." At the other end of the continuum of social control, programs that filter out files with naughty words or suggestive pictures are available for concerned parents who want to censor their own young web surfers.

Such efforts sometimes yeild unintended, even comical, results. For example, Germany's ban on the word "breast" blotted out information on breast cancer as well as *Playboy* pictorials. One popular Internet filtering program cut off access to the White House home page because it used the word "couple"—also often found in ads soliciting sexual encounters—when referring to the President and his wife.

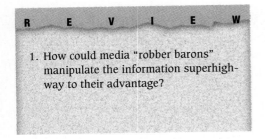

R E V I E W

1. How could media "robber barons" manipulate the information superhighway to their advantage?

However, the implications of censorship in free societies are not always so humorous. By banning "indecency" as opposed to outright "obscenity" on the Internet, many believe the U.S. Congress significantly—and unnecessarily, given the availability of cheap filtering software—encroached on the First Amendment rights of adults. And at what point do censors on college campuses chill the free exchange of ideas in the name of political correctness, as the Supreme Court ruled had happened in the case of the salacious E-mail?

Privacy

The censorship issue also reminds us that although the information superhighway has thus far resisted attempts to control it, the potential exists for it to become an instrument of privacy invasion such as the world has never known—offering the opportunity to monitor virtually every communication and every transaction made by anyone, anywhere, at any time. Another significant privacy threat is posed by the relative ease with which interchanges on the Internet—ranging from commercial transactions to simple requests for information—can be recorded, traced back to their origin, and collated with other data. In Chapter 5, we saw how existing means of matching consumers to computer data are a serious privacy concern. The expanded use of the Internet could make this process ruthlessly efficient and extend the snooping to new lows—such as spying on our media habits and personal affiliations.

Is your E-mail private? According to the Electronic Communication Privacy Act of 1986, it is, but operators of private E-mail networks can, and often do, monitor your mail. There is also the danger that your messages will be copied from your computer—or from the recipient's computer—without your knowledge. To preserve privacy, you can **encrypt** your messages in a secret code and give decoding "keys" only to the intended recipients.

Encryption means to write a message in a secret code.

Law enforcement officials would like you to "file" a copy of your encryption key with a federal agency so that officials would be able to decode your messages—under court order, of course—to check for criminal or national security violations. Internet users and civil liberties groups are up in arms over the proposal, claiming that it is an unreasonable invasion of privacy by the government and makes all users vulnerable in the likely event that someone eventually "cracks" the secret code key. Others believe that this system will be unnecessarily costly and, ultimately, ineffective as sophisticated users apply their own secret codes to messages before they are run through the encryption chip (Davis, 1994). However, in the absence of a workable security plan, commercial and government users may avoid using the Internet and the future information superhighway as well, impairing its economic viability.

SUMMARY & REVIEW

How Did the Information Services Industry Evolve?

How did common carriers originate?
The common carrier concept grew out of nineteenth-century railroad regulation designed to curb the monopolistic practices of industrial "robber barons" who used their control of transportation networks to dominate the businesses that relied on the railroads to transport their goods. Common carriers must provide their services on an equal basis to all customers according to a published schedule of rates. Communication carriers may not own a financial interest in the information service providers who create the content. The Mann-Elkins Act and the Communications Act of 1934 were important legislative milestones in the evolution of communications common carriers.

What were the first information services?
As opposed to common carriers, which provide the networks on which information is carried, information service providers create the content that is carried. Newspaper wire services, beginning with the Associated Press in 1850, were the first electronic information services. Audio information services are as old as the telephone itself, but they first emerged in their modern form as time announcements in 1927. The AT&T divestiture created the audiotext industry as it exists today by opening up the public telephone network to independent information service providers. Videotex and teletext are computerized text services delivered over telephone and broadcast networks, respectively. They originated from experiments with consumer data services carried out by the British Post Office in the 1970s. The French Minitel was the first successful videotex service.

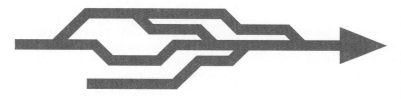

What Technologies Are Important to the Information Services Industry?

How do videotex systems work?
Consumer videotex systems such as Prodigy and CompuServe are usually accessed via a personal computer attached to a modem. A connection is then established through the local telephone office to a local node on a packet-switched network. Information requests are forwarded to a central computer that stores the videotex information. Sometimes local nodes and the user's own computer store supplementary text and graphics. Graphical information is still a problem, since it requires a great deal of computer storage and slows down the delivery of information to the user.

What is the information superhighway to the home?
The information superhighway is a concept for a broadband, intelligent digital network that will integrate voice, text, and video delivery to the home. It will offer many more channels, improved transmission quality, and advanced interactive and multimedia capabilities. Users will be able to order up just the content and the degree of transmission quality they desire. In the near term, the integrated services digital network (ISDN) will be used to upgrade digital telephone networks in the home. Asynchronous transfer mode (ATM) networks will offer high-capacity transmission of voice, data, and video over a single network.

How Is the Information Services Industry Organized?

What are the main elements of the information services industry?
Common carriers operate the networks, while information service providers create the content that is carried on the network. Value added networks (VANs) and database service providers act as intermediaries, providing enhanced network services and packaging for information services. Audiotext and bulletin board systems are highly fragmented indus-

tries, while major corporations dominate the videotex and teletext industries.

How Are Information Services Used?

What is on audiotext?

Adult entertainment was the most popular form of audiotext service until local phone companies began to refuse billing for them. There are thousands of active audiotext programs, including credit services, promotions and contests, information and entertainment programs, children's services, and interactive polls. About an eighth of telephone subscribers use 900 or 976 numbers.

What do videotex services have to offer?

Consumer videotex services have evolved into interactive media featuring electronic mail, transactional services, and computer games. There are thousands of business-oriented videotex services, including electronic versions of trade and technical journals and reference indexes. There are tens of thousands of bulletin board systems that serve the needs of small communities of computer users. There are about 4 million consumer videotex subscribers in the United States. Increasingly, videotex and DBS systems are being merged into the Internet.

What is the Internet?

The Internet is a "network of networks" that connects millions of computer users from all over the world. Some of its more popular features are electronic mail, a user-supported on-line "news service," access to libraries of computer programs and electronic documents, and multiuser computer games, features also found on popular consumer videotex services. The Internet is much more extensive than any of the commercial services and gives free access to a wide variety of public data files supplied by academic institutions and government agencies.

How can I access the Internet?

Most of the national consumer videotex services now offer access to the Internet for a fee. There are also a growing number of independent Internet access providers, including some telephone and cable television companies. Home access is complicated by the need to use computer modems, which greatly slow the speed of communication, especially when accessing files with audio or pictures. However, in some areas, cable TV connections or new digital telephone lines can speed the conversation. Students and employees of many academic and government institutions and a growing number of private businesses can obtain "free" high-speed Internet connections, although their organizations are really paying the cost. Internet users need to take advantage of the various search tools and personal computer programs that greatly increase the ease of access to the network.

What Issues Will Shape the Information Superhighway?

What are the main concerns about how the information superhighway will develop?

There is growing concern over the presence of objectionable content on the superhighway, including pornography, sexist and racist language, and content that might provoke antisocial behavior. A workable plan for protecting the privacy of communication on the Internet is also needed.

How will the information superhighway be funded?

Although today's Internet is funded largely through public agencies like the National Science Foundation and major universities, it is unlikely that the future information superhighway will be a government project. Private businesses, including telephone companies and cable television operators, will fund the network from the proceeds of customer subscription fees. While relieving the taxpayers of the financial burden, this approach raises the question of how the network will be extended to areas that may be economically unattractive to business interests, such as rural areas and impoverished inner-city neighborhoods. Another concern is that Information Age "robber barons" could use their ownership of the network to gain control of the content of the information the networks carry and of the transactional services that will be offered over the information superhighway.

REFERENCES

Andrews, E. L. (1992, March 19). Cable TV battling phone companies. *The New York Times,* pp. A1, A16.

Andrews, E. L. (1993, April 12). Cable company plans a data superhighway. *The New York Times,* pp. C1, C5.

Bouman, H., & Christofferson, M. (Eds.). (1992). *Relaunching videotext.* Boston, MA: Kluwer Academic Publishers.

Brooks, J. (1976). *Telephone: The first hundred years.* New York: Harper & Row.

Davis, B. (1994, March 22). Clipper Chip is your friend, NSA contends. *The Wall Street Journal,* pp. B1, B2.

Dordick, H., & LaRose, R. (1992). *The telephone in daily life.* East Lansing: Department of Telecommunication, Michigan State University.

Elmer-Dewitt, P. (1993, April 12). Electronic superhighway. *Time,* pp. 50–55.

Flynn, L. (1994, November 20). Getting on-line the Microsoft way. *The New York Times,* p. 10F.

Gelerman, S. (1994, March). Herd not obscene: How the Supreme Court might debate the constitutional implications of a case when VR meets kiddie porn. *Wired,* pp. 66–70.

Glascock, J., & LaRose, R. (1992, March). A content analysis of 900 numbers: Implications for industry regulation and self-regulation. *Telecommunications Policy,* pp. 147–155.

Greenberg, B. S. (1989). Teletext in the United Kingdom: Patterns, attitudes, and behaviors of users. In J. L. Salvaggio & J. Bryant (Eds.), *Media use in the information age.* Hillsdale, NJ: Erlbaum.

Hahn, H., & Stout, R. (1994). *The Internet complete reference.* New York: McGraw-Hill.

Kessler, J. (1992). *Directory to fulltext online resources.* Westport, CT: Meckler.

LaRose, R., & Atkin, D. (1992, Spring). The Reinvention of the telephone as a mass medium: Audiotext in the information environment. *Journalism Quarterly,* pp. 413–421.

Levine, J., & Baroudi, C. (1993). *The Internet for dummies.* Boston, MA: IDG Books.

Littlefield, S. (1994, November). Connect with the Internet via SLIP or PPP. *Online Access,* pp. 17–18.

Marcaccio, K. (Ed.). (1991). *Computer-readable databases: A directory and data source book* (7th ed.). Detroit, MI: Gale Research.

Mayer, R. (1986). The French videotex system: Success story or "Edsel of the eighties"? Salt Lake City: Family and Consumer Studies, University of Utah.

McGraw-Hill, Inc. (1993). A history of telecommunications regulation. In *Managing Voice Networks.* Delran, NJ: McGraw-Hill Datapro Information Services Group.

McQuillian, J. (1993, February). Why ATM? *Business Communication Review,* pp. 137–138.

Merit (1995). Merit statistics (ftp:// nic.merit.edo/statistics/nsfnet).

Morse, R. C. (1985). Videotex USA. In P. I. Zorkoczy (Ed.), *Oxford surveys in information technology* (Vol. 2). New York: Oxford University Press.

Network World. (1992, November 4). The 1991 900 services market at a glance. p. 13.

Quittner, J. (1994, March). Johnny Manhattan meets the Furrymuckers: Why playing MUDs is becoming the addiction of the 90s. *Wired,* pp. 92–93, 138.

Sandberg, J. (1994, December 21). AT&T is ready to acquire Ziff unit, jumping into crowded on-line arena. *The Wall Street Journal.*

Sloan, W., Stovall, J., & Startt, J. (1993). *Media in America.* (2nd ed.). Scottsdale, AZ: Publishing Horizons.

Treese, W. (1994). The Internet index. (httpillwww.openmarket.com/info/internet-index/curren-sources.html).

U.S. Department of Commerce. (1993). *U.S. industrial outlook 1993.* Washington, DC: U.S. Government Printing Office.

Weber, T. (1994, March 21). Button down: The remote control of the future should be a lot more versatile—and a lot simpler. *The Wall Street Journal,* p. R10.

Chapter 14

COMMUNICATIONS MEDIA IN THE WORKPLACE

C H A P T E R   P R E V I E W

any workers spend almost all their time on the job using computers and telephones. In addition, the workplace offers numerous opportunities to consume mass media in print, audio, and video forms. Communication technologies in the workplace also often foreshadow developments in consumer communications media.

This chapter will focus on industries that are users of communications media. Recall from our earlier discussion of the information economy that these organizations make up the secondary information sector—those that do not have information production as their primary function but that do create, transmit, and manipulate information in the course of their daily operations.

In this chapter we will examine the multimedia communications technologies that are used in the business world. We will see that the array of technologies and services available to organizational users differs dramatically from those found in the home. We will also describe typical applications of communications media at work and discuss some important social and policy issues that surround the use of information technologies on the job.

THE FUTURE OF WORK: TWO SCENARIOS

Sand Box City, Hawaii, 2010

The noon sun glistens on the lagoon as you send your last E-mail message of the day to your virtual office. The paper umbrella in your drink pokes your cheek gently as you end another day far from the stresses of the workaday world. Only two hours to clear out the old in-box today, which left you plenty of time for the appointment with the specialist about your tennis elbow. It's after five in New York, and no one will be looking for you until tomorrow. It's time to pull the kids away from their multimedia educational program and head for the beach for a nap in the sun!

Treadmill, New Jersey, 2010

Your computer flickers in the light of the bare bulb as you send the latest batch of insurance claims to the data broker in Manhattan. Sixteen hours of work without a break, and you had to underbid the offshore data factory in Mogadishu, but now at least you can buy more painkiller for the shooting pains in your palms. Time to call the kids in from their "playground" on the deserted freeway and get them to work on the stack of airline coupons that just came in while you catch some sleep!

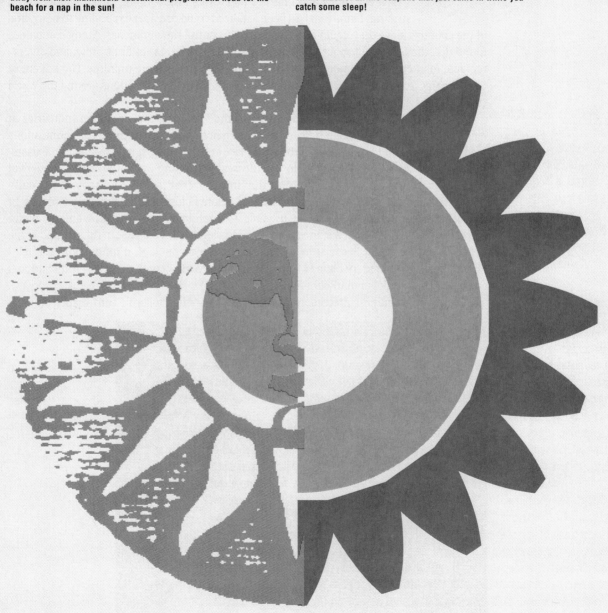

ommunications media specifically adapted to the needs of commerce date back at least to the clay tablets of ancient Sumer, which were used to keep track of trade transactions. Before telecommunications, transportation was the main means of business communication. Businesses used stagecoaches, horses, ships, runners, railroads, and even passenger pigeons to complete transactions and to obtain critical intelligence.

The establishment of telegraph service by Samuel F. B. Morse in 1844 transformed the world of business, making it possible to communicate instantly with farflung business associates and branch offices. Historian Daniel Czitrom (1982) calls the telegraph "lightning lines" for the speed with which communication moved and for its transforming effect, like lightning striking. Firms that had been localized could consider expanding to new parts of the country, since they could now more closely control their branches. Many companies found that the barriers of space and time were reduced. The size of firms grew, and diverse regional markets became more standardized and their prices more uniform. The advent of transoceanic telegraph service in 1866 made it possible to link operations around the world (see Table 14.1).

We have already recounted the histories of the telephone and computer industries at length and will not retell them here, other than to note that both of these communications media initially found applications in the workplace and then later spread to residential users. Most early phones were located in businesses, beginning with the first commercial installation at a burglar alarm firm in Boston in 1877 (Fagen, 1975). Many of the early residential phones were themselves business related, installed in the home offices of physicians. The telephone made it possible to coordinate the activities among many employees and across great distances, and it made a significant increase in the size and scope of businesses possible. Perhaps more than any other technological innovation, the telephone could be credited (or blamed, depending on one's view) with the rise of transnational corporations and global markets (de Sola Pool, 1983).

Likewise, the earliest precursors of the computer—the Hollerith card reader and the

THE TELEGRAPH TRANSFORMED COMMUNICATIONS IN THE BUSINESS WORLD IN THE LATE 1880S. HERE TELEGRAPH WIRES SPAN A BUSY NEW YORK CITY STREET.

TABLE 14.1. WORKPLACE COMMUNICATIONS MILESTONES

Year	Event
1844	Telegraph service
1866	Transatlantic telegraph service
1877	First business telephones
1879	First PBX
1890	Hollerith card tabulator
1951	UNIVAC—first commercial computer
1962	First commercial time-sharing computer system
1964	First local area network
1968	Group II facsimile machines
1981	IBM Personal Computer

adding machine—were very much business machines. The first (nonmilitary) commercial computer was UNIVAC, delivered to the U.S. Census Bureau in 1951. It took over twenty years after that for the computer to reach the home. As with the telephone, many of the earliest uses for the home computer also involved the extension of work activities into the home.

TECHNOLOGY TRENDS

Although many of the information technologies found in the work environment have their parallel in the home environment—the telephone and the personal computer, for example—some distinctive communications media have also evolved in the workplace.

Office Telephone Systems

Large organizations quickly realized that they could improve their internal communications with the telephone and instituted their own private telephone switching systems, the first of which was installed in 1879. The largest corporations have their own **private branch exchanges (PBXs),** scaled-down versions of the switching equipment that telephone companies have in their central offices. A PBX system connects all the internal phones within the organization to each other and also makes connections to outside lines. (See Rowe, 1991, and Briere, 1993, for descriptions of business telecommunications technologies and services.)

Organizations buy PBXs to save money on communications and to get access to advanced system features. Business users have to pay for each of their local calls so they can save money by making intraorganizational calls on the PBX. Because not all employees make outside calls at the same time, as many as ten employees can share one outside line through the PBX, yielding further cost savings. The various custom calling services that residential subscribers can obtain for an extra fee, such as call waiting and **Caller ID,** are built into PBX systems.

Other PBX features are not usually found on the public network, including a "camp on" feature that automatically notifies callers when a busy line they have been trying to reach becomes free. To help users cope with all the added options, PBX phones have dedicated feature buttons so that corporate users do not have to remember activation codes to access the special functions. Other buttons allow users to handle calls that come in to other phones in the office. Many PBX phones have miniature data displays to support Caller ID and other user information features. Another option can flash a "Do not disturb" message on the caller's display. The counter to this is "Barge in," which allows a supervisor to override the do not disturb, or even to interrupt a phone conversation. Advanced PBX systems integrate voice and data communications and incorporate **wireless** extensions that work like cellular telephones.

PBXs can also be programmed to manage employee communications by monitoring conversations or by preventing calls to certain numbers (such as long-distance or 900-number calls). In telemarketing operations, they are used to distribute calls evenly to all of the attendants and provide detailed reports on each worker's call completion rates. Sometimes these call management functions are contained in stand-alone systems, known as **automatic call directors (ACDs).**

Private branch exchanges (PBXs) are privately owned telephone switches.

Caller ID displays the number of the party who is trying to call on a small screen.

Wireless communication takes place through radio or light beams.

Automatic call directors (ACDs) are systems that manage and distribute calls to work groups, as in telemarketing centers.

Small companies use **key systems.** Old-fashioned key systems were readily identifiable by the row of lighting plastic buttons across the bottom of each set and the thick cables interconnecting all of the telephones in the office. Modern key systems are more like PBXs, have all of the same features, and run on standard telephone wiring. They are just packaged and priced differently for smaller offices.

Many office telephone systems also have their own **voice mail** system. The purchase of such a system is usually justified by replacing human telephone operators or by reallocating clerical staff to other, more productive, duties. Voice mail is much cheaper than putting a dedicated answering machine on each employee's desk, since the recording system is shared among all employees. The latest office systems combine voice and text messaging, giving users a text-based menu that lets them scan and prioritize incoming calls. Voice mail systems are also often integrated with automated attendant systems—the proper name for the mechanized voices that instruct us to "Press 1 for customer service, press 2 for sales, press 3 . . ."

Facsimile machines are another mainstay of modern corporate communications. Facsimile transmission actually predates the invention of the telephone, but before 1968 it was limited to a few highly specialized applications such as transmitting photographs and fingerprints for criminal investigations. That year saw the introduction of the so-called Group II machines that could transmit a page in four to six minutes using special chemically treated paper. Today's Group III machines can transmit a page of text in well under a minute and use low-cost thermal paper to record the image. Group IV machines, which must be attached to ISDN lines, transmit a page in under five seconds and match the print quality of computer laser printers. Advanced features allow users to automatically "broadcast" the same fax to multiple locations and to delay transmissions to times of the day when the telephone rates are lowest. Many fax machines are now really computer cards located inside personal computers, which allow users to transfer documents in electronic form and completely avoid the step of transferring them to paper.

F A S T   F A X   F A C T S

The basics of fax machine operation are simple to understand. Suppose you were to take any of the illustrations that appear in this text and use a ruler to overlay a fine grid of lines on it—say, a sixteenth of an inch square. You could "fax" the picture to someone across the room by moving from square to square in a prearranged sequence and simply saying "light" if the square is mostly white and "dark" if the square is black. Your confederate could then reconstruct the picture by filling in light and dark spots on a similarly constructed grid.

A facsimile machine works in much the same way, except that a photosensitive cell is used to detect the light and dark spots instead of the human eye. The "grid" is much finer than you could draw with your ruler—200 lines per inch with today's Group III machines. Computer-readable 1's and 0's encode the information. A simple data compression technique known as run length encoding is used to speed the transmission. When large patches of white space are encountered, such as in the margin at the top of a page, the system transmits an abbreviated data stream that signals the receiver to insert the required number of blank lines instead of transmitting all of the white area point-by-point. A computer modem inside the fax machine then transmits the digital data to a modem in the receiver's fax. Instead of blackening squares with a pencil, most fax machines use tiny heating elements to

darken spots on specially treated paper. There are also "plain paper faxes" that reproduce the image on standard office stationery using the same electrostatic process as office copying machines.

Local Area Networks (LANs)

Local area networks (LANs), first developed in the early 1970s, are high-speed data networks that cover a relatively confined area—say, the size of a large office building or a campus of buildings. LANs offer significant advantages over telephone transmission in that the data can be kept in digital form, data can be transmitted at much higher speeds than is possible over telephone lines, and a single transmission path can be shared among many users (see Figure 14.1). These advantages can translate into significant cost savings and performance benefits.

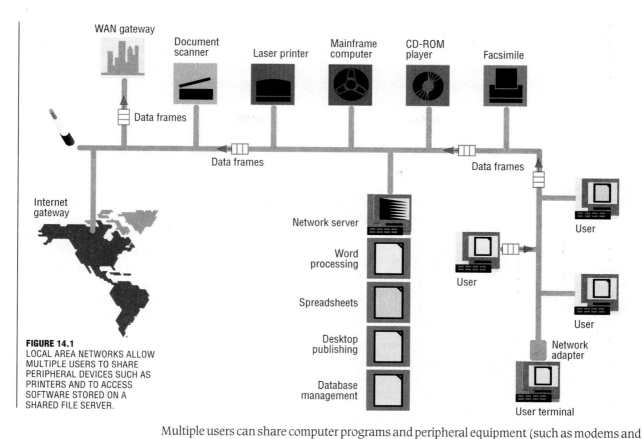

FIGURE 14.1
LOCAL AREA NETWORKS ALLOW MULTIPLE USERS TO SHARE PERIPHERAL DEVICES SUCH AS PRINTERS AND TO ACCESS SOFTWARE STORED ON A SHARED FILE SERVER.

WANs are wide area computer networks that are national or international in scope.

Wireless LANs are local area networks that send computer data via radio waves or infrared radiation instead of over wires.

Electronic mail is a written message sent over a computer network.

Computer-mediated conferences are discussions on a computer network.

Multiple users can share computer programs and peripheral equipment (such as modems and laser printers), basic business tasks from report printing to electronic component manufacturing can be monitored and controlled from remote locations, and files can be shared, allowing users to work collaboratively on group projects and to access common databases.

LAN technology is progressing rapidly. Current developments greatly increase LAN transmission speeds while enabling LANs to extend across wide areas (**WAN**) and encompass voice and image communication as well as text and data. LANs are also becoming wireless and are on a path to converge with public cellular radio networks. **Wireless LAN** users can interface with their networks through radio transceivers built into their portable computers, thus allowing the user to go anywhere in a building or office park and gain instant access to the corporate network without having to connect a cable to a computer.

Increasingly, LANs are being used as instruments for computer-mediated office communications. Linking all the personal computers in an office allows for computer messages to be sent over **electronic mail** (E-mail) systems. E-mail supplants not only paper memos but also some face-to-face communication. E-mail lets users broadcast messages to a large number of people simultaneously and to communicate asynchronously—that is, to conduct exchanges with communication partners who may not be available at the time one wishes to communicate with them. **Computer-mediated conferences** are used to discuss and debate organizational issues with the assistance of network software that helps structure the exchanges. Another trend in computer-mediated communication is to automate the laborious process of calendar coordination among employees when in-person meetings are still required.

Teleconferencing Systems

Computer conferencing systems are but one type of **teleconferencing** system. Teleconferencing systems include any electronic system that allows three or more people to communicate simultaneously; they come in three basic varieties: audio, audiographic, and video (Svenning & Ruchinskas, 1984).

Audio Conferencing. A telephone call with a speakerphone on one end that allows three people to communicate at the same time is the most basic form of teleconference. When more than a few people participate at one location, specialized—and expensive—speakerphone units are needed to cancel out the effects of echoes and background noise. For audio conferences involving more than a handful of locations, special devices called **bridges** are used to equalize the sound levels on the different telephone circuits.

Audiographic Conferencing. If we added a fax interchange to our basic speakerphone teleconference, that would be a crude form of **audiographic teleconferencing.** Computers can also be linked using modems and a special variety of communication software, known as remote control software, to share screens of information over a distance. Pressure-sensitive **electronic blackboards** let viewers at remote locations see what the conference leader writes on the board. **Light pens** allow conference participants to annotate shared computer screens by touching the surface of their computer screens with a penlike pointing device.

Video Teleconferencing. The greatest barrier to video teleconferencing is the limited capacity of today's public telephone network. It is not (as yet) possible to squeeze moving video into the telephone lines coming into our homes and offices. Corporate videoconferencing often takes place on corporate networks that use satellite, microwave, or fiber optic systems. A growing number of videoconferences do go through the public network, but they have to use special high-speed data lines, which are not available on an as-needed basis. Videoconferences also require specialized network interface devices, called **codecs** (short for coder-decoder). Codecs digitize and compress video to reduce transmission costs, using techniques similar to the advanced HDTV systems and cable systems that may soon be coming to our homes.

To save on the cost of videoconferences, compromises with transmission quality are often made. Broadcast television updates its pictures thirty times

UNDERSTANDING LANS

LANs have a bewildering array of variations, but (almost) all have a few things in common. They represent text, numbers, and images as pulses of electricity corresponding to the 1's and 0's of computer data. They specialize in high-speed transmission, on the order of millions of bits per second, or several textbook chapters per second. Most share a single transmission medium among many users, usually a coaxial cable, the same kind of wire that comes out of your cable TV converter.

When multiple users share a wire, some obvious problems crop up. What if two users want to send data at the same time? What if someone sends a very long file that ties up the network? How do we sort out which data go where? First, we break up the data streams from each computer into manageable chunks, say a thousand bytes each, to keep the network from getting tied up by long data streams. We call these chunks "frames." We have to add some extra data bits to each frame of data to provide address information about the sender and the receiver so that we can send the data chunks to the proper destination and reassemble them in their proper order. We also have to add bits that tell us where each frame belongs in the sequence and others that notify us if there has been an error in the transmission. Then we work out some method of taking turns so that the data streams do not collide with one another. Here, there are many approaches. Some involve allocating time slots to users; others entail getting an electronic "permission slip," or token, before entering into the data stream. The most common access method is to simply let collisions take place and arrange for orderly retransmissions.

Within a building or office park there may be dozens of independent LANs that occasionally need to share data, such as E-mail messages. Bridges, routers, and gateways are the devices used to extend and interconnect the networks. LANs are also being connected to distant locations via telephone lines. Wide area networks (WANs) connect networks across city, state, or even national borders, as in the case of the Internet.

TELECONFERENCING SYSTEMS ARE BECOMING A COMMON BUSINESS TOOL.

a second, giving us the illusion of natural continuous motion. Videoconferencing systems can slow down to 15 or even 5 frames per second. At 15 frames per second, there is likely to be a perceptible blurring of sudden movements. At 5 frames per second, all motion seems jerky and it is not possible to closely follow lip movements or changes in facial expression, giving a **freeze-frame** effect. Another way to save money is to cut down on the number of video feeds that are used, such as by originating video from one location only and restricting the other locations to interactions by computer or telephone.

Public networks are rapidly evolving to increase the amount of transmission capacity available to corporate users and to make the usage more flexible. The advent of ISDN makes it possible to summon the exact amount of bandwidth desired at the time of the conference. Rapid strides in codec technology are also being made, reducing these complex and expensive devices to a single computer chip so that they can be built into low-cost expansion cards for personal computers.

Freeze-frame video teleconferences use a sequence of still images that do not convey a sense of continuous motion.

Business videos are programs created by organizations for their employees and customers.

The Multimedia Corporation

Not all of the video in the workplace is in the form of live videoconferences. Many corporations maintain extensive in-house production facilities that rival those of commercial production houses or television studios. Most of the **business videos** produced by these studios are educational, ranging from orientation tapes for new employees or new products to full-length courses on management practices or technical topics. Some corporate video is quite elaborate indeed, with production values, actors, and production costs that rival those of broadcast television. These big-budget spectaculars are usually reserved for performances that are intended to have a strong motivational impact, such as annual meetings of sales representatives. They are transmitted to branches across the country by satellite hook-ups. Other companies routinely use business video to replay management briefings or to create video versions of the old stand-bys of corporate communications: the company newsletter and the press release.

Desktop publishing prepares documents "on a desktop" with a personal computer.

Desktop video is using personal computers to "play" video presentations or display video teleconferences.

The spread of **desktop publishing** and **desktop video** technologies is making multimedia presentations commonplace in many large organizations. Sales and marketing departments are making sales presentations that incorporate video and lively color graphics that can be presented on personal computers during sales visits to customer locations. Engineering design departments may use virtual reality software to help design and evaluate products "inside the computer" without constructing costly prototypes. Human relations and training departments may have advanced multimedia players that provide interactive training to employees. Multimedia kiosks provide interactive presentations in the company's lobby area, in the corporate media center, or even in the corporate museum or employee credit union. Advanced local area networks make it possible to store all these materials on centrally located video servers, where they may be accessed by anyone in the corporation (IBM Coroporation, 1994).

Private Networks

As the name implies, **private networks** are owned and operated for the exclusive use of an organization. Private networks link up all the information technologies in the firm, from desktop personal computers and telephones to teleconferencing systems and mainframe computers. Since these networks are frequently national or even international, they are also commonly referred to as wide area networks, or WANs.

Corporate networks often include transmission links and network control centers that are owned and operated by the company itself rather than leased from telecommunications carriers. These facilities include PBX, key and voice mail systems, and communications interfaces for mainframe computers. Microwave, satellite, and fiber optic systems link locations with the highest traffic volumes. An increasingly popular option is a unique satellite system, **very small aperture terminal (VSAT),** that interconnects hundreds of small satellite earth stations with a central location. In other cases, the links are lines leased from carriers for a flat monthly rate rather than being usage-sensitive lines. Other dedicated transmission facilities complete the last mile of connection with long-distance networks. These are known as **bypass** networks, since they go around, or bypass, local telephone companies entirely in an effort to economize on monthly telephone service charges.

Private networks offer several important advantages: (1) They economize on communications costs by substituting the company's own facilities for common carrier services, (2) they offer a degree of security and a backup capability not found in public networks, and (3) some private networks also have capabilities that the public network cannot provide, such as broadband circuits for videoconferences.

Mobile Communications

Most cellular radio telephone users today are business users. Senior managers often have cellular phones so that they can stay in touch with the office in their travels. To some extent, a cellular phone is also a valued "perk" for the modern executive on the move. Many cellular phones are also found in the hands of lower-level employees whose daily tasks take them outside the office. These workers include outside salespersons and roving maintenance and equipment repair technicians.

Pagers used to be an executive perk, but nowadays executives on their way up the corporate ladder regard getting rid of their beepers as a step upward. About three-fourths of the active 12 million paging units in the United States are used for business purposes. About a third of these are found on outside salespersons, and most of the rest are for health care, construction, and emergency service workers. Only about 1 percent of the pagers are on the belts or in the purses of top executives and administrative personnel.

Outside the office, cellular radio networks can accommodate **cellular data** users. All that is required is a special modem that converts the computer data to signals in the cellular radio communications band. There were about 50,000 cellular data users by 1992. These systems are used extensively by express mail delivery services to track packages (Calem, 1992).

Ultimately, this is all leading toward a new concept in business communication systems, the personal data assistant (PDA). Still in their formative stages, PDAs are intended to be a sort of "universal telecommunications appliance" that will allow busy executives to receive all manner of messages—fax, E-mail, voice mail, pages—from

R E V I E W

1. Historically, what was the impact of the telegraph and the telephone on business operations?
2. What are LANs used for?
3. What are three basic types of teleconferencing?
4. How are large organizations using multimedia technology?

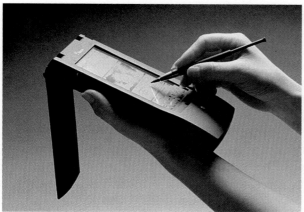

STILL IN THEIR EARLY STAGES, PERSONAL DATA ASSISTANTS (PDAS) PROMISE TO MAKE COMPUTING AND DIGITAL COMMUNICATIONS MUCH MORE PORTABLE IN THE NEAR FUTURE.

Centrex is a portion of a telephone company's switch dedicated to a particular group of users.

Leased lines are dedicated to a particular user for a flat monthly rate.

Wide area telecommunications service (WATS) lines, also known as 800 numbers, bill the cost of a long-distance call to the party called instead of the caller.

Automatic number identification (ANI) is an intelligent network service that identifies the number of the party who is placing a call.

Virtual private networks are private networks defined by software in the intelligent network instead of by full-time physical connections.

all communications sources. The PDA will thus be a sort of "pocket secretary" that will help business users manage their communications more effectively.

BUSINESS COMMUNICATION SERVICES

Businesses also have access to a wide range of information services that are unfamiliar to residential users. For starters, business phone lines are priced differently from consumer lines. Businesses have higher monthly charges and are usually charged a few cents for each local phone call.

Centrex (short for CENTRal EXchange service) is a special service package offered by the phone company to organizational users who do not choose to buy their own PBX systems. The telephone company reserves a block of lines in its central office for a corporate office location. Calls made within this group do not incur the per-call charges that normally apply to business lines and are dialed with three, four, or five digits instead of the usual seven. Centrex users also have access to many PBX special features and enjoy bulk discounts on monthly telephone services that make it an attractive alternative to standard business lines. Centrex is particularly appealing to large public institutions that do not have the financial resources to purchase large PBX systems and do not enjoy the tax breaks that private corporations get when they buy new equipment. The intelligent network is bringing significant improvements in Centrex service. With it, Centrex customers can make their own service changes, connect multiple locations in the same metropolitan area, and have access to just about all of the special features that PBX users have.

Leased lines may connect a user to one other location or to an entire telephone exchange on a dedicated basis. Leased lines differ from regular telephone lines in that they are dedicated to the user—they never get a busy signal. They are also priced on the basis of a flat monthly charge. No matter how much the line is used, the charge is the same. By aggregating large volumes of traffic on such dedicated lines, corporations can realize significant savings.

800 numbers have many applications outside the toll-free customer service and telemarketing lines familiar to most consumers. These numbers, more properly known as **wide area telecommunications service (WATS)** lines, can also be used to interconnect high-volume nodes on corporate networks. WATS lines are also used for outbound applications, such as when telemarketers or survey researchers place calls from centralized phone banks. When a call comes in on an 800 number, the number of the calling party is often forwarded via an intelligent network service, known as **automatic number identification (ANI),** to the calling center. There, the number is matched with computer files so that when the agent picks up the phone the customer's file is already on the agent's computer screen. One common misconception about WATS lines is that they are "free." It is true that the calls are not charged to the calling party. They are, of course, charged to the company that receives the call, using a special discount that lets them pay up to 50 percent less than residential users.

Virtual private networks are the latest wrinkle in private corporate networks. Instead of physically connecting locations with pieces of wire, as is done for dedicated leased lines, telecommunications carriers use intelligent switching to reserve capacity for large customers. To the corporate user, the system appears to operate the same as a leased line network. Communications can be integrated across the entire corporation, even at locations too small to justify their own "hard-wired" dedicated connections, while still achieving substantial cost savings. Employees can also dial into an 800 number from anywhere in the country, get access to the network, and place "free" long-distance calls. Special pricing schemes for the very largest corporate customers enable them to make long-distance calls for as little as a fourth of what residential users pay.

Digital data services (DDS) are special dedicated lines for high-speed communication between computers. Unlike standard telephone lines, DDS lines are able to accept data in digital format without converting them into analog form with a modem. This allows much higher transmission speeds and much more reliable transmission. The transmission rates are in incremental sizes: 1200, 2400, and 9600 bits per second (bps) lines are available just about anywhere. Lines that can run at 56,000 bps are also available in most urban areas. This is also the highest rate of speed that is commonly available on a dial-up basis, which allows billing just for the amount of time actually used.

For higher data transmission speeds, users have to install dedicated lines, for which they pay a flat monthly fee. Another popular transmission rate is 1.5 million bps, a service arrangement known as a **T1.** The next step up is the T3, capable of sending data at 45 million bps, or about three copies of this textbook per second. This is also the lowest speed at which full-motion, uncompressed video may be transmitted. T3 lines are sometimes used by the TV networks for "feeds" to their control centers in New York. Such lines are not cheap, however—a T1 line from New York to San Francisco can cost thousands of dollars per month.

Digital data services for business users are evolving rapidly in the direction of higher capacity, greater flexibility, and lower cost. ISDN is the master blueprint for future network development. Consumers and small businesses will have a three-channel telephone service allowing simultaneous voice, data, and video. Corporate users will opt for a service combining twenty-three channels for voice, video, and data with one channel that will exchange control information with the central office switch, for a combined capacity of 1.5 million bps. Future improvements will up that to 150 million bps and more.

> Digital data services (DDS) are dedicated, all-digital lines.
>
> T1 carriers transmit telephone calls and text in digital form at the rate of 1.5 million bits per second.

R E V I E W

1. What are some specialized communications services just for large organizations?

2. If an organization wanted to avoid paying for its internal telephone calls but could not afford a PBX, what telephone service could it use?

3. When you call "toll free" to place an order, what type of network service are you using? Is it really a "free" call?

4. Name three options that large corporations have for transmitting data.

ORGANIZATIONAL STRUCTURE

Large organizations must devote considerable resources to the management of information technologies. In information-intensive industries such as banking and insurance, the annual cost of information technologies and telephone services may be the single largest item in the annual budget. The largest corporations have hundreds of workers who specialize in communications and computing.

A variety of organizational structures are used to manage these resources. In the past, telecommunications was managed as if it was a corporate telephone utility, with an emphasis on reliable service at the lowest possible cost. The telecommunications manager usually reported to the senior executive in charge of office administration or facilities management, a relatively lowly position in the corporate hierarchy.

Computers entered many corporations as "number crunchers" for corporate accounting departments. As such, they naturally fell under the authority of senior financial officers, who are very prestigious members of the modern firm. As computers assumed an expanded role across the corporation, **management information system (MIS)** departments were organized to manage them, still under the aegis of the chief financial officer.

Recognizing the growing convergence of computer and communications technologies, many large organizations are now combining the telecommunications and computer

---

INFORMATION TECHNOLOGIES AND THE FACTORY OF TOMORROW

Computer manufacturers can now order customized computer circuit boards by simply placing a phone call to Tektronix, an Oregon-based manufacturer. All of the administrative and production departments in the company's circuit board division are linked via a local area network to a minicomputer. This makes it possible to link information in all of the departments and to update it automatically as each order moves through the system (Eckerson, 1993).

How It Works

Customers send their orders via an electronic data interchange (EDI) system that puts all order forms and invoices into a common electronic "language" that both Tektronix and its customers can read inside their own computer systems. The EDI orders feed directly into a materials planning system that specifies the component parts needed to make the boards, then forwards that information to a control system on the factory's floor that plans the manufacturing process. The customer's engineering department sends computer-assisted design (CAD) files to the Tektronix sales department, which forwards them to Tektronix engineers who use the plans to program machines on the shop floor that manufacture the parts. Once manufacturing is underway, the control system on the assembly floor updates inventory and production information so that management can get daily reports on productivity and costs. The cost information is compared to the quoted price and those data are used by the sales department to prepare future price estimates.

The Bottom Line

This process improves on the conventional manufacturing cycle in several important ways. First, the amount of time it takes to retool the plant—to change the configuration of machines and the sequence of steps required to manufacture each part—is dramatically reduced by the ability to directly interface design information with production control. The sales and marketing end of the business is also much more efficient, since the interchange of electronic

files reduces errors and managers have much more reliable and up-to-date information about their actual costs.

Tektronix's computer-integrated manufacturing (CIM) system has delivered some important benefits to the company's bottom line, stemming from a 30 percent reduction in the lead time required to produce a new circuit board. The amount of materials wasted in the production process and the inventories of parts that the company has to keep on hand have also declined substantially. Most important, the CIM system is an example of an information system that provides a competitive edge, allowing Tektronix to beat competitors who have longer turnaround times in the production process.

Coming Soon to a Factory Near You

Although the Tektronix system has received recognition as a "cutting edge" CIM application, this technology has been adopted by many large manufacturers of industrial products. During the 1992 Persian Gulf War, CIM systems made it possible to order replacement parts and have them delivered in the war zone in a matter of weeks, a process that formerly took many months and would have outlasted the war itself.

CIM also has the potential to revolutionize the manufacture of consumer products. Some automobile makers have terminals in their showrooms that communicate customer orders directly to their factories, reducing the lead times for new car orders while improving the efficiency of the production process. Gone are the days of "too many green Oldsmobiles," when cars with last season's most popular color glutted the new car lots at the end of the model year. Car buyers might soon be able to customize their own cars in various ways, such as matching paint jobs to their favorite suit, mating car seats to their posterior dimensions, or  defining their own options for the coming generation of computer-controlled "active" components ("Make my stationwagon's muffler sound like a sports car's, the horn sound like an 18-wheeler's, and let me take speed bumps at 50 mph"). No word yet on when we will get our hands on the CAD/CAM systems so we can "make it look like a '56 T-Bird only without the fins."

---

management functions under organizational titles such as "information systems" and "information technologies." As we shall soon see, many organizations are starting to look at information technologies more as a strategic business resource rather than as a corporate utility. These companies are establishing new top-level management positions, **chief information officers (CIOs)**, who are charged with using computers and telecommunications to create new business opportunities (Toffler, 1990).

Corporate communications also means advertising and public relations, topics covered elsewhere in this text. Additionally, many large organizations now have their own in-house video/multimedia production units where support materials for external advertising and public relations campaigns, as well as internal training and employee relations activities, are produced.

USING INFORMATION TECHNOLOGY

Information technologies and services are only the basic building blocks for what really matters to organizational communication users: the applications that help them succeed in businesses. Peter Keen (1988), a noted author and consultant on the topic of information technologies in organizations, points out three basic ways to use information technologies in an organization: to run the business better, to get a competitive edge, and to innovate with new products or services.

Running the Business Better

Running the business better involves improving productivity, improving internal communication, improving executive information, linking field units, and managing inventories.

Improving Productivity. Information technologies can be used to increase **productivity**, the amount of productive output relative to the inputs—workers, machinery, and other resources—expended to create products. We can use information technologies either to up the output of the workers and factories already in place or to reduce the money we spend on the workers, factories, and other facilities in the future.

Productivity is the amount of output relative to input, often expressed in terms of the number of units produced per hour of work.

The earliest computer applications are an example of this approach. Roomfuls of mechanical calculators and data clerks were replaced by the first electronic computers. Artillery designers using computers were able to turn out more statistical tables per unit time with far fewer workers involved, so productivity improved. Common personal computer applications can also increase efficiency. For example, the productivity of report production increases when word processing is used, because there is no need to continually retype drafts. The number of reports produced per hour therefore increases. Likewise, a PBX system can cut monthly telephone line charges by 90 percent, yet workers still produce the same output. This also increases productivity, since the cost of creating the firm's output decreases. The application of information technologies in the office is known generally as **office automation**.

On the factory floor, **computer-assisted design/computer-assisted manufacturing (CAD/CAM)** systems have been developed in an effort to increase manufacturing productivity. With these systems, the designs of new products can be visualized and their performance simulated inside computer workstations, greatly shortening the cycles of design, prototyping, and testing that were once required. The output of the design process can be interfaced directly with computerized machining and even robotized assembly lines.

IN JAPAN, FACTORIES SUCH AS THIS NISSAN PLANT ARE CONTROLLED BY COMPUTERS. HERE A HUMAN EMPLOYEE MONITORS THE PERFORMANCE OF A ROBOTIC WELDING MACHINE.

In the most advanced systems, the entire production process is controlled by computer and telecommunications systems, a development called **computer-integrated manufacturing (CIM)**.

Computer-integrated manufacturing (CIM) is putting the entire manufacturing process under the control of computer and telecommunications systems.

Improving Internal Communication. The so-called "flattening" of the organization has been made possible by electronic mail and other computer-mediated communications systems. This means that the layers of middle management that filter directives down to the shop floor are no longer needed, thereby removing a layer of corporate hierarchy, or flattening it. Improvements in communication also make it possible to eliminate lower-level employees as well. For example, the installation of LANs in television news operations has meant the elimination of many junior "copy persons" who were once employed to help edit and coordinate news stories. Hollywood studios are among the organizations that have followed the E-mail trend. Disney Studios, for example, maintains communications among an elite core of two dozen top executives with an E-mail system dedicated just to them (Thompson, 1993).

Improving Executive Information. Now senior managers can maintain direct contact with the shop floor and obtain vital business information from on-line services themselves. Automated systems provide vital monitoring and control information automatically without the mediation of middle managers.

Organizational planning and budgeting cycles can be greatly shortened, and the organization can respond more quickly to changing markets. For example, the head of an insurance company can track claims activities and staffing on a day-to-day basis without waiting months for quarterly reports to trickle up from corporate staff.

Linking Field Units. Wide area networks can solve another chronic problem of corporate management: coordinating the activities of farflung branch offices. For example, Home Box

Office has a network that links its seven regional offices with headquarters in New York so that regional managers can share database information about program scheduling and cable systems that carry HBO's pay television service (Mulqueen, 1992).

Managing Inventories. Japanese automakers and electronics manufacturers were the first to innovate with the **just-in-time** (JIT) inventory method that reduces the number of components that factories have to keep on hand. Information systems are used to coordinate component suppliers, who deliver the required parts just in time for assembly. This method reduces the number of parts that must be kept in inventory from several weeks' supply to only several hours' worth. In the mass media industry, similar methods are being used by record, book, and videotape stores to help manage inventories more efficiently.

Getting the Competitive Edge

Information technologies can also make a critical difference in the competitive race to expand existing markets at the expense of the competition. Some popular strategies are to improve access to the firm, to extend the corporate network to the customer, and to differentiate existing products through information technologies.

Improve Access. Banks have lured new customers on the basis of the convenience of their automatic teller machine (ATM) networks. ATMs have extended bank hours of operation and have opened up many new locations.

Just-in-time systems use computerized inventory management systems to reduce the inventory by coordinating deliveries from suppliers.

Electronic data interchange (EDI) is an electronic system for placing and tracking transactions between firms.

WALK-UP INFORMATION BOOTHS OR KIOSKS ARE BECOMING WIDELY USED FOR GIVING INFORMATION TO CUSTOMERS OR CLIENTS.

Extend the Network to the Customer. The ultimate in improved access is to bring services to the customer's home or desktop. The idea of putting a terminal on the customer's desk first occurred to American Airlines in the 1960s, which instituted the Sabre system so that travel agents could receive instant updates of airline schedules and seat availabilities and make ticket reservations instantly. American Airlines was able to expand its share of the domestic airline market by being the first with the new system (and also possibly because it was usually first in the alphabetical listings of flights). Consumer videotex services are extending this strategy to the ultimate end users of the air travel system. Home computer users can place their own airline reservations and split the travel agent's fee with the on-line service provider. In the business world, the push is on to create **electronic data interchange (EDI)** so that corporations and their customers and suppliers can freely exchange product orders, invoices, and payments in a standardized electronic format.

Product Differentiation. Another way to gain a competitive edge is to differentiate standard products with "added value" made possible by information technologies. Companies that use 800 numbers for customer service and product support are the prototypical example. In the media realm, the broadcasting networks have attempted—unsuccessfully, so far—to differentiate their standard product, a video entertainment service, with teletext, a digital information service containing electronic program listings. Interactive television programs are another example of the product differentiation strategy.

R E V I E W

1. What is productivity and how might communications media affect it?
2. What are three basic purposes that businesses use communications media for?
3. Name two examples of new products or services made possible by communications media.
4. How could the concept of computer-integrated manufacturing be applied in the music recording business?

Innovating with New Products

Unfortunately, new ways of running a business better or of edging out the competition are soon copied by one's competitors, erasing the advantage. More and more, organizations are looking to innovations in information technologies as a way to redefine existing markets or to create entirely new information-based products. In these applications, the new systems almost always represent incremental costs rather than cost savings but are desirable because they develop new and profitable lines of business. For example, the Boeing Corporation developed an extensive private telecommunications network to support its farflung aerospace business and then converted the network into a profitable data service. Likewise, American Airlines's Sabre system has become an important business in its own right, enabling its parent corporation to turn a profit despite setbacks in its traditional air passenger service business.

The publishing business offers some prime examples of innovation with new products. Large trade press publishers such as McGraw-Hill now offer on-line services derived from the databases they compile to create their conventional print publications. Textbook publishers have begun to offer "customized publishing" of textbooks composed of pieces from several different authors. This, coupled with a favorable court ruling on copyright clearances for course packets, has positioned the textbook publishers to win back a major share of college course publication revenues that were going to photocopying companies. The newspaper industry is also innovating, with audiotext and videotex services that supplement newspaper readership and contribute new revenues.

POLICY AND SOCIAL ISSUES

Among the controversial issues related to telecommunications in the workplace are challenges to the value of information systems, the death of hierarchical structures, and privacy on the job.

Debunking the Myth of Information Systems

Although the stated objective of information systems in the workplace is to increase productivity, such increases have proved somewhat elusive. This is an important issue both for individual businesses and for the economy as a whole, as a great deal of human and capital resources are being expended on information technologies.

Why are productivity gains hard to find? For one thing, the assistance that in-house technicians and unofficial "computer gurus" give their co-workers may more than triple the officially budgeted expenditures for maintaining personal computers. The full capital and operating costs of advanced teleconferencing systems are sometimes not factored in, and the existence of such systems may lead to more meetings than are really necessary in an effort to justify the ongoing expenses. Executives may spend more time playing with type fonts, videoconference production techniques, presentation graphics, and electronic databases than is necessary to make sound business decisions. Organizations sometimes abandon efficient information systems in favor of yet newer technology before the older ones have paid for themselves in terms of cost savings. In addition, many information systems never work properly or are abandoned before they are completed (Bulkeley, 1992; McGovern, 1993; Zachary, 1991).

Over 6 million American telecommute and two-fifths of U.S. homes have some type of home office. Telecommuting helps employers retain valued employees with child-care or elder-care responsibilities or personal disabilities. Job satisfaction rises as workers are relieved from the stress of solving problems at home and from two-hour commutes. Improved employee satisfaction could translate into increased productivity.

Some employees are indeed unable to avoid the temptation of the five-hour lunch. Some report increased stress from juggling work and family crises at home. Others fear that telecommuting leads to isolation and lack of support at work and will throw them off the corporate "fast track." After factoring in the equipment and the cost of training each employee to be a computer troubleshooter, productivity gains go down the drain.

Since commuting costs are absorbed by the employee, these do not factor into the employer's "bottom line," and neither party weighs the costs of air pollution or highway construction. Most telecommuters today still have office space downtown, which sits empty most of the time. The integrated services digital network (ISDN) could greatly increase the quality and ease of access to corporate computer networks. Advances in desktop videoconferencing, in conjunction with ISDN lines, will make it possible for remote employees to have more of a sense of "being there" in the office. Multimedia computers could make it possible to replicate a wide range of office tasks and to facilitate cooperative projects on a computer network (Violino & Stahl, 1993).

The Global Sand Box?

Telecommuting has the potential to radically transform the world of work and even society as a whole. Service sector companies from banks to movie studios could become "virtual corporations," little more than a collection of nodes on a worldwide digital network. Downtown office buildings might empty and freeways turn into greenbelt parks. Employees could enjoy a permanent "working holiday," rambling freely about the globe, E-mailing their work from wherever their travels may take them. We could all live the life of Steve Roberts, a computer consultant who pedals around the country on a bicycle equipped with four computers, a cellular radio modem, and an on-board satellite link (Carroll, 1992). Employers would benefit, since they would no longer have to maintain expensive office facilities. Upward pressure on salaries might ease, as employees experience lower housing, transportation, and family care costs. With an end to air pollution, and global warming, and the restoration of the ozone layer, we could all go out and enjoy the sun!

Or the Electronic Sweatshop?

Telecommuting could replicate the horrors of the Industrial Revolution, when workers toiled long hours for starvation wages at spinning wheels in their homes. When workers supply their own offices and equipment, they are making a capital investment in their employer's corporation. Isn't this tantamount to a massive transfer of wealth from the poor to the rich? Employers may treat such employees as private contractors and eliminate health and retirement benefits. Employers might no longer make commitments to employees if they never have to incur moving costs and can replace anyone by putting out a work order "on the net." Bank clerks in New York City and screenwriters in Hollywood could suddenly find themselves in direct competition with contractors in Bombay. And how would the downtrodden information workers fight these injustices? Without a common physical gathering place they might be unable to organize themselves into unions or professional associations. And what will happen to those empty cities and the people too poor to move out of them?

A 1969 study that examined the impacts of eighteen cases of industrial and office automation found that the majority did increase the productivity of labor (Crossman & Laner, 1969). A later review of some thirty office automation studies by communication researcher Ron Rice revealed a wide range of productivity-enhancing effects (Rice & Bair, 1984). These included increases in document production rates, decreases in the number of separate tasks per activity (such as the elimination of typesetting), fewer media transformations (such as from handwriting to typescript to computer text), lower document production costs, and the elimination of "shadow functions" such as telephone tag, which do not contribute directly to the finished product. Teleconferencing systems also seem to improve productivity by lowering travel expenditures and increasing the efficiency of meetings.

However, it is difficult to sort out the effects of information technologies from those of other changes that are often introduced at the same time, such as job redesign, alterations in employee reward systems, new supervisors, and even new office furniture. Industrial psychologists long ago learned that when it comes to tinkering with worker productivity, "everything works." That is, just about *anything* done in an effort to increase productivity will seem to have an effect, if for no other reason than the workers who take part in the experiment feel they are receiving special treatment and respond with higher levels of production.

One recent economic analysis concluded that, at an aggregate level, investments in information technology are not related to increases in productivity (Morrison & Berndt, 1991). This does not mean that all information technology installations are unproductive, but it does appear that overall the successes are balanced by the failures. Other recent studies suggest that it is only in the last few years that productivity gains have been registered. However, traditional productivity measures may overlook the primary contributions of information technology, such as increased product variety and quality.

If information technologies do not unequivocally contribute to the corporate "bottom line," why are corporations so eager to adopt them? Factors other than rational systems analysis can enter into the decision-making process: hidden personal agendas, corporate politics, and the need to maintain a certain "corporate image" or to "keep up with the Jones Corporation." According to sociologist Rob Kling (1980), modernization waves in computer technology seem like **computerization movements,** complete with the prophets, zealots, and true believers found in political movements. Communications researchers have found a similar phenomenon when it comes to making corporate decisions about telecommunications technologies. The **social influence model** takes note of the personal attitudes and interpersonal relationships that intrude on the rational evaluation of new technologies (Fulk, Schmitz, & Steinfield, 1990).

The Structure of Work: The End of the Corporate Pyramid

The pyramid-shaped hierarchical structures of Industrial Age organizations are being swept aside (Toffler, 1990). Two new metaphorical images are emerging to describe this transformation. The term **flattened pyramid** describes an organization where the middle layers of management have been stripped away, leaving the high-level executives at the point of the pyramid resting on a wide base of lower-level employees (see Figure 14.2). In the **core and ring** model, a small core of key employees preserves the essential knowledge of the business, and "disposable" temporary employees are added to or subtracted from the ring as fluctuations in the marketplace and new business opportunities may dictate.

Information technologies have made these changes possible by reducing the amount of

Computerization movements are social movements promoting the adoption of information technologies within organizations.

The **social influence model** recognizes that social dynamics within an organization are involved in the decision to adopt communications media.

The **flattened pyramid** is an organizational structure in which the layers of middle management have been stripped away.

The **core and ring** is a structure in which a small group of permanent professional employees manages a fluctuating temporary work force.

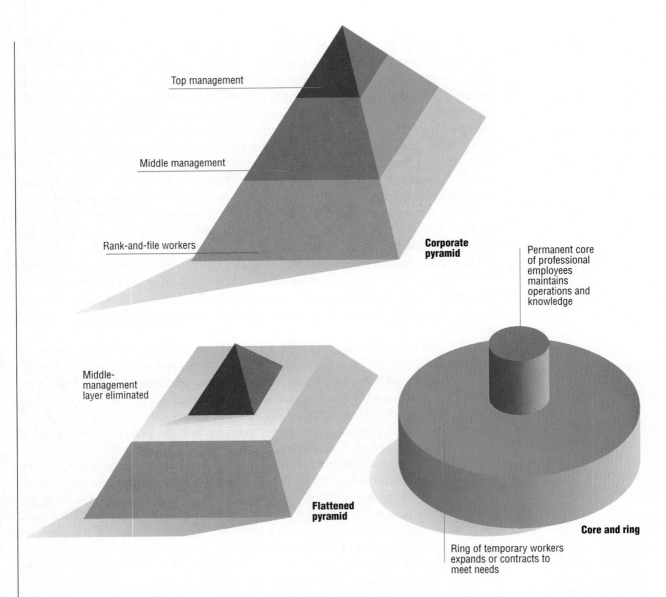

Top management

Middle management

Rank-and-file workers

**Corporate
pyramid**

Permanent core
of professional
employees
maintains
operations and
knowledge

Middle-
management
layer eliminated

**Flattened
pyramid**

Core and ring

Ring of temporary workers
expands or contracts to
meet needs

FIGURE 14.2
THE TRADITIONAL CORPORATE
PYRAMID IS BEING REPLACED
BY THE FLATTENED PYRAMID
AND THE CORE AND RING
STRUCTURE.

midlevel management required to fulfill essential communication and coordination functions. Data collected directly from purchasing and ordering systems, for example, can be digested by computer and supplied directly to senior management, a process that once took a corps of executive report writers. Likewise, directives can be distributed and feedback gathered directly from line employees through electronic mail systems, eliminating platoons of corporate memo writers.

Sociologist Shoshana Zuboff (1984) concluded that part of the reason for dissolving corporate hierarchies is that information technologies alter the basis of power in organizations. The knowledge base of midlevel managers no longer differs much from that of rank-and-file employees, undermining the authority of the middle managers and transforming corporate structure into a more collaborative model. Thus, electronic mail and computer conferencing do not "automate managers out of a job" but rather transform work by sharing information instead of hoarding it and by substituting autonomy and learning for subordination and obedience.

REVIEW

1. What are some of the reasons why communications media often fail to increase productivity?
2. What effect have communications media had on privacy in the workplace?
3. What new corporate structures are emerging through the application of communications media?

Monitoring is the practice of tracking employees' performance through their interactions with communications media.

Privacy on the Job

Quite simply, there is no privacy at work. Employers are free to monitor telephone conversations and inspect E-mail messages at will, and only a few firms have corporate privacy policies that voluntarily prohibit such practices or even notify employees that they are subject to monitoring. There have been cases of employee dismissal for the offense of exchanging personal messages, and even for the receipt of unsolicited personal messages.

Information technologies have greatly expanded the scope of employee **monitoring** and surveillance. Computerized systems track the time required to complete each task, and the data are collated and reported upward so that senior managers can use the information to manage the productivity of not only the low-level employees but also their supervisors and middle managers. In the modern organization, the motto on the chief executive's desk could well be "The information stops here," rather than "The buck stops here" (Rifkin, 1991).

SUMMARY & REVIEW

What Are Important Trends in Communications Media in the Workplace?

What is the historical relationship between communications media and organizational structure?
Innovations in communications media, from the telegraph to the telephone to the computer and modern integrated communications networks, have made it possible for organizations to continually increase the size and scope of their operations. Communications media are used to solve the problems of coordination across national and international boundaries and across time zones.

What are important components of modern corporate communications networks?
Organizations use PBXs, key systems, or Centrex service to save on their local telephone bills. For data communications, they use local area networks to move information within buildings or campuses. Wide area networks connect farflung business locations over specialized facilities, including leased lines, virtual private networks, T1 carriers, DDS lines, and VSAT networks. Large organizations maintain private networks that give them access to advanced services, such as teleconferencing, and that save them substantial portions of their telecommunications costs. Many also have their own in-house business video studios so that they can produce television programs for their employees and customers.

What are three basic types of teleconferencing?
Audio teleconferences can be implemented with the most rudimentary technology, such as a speakerphone. Large audio conferences require the use of special bridging equipment so that all participants can be heard clearly. Audiographic teleconferences add text or still graphics to the discussion, with the assistance of computer transmission, facsimile, or specialized graphics display devices, such as electronic blackboards or light-sensitive computer screens. Videoconferencing adds moving pictures to the conference. Some videoconferences match broadcast television quality, but most use more economical forms of video transmission, leaving a somewhat blurred or jerky picture.

What is the multimedia organization?
Many large organizations have elaborate audio and video production facilities, which are now undergoing a transformation to keep pace with new technology. Multimedia presentations—involving audio, text, computer graphics, and video—are found in a growing number of departments in large organizations. They are used extensively in training applications, where interactive multimedia presentations sometimes substitute for live instructors. Employee communications, customer sales presentations, and engineering departments are other areas where multimedia technology is likely to be found.

How do organizations save money by using specialized telecommunications services?
Centrex is a special telephone service that local telephone companies provide for large organizations that allows employees to make "free" calls to other employees at the same location and gives users the benefit of many of the same time- and money-saving features found on advanced PBX systems, without having to incur the up-front cost of buying a PBX. Organizations make use of leased lines, which they obtain for a flat monthly rate, to save money on usage-sensitive charges for calls between locations with high call volumes. 800 numbers are the "toll free" numbers that consumers use when they call to place orders for products they see advertised. The calls are charged to the company that receives them, but heavy volume discounts apply, and the 800 numbers save the companies the cost of having retail outlets in every city or town. Large organizations can also get bulk discounts on telephone services through the use of virtual private networks, while special digital lines provide them with cost-effective, high-capacity connections that can be used to transmit data between computers and teleconferencing units.

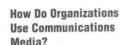

How Do Organizations Use Communications Media?

How are communications media managed?
Computers and data communications are usually the province of the MIS department under the authority of an organization's top financial officer. Telecommunications was usually treated as a corporate telephone utility, under the control of the head office administrator. More and more organizations are integrating the two functions and giving overall direction to a new breed of senior executive, the chief information officer.

What are some important communications media applications?
Organizations use communications media for three generic purposes: to run their businesses better, to get the edge on their competition, and to innovate with new products. Office automation and computer-integrated manufacturing are terms that describe the use of computerized systems to

run the office and the factory floor more efficiently. Automated teller machines and emerging electronic data interchange systems are examples of efforts to gain the competitive edge. On-line airline reservation systems and custom textbook publishing are examples of new product innovations made possible through advanced applications of communications media.

How have information technologies changed manufacturing?
Computer-integrated manufacturing is a term that describes the use of integrated information systems to improve the manufacturing process. With these systems, ordering information collected from the customer can be directly translated into product specifications, and automated design, manufacturing, and distribution systems can speed the delivery of the product to the customer while greatly expanding the ability to customize products for special user needs.

What Are the Broader Implications of Communications Media Use by Organizations?

Do communications media improve productivity?
Although the stated purpose of acquiring new communications media for the workplace is to increase productivity, or average worker output, this goal is often elusive. The pace of technological change is so rapid that the promised benefits are often not realized before the next computerization movement hits. There are also many hidden costs associated with communications media that mitigate against productivity gains.

Is there privacy in the information workplace?
Workers have limited rights to workplace privacy to begin with. The spread of information technologies further threatens workplace privacy by making it easy to inspect employee communications over E-mail systems and to precisely monitor work activity in automated systems.

How are communications media affecting the structure of work?
Communications media have triggered a radical transformation in the structure of organizations. Entire layers of middle management have been stripped away as more and more senior executives use communications media to coordinate

rank-and-file employees themselves, creating a flattened pyramid. Other corporations retain only a small core of permanent professional employees and then expand or contract a large "ring" of temporary employees as market conditions dictate. Yet other firms are becoming virtual corporations, in which a small group of managers subcontract virtually all corporate functions to outside suppliers or to a force of telecommuters.

REFERENCES

Briere, D. (1993). Communications services: An overview. In *Managing voice networks*. Delran, NJ: McGraw-Hill Information Services.

Bulkeley, W. (1992, November 2). Study finds hidden costs of computing. *The New York Times*.

Calem, R. E. (1992, November 8). Look, no wires! But the pages fly. *The New York Times*, p. F9.

Carroll, P. B. (1992, April 21). A restless loner on a custom bike: It's HAL on wheels. *The Wall Street Journal*, pp. A1, A5.

Crossman, E. R. F. W., & Laner, S. (1969). *The impact of technological change on manpower and skill demand: Case-study and policy implications*. Department of Industrial Engineering and Operations Research, University of California, Berkeley.

Czitrom, D. (1982). *Media and the American mind: From Morse to McLuhan*. Chapel Hill: University of North Carolina Press.

de Sola Pool, I. (1983). *Forecasting the telephone: A retrospective technology assessment of the telephone*. Norwood, NJ: Ablex.

Eckerson, W. (1993, April 15). Tektronix profits from CIM initiative. *Network World*, pp. 1, 11, 47.

Fagen, M. D. (Ed.). (1975). *A history of engineering and science in the Bell System: The early years 1875–1925*. Murray Hill, NJ: Bell Telephone Laboratories.

Fulk, J., Schmitz, J., & Steinfield, C. (1990). A social influence model of technology use. In J. Fulk & C. Steinfield (Eds.), *Organizations and communication technology*. Newbury Park, CA: Sage Publications.

IBM Corporation. (1994, March 14). The multimedia company. *Information Week*, pp. IBM1–6.

Keen, P. (1988). *Competing in time*. New York: Harper Business.

Kling, R. (1980). Social analyses of computing: Theoretical perspective in recent empirical research. *Computing Surveys*, *12*(1), 61–110.

McGovern, P. (1993, August 6). Plug in for productivity. *The New York Times*, p. F7.

Morrison, C. J., & Berndt, E. R. (1991). *Assessing the productivity of information technology equipment in U.S. manufacturing industries*. Washington, DC: National Bureau of Economic Research, Working Paper No. 3582.

Mulqueen, J. J. (1992, November 8). HBO tunes new net. *Communications Week*, pp. 1, 80.

Rice, R. E., & Bair, J. H. (1984). New organizational media and productivity. In R. E. Rice & Associates (Eds.), *The new media*. Beverly Hills, CA: Sage Publications.

Rifkin, G. (1991, December 8). Do employees have a right to electronic privacy? *The New York Times*, p. F8.

Rowe, S. (1991). *Business telecommunications*. New York: Macmillan.

Svenning, L., & Ruchinskas, J. (1984). Organizational teleconferencing. In R. E. Rice & Associates (Eds.), *The new media*. Beverly Hills, CA: Sage Publications.

Thompson, A. (1993, May 8). Forget doing lunch—Hollywood on E-mail. *The New York Times*, p. B3.

Toffler, A. (1990). *Powershift*. New York: Bantam Books.

Violino, B., & Stahl, S. (1993, February 8). No place like home. *Information Week*, pp. 22–29.

Zachary, P. (1991, November 11). Computer data overload limits productivity gains. *The Wall Street Journal*, p. B1.

Zuboff, S. (1984). *In the age of the smart machine*. New York: Basic Books.

Chapter 15

THE ADVERTISING INDUSTRY

C H A P T E R   P R E V I E W

s we saw in an earlier chapter, advertising is an important economic basis of conventional mass media. The advertising industry provides an important linkage between the secondary information sector—providers of products and services that are not directly information related— and the communications media that they use to promote the sale of their wares. This chapter addresses the evolution of advertising, not only in its current context as an economic powerhouse that uses persuasion to accomplish its goals, but also as an institution experiencing growing pains as it attempts to grapple with the technological advances occurring in the area of the mass media. We will also see how information technologies such as the telephone and the computer are being used to revive an old type of mediated sales technique, direct marketing, that seeks immediate responses from consumers.

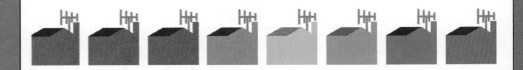

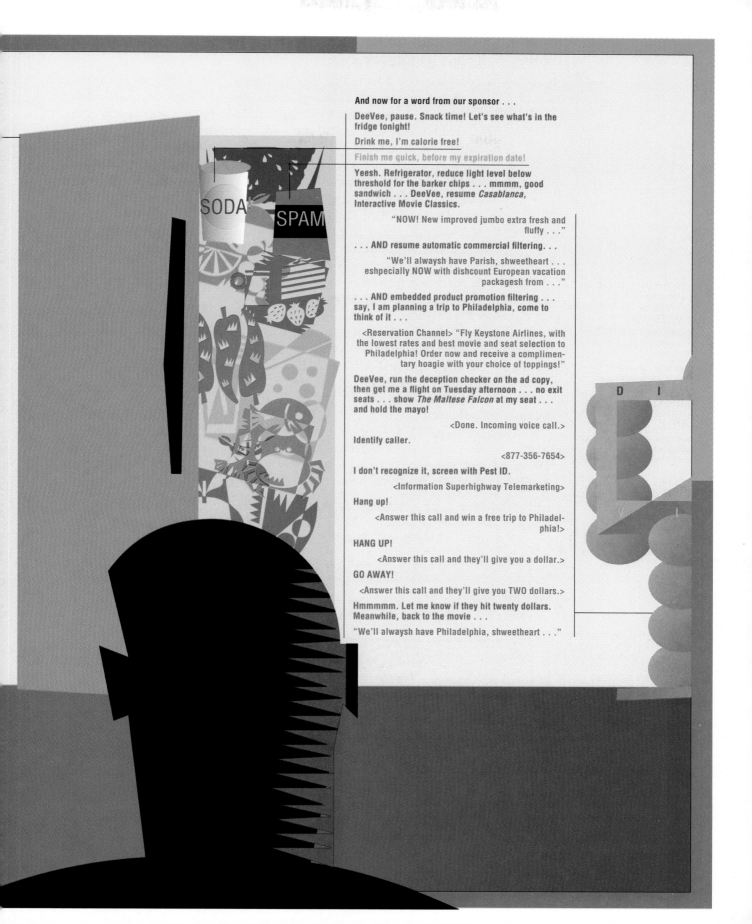

And now for a word from our sponsor . . .

DeeVee, pause. Snack time! Let's see what's in the fridge tonight!

Drink me, I'm calorie free!

Finish me quick, before my expiration date!

Yeesh. Refrigerator, reduce light level below threshold for the barker chips . . . mmmm, good sandwich . . . DeeVee, resume *Casablanca*, Interactive Movie Classics.

"NOW! New improved jumbo extra fresh and fluffy . . ."

. . . AND resume automatic commercial filtering . . .

"We'll alwaysh have Parish, shweetheart . . . eshpecially NOW with dishcount European vacation packagesh from . . ."

. . . AND embedded product promotion filtering . . . say, I am planning a trip to Philadelphia, come to think of it . . .

<Reservation Channel> "Fly Keystone Airlines, with the lowest rates and best movie and seat selection to Philadelphia! Order now and receive a complimentary hoagie with your choice of toppings!"

DeeVee, run the deception checker on the ad copy, then get me a flight on Tuesday afternoon . . . no exit seats . . . show *The Maltese Falcon* at my seat . . . and hold the mayo!

<Done. Incoming voice call.>

Identify caller.

<877-356-7654>

I don't recognize it, screen with Pest ID.

<Information Superhighway Telemarketing>

Hang up!

<Answer this call and win a free trip to Philadelphia!>

HANG UP!

<Answer this call and they'll give you a dollar.>

GO AWAY!

<Answer this call and they'll give you TWO dollars.>

Hmmmmm. Let me know if they hit twenty dollars. Meanwhile, back to the movie . . .

"We'll alwaysh have Philadelphia, shweetheart . . ."

A BRIEF HISTORY OF ADVERTISING

THIS CHAPTER WAS WRITTEN BY STEPHEN PHELPS, SOUTHERN ILLINOIS UNIVERSITY.

The origins of **advertising** were unearthed by archaeologists who found **signage** on the walls of ancient cities in Greece and Rome inviting travelers to stop by local establishments to sample their wares. These wares ranged from tangible goods, such as wine and food, to the less tangible variety such as overnight accommodations.

Another ancient form of advertising was the **town crier,** who told the citizenry about the "good deal" to be found "just around the corner." Unlike the signs, which contained only information regarding the merchant, the criers also informed the citizens of the news of the day. Because the crier, or his agent, was compensated for his assistance in getting the advertising message out in the context of the news, there are interesting parallels with the newspaper of today (Applegate, 1993; Roche, 1993; Schramm, 1988).

With the introduction of the printing press in Europe in 1455, businesses accessed ever-larger markets for their goods. With the printing press also came a new form of advertising, the **handbill.** The advantage of handbills over signs and town criers was that the message could be efficiently copied and distributed to many people in a relatively short time span and the content could be expanded to include as much description as thought necessary to effect the transaction. Flyers and hand-distributed leaflets are still much in use today, particularly by local retailers and candidates for political office.

Advertising is media selling audience access to those who wish to put their sales message before the audience.

Signage refers to signs and billboards used for advertising purposes.

Town criers announced the news of the day before the advent of the newspaper.

Handbills are printed advertisements distributed by hand.

Classified ads are brief newspaper advertisements, usually a single column wide.

Advertising in America

The earliest newspaper ads in America were in the form of **classified ads** published in the Boston *News-Letter* in 1704 (Sandage, Fryburger, & Rotzoll, 1989). An example of advertising from the colonial period is the following ad, which appeared in Benjamin Franklin's newspaper, the *Pennsylvania Gazette*:

> To Be SOLD   A Plantation containing 300 acres of good Land, 30 cleared, 10 or 12 Meadows and in good English Grass, a house and barn lying in Nantmel Township, upon French-Creek, about 30 miles from Philadelphia. Enquire of Simon Merideith.

Franklin also expanded the space devoted to advertising and was the first to apply creative writing skill to advertising copy. He was also the first to include illustrations alongside the copy.

In the early nineteenth century economic forces were at work that would eventually give

DURING THE EIGHTEENTH CENTURY, ADVERTISING INCREASED AS MORE PRODUCTS WERE MASS PRODUCED AND MORE PEOPLE BECAME POTENTIAL CONSUMERS. HERE IS AN AD FOR COOK'S VIRGINIA TOBACCO, WHICH APPEARED AROUND 1720.

the average citizen the ability not only to read about but also to purchase the "new," "revolutionary" products. Chief among these forces was the Industrial Revolution, which witnessed such innovations as steam power and mass production and developments in modes of travel that would eventually extend markets—and the advertising message—from "sea to shining sea."

Benjamin Day's *New York Sun* originated the concept of the mass circulation newspaper, or penny press, in

TABLE 15.1. ADVERTISING MILESTONES

Year	Event
1455	Gutenberg introduces printing press to Europe
1704	First classified ads
1833	Penny press originates
1849	Palmer first media representative
1865	Rowell's first ad agency
1875	Ayer starts free contract system
1905	Lasker originates salesmanship in print
1914	Federal Trade Commission established
1926	First commercial radio network
1948	First commercial TV network

1833 (see Table 15.1). From that point, we see advertising emerging both as a form of persuasive communication, bought and paid for by the advertiser, and as an economic engine capable of financially supporting the media enterprise. Another important influence in the penny press era was Robert Bonner, whose *New York Ledger* innovated with large display advertisements in the 1850s that broke the bounds of the newspaper column format. However, the continuing reluctance of many newspapers to carry display ads left the door open to the first magazine advertising in the 1860s.

The Rise of the Advertising Profession

In examining the history of advertising, it is also necessary to acknowledge the work done by its practitioners. These include **media representatives, advertisers,** and **advertising agencies.** The earliest advertising professionals were essentially media agents, who wholesaled advertising space on behalf of publishers. The best-known advertising agent from this era was Volney B. Palmer, who started in the advertising business in 1842 and coined the term "advertising agency" in 1849. Palmer represented some 1,300 newspapers and originated the **commission** system, under which publishers paid a fee on completion of a sale. Palmer also offered a wider range of services than other agents. He not only sold advertising space but also produced the ads, delivered them to the publishers, and verified their placement.

In 1865 George P. Rowell, considered to be the founder of the advertising agency as we know it today, began contracting with local newspapers for a set amount of space, then brokered the space to clients. This made Rowell something of an independent "middleperson" who had to cater both to publishers and to advertising clients. Rowell published an influential newspaper advertising directory, *Rowell's American Newspaper Dictionary,* in 1869 and advised his clients on which newspaper to select for their needs.

Another advertising pioneer of the nineteenth century was Francis Wayland Ayer, founder of the firm N. W. Ayer & Son (F. W. was the "son"). Ayer's most important contribution was to change the role of the advertising agency by making it the servant of the advertiser, rather than the publisher. He originated the **open contract plus commission** system in 1875, under which he contracted with the advertiser to place an advertising campaign in exchange for a commission on the advertising sales, but the fee was paid by the advertiser rather than by the publisher. Under this arrangement, Ayer also had the freedom to change publications, making it possible to negotiate the best possible advertising rates for the client. Ayer was an important voice in the evolution of advertising ethics, promising to always work in the best interest of the advertiser—and refusing ads for products that he considered harmful or deceptive.

On the client, or advertiser, side John Wanamaker stands out. A Philadelphia merchant, Wanamaker discovered that he could distinguish his store from other department stores in the city by setting a fixed price on his goods—which was not the practice of the day—and by offering a money-back guarantee. He also found that when he informed the public of these policies via newspaper ads his sales increased on the day following the announcement. This led him to increase the size and frequency of these messages and to employ someone on his staff to create the advertisements. This writer was John Powers, who in 1880 became one of the first professional **copywriters.**

Media representatives work on behalf of media outlets to help sell their advertising.

Advertisers are the organizations that commission advertising campaigns to help sell their products.

Advertising agencies are organizations that create and place commercial messages for advertisers.

A commission is a percentage fee paid to an agent as a reward for completing a transaction.

Open contract plus commission is a business arrangement between advertiser and advertising agency that allows the agency to collect a commission on the advertising it places.

Copywriters write the text of advertisements.

Wanamaker was also the first to publicly question the value of advertising. When asked to comment on the how he felt about the large sums of money he was expending on newspaper advertising, he responded, "I know that half of my advertising expenditure is wasted; the problem is, I don't know which half." This comment continues to haunt the advertising profession today—although it also benefits the many advertising research companies that have used it as their own sales pitch since the turn of the century.

The Origins of Modern Advertising: Hard Sell Versus Soft Sell

Another defining moment in advertising took place in 1905 when John E. Kennedy, a copywriter working in partnership with Albert Lasker at the Lord & Thomas advertising agency in New York, redefined advertising as "salesmanship in print." Before then, advertising copy was usually brief and hyperbolic, and most ads sought a mail-in response from the reader, a variety of advertising that we now call **direct marketing.** Kennedy, an experienced salesperson, felt that advertising copy should offer consumers reasons that they should go out and buy the product by presenting arguments much as a live salesperson would do. This "hard sell" approach to advertising as a mediated sales tool helped to focus the creative message and introduced the "reason why" philosophy to copy preparation (Wells, Burnett, & Moriarty, 1992), a philosophy which Lasker championed throughout a long and distinguished career that lasted until 1942.

The "soft sell" approach was pioneered at about the same time by Stanley Resor and his copywriter, Helen Lansdowne, at the J. Walter Thompson agency. This approach tended toward an emotional rather than a rational appeal. Resor also introduced the study of consumer psychology into the advertising practice and sought to make advertising an integral part of his clients' overall sales efforts.

Direct marketing is a form of advertising in which an immediate response is requested of the receiver.

DURING WORLD WAR I, ADVERTISING TURNED FROM PROMOTING CONSUMPTION OF GOODS TO GETTING CITIZENS INVOLVED IN THE WAR EFFORT BY BUYING WAR BONDS.

The early twentieth century was also a time when the business practices of many American industries—the advertising industry included—were coming under increasing public scrutiny. Advertisements for patent medicines that promised miracle cures "for all that ailed you" sowed doubt about the honesty of all advertising. This led to the establishment of the Federal Trade Commission in 1914 to regulate advertising practices and also to the creation of professional associations, notably the American Association of Advertising Agencies in 1917.

During World War I, advertising found its voice directed away from the materialistic needs of the average citizen and toward the good of the country as a whole. This campaign—in which Albert Lasker played an important role—included activities to build public sentiment for the war effort as well as appeals to the home front to curtail unnecessary consumption and to "Buy War Bonds" instead. The program also had a side benefit to the industry, in that it gave new evidence of the power of advertising to affect public opinion and placed what had previously been a somewhat suspect marketing tool into a more favorable light—and led to the use of advertising methods in future political campaigns.

The 1920s saw the rise of a powerful new mass medium for advertising: the radio. Radio came of age as an advertising

R E V I E W

1. Who was the founder of modern advertising?
2. Describe three steps in the evolution of the nature of the advertising agency.
3. How did Harold Lasker and Stanley Resor differ in their approach to advertising?

medium in 1926 when RCA purchased a chain of radio stations from AT&T, including WEAF in New York, and established the National Broadcasting Company. The creation of the radio network concept provided national advertisers with an unprecedented means to distribute their message to prospects across the nation simultaneously (Vivian, 1991). The new medium resembled the penny press in that it was designed to bring news, information, and entertainment to the public at large. To an even greater degree than the press, the radio medium depended on revenues received from advertisers.

The Great Depression of 1929–1938 saw advertising expenditures drop dramatically and led many critics to question the social value of advertising itself. It took another world conflict to revitalize advertising's image. The War Advertising Council of World War II organized advertising campaigns for government agencies, military recruiting, and war bonds once again. This time around, the organization continued beyond the war years and is known today as the Advertising Council. Its efforts are now focused on **public service campaigns,** such as "Take a Bite out of Crime" and "Just Say No to Drugs."

The years following World War II saw the explosive expansion of television as an advertising medium, especially following the establishment of national television networks in 1948. Television quickly grew to eclipse all other forms of mass communication as the medium of choice for national advertisers. At first, television advertisers followed the practice prevalent in the radio industry of sponsoring entire programs. However, by the 1970s program sponsorship had given way to the purchase of advertising time in 60- or 30-second (and, later, 15-second) increments. In the early 1980s, cable television emerged as yet another new advertising medium. By 1994 the once-dominant broadcast television networks had seen their piece of the evening television audience slip to under 60 percent.

TECHNOLOGY TRENDS

The technology of advertising has developed side by side with the technology of the mass media. We will not recount those developments here but instead will focus on the ways that information technologies are starting to transform conventional advertising forms.

Print media now use computer and telecommunications technologies extensively and may even claim to be the first mass medium to enter the computer age. Many of these developments are behind-the-scenes advances in the creation, production, and distribution of print publications using computer platforms that do not directly affect the advertising process. One meaningful contribution of the computer to print advertising is **selective binding.** This automated technique enables the publication to build unique versions of each issue for selected groups of readers. For example, *Newsweek* has some 160 separate editions targeted by geographic location and the characteristics of their recipients. This technique makes it possible for advertisers to reach their intended audiences more efficiently.

Another electronic trick of the trade is the ability to print information that has reference to an individual reader. Not only do you see your name printed in the text of a mailing from a marketer such as Publishers Clearinghouse, but you can also read it in the pages of a magazine in the text of an advertisement ("Hey, Ms. Jones, have we got a computer for YOU!").

Another interesting use of the computer is **database marketing,** which has typically been the domain of the direct marketers, who maintain lists of specific consumers. An

Public service campaigns are advertising campaigns intended to promote desirable social behavior or ideas rather than to sell specific products.

Selective binding allows publishers to create multiple versions of the same publication.

Database marketing is used when advertisers maintain computerized lists of consumers so they can contact them directly.

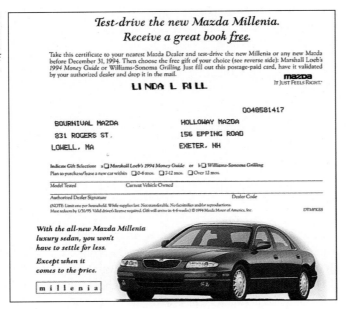

example is the Land's End Company, which sells clothing and related merchandise via catalog. The customer listing is so exact that when an order is phoned in the operator is able to "call up" the individual from the database and identify all the items he or she has ever purchased from the company.

This approach has also been explored for controversial products with mass appeal, such as tobacco and alcohol. Because of the restrictions that apply to their advertising use of the broadcast medium, some firms in these industries have turned to database marketing to maintain a dialogue with their customers. One example is R. J. Reynolds, which encourages buyers of Camel cigarettes to send in packages or coupons in exchange for branded apparel such as jackets, visors, and sweaters. Besides encouraging repeat purchasing and creating "walking billboards" for their product, the company is building a mailing list of its most loyal users against the day that further restrictions may be placed on cigarette advertising.

Advertising has also made its appearance on computer networks. Prodigy, a joint venture of IBM and Sears, inserts ads at the bottom of the "pages" of videotex that it transmits to its subscribers via telephone lines. Cable and television networks are also aligning themselves with consumer videotex services. CBS Television struck a deal with Prodigy to bring some aspects of its 1994 Winter Olympics coverage on-line (Mandese, 1994). Also in 1994, cable giant TCI and computer software behemoth Microsoft announced a new cable network aimed at personal computer owners, with a simultaneous videotex feed that allows users to order computer software and hardware that they see on the channel.

The oldest form of advertising, the outdoor sign, is also slated for a high-tech makeover. According to an article in *Mediaweek,* "At least two regional cable sports networks are considering the purchase of new technology that can impose signage onto stadium and arena walls and floors on live sports telecasts—in effect, creating signage where there is none" (Burgi, 1994, p. 1). Then the reality for the home viewer will be decidedly different from that experienced by the fan attending the sports venue, and a new advertising selling opportunity will be born. This innovation could also effectively "block out" advertisers that have ads posted in the venues but are not affiliated with the commercial broadcast of the event.

Will there be "billboards" on the information superhighway of tomorrow? There are few on the information superhighway of today, the Internet. The Internet's original purpose was education and research, not commerce, and the community of Internet users takes a dim view of advertising, indeed. Firms that try to publicize their wares on the net are quickly inundated with abusive electronic mail from purists who want to keep the Internet free of commercials.

However, as cable and telephone companies build their own advanced versions of the Internet, the siren call of advertising revenues will no doubt prove irresistible. Some in the advertising industry are gleefully anticipating the advent of interactive ads. Some of the possibilities include (see Arlen, 1993; Stefanae, 1994):

- *Impulse ads* that will let you buy products you see advertised—or even products that you see actors using in the "entertainment" portion of the program—at the touch of a button.

- *Personalized ads* that include the name and phone number of the retailer nearest you, TV commercials that address you personally by name, perhaps followed someday by ads that insert your voice and your face in the product demonstrations.

- *Ads on demand* that will let you review ads, browse electronic catalogs, or request additional product information—but just for the products you are interested in.

- *Instant coupons* delivered into your living room via a set-top printer.

- *Multimedia "junk mail"* with nearly irresistible pitches tailored to your personal tastes, made possible by monitoring and matching all of your transactions on the information superhighway.

These developments could technically spell the end of advertising—at least as we know it today and as practiced by today's advertising and mass media industries—since they are really direct marketing techniques rather than advertising in the currently accepted sense. A more sanguine view is that they are just a case of "back to the future," a return to the early twentieth century when most ads included a direct response component, and that the advertising industry will readily adapt to the new forms.

However, at least some of the new advertising technologies now on the horizon pose a direct threat to the livelihood of advertising agencies, media representatives, mass media, and all the other "middlepersons" that stand between the advertiser and the consumer. Interactive home shopping channels would give marketers a direct pipeline to the consumer that eliminates today's advertising agency and media representative middlepersons entirely. Home shopping could also evolve into a computer medium, in which consumers view digital catalogs stored on high-capacity computer storage media—or receive interactive "junk mail" sent to them on computer disk—in which case the broadcast media would also be left out of the picture.

Other advertisers are experimenting with kiosks—standalone videotex terminals that provide in-depth product information right at the point of sale. The "intelligent shopping cart" has made its appearance, complete with a computer display that directs the con-

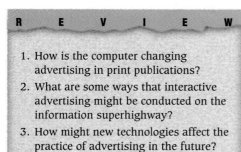

REVIEW

1. How is the computer changing advertising in print publications?
2. What are some ways that interactive advertising might be conducted on the information superhighway?
3. How might new technologies affect the practice of advertising in the future?

sumer to product locations and special promotions throughout the supermarket. Some grocery chains are installing television monitors over their checkout lanes that telecast news of in-store specials and messages from brand advertisers. And the cost of computer chips that can synthesize the human voice is dropping quickly, raising the specter of the "talking cereal box" shouting advertising slogans at us as we walk down the aisles of our local supermarket. At the same time, digital multimedia systems should make it possible to "zap" commercials and (electronic) print ads more effectively, to filter them out automatically, or even to jam the advertiser's computer network with abusive E-mail messages in retaliation for an especially intrusive commercial, perhaps neutralizing the power of conventional advertising forms.

INDUSTRY ORGANIZATION

Advertising media are the communications media used to deliver the advertising message.

Research organizations compile statistics about consumers and their media habits and evaluate advertising presentations.

Vehicles are the specific media programs or publications in which advertisements are carried.

Someone or some organization must identify the need for an advertising message—and foot the bill for the campaign that results. This initiator is the advertiser. Then the message must be created. Here the responsibility may either be retained by the advertiser or be subcontracted to an advertising agency. Next, the message must be placed in one or more of the **advertising media,** each of which has its own organizational form and structure. Weaving in and around this process are **research organizations** that help all concerned evaluate and measure the target group, the message content, and the media **vehicles** under consideration. As a means of understanding the structure of the industry, we will follow the development of an advertising campaign from the moment of its conception by an advertiser to its presentation to the public through the media (see Figure 15.1).

FIGURE 15.1
THE ADVERTISING PROCESS DEPENDS ON MONEY (GREEN ARROWS) AND INFORMATION (RED ARROWS) FLOWS BETWEEN ADVERTISERS, THEIR AGENCIES, THE MEDIA, AND CONSUMERS.

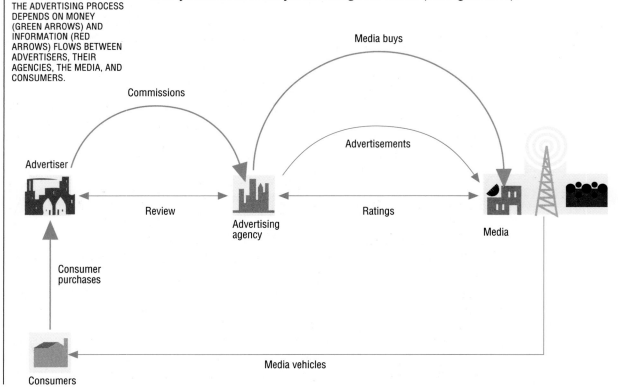

Advertisers

In 1991 *Advertising Age* reported that combined advertising expenditures placed by the top 476 advertising agencies on behalf of their clients was slightly less that $34 billion. Leading national packaged goods companies such as Proctor & Gamble and the major automotive companies lead the list of major advertisers.

In the past, it was not unusual to find the chief executive officer of a leading consumer goods firm involved in the advertising budget decision-making process. This is less common in today's age of product segmentation. To cope with the myriad duties involved in getting a brand to market, companies typically assign the advertising, budgeting, and executional responsibilities to a **marketing manager** in charge of a family of brands, who in turn delegates the advertising duties for a specific family of products to a **brand manager.** While the day-to-day advertising operation is normally handled by the brand manager, ultimate advertising budget approval is typically held at the marketing manager level or higher.

In a large packaged goods company, the advertising process begins when the marketing manager calls for a meeting with the **advertising manager** of the firm to discuss advertising goals, deadlines, and expectations for the coming year. The creation of the advertising message will generally not be performed by the organization itself, but instead delegated to an advertising agency. The advertising manager acts as liaison when a firm uses more than one advertising agency. The brand manager then calls for a meeting with the agency's representative to discuss the coming year's advertising needs.

In those instances where the advertiser is a local retailer, the process is much simpler. Typically the owner determines approximately how much to spend on advertising in the coming year, writes the ads herself or himself, and arranges to have the ad placed in local newspapers as needed. This is not to say, however, that the thought process that goes into the selection of the target for the ad or that the development of the message itself is any less important. It is just that the process takes place on a somewhat reduced scale when compared to a national program.

Inside the Advertising Agency

Most major advertisers do not want to plan and produce advertising campaigns themselves. Their business is to produce and sell a product, whether tennis shoes, soft drinks, or dog food. So, a variety of advertising agencies have grown up at local, national, and international levels to plan and produce ad campaigns for them.

The advertising agency working on an account normally assigns a single individual to work on the brand and see it through all phases of the advertising process. This individual, typically referred to as the **account executive,** in many respects is a mirror image of his or her brand manager counterpart on the client side. Both individuals typically come equipped with a business school frame of reference and tend to view the brand in the context of its overall position in the competitive marketplace. The difference is that the account executive's duties typically begin where the brand manager's end.

The account executive acts as the manager of the assignment as it progresses through the agency. She or he sees to it that the assignment is first translated into a set of working papers for the creative department. Although this step can go by various names—creative work plan, creative assignment, preliminary analysis—its function is the same: making sure that there is no misunderstanding about the expectations of the account. Key items in this document include the brand's position relative to the competition, the advertising objective,

Marketing managers are in charge of a family of products for an advertiser.

Brand managers are in charge of one specific product.

Advertising managers coordinate the advertiser's efforts across all of its products.

Account executives supervise advertising campaigns for clients inside the advertising agency.

a clear definition of the intended target group for the message, and any mandatory elements that the client might have established as integral parts of the advertisement.

This information is then shared with the **creative department.** Normally a **creative director** has overall responsibility for the brand and helps prepare a second document called a **copy platform.** This document is a critical link in the advertising creative process because it specifies what the creative department sees as the most important issues to be addressed in the advertising. The copy platform looks at the product and its benefits through the eyes of the consumer, instead of through the eyes of the advertiser. Because this step might result in the creative direction being somewhat off track from the brand manager's original conception, the document is presented to the client before proceeding any further.

Once the advertising agency has been given the green light to proceed, the assignment is turned over to a creative team, including a copywriter and an **art director** who identify the best possible words and pictures for addressing the issues identified in the copy platform. A variety of creative professions may be involved in the ad's execution: writers, artists, art directors, musicians, graphic designers, content or subject experts, and research people. What emerges after a period of creative incubation is not a single clear-cut solution to all of the client's problems, but rather several executions, one of which will be able to survive the critical **client review** process. Once an execution gets approval from the client, the assignment is given back to the creative department for final production.

Meanwhile, the agency's **media department** is hard at work selecting media to carry the client's advertising message, given the budget available. The account executive works constantly to keep all parties up-to-date on one another's progress. Once the creative and media recommendations are approved by the client, the **media buyer,** a specialist within the media department, initiates negotiations with media suppliers for purchase of specific media vehicles that will carry the advertising message. The initial media document and budget recommendation prepared by the media department contained only the type of media recommended and not specific newspapers, magazines, or broadcast programs. This is by design, as the media plan is normally prepared up to a year before the ad is produced.

Media

The main economic base of many American media is advertising. For commercial radio and television stations, it is by far their most important source of revenue, while newspapers and magazines depend on a combination of newsstand sales, subscriptions, and advertising. Advertisers select media depending on whom they want to reach, what kind of message or information they want to communicate, and the costs of various media.

In an advertising campaign, the media swing into action at the behest of the advertising agency's media buyer. On notification that the media plan has been approved by the client, the ad agency's media buyer contacts the appropriate **media representative** firm to find out the current costs and availability of media vehicles under consideration. The media representative identifies current **inventory** that meets the buyer's general criteria. For television, this criterion is usually in the form of the number of members in the target group that the vehicle can deliver at the time of day in which the buyer wishes to advertise. The "media rep" counsels with station salespeople to determine what price will be charged for commercial time in the identified programs. Finally, a package of programs is delivered by the rep to the buyer at the agency.

The buyer examines the list of programs, their prices, and the audience delivery estimates. Advertisers try to reach the largest number of people in the target audience at the

---

Creative departments produce the copy and artwork that go into advertisements.

Creative directors coordinate the activities of the creative department on behalf of a specific product.

The copy platform describes the creative issues to be addressed in advertising from the perspective of the consumer.

Art directors coordinate the graphic artists and video and film producers who make the visual elements of an ad.

Client review is the process of obtaining approval from the advertiser for the advertising campaign.

The media department selects the media that will be used to carry an ad.

Media buyers negotiate on behalf of the advertiser and the agency to buy advertising space from the mass media.

Media representatives are intermediaries between advertising agencies and media outlets.

Inventory is the stock of unsold advertising space that is still available.

TABLE 15.2. STRENGTHS AND WEAKNESSES OF ADVERTISING MEDIA

Medium	Strengths	Weaknesses
Newspapers	Intense coverage	Short life
	Flexibility	Hasty reading
	Prestige	Moderate to poor reproduction
	Dealer or advertiser coordination	
Magazines	Market selectivity	Inflexible area coverage/time
	Long life	Inflexible to copy changes
	High reproduction quality	Low overall market penetration
	Prestige	Wide distribution
	Extra services	
Television	Mass coverage	Fleeting message
	High impact	Commercial wearout
	Repetition	Lack of selectivity
	Prestige	High cost
	Flexibility	
Radio	Audience selectivity	Fragmentation
	Immediacy	Transient quality of listenership
	Flexibility	Limited sensory input
	Mobility	

Source: Adapted from Lavine & Wackman (1987).

lowest possible price. The costs of various media depend on several factors: the size of the audience, the composition of the audience (age, wealth, education, and so on), and the prestige of the medium. In general, media with larger audiences can charge more for accepting and carrying advertisements. However, a smaller, more specifically focused audience can sometimes be even more valuable to an advertiser than a larger, more heterogeneous one. Comparisons between vehicles are made on a **cost per thousand (CPM)** basis—that is, on the basis of the cost for reaching a thousand members of the target audience for the ad. This efficiency comparison is determined by dividing the cost of each program by the audience it delivers, in thousands. While the general goal is to try to reach the largest number of the target audience for the lowest dollar investment (Sissors & Bumba, 1993), many other factors may be considered, including the inherent characteristics of different media. Table 15.2 lists some of the strengths and weaknesses of various advertising media.

> **Cost per thousand (CPM)** is a way of comparing advertising costs in terms of how much it costs to reach 1,000 members of the target audience for an ad.

The nature of the target audience also affects media selection. Often media advertisers want to reach a broad **general audience.** Some advertisers want to sell products, such as soap or soft drinks, that might interest virtually everyone in a mass audience. Other advertisers might use a general audience medium if it has a high impact on a particular group they want to reach. For example, while a very broad audience watches prime-time network television, ads are often placed there for products aimed primarily at older people, such as denture adhesive cream. Television may reach a larger group of older people than any other medium, so the added cost may be worth it. Other advertisers want to reach a narrower **audience segment.** An advertiser that wants to sell athletic shoes to teenagers will pick just the television shows and radio stations that appeal selectively to teenagers.

> **General audience** means that the audience is made up of a large group of people from all walks of life.
>
> **Audience segment** is a subgroup of consumers with specialized tastes and media habits.

Advertisers also take into account the nature of the media and the kinds of ads they can carry. A television ad with the style of a music video may be important in capturing the interest of young men to tell them about a new athletic shoe. Television carries a certain kind of punch that just sound on a radio station, or a still image in a magazine, may not be able to achieve. The advertiser might decide to run a few television commercials to capture attention, then remind people of the product with radio ads, billboards, magazine ads, and so on. Usually an advertiser will try to mix media to make sure that everyone in the target group gets their pitch in one form or another, several times. For sports shoes, that mix might include ads on network television shows popular with young people, ads on MTV to catch those who do not watch much network television, ads on FM stations aimed at young men (which may be different from stations targeting young women), and ads in magazines about team sports, music, outdoor activities, cars, and other pursuits of interest to young men.

Following this analysis, the buyer recontacts the media representatives and the negotiating process begins in earnest. At its conclusion, the media buyer informs the client about the buys via the media planner or account executive, notifies the agency's accounting department to prepare the necessary billing documents, and contacts the execution arm of the creative department (sometimes called the **traffic department**) to deliver the finished ads to the proper media organization at the appropriate time.

Research

An integral part of the entire advertising process is research. Those involved with **marketing research** collect and analyze data about product sales and factors that affect the opinions that consumers have about products. Market researchers often work directly with the advertisers.

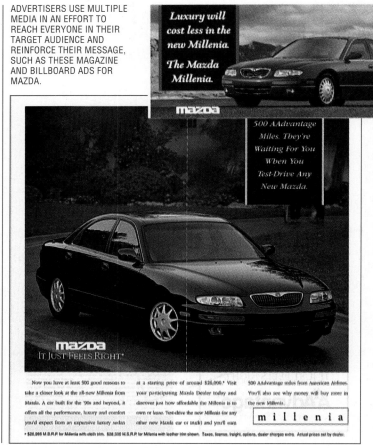

ADVERTISERS USE MULTIPLE MEDIA IN AN EFFORT TO REACH EVERYONE IN THEIR TARGET AUDIENCE AND REINFORCE THEIR MESSAGE, SUCH AS THESE MAGAZINE AND BILLBOARD ADS FOR MAZDA.

Traffic department is the part of an advertising agency that coordinates the delivery of the finished advertising message to the media.

Marketing research compiles data about sales and consumer attitudes, usually for the advertiser.

Media research compiles data about media consumption for the advertising industry.

Media research experts work for the media and the media departments of the advertising agencies to give them information about patterns of exposure to the mass media. Media research encompasses:

- Target audience delivery information for radio and television broadcasts
- Circulation figures for magazines and newspapers
- Profiles of the users of consumer products
- Media usage habits
- Qualitative studies that gauge audience reactions to specific media vehicles
- Reports on annual advertising expenditures levels of the leading national brands
- Copy tests that evaluate the effectiveness of ads that are under development

Examples of research companies and the audience information they provide are shown in Table 15.3.

TABLE 15.3. RESEARCH SERVICES AND THE AUDIENCE DATA THEY PROVIDE

Medium	Company	Audience Report Content
National television	A. C. Nielsen	Audience delivery (ratings) for programs on the national TV networks
Local television	A. C. Nielsen	Audience delivery (ratings) for programs broadcast by local TV stations
National radio	RADAR	Audience delivery (ratings) for network programs by local radio stations
Local radio	Arbitron	Audience delivery (ratings) for stations broadcasting in the local market
Newspapers	Audit Bureau of Circulation	The number of newspaper copies sold
Magazines	Simmons/MRI Research	Audience delivery (ratings) for the top magazines in the U.S.

Television households are homes with working TV sets.

Households using television (HUTs) are homes that have their TVs turned on at a given time.

Ratings are the percentages of TV households watching particular programs.

Shares are the percentages of HUTs watching particular programs.

Audimeters are automatic devices for measuring household television viewing.

People meters are electronic devices that register individual television viewing.

Each medium has its own audience measurement "language," but television's is perhaps the most widely used—and the most arcane. In this lexicon, a **television household** is a home with a (working) television set. There are about 90 million of these households in the United States. A **HUT** is a **household using television,** an estimate of all of the households in the United States that are using television during a particular time period. A **rating** is the percentage of all television households tuned in to a particular program. Each rating point is one percentage point, representing about 900,000 households. A **share** is the percent of HUTs watching a program; thus, it is based only on the number of homes actually watching television. It is this measure that is of greatest interest to advertisers (see Figure 15.2).

The A. C. Nielsen Company compiles ratings and share data by distributing diaries to random samples of homes, in which family members record all the programs they watch. National TV ratings are derived from **audimeters,** electronic devices attached to the television that record each move of the television dial. **People meters** are electronic devices that record *who* is watching, as well as what is being watched, by getting family members

FIGURE 15.2
RATINGS ARE COMPUTED BY DIVIDING THE NUMBER OF HOMES WATCHING A SHOW BY THE TOTAL NUMBER OF HOUSEHOLDS. SHARES ARE COMPUTED BY DIVIDING BY THE NUMBER OF HOUSE- HOLDS USING TV AT A PARTICULAR TIME.

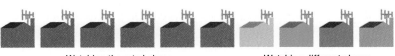

Watching the rated show   Watching different shows   **10 HUTs**

Households using television (HUTs)

+

10 not using

Households not using television

= 20 TV households (TVHH)

$$\text{Rating} = \frac{\text{Number watching rated show}}{\text{TVHH}} = \frac{6}{20} = 30\%$$

$$\text{Share} = \frac{\text{Number watching rated show}}{\text{HUTs}} = \frac{6}{10} = 60\%$$

to push buttons periodically to indicate who is in the room. The search is now on for "passive" people meter techniques that will record individual viewing without requiring viewers to touch buttons—such as by sensing their body heat or by "recognizing" their faces with digital pattern recognition devices. Advanced systems may even tell advertisers when viewers are paying attention to the TV set, are smiling at the program (or nodding off to sleep), or are attending to specific commercial segments.

Audience measurement studies are sufficient to tell us whether the advertising message is being exposed to a target group and roughly what numbers are involved, but it does not provide insights into how or why the advertising is able to communicate successfully. For this purpose, we need a second dimension of audience research, one that enables the advertiser to talk directly with the target group. Because this research focuses on individuals and what "drives" them, it is often referred to as **motivational research.** Examples of this form of audience research include focus groups and mall intercepts.

Focus groups are small groups of eight to twelve people who fit the profile of the target audience. A moderator leads the group through a series of open-ended questions relating to one or more advertising issues of interest. The purpose of the session is to derive insights into how the advertising campaign may be ultimately received by the target group.

Mall intercepts involve contact with members of the target group at shopping malls. This approach, while useful for gauging initial reaction to or awareness of an advertising campaign, provides less insight than the focus-group technique. However, the results from mall intercepts can be mathematically analyzed, whereas the focus-group discussion is less structured and produces results that are more qualitative than quantitative. Mall intercepts are also a useful means for letting consumers sample products and obtaining their reactions to products.

Copy testing is another form of advertising-related research, the purpose of which is to assess the effectiveness of advertisements while they are still under development. For example, test ads might be inserted in television programs in selected markets, and researchers might contact respondents by phone to determine if they can still recall seeing the ad on the day after it appeared. More sophisticated methods allow direct comparisons of ads by doing "split runs" of magazines in which alternate versions of the same ad are sent to different households. Cable television systems can also be used in this way to provide comparisons of alternate treatments for television commercials.

Direct Marketing

Although direct marketing was an aspect of most ads in the last century, more recently it has become a discipline unto itself, more closely linked with the practice of interpersonal salesmanship than with advertising. More and more, direct marketing techniques and advertising techniques are beginning to converge, especially as the advertising industry turns to new, more interactive forms. Many advertising agencies now have direct marketing departments, whose activities are rapidly growing in importance.

Direct marketing differs from advertising in that it concentrates the marketer's resources on the most likely prospects rather than sending a message to a wide audience in the hopes that at least some of the prospects will receive it (see Nash, 1982, 1992). Direct marketing also has a quality of immediacy, in that recipients of the message are asked to take immediate action, such as placing an order over the phone or returning a printed order blank by mail. Although direct marketing messages do not have the same "glitz" as mass media

Motivational research examines the reasons that people consume the products and media they do, rather than how much they consume.

Focus groups are small-group interviews intended to explore consumer reactions in depth.

Mall intercepts are consumer interviews conducted in shopping centers.

Copy testing evaluates the effectiveness of advertisements.

advertising, they do have two major advantages over other forms of advertising: (1) They can be customized to individual consumers, using personal forms of address and bits of personal information gleaned from computer databases, and (2) their effectiveness can be measured so that they can be continually fine-tuned.

Direct marketing encompasses a wide variety of communications media and marketing needs. It has long been popular with book publishers, record clubs, and magazines, but now it is coming into favor with a wide range of advertisers. **Direct mail** ("junk mail") solicitations, **catalog** sales, and **telemarketing** are perhaps the most obvious forms of direct marketing activities. However, anyone who as ever called an 800 number to order the "greatest hits of the sixties," dialed a 900 number, returned a magazine subscription form, entered a magazine contest or sweepstakes, sent in a donation to a TV telethon, or redeemed a coupon clipped from the newspaper has also responded to a direct marketing appeal. **Infomercials** are a new form of broadcast direct marketing. These are program-length, made-for-television presentations whose sole purpose is selling the featured product or service. The infomercial concept has been taken to its logical conclusion in the form of entire cable networks devoted to hawking products through 800 numbers—the **home shopping channels.**

The direct marketing industry relies on many of the same media and creative professions that advertising does but has some unique disciplines of its own as well. For example, there are firms that specialize in compiling and matching computerized telephone and mailing lists,

Direct mail refers to direct targeting of customers with mailed catalogs, advertising, or other materials.

Catalogs are compilations of advertisements mailed to the consumer in booklet form.

Telemarketing is using the telephone in direct marketing to solicit or receive sales responses.

Infomercials are program-length direct response commercials.

Home shopping channels are cable or broadcast television channels that carry nothing but direct response advertisements.

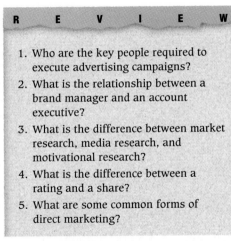

R E V I E W

1. Who are the key people required to execute advertising campaigns?
2. What is the relationship between a brand manager and an account executive?
3. What is the difference between market research, media research, and motivational research?
4. What is the difference between a rating and a share?
5. What are some common forms of direct marketing?

others that specialize in assembling direct-mail packages, others that just make telemarketing phone calls, others that only receive 800-number calls, and others still that just open return mail and complete (or "fulfill") the orders.

Research also takes on a distinctive character in direct marketing campaigns. Direct marketers are able to directly gauge the results of their advertising appeal, as well as the appropriateness of the media chosen, by counting the dollars in the cash register at the end of the day. This direct cause-effect measure allows the advertiser to try out various approaches and see immediately their results without resorting to the various media research services.

GENRES, FORMS, AND AUDIENCES

The genres of advertising are the various ways in which advertising can be used to attempt to affect the action taken by the target group:

- *Give new information.* This includes announcements by advertisers regarding new products or product improvements, sweepstakes or contest announcements, and other items of a newsworthy nature about the product or service. The government-funded advertising campaign on the use of condoms to help prevent the spread of the AIDS virus is also an example of this genre.

- *Reinforce a current practice.* This type of message is used primarily by advertisers that currently enjoy a dominant position in a product category and need to make consumers less sensitive to competitive appeals. This is one of the most efficient uses of advertising, as it addresses the "heavy user" of the product who does not need to be convinced of its merits. In this case, the advertiser tries to increase **brand loyalty,** the propensity to make a repeat purchase of a product. A popular example of this type of ad is Coca-Cola's animated polar bears.

- *Change a predisposition.* The third genre of advertising is the most visible, in the form of the often-annoying ads that take on a competing product head-to-head. It is also the most difficult genre to execute successfully because it needs to both address and change the purchase habits of the competitor's regular users—which the competitor answers with its own campaign. Advertisers are often satisfied when they succeed in raising **brand awareness,** or the consumer's ability to identify the product. An example is a Red Roof Inns campaign in which business travelers who frequent mid-priced motels are invited to stay at Red Roof Inns and save the money they would have spent on amenities that they don't really want, such as mints on the pillow, a postage stamp–sized swimming pool, and a dingy bar.

Brand loyalty is the consumer's propensity to make repeat purchases of a specific brand of product.

Brand awareness is the consumer's ability to recall the name of a specific brand of product.

TABLE 15.4. MASLOW'S NEEDS HIERARCHY APPLIED TO ADVERTISING

Need	Product	Appeal/Visual
Hunger	Seafood restaurant	Shrimp steaming on a plate
Safety	Smoke detector	Home in ashes, burned toys
Love	Roses	Couple embracing
Prestige	Gold watch	Pro golfer wearing watch
Self-actualization	Golf clubs	"Duffer" receiving congratulations from peers

The hierarchy of needs is a way to categorize the "pecking order" among human needs.

Creative approach refers to the type of appeal that a copywriter incorporates into an ad.

Positioning is the process of comparing a brand with competing products.

Brand imagery is an advertising approach that seeks to give a product a personality of its own.

A unique selling proposition is a unique attribute that a product has that its competitors do not.

Target audience is a narrow, specifically defined audience that an advertiser or communication medium wants to reach.

With these uses of advertising in mind, the challenge to the copywriter is to select an appeal that will be sufficiently engaging to elicit the desired response from the designated target group. One accepted method for categorizing appeals is a conceptual tool borrowed from psychology: Abraham Maslow's **hierarchy of needs.** The essence of the Maslow hierarchy is that individuals must satisfy lower-order needs, beginning with their most basic survival needs, before they are in a position to attend to needs of a higher order, such as prestige. Table 5.4 provides an illustration of how these needs would correspond to advertising appeals. The copywriter selects a **creative approach** that is unique to the product and that accomplishes one or more of the advertising tasks outlined earlier. An interesting example—which demonstrates that this approach is anything but new—is the accompanying ad for Philco Batteries. It is easy to tell from the picture of the car stalled on the train tracks, along with the headline "Stop! Look! Think!" that unless the current safety needs of the people in the car are taken care of, there is no need to be concerned about much else. In addition, in the body copy we are told that "Thousands upon thousands of car owners today—in record breaking numbers—are replacing their ordinary batteries with dependable long-life super-powered Philco Batteries." This ad uses a safety appeal to change the predisposition of the target group to use the product. It is also an example of the "hard sell" school of advertising championed by Albert Lasker.

THIS CLASSIC AD USES A "HARD SELL" APPROACH TO APPEAL TO BASIC SURVIVAL NEEDS.

An alternative approach to setting the creative strategy is one of **positioning** the product relative to the competition. Rather than identifying an appeal based on the consumer's needs or wants, the copywriter focuses on the makeup of the brand, with emphasis on the advantages the brand has over its chief competitor.

When the focus is on the brand to the extent that it takes on a personality of its own, it has developed **brand imagery.** Creative approaches that use this device often have a continuing spokesperson for the product, such as the Maytag Repairman, or an animated figure, such as Tony the Tiger.

Another approach is to identify a single physical characteristic the brand enjoys that its competitor does not. This is often referred to as a **unique selling proposition.** The tail fins that sprouted from the hind quarters of American automobiles in the late 1950s are an example.

Types of Audiences

Advertisers tend to think of audiences in terms of group characteristics so they can be divided into relatively homogeneous segments, or **target audiences** that are alike in their consumer and media use characteristics. Defining the audience for an advertising message typically starts with a profile of those individuals who would be the most likely prospects for purchase of the product. This profile can be developed from studying

current users of the product or by examining users of competitive products in the category. There are several different approaches to segmentation.

Usage-based segmentation divides consumers according to their amount of consumption. Usage information can be gleaned from internal sales records or from research services. A leading supplier of product usage information is Simmons Research Services, which maintains a database of 20,000 consumers who report on their product consumption habits for a wide array of goods and services. From these sources the advertiser can determine the relative size of heavy, medium, and light user groups, and their geographic distributions. Long-distance telephone ads that emphasize volume discounts for heavy telephone users are an example of advertising based on this approach.

Demographic segmentation categorizes people on the basis of the personal and household characteristics that the U.S. Census tabulates, such as age, sex, ethnicity, and income. This form of segmentation is especially popular, since most of the market research and audience research reports used in the advertising industry are indexed by these categories. For most advertisers of consumer products, women between the ages of eighteen and forty-nine are the primary target group, since they make the most purchases in supermarkets and department stores.

Lifestyle segmentation groups audiences according to their attitudes, interests, and opinions. For example, two consumers may have identical demographic characteristics—say, male, age 42, living in an urban area, with a professional occupation. However, based on their attitudes, interests, and opinions, one might be categorized as a "yuppie" and the other as an "aging hippie." The former probably reads *GQ* and would be an ideal target for an ad for a new BMW, while the latter reads *High Times* and might only consider buying a used Volvo.

Geodemographic clustering, the latest wrinkle on demographic segmentation, is made possible by applying high-powered statistical analyses to census data so that advertisers can characterize people by the areas (usually postal zip codes or census tracts) that they live in (Weiss, 1988). For example, much of Michigan falls into a "shotguns and pickups" cluster, while some of the wealthy suburbs around its major cities fall into the "blueblood estates" category. This approach is beloved by direct marketers, since they can use it to target their mailings and phone calls. If our "aging hippie" lived in shotguns and pickups territory, we might send him ads for a country music compact disc club, but one living in a blueblood estate would get an ad for New Age Celtic music.

Usage-based segmentation divides consumers according to their amount of consumption.

Demographic segmentation is based on social or personal characteristics such as age, sex, education, or income.

Lifestyle segmentation categorizes people on the basis of their attitudes, interests, and opinions.

Geodemographic clustering categorizes consumers based on the demographic characteristics common to the area in which they live.

R E V I E W

1. What are three basic genres of advertising?
2. What is the relationship between brand loyalty and brand awareness?
3. What are four ways of segmenting advertising audiences?
4. If we design a commercial to appeal to heavy consumers of beer, what type of segmentation are we using?

Linking the Medium to the Audience: The Media Evaluation Model

The audience for advertising is thus a predesignated target group. While this process may seem simple enough, one problem has persisted: that of "linking" the target group to the media vehicle itself (see Figure 15.3). That is, not all media channels are universally available to all members of a target audience, not all members are exposed to any particular vehicle carried on the channel, and not all of them see the ads in the vehicle, recall those ads, or are affected by them.

ISSUES IN THE ADVERTISING INDUSTRY

Issues of concern when it comes to advertising include the use of deception, intrusiveness, and matters of taste.

Deceptive Advertising

Most advertisers go to great lengths to avoid deceptive advertising in order to preserve their good name and reputation. However, blunders can happen, particularly when the advertising message is prepared by a third party—the advertising agency.

Just such a problem occurred in 1990 when the Volvo Company was found to have "rigged" a commercial that apparently demonstrated Volvo's ability to stand up to the weight of a heavy truck placed on its roof. Other vehicles were not so fortunate and suffered severe damage. However, the production company hired to film the spot had reinforced the Volvo, while weakening the other vehicles. When this fact came to light, Volvo was forced to pay a fine, but more important, the company suffered immeasurable damage to its credibility.

This was a fairly clear-cut example of what can happen when advertising crosses the line.

FIGURE 15.3
ADS HAVE TO CLEAR THE "BARRIERS" OF DISTRIBUTION, EXPOSURE, AND PERCEPTION BEFORE THEY "COMMUNICATE" WITH THE AUDIENCE. ONLY THEN DO THEY HAVE A CHANCE OF PROVOKING A RESPONSE.

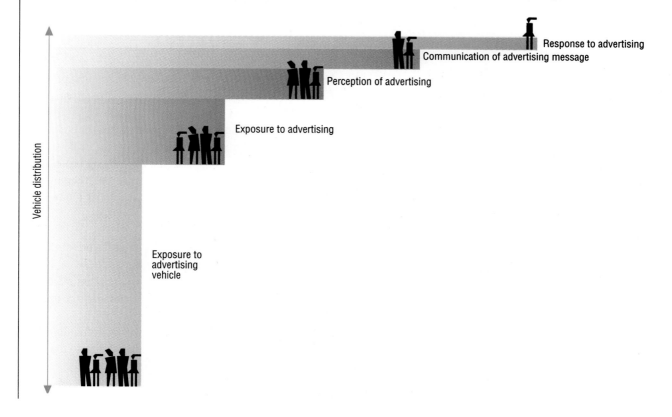

Response to advertising
Communication of advertising message
Perception of advertising
Exposure to advertising
Exposure to advertising vehicle
Vehicle distribution

Many products are unable to clearly differentiate themselves from the competition and are left with the challenge of "creatively" establishing a point of difference in the mind of the consumer, a challenge that often invites exaggeration. What constitutes acceptable creative appeals is a question that the advertiser has to grapple with, oftentimes aided by a staff of attorneys.

In question is the extent to which advertising is granted protection under the First Amendment, which guarantees freedom of speech and press in the United States. Specifically, does the right to a free press extend automatically to those utilizing the press to carry their commercial messages in the same way that it encompasses the editorial content?

The answer has been a fairly consistent "No." In the 1942 case of *Valentine* vs. *Christensen* it was ruled that the First Amendment does not protect purely commercial speech (in the form of advertising) because this particular form of communication does not contribute to decision making in a democracy—the original object of First Amendment protection. When the tobacco industry challenged a government ruling prohibiting cigarette ads in broadcast media, the Supreme Court found that the intention of the framers of the Bill of Rights was to protect the free speech of the average citizen and did not automatically extend to all commercial enterprises.

Intrusiveness

Many direct marketers rely on mail and the telephone, communications media that are by their very nature more intrusive than the mass media. While we can ignore direct-mail solicitors by consigning their missives to the trash, it is difficult indeed to avoid that dinnertime phone call.

The annoying nature of these intrusions may cast a negative pall over the entire advertising industry. It also puts consumers into the habit of "turning off" the efforts of advertisers. These practices also raise consumer skepticism regarding the content of advertising messages. Although many state legislatures have made it a requirement that direct marketing firms divulge the "catch" in their offers, the important details are often found only in the fine print.

Infomercials, which resemble broadcast programming (often a newscast or talk show), also pose a problem. If the viewer is unable to distinguish between editorial and commercial messages, the commercial may be accorded a higher degree of credibility and therefore be accepted as the unquestioned truth. The danger to the advertising profession is that the advertisers using this approach are in a sense "mortgaging" their credibility in the long run in order to make a quick dollar today.

> **R E V I E W**
>
> 1. What do we mean by deceptive advertising?
> 2. How are advertising messages covered under the First Amendment regarding freedom of speech?
> 3. What are some ethical concerns about direct marketing campaigns?

Offensiveness

Controversy also surrounds advertising for products that are designed for private use by consumers, such as feminine hygiene products, adult diapers, denture adhesives, hemorrhoid treatments, and condoms. The problem is that these messages are often exposed to audiences for whom they were not intended, some of whom may be offended by the message content.

This quandary of getting the message out to the proper group without offending other groups is encapsulated by the federal government's recent campaign to educate the public on the use of condoms to prevent the spread of AIDS. While the vast majority of the populace no doubt appreciate the threat that AIDS presents to our society, there are those who believe that the ads should be focused only on those groups with the greatest risk of contracting the disease. The major television networks have also been reluctant to air ads for condoms.

SUMMARY & REVIEW

How Did the Advertising Industry Develop?

What are the early origins of advertising?
Advertising dates back to the shop signs and town criers of ancient times. The advent of mass circulation newspapers in nineteenth-century America gave advertising its initial boost. At first, advertising professionals worked on behalf of the media rather than the advertiser. Volney B. Palmer was the most influential advertising professional of that era. George P. Rowell, the founder of modern advertising, was the first to represent the interests of the advertiser as well as the publisher. The evolution of the modern advertising agency was completed by F. W. Ayer, who made the agency the servant of the advertiser rather than the publisher.

What influenced the development of advertising in the twentieth century?
In the early twentieth century advertising turned away from the direct marketing approach, which demanded an immediate response from the receiver. Two new approaches emerged. The hard sell approach, championed by Harold Lasker, sought to convince consumers to buy products much as a salesperson would. The soft sell, pioneered by Stanley Resor, emphasized the emotional appeal of the product. Advertising was pressed into service during times of war and economic crises, inspiring advertising campaigns on even grander scales. Radio and television emerged as important new advertising forms.

Millenia

How Are New Technologies Changing the Practice of Advertising?

What has been the impact of the computer on advertising?
Computerized selective binding now makes it possible to create dozens of special editions of a print publication, each with its own specially tailored editorial content and advertising layouts. The same technology makes it possible to print personal messages to individual readers in the advertising copy. Consumer videotex services also afford new advertising availabilities.

What might interactive advertising be like?
The advent of the information superhighway could make it possible to order goods and services directly from our home at the touch of a button. We will also be able to call up advertisements on demand, and ads will be much more personalized to our unique identities and interests. Other forms of advertising might radically change the nature of the advertising industry, placing more reliance on direct marketing techniques and new channels that are not part of existing mass media systems.

How Are Advertising Campaigns Conducted?

How are advertising campaigns initiated?
Marketing managers and brand managers who work for major advertisers budget and plan advertising strategies that will help them introduce new products or increase the sales of existing products. They work with an in-house advertising manager to coordinate their companies' overall advertising effort. Once a campaign is planned, they contact one or more advertising agencies to execute the plan.

How are campaigns organized inside an advertising agency?
The account executive is the liaison between the advertiser and the advertising agency staff. The account executive coordinates the activities

of the creative department, which creates the ads, and the media department, which determines where the ads will be placed. The creative director, copywriters, and art directors take charge of the execution of the ads. The agency's media buyer negotiates with the media.

How do advertising agencies work with the media?
The media buyer may negotiate directly with media outlets or may work through an intermediary media representative firm. Alternative advertising placements are evaluated by comparing them on a cost per thousand basis, although other factors relating to the qualitative nature of the medium and a specific advertising vehicle may also be considered. The agency's traffic department takes charge of delivering the finished advertisements to the media.

What is the role of research in the advertising process?
Advertisers rely on market research to help them identify advertising and new product opportunities. Media researchers provide advertising agencies and media organizations with data about the number of people who are exposed to various media vehicles and the characteristics of those audiences. Motivational researchers provide additional insight into consumer behavior with the help of focus groups and mall intercept techniques.

How are broadcast audiences measured for advertising purposes?
Media research companies provide two basic types of statistical measures that advertisers use to compare the programs, or vehicles, in which their ads are carried. Using television as the example, a rating indicates the percentage of all homes with televisions tuned to a particular program. A share indicates the percentage of all homes actually using television at a given time that are tuned into the program. Ratings and shares may further be classified according to demographic characteristics such as age and sex. Advertisers evaluate advertising on the basis of the cost of reaching a thousand members of the target audience (CPM).

How Are Ads and Audiences Categorized?

What are the different types of advertising?
Advertising is generally designed to achieve one of three basic goals: to provide new information (brand awareness), to reinforce a current

practice (brand loyalty), or to change an existing predisposition. Advertising genres are further categorized according to the type of need they appeal to, using a hierarchy of needs. In this hierarchy, basic survival needs must be satisfied first before higher-level needs for self-actualization can be realized.

What is direct marketing?
With direct marketing, the recipient of the advertising message is asked to make a direct and immediate response to the ad, such as by mailing in a printed order blank or dialing an 800 number to place an order. Telemarketing, home shopping channels, infomercials, and catalog sales are other common examples. The popularity of direct marketing is likely to increase in the future as the spread of interactive technologies such as videotex and two-way cable television make it easier to place orders in direct response to advertising.

How are advertising audiences categorized?
While some advertisements are directed to a general audience, most are tailored to a specific market segment or target audience. These subgroups may be categorized in a variety of ways. Common approaches include product usage, demographic (social and personal) characteristics, lifestyles (predicated on attitudes, interests, and opinions), or geographic area (geodemographic clustering).

What Are the Important Issues Facing the Advertising Industry Today?

What are the effects of deceptive advertising?
Advertisers and their agencies must constantly strive to avoid dishonest advertising practices, such as deceptive claims. Laws against deceptive advertising can be used against advertisers. Worse, they suffer from a loss of consumer confidence, which can damage future sales.

What other issues are of concern when it comes to advertising?
The growing use of mail and telephone marketing, infomercials, and home shopping channels could potentially harm the credibility of conventional advertising. There is also a continuing controversy over how to handle advertisements for personal products such as condoms and feminine hygiene products.

REFERENCES

Applegate, E. (1993). The development of advertising, 1700–1900. In W. D. Sloan, J. G. Stovall, & J. D. Startt (Eds.), *The media in America* (2nd ed.). Scottsdale, AZ: Publishing Horizons.

Arlen, G. (1993, Fall). Interactive advertising. *Convergence*, pp. 32–35.

Burgi, M. (1994, February 7). It's the time of the signs: Virtual reality meets TV sports. *Mediaweek*, p. 1.

Lavine, J. M., & Wackman, D. B. (1987). *Managing media organizations*. New York: Longman.

Mandese, J. (1994, February 7). NBC, CBS Forge on-line deals. *Advertising Age*, p. 1.

Nash, E. L. (1982). *Direct marketing*. New York: McGraw-Hill.

Nash, E. L. (1992). *The direct marketing handbook* (2nd ed.). New York: McGraw-Hill.

Roche, B. (1993). The development of modern advertising, 1900–present. In W. D. Sloan, J. G. Stovall, & J. D. Startt (Eds.), *The media in America* (2nd ed.). Scottsdale, AZ: Publishing Horizons.

Schramm, W. (1988). *The story of human communication: Cave painting to microchip*, New York: HarperCollins.

Sandage, C. H., Fryburger, V., & Rotzoll, K. (1989). *Advertising theory and practice.* New York: Longman.

Sissors, Jack S., & Bumba, L. (1992). *Advertising media planning.* Lincolnwood, IL: NTC Business Books.

Stefanae, S. (1994, April). Interactive advertising. *New Media*, pp. 43–52.

Vivian, J. (1991). *The media of mass communication.* Old Tappen, NJ: Allyn & Bacon.

Weiss, M. J. (1988). *The clustering of America.* New York: Harper & Row.

Wells, W., Burnett, J., & Moriarty, S. (1992). *Advertising: Principles and practice.* Englewood Cliffs, NJ: Prentice-Hall.

Chapter 16

THE PUBLIC RELATIONS INDUSTRY

C H A P T E R   P R E V I E W

This chapter describes the practice of public relations, the organized effort to gain favorable action on behalf of one or more goals or objectives. Along with advertising, public relations typifies the concept of "information within markets" in the media industry itself. In this chapter we will trace the origins of the public relations profession, examine the current structure of the industry, and describe the technological trends that may transform the public relations industry within the information society.

A Conversation with the Personal Re-editor (PR)

Why don't people *like* me? I want them to *like* me.

Candidly, sir, it's hard to like anyone as rich, powerful, and ruthless as you are. You need Personal Re-editor™!

If you weren't a computer, I'd fire you for saying that!

Let's start right there. I'm going to put my Nasty Filter™ on all of your electronic communications. From now on, whenever you yell "You're fired" it will come out "We're not communicating too effectively."

You @!!!#% computer, I'm going to kick your keyboard down the stairs for being so impertinent!

"You're a nice computer, please tell me more!" See how it works? You sound more likable already!

Oh, all right, as long as I don't have to listen to my own twaddle. What about my yellow fangs? My own children cringe when I smile.

I'm going to completely reedit your video image. No more fangs, no more steely glare, no more snarl.

So how's this going to help me slip the AT&T deal by Congress? They're the last piece, then I'll own everything, *everything*, I tell you!

I'll synthesize a flattering DeeVee biography out of your new image and send it as electronic mail to every registered voter. The news media will get a likable interactive news release that they can interview themselves. Viewers will be able to send a personalized video call to their senators demanding that they okay the deal.

But what if they *still* don't like me?

Don't worry, sir, the bio will remind everyone that you own controlling interests in several consumer credit databases and tactfully mention their outstanding credit card balances. If you just give people a chance to like you, they will, sir, believe me, they will!

How much will my lawyers charge for this?

"Isn't this unethical?" No sir, computers don't have any ethics!

HISTORY AS PUBLIC RELATIONS

THIS CHAPTER IS BY DON BATES, EXECUTIVE VICE-PRESIDENT AND CHIEF OPERATING OFFICER, SUMNER RIDER & ASSOCIATES, NEW YORK, NY.

Public relations is any organized effort to gain favorable action.

Edward Bernays, considered by many as the founder of modern public relations, wrote:

> The three main elements of public relations are practically as old as society: informing people, persuading people, or integrating people with people. Of course, the means and methods of accomplishing these ends have changed as society has changed. In a technologically advanced society, like that of today, ideas are communicated by newspaper, magazine, film, radio, television, and other methods. (Bernays, 1961, p. 12).

For Bernays and other historians of the practice, **public relations** has always gone hand in hand with civilization; in their eyes, much of re-corded history can be reinterpreted as the practice of public relations. Whereas primitive societies were ruled almost exclusively through fear and intimidation, more advanced cultures learned to depend on discussion and debate. Persuasion became less and less grounded in force and more and more grounded in words as rulers sought to build consensus. With the invention of writing, public relations began to take shape.

Whether they were promoting their image as warriors or kings, leaders of ancient civilizations such as Sumeria, Babylonia, Assyria, and Persia used poems and other writings to promote their prowess in battle and politics. In Egypt much of the art and architecture (statues, temples, tombs) was used to impress on the public the greatness of priests, nobles, and scribes.

In ancient Israel, the Bible and other religious texts became one of the most powerful means in history for molding the public mind. With the growth of the Hellenic world, the word, both written and spoken, exploded as a force for social integration. The Athens marketplace became a center of public discussion concerning the conduct of business and public life. Oratory flourished, and the public interest became a central tenet of philosophical speculation.

Hail, Caesar!

In ancient Rome the force of public relations was evident in phrases such as *vox populi, vox Dei* ("the voice of the people is the voice of God") and *res publicae* ("public affairs"), which means "republic." Julius Caesar carefully prepared the Romans for his crossing of the Rubicon in 49 B.C. by sending reports on his epic achievements as governor of Gaul. Most historians agree that he also wrote his *Commentaries* as propaganda for himself. Recognizing the power of news to mold public opinion, Caesar published a daily paper called *Acta Diurna* ("daily acts" or "daily records"), which continued for 400 years. Besides notices of births, deaths, and marriages, it contained government decrees and accounts of fires and severe weather.

Propaganda is media content aimed at persuading people to accept an idea or ideology.

When Christianity emerged at the height of Roman hegemony, the teachings of Jesus Christ and his apostles took center stage in the battle for religious dominance in the public mind. Once the Christian church took shape, Bernays explains, it relied on eloquent speeches to win converts and to guide the faithful. Indeed, the word **propaganda** was originated by the Catholic Church when, in the seventeenth century, it set up its *Congregatio de propaganda*, the "congregation for propagating the faith," explicitly acknowledging the need for a third party to facilitate communication between the government and the people (Bernays, 1961).

TABLE 16.1. MILESTONES IN PUBLIC RELATIONS

Year	Event
49 B.C.	Julius Caesar promotes himself to emperor of Rome
1792	French propaganda ministry
1897	The term "public relations" coined
1900	The Publicity Bureau established
1923	*Crystallizing Public Opinion* published
1954	PRSA code established

Public opinion is the views held by large numbers of people on politics or political issues.

The Origins of Modern Public Relations

Public relations continued to develop even during medieval times but it was not until the Renaissance and Reformation that the foundation of the modern world arose and with it the underpinnings of the kind of public relations that has become integral to the management of public and private institutions today. Great documents of liberty crystallized the power of public opinion; the Magna Carta, for one, was the inspiration for the U.S. Constitution.

With the spread of new knowledge in new forms—such as translations of the Bible from Latin into everyday languages and mass-printed books and newspapers in the fifteenth century—came an explosion of **public opinion.** When the French Revolution arrived, the stage was set. In their Declaration of the Rights of Man and Citizen (1789), the leaders of the French Revolution proclaimed the right of citizens to express and communicate thought freely. In 1792 the National Assembly of France created the first propaganda ministry (see Table 16.1). Part of a section of the Ministry of the Interior, it was called the Bureau d'Esprit, or "Bureau of the Spirit." It subsidized editors and sent agents to various parts of the country to win public support for the French Revolution.

The American Way

England's rebellious American colonies produced a host of public relations experts who used oratory, newspapers, meetings, committees, pamphlets, and correspondence to win people to their cause. Included among them were Benjamin Franklin, John Peter Zenger, Samuel Adams, Alexander Hamilton, James Madison, and John Jay. Adams has been called the great press agent of the American Revolution for fashioning the machinery of political change. Hamilton, Madison, and Jay are credited with winning ratification of the Constitution by publishing letters they had written to the press in 1787–1788. Today, they are known as the Federalist Papers.

AN EARLY PUBLIC RELATIONS SUCCESS IN THE UNITED STATES WAS DAVY CROCKETT, MANY OF WHOSE FEATS WERE INVENTIONS OF HIS PRESS AGENT, MATTHEW ST. CLAIR.

In the same light, the other great documents produced by the founders of the United States—the Declaration of Independence, the Constitution, and the Bill of Rights—may all be seen as masterworks of public relations. These documents, so essential to the notion of tying one's destiny to the public interest, also helped establish the United States as the breeding ground for pursuing public relations in an unheard-of fashion—as a business as well as a profession that represented the diverse interests of democracy and free enterprise.

Many American legends are the result of public relations campaigns. For example, the legend of Daniel Boone was created by a landowner to promote settlement in Kentucky. Davy Crockett's exploits were largely created by his press agent, Matthew St. Clair, in an effort to woo votes away from President Andrew Jackson. The master of all nineteenth-century press agents was Phineas T. Barnum. Showman par excellence, he created a wave of publicity stunts and coverage that made his circus, "The Greatest Show on Earth," an irresistible draw in every city and town it visited. Press agentry was so successful that it became an essential undertaking for companies that depended on the public's attention. Indeed, the success of Barnum and his colleagues in manipulating the press was so great that the media to this day still harbor skepticism toward anything that suggests commercial promotion.

Public Relations in the Age of the Robber Barons

It was in the last two decades of the nineteenth century and the early years of the twentieth century that public relations bloomed in the fullest sense. This was the era of America's wild and woolly development as the center of capitalist enterprise, when industry, the railroads, and utilities exploded across the face of the nation.

The hard-bitten attitudes of businessmen toward the public were epitomized in 1892 by the brutal methods of Henry Clay Frick to crush a labor union in the Carnegie-Frick Steel Companies plant in Homestead, Pennsylvania. The employees' strike was ultimately broken and the union destroyed by the use of the Pennsylvania state militia. Cold-blooded might won that battle, but the employees would eventually win the war of public opinion. Much of public relations history is woven into this unending struggle between employer and employee that today, fortunately, is fought with public relations professionals, not physical force (Cutlip, Center, & Broom, 1985).

Corporations quickly learned the value of combating hostility and courting public favor through professional public relations. Corporations also learned the value of publicity in attracting customers. Companies across America established press bureaus to manage the dissemination and coverage of news favorable to themselves and unfavorable to their competitors. The "battle of the currents" between Westinghouse (advocates of alternating current power transmission systems) and Thomas A. Edison's General Electric (direct current) is one of the earliest examples of how public relations was first conducted in the United States by powerful economic interests. Using former newspapermen as their publicists, the companies fought each other tooth and nail for media attention, political influence, and marketing advantage.

Trade associations also got the bug for public relations in the late 1800s. The Association of American Railroads claims it was the first organization to use the term *public relations*—in 1897 in the *Year Book of Railway Literature*.

The Publicity Bureau

In the 1900s, public relations came of age with the evolution from individual press agents and publicists to counseling firms of experts in the field. The nation's first publicity firm, The Publicity Bureau, was founded in Boston by George V. S. Michaelis, Herbert Small, and Thomas O. Marvin. In 1906 the bureau came into prominence when it was hired by the nation's railroads to defend against adverse regulatory legislation then in Congress. The firm failed in its efforts, but soon after most railroads established their own public relations departments.

Ivy Lee was perhaps the most famous of the early public relations practitioners, and with good reason. Although he did not use the term *public relations* himself until 1919 or so, he helped develop many of the techniques and principles that practitioners follow today. He believed in open communications with the media, and he was candid and frank in his approaches to the press. He understood that good corporate performance was the basis of good publicity. Many believe that his major contribution was to humanize wealthy businessmen and to put big business in a more positive light.

Among those competing with Lee for prominence during this time were Edward L. Bernays and his associate and wife, Doris Fleischman. Bernays is credited with coining the term **public relations counsel** in the first book on the subject, *Crystallizing Public Opinion*, originally published in 1923. In his practice and in his many books, Bernays saw public relations as an art applied to a science, the art of communications and social science. He and his colleagues went well beyond publicity in their roles as consultants to business, government, and nonprofit enterprises. Another pioneer was Arthur W. Page, who integrated public relations throughout the Bell System. He saw its role as critical to business success (Cutlip, Center, & Broom, 1985).

The **press release** was also invented in the 1920s. A press release is written in the form of a news story but presents only the point of view of the organization that produces it. Newspaper reporters sometimes use information from press releases to help them write their own stories. The story goes that Ohio Bell Telephone discovered that if it handed out "canned" news in this form, newspaper reporters would stop going to telephone rate hearings (Bleifuss, 1994).

During World War I, the Committee on Public Information was organized to help sell war bonds and to generally promote the war effort. Edward Bernays was among those who lent his talents to the war's "publicity front." World War II had the Office of War Information, which organized one of the largest public relations campaigns in history to muster support for America's entry into the war. Between world conflicts, the Roosevelt administration relied heavily on public relations techniques to promote its New Deal legislation.

The Rise of Public Relations Ethics

The contributions of Bernays, Lee, and Page did much to inject a spirit of professionalism into the practice of public relations. They were firmly opposed to Barnum's credo "There's a sucker born every minute." However, throughout history critics have charged that public relations too often manipulates the public interest for private gain, using the press, special events, and other activities merely to sell more products or to create an image that masks or sugarcoats an otherwise problematic reputation.

At the macro level, critics like Marvin Olasky (1987) say that public relations in the late nineteenth and early twentieth centuries worked to restrict economic competition. At the micro level, some critics, particularly in the media, think that what public relations people do every day is frivolous, concocted, inaccurate, superficial, even dangerous to liberty and freedom. Frequently, practitioners are called "flacks" to denigrate their communications contributions.

Public relations counsel is a person or organization who advises others about public relations matters.

Press release is the means by which public relations professionals distribute information to the mass media.

WORLD WAR I SHOWED THE POWER OF PUBLIC RELATIONS IN GETTING CITIZENS INVOLVED IN THE WAR EFFORT.

Are these criticisms valid? In some instances, yes. In one noted case, a Hollywood publicist concocted a story about a fictitious "best dressed" contest to promote the career of an unknown by the name of Rita Hayworth to movie stardom. In another incident that wound up before the Supreme Court, railroad publicists created phony organizations to criticize the rival trucking industry. Incidents like these led to the Public Relations Society of America's first code of ethics in 1954 and to a Declaration of Principles in 1959.

TECHNOLOGY TRENDS

Throughout most of the history of public relations, practitioners depended on a pen or pencil and a printing press to do their jobs. All they needed was something with which to write down their thoughts and some means with which to distribute what they had written to the audiences they wanted to reach. With the invention of electricity, technology in the larger sense became more important. Mass media and mass communications became the norm in public relations activities. Radio and television became powerful new carriers of the public relations "message." The telephone, electric typewriter, and photocopier also became ubiquitous as public relations tools. But perhaps the most significant technological advances of all were television and the personal computer.

New Mass Media in Public Relations

Only in the last twenty years has television been harnessed as a new technology for public relations purposes. Using in-house and commercial facilities for production and distribution, public relations practitioners in companies, government agencies, and nonprofit organizations began creating their own broadcast-quality television programs and products.

The most popular applications came in the form of promotional videos, **video news releases,** and **videoconferencing.** Practitioners wired themselves to the exploding public addiction for television and film. Television brought them closer to their audiences and gave them increasing control over the content and delivery of communications.

Technology also affected print media. Local newspapers shrank in numbers, but trade and consumer magazines grew, as did weekly community tabloids. Reflecting the "television mentality" of the public, these publications paid greater attention to graphics and design to make them more visually dramatic and engaging. The advent of **desktop publishing** also made it possible to expand the number of media "outlets," especially in-house publications for large organizations.

The increasing number of outlets expanded the venues for public relations material. Whereas practitioners once directed their publicity at a few tightly controlled national media outlets, they now had scores of channels to work with, providing many more opportunities for their clients and employers to be seen and heard. And public relations spokespersons have many more opportunities to appear on news and talk shows, whether on satellite-delivered national channels or local channels and leased access channels. Thus, for public relations the explosion of nontraditional outlets means greater opportunities for publicity and promotion. It also means complications. Whereas in the past practitioners only had to concentrate on a few well-established venues, they now have to consider hundreds, if not thousands. They have to be more sophisticated in knowing when and how to use technology more efficiently and effectively in order to avoid problems such as overcommunicating

Video news releases are press releases distributed in video form.

Videoconferencing is a teleconference with moving images.

Desktop publishing prepares documents on a "desktop" with a personal computer.

(going to too many people with too many messages) and adding unnecessary time and expense to the process. Cost-benefit ratios become more critical in making communications decisions.

Satellite Broadcasting

Satellite videoconferencing has become especially effective, with audiences at different sites being able to see each other on TV and listen and talk by phone. Today, many large corporations have their own in-house television networks that broadcast internally produced meetings, employee relations programs, and special events. These networks are used to inform, train, and motivate sales staff, executive management, and others. Similar facilities can be rented through major hotel chains and private videoconferencing suppliers.

Satellites are now used to transmit special events, video news releases, training programs, panel discussions, annual meetings, and news conferences. An early example was in 1982 when Johnson & Johnson used this new technology to reach hundreds of reporters in thirty cities with information about the Tylenol product tampering scare. Another early example was Emhart Corporation's New York–to–London investor relations presentation in 1983. During the broadcast, the company's chairman and other officials saw and talked with European investors and financial analysts. Emhart also pioneered the televised annual meeting, broadcasting several hours of the meeting to groups of investors in major markets around the United States and overseas. Coca-Cola staged an international celebration of its 100th anniversary with a live, two-day satellite broadcast linking its U.S. event site in Atlanta with simultaneous events in London, Sydney, Tokyo, Nairobi, and Rio de Janeiro as part of a spectacular global party. Satellite broadcasting is growing in popularity because of its impact, speed, spontaneity, and cost effectiveness.

Satellite media tour is held when a public relations spokesperson is interviewed by media outlets via satellite.

In a **satellite media tour,** spokespersons spend a few hours in a broadcast studio being interviewed by reporters who are receiving the video and sound via satellite in their own studios. Interviewers may broadcast the session live, edit it into a larger news or talk show, or tape it for later use. A good spokesperson can handle up to twenty-five interviews in a day.

Video News Releases

Video news releases are one of the newest and hottest public relations tools. Developed from television and VCR technology, these are the video equivalent of print news releases except that they are written and designed to be seen and heard, not read. They have become an especially important tool for public relations professionals who want to reach large audiences via television. Video news releases can be expensive, but since the coverage they receive is often extensive, they are usually well worth the expense. Video releases have proven to be an effective means of getting public relations material into the visual medium of television and to spread the message to local television outlets (Feurey, 1986). They are usually carefully crafted to make it easy for television stations to include them in their news broadcasts (McGowan, 1994).

Video news releases have generated a great deal of controversy, "usually initiated by newspaper and magazine articles decrying in shocked tones that some television news stories are actually produced by public relations people," says McGowan (1994). Public relations people, on the other hand, argue that a video release can supply visuals and an in-depth approach to a subject, beyond the reach of rushed daily news shows. Despite the division of opinion, there is general agreement that the people producing video news

- The narrator of "reporter" is heard, not seen, because stations prefer to show their own reporters on air, usually holding a microphone with the station's logo.
- The unseen narrator or reporter is recorded on only one of the videotape's two soundtracks so that stations can have their on-air reporters renarrate the track without losing other essential sound. When a release is delivered via satellite, versions with and without a narrator may be fed.
- Titles identifying spokespersons, experts, and others who speak in the video or on-air are left for stations to do in their own graphic style. The information for titles may be put on a printed transcript accompanying the tape or in the opening titles of the satellite feed.
- A suggested "lead-in" or script for a station's on-air reporter or anchor may also be put in the transcript or opening titles, as well as an "anchor graphic" (the picture seen over the shoulder of an anchor introducing the story in the videotape).
- To facilitate editing by stations, the printed transcript may include precise timings for each scene in the release or in accompanying additional footage.
- Raw footage is included so that stations can have additional video to work with when and if they edit the release.

Example: Neutrogena Soap

The main body of the video news release concentrates on debunking the myth that expensive lotions and moisturizers can keep skin from aging. A third-party spokesperson—a noted dermatologist—states that the best way to take care of facial skin is to wash with warm water and a mild soap like Neutrogena. The product is mentioned only once, and then in passing. While the announcer talks about expensive products that do not really work, the video shows cosmetics counters in department stores. It shows the doctor examining a patient's skin and, while he is talking, a woman 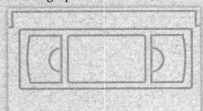 washing her face. While the Neutrogena packaging is not seen at any point, the soap being used is the clear, amber-colored bar that has become synonymous with the product.

releases should do them professionally, identifying their source, and that stations receiving them should judge their suitability for broadcast on the basis of whether they represent their subjects objectively.

Public Relations in the Information Age: The Personal Computer

Today, all public relations firms or departments have personal computers, often linked by internal and external networks. Whereas only a few years ago press lists were manually typed on envelopes and labels, or imprinted from metal addressograph plates, they are now routinely maintained on computer. Documents that once took hours to produce can now be put together in a matter of minutes. Similarly, the labeling and mailing can be handled within a few hours instead of a couple of days. More recently, computers have become the gateway to a booming array of on-line and in-house databases that put valuable research and information at the practitioner's fingertips in seconds. The most common applications are word processing, time and activity reports, accounting and billing, telecommunications, tracking issues, financial planning and budgeting, media list development and management, and project management and scheduling.

Until recently, public relations professionals depended on general software such as Lotus 1-2-3 or Microsoft Word for these applications. Today, however, a growing number of companies are offering PR-specific products, most of them related to the dominant task in most public relations operations: publicity and media relations. Most come with a small database of media information.

One such program, Targeter, shows where media management software is moving. It contains the names and addresses, plus phone and fax numbers, of over 150,000 reporters and editors at the more than 40,000 print and broadcast media in the United States and Canada, plus thousands more internationally, including all daily newspapers around the globe. The Targeter database is categorized by more than 2,500 classifications of editorial interest and includes information on audience demographics, usage of photos and artwork, market statistics, nine-digit zip codes, and congressional districts. Most important, the software is automatically updated each day by electronic mail.

Besides media management software, public relations practitioners can buy computerized disks of preselected media from major media mailing list suppliers. They can also take advantage of fax services such as Fast Fax and well-known public relations news services such as PR Newswire and Business Wire, which send news releases and other information directly to their printers in the newsrooms of major newspapers and other outlets. These services are particularly valuable for timely dissemination of breaking news and business transactions of publicly traded companies.

Software has also been created for analyzing press clippings and news coverage. These services tabulate and analyze a customer's publicity for message content, audience exposure, competitive share, geographic distribution, return on investment, positive versus negative impressions, and other factors. They can evaluate the effectiveness of media campaigns.

For tracking and billing time and expenses, other software packages have been adapted to the needs of public relations practitioners. These products record and invoice time, purchases, and out-of-pocket expenses. They automatically generate financial reports and profitability analyses. Some also permit instant on-line review of current figures. Usually, they require minicomputers or high-end microcomputers to do their work.

More sophisticated setups, designed as **integrated systems,** encompass a full range of management communications interests (see Table 16.2). These systems can be organized in a hierarchical form, resembling a family tree or file cabinet approach to information, or as a **relational database** in which data are stored in cross-referenced tables for easier search and find capabilities, along with easier information management. Edward Grefe (1986), a pioneer in developing relational databases for public relations, recommends them because of their ability to automatically send and track letters with personalized copy addressed to members of groups selected from databases.

Relational databases are particularly effective, Grefe stresses, for press relations, grassroots lobbying, issues management, and new product launches.

TABLE 16.2. PUBLIC RELATIONS MANAGEMENT SOFTWARE FUNCTIONS

Contributions
Grants
Matching gifts
Political action committees
Dinners
Volunteers

Tracking
Legislative tracking
Regulatory tracking
Executive orders
Judicial opinions

Player Profiles
Mailings lists
Coalition building
Allies and adversaries
Contact lists
Individuals (e.g., shareholders, elected officials)
Organizations (e.g., nongovernmental, legislative committees)

Issues Management
Trend analysis
Issues analysis

Subjects
Events
Programs

Media
Speakers bureau
Speech writing
Press releases
Publications
Graphics
Financial communications
Advertising campaigns

Research
Statistics
Polling

Utilities
Text retrieval
Word processing
Spreadsheet and analysis
Personal card file

Integrated systems are computer programs for public relations professionals that combine a wide range of management functions in one package.

Relational databases are computer programs in which data may be cross-referenced by key words and categories.

On-Line News and Information

Along with the growth in computers has come a growth in on-line databases through which public relations practitioners can improve their ability to research subjects, monitor media coverage almost instantly, and retrieve important information in a timely fashion. Among the many services available are NEXIS, DIALOG, DataTimes, CompuServe, Dow Jones News Service, AP Alert, Burrelle's News Express, and Wall Street By Fax. They are accessed by phone and computer. For broadcast media, companies such as Radio/TV Reports' Broadcast Retrieval and the Video Monitoring Service offer "clips" from on-air audio and video. As the evaluation of public relations results grows in importance, these and related services will become increasingly essential. As their prices drop, they will become more and more accessible to larger numbers of practitioners.

Many organizations are developing their own internally generated information services. The White House, for example, maintains a bibliographic file of remarks made by the president in all of his speeches. The public utilities industry keeps a database of information on rate and regulatory issues affecting its members. These databases are a ready source of assistance for staff, researchers, writers, reporters, and others. They make it easier to use information efficiently and effectively and can include everything from simple mailing lists to detailed analyses of issues.

Public Relations on the Information Superhighway

New interactive technologies afford public relations professionals some new tools of the trade. "New media" such as electronic mail, fax, and interactive television, and some not-so-new media such as the mail and the telephone, are starting to supplant the conventional mass media as the essential communication links in modern democracy.

Some interesting examples emerged from the 1992 U.S. presidential campaign. Democratic presidential hopeful Jerry Brown abandoned traditional fund-raising efforts in favor of a "grassroots" campaign supported by pledges made through calls to an 800 number. Brown also eschewed conventional campaign "spots," producing program-length "infomercials" for cable TV instead. Billionaire independent candidate Ross Perot adopted some of the same tactics, although he used the 800-number calls more as a type of electronic referendum to validate the legitimacy of his candidacy. He also used "closed circuit" satellite teleconferences to reach out to his supporters. Perot also proposed a scenario wherein, when he was elected, citizens would engage in an electronic dialogue with him using dial-in telephone polls.

Special-interest groups soon turned to high-tech methods. In the first month of the new congressional session that followed the 1992 election, the volume of telephone calls to the Capitol doubled, reaching over 4 million per month. One flood of calls, apparently triggered by revelations that Justice Department nominee Zoe Baird had hired an illegal alien as a babysitter, was credited with torpedoing her nomination. Another torrent of voter feedback was unleashed by the National Rifle Association (NRA) in a bid to preserve the right to keep and bear automatic assault weapons. NRA members placed calls to a 900 number, which automatically generated a letter to Congress in the caller's name. Another tactic is the "patch through." Political consultants scan computerized mailing lists for likely supporters of a cause. Computers automatically identify and place calls to likely prospects, then live operators explain the issue and offer to patch the caller through directly to his or her congressional representative or to the White House. At the U.S. Chamber of Commerce a computerized dialing system places calls to members when an issue of vital importance is before Congress. They then press 1 to send a Mailgram, press 2 for voice mail, or press 3 for electronic mail (Engleberg, 1993; Houston, 1993; Kelly, 1992).

Some politicians have turned to their own high-tech methods to stem the flow of electronic public relations. Congressional staffers retaliated for one unwanted flood of communications by sending junk faxes that jammed the offending special-interest group's fax machines. The Clinton administration installed an interactive voice mail system that allows callers to "vote" on the president's economic plan before recording a brief message for the president. You can also send electronic mail to the president (President@White.house.gov) and download files containing the texts of his latest speeches or graphic images of the president striking inspiring patriotic poses.

INDUSTRY ORGANIZATION

Public relations activities are addressed to one or more of the many **publics** that can influence an organization's success—customers, employees, shareholders, donors, the press, and so on (see Table 16.3). Definitions of public relations abound. Here are a few:

> Public relations is the management function that identifies, establishes and maintains mutually beneficial relationships between an organization and the various publics on whom its success or failure depends. (Cutlip, Center, & Broom, 1985)

> [It's] the management function which evaluates public attitudes, identifies the policies and procedures of an individual or an organization with the public interest, and plans and executes a program of action to earn public understanding and acceptance. (*Public Relations News*)

> Public relations helps our complex, pluralistic society to reach decisions and functions more effectively by contributing to mutual understanding among groups and institutions. It serves to bring private and public policies into harmony. (Public Relations Society of America)

In more practical terms—on the job—the public relations unit, whether one person or many people, has a wide range of responsibilities. Here are a few of the most important:

- Advises and counsels the organization on communications questions affecting its publics

- Serves as an early-warning system on emerging issues related to the organization's success

- Provides technical support for other management functions with an emphasis on publicity, promotion, and media relations

- Acts as a gatekeeper between the company or organization and its many publics, most conspicuously representatives of the press, legislators, and government officials

TABLE 16.3. THE MANY PUBLICS IN PUBLIC RELATIONS

For Businesses
Shareholders
Customers/consumers
Employees
Suppliers
Financial institutions
Legislators
Community activists
Print/broadcast media

For Nonprofit Enterprises
Contributors/donors
Clients/consumers
Volunteers
Employees
Members
Suppliers
Legislators
Community activists
Print/broadcast media

For Government Agencies
Taxpayers/voters
Legislators
Related government agencies
Employees
Community activists
Print/broadcast media

Good public relations has many benefits: improved credibility and accountability, stronger public identity, more favorable press coverage, greater sensitivity to public needs, improved employee morale, larger market share, increased sales, and better internal management. Bad public relations can exist as well, often because the people in charge of the function did not do their jobs or because the company or organization operated outside the bounds of the public interest. Perhaps management allowed the production of faulty products, or permitted pollution of surroundings, or illegally manipulated the price of the company's stock. Public relations might help to soften the fallout from such an event (negative press coverage, public outrage, regulatory punishment), but only a change in management policy or practice will truly make a difference. If one cliché dominates public relations thinking, it is this: "You can't make a silk purse out of a sow's ear."

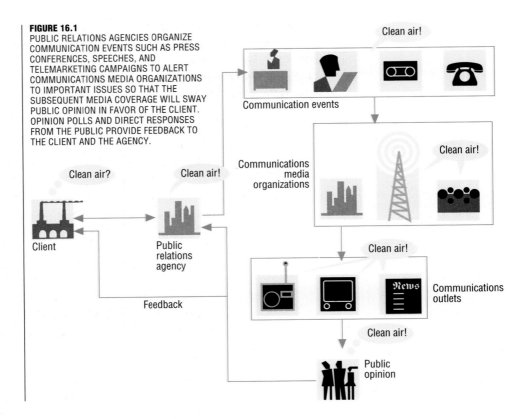

FIGURE 16.1
PUBLIC RELATIONS AGENCIES ORGANIZE COMMUNICATION EVENTS SUCH AS PRESS CONFERENCES, SPEECHES, AND TELEMARKETING CAMPAIGNS TO ALERT COMMUNICATIONS MEDIA ORGANIZATIONS TO IMPORTANT ISSUES SO THAT THE SUBSEQUENT MEDIA COVERAGE WILL SWAY PUBLIC OPINION IN FAVOR OF THE CLIENT. OPINION POLLS AND DIRECT RESPONSES FROM THE PUBLIC PROVIDE FEEDBACK TO THE CLIENT AND THE AGENCY.

Elements of Successful Public Relations

The practice of public relations is based on research and evaluation, including public opinion polls, readership surveys, mail questionnaires, telephone interviews, focus groups, and literature searches. Of necessity, then, good public relations begins with a serious assessment of public attitudes. Without adequate background on who you are trying to reach and how they think, it is next to impossible to communicate effectively. More specifically, without research and evaluation, you cannot really design programs that will change or modify your relations.

PRODUCING AN INVITING ANNUAL REPORT IS PART OF THE PUBLIC RELATIONS EFFORT.

Second, public relations is a planned effort, not a hit-or-miss proposition (see Figure 16.1). Planned means managed. Managed means based on overall organizational objectives, not just the public relations unit's views. Planned effort begins with a written action plan for a year or more ahead that allows for changes and contingencies along the way. This plan must have the approval of top management. It schedules needed publications and communications, such as a monthly newsletter, the annual report, and special event speeches and presentations. More important, the plan organizes a timetable and strategies aimed at achieving overall goals for the program.

Third, public relations has the goal of public support. In a for-profit organization, this might translate into one or more actions, among them purchase of products, purchase of stock, or votes for or against specific trade regulations. For a nonprofit organization, public support might take the form of donations of money or material, volunteer assistance, or paid memberships. For a government agency, it might mean legislative influence, taxpayer cooperation, or public participation.

Finally, public relations has a communications focus. Over time, the public relations unit makes use of most of the print, electronic, and face-to-face communications available in our society. These are the tools and techniques (see Table 16.4) that help organizations to reach their publics. They are the vehicles that carry information back and forth between private and public interests.

It is also important to realize what public relations is not. To do the work of public relations, practitioners often make use of the full range of mass communications—advertising, marketing, opinion research, print and broadcast media—but these functions have their own principles and practices and the people involved are experts in their own right with their own bodies of knowledge and experience. What they do and how they do it is substantially different from what public relations practitioners do. Understanding these differences helps keep the public relations function in perspective, avoiding management and client misunderstandings about what to expect from its application and what to pay for the services involved.

TABLE 16.4. PUBLIC RELATIONS ACTIVITIES

Annual reports
Brochures, flyers, circulars
Press kits
Press conferences
News releases
Editorials
Speeches
Feature articles
Video news releases
Satellite broadcast media
Tours
Videoconferences
Teleconferences
Exhibits and displays
Photographs
Videotapes and films
Audiotapes and compact discs
Advertorial programming
Paid advertisements
Public service advertisements
Legislative testimony
Sports sponsorships
Event sponsorships
Plant tours and open houses
Technical seminars
Public demonstrations
Slide shows
Speakers' bureaus
Opinion polls and surveys
VIP visits
Novelties
Meetings and conventions

Public Relations Organizations

Although "public relations" is the preferred generic term in most corporations, the overall function is also known by other designations that might appear in an organization chart or in the titles of practitioners. Among the most popular: public affairs, corporate communications, and corporate relations. In specific industries such as public utilities you might find the terms "consumer affairs" or "community relations"; in nonprofit and government organizations, "public information" or "marketing communications." In addition, the overall term might be subdivided further to reflect specific jobs, such as investor relations, financial relations, or media relations.

Today, all leading corporations have public relations departments of one sort or another. The same goes for major nonprofit organizations such as colleges, hospitals, and national charities. And government has similar operations, although they are called "public affairs" or "public information" offices.

To assist these entities, there are some 4,000 independent public relations firms, most with one or two people, but several score with fifty or more. The largest firms, such as Hill and Knowlton or Burson Marsteller, have several hundred employees worldwide (U.S. Department of Labor, 1993).

The Public Relations Profession

Some 155,000 people work full time in public relations. Aside from their job titles, public relations professionals are also defined by the organizations they belong to and the publications they read. The Public Relations Society of America (PRSA) is the largest and most influential professional organization. Others include the International Association of

Business Communicators (IABC) and Women in Communication (WIC). For the highest-level practitioners, there are private, invitation-only associations, such as the PR Wiseman, the PR Seminar, and the Arthur W. Page Society.

Among the most important magazines and journals in the field are the *Public Relations Journal, Public Relations Quarterly, Public Relations Review, Communications World, PR Services,* and *Inside PR.* Probably the most famous publications are *Jack O'Dwyer's Newsletter* and his company's directories, which carry the names, addresses, and other information for corporate practitioners and consultants. Other newsletters include *PR Reporter, Public Relations News,* and *Bulldog Reporter.*

Internationally, there may be another 150,000 professional practitioners, and almost every major country has a public relations society, most of which affiliate in one way or another with the International Public Relations Association (IPRA). The IPRA publishes a journal of research and opinion. Most of the local societies have periodic newsletters.

For most of the history of modern public relations, those doing the day-to-day work came from the ranks of the press—newspaper reporters and editors. Today, the field attracts individuals from a wide variety of backgrounds, virtually all of them college graduates with degrees (both undergraduate and graduate) in the liberal arts, large numbers of whom studied journalism, marketing, mass communications, and English. Several thousand have majored in public relations at one of more than 100 colleges and universities offering such programs.

The management ranks in public relations are still overwhelmingly male dominated. The situation is changing, of course, but slowly, perhaps more slowly than in other pursuits such as accounting, human resources, and business management generally. Public relations is also overwhelmingly white in its racial composition, although efforts are under way to attract nonwhite practitioners to the field. Within PRSA, committees and task forces are working on the challenge.

Salaries in public relations begin at around $18,000–$25,000 and rise to as high as $200,000–$400,000 or more in the largest corporations and public relations firms. Currently, the average salary is probably in the $50,000–$100,000 range, with the larger salaries being found in the corporate world and at the higher echelons of public relations firms. In 1993, the median salary was over $46,000.

Beginning practitioners cut their teeth in the area of publicity and media relations, writing and editing news releases, contacting reporters and editors, and generating press coverage. Seasoned practitioners, on the other hand, are more involved in planning and management. When they do write, it is most often speeches, proposals, and presentations. When they work with the media, it usually involves broader editorial issues and higher-level contacts.

R E V I E W

1. How does public relations differ from advertising?

2. What are some of the audiences for public relations?

3. What are four elements of successful public relations?

4. Name professional organizations that serve the public relations field.

5. What are the different categories of public relations?

6. What are some important tools of the public relations profession?

7. What are the qualifications for the public relations profession?

In addition to their education and experience, practitioners are supported by active PRSA and IABC programs of continuing education and accreditation. To become accredited, practitioners must pass complete oral and written examinations. Half of those who take the PRSA test fail. PRSA also has a four-stage career track to help practitioners develop their skills and abilities.

Overall, the public relations field is growing and will continue to grow as society becomes more complex and as larger numbers of individuals and organizations seek public support for their endeavors. The influence of public relations will expand as well, as larger numbers of practitioners become part of traditional top management teams, applying their communications skills and knowledge across all management functions.

Forms of Public Relations

Most of the work handled within the public relations function requires hands-on activity day in and day out. Practitioners spend long hours writing, editing, phoning, and meeting. They also devote considerable time to coordinating the design, printing, and dissemination of printed promotional materials ranging from one-page flyers to feature-length films. Their principal focus is helping clients or employers to communicate better with their publics.

Public relations is usually organized into several key categories:

- *Publicity or media relations* —Gaining press coverage through news releases, press conferences, and other materials

- *Promotion or selling*—Developing and disseminating print and audiovisual materials, arranging exhibits and displays, and providing promotional giveaways

- *Community relations*—Working with community groups and other key community interests that can influence public attitudes, and public policies

- *Government relations*—Assisting or influencing state, local, or federal government action on problems involving legislation, regulation, and related activity

Political action committees (PACs) are organizations that collect donations for political candidates on behalf of an organization or cause.

- *Public information*—Developing and disseminating print and audiovisual materials whose purpose is to inform, educate, and assist

- *Special events*—Planning and managing internal and external events such as groundbreakings, ribbon-cutting ceremonies, tours, and open houses aimed at attracting public attention

- *Employee relations*—Assisting management in informing staff at all levels about personnel policies and practices, labor relations, contracts, benefits, and other issues involving the health and welfare of the labor force

- *Issues management*—Identifying and helping to manage the big issues affecting institutional success, such as air and water pollution (the environment), foreign competition, ethnic diversity, and plant closings or relocations

- *Lobbying*—Working with legislators and their legislative aides to influence the content and course of legislative action affecting institutional practices, through contributions to **political action committees (PACs),** campaign contributions, and other direct assistance not included as part of more conventional government relations efforts

How much time and money an organization puts into each of these functions depends on the degree of need. Employers and clients with big issues and big problems tend to do more. Organizations with less of a need might devote the lion's share of their energies to one or two areas. Over time, however, every organization makes use of all these functions, except perhaps for lobbying, which is often too political and legalistic for smaller, less visible enterprises. And there are distinctions based on purpose. Government agencies, for example, tend to favor public information because of their public service orientation. Nonprofit organizations might also lean toward public information, in addition to public relations activities that support fund-raising.

ISSUES IN THE PUBLIC RELATIONS PROFESSION

Issues affecting public relations include credibility and accountability; ethical behavior; professional development; and the uses of research and evaluation.

Credibility and Accountability

Public relations exists in the context of a constant struggle with the companion issues of credibility and accountability. Every day practitioners must ask themselves and those they work for, directly and indirectly, whether what they are doing and saying is believable and whether what they earn and spend is in keeping with the best interests of the publics they serve. The answers affect what and how practitioners write, speak, plan, and program their activities. The answers also influence results. To be uncredible or unaccountable is a surefire recipe for failure.

Ethical Behavior

Allied to credibility and accountability is the issue of ethics—the ethics of personal behavior as well as the ethics of public relations strategies and messages. Practitioners must continually ask themselves whether what they do to generate public attention is within the bounds of reasonableness, good taste, and truth. They must make a concerted effort to eliminate (to whatever degree possible) public relations initiatives that are false and misleading. This is especially difficult for practitioners hired as promotional mouthpieces rather than as communications strategists. Both the PRSA and IABC have codes of ethics and standards to help focus the responsibility of practitioners (see box). In addition to its code of ethics, the PRSA has a Board of Ethics and Professional Standards with procedures for handling breaches of the code. Violations can lead to expulsion from membership. Unethical behavior often also leads to public censure when the circumstances of the infraction become known in the press.

FROM THE PRSA CODE OF PROFESSIONAL STANDARDS FOR THE PRACTICE OF PUBLIC RELATIONS

- A member shall conduct his or her professional life in accord with the public interest.

- A member shall exemplify high standards of honesty and integrity while carrying out the dual obligations to a client or employer and to the democratic process.

- A member shall deal fairly with the public, with past or present clients or employers, and with fellow practitioners, giving due respect to the ideal of free inquiry and to the democratic process.

- A member shall adhere to the highest standards of accuracy and truth, avoiding extravagant claims or unfair comparisons and giving credit for ideas and words borrowed from others.

- A member shall not knowingly disseminate false or misleading information and shall act promptly to correct erroneous communications for which he or she is responsible.

- A member shall not engage in any practice which has the purpose of corrupting the integrity of channels of communications for which he or she is responsible.

- A member shall scrupulously safeguard the confidences and privacy rights of present, former, and prospective clients or employers.

Professional Development

Other issues for practitioners involve professional development and personal growth. Clearly, there is a need for practitioners to become more sophisticated about how to use new technology for communications purposes. They also have to learn more about the basics of business—how it is structured, and how it is managed. Since most practitioners enter the field after studying liberal arts or after having worked in journalism and publishing, they have little knowledge of how corporations and small businesses operate. To communicate profit and loss issues, they need to get up to speed as quickly as possible.

There is also a great concern in the field about a perceived weakening in the writing and thinking skills that have been the foundation of the practice's success over the years. Senior practitioners, in particular, complain about how difficult it is to find employees who are strong, journalistically oriented writers.

Use of Research and Evaluation

Practitioners need to apply more research and evaluation to what they do for clients and employers. Although both are inherent in the traditional public relations planning process, they are still used scantily in helping to define the goals of programs and activities and later in measuring their effectiveness.

Part of the reason for not using more research and evaluation is money. Most public relations budgets are bare bones—there is little money beyond the essentials needed for the process. These budgets focus largely on how-to, not why-to, thinking. To move forward in this area, practitioners need to integrate research and evaluation into their plans and budgets. They also need to educate top management on the value of research and development in designing and delivering more effective messages and programs.

In addition to providing clearer direction for programs, research helps build the theory and practice of public relations, linking the field to other mass communications functions in the process. Major research techniques in public relations include environmental monitoring (assessing the corporate climate), audits (evaluating an organization's standing with its publics), and readability studies (analyzing a publication's effectiveness).

Evaluation studies are aimed at assessing the effectiveness of public relations itself (Swinehart, 1979). Among the methods used are:

1. Description and subjective appraisal by persons directly involved in program operation

2. Counts of activities—such as number of materials produced, amount of material placed, films shown, inquiries answered

3. Appraisal of activities or products by content specialists and media personnel

4. Reactions of audiences or recipients of information—volunteered self-reports on usefulness of materials

5. Audience reactions solicited from an appropriate sample of users rather than those volunteered by some users

6. Small-scale studies to obtain results of actual and potential audiences, with assured exposure and immediate assessment or reactions (e.g., small-group studies of films, pamphlets, or TV/radio spots)

7. Controlled field experiments or panel studies, to assess actual impact of programs or materials

In the absence of research and evaluation, public relations effectiveness is compromised and the practice's credibility and accountability suffer. Unless you know where you are going and have some expectation of results, you will never really know whether you have succeeded. Unless you can point to hard data substantiating the impact of your programs, the client or employer will always be suspicious of promises or rationalizations.

Public Relations and Society

More broadly, public relations practitioners are faced with two sets of issues: those related to the public interest and those related to how and why they practice their particular art of communication. They have to worry about what the public wants as much as what their employers want. Consequently, they live with a divided sense of self. They are both makers of messages and messengers. But most practitioners seem to relish their role despite its

1. What are some of the important elements of ethical behavior in public relations?
2. What is the role of evaluation in public relations?
3. Why is professional development especially important in the public relations field?
4. What are some techniques for evaluating public relations?

inherent difficulties. They understand the importance of public relations' role in society, and they are willing to tolerate the criticism in order to accomplish their goal.

In a speech before the Arthur W. Page Society titled "The Truth Is in the Consequence," public relations pioneer Allen Center (1983) addressed the implications of the changing role of public relations in society:

There is no longer a serious question about the essentiality of the public relations function, or the expertise with which it is carried out most of the time. . . . At no period in my lifetime have the basic abilities to monitor and interpret information, to respond effectively, to relate public opinion to an organization's affairs, and to communicate persuasively been of more critical importance in the successful management of all kinds of enterprises.

Similarly, at no time in my life has there been a greater need to use these abilities in ways that can help produce empathy, compromise, reconciliation, dialogue, and understanding rather than contention, controversy, animosity, prejudice, or misunderstanding. . . . Work to change and to improve things for the future within the framework of a free, open, democratic, and competitive society—on the payroll. You can't change much of anything by brooding, or getting into a big argument, being fired, or sitting on the sidelines. You have to stay in the game.

SUMMARY & REVIEW

What Are the Origins of Public Relations?

How did public relations develop?
In a sense, public relations is as old as history itself. The rulers of ancient empires, political propagandists, and the propagators of the world's great religions were among the first to successfully use public relations techniques. In this light, the Federalist Papers, the Bill of Rights, and the popularization of frontier heroes like Daniel Boone and Davy Crockett may be seen as examples of successful public relations campaigns. Modern public relations evolved in the late nineteenth century as large corporations sought to defend their interests in the arena of public opinion. The first independent public relations counsel was established in the early 1900s. Ivy Lee was an early practitioner who worked to improve the image of the industrialists of the late nineteenth century. Edward Bernays is widely regarded as the originator of the current professional practice. Mass persuasion propaganda campaigns during both world wars were also influential in expanding the scope and effectiveness of public relations.

What are some criticisms of public relations?
Critics contend that public relations is an organized attempt to mislead the public and to represent the interests of large corporations at the expense of the public good. In the past public relations campaigns have stooped to such tactics as concocting fictitious news events and creating phony organizations to promote their causes. Now public relations professionals subscribe to the Public Relations Society of America's code of ethics to avoid such abuses.

How Have Technological Changes Affected Public Relations?

How are changes in communications media altering public relations?
Expansion in the number of media outlets, especially in newspaper publishing and cable television, has expanded opportunities for public relations professionals to present their message to the public. Video news releases were developed to help place public relations stories in television newscasts. Satellite networks and videoconferences afford new

opportunities to deliver highly targeted press briefings. Electronic mail, mass calling, and facsimile are also being applied in modern public relations practice. Meanwhile, the internal operations of public relations organizations are being transformed by the adoption of personal computers to automate many routine public relations tasks and to gain access to relational databases and on-line information services with public relations information. Public relations techniques used in political campaigns are also taking advantage of advances in computer and telecommunications technology, giving politicians new opportunities to state their case directly to the public, circumventing mass media channels.

What are the key elements of successful public relations?
Public relations campaigns succeed to the extent that they promote mutual understanding between the organization that sponsors the campaigns and one or more of the publics on which the organization depends to achieve its goals. Successful public relations campaigns are based on research and evaluation of public attitudes, employ careful planning, have the goal of winning public support in some tangible way, and use communications media to achieve their ends. Public relations campaigns thus rely on the successful execution of related advertising, marketing, opinion research, and media

campaigns, but the public relations function is distinct from all of these.

What are some of the techniques used in public relations?
The techniques used to reach the public depend on the nature of the public relations message and on the nature of the public, or publics, to which they are addressed. For businesses, some of the important audiences include shareholders, customers, employees, suppliers, the financial community, community activists, legislators, and the media. Annual reports, press releases, speeches, teleconferences, news conferences, "advertorials," and public tours are some techniques commonly used on behalf of corporate public relations clients. Nonprofit groups and government agencies must address many of the same publics but also must reach volunteers and members of the general public. They rely more on nonpaid forms of promotion in their public relations campaigns, such as public service announcements and door-to-door canvassing by volunteers.

What Is the Public Relations Industry Today?

How is the public relations industry organized?
Most large organizations have their own public relations departments, although they go by various names, including public affairs and public information. There are also thousands of independent public relations firms that supplement corporate PR departments or that perform these functions for smaller firms. Additionally, public relations may be categorized in terms of functions, including media relations, promotion, community relations, government relations, public information, special events, employee relations, issues management, and lobbying. The public relations profession is also defined by membership in organizations such as the Public Relations Society of America and the International Public Relations Association.

What are the standards for ethical conduct in public relations?

Continuing growth and change in the practice of public relations require continuing attention to the issue of ethical conduct. Public relations professionals face conflict between the interests of their clients and standards of conduct defined by the Public Relations Society of America's Code of Professional Standards. These standards require practitioners to maintain high standards of honesty, and fair play and to always operate in the public interest while serving the interests—and maintaining the confidence—of their employers.

What does it mean to be a public relations professional?

Today's public relations professionals hold college degrees in fields such as liberal arts, journalism, marketing, mass communication, or English. Also, more than 100 colleges offer programs in the field of public relations. Practitioners seek accreditation from profes-

sional societies such as the Public Relations Society of America and follow the society's ethical standards. They keep up to date with professional publications aimed at the public relations field. They also participate in continuing education programs to develop their abilities throughout their careers.

What is the role of research and evaluation in public relations?

Research helps public relations practitioners improve the effectiveness of their activities, while evaluation helps them determine how effective they have been. Environmental monitoring, audits, readability studies, and evaluation activities such as feedback from public relations clients and publics are examples of research and evaluation methods. The role of research and evaluation must expand if public relations professionals are to maintain a high degree of credibility and accountability for their actions.

REFERENCES

Bernays, E. (1961). *Crystallizing public opinion*. Norman: University of Oklahoma Press.

Bleifuss, J. (1994, March 20). New angles from the spin doctors. *The New York Times*, p. F13.

Center, A. (1983, April 15). *The truth is in the consequence.* Address to the Arthur W. Page Society, University of Texas at Austin.

Cutlip, S., Center, A., & Broom, G. (1985). *Effective public relations* (6th ed.). Englewood Cliffs, NJ: Prentice-Hall.

Engleberg, S. (1993, March 17). A new breed of hired hands cultivates grass-roots anger. *The New York Times*, pp. A1, A11.

Feurey, J. (1986). Video news releases. In *New technology and public relations.* New York: Institute for Public Relations.

Grefe, E. A. (1986). Relational data base management. In *New technology and*

public relations. New York: Institute for Public Relations.

Houston, P. (1993, March 16). Phone frenzy in the Capitol. *The Los Angeles Times*, pp. A1, A12.

Kelly, M. (1992, June 6). Perot's vision: Consensus by computer. *The New York Times*, pp. A1, A8.

McGowan, A. (1994, March 6). Private communication with author.

Olasky, M. (1987, April). The development of corporate public relations. *Journalism Monographs*, No. 102.

Swinehart, J. (1979, July). Evaluating public relations. *Public Relations Journal*, pp. 13–16.

U.S. Department of Labor. (1993). *Occupational outlook handbook, 1992–93 edition.* Washington, DC: U.S. Government Printing Office.

Chapter 17

EFFECTS OF MASS MEDIA

C H A P T E R   P R E V I E W

n the preceding chapters we documented patterns of consumption of the mass media and discussed the content of media systems. In this chapter we will examine the social implications of media consumption. We will gain an understanding of what mass media effects are and how these effects are studied. We will also review important categories of effects, including effects on both antisocial and prosocial behavior and studies of the effects of political communication and advertising. We will also look briefly at critical theories of the mass media that focus on the broad cultural implications of the mass media.

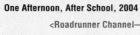

<Roadrunner Channel—Enter parental authorization code>

[8523456]

<INVALID CODE—ACCESS DENIED>

Darn!

<Interactive Mud Wrestling—Enter parental authorization code>

[8523465]

<INVALID CODE—ACCESS DENIED>

Drat!

<Dirty Joke Channel—Enter parental authorization code>

[8523546]

<PARENTAL CODE RECOGNIZED—PLEASE WAIT>

Yesssss! I knew it had to be one of her phone numbers!

<Dialing Ajax Multimedia Corp. 852-3546>

Uh oh . . .

So! You've been trying to crack the parental advisory channels again, I see. Just for that, I'm cutting you off from everything except the Homework Channel, and if the DeeVee has to call me one more time at work you're going to be sorry—*and* I'm going to have it monitor your keystrokes, so you'd better get busy, young lady!

<Click!>

Gee whiz, Mom, I was just trying out a new program!

[Running . . . homework keystroke emulator]

Gosh darn! Where did she come up with that new parenting software?

edia bashing" has become a popular, if somewhat predictable, sport. First media critics find new evidence of negative media effects. Then the media produce their own experts to refute the claims. The talk shows and editorial columns buzz for a while, public hearings are held, calls for action are heard. Then the media retreat behind the First Amendment protections of free speech, they promise to regulate themselves, and the debate quiets down until the next controversy arises (Jensen & Graham, 1993).

The sources of concern may be seen at every turn of the page or flip of the dial. The media are suspected of encouraging antisocial behavior, including violence, sex crimes, drug abuse, racism, and sexism. The mass media have also been implicated in the destruction of the family, religion, schools, political institutions, and cultural identities. They are accused of fostering a consumer society that denigrates authentic human relationships and replaces them with nonstop material consumption, all for the profit of multinational corporations.

With each new controversy come cries for action: Ban the offending content. Force the media to police themselves. Boycott the offending media or their advertisers. Enact laws that will change ownership and employment practices so more socially responsible people make media content decisions. Produce more positive media to counteract the harmful effects.

Media executives often defend themselves by pointing out that society's ills have deeper causes, such as the disintegration of the family or economic and racial oppression, that are unlikely to be much affected by an evening's entertainment. The media merely reflect society, not shape it, they argue.

Public policymakers hold hearings, have experts testify, propose legislation, and hold high-level meetings with media executives, but ultimately their hands are tied. The First Amendment protects the free speech rights of the media, even when that "speech" consists of off-color humor or prime-time shoot-outs. Sometimes behind-the-scenes pressure tactics result in industry self-regulation, but the voluntary standards are often eroded by competition among media outlets, the media critics go on alert, and the cycle begins anew.

The tragedy is that in the process, the First Amendment rights of the media must be pitted directly against the health and welfare of society, for a great deal of research indicates that the concerns of the media critics are well founded. Unfortunately, the voices of the researchers are too often drowned out in the heat of the public debate. The tragedy is compounded by the fact that those who suffer most are innocents—young children who consume mass media in extremely large doses.

RESEARCH ON MEDIA EFFECTS

Most social scientists begin with theoretical models of how media consumption interacts with human behavior through a process of cause and effect, deduce predictions about media effects from these theories, and test these predictions through systematic observation. The results of their research are used to further bolster their theories or to demolish them, leading to new theoretical paradigms. For social scientists studying media effects, mass media exposure is usually the "cause," or **independent variable.** Exposure to media content triggers mental processes and behaviors that are the "effects" of the media—antisocial or prosocial behaviors, for example. These are called **dependent variables.**

Another approach taken by some social scientists is to observe people's interactions with

Independent variables are the causes.

Dependent variables are the consequences.

media and with each other, then *induce* explanations or theories about what causes might be leading to what effects from the concrete situations that observers see.

While many social scientists use quantitative methods that allow them to enumerate their findings and analyze statistical relationships between the independent and dependent variables, others infer the relationships from qualitative methods, such as by studying the symbols in media content or observing behavior in natural settings (Wimmer & Dominick, 1991). It is important to understand the methods used to study media effects, as their relative strengths and weaknesses help us evaluate their contributions to the media effects debate. For example, media executives who oppose policy proposals based on media effects research often critique methodological shortcomings in the research as an argument against the policy proposals.

Content analyses are quantitative descriptions of the content of media systems.

CRITICAL COMMUNICATION THEORY

Paul Lazarsfeld (1941), one of the pioneers of communications research, was the first to point out the difference between what he called *administrative research,* which takes existing media institutions for granted and documents their use and effects, and *critical research,* which criticizes media institutions themselves from the perspective of the ways that they serve dominant social groups. All of the communications effects research described elsewhere in this chapter, even that which results in "criticism" of the media for excessive sex or violence, falls into the administrative research category, since it fails to critique the basic foundations of existing media institutions. Critical theorists reject these administrative approaches to communication theory and the underlying source-message-channel-receiver model (which critical theorists have redubbed the "linear model" or "transmission paradigm") on which they are based. Instead, they use theoretical approaches drawn from such fields as history, feminist studies, Marxist political economy, and literary criticism to examine the power relationships and hidden ideologies expressed in media content and media institutions (Chomsky & Herman, 1988). In so doing, they hope to expose and eliminate patterns of cultural oppression and domination predicated on social class, ethnicity, and gender (Grossberg, 1993; McChesney, 1993; Steeves, 1993).

Critical theorists have their own methods and their own vocabulary to further distinguish their approach. Critical theorists reject the methods of administrative research, including the quantitative content analytic, experimental, and survey research methods described in the text, and indeed some reject the scientific method on which many communication studies are based. Instead, critical theorists favor interpretative and inductive methods such as semiotics, historical research, and ethnography. Rather than talking about how communication effects are limited by selective perception, some critical theorists would state that audiences are active "readers" of media "texts," which in their view better characterizes the prominence of the audience instead of the source (Morley, 1992). Likewise, critical theorists talk of "group mediation" (for example, Barbero, 1993) or "interpretive communities" (Lindlof, 1994), whereas social scientists use the term *multistep flow* to describe the way in which social interactions affect perceptions of the media.

Content Analysis

Content analyses quantify the nature of the content found in media systems. Researchers begin with systematic samples of media content and then apply objective definitions to classify the content. For example, if researchers wanted to find out whether television has gotten more violent over the years they might select a representative "composite week" of prime-time programming. They would develop objective definitions of "violent," such as sequences in which characters are depicted as targets of physical force. Trained observers would then classify each of the scenes in the sample of shows and compare notes to make sure that the definitions are consistent and produce the same results regardless of the observer. Then the researchers enumerate the number of violent acts per hour and can compare the statistics with previous studies (Gerbner & Gross, 1976).

Content analysis studies can create detailed profiles of the media they examine and are a useful means of identifying trends in media content over time. However, they cannot be used as a sound basis for inferring the effects of the media. For that, we must conduct research that involves the audience itself for, as we shall see, the audience often perceives the media in a different way than the researchers—or the producers of the content for that matter—do. Because content analysis is a time-consuming task, researchers sometimes take only a small sample of content (such as one week's worth of prime-time television shows, just on the three biggest broadcast networks) that may not completely reflect the full range of programming. In addition, the definitions used can sometimes be problematic. For example, if a character in a situation comedy slaps another character on the back and they begin laughing, is that violence? According to some definitions, it is; according to others, it is not.

Experimental Research

Experimental studies examine the effects of media under carefully controlled conditions. Typically, a small group sees a media presentation that is loaded with the type of content under study, and their responses are compared with those of people exposed to media without the "active ingredient." Although the subjects for experimental studies do not usually represent society as a whole in a statistical sense, subjects are randomly divided between the two groups to minimize the impact of their individual differences.

Perhaps the most influential experiments in the annals of media effects studies are those conducted by Albert Bandura (1965) and his colleagues at Stanford University in the 1960s. They exposed children to a short film in which a "model" acted aggressively toward a Bobo doll, a large inflatable plastic doll with the image of a clown printed on the front and sand in its base so it rocked back and forth when hit. The model punched the doll in the nose, hit it with a mallet, kicked it around the room, and threw rubber balls at it. This sequence was repeated twice.

All of the children in the study, tots from a local nursery school, saw this part of the action. However, the ending of the film was varied to conform to three experimental conditions. In the *model-rewarded* condition, a second model appeared and rewarded the aggressor with

verbal praise, soda, candy, and Cracker Jacks. In the *model-punished* condition, the second model scolded the first and spanked him. A third group of children, or the *no consequences* condition, saw only the opening.

After the show, which the children were told was a TV program, subjects were led to a playroom equipped with a Bobo doll, a mallet, some rubber balls, and assorted other toys. As adult observers watched, many of the children in the model-rewarded and no consequences conditions replicated the aggressive acts they had seen, although those in the model-punished condition tended not to. Subsequently it was verified that all the children had learned the behaviors—when adults offered them rewards they could all reproduce what they had seen.

The researchers concluded that the punishment the children experienced *vicariously* in the model-punished condition inhibited their aggressive behavior. However, the most important finding of the study was that the no consequences condition also produced a great deal of imitation. This suggested that mere exposure to television violence—whether or not the violence was ultimately rewarded—could spur aggressive responses in young children.

The value of such a carefully controlled design is that it rules out competing explanations for the results (e.g., subjects who saw the violent films were already violent children). Only the experimental treatment is varied between groups, so that any subsequent differences between them (such as the beatings the subjects inflict on their own Bobo dolls) can be ascribed to the media content in question.

However, the small and unrepresentative samples used in such studies—often consisting of college students in introductory classes or the small children of university professors— raise questions about **generalizability,** the degree to which the results apply to other populations and settings. In addition, the measures that are used (often written responses to a questionnaire or highly structured experimental tasks) and the conditions under which the experiments are conducted do not adequately reflect the real-world situations of ultimate interest, such as behavior in an actual child's playroom or on a school playground. This is the issue of **ecological validity.**

Generalizability is the degree to which social science studies can be applied to the real world.

Ecological validity is the extent to which conditions under which studies are conducted adequately reflect real-world situations.

The experimental treatments may also be unrealistic, in that they often involve much longer and much more "intense" sequences of the content in question than are likely to be encountered in the real world—and they are often presented as disjointed segments that do not show the ultimate consequences of the actions portrayed. Moreover, experimental subjects may be forced to expose themselves to content that they might not normally see, so that the effects that are observed may be exaggerated (Anderson & Meyer, 1988).

Surveys

Survey studies are familiar to most of us, since they employ the same basic methods as public opinion polls. For example, researchers interested in finding out the effects of violent video games could administer a survey to a random sample (see box on page 416) of college students at universities all over the country. Media effects are inferred by statistically relating the independent media exposure measures ("How many violent video games have you played in the last week?") with the dependent variable of interest (e.g., attitudes toward violence or self-reports of violent behavior).

Survey studies make generalizations about a population of people by addressing questions to a random sample of that population.

Survey studies are more generalizable than experimental studies, in that the samples are often representative of larger populations (such as all U.S. college students). They can also attempt to account for a wider range of factors than just the experimental manipulation (such as peer pressure to play violent games or religious beliefs that prevent playing such games).

Did you ever hear yourself say this after an election? "How could that candidate lose? All of my friends voted for her." The answer to this riddle is the key to understanding the science of survey sampling. The obvious answer is that your circle of friends does not adequately represent the opinions of the entire electorate. How do you avoid the same error in future elections? Well, you could simply ask more people outside of your inner circle, but that takes time and effort. What types of people should you ask? How many? How should you select them?

Survey sampling methods have evolved as a reaction to some classic blunders encountered in answering these very same questions. The most famous blunder of all was committed by *Literary Digest,* which had a good record of predicting the outcome of presidential elections in the 1920s and early 1930s. The magazine collected "ballots" from its readers, supplemented by lists compiled from telephone subscriber records. Tens of thousands of responses were received, but in 1936 the poll picked Alf Landon, who was soundly trounced by Franklin Roosevelt. In the aftermath, researchers realized that there was an inherent bias in the telephone subscriber lists that were used. During the Depression, only about a third of homes had phones, and these were mostly upper-income homes, where Roosevelt had little support.

By applying the science of probability sampling, researchers found that they could get more accurate results using far fewer respondents. One key is to start with a list that includes all members of the population under study. In the case of election polls, this means using voter registration lists. However, unlike in the Depression, 94 percent of homes now have telephones, so the bias involved in polling by phone is a great deal less than it was then, providing we take care to screen out potential respondents who are unlikely to vote.

The other important point is to randomly sample the list, so that everyone on the list has an equal chance of being selected. One way to visualize this would be if we cut up all of the phone books in the country, placed the individual listings in a giant revolving metal drum, and started picking numbers. This would obviously be quite cumbersome and would overlook the many homes (about 30 percent) with unpublished numbers. Most survey firms therefore use a random digit dialing technique in which a computer generates random numbers to fill in the last two digits of the listed numbers.

If we follow these simple rules, we can get an accurate response from only a few hundred respondents. For example, a sample of 400 respondents can adequately represent the entire country with only a 5 percent margin of error.

So why do polls still come out wrong, and why do different polls so often disagree? One problem is the volatility of public opinion. People can simply change their minds between polls or between the last poll and election day, and political preferences are a lot less stable than they once were. Another problem is accurately determining who the likely voters are when qualifying them for the survey. The response rate to surveys is another problem. Americans are inundated by surveys of all types, and in some areas fewer than a third of the households contacted will be reached and agree to participate. If certain types of respondents refuse more often than others, the results of the poll may be biased.

Ethnographic Research

Ethnography is a naturalistic research method in which the observer obtains detailed information about human behavior from personal observation or interviews over extended periods of time.

Ethnography provides a naturalistic way of looking at the effects of media in a specific time and place. It adapts the techniques used by anthropologists for looking at the cultures of people in a broad, holistic way. Ethnography stresses placing media and media use in a broad context of other aspects of media users' lives and cultures. It tends to gather a great deal of information about a limited number of people in a specific place and time.

Ethnographers tend to use more open-ended, longer interviews, to let people express themselves in their own words rather than respond to standard questions using preset categories, and observe their behavior over extended periods of time as well. Media ethnographers often stress watching or reading media with people at home to observe interactions, record their discussions about media, see how they use and make sense of media, and try to discern effects of media on their lives.

For instance, an anthropologist who had been studying the same Brazilian village for thirty years, since before television, observed effects in village life and in villagers' knowledge and attitudes about the world and their village that seemed to stem from television. He observed how people used television, watched it with them, and then systematically interviewed the villagers about it, using both in-depth, open-ended interviews and survey questionnaires. His results showed a considerable broadening of information about the outside world, a notable liberalization of attitudes about gender and racial roles, and a rise in material aspirations, along with some loss of local culture as expressed in local holidays, festivals, and traditional ways of doing things (Kottak, 1990).

Although ethnographers sometimes use questionnaires, ethnography is often seen as an alternative to surveys. Surveys permit the comparison of many people with standardized questions and more reliable statistical inference about effects, but survey questions impose a structure of meaning and specific response categories for the respondents. While that is extremely useful for standardizing responses so they can be compared, ethnographers often see an equal value in letting people speak in their own words, using their own concepts and categories, to make sure the researcher is not imposing ideas on them.

However, while ethnographies can yield great depth of information about the particular place and time being studied, they do not permit much generalization. Although ethnographers try to accurately record information in such a way that other ethnographers could reach the same observations and establish the reliability of the observations and conclusions, such reliability or reproducibility is a serious issue. The anthropologist in Brazil did similar studies in several other villages and cities, but to try to create generalizations about the effects of television in Brazil, he had to use survey techniques of standardized questions and samples.

The different types of studies tell us different things. Content analyses often show that the media are suffused with violence and sex, for example, but tell us nothing about the actual effects on the audience. Experimental studies often find evidence of effects, even from extremely short exposures of 15 minutes or less, but cannot assess how other factors may reduce or enhance those effects. Survey studies tend to show weak media effects but are subject to criticism about the soundness of their findings. Nor do these three basic methods exhaust all the possibilities. Ethnographic research and semiotic studies also can make important contributions to our understanding of the implications of mass media using qualitative rather than quantitative methods. It is important to explore the issue with a variety of different methods.

REVIEW

1. What are some of the things we blame on the mass media?
2. How do social scientists and critical theorists differ in their approaches to understanding the media?
3. What is a media effect?
4. In what ways are experimental studies superior to survey studies? In what ways are they inferior?
5. What do ethnographers do?

Theoretical model	Example	Audience response
Hypodermic	War! / Do exactly what media say	We want war!
Multistep	This means war / Follow opinion leaders who interpret media	People are saying this means war
Selective process	It's the moral equivalent of war / Interpret their own way	War? What war?
Social learning	Let's go get 'em! / Imitate behavior shown in media	Let's play war!
Cultivation	It's war on the streets / Think real world works like TV world	It's a scary world out there

THEORIES OF MASS MEDIA EFFECTS

Theories about the way the media influence us are the other crucial ingredients to understanding media effects. These theories represent explanations of how the effects take place and allow media researchers to make predictions about the types of presentations that are likely to have effects, and on whom (see Figure 17.1).

Early observers of mass media believed that they were extremely powerful, capable of swaying minds with the impact of a speeding **bullet** or a **hypodermic needle,** leading to theoretical models by the same names. These theorists were struck by the apparent power of wartime propaganda to whip entire nations into a frenzy and also by the seeming ability of advertising to manipulate consumer behavior. Experimental studies of **persuasion** begun during World War II focused on identifying the types of verbal arguments (one-sided versus two-sided, and fear appeals versus emotional appeals) that are the most convincing in various situations and with different types of people (Hovland, Lumsdane, & Sheffield, 1949).

However, survey studies of the processes of social influence conducted in the late 1940s presented a very different view, in which a **multistep flow** of media effects was found. That is, most people receive media effects secondhand, through the influence of **opinion leaders** (Katz & Lazarsfeld, 1955). The opinion leaders in turn are influenced by more elite media rather than by everyday mass media channels. For example, political opinion leaders might take their cues from *The New Republic*, not from *Time* magazine, and pass them along to

The **bullet or hypodermic** model posits powerful, direct effects from the mass media.

Persuasion is the use of convincing arguments to change people's beliefs, attitudes, or behaviors.

The **multistep flow** model assumes that media effects are indirect and are mediated by opinion leaders.

Opinion leaders are people in our daily lives who influence our opinions on certain topics.

members of their immediate social circle, but only after some modification and adaptation to the norms of that circle.

The multistep flow idea is expanded by two key concepts from recent critical research. One is that people within different social classes make very different interpretations of media. People tend to talk about media to people similar to themselves in education, occupation, wealth, and family background. Going beyond the idea of opinion leaders, people tend to interpret media content through discussion with key groups of people called "interpretive communities" (Lindlof, 1994). These are often natural communities such as families, neighborhoods, unions, and churches, but they also include people who find like-minded people and form a group to interpret and reinforce media messages, such as campus Rush Limbaugh fan clubs.

The selective reception of mass media reduces their impact somewhat. People have a tendency toward **selective exposure**—that is, they avoid messages that are at odds with their existing beliefs. Thus, those who take the "pro-life" position in the abortion debate are unlikely to watch a television program featuring pro-choice advocates. Even when people expose themselves to discordant content, they tend to distort it through the process of **selective perception.** Thus, pro-choice supporters who watch a TV interview with a leader of a right-to-life group would be more likely to find additional "proof" that their position is correct than to be converted to the pro-life cause. **Selective retention** refers to the fact that people's memories of media presentations are also distorted, so that months later someone may remember that "his" side won an abortion debate when in fact his side was humiliated (Sears & Freedman, 1972).

In 1960 Joseph Klapper published an influential review of research on the effects of the mass media. Klapper concluded that the media were weak, able to deliver only a few percent of the voters in an election, or to gain only a few points' worth of market share for advertisers. Even these effects registered only at the margins, he said, primarily among the uninterested or the uninformed.

In the 1960s social critics cast about for explanations for mounting violence, increased political unrest, and a perceived decline in public morality, particularly among college students. Television was seen as a possible cause, since the same generation was also the first TV generation and TV was loaded with images of violence and sex. About the same time, a new theory of mass media effects, **social learning theory,** emerged that lent credence to these claims. Based on Albert Bandura's research, the theory explained that viewers imitate what they see on TV through a process known as **observational learning.** The "rewards" that television characters receive for their antisocial behavior—including their very appearance on a glamorous medium such as television—encourage imitation (Bandura, 1986).

Another explanation for violence in America emerged from a group of researchers led by George Gerbner. They theorized that heavy exposure to television cultivates a worldview that is consistent with the "world" of television (Gerbner & Gross, 1976). According to **cultivation theory,** heavy television viewers are likely to overestimate their own chances of being victims of violent crime, owing to their heavy exposure to programs in which violent crime is commonplace.

However, other theoretical perspectives call into question the effects of the media. Social learning theory itself stresses the importance of punishments as well as rewards in media portrayals. When the bad guys on TV get caught and go to jail, this presumably inhibits viewers from imitating them. The **catharsis hypothesis** argues that media portrayals of sex and violence can actually have positive effects by allowing people to live out their antisocial

R E V I E W

1. What are three theories that posit relatively strong effects from the mass media?

2. What are some processes that attenuate effects of the mass media?

3. What are examples of media effects that are best explained by persuasion? By social learning theory? By cultivation theory?

desires in the fantasy world of the media rather than in the real world (Feshbach & Singer, 1971).

These theories are by no means the only approaches that researchers use to understand the social implications of media use. In fact, in recent years some scholars calling themselves critical theorists have called into question the value of all such attempts to examine media effects, believing that they focus too narrowly on individual behavior, leaving out the broader social implications. The critical theorists also object to what they view as a mechanistic cause-and-effect process that they feel does not adequately reflect the relationship between media and society.

MASS MEDIA AND ANTISOCIAL BEHAVIOR

Antisocial behavior is behavior contrary to prevailing norms for social conduct, such as racism, sexism, or violence.

Antisocial behavior refers to behavior that is contrary to prevailing norms for social conduct. It can include unlawful behaviors, such as murder, hate crimes, rape, and drug abuse, as well as behaviors that most members of society find objectionable even if they are not illegal, such as racism and sexism, drunkenness, and sexual promiscuity.

Violence

The effects of violence on television have probably received more attention than any other type of media effect. Effects on children are a special concern, since youngsters have trouble distinguishing between the "real world" and the "television world." To the child's mind, if the Coyote recovers instantly from a bash on the head, then the same should be true for little brother. With their short attention spans, young children are unlikely to associate the legal consequences of violent behavior that emerge in the dull courtroom scenes with the eyecatching shootout at the beginning of the show. Given that children spend so much time with television and that much of this time is unsupervised by parents, the potential exists for great harm to impressionable young minds. (See Atkin, 1985; Jeffres, 1986; Liebert & Sprafkin, 1988; and Wimmer & Dominick, 1991 for overviews of the media effects literature.)

Television is indeed packed with violence. According to content analysis studies conducted over the years, the average prime-time action drama contains six violent acts per hour. Comedies contain violence, too, at the rate of about one act of violence per hour—to researchers, a pie in the face counts just as much as a fist in the face. Children's programs, such as cartoons and music videos, are also laced with violence. A recent concern is so-called "reality programming" that inserts the camera into real-life police operations. By the time an American child reaches adulthood, he or she has probably witnessed over 10,000 acts of murder on television.

Nor are prime-time television programs the only source of media violence. Popular movies from *The Great Train Robbery* to *Jurassic Park* have featured violent action. Children can view many of these violent films on cable television channels in their bloodiest, uncut forms. In the early 1950s there was such an uproar over the violence in comic books such as *Tales from the Crypt* that the comics industry instituted the Comics Code, which put an end to violent comics for a while. A glance at any comic book rack today, however, reveals that this code has long since lost its force, and many violent comics (including *Tales from the Crypt*) are again being published, some of which have been turned into equally violent television programs and movies. Traditional children's literature such as *Grimm's Fairy Tales* is rife with violence, too, as is the Bible.

Numerous experimental studies, many patterned after Bandura's, have demonstrated that children can imitate violence from the mass media. Televised violence not only prompts children to carry out parallel acts of aggression but to perform other, novel, forms of violent behavior, and it predisposes them to select violent resolutions to conflicts in their daily lives.

Children will imitate violence even if it is not explicitly reinforced on television. In one long-term study (Lefkowitz et al., 1972) it was found that children who were exposed to high levels of television violence at an early age tended to be more violent people ten or twenty years later compared to those who watched relatively little television as children. Other experimental studies have found little or no evidence of a "catharsis effect" that reduces violent tendencies through exposure to fantasy violence. The effects of violence are not limited to children. Consistent with cultivation theory, research shows that adult viewers who watch violent programs are likely to modify their own worldviews to match the TV portrayals they see.

Studies that examine a broad cross-section of the population also tend to show a relationship between violent behavior and viewership of violent television. That is, heavy viewers tend to be no more violent than relatively light viewers. However, these relationships are relatively weak compared to the experimental findings, and some argue that they may be explainable by statistical artifacts or by factors other than exposure to television violence. Others reject the findings of experimental studies on the grounds that they are unrealistic (see, for example, Anderson & Meyer, 1988; Freedman, 1984; Hirsch, 1980; Milavsky et al., 1982). These criticisms notwithstanding, it is probably safe to conclude that exposure to antisocial television portrayals can cause antisocial behavior.

Prejudice

Sexism, racism, and other forms of intolerance of social groups may also be abetted by the media. Media portrayals encourage **stereotyping,** or the formation of generalizations about a group of people based on limited information. Stereotypes are harmful when used to define one's images of other groups, particularly when they become rationalizations for treating others unfairly. Stereotypes may be internalized by members of the groups to which they are applied, undermining self-respect. Mass media can create stereotypes because they are sometimes the only source of information about people who are different from oneself and because they often present a one-sided or distorted view.

For example, content analysis studies show that women and minorities are underrepresented in mass media portrayals and that they usually appear in subservient, low-status roles. To the white male viewer, this might somehow make it seem "acceptable" to treat women and minorities as inferiors. For their part, women and minority viewers also get

VIOLENCE IN THE MEDIA—BOTH IN ENTERTAINMENT AND NEWS PROGRAMMING—IS A MAJOR CONCERN OF PARENTS, SOCIAL SCIENTISTS, AND POLICY-MAKERS.

Stereotyping is the formulation of generalizations about groups of people based on limited information.

the sense that their group is somehow less important than the dominant group because of their underrepresentation, and they may internalize the stereotypes pressed upon them by the media—for example, that women are supposed to look beautiful and give up their careers for their families.

Some experimental studies have shown that young girls exposed to a heavy diet of TV shows with women in traditional sex roles do tend to limit their own career aspirations to traditionally female occupations—secretary, nurse, housewife (Beuf, 1974; Freuh & McGhee, 1975). There has been relatively little research on the effects of media stereotypes on minority children, but scholars believe that their life aspirations are affected by the limited media portrayals of minority actors (Clark, 1972). These negative effects may occur even when the media attempt to reduce people's prejudices and expose their stereotypes through satire. The 1970s TV series *All in the Family* was an attempt to poke fun at the Archie Bunkers of the world who were prejudiced toward women, minorities, and indeed anyone not just like themselves. Unfortunately, the real-life "Archie Bunkers" who tuned into the program found Archie to be a sympathetic character. They thought the minorities, women, and wiseguy college students in the program were the butts of the jokes, not Archie. Selective perception was evidently very much at work.

Media stereotyping is by no means limited to women and ethnic minorities. Blue-collar families are also underrepresented in the media, for example, and when present are often portrayed in an unfavorable light that denigrates their lifestyles (for example, *The Simpsons, Roseanne*). The same is true of representations of homosexuals, the physically and mentally challenged, the homeless, the mentally ill, and seemingly any group that deviates from mainstream society.

Media stereotypes also apply to many other groups. We can easily summon to mind stock images of serious college students (invariably known as "nerds" in media lexicon), millionaires, lawyers, doctors, business executives, and law enforcement professionals that have little in common with their real-world counterparts. To some extent, the media cannot function without stereotypes. They are the stuff that stories are made of, a type of conceptual shorthand that allows viewers to immediately recognize characters and connect with their situations. It is when the stereotypes spill over from the flickering screen into our daily lives that they become a concern.

Sexual Behavior

Sex in the mass media erupted as an issue in the 1920s, in the aftermath of a wave of Hollywood sex scandals. Hollywood imposed strict self-censorship standards on itself that now seem ludicrous in retrospect: no cleavage, no navels, separate beds for married couples,

---

A CRITICAL VIEW OF MEDIA, VIOLENCE, AND CULTURE

A critical analysis of John Hinckley's attempted assassination of Ronald Reagan examined the way in which Hinckley "read the text" of a violent movie (*Taxi Driver*) and mingled it with his fantasies about actress Jodie Foster and former actor Ronald Reagan (Real, 1989). By noting that Hinckley committed his act of violence on the eve of the Academy Awards ceremony, Real wove an explanation of how the would-be assassin was trying to "communicate" his unrequited love for Foster. Critical approaches to the study of advertising emphasize the ways that it promotes a general pattern of consumption—as opposed to the consumption of specific products, which is the focus of administrative research on advertising—in a way that reinforces the economic domination of the large corporations that pay for the advertising. Likewise, a critical look at the political effects of mass media might bypass campaign advertisements entirely and instead examine the hidden political messages about obedience to authority, class structure, and gender relations contained in such "nonpolitical" programs as *Sesame Street* and *Married . . . with Children.* Thus, the critical theorist is able to examine broad questions about the relationship between culture and society that may elude the social scientist.

no kisses longer than four seconds, cutting to the clouds overhead when sex was imminent. When Elizabeth Taylor said the word "virgin" in a 1954 movie, it caused a sensation. Over the next three decades, producers and publishers vied to see who could push the limits of prurience to new heights—and reap the financial benefits at the box office.

The last decades have seen a dramatic increase in the accessibility of highly explicit pornographic material through home video and adult entertainment telephone services. At the same time, social norms about appropriate sexual conduct have been evolving rapidly to exclude such behaviors as date rape and sexual harassment. These two trends are clearly on a collision course, raising anew the question of whether exposure to pornography fosters inappropriate sexual behavior.

Experimental studies offer a qualified "yes" to this question. When male college students are exposed to explicit pornography, they are more likely to express negative attitudes toward women, are more likely to think that relatively uncommon sexual practices (such as fellatio and anal intercourse) are widespread, and are likely to be lenient with rape offenders in hypothetical court cases. They are also more likely to administer (simulated) electric shocks to females (who are actually confederates of the researchers) in experimental studies. The main caveat to this last finding is that it applies only to violent pornography, in which the female models are subject to coercive or violent behavior. Acting on this research, a presidential commission under the Reagan administration (the so-called Meese Commission) spearheaded a clean-up of the pornography industry to remove coercive and violent portrayals (Attorney General of the United States, 1986).

Did the Meese Commission go far enough? Some don't think so. Feminists campaign against pornography that is demeaning to women including, for example, anything that portrays women as subservient or unequal sex partners, shows them as disembodied sex organs, or involves bodily invasion by infrahuman species or inanimate objects. Thus far, the research shows that nonviolent, noncoercive pornography does not stimulate aggression against women, although it may contribute to callousness toward women (Zillman & Bryant, 1982). Researchers have yet to fully explore the subservience issue. They have also not as yet addressed the types of effects that many are concerned about now, such as sexual harassment and date rape.

MANY SOCIAL COMMENTATORS FEEL THAT CIGARETTE AND ALCOHOL ADVERTISING IN CONSPICUOUS PLACES CAN INFLUENCE IMPRESSIONABLE MINDS.

Drug Abuse

A generation ago there was concern that movies like *The Trip* and *Easy Rider* glorified the drug scene and contributed to an epidemic of illegal drug use among college students. With the exception of a few "alternative" publications such as the magazine *High Times*, the media heeded the public concerns. Even in drug crime dramas, such as *Miami Vice*, viewers saw the mirror and the white powder and heard a little sniffle but never actually saw the powder going up the straw into the nose.

The abuse of legal drugs is quite another story. Cigarette and hard liquor ads have long been banished from television, but they still appear in print. Beer and wine commercials remain one of the leading sources of advertising revenue for television, and ads for over-the-counter drugs are another leading category. Advertisers claim that these ads do not promote the consumption of these products and only affect the relative share of the market enjoyed by the various brands. However, studies of children and adolescents provide some evidence that exposure to "soft" liquor and cigarette ads is related to their consumption among these groups. Meanwhile, young children exposed to over-the-counter drug commercials look on drugs as a way to solve their personal problems, a habit that might carry over to illicit drugs somewhere down the road. Critics contend that some of the ads are secretly targeted to young viewers through characters (such as Old Joe in the Camel cigarette ads) that are carefully crafted to appeal to impressionable young viewers at an age when they are initiating lifelong addictions.

Mass Media and Prosocial Behavior

Prosocial behavior is in a sense the opposite of antisocial behavior. It includes all of those behaviors and positive qualities that many people want to encourage in their children and their society: cooperation, altruism, sharing, love, tolerance, respect, balanced nutrition, personal hygiene, safe driving, improved reading skills, and so on. We can also include here the discontinuance of antisocial behaviors, such as when individuals decide to renounce unsafe sex, smoking, drinking, or reckless driving. Prosocial media attempt to foster prosocial behavior. They fall along a continuum based on the relative mixture of entertainment and informational content. They range from heavily sugar-coated messages to explicit, hard-core education.

Information Campaigns. **Information campaigns** use the techniques of persuasion and advertising to "sell" people on prosocial behaviors. They differ from other types of public affairs activities in that they seek to achieve specific objectives among their audience, such as heightening their awareness of a health or social problem and changing related attitudes and behaviors. Unlike educational television, they usually adopt an informal and entertaining style to attract an audience. Perhaps the most familiar manifestations of information campaigns are the public service announcements that populate late-night television ("This is your brain. This is

Prosocial behaviors are those that a society values and encourages, such as tolerance, sharing, and cooperation.

Information campaigns use the techniques of advertising in an attempt to convince people to adopt prosocial behaviors.

PUBLIC SERVICE CAMPAIGNS, LIKE THIS ONE FROM THE AD COUNCIL, ARE DESIGNED TO ENCOURAGE PROSOCIAL BEHAVIOR.

drugs. This is your brain on drugs."). However, information campaigns take many other forms, including orchestrated celebrity appearances on radio and television talk shows, the pamphlets you find in your doctor's office, and public service advertisements in print media.

Information campaigns have a spotty record of success. Experimental studies show that campaigns sometimes do affect the awareness, attitudes, and even the behavior of their audience. Campaigns can succeed if they have clear objectives and target audiences and find relevant ways to overcome the indifference of the audience (Mendelsohn, 1973). To take one example, in the 1970s the United Methodist Church created a campaign aimed at young children to counteract television violence by stressing cooperation. Research showed that children who saw a "prosocial commercial" called "The Swing" did indeed imitate the cooperative behavior that was shown (Liebert & Sprafkin, 1988).

Even when well designed, information campaigns seldom have much impact. Since they rely on free advertising space, they have difficulty reaching their intended audiences and never with the same impact as a political campaign or product promotion. "The Swing" rarely appeared alongside programs frequently watched by children, often airing in the wee hours of the morning—the only hours in which broadcasters were willing to contribute free air time. The public interest groups that produce information campaigns usually expend all their resources in developing the media materials, leaving little for paid media placements that might bring the campaigns to the attention of their true target audiences.

But few information campaigns are effective to begin with. They are often created by advertising professionals who contribute their time in exchange for a chance to showcase their skills. The results are often eyecatching and memorable ("This is your brain . . .") but seldom achieve their stated goals, because they fail to take into account the ability of the audience to selectively process information or else fail to activate the social networks that apply personal influence. A common mistake is to use strong fear appeals in an effort to dissuade adolescents from illicit behaviors. Unfortunately, the teens who are most susceptible to these behaviors are also likely to have low self-esteem, meaning that they will discount or deny the message rather than taking it to heart. The adults who are behind the campaigns think they are great ("Yeah, hard hitting—that'll teach them!"), but the target audience just shrugs them off.

In other cases, campaigns either have no specific objectives or target audiences or have too many, trying to satisfy multiple agendas ("We want users to stop using, potential users to stop thinking about it, and their parents to drum it into their heads"). Developers of information campaigns seldom have the resources for the detailed background research that goes into successful product commercials. What is more, they try to achieve much more than product advertisements, which merely aim to increase awareness of a brand name or a new product. Information campaigns often target deeply ingrained habitual behaviors, a goal that the advertising executives who create the public service spots usually admit they cannot readily achieve in their "day jobs."

Informal Education. **Informal educational** media focus more on enhancing the knowledge of the audience rather than changing its beliefs or social behaviors. These media are usually consumed in the home rather than in an educational institution. Without a "captive audience," they must artfully combine the elements of education and entertainment. The best-known example is *Sesame Street*. Since its inception in 1972, *Sesame Street* has proved to be both popular and a highly effective means of readying young children for school.

Sesame Street is also an example of another phenomenon that plagues prosocial media,

Informal education is entertaining educational programming consumed outside of a school setting.

Unintended effects are effects counter to those that the designers of a prosocial program hope for.

the **unintended effect.** *Sesame Street* was originally designed to close the gap in school readiness between minority and majority children. Unfortunately, it does just the opposite. White, middle-class children who watch the show get more out of it than low-income minority children, and the knowledge gap between the two widens as a result (Cook et al., 1975). Antidrug campaigns also have a habit of backfiring by inadvertently glamorizing abuse or by supplying information that encourages use ("Drugs only *fry* your brain? I thought they *incinerated* your brain!").

Distance learning refers to formal education programs delivered through communications media.

Distance Learning. Further along the continuum from informational entertainment to entertaining information are **distance learning** courses. These are media presentations that are fully integrated into formal academic curricula, in most cases little more than mediated versions of classroom instruction. Television is the most familiar distance learning medium for most college students. However, television is by no means the only medium for distance learning. The Open University in Great Britain relies on radio and print materials. Advanced teleconferencing technologies combine elements of audio, video, and computer graphics.

As deadly as televised lectures sometimes seem, they do seem to work. Hundreds of research studies have shown that they are as educationally effective as "live" classroom instruction (Chu & Schramm, 1975)—although they are usually tested under conditions that make it impossible to fall asleep or channel hop to MTV. When shown to "nontraditional" students who cannot come to campus for lectures, telecourses sometimes prove more effective. That is probably because adult learners are often better motivated than on-campus students and may be taking only a single course at a time.

Incidental learning refers to the positive educational side effects of mass media consumption.

Incidental Learning. What about the prosocial effects of entertainment media? Do couch potatoes soak up valuable information from TV quiz shows? Do children imitate altruistic behavior from the Smurfs as readily as they pick up violent behavior from the Coyote? Do they learn about anthropology from watching *The Flintstones* or acquire reading skills from *Wheel of Fortune,* as the TV networks sometimes like to claim? We call these effects **incidental learning,** since they are incidental side effects from the consumption of entertainment media that are otherwise devoid of instructional purpose.

Compared to the antisocial effects, little research has been done on the prosocial effects of entertainment media. Content analyses of television entertainment programming reveal frequent examples of prosocial behavior, although these instances may be overwhelmed by glorified depictions of mayhem and aggression (Greenberg et al., 1980). In general, prosocial programs can be highly effective (Hearold, 1986), although prosocial effects do not seem to be as predictable and long lasting as antisocial effects (Liebert & Sprafkin, 1988).

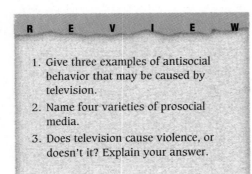

R E V I E W

1. Give three examples of antisocial behavior that may be caused by television.
2. Name four varieties of prosocial media.
3. Does television cause violence, or doesn't it? Explain your answer.

THE EFFECTS OF ADVERTISING

If the mass media have mixed success in influencing behavior, why is there so much advertising? The answer is that advertisers are happy to achieve far more limited effects than those that concern media watchdog groups. Most advertisers take our consumer behavior as a given and merely seek to influence the particular brand we purchase. First, they seek to increase our **brand awareness** so that we think of their product when we are in the store.

Brand awareness is the ability of a consumer to remember the name of a product.

Once they have us sold, they try to maintain **brand loyalty** so that we will keep coming back for more. Thus, automobile manufacturers do not waste their money convincing us that we need a new car. But they *do* try to make us think of their product when we are out shopping for a car and to come back to them for our next one.

Does Advertising Work?

Even with these relatively modest goals, many advertising campaigns are a flop. Sometimes they are outgunned by more powerful campaigns from competitors. In addition, many other factors influence consumer purchases, including the price of the product, special promotional offers, its availability, the way it is packaged, and—let us not forget—the true needs of the consumers and the objective merits of the product itself. Any of these can negate an effective advertising campaign.

Sometimes the campaign itself is ineffective or backfires. Part of the problem lies with the way that commercials are tested before they go on the air. If they are highly memorable, they are deemed successful. Only much later do the advertisers find out whether they sell more hamburgers or athletic shoes.

There are many highly successful advertising campaigns, with the best ones capable of producing substantial increases in market share. However, the average commercial campaign is likely to register an increase in sales of only a few percent. These modest gains nonetheless translate into millions of dollars for mass market products. That, and the hope of the occasional blockbuster campaign, is what keeps the whole system of commercial advertising and mass media afloat.

Social Effects of Advertising

What are the overall effects of advertising? One effect is on the consumer's pocketbook. Overall, about 3 percent of the total amount that consumers spend for goods and services goes into advertising. There are some product categories—cigarettes and soft drinks, for example—where much of the cost of the product is advertising cost. To the extent that their manufacturers establish brand loyalty, they can charge more for their products. However, advertising also makes consumers aware of alternative products and special offers and generally promotes competition, which helps to keep prices down at the retail level. Overall, it appears that advertisements are a slight "bargain." That is, they return slightly more to the consumer than they take away.

While ads are not very successful at altering fundamental patterns of consumer behavior—such as "making" us buy a new car when we really don't need one—it is possible that they raise overall levels of consumption. If we are continually exposed to ads with sensuous pictures of gleaming new cars and see films and TV shows with glamorous Hollywood stars tooling around in the newest Bulgemobile, doesn't that make our old rust bucket seem all the more shabby to us?

On a broader scale, the advertising barrage may cultivate materialistic values, subtly convincing us that the key to our happiness lies in the consumption of consumer goods. The noted economist John Kenneth Galbraith (1967) argues that advertising is a type of propaganda that places consumers on an endless treadmill of work to fulfill wants created by ads, all in the service of large corporations who need to keep their factories running at capacity. However, it is also possible that consumption causes advertising—that advertising expenditures rise along with disposable income and the demand for consumer products, for reasons that have nothing to do with advertising.

The effects of television advertising on young children have received a great deal of attention, as it is through TV that most children first come into contact with the consumer society. Young children have a difficult time understanding commercials. They confuse the commercials with the programs and react uncritically to the advertising messages. In the past, advertisers exploited the gullibility of young viewers by using the hosts of children's shows to hawk their products, selecting deceptive camera angles to make tiny toys appear child-sized, and prompting children to wear down their parents by parroting annoying advertising slogans. Cereal commercials were the worst offenders, promoting unhealthful confections by placing toys in the packages instead of nutrition. The Federal Trade Commission issued guidelines that curbed some of the worst practices. Hosts no longer appear in commercials—although ancillary merchandising has made some cartoon shows into little more than program-length commercials for "action figures" and other spinoff products—and commercial announcers now have to mumble caveats such as "Some assembly required" and "Part of this nutritious breakfast" as they deliver their spiels. The FTC has not figured out a way to crack down on pestering, however.

THE EFFECTS OF POLITICAL COMMUNICATION

Increasingly, political campaigns have devolved into advertising campaigns, with the candidate as the product. The techniques of market research and mass persuasion have been applied with a vengeance to the political process. The political caucus has given way to the focus group, a type of open-ended interview in which small groups of consumers/voters are prompted by market researchers to reveal their innermost feelings about the candidates for the benefit of a hidden TV camera.

Political Commercials

What is the net effect of the political ads that clutter the airwaves before an election? Surprisingly little, if we look just at the direct effects of the ads on voting behavior. Like ads for commercial products, campaign ads have relatively modest effects, especially those that appear in the final days of the campaign. By that time, most voters have made up their minds,

THIS "ATTACK AD" FROM THE 1984 PRESIDENTIAL CAMPAIGN IMPLIED THAT DEMOCRATIC CANDIDATE MIKE DUKAKIS WAS "SOFT ON CRIME." THE AD WAS CREDITED WITH SWINGING VOTES TO GEORGE BUSH.

Many are still at large.

and the processes of selective exposure, selective perception, and selective recall attenuate the effects. Political commercials cannot "convert" many voters to the other side at that stage. That leaves the undecided voters, many of whom are likely to simply stay home. According to the multistep flow model, the undecided voters who do vote are more likely to be swayed by the people around them than by the candidates' campaign spots.

It is ironic that the less important the election, the more important political ads become. This is because, aside from the presidential race and one or two other top-of-the-ballot contests, voters are unlikely to be familiar with the candidates. Many Americans cannot name their own member of the House of Representatives, let alone the name of the challenger or the positions either one takes on the issues. Since people are naturally unwilling to vote for an unknown quantity, this often gives incumbents—and candidates with names like "Kennedy" or "Trueheart"—a natural advantage. A generation ago, the party label was the accepted way to sort through a field of unknown candidates, but now party loyalty and discipline are in decline. Issues are also passé. In this vacuum, a little bit of advertising can be very effective. After all, this is one of the things that advertising is good at, establishing "brand awareness."

Campaign Coverage

What about the other campaign coverage that appears in the media, such as news stories, public opinion polls, public appearances by the candidates, debates, and editorial endorsements? Campaign coverage is inherently more effective than political advertisements because authoritative media sources are generally more credible, or believable, than politicians, and credible sources are more persuasive.

Media coverage sometimes makes political ads effective when the ads become news stories in themselves. The classic example was a television spot run by Lyndon Johnson in the 1964 presidential campaign. The ad showed a little girl picking wildflowers, followed by a picture of a mushroom cloud of a nuclear explosion, implying that opponent Barry Goldwater's "hard line" military policies would have dire consequences. The ad only ran once, but the print and electronic media publicized it in their campaign coverage, greatly extending its reach and lending credibility to the message.

However, selective processes also limit the effectiveness of campaign coverage, just as they limit the effects of campaign ads. Nowhere is this more evident than in presidential debates. Debates are seen through the distorted lens of selective perception to such a degree that who one sees as the "winner" of a debate depends almost entirely on which candidate one favored going in. Very few voters are converted to the other side by debates, with most of the movement in candidate preferences found among those who are undecided or relatively uninterested in the election.

The impact of election polls is also dulled by selective perception, with a candidate's "true believers" likely to discount the credibility of polls rather than to change their preference. This is not to say that polls do not play an important role in the political process. The candidates themselves follow them religiously, constantly reformulating their message and their image to increase their popularity among key blocs of voters. Political contributions also flow in on a rising tide of positive poll numbers and recede when the polls take a downturn. As with paid advertising spots, coverage is likely to be more influential in the less important elections. Editorial endorsements in newspapers follow this rule. They have relatively little impact on elections for national or statewide offices but may be the deciding factor for local candidates.

The mass media are by no means powerless bystanders in the electoral process; it is just that the effects do not flow directly from the mass media sources that most of us are familiar with. Recalling again the concept of the multistep flow, opinion leaders in our own circle of friends, family, and acquaintances are the true sources of personal influence. In turn, they are influenced by opinion leaders of their own and by their exposure to elite media sources that most of us do not see. They are the "C-SPAN junkies," the people who watch the Sunday newsmaker interviews while the rest of the population tunes into the football game. Increasingly, politicians seek to circumvent journalists and media pundits to speak directly to opinion leaders. Using such channels as electronic bulletin boards and closed group teleconferences, they deliver their message directly to the influentials, bypassing the media gatekeepers entirely.

Voter Participation

Media coverage also affects voter participation. In minor elections where as few as 10 percent of the eligible voters turn out, if the media turn their attention to an otherwise obscure race, voter participation may soar. If the coverage selectively galvanizes unified blocs of voters, this can have a major impact on the election results as well.

Since 1952 television networks have used computers to "call" presidential elections at an early hour on election night. In every national election since then, complaints have been heard about the potential of media coverage to reduce election turnouts, particularly when networks interview voters outside the election booths and pick the winners long before the polls are closed. It is difficult to prove that any such effect exists or, if there is one, that it helps or hurts one side or the other. The presumption is that West Coast voters will not turn out to vote for a candidate who has already lost, possibly threatening the chances of state and local candidates who still have a chance to win. However, it could also be argued that supporters of the winner will not turn out in equal numbers, since they feel their vote is no longer needed. In postelection surveys, it appears that only a tiny percentage of voters are affected.

Mass Media and Public Opinion

The mass media may have more important effects between elections than during them. In earlier chapters we saw how the media have an agenda-setting function. That is, by the topics they choose to cover, they define the set of issues that people talk about among themselves and that they are likely to perceive as important in future elections. The media are not in complete control of this process, however. They must respond to feedback from their audiences in the form of newsstand sales, ratings, letters to the editor, and their own polls. Some issues resonate with the audience, while others fall flat, and the media have to respond if they want to continue selling products for their advertisers. The public agenda is also shaped by a marriage of convenience between politicians, special interests, and the press, wherein the press caters to the agendas of the pols and the interest groups in order to maintain access to newsmakers.

The set of commonly held beliefs, attitudes—and misconceptions—about the issues of the day that arise out of this process is what we call **public opinion.** Like candidate preferences, public opinion is also shaped through interpersonal influence. The publicity attached to polls

Public opinion is the set of commonly held beliefs about the issues of the day.

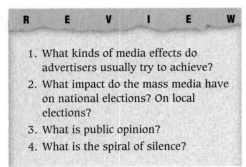

R E V I E W

1. What kinds of media effects do advertisers usually try to achieve?
2. What impact do the mass media have on national elections? On local elections?
3. What is public opinion?
4. What is the spiral of silence?

may help mold public opinion through a process called the **spiral of silence.** That is, when we believe that our opinions match the rising tide of public opinion—for example, when we see opinion poll results that support our own opinions—our beliefs are strengthened. Conversely, when we sense that we hold an unpopular belief, we remain silent. Since one of the ways we gauge how popular our own opinions are is by hearing the same opinions voiced by others, a self-perpetuating cycle begins that eventually suppresses the less popular view.

SUMMARY & REVIEW

What Are Some of the Methods Researchers Use to Assess Media Effects?

What is meant by a media effect?
Media effects are changes in knowledge, attitude, or behavior that result from exposure to the mass media. Exposure to media content is treated as the causal, or independent, variable that leads to the effects, or the dependent variable. Some examples of media effects that have been examined extensively by social scientists include impacts on violent behavior, sexual behavior, voting behavior, consumer behavior, racism, and sexism.

What are the three basic methods of media effects research?
Content analysis is used to characterize the content of media systems by enumerating the types of behaviors, themes, and actors that appear in the media, although they cannot be used to make inferences about the actual effects of the media. Experimental research studies the relationship between exposure to media content and audience effects under tightly controlled laboratory conditions that make it possible to rule out competing explanations for the effects that are observed. Survey studies administer questionnaires to large representative samples of subjects in an effort to examine relationships between media exposure and media effects, but taking into account a wider range of factors than experimental studies.

What other methods are used to explore the implications of mass media for society?
Other methods are more qualitative and less quantitative. Semiotics is the study of the symbols and underlying meanings contained in media presentations. In ethnographic studies researchers maintain extended contact with subjects so that they can gain deep insight into social processes and the significance of the media in social systems. Qualitative methods such as these are often capable of yielding insights into human behavior that are unavailable to practitioners of the other methods.

What is a sampling?
Sampling is a technique that is often used in survey studies. Its goal is to collect responses from a relatively small group of respondents who will be statistically representative of the larger population from which the respondents are drawn. The key to good sampling is random selection—that is, giving each member of the population an equal chance of being chosen for study and seeing to it that the sample is drawn from a list that includes all members of the population being studied.

What Are Some Theories for Understanding the Implications of Mass Media for Society?

How have theories of mass media effects changed?
Theories of mass media effects have evolved over the years. Early theorists believed in very powerful mass media, which could have immediate and profound effects on their audiences after the fashion of a speeding bullet or a hypodermic injection. Later researchers learned that the influence of the mass media is weakened by the intervention of social groups in a multistep flow process and by the audience's ability to avoid and misinterpret content with which they disagree. Social learning theory describes how people can learn behavior from visual media, while cultivation theory illustrates how people's understanding of the world around them is shaped by media images. These theories led to a restoration of the perception that mass media are relatively powerful influences on society.

What Are Some of the Effects of the Mass Media?

What is the impact of the mass media on antisocial behavior?

Experimental studies have shown that even relatively short exposure to TV programs featuring violence can provoke violent behavior in viewers, particularly young children. Men exposed to violent pornography harbor more violent feelings toward women. Media also can reinforce sex-role and racial stereotypes that lead to sexism and racism. In general, the mass media can cause a wide variety of antisocial behavior, although these effects may be moderated by interpersonal influence and by the sometimes inconsistent nature of media portrayals of such behavior.

What is the impact of the mass media on prosocial behavior?

Prosocial behaviors are socially desirable acts such as cooperation, sharing, and racial tolerance. Information campaigns seek to convince mass audiences to adopt socially desirable behaviors. While such campaigns are sometimes effective, they often suffer from poor planning and execution and limited audience exposure and must contend with resistance from social influence and selective perception among their audiences. Other varieties of prosocial media combine varying degrees of entertainment and educational content, ranging from distance-learning classes to incidental learning from entertainment programs. Overall, there is far more emphasis on antisocial

behavior than on prosocial behavior in the media, making it difficult to demonstrate positive effects.

What are the effects of advertising and political campaigns?

Despite the huge sums of money expended on commercial and political advertisements, their effects are relatively modest, directly affecting perhaps only a few percent of the audience. Those who are affected by advertisements are likely to be those who are relatively uninformed or uninterested in the product or the candidate to begin with. Interpersonal influence and selective perception processes act to reduce the impact of advertisements on most audiences. Still, those few percent can translate into millions of dollars in a successful advertising campaign, or into crucial deciding votes in a political race.

Why doesn't someone "clean up" the media if they have so many negative effects?

Efforts by the U.S. government to reduce the amount of antisocial media content inevitably conflict with the free speech rights of the media. The media sometimes agree to adopt their own guidelines, such as content ratings or program standards. However, these are voluntary standards that are usually eroded by pressures to make sensational programming in an attempt to reach the largest possible audience. Media spokespersons often question the research that shows harmful effects, on the grounds that the studies are conducted under highly controlled conditions that do not adequately reflect the real world.

REFERENCES

Anderson, J. A., & Meyer, T. P. (1988). *Mediated communication.* Newbury Park, CA: Sage Publications.

Atkin, C. (1985). *The effects of mass media: Readings in mass communication and society.* East Lansing: Department of Communication, Michigan State University.

Attorney General of the United States. (1986). *Final report of the Attorney General's Commission on Pornography.* Washington, DC: U.S. Government Printing Office.

Bandura, A. (1965). Influence of models' reinforcement contingencies on the acquisition of imitative responses. *Journal of Personality and Social Psychology, 1,* 589–595.

Bandura, A. (1986). *Social foundations of thought and action: A social cognitive theory.* Englewood Cliffs, NJ: Prentice-Hall.

Barbero, J. (1993). *Communication, culture, and hegemony: From the media to the mediations.* Newbury Park, CA: Sage Publications.

Beuf, A. (1974). Doctor, lawyer, household drudge. *Journal of Communication, 24*(2), 142–145.

Chomsky, N., & Herman, E. (1988). *Manufacturing consent: The political economy of the mass media.* New York: Pantheon.

Chu, G. C., & Schramm, C. (1975). *Learning from television: What the research says.* Washington, DC: National Society of Professionals in Telecommunications.

Clark, C. C. (1972). Race, identification and television violence. In G. A. Comstock, E. A. Rubenstein, & J. P. Murray (Eds.), *Television and social behavior* (Vol. 5). Washington, DC: U.S. Government Printing Office.

Cook, T. D., Appleton, H., Conner, R. F., Shaffer, A., Tamkin, G., & Weber, S. J. (1975). *Sesame Street revisited: A case study in evaluation research.* New York: Russell Sage Foundation.

Feshbach, S., & Singer, R. (1971). *Television and aggression.* San Francisco: Jossey-Bass.

Freedman, J. L. (1984). Effect of television violence on aggressiveness. *Psychological Bulletin, 96*(2), 227–246.

Freuh, T., & McGhee, P. E. (1975). Traditional sex role development and the amount of time spent watching television. *Developmental Psychology, 11*(1), 109.

Galbraith, J. K. (1967). *The new industrial state.* Boston: Houghton Mifflin.

Gerbner, G., & Gross, L. (1976). Living with television. *Journal of Communication, 26,* 173–199.

Greenberg, B. S., et al. (1980). Antisocial and prosocial behaviors on television. In B. S. Greenberg (Ed.), *Life on television: Content analysis of U.S. TV drama.* Norwood, NJ: Ablex.

Grossberg, L. (1993). Can cultural studies find true happiness in communication? *Journal of Communication, 43,* 89–97.

Hearold, S. (1986). A synthesis of 1043 effects of television on social behavior. In G. Comstock (Ed.), *Public communication and behavior: Vol. I.* New York: Academic Press.

Hirsch, P. M. (1980). The "scary world" of the nonviewer and other anomalies: A reanalysis of Gerbner et al.'s findings on cultivation analysis. *Communication Research, 7,* 403–456.

Hoveland, C., Lumsdane, A., & Sheffield, F. (1949). *Experiments on mass communications.* Princeton, NJ: Princeton University Press.

Jeffres, L. (1986). *Mass media processes and effects.* Prospect Heights, IL: Waveland Press.

Jensen, E., & Graham, E. (1993, October 26). Stamping out TV violence: A losing fight. *The Wall Street Journal,* pp. B1, B9.

Katz, E., & Lazarsfeld, P. F. (1955). *Personal influence.* New York: Free Press.

Klapper, J. T. (1960). *The effects of mass communication.* New York: Free Press.

Kottak, C. (1990). *Prime time society.* Belmont, CA: Wadsworth.

Lazarsfeld, P. F. (1941). Remarks on adminstrative and critical communication research. *Studies in Philosophy and Social Science, 9,* 2–16.

Lefkowitz, M. M., Eron, L. D., Walder, L. O., & Huesmann, L. R. (1972). Television violence and child aggression: A follow-up study. In G. A. Comstock & E. A. Rubenstein (Eds.), *Television and social behavior* (Vol. 3). Washington, DC: U.S. Government Printing Office.

Liebert, R., & Sprafkin, J. (1988). *The early window.* New York: Pergamon Press.

McChesney, R. W. (1993). Critical communication research at the crossroads. In M. R. Levy & M. Gurevitch (Eds.), *Defining media studies.* New York: Oxford University Press.

Mendelsohn, H. (1973). Some reasons why information campaigns can succeed. *Public Opinion Quarterly, 37,* 50–61.

Milavsky, J. R., Kessler, R., Stipp, H., & Rubens, W. S. (1982). Television and aggression: Results of a panel study. In D. Perarl, L. Bouthilet, & J. Lazar (Eds.), *Television and behavior: Ten years of scientific progress and implications for the eighties* (Vol. 2). Washington, DC: U.S. Government Printing Office.

Morley, D. (1992). *Television audiences and cultural studies.* New York: Routledge.

Real, M. (1989). *Super media.* Newbury Park, CA: Sage Publications.

Sears, D. O., & Freedman, J. L. (1972). Selective exposure to information: A critical review. In W. Shramm & D. Roberts (Eds.), *The process and effects of mass communication.* Chicago: University of Illinois Press.

Steeves, H. L. (1993). Creating imagined communities: Development communication and the challenge of feminism. In M. R. Levy & M. Gurevitch (Eds.), *Defining media studies.* New York: Oxford University Press.

Wimmer, R. D., & Dominick, J. R. (1991). *Mass media research* (3rd ed.). Belmont, CA: Wadsworth.

Zillman, D., & Bryant, J. (1982). Pornography, sexual callousness, and the trivialization of rape. *Journal of Communication, 32,* 10–21.

Chapter 18

THE SOCIAL IMPACTS OF INFORMATION TECHNOLOGIES

C H A P T E R   P R E V I E W

This chapter assesses the social effects of information technologies. Because the telephone was invented before researchers started to study social impacts, we begin with a retrospective assessment of its possible effects. Next we examine the effects of today's information technologies on consumers, focusing on such issues as social equality, privacy, and criminal behavior. Finally, we consider the effects of information technology in the world of work, including their impact on the amount and quality of employment.

Detroit, Michigan, 2010

Hello, is anyone in there?

> You can call me DeeVee if you want. You must be Dantaya.

Mr. D.V., Dad says I can play you when he doesn't need you for his new job.

> That's right, and I have over 5,000 channels and 10 million databases and we can call anywhere in the world!

Well, I could use a little help with my arithmetic homework. Dad's so busy now . . .

> I have the U-M Elementary Math Tutor Channel, or I can download the MIT Math Buddy program directly to your own computer.

I don't have a computer, so let's try that You'M tutor.

> That's Yew-EM, short for the University of Michigan, and it's only twenty dollars an hour for a live interactive feed . . .

No, I don't think Dad can afford that. I know, let's call my gramma in Atlanta. She's real good at math. I'll need to show her my paper, though. Can you do that?

> <Dialing, Mrs. Janetta Johnson, Atlanta, Georgia.> That will be 50 cents a minute for the video.

No! That's *thirty* dollars an hour! Don't you have anything for kids that's for free?

> Certainly! <Roadrunner Channel—Sugar Frosties Theater—Beavis & Butt-Head Classics—Pee Wee Herman Channel—Michael Jackson Network—Interactive Power Rangers—Toy Store Channel—Child Abuse Victim Support Channel>

I guess I'll just have to try to do my own arithmetic, MISter DataVision.

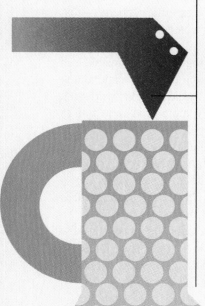

Although the telephone has been with us for over a hundred years, we know surprisingly little about the impact it has had on society. The fields of study most concerned with the impacts of media on society today—sociology, social psychology, and communications studies—were not yet developed back in the 1870s. The task of assessing the effects of the telephone fell to the journalists and technologists of three generations ago. These predictions were collected by the late telecommunications scholar Ithiel de Sola Pool (1983). This exercise in "retrospective technology assessment" gives us a perspective on the social impacts of the telephone from a time before it was a fixture of daily life.

One prediction was that the telephone would reduce the literacy level. Once relieved of writing letters and thank-you notes (then used in conjunction with virtually all social interactions), people would let their writing skills atrophy. In actuality, the literacy level improved, a result of the expansion of public education. Most agree that literacy levels are declining today, but television, not the telephone, now gets the blame.

The telephone was also expected to revitalize rural areas by enriching the life of the farm family. Instead, the farm population declined dramatically, although as a result of improvements in agricultural technology and the progressive transition from an agricultural to an industrial economy.

Women were also expected to benefit, particularly socially isolated rural women. As we shall see, the feminist critique of the telephone argues that just the opposite happened—that the spread of the telephone became a means of further confining women in their homes and of oppressing them when they left home.

Other early predictions clearly did come true. It was thought that telephones would lead to suburbanization, making it convenient to move to the suburbs while maintaining employment and social contacts in the city. Suburbanization clearly did take place, although the automobile, and the streetcar before it, probably played a more prominent role in fostering this social trend.

Telephones were also predicted to increase the size of cities, and in one respect that may be true. Prior to the telephone, office communications were transmitted by messengers. Without the telephone, the sheer number of elevators required to hold all the messengers would have made urban skyscrapers economically unattractive. However, pneumatic tubes or more efficiently organized office mail systems might have also filled the bill.

These examples show that it is difficult to trace causal relationships between new technologies and social change. When the anticipated impacts do not take place, it may be because of other forces that overwhelm the effects of the technology. Likewise, when the predictions *do* come true, it may turn out that they have little to do with the technology in question.

These examples also remind us that if we wait long enough, any prediction can come true—or can be falsified. Take the prediction that the telephone would become a mass medium. If we had examined it in 1900 before commercial radio service but when "telephone broadcasting" experiments were under way, we might have concluded that the prediction was accurate. By the 1930s, when national radio networks were in full swing, that prediction looked ridiculous. In the 1990s, as we observe the growth of audiotext and videotex services and experiments with telephone video services, that prediction is beginning to look positively clairvoyant.

CURRENT ISSUES IN THE SOCIAL EFFECTS OF INFORMATION TECHNOLOGIES

Among the social effects of information technology, those of greatest concern involve social equality, personal relationships, privacy, criminal behavior, cultural effects, and health and environmental effects.

Social Equality

Information technologies are not equally accessible to all social groups. Many members of minority and low-income groups do not have telephones, for example. Whereas about 95 percent of all homes have telephones, the figure is only about 85 percent for African American homes (Belinfante, 1989). Before 1940, telephone companies sometimes avoided pockets of poverty, believing that these areas would prove unprofitable. Today, Telephone Assistance Plans are available to subsidize telephones for low-income households. Nevertheless, many families still cannot afford them and are disconnected from the world of work, from public assistance agencies, and from family and friends.

According to a national study of school-aged children conducted by the Educational Testing Service, white students have higher levels of **computer literacy** than African American or Hispanic students, and the gap between the groups widens at the higher grade levels (Kominski, 1988). Differential exposure to computers in the home may explain the gap. White students are far more likely to have a home computer. The same study showed that while computer competence is about equal for boys and girls in the lower grades, by the seventh grade boys are far ahead. Once again, the availability of computers in the home is a key factor.

Some contend that computer education is really fulfilling a **hidden curriculum** that imposes the values of the dominant culture by teaching young women and minorities to obey commands and to acclimatize them to repetitive tasks. It also teaches students to accept authority, personified by the adult authority figures who define the computer applications and provide user assistance. According to this argument, well-intentioned efforts to close the computer gap by pushing computer literacy for minorities and women only exacerbate the problem by further conditioning them to accept their "place" in a system of economic exploitation (Roszak, 1986).

The computer gap for minorities and women persists into adulthood. The industries that provide information technologies and the occupations that use them are largely dominated by white males. According to the National Science Foundation, in the 1980s only 3 percent of computer specialists were African American. Although women such as Lady Ada Byron Lovelace (patroness of Charles Babbage and the world's first computer systems analyst), Grace Hopper (developer of the COBOL programming language), Ellen Hancock (vice-president of network services for IBM), and Lore Harp (founder of Vector Graphics) have played prominent roles in the computer industry, women are seriously underrepresented in computer science fields. The Bureau of Labor Statistics indicates that women in computer professions earn considerably less than their male colleagues, although this gap is somewhat smaller than the national average across all lines of work (see Davidson & Cooper, 1987; Werneke, 1985; Zientara, 1987; Zimmerman, 1990).

Women have also borne the brunt of job losses resulting from the office automation trend, while minority blue-collar workers fill many of the jobs slated for robotization. The one computer-related occupation that does have a relatively high percentage of females, computer programmer, is also headed for automation with the advent of computer-aided

Computer literacy is the basic understanding of computers.

Hidden curriculum is the notion that by learning information technologies, students adopt the dominant culture.

WOMEN AND TELEPHONES: A FEMINIST CRITIQUE

In the words of feminist scholar Lana Rakow (1992), the telephone is a "gendered technology" through which women sustain themselves as women (Moyal, 1988) but also through which they complete gendered work—work that is culturally assigned to women. It is a technology that is embedded in patterns of a social hierarchy that relegates women to certain narrowly defined roles, including that of the household "communications specialist" who maintains social relationships over the telephone. In this view, women's mythic propensity to chatter on the phone is in fact the consequence of carrying out stereotypical female family functions and also of a society that denies access to meaningful activities outside the home.

Women have influenced the development of information technologies in other, more subtle, ways. The telephone was intended as an instrument of communication for the (male-dominated) business world. At first, telephone companies discouraged trivial "social use" of the telephone (mostly by women) to keep the lines clear for important (male-originated) business calls. However, women staged a quiet rebellion against these restrictions, forcing the redesign of the telephone system. The telephone may have given women new freedom to communicate with the world beyond the home, but at the same time the communication took place inside the home, perhaps diminishing opportunities to make new social contacts outside of it.

During the 1880s, the job of telephone operator became women's work. Employers believed that women were more docile than men and would be more polite to telephone subscribers—and also more willing to work for low wages. At first, telephone operators enjoyed greater status—and also better pay—than their sisters who worked as retail clerks and factory workers. The Bell System required that their operators be high school graduates, which also contributed to the status of the job. Before 1900, the telephone operator had some autonomy, enjoying the freedom to set her own pace and to frame her own personal greeting for callers.

This changed swiftly in the early twentieth century as efficiency experts made the operator's job highly structured and routinized. Operators now had to answer 90 percent of all calls within four seconds, and their conversation was limited to some 100 specific expressions in the company rule book. Work shifts lasted eleven hours without a break, all the time encumbered by a "headset" the size of a toaster that weighed several pounds. Sexual harassment by male supervisors was rampant. In those days, the "glass ceiling" was more like a "brick roof." Women were never promoted beyond the level of floor supervisor and could work for the phone company only until their mid-twenties, after which time it was assumed they would all get married and start families (Martin, 1991).

In response, female operators got active in the labor movement, forming the only international union directed by and composed entirely of women, the Telephone Operator's Department, in 1919. Under the leadership of Julia O'Connor, the Telephone Operator's

Department succeeded in winning improvements in working conditions. A strike against New England Telephone broke the back of the union when the other, male-dominated telephone unions refused to honor picket lines and male college students were hired as strike-breaking scabs. The status and pay of the telephone operators declined as they were replaced by automatic switching equipment. The replacement of telephone operators by automatic switching equipment stands today as one of the premiere examples of job displacement by auto-mated systems (Norwood, 1990).

software engineering (CASE) systems. The new, high-paying jobs created by information technologies are usually in technical fields dominated by white males.

Women, many of them recent immigrants from Latin America, also populate the "clean rooms" in semiconductor factories. Others work for piece-rate wages, assembling computer components in their own kitchens. Silicon Valley employers say that they prize the maternal instincts, agility, and work ethic of the female workers—but perhaps also their seeming willingness to accept low wages. The consequences reach beyond economic exploitation, however. The rooms are designed to keep the semiconductor components clean, not the employees' lungs. The solvents used on the chips are highly toxic and are the chief suspects in the extremely high incidences of immune system disorders, birth defects, and miscarriages among clean room workers (Hayes, 1989). The telephone industry has an equally dismal record of exploitation of women (see box on page 438).

The **information gap hypothesis** makes a parallel and equally gloomy statement about the effects of information technology. This perspective makes a distinction between the "information rich" and the "information poor." The information rich are those with superior levels of education and access to resources such as libraries and home computers. The information poor have inferior levels of education and resource access—and tend to be the economically poor as well (see Figure 18.1). The hypothesis states that the introduction of new information technologies in the population will benefit both groups but that it will benefit the information rich more. Why? The information rich have advantages that help them master the new technologies more quickly (Ettema, 1989).

This means that over time the gap between rich and poor will inevitably widen, perhaps creating a two-layered society with no middle class. Demographers and economists see a slight trend in this direction. However, factors other than information technologies, such as a prolonged economic recession, the decline of public education, and changes in the tax laws in the 1980s, may be responsible for this perceived tend.

The Structure and Quality of Personal Relationships

Canadian communications scholar Marshall McLuhan (1964) coined the term "the global village" to describe the changes in communications technology that, to him, seemed to be

The information gap hypothesis posits that the "information rich" benefit more from new information technologies than the "information poor."

FIGURE 18.1
ACCORDING TO THE INFORMATION GAP HYPOTHESIS, THE INTRODUCTION OF NEW INFORMATION TECHNOLOGIES WILL HELP THE INFORMATION RICH GET RICHER, AND THE INFORMATION POOR GET RICHER, BUT THE RICH GET RICHER FASTER, CAUSING THE INFORMATION GAP TO WIDEN.

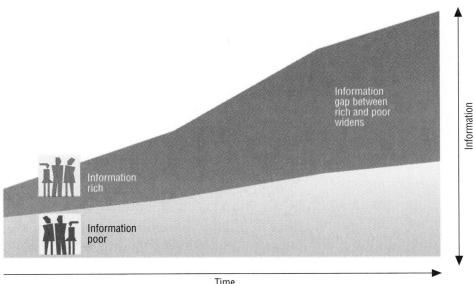

drawing the entire world together into a kind of electronically mediated small town. "By electricity we everywhere resume person-to-person relations as if on the smallest village scale" (p. 255).

On the one hand, electronic communication makes it easy to create "psychological communities" that extend our relationships across time and distance, even to create "virtual communities" of people that we know only through communication networks. The potential downside is that this trend could lead to a "postmodern" society (Lyotard, 1984) in which nation states dissolve in chaos, as people become less interested and involved in the events in the immediate world around them. The opposite could also happen. Information technologies might also intensify people's relationships in their local communities by opening new channels of communication and affording new ways to coordinate activities and maintain relationships.

When sociologist Claude Fischer (1992) examined the initial introduction of the telephone in Northern California in the early twentieth century, he concluded that it had augmented some forms of local activities, such as the coordination of functions for local clubs and service groups, while disrupting others, such as neighborhood political organizations. To the extent that information technologies have disrupted the fabric of community life, they share the blame with other technologies—the automobile and urban transportation systems—and other social forces, such as economic and racial oppression.

It is certainly true that there is "something missing" when we use mediated communication: nonverbal cues—gestures, facial expressions, body posture—that help us to understand the deeper meanings of words. This is the concept of **social presence,** or the relative presence or absence of sensory cues that help convey hidden meanings. **Computer-mediated conference** systems have low levels of social presence, and telephone calls are not much better. This makes electronic media an inferior means of establishing interpersonal relationships. However, they are useful for maintaining relationships once they have been established and for conveying information. Most people say they prefer direct face-to-face contact when they have something important to say but prefer the telephone to seek out information. More people save bad news for in-person contacts than they do good news (Dordick & LaRose, 1992). This is consistent with the findings of Short, Williams, & Christie (1976), which show that media with low social presence are adequate for information seeking and problem solving but less effective when resolving conflicts or forming impressions of new acquaintances.

> **Social presence is the degree to which sensory cues are present that convey hidden meanings.**
>
> **Computer mediated conferences are discussions on a computer network.**

Privacy

It is useful to distinguish between two dimensions of privacy: freedom from unwanted intrusions and control over personal information.

Electronic Intrusions. Almost 20 million calls are placed by telephone solicitors each day (Ingersoll, 1991). According to one recent survey, seven-eighths of all households receive at least one unwanted call during the course of a month (Dordick & LaRose, 1992). About three-fifths of American homes receive pitches from telemarketers and charitable organizations each month. However, callers who hang up when someone answers the phone are even more prevalent, and not all of these are "innocent mistakes" on the part of people who realize that they have misdialed. Many of the hang-ups are generated by telemarketers or survey researchers searching for a particular type of person (such as female consumers) and who hang up when the "wrong" person answers the phone. Others are automated calling machines looking for facsimile machines to which to send unsolicited "junk faxes" or for computer access lines to crack. Unwanted personal calls and telephone surveys reach about a quarter of all homes, and over 10 percent receive an abusive or obscene call each month.

Electronic Disclosure. Consumer credit databases maintain extensive files on the credit histories of virtually everyone (Rubin, 1988; Wessells, 1990). These files can be accessed by anyone who pays the subscription fee, and no notification of the subject of the files is necessary. Complete details on every check you ever bounced and every loan payment you ever missed can be obtained with the right computer access code. Records of recent credit card purchases can be obtained from some sources—even records of food purchases if you present a supermarket ID to cash a check or get a discount. The National Crime Information Center contains tens of millions of files on Americans who have run afoul of the law, many for minor infractions (Johnson, 1990). Other databases deal in innuendo. In one infamous case, a newspaper editor was denied car insurance because he had once had long hair and a beard and attended political demonstrations, giving him a reputation as a "hippy type."

A great deal of the information may be incorrect, may be out of date, or may even apply to another person with a similar name or address. Even if you find out, the errors can keep cropping up for years. The database providers trade files with one another, and the error you correct in one file may remain in another, and even recycle back to its original source years later. The social effects of erroneous consumer credit information can be traced in ruined reputations and broken lives. There are numerous horror stories of consumers losing their credit ratings and of innocent citizens going to jail because of mistaken database information.

Computerization of criminal records is a serious concern, as many employers discriminate against anyone with a criminal background. The offenses involved may be minor ones and the offenders may have paid their debts to society, but their crimes live on in computer databases. According to a Harris poll, about a fifth of all adults in the United States believe that they have been the victim of an invasion of privacy by computer (Harris & Associates, 1983).

The growing store of transactional information facilitates sophisticated **matching** between databases. Every time you use a credit card, write a check, or call an 800 number, you leave an electronic record behind. Whenever your purchases are processed by a scanner or a computerized point-of-sale terminal, chances are that transaction also winds up in a database somewhere. In some cases, personal information can be matched so that, for example, marketers of diaper services can compile lists of specific persons who have made a purchase of baby supplies by credit card in the last thirty days and who live in high-income neighborhoods. In other cases, the exact identity of the individuals is not even necessary. High-tech marketers can blanket zip code areas that census data tell them are

Matching is the cross-correlation of consumer databases.

SUPERMARKET SCANNERS MAKE IT POSSIBLE TO COLLATE AND MATCH LARGE VOLUMES OF CONSUMER DATA.

FIGURE 18.2
THE RIGHT TO PRIVACY IS
PROTECTED IN A NUMBER OF
AREAS.

The right	What it means
Inspection	You have the right to inspect information contained in credit agency files (Fair Credit Reporting Act of 1970)
Challenge	You have the right to challenge the accuracy of the files and to append your own explanations
Update	Credit agencies must purge items that are more than seven years old
Control	Inquiries for purposes other than hiring, insurance investigations, or credit checks can be made only with the permission of the subject or under a court order; federal agencies may not transfer information without consent or use information for purposes other than that for which it was originally collected (Privacy Act of 1974)
Refuse	Citizens can refuse to disclose their social security number except where required by law, to prevent computer matching (Privacy Act of 1975)
Notification	Federal law enforcement agencies must notify individuals whose financial records are subpoenaed (Right to Financial Privacy Act of 1979); secret files are prohibited and government agencies must publish descriptions of the files they keep each year (Privacy Act of 1974)
Electronic piracy	Telephone wiretaps are allowed only with a court order, and this extends to electronic mail messages (Electronic Communication Privace Act of 1986)

likely to have large concentrations of young families, or they can look for neighborhoods where exceptionally heavy purchases of paper diapers have been recorded on nearby supermarket scanners.

Interactive media pose a new privacy threat in this vein. Records of your transactions with on-line services, even records of the entertainment programs you consume, could be turned against you in the form of high-powered advertising campaigns or direct marketing appeals that could be so finely tuned to your needs that you might find them irresistible.

The law *does* protect your right to privacy in a number of ways, as Figure 18.2 indicates. For more on protecting your rights, see the appendix.

Information Technologies and Criminal Behavior

Information technologies have given rise to their own unique forms of criminal behavior (Mandell, 1990; Sieber, 1986). **Hacking** has been widely used in the media in recent years to refer to several distinct categories of computer crime:

Hacking is the use of information technology for unlawful purposes.

- *Sabotage* involves acts of willful destruction such as flooding the computer room, shooting the computer with a revolver, and erasing files with a powerful electromagnet. Saboteurs now enjoy using software to erase stored programs or to jam computer memory with replicated files—viruses, worms, and so on. A graduate student at Cornell, Robert Morris, brought down research computers all over the country by injecting a self-replicating, self-propagating program into the Internet.

- *Theft of service* involves gaining unauthorized access to computer time. Computer criminals sometimes obtain access codes from insiders. More usually, they uncover telephone access codes from on-line systems and try identification codes until they find one that works.

- *Software piracy* includes unauthorized duplication of programs owned by legal users and the obtaining of illegal copies from computer bulletin boards. In the mid-1980s it was estimated that half the software in use was pirated, which was costing the software publishing industry tens of billions of dollars. This figure has dropped to about 20 percent, but the problem still persists.

- *Data brokering* is a polite term for gaining unauthorized access to confidential information for gain. Want to see Dan Rather's credit card bills? Slip $50 to someone who has an illegal access code to a consumer credit database and you can find out.

- *Financial fraud* has gone high tech. In one case a rogue computer consultant for a bank rigged a transfer of $10 million to his private Swiss bank account. The Harris Gang infiltrated a consumer credit bureau and created phony credit reports to obtain loans for fictitious people. Another popular scheme is to make minute deductions from thousands of accounts and divert them to a hidden account. Raiding automatic teller machines with stolen access cards is another popular variation.

- *Cracking* uses many of the same techniques as other forms of hacking but is done just for "fun" rather than for financial gain. In 1983 the 414 gang (named for their telephone area code) made headlines by breaking into computers at banks and national defense installations. The "fun" is not harmless, as the entries often cause damage and the crackers wind up in jail.

- *Telephone hacking* involves using "blue boxes" that defeat the inner workings of telephone switching systems and allow telephone calls to be placed for free. Stephen Wozniac and Steve Jobs, founders of Apple Computer, gained their first experience with consumer electronics by selling blue boxes to their classmates at the University of California. Now the most popular scams involve the theft of telephone credit card account numbers and selling cellular radios with authorization codes that duplicate those of legal users.

While information technologies do not "cause" crime, they have changed the venue of crime from convenience store cash registers and branch bank counters to the living room. In the process, they have eliminated some of the worst risks that criminals face and created a new category of white-collar crime that is somehow more acceptable, and entails lesser penalties, than "common crime." In the Information Age it is indeed easier and even somehow more respectable to steal $2 million with a computer terminal than $200 with a pistol.

On the other side of the ledger, information technologies are being used to curb criminal behavior. Over 10,000 convicted criminals in the United States now live in "electronic

prisons" inside their own homes (Malcolm, 1990). Some systems place telephone calls to residences and workplaces at random intervals, while other systems require prisoners to wear a transmitter on their ankle. High tech has also come to the telephone wiretap. "Roving wiretaps" make it possible to sweep entire telephone exchanges listening for individual voices so that calls can be traced from any phone, not just a single location (Johnson, 1990).

Psychological Effects of Information Technologies

The telephone is often credited with a positive psychological effect on relieving loneliness, particularly for women living in remote areas. The phone can also be an instrument of everyday social pleasure. In one recent survey, two-fifths of a national sample of telephone users said that they used the telephone for enjoyment (Dordick & LaRose, 1992).

For others, the telephone is an instrument of terror. In the same survey, over a third said that making a call to a stranger made them tense, and about 10 percent became tense even when calling an acquaintance. Ironically, many of those who experienced anxiety about using the telephone were in fact heavy phone users. They also used a wide array of telephone technologies, including answering machines and cellular telephones.

Another malady of our times is **computer anxiety,** also known as cyberphobia, or computerphobia, a debilitating fear of the computer (Howard, 1986; Meier & Lambert, 1991). By some estimates, it afflicts up to a third of the adult population; people with the most extreme cases suffer from nausea, vertigo, and cold sweats. Their anxiety has several possible origins, including the fear that they will cause damage by pushing the wrong key, concern over the social effects of the computer (such as on privacy), fear of personal failure, and an "out of control" feeling that nontechnical persons experience when faced with a complex technical system. Women and people with relatively low mathematical skills are especially likely to suffer from computer anxiety. Computerphobes do poorly on computer tasks and in computer classes and are dissatisfied computer users. Training, user-friendly computer system designs, and experience with computers may help to dispel their anxiety.

At the other end of the spectrum are those who might justifiably be called **computer addicts.** The computer has an interactive quality that makes it seem as though it responds

Computer anxiety is a debilitating fear of computers.

Computer addiction is the compulsive use of the computer.

to the user's every move. It does not always reward users with the response they hope for, however, creating a sort of variable reinforcement schedule—just the kind known to prompt obsessive "addictive" behavior. Video games are often cited in this regard—parents complain about children who seemingly become addicted to a particular game. There is also anecdotal evidence of adults who have lost everything they own playing trivia games on videotex services or calling dial-a-porn numbers. The potentially addictive qualities of information technologies have actually been noted with anticipation by some promoters of artificial reality systems, who promise a "better high than drugs."

Psychologist Sherry Turkle (1993) prefers the metaphor of "seduction" to that of addiction. She stresses that the holding power of the computer does not come from what is external (like a drug) but rather from what is within people—what they learn about themselves through their infatuation with the computer. What attracts people to the computer is its ability to provoke self-reflection, to extend their minds into artificial worlds, and to adapt itself to the needs of each user. In this view, habitual computer users are drawn by the ability to control the world inside the computer, to achieve the illusion of intimacy, to gain confirmation of a sense of selfhood, and to express themselves in the style of their own choosing.

Cultural Effects

Cultural analyst Neil Postman (1992) argues that computers foster a state of mind and a state of culture that he calls **technopoly,** in which technology is deified and extends its control to all aspects of life. Technopoly greatly exceeds the worst excesses of **technocracy,** in which the scientific method is applied to the improvement of life and also, some think, to the destruction of culture. The same theme is echoed in the writings of French sociologist Jacques Ellul (1964), who argues that the relentless pursuit of technological improvement leads to the development of a technological elite of scientists, engineers, and managers for whom technology becomes an end in itself, devoid of moral foundation.

Another view of the compelling nature of information technologies comes from critical theorist Vincent Mosco (1982). He gives a Marxist explanation of leisure activity, that its function is to resuscitate weary workers to prepare them for a return to their labors. Thus, the intensity with which we play at our home computers is in direct proportion to the trivialization of our labors on the job—and at school—by the unrelenting onslaught of information technologies.

Health and Environmental Effects

Information technologies are sometimes heralded as "clean" technologies that eliminate the belching smokestacks of the Industrial Age. The residents of Silicon Valley and other high-tech corridors might dispute this claim, now that they find high levels of toxic industrial solvents in their drinking water.

Computer disposal is also a growing problem. According to one study, there will be 150 million computers in landfills by 2005, enough to cover an acre of land three and a half miles deep. Computer recyclers now mine discarded computers for valuable materials and reusable computer chips, but there is an increasing need for a "green" computer whose casing and packaging can be recycled. The German government now requires computer makers to reclaim abandoned machines (Lohr, 1993).

Computer power consumption is also significant. In 1993, the Environmental Protection Agency (EPA) began issuing "Energy Star" stickers for machines that "sleep" when they are

Technopoly is a culture in which technology controls all aspects of life.

Technocracy is application of the scientific method to all aspects of life. **Technopoly** is its most extreme form.

R E V I E W

1. What were some of the effects of the telephone on society?
2. What does the information gap hypothesis predict about the effects of new information technologies?
3. What implications do information technologies have for women?
4. What impact do information technologies have on personal relationships?
5. What danger does computer matching pose to our personal privacy?
6. What are some novel types of criminal behavior that have been made possible by the spread of information technologies?
7. What is computer anxiety?
8. What are some of the potential health effects of information technologies?

Repetitive stress injury is a debilitating pain caused by excessive use of computer keyboards.

turned on but not being actively used. This program could save enough energy to power a couple of small states for an entire year.

Extremely low frequency (ELF) radiation—the kind that electrical power lines emit—also poses an environmental threat. At one point, EPA scientists concluded that ELF was as dangerous as suspected cancer agents, although this finding was overruled by EPA administrators. Computer video display terminals (VDTs) emit the same type of radiation and are suspected by some of causing cancer and miscarriages in heavy users. Lately, portable telephones have also been implicated. Microwave and satellite communication systems are also sources of electromagnetic radiation with possible health effects. However, there is no proven theory about how electromagnetic fields interact with living tissue. Without this "missing link," scientists are reluctant to blame electromagnetic radiation for health effects or to establish "safe" exposure levels (Lewis, 1990).

There is far less dispute about **repetitive stress injuries,** such as the shooting pains caused by tapping a keyboard for hours on end, day after day. Several thousand cases of short- or long-term disabilities resulting from heavy computer use are reported each year. Computers are also responsible for eyestrain, sometimes resulting in permanent eye damage. Flickering from the interplay of the computer screen's scanning pattern and fluorescent lights is most often the culprit.

EFFECTS OF COMMUNICATION TECHNOLOGY ON THE WORLD OF WORK

If we do succeed in improving productivity through information technologies, does that just mean more unemployment? Not necessarily (see Kilborn, 1993; National Commission for Employment Policy, 1986; Perrolle, 1987; Schiller, 1981; Wessells, 1990). Information technology can reduce costs and increase product quality, which, in turn, creates demand for more products and thus higher employment. Another possibility is to increase productivity in labor-intensive industries and free up societal resources to invest in research and development or in new labor-intensive occupations in the service sector, thereby increasing total employment.

Historically, fears about higher unemployment resulting from automation have proved unfounded, whether the "new technology" was the machine-driven textile machinery of the 1780s or computers of the 1980s. Even the replacement of humans by robots may increase employment in the final analysis, once the new employees required to manufacture and maintain the robots are counted and the indirect effects on employment that result from productivity increases are assessed.

Job displacement occurs when a job is eliminated by automation.

Of course, this information provides little comfort to individual workers who find themselves "automated out of a job." Indeed, entire classes of workers have been "automated out of an industry," such as the newspaper typesetters whose occupation has been made obsolete by computerized typesetting equipment. This phenomenon is euphemistically called **job displacement** by labor economists. Since World War II, the percentage of industrial employees in the U.S. work force has been halved. As the transition to an information economy continues, more industrial workers will have to become information workers or service workers.

Contingent employees are temporary employees who can be hired or fired at will.

However, not everyone can make the transition, and many of the new service jobs are low paying and lack benefits and job security. About half of the new jobs are part-time jobs, double the level of a decade ago, and nearly a third of U.S. workers are now **contingent employees** without long-term employment agreements.

At last we arrive at the bottom line for workers in the Information Age. The United States has seen the virtual elimination of a blue-collar middle class in the span of a single generation. In terms of mass media icons we have gone from *The Life of Riley* to *All in the Family* to *Roseanne*. Gone are the days of a comfortable existence with job security and benefits resulting from trade union membership. Today's blue-collar workers must survive bouts of unemployment and need two paychecks to make ends meet. Rapid obsolescence occurs in white-collar technical occupations, too. Thousands of middle managers who once were needed to coordinate communications and operations have been replaced by office information systems.

How extensive is job displacement? According to a study by the National Commission for Employment Policy completed in the mid-1980s, between 10 and 20 percent of all unemployed workers have been displaced by computer technology. Future job displacements are likely to be concentrated in two areas. Assembly-line workers such as welders, assemblers, painters, and materials handlers—the remnants of the blue-collar middle class—are likely to be replaced by robots. They account for about 3 percent of all U.S. workers and are largely middle-aged white males living in the Midwest. The other group makes up about 20 percent of the work force, mostly female "pink-collar" employees in clerical occupations targeted for replacement by office automation—bank tellers, postal clerks, secretaries, and so on. However, the estimates of actual job losses in these categories vary wildly: between 100,000 and 800,000 jobs lost to robotic assembly lines, from 250,000 clerical jobs lost to 50,000 clerical jobs *gained* as a result of office automation.

Careers in the Information Society

What about *your* career? Will you be one of the displaced? The U.S. Department of Labor compiles annual employment projections in its *Occupational Outlook*. Table 18.1 shows the number of people employed in some representative communications media occupations, "average" salaries (actually, either the mean or the median in each field), the outlook for growth in the category by the year 2005, and explanations for growth or decline.

Generally, the news is worst for blue-collar jobs, such as line installer, broadcast technician, and repair technician, and for pink-collar occupations, such as telephone operator. Reliability improvements in information systems and automation are threatening their livelihoods. Some of the lower levels of the white-collar ranks are also threatened. Fewer computer operators will be needed as organizations decentralize their computer operations, for example. According to these estimates, demand for clerks and typists will not decline, because of the explosion in information handling that has hit the office in the wake of automation.

In white-collar occupations, the outlook is generally rosier. New technologies will keep demand for technical graduates at high levels, especially for electrical engineers in communications and computer specialties. However, many engineers will find higher-level technical and engineering management jobs to be in short supply relative to the large numbers who enter the profession. The outlook in computer-related occupations such as systems analyst and programmer remains upbeat, owing to the continuing need to integrate information systems into business applications.

TABLE 18.1. OCCUPATIONAL OUTLOOK IN COMMUNICATIONS MEDIA

Occupational category	Number of jobs	Typical salary	Growth by 2005	Explanation
Engineering/science/data managers	313,000	$100,000+	Above average	More R&D, but competitive
Electrical and electronic engineers	426,000	$ 50,000	Above average	Excellent in computers and communications
Computer systems analysts	436,000	$ 38,700	Well above average	Computer technology spurs growth
Radio/TV announcers	57,000	$ 27,000 (sm mkt TV) $129,000 (lg mkt TV)	Average	Many more applicants than jobs
Reports and correspondents	67,000	$ 33,000	About average	Small daily papers proliferating
Photographers and camera operators	120,000	$ 33,000	Average	Slow growth in photojournalism
Actors, directors, and producers	95,000	$ 12,000 (actors)	Well above average	Cable TV and home video expanding
Broadcast technicians	33,00	$ 16,000 (sm mkt TV) $ 32,000 (lg mkt TV)	None	Automation will cut jobs
Computer programmers	160,000	$ 34,000	Well above average	Data communications, expert systems hot
Computer operators	282,000	$ 19,400	Below average	Computer systems "downsizing"
Telephone operators	325,000	$ 16,600	Decline	Voice mail and voice recognition cut jobs
Typists and data entry	1,448,000	$ 16,700	No growth	Info explosion offsets automation
Computer/office machine repair	156,000	$ 23,500	No growth	Quality improvements offset growth
Line installers and splicers	232,000	$ 31,000	Decline	Digital means less maintenance

Source: U.S. Department of Labor, *Occupational Outlook Handbook, 1992–1993 Edition* (Washington, DC: U.S. Government Printing Office).

No general expansion of employment in mass media fields is predicted in these forecasts, with the exception of jobs for writers and producers, which are expected to increase with the multiplication of cable channels and home video production. Mass media fields are generally highly competitive at the entry level, with tens of thousands of new graduates of media, communication, and journalism programs hoping to enter relatively small fields of employment each year. High turnover rates in media occupations, rather than expansion in the number of jobs available, provide most of the openings. Why the high turnover? Although media stars get well-publicized multimillion-dollar salaries, rank-and-file actors and television announcers have salaries that place them near the bottom of the white-collar hierarchy.

For those who are anxious about their own occupational outlook, the best advice is to be adaptable and to acquire an education that is both broad and deep. Most people entering the work force today can expect to change their careers several times, rather than stay with one line of work—let alone one company—for life. It is also important to learn how to use information technologies in the job marketplace (see box on facing page).

The Quality of Work: Deskilling, Taylorism, and Fordism

The ability of information technology to reduce skill requirements for the average worker, a process known as **deskilling,** was known from the start. Charles Babbage was the first to speculate about using computers to simplify work tasks to the point where less-skilled— and more lowly paid—workers could complete them (see Braverman, 1974; Schement & Lievrouw, 1987).

Had Babbage succeeded in constructing his computer in the early nineteenth century, we

Deskilling is reduction of the skill requirements of a job through mechanization or automation.

Many college students have discovered a new application for desktop publishing: mass production of résumés. Most word processing packages include a mailing list function that makes it easy to create generic cover letters that can be customized with the address of each employer. Some savvy grads pool their resources to create databases of employer contacts, yielding dozens or hundreds of job-seeking letters.

For the most part, they are wasting their postage. Only a few jobs are found in response to mailing out résumés. Personnel departments screen out most of them and function more to prevent you from getting a job instead of help you to get one. Most jobs come through personal contacts and a few from responding to want ads, but unsolicited résumés hardly ever work. The cover letter is probably more important than the résumé, especially for new entrants in the work force. Better yet is to use the telephone first to see whether anything is available and to "network" with the line managers who actually have the jobs to fill.

There is now a high-tech approach to employment recruiting. Management Recruiters International, for example, has a network of videoconferencing systems in major cities that allows employers to screen potential candidates without incurring travel expenses. Using videoconferences, they screen applicants and evaluate "intangibles" about character and oral communication skills. The video interviews cost employers about a fifth of what it costs for face-to-face interviews (Cummings, 1993).

On-line résumé screening systems are another approach. The National Engineering Consortium, a professional organization serving the telecommunications industry, has an on-line system that lets college students create an electronic version of their résumés. Employers can then search the applicant database with a variety of selection criteria (e.g., Rhodes Scholar, 4.0 average, course work in network routing algorithms, plays golf). Now colleges and universities are getting on the network, too. Ball State University in Indiana offers an alumni database that includes electronic résumés of its graduates. Northwestern University's AlumNet database is designed to put its grads in touch with alumni volunteers who help them hunt for jobs or change careers.

The high-tech job hunter can also log into one of the several on-line jobs conferences offered on computer bulletin board systems around the country. These conferences offer tips on job-seeking strategies as well as job postings. Only the "host" systems are listed. You may find the conferences are carried on a local bulletin board in a community near you (Motley, 1992).

Conference	Host System	Contact Number
Employment	Writer's Block BBS	410-945-1540*
U.S. Office of Personnel Management	Personnel Management	313-226-4423*
Résumé Exchange	Résumé Exchange BBS	602-258-8347*
Get That Job	Halls of Ivy BBS	404-936-9831*
Job Mart (arts and entertainment employment)	Rock N Roll Atlanta BBS	404-982-0960*
National MediaNet	MediaNet Pro-Line	317-547-6204*
Peterson's Connexion	CompuServe	800-338-3282

*You will need a computer and a 1200 bps modem to access these numbers!

Taylorism refers to the process of scientific management, which seeks to improve the efficiency of work by routinizing it.

Fordism is the application of the assembly-line process, reducing work to the endless repetition of a single task.

might have called this process "Babbagism." Instead, we call it **Taylorism,** after Frederick Winslow Taylor, who first articulated the principles of *scientific management.* Scientific management seeks to improve efficiency by routinizing each task so that there is only one "right" way to do it and by setting job standards that dictate exactly how many operations should be performed in a set amount of time. **Fordism,** after Henry Ford, took the systematization of labor one step further by introducing the assembly-line system, in which each employee performs only a single, narrowly defined task, over and over again. Unlike the nineteenth-century craftsmen that preceded them, Taylorized and Fordized workers do not know how to "make" anything. Their knowledge is limited to one small task, so that upward mobility is impossible. Only the owners and their white-collar managers know how to organize those tasks to produce goods and services.

Information technologies can amplify Taylorism and Fordism in some distressing ways. First, they make it possible to monitor employees more closely, such as by counting the number of keystrokes made by clerical employees in each hour. Second, they extend the precepts of scientific management from the assembly floor to the office. The advent of expert systems and artificial intelligence may extend this reduction of labor to the white-collar executive as well.

Post-Fordism deskills jobs to the point where workers no longer need to be paid a decent living wage.

Deskilled workers can be paid less and replaced at will. In the lexicon of the critical theorists, this trend is known as **post-Fordism.** That is, it invalidates the basic social contract initiated by Henry Ford in the 1920s, which was to pay industrial workers a decent living wage so that they could afford to purchase the very products that they produced. In the post-Fordist society, jobs are deskilled and pay is cut to the point that workers can no longer participate in the consumer economy.

Upskilling and Reskilling

Another dismal possibility is that skill requirements will be upgraded to the point that much of the work force does not qualify for them. This process is known as **upskilling.** For example, displaced typesetters are unable to qualify to operate the new automated systems because a college degree and experience with computer systems are required.

Upskilling means raising the educational requirements of a job through the application of automation.

Reskilling is redesigned jobs so that they entail a wide range of skills.

Counterexamples can be found, though, such as the redesign of insurance claims-processing departments to make each employee a responsible account representative instead of a small cog in a large Taylorized office. Some call this **reskilling:** reassembling tasks that were formerly parceled out to specialized workers while keeping the overall mix of skills required within the scope of the incumbent employees. This process once again makes the employee the repository for all the information necessary to "make things," reclaiming the role of the preindustrial craftsperson. Sociologist Shoshanna Zuboff (1984) argues that the success of industrial enterprises today requires that employees regain an understanding of the theoretical principles behind the work process, since the operation of machines now depends on the ability to manipulate symbolic information rather than to perform finite, atomized tasks.

This is consistent with Daniel Bell's (1973) view that knowledge has replaced capital as the cornerstone for economic enterprise and social relations. These changes could rock the very foundations of industrial capitalism by recentering control in industrial production in the workers themselves. It is ironic that information technologies, the final product of industrial capitalism, may yet fulfill Karl Marx's prophecy. It was he, after all, who pointed out that capitalism creates the contradictions that inevitably lead to its own destruction.

In one study of changes in skill requirements in jobs that had been automated, conducted in the 1960s, it was found that there was a slight increase in skill levels overall, although some examples showed a slight decrease while others showed an increase (Crossman & Laner, 1969). In Zuboff's view, what we may be seeing is a process of reskilling occurring simultaneously with deskilling. Information technologies do not invariably entail deskilling—it all depends on the nature of the application.

The Decentralization of Work

Work decentralization is taking place at several levels. Many corporate "backroom operations"—mostly clerical and data processing jobs—are being relocated from corporate headquarters in large cities to the suburbs. Telemarketing and customer service operations are also being exported to rural and semirural locations in the Great Plains states. A great deal of information processing now goes offshore; for example, used airline ticket coupons are shipped to less developed countries for data entry. Other companies eliminate their backroom operations

R E V I E W

1. Do information technologies increase or decrease the quantity of work? Explain your answer.
2. What are some careers that are likely to expand in the next ten years?
3. What are the differences between Taylorism, Fordism, and post-Fordism?
4. Give examples of jobs that have been deskilled, upskilled, and reskilled.
5. What new organizational structures are emerging?

Outsourcing is the practice of subcontracting tasks to outside firms instead of performing them "in-house."

Telecommuting occurs when work is performed in the home and workers are linked together by telecommunications networks.

entirely and subcontract, or **outsource,** to suppliers that specialize in transactions processing, data entry, or telemarketing. Computer networks make it possible to integrate the work products of suppliers and farflung backroom operations.

The ultimate in work decentralization is **telecommuting,** in which the employee's home office is linked to the workplace via telephone, electronic mail, facsimile, and teleconferencing systems. Telecommuting dovetails neatly with the "core and ring" corporate structure, since the expendable, temporary workers who make up the ring can complete their labors from their homes, with minimal expenditures for employee recruitment, relocation, or office space. Some see telecommuting as the answer to the problems of urban blight and worker alienation, while others see it as the ultimate threat to information workers.

SUMMARY & REVIEW

How Do Information Technologies Affect Our Daily Lives?

What were the social effects of the telephone?
The telephone was invented before social science was, so we can only engage in retrospective technology assessment in an attempt to understand its effects. Early observers believed that the phone would increase illiteracy, revitalize rural life, improve the life of women, increase suburban sprawl, and make cities grow, among other things. However, many of the predictions did not come true, and other technological and social changes may have accounted for the predictions that did come to pass.

How do information technologies affect society today?
Information technologies do not benefit all groups in society equally. Women and African Americans may be left behind in the transition to the information economy. The information gap hypothesis predicts that efforts to improve the plight of the disadvantaged through information technologies will instead result in

widening the gap between rich and poor. The compilation of vast databases of consumer information and the practice of matching data between files poses the privacy threat of unwanted disclosures of personal information. Information technologies also foster entirely new forms of criminal behavior, ranging from sabotage and theft to hacking. An overall increased reliance on technology creates the threat of technocracy, a totalitarian system in which all aspects of life are under cybernetic control.

How do information technologies affect personal relationships?
History shows that new communications technologies augment some forms of interpersonal communication while disrupting others. The advent of the information superhighway has the potential for bringing about a "global village" in which everyone is our neighbor in a small electronically mediated village. The "virtual communities" that have formed on the Internet are an initial indication that new types of human relationships may be created. However, there is also the danger that the world could evolve into an extremely fragmented "postmodern" society in which chaos reigns. Information technologies may also

degrade the sense of social presence we experience when we talk to people face to face.

Are information technologies harmful to human health?

Contacts with information technologies may produce a variety of psychological and physical afflictions. Computer anxiety is a debilitating fear of computers that affects many users. Others may become addicted to computer use. Industrial pollution and waste disposal problems connected with information technology pose growing environmental hazards. The electro-magnetic radiation emitted by electronic devices and repetitive stress injuries resulting from excessive use of computer input devices may pose threats to personal health.

How Do Information Technologies Affect the World of Work?

Do information technologies cause unemployment?

Improvements in productivity brought about by applications of information technology have the potential to displace large numbers of jobs. Historically, new waves of industrial technology have increased employment in the long term, and the same is likely to hold true today. However, in the short term entire categories of workers will be eliminated, and workers may find themselves with useless skills or forced to seek unstable contingent employment. Some careers, such as computer systems analyst, actor, director, and producer, will grow rapidly, while other categories, such as telephone operator and computer operator, will suffer.

Do information technologies make work less satisfying?

In some applications, information technologies increase the twin tendencies of Taylorism and Fordism, deskilling work to meaningless, repetitive assembly-line tasks. In the extreme, jobs are so degraded that workers no longer command a decent living wage, a condition called post-Fordism. In other instances, information technology upskills jobs, displacing workers whose skills no longer match job requirements. This is what sometimes happens when factories are automated and low-skilled assembly-line workers are replaced by computer technicians. However, information technologies can also be applied in ways that reskill jobs, restoring work to a meaningful and dignified pursuit. For example, insurance industry claims adjusters may oversee the processing of a claim from start to finish, whereas previously they worked on only one aspect of the process.

How are information technologies changing the structure of organizations?

The spread of personal computers and high-speed communications networks is resulting in the decentralization of work in a variety of ways. "Backroom" data processing operations that were maintained at corporate headquarters are being relocated to remote areas—sometimes outside the United States—to reduce informa-tion processing costs. Other companies outsource operations to independent suppliers, gathering their output and coordinating their efforts with advanced information systems. Telecommuting relocates the workplace to the home environment.

REFERENCES

Belinfante, A. (1989, May). *Telephone penetration and household and family characteristics.* Washington, DC: Federal Communications Commission.

Bell, D. (1973). *The coming of post-industrial society.* New York: Basic Books.

Braverman, H. (1974). *Labor and monopoly capitalism.* New York: Monthly Review Press.

Crossman, E. R. F. W., & Laner, S. (1969). *The impact of technological change on manpower and skill demand: Case-study and policy implications.* Berkeley: Department of Industrial Engineering and Operations Research, University of California.

Cummings, J. (1993, March 1). Videoconferencing gives recruiter edge. *Network World,* p. 25.

Davidson, M. J., & Cooper, C. L. (1987). *Women and information technology.* New York: Wiley.

de Sola Pool, I. (1983). *Forecasting the telephone: A retrospective technology assessment of the telephone.* Norwood, NJ: Ablex.

Dordick, H., & LaRose, R. (1992). *The telephone in daily life: A study of personal telephone use.* East Lansing, MI: Department of Telecommunication.

Ellul, J. (1964). *The technological society.* New York: Knopf.

Ettema, J. (1989). Interactive electronic text in the United States: Can videotex ever go home again? In J. Salvaggio & J. Bryant (Eds.), *Media use in the information age.* Hillsdale, NJ: Erlbaum.

Fischer, C. (1992). *America calling.* Berkeley: University of California Press.

Harris, L., & Associates. (1983). *The road after 1984: A nationwide survey of the public and its leaders on the new technology and its consequences for American life.* Washington, DC: Eighth International Smithsonian Symposium.

Hayes, D. (1989). *Beyond the silicon curtain.* Boston, MA: South End Press.

Howard, G. S. (1986). *Computer anxiety and the use of microcomputers in management.* Ann Arbor, MI: AMI Research Press.

Ingersoll, B. (1991, November 27). Congress closer to restricting auto-dialing. *The Wall Street Journal,* pp. B1, B3.

Johnson, C. (1990, November 11). Police tools of the 90s are highly advanced, but privacy laws lag. *The Wall Street Journal,* pp. A1, A10.

Kilborn, P. T. (1993, March 15). New jobs lack the old security in time of "Disposable Workers." *The New York Times,* pp. A1, A6.

Kominski, R. (1988). *Computer use in the United States: 1984.* Current Population Reports, Series P-23, No. 155. Washington, DC: U.S. Government Printing Office.

Lewis, P. H. (1990, July 8). Worries about radiation continue, as do studies. *The New York Times,* p. F8.

Lohr, S. (1993, April 14). Recycling answer sought for computer junk. *The New York Times,* pp. A1, C5.

Lyotard, J. (1984). *The postmodern condition.* Manchester, England: Manchester University Press.

Malcolm, A. H. (1990, February 22). For some convicts, wires replace bars. *The New York Times,* pp. A1, A13.

Mandell, S. L. (1990). Computer crime. In M. D. Ermann, M. Williams, & C. Gutierrez (Eds.), *Computers, ethics and society.* New York: Oxford University Press.

Martin, M. (1991). *"Hello, central?" Gender, technology and culture in the formation of telephone systems.* Montreal: McGill-Queen's University Press.

McLuhan, M. (1964). *Understanding media.* New York: McGraw-Hill.

Meier, S. T., & Lambert, M. E. (1991). Psychometric properties and correlates of three computer aversion scales. *Behavior Research Methods Instruments and Computers, 23*(1), 9–15.

Mosco, V. (1982). *Pushbutton fantasies: Critical perspectives on videotex and information technology.* Norwood, NJ: Ablex.

Motley, L. (1992). *Modem USA.* Takoma Park, MD: Allium Press.

Moyal, A. (1988). *Women and the telephone in Australia: Study of a national culture.* Paper presented to the International Communication Association, Dublin, Ireland.

National Commission for Employment Policy. (1986). *Computers in the workplace: Selected issues*. Washington, DC: U.S. Government Printing Office.

Norwood, S. (1990). *Labor's flaming youth*. Urbana: University of Illinois Press.

Perrolle, J. (1987). *Computers and social change: Information, property and power*. Belmont, CA: Wadsworth.

Postman, N. (1992). *Technopoly*. New York: Knopf.

Rakow, L. F. (1992). *Gender on the line*. Urbana: University of Illinois Press.

Roszak, T. (1986). *The cult of information*. New York: Pantheon Books.

Rubin, M. R. (1988). *Private rights, public wrongs: The computer and personal privacy*. Norwood, NJ: Ablex.

Schement, J. R., & Lievrouw, L. (Eds.). (1987). *Competing visions, complex realities: Social aspects of the information society*. Norwood, NJ: Ablex.

Schiller, H. I (1981). *Who knows: Information in the age of the Fortune 500*. Norwood, NJ: Ablex.

Short, J., Williams, E., & Christie, B. (1976). *The social psychology of telecommunications*. New York: Wiley.

Sieber, U. (1986). *The international handbook on computer crime*. New York: Wiley.

Turkle, S. (1993). Computational seductions: The roots of computer holding power. In J. V. Pavlik & E. Dennis, *Demystifying media technology*. Mountain View, CA: Mayfield.

Werneke, D. (1985). Women: The vulnerable group. In T. Forester (Ed.), *The information technology revolution*. Cambridge, MA: MIT Press.

Wessells, M. G. (1990). *Computer, self and society*. Englewood Cliffs, NJ: Prentice-Hall.

Zientara, M. (1987). *Women, technology and power*. New York: American Management Association.

Zimmerman, J. (1990). Some effects of the new technology on women. In M. D. Ermann, M. B. Williams, & C. Gutierrez (Eds.), *Computers, ethics and society*. New York: Oxford University Press.

Zuboff, S. (1984). *In the age of the smart machine*. New York: Basic Books.

Appendix

CONSUMER ISSUES IN THE INFORMATION SOCIETY

This appendix examines issues that affect us as consumers of communications products and services in the information society. We will review some important consumer controversies, identify resources that will help you become a knowledgeable consumer of information services and products, and outline strategies for dealing with common communication consumer problems.

MASS MEDIA CONSUMER CONTROVERSIES

Because so much of the mass media come to us "free," or at least heavily subsidized through advertising sales, it is sometimes difficult to conceive of mass media consumption as a consumer issue. After all, what right do we have to complain about something we do not pay for?

In fact, the mass media are supported by our consumer behavior, although indirectly. The programs, articles, and advertisements are all paid for through the prices we pay for the mass market products that are advertised in the media. In some product categories, the cost of advertising accounts for as much as half the price we pay.

Does this mean that advertising unnecessarily adds to the cost of goods and services, a kind of hidden "tax" that supports media interests? Not always. In the long run, advertising can actually reduce the prices we pay for consumer goods by promoting competitive pricing, attracting our attention to product improvements that add value, and informing us about where to get the best buys.

It is difficult, however, to make this argument for products like sugary children's cereals, beer, and cigarettes, for which there are few meaningful distinctions between brands and a large proportion of the cost is for advertising—and which can have harmful effects on their consumers. In these cases, restrictions or even outright bans on advertising may be justified, such as the prohibitions on cigarette and hard liquor advertisements on television.

Deceptive Advertising

Deceptive ads are those that are likely to mislead a reasonable consumer. These include such flagrant deceptions as making false claims about the effects of patent medicines, promoting phony sales on items that are already out of stock, and faking product demonstrations. Important omissions can also be deceptive, as when bread makers claim that their product "helps build strong bodies" while failing to add that all breads contain pretty much the same ingredients. The Federal Trade Commission enforces federal rules about false advertising, and many states and cities have consumer affairs offices or ombudspersons to investigate consumer complaints.

Mass Media Content

Because we pay for the programs as well as the ads through the products we buy, the content of the mass media is also a consumer issue. Under the Communications Act of 1934, broadcasters are required to operate in the public interest. Since the 1960s citizens' groups such as Action for Children's Television (ACT, now defunct), the national Parent Teachers Association (PTA), the United Church of Christ, and the American Family Association have taken active roles as mass media consumer groups. These groups monitor the media for content of concern to their members—sex, violence, drug use, and so on—and testify at the periodic public hearings that examine curbs on objectionable programming. Some citizens' organizations use their consumer power more directly by calling for boycotts of advertisers who support programs that the groups object to.

The Cost of Cable Service

There is one mass medium in which the consumer directly pays for a substantial share of the total cost of service: cable television. How much should cable cost? In past years, cable operators had a captive audience. If you wanted to receive television in most small towns, you had to have cable. It was a bargain at any price. When cable entered the suburbs and the cities, cable operators promoted their product as a cost-effective alternative to movies: For the cost of one night at the movies with the family, you could have a month's worth of pay cable with basic service thrown in. Home videos gave consumers another money-saving alternative to a "night on the town" at about the same time that cable deregulation allowed rates to rise steeply in many areas. This competition led many consumers to question anew the value of basic cable service.

Until recently, cable television enjoyed something of a unique status as an unregulated monopoly. Other monopolies, such as local telephone and electrical power utilities, had long since been subjected to strict rate of return regulation that allowed them only a fixed percentage rate of return on their capital investments. Cable had escaped classification as a public utility and was usually regulated at the municipal level. There was no consistent public scrutiny of cable operators' books to ensure that they were not making "excessive" profits. More recent legislation established benchmarks for cable rates based on such factors as the size and capacity of systems and the nature of the equipment they had on hand, but ironically this legislation actually raised rates in many areas, stirring the controversy anew. At least now, if you have a complaint about your cable rates, you may have recourse to your local cable franchise authority.

TIPS FOR MASS MEDIA CONSUMERS

• If the products you buy are not as advertised, contact your local consumer affairs or Better Business Bureau.

• The Federal Trade Commission in Washington, D.C. is responsible for handling consumer complaints about deceptive advertising.

• Citizens' groups can help you take action to influence mass media content.

• Ask your cable operator about its policy regarding the privacy of subscriber lists and transaction information.

Audience Privacy

The prospect of interactive cable—and other versions of the information superhighway—raises an entirely new set of issues for mass media audiences. Interactive systems have the ability to keep complete records of all program choices—records that could be used by advertisers and telemarketers against the best interests of the consumer. Interactive systems could also be used to infringe on civil liberties, such as by allowing some future J. Edgar Hoover to identify "subversives" from records of who watches, for example, public television. Cable companies are supposed to keep subscriber records confidential and must notify subscribers about privacy protection policies. Today, cable operators have little to gain from selling their subscriber lists to telemarketers, but the potential value of detailed interactive viewing data to advertisers could change that.

UNDERSTANDING YOUR PHONE BILL

The choices facing telephone consumers are growing more complex as new technologies and changes in public policy create new options. A variety of special charges, new service options, and changes in the way telephone rates are set have a major impact on what consumers pay for telephone service.

Special Charges

In many states special charges on the phone bill appear as line items that are unfamiliar to the average consumer. These charges help subsidize key elements of telephone universal service that make the phone system accessible to (almost) all.

> *Telephone assistance programs,* sometimes known as "lifeline services," are available in most states to help subsidize service to low-income households. All subscribers are assessed a small monthly charge to cover the cost of the program.

> *911 service fees* defray the costs of the center where emergency calls are received and the computer and telecommunications equipment used to dispatch emergency response teams.

> *Telephone devices for the deaf,* or *TDDs,* are provided at public agencies and large firms through another small fee so that hearing-impaired persons with TDD terminals can communicate with these organizations. Many states assess fees for telephone relay services so that those without TDDs can communicate with the hearing-impaired persons through a live operator equipped with a TDD.

> The *access charge* was established by the Federal Communications Commission after the AT&T divestiture to help compensate local telephone companies for the costs they incur in relaying calls to long-distance carriers.

Understanding Local Phone Rates

Ever wonder why it costs more to call someone on the other side of the county than it does to call someone on the other side of the country? Local long-distance calls—those that are made within your local access and transport area (LATA) but outside your local calling area—usually cannot be handled by long-distance carriers, only by your local telephone company, so you are paying a monopoly price for such calls. Some inter-LATA calls that stay within the borders of a single state are also expensive if they are protected from competition by state-level regulation.

Many local telephone companies are trying to convert consumers to usage-sensitive pricing—that is, per-minute or per-call charges for local calls. Historically, unlimited local calls were included in the basic monthly fee. Now telephone companies are instituting a variety of calling plans that offer discounted monthly rates to users who make fewer than a certain number of calls, then institute per-call charges after that limit is exceeded.

Directory assistance calls are no longer free. Local directory assistance charges vary from state to state, usually giving you some number of free directory calls per month, with a per-call charge after you reach the limit. Long-distance information calls cost 65 cents each.

Local telephone rates are set through public hearings conducted by state-level public utilities commissions, but in recent years they have been affected by industry restructuring and the imposition of access fees, a federal levy. Local telephone rates have about doubled since the AT&T divestiture. The savings in long distance have been offset by higher local rates, but the shift did not affect all users equally. Low-income households, which make relatively few long-distance calls, wound up paying more for telephone service, while the heavy long-distance users in affluent homes pay less. Small businesses also saw their overall telephone costs go up. However, the quality of local service has improved, so perhaps it is worth more. According to data compiled by the FCC, customer satisfaction, transmission quality, dial tone speed, and call completion rates have all improved.

Technological improvements in the local phone system, such as digital switching and fiber optic transmission, also accelerated after divestiture. In some states, the rates that telephone companies charge are primarily a function of the investment that they make in capital improvements in the telephone plant, so there is a direct tradeoff between the quality and cost of service for the consumer. In hopes of spurring investment in the telecommunications infrastructure, many states are switching to a new type of price control for local telephone service that allows rates to rise in relation to inflation and overall improvements in the productivity of telecommunications firms.

Optional Services

Telephone companies now offer a variety of optional services. While many of the options are helpful to heavy telephone users, they also add significantly to the monthly bill.

Custom calling services are sometimes sold to consumers using high-pressure telemarketing tactics that push packages of multiple services, rather than just the specific services individual users might really need, such as call waiting and Caller ID service. Consumers should carefully consider the usefulness of other custom calling features (such as call forwarding and speed dialing) before ordering them.

Telephone maintenance plans have also provoked controversy. Since the AT&T divestiture, the maintenance responsibilities of the phone company end at your front door. If inside wiring is the problem, you pay hefty hourly rates to have the problem fixed. Telephone maintenance programs are a type of insurance policy that you pay for in small monthly installments. However, these plans usually wind up costing you more money than they are worth in the long run. Most inside wiring jobs involve moving or adding phones, and these tasks are not covered by the maintenance plans.

Touch-tone dialing is essential for interacting with the automated attendant systems that greet callers to many businesses and public offices. In most states consumers still face an extra charge, even though the touch-tone interface equipment has long since been paid for, and it now actually costs less to handle touch-tone calls than rotary-dialed calls. The charges persist because they are an important revenue source for local telephone companies, and their elimination would increase the cost of basic local service.

Long-Distance Service

Do discount long-distance plans really save you money? Those TV commercials that make side-by-side comparisons of "our network" versus "their network" often highlight the biggest differences between the two companies' rates. You might call the same location at a different time of day or a slightly different location at the same time and find that "their" network is actually the cheaper one. Many special rate plans are available, predicated on the amount of calling you do and where you call. However, if your calling patterns change significantly, the savings may disappear. You may be able to save more than the discount plans will by simply taking better advantage of time-of-day discounts. Usually after 5 P.M. and after 11 P.M. are the break points for significant rate reductions. You can also save on weekend calls (although Sunday afternoon calls may return to the daytime weekday rates).

Other aspects of long-distance billing can make as much difference in your bill as the rate plan. You are not supposed to get charged for "busies" or "no answers" or even for failed connections to computers and fax machines. Long-distance companies vary in the accuracy of their billing when it comes to these matters—and in the ease of getting credits for incomplete calls. For example, one company might charge you for a call that is so garbled that a fax cannot be sent, another gives you credit simply for the asking, another demands to see your fax log before the credit is issued. The time increments used in billing also make a difference. Some companies have one-minute billing increments, so that if you make a call that lasts a minute and one second you get charged for two full minutes. Others have increments of as little as six seconds. Different policies may apply to the first minute of the call, which is always the most expensive. If you make a lot of short calls, the billing increments can make a big difference. Rates for credit card and operator-assisted calls also vary widely and are always more expensive than calls you dial directly from your home.

To compare, get competitive prices on some of your most frequent calls or ask a prospective new carrier to audit a typical monthly bill for you. New "flat rate" pricing plans (the same rate for all calls regardless of distance) will also help you compare. If you do decide that another company is cheaper, you can easily change your carrier by contacting your local phone company. There is a charge, but your new long-distance company will usually pay it for you.

Another option is to bypass your selected long-distance carrier for individual calls. You may find certain locations that are cheaper on another network or all your carrier's lines may be busy at a particular time. You can reach other long-distance carriers by dialing a five-digit prefix unique to each carrier (for example, 10288 = 10ATT).

T I P S   F O R   T E L E P H O N E   C O N S U M E R S

• If your income is limited, check with your phone company to see whether you qualify for a telephone assistance program.

• Carefully evaluate your need for custom calling services and telephone maintenance programs.

• Keep a diary of your local calls so you can decide which optional calling plan will save you money.

• If your phone company cannot answer your billing questions, contact your state public utilities commission.

• Ask your phone company about your Caller ID blocking options.

• Have long-distance carriers audit an actual bill and compare charges.

• Use direct dialing for all your domestic and international long-distance calls.

• Use a long-distance charge card whenever possible when you are away from home.

• Take advantage of time-of-day and day-of-week long-distance discounts whenever possible.

• Use your telephone directory whenever possible to avoid directory information charges.

Long-distance calling away from home can cost you plenty. Hotels and motels sometimes charge exorbitant premiums on long-distance calls, which can double the cost. Toll calls placed from coin-operated telephones are sometimes connected through long-distance companies that charge premium rates. When traveling, your best bet is to always use a telephone credit card.

Services also vary in quality, which may make a difference to you. Quality of services includes live operator assistance as needed, credit cards, international calling, and the ability to "hear a pin drop."

Information Services

Information services via phone lines also have traps for the unwary consumer. Even at a few cents per minute, videotex fees quickly mount for the "addicted" user. In one U.S. videotex trial, some callers became so addicted to an on-line trivia game that they ran themselves into bankruptcy. Charges from 900 and 976 lines may run a few dollars per minute rather than a few cents, so callers get into trouble even faster. Telephone companies may (or may not) "forgive" one month's worth of information service charges if you can convince them that a child is responsible or have some other compelling excuse—but after that you pay.

There are some common audiotext scams to watch out for, such as advertising one rate (or no rate at all) and charging a higher rate to your telephone bill. Another scheme is to get you to call one 900 number at a low rate but then switch you to another, higher-priced service after you are on the line. Some interactive 800 numbers switch you to expensive 900 numbers, too. Other audiotext services specialize in pleading tactics that lure you to stay on the line just long enough to get charged for the next minute.

The value of the information available through audiotext services is also an issue. Many college students are victimized by 900 services that promise jobs but that deliver listings from newspaper "help wanted" sections, at a hundred times the cost. This is unfortunately indicative of many audiotext services, which charge users for information that is already publicly available at a fraction of the cost.

The abuse of information services by minors is another concern. Calls to adult entertainment services are hard to monitor, at least until the phone bill arrives. In one case an information service provider switched programs suddenly between a Santa Line (Call Santa and place your order) and a phone sex line. Promoters of another Santa Line invited children to hold their telephone receivers up to the television while the commercial's soundtrack played the touch-tone digits that dialed Santa! Teens are susceptible to chat lines, where anonymous groups of callers talk about whatever comes to mind—usually sex. More than one "chat line romance" has turned into an ugly case of rape or child molestation. Videotex is somewhat more childproof than audiotext, requiring some degree of computer skill, but computer literate youngsters have no trouble finding pornographic computer files and X-rated computer conferences on the Internet.

TIPS FOR INFORMATION SERVICE CONSUMERS

- Always be sure of the cost of the service before you call.
- If the service provider does not announce the cost when you call, or indicate the passage of time, hang up.
- Do not allow your audiotext calls to be passed on to another service. Just hang up.
- Buy a telephone lockout device if you have concerns about children accessing 900 and 976 numbers.
- Use ad-supported audiotext services that are free to the user whenever possible.
- Your phone company may forgive you once for excessive charges, but not twice.
- Shop around for consumer videotex services with low—or no—usage-sensitive charges.
- Change the password on your videotex service periodically to prevent unauthorized access, avoid common words and names.
- Check with your local library to see if the information you are paying for is already available for free.

Some consumer protection is available for audiotext users. Chat lines are now required to have monitors to steer the conversations clear of impropriety. Service providers must declare the cost of their service in their advertising and again when you call if the calls cost over $2 per minute. There is a "grace period" of 30 seconds during which you may hang up without incurring a charge. Users must be apprised of the passage of time with an audible tone or voice message. Another way to avoid excessive audiotext charges is to call only advertising-supported services with no usage charges. One security measure available to parents is a mechanical lockout device that covers the telephone dial or keypad. Some telephone companies also make it possible to automatically block calls to 900 and 976 calls.

COMPUTER CONSUMER ISSUES

Some important issues for home computer consumers are figuring out which computer and which software to buy, how to get the most value for their dollar when they buy, and how to get help after they open the carton.

Which Computer?

The question of which computer to buy divides the world into two seemingly irreconcilable camps: Apple users and IBM (and IBM-compatible) users. Apple users extol the user-friendliness, attractive interfaces, and multimedia capabilities of their machines. IBM users say that their machines rule the "real world" of work; that they get the job done faster, cheaper, and better—even if not "friendlier"—and that new software (especially Windows) and hardware options make IBM machines as accessible and versatile as Macintoshes. It is up to each person to decide whether he or she is a "Mac person" or an "IBM person."

The next step is to identify the features you need. Here is where many consumers go astray, buying systems loaded with options and performance capabilities they will never use. For simple word processing and spreadsheet applications, the most basic and low-cost systems will suffice. The only really essential peripherals are a printer (a cheap dot matrix printer will usually do) and a modem. The most demanding home applications are video games, which require large amounts of random access memory (RAM), advanced interface devices, CD-ROM players, and the fastest internal processors to perform at their best. If you want a slick video game player, you might consider a separate video game system for your TV instead of loading your personal computer with expensive options. You can easily buy both a basic home computer and a fancy game player for the cost of configuring a home computer system for high-tech game playing.

Where to Buy

If you decide that you are a "Mac person," you'll need to decide which model you want. To buy it, call local computer dealers listed in the Yellow Pages to find out who has the best price, then check with reliable mail-order companies for their prices (and you can save on sales tax from out-of-state firms). Apple offers substantial educational discounts, so if you are attending school, or know someone who is, inquire about special purchase plans through academic institutions.

If you are an "IBM person," you have hundreds of brands to choose from, and you might get rewarded with a real steal—or burned by a real sting. Read product reviews in the personal computer magazines at your local newsstand and check out the systems featured by local computer dealers before you decide. Don't be afraid to go mail order, especially with some of the more established direct-mail dealers, who also are reviewed periodically in consumer computer publications.

Whether you are buying from a dealer or a mail-order company, always check out the warranty and customer service. Look for a warranty of at least one year; some last two years or more. If you buy through a local dealer, ask about its repair capability. Does the dealer have a factory authorized technician who performs the repairs on site, or does the technician pack your computer into a box and send it to a repair depot? If the latter is the case—and it most often is—you could save some money by buying via mail order and sending the broken computer in yourself. Also ask whether your dealer has a help line you can call. Chances are, a technician can "talk you through" most of the problems you will have setting up your computer. Increasingly, software companies are charging for help-line service, so be sure your dealer can help you.

Used computers are another avenue to explore. Used computers are very inexpensive, and most will run the home computer applications you are likely to need. Computers are solid-state devices and never really wear out. The most troublesome components are the

Computer software piracy is probably the most common crime in America next to cheating on taxes. What computer user hasn't at least been tempted to copy a software program from a friend or download the latest version of a program from a computer bulletin board? In the corporate environment, the temptation to "share" a single copy of a program among many users or to load a package onto a network must be irresistible to many a manager facing a budget crunch. The rationalizations abound: "We only use one copy at a time"; "I am just a poor student and that software is sooooo expensive"; "I don't use it very much"; "I can copy a book on a Xerox machine, why can't I copy a program?"; and the old stand-by "Everybody else is doing it, why not me?" After all, about a fifth of all the personal computer software in the United States is illegal, and it wasn't too long ago that half the software in use was illegal.

The only problem is that as of December 1992, unauthorized copying of computer software is a felony offense. Copy a software package, go to prison. Specifically, if you copy more than 10 programs in an eighteen-month period or any software worth more than $2,500, you are looking at a felony rap. If you are a supervisor and your employees copy software illegally, you are responsible, even if you have no knowledge of what is going on, even if you have a no-copying policy, even if you get a lawyer to write a letter to your employees telling them that you are not responsible.

But what are the chances of getting caught? Even now that piracy is a felony it is unlikely that the police will break down your door and search your home computer. However, if you are engaged in wholesale copyright fraud, such as downloading illegal software to others for a fee over your computer bulletin board system, you are taking a big risk. At work, you are vulnerable to colleagues and disgruntled employees who might want to settle a score with you by dialing the 800 number for the Software Publisher's Association (SPA), an industry group that roots out copyright violations.

The SPA Is Watching YOU!

The Software Publisher's Association does have some enforcement staff, although they confine themselves to making a few highly visible examples of corporate copyright abusers. If the SPA "police" visit you, they can make you shut down all your computers, immediately come up with the money to buy legal copies at the full retail price, and impose fines for triple damages on top of that. Now that software piracy is a felony, they could conceivably use the federal antiracketeering statutes to confiscate your computers, even your entire business! If you work at home, that could mean losing your house. If the SPA does visit you, it might be hard to avoid a fine even if you are innocent. Strictly speaking, you need to produce the master disks, manuals, licenses, and purchase documents for all of the copies of all the software packages on all of your computers. For a large corporation, this could add up to warehouses full of empty Lotus 1-2-3 boxes! If any of your employees have "donated" software they brought from home to their office computers, they could nail you for that, too.

Technology Fixes

There are some technology solutions to the piracy problem in the corporate network environment, although some of them are rather drastic (Paul, 1993; Stang, 1993). One possibility is to make employees use "diskless workstations" that have no floppy disk drives at all. Instead, employees have to download each application from the corporate network every time they use it. Of course, if the network ever crashes, you have to lock up and go home for the day—or for the week. Or, you can force all users to access software through a "menu system" that prohibits the copying of files from software directories. Network managers can also search through the local hard drives of all of the computers on a network to look for illegal software. The problem is, the same procedure facilitates searches of personal directories for other reasons—say, looking for critical memos about company supervisors. New versions of network management software will have features that automatically administer copyrights. For example, the use of a program could be limited to an individual workstation or group of workstations, or fees could be charged according to the amount of use a package gets. Another option is to limit the number of simultaneous software users to that which the purchase agreement allows. When that number is reached, the next user has to wait, sort of like getting a "busy" signal on the telephone. "Sorry, all of our Word Perfects are busy, please try your word processing again later."

- Buy the minimum configuration that will meet your needs.

- Consider a stand-alone game machine instead of configuring your personal computer with expensive game gear.

- Check mail-order and used-computer outlets.

- Compare the warranty and customer support offers of prospective computer dealers.

- Find out whether your dealer has her or his own factory-authorized repair technician or merely forwards your computer to one by mail.

- Look for low-cost "clones" of popular computer and software brands.

- Obtain freeware and shareware through computer bulletin boards.

ones with moving parts: the disk drives and the power supplies. These can easily be checked out and replaced by a qualified technician. Many areas have stores that sell used equipment on consignment or that hold auctions for used computers. If you are a first-time computer purchaser, take someone with you who is familiar enough with computers to know how to "kick the tires." Classified ads in newspapers are another option, as long as you follow the same precautions you would take when buying a used car: Make the sale contingent on the unit passing an inspection at a local computer dealer. Also have the dealer inspect the internal components to make sure that you are getting original equipment or quality substitute components.

Buying Software

When it comes to software, home users are often unaware that there are low-cost ways to acquire software other than stealing it ("stealing" is not too strong a word, as software piracy is now a felony—see box). One option is to look for special deals that "bundle" popular software into the purchase price of a new computer. Most popular packages have low-cost "clones" that offer the same features at a much lower price. These packages can be found by shopping around a bit at the local computer store or by reading consumer computer magazines. Another route is "freeware" or "shareware." These packages do not have much of the look and feel of the commercial products, and their documentation is often minimal or poorly executed, but they still get the job done. Local computer bulletin board systems are a source of these packages, and subscribers to on-line services such as CompuServe and GEnie can also access them. Your public library probably has a catalog of free personal computer software. Table A.1 lists some of the most popular shareware packages. Each of the packages listed costs less than $100.

TABLE A.1. SHAREWARE'S GREATEST HITS

Program	Type	Contact
PROCOMM	Communications	Datastorm 1-314-474-8477
PC-File	Database manager	ButtonWare 1-800-JBUTTON
PC Write	Word processing	Quicksoft 1-206-282-0452
Automenu	Menu program	Magee Ent. 1-404-446-6611
PC Calc	Spreadsheet	ButtonWare 1-800-JBUTTON
PC Key Draw	Drawing	OEDWARE 1-301-997-9333

Source: De Maria & Fontaine (1988).

CONSUMER PRIVACY

Earlier in this text we detailed the effects of information technologies on consumer privacy. Here we consider the privacy rights that people have as consumers. At the core of the matter is the question of whether individuals have a fundamental right to privacy. The U.S. Constitution is silent on this issue, perhaps because the framers of the Constitution could not foresee the threat of information technologies whose invention was a hundred years in the future. Nonetheless, a right to privacy has been articulated in a series of decisions by the federal courts and has been extended to information privacy by several pieces of legislation over the last twenty-five years. All consumers should be aware of their rights under these laws:

The right to inspect. Under the Fair Credit Reporting Act of 1970, consumers have the right to inspect the information contained in a credit agency's file.

The right to challenge. Consumers have the right to challenge the accuracy of the information and to append their own explanations.

The right to updates. Credit agencies must purge items that are more than seven years old, including records of old arrests and lawsuits.

The right of control. Inquiries for purposes other than hiring, insurance investigations, or credit checks can only be made with the permission of the subject or under a court order. The Privacy Act of 1974 constrains federal agencies— although not state and local government or private companies—from transferring information without consent or from using information for purposes other than that for which it was originally collected.

The right to refuse. The Privacy Act of 1974 stipulates that citizens can refuse to disclose their social security number except where required by law. This limits the use of social security numbers to match data between sources.

The right to notification. The Right to Financial Privacy Act of 1979 requires that federal law enforcement agencies notify individuals when their financial records are subpoenaed. The Privacy Act of 1974 prohibits secret files and requires government agencies to publish descriptions of the files they keep and the types of information they contain each year.

The right to electronic privacy. A 1967 Supreme Court decision held telephone wiretaps unconstitutional, although Congress later legalized wiretaps conducted under court order. The Electronic Communication Privacy Act of 1986 extended this protection to electronic mail messages.

It is also important to be aware of the privacy rights that you do not have. Aside from federal law enforcement agencies, no one has to notify you that he or she has a computer file on you nor let you have access to the files unless you are denied credit. Some consumer credit bureaus will let you see your files, for a "nominal fee," but you have no legal right to the information if they choose not to release it. You also have no right to control the further release of information about you, other than by federal government agencies. The Privacy Act of 1974 does not prohibit "routine" information transfers between government agencies, and just about all transfers may be deemed "routine"—a huge loophole in the law. When you do catch an error, you cannot force the database company to correct all past transmissions of the erroneous data. Since verification of consumer information files is accomplished through cross-checks with other databases, it is entirely possible that the error will creep back into your file at a later date.

When talking on the phone or using electronic mail from your home, you do have privacy protection, but your communications in the workplace are not protected. Regardless of the setting in which the call is made, the other party to the communication is free to make a recording of it and may do so without your consent. You have no privacy protection when you are talking on a cordless phone. It is so easy to intercept such conversations that no one has an expectation to a right of privacy when using them. It is unlawful to intercept cellular telephone transmissions, although anyone with a special radio device called a scanner can do so; at least you do have some grounds for seeking legal redress if your calls are scanned.

While you can decline to give out your social security number if you want to avoid being "matched" in computer databases, your telephone number may be used for the same purpose. This is part of the reason why Caller ID (see box) has provoked a firestorm of

For a few dollars a month, Caller ID gives telephone subscribers the ability to see the numbers of incoming calls displayed before they pick up the phone. This may sound innocuous, but to hear consumer and civil liberties advocates tell it, it is the worst threat to privacy since the invention of the wiretap. With Caller ID, telemarketers have the ability to match incoming calls with computerized files containing personal information about the caller. In the twinkle of a computer screen, all that information is displayed for the telemarketing agent and can even be used to summon a customized sales script tailored to the caller's personal characteristics or purchase history. The fear is that this will help telemarketers craft sales pitches that will be virtually irresistible. Even innocent calls to local retailers could be correlated in market research databases that could be turned against the unsuspecting consumer. Worse, the technology could be used to create electronic "pigeon lists" of gullible consumers who respond to telemarketing scams ("Call this number for a free trip to Florida") by trapping their numbers and reselling them. The telephone number could also help telemarketers match data in different computer files.

Law enforcement agencies could set up Caller ID–based sting operations ("Need money fast? Got something to sell? Call this number"). Will battered women feel safe calling shelters if they know that their identity might be revealed? And would you want the IRS to keep a record of your phone number from the time you called to see whether a lost weekend in Miami qualified as a business travel expense? Clearly, caller ID has the ability to encroach on an important type of privacy right that is imperiled in the Information Age—the right to control personal information.

However, Caller ID also has the ability to offer high-tech consumer protection. Abusive calls drop sharply in areas where Caller ID is available. Alert victims can help consumer protection agencies track down telemarketing scams more efficiently by noting the numbers of calling parties or by activating a call trace feature that automatically reports problems calls to the authorities. Caller ID can also help the consumer duck repeated calls from collection agencies and market researchers. The intelligent network could also make it possible to set up consumer databases of numbers used by fraudulent telemarketers, which consumers could query when a call from an unknown number is received. Thus, Caller ID could enhance another form of privacy right—the right to avoid unwanted intrusions. Some even argue that the service is merely the electronic version of the peepholes that we have in our front doors—that it restores to us a measure of privacy that has been denied us ever since Mr. Watson invented the telephone bell.

Further technology advances could raise the intensity of the battle. Caller ID blocking lets callers block the transmission of their number on a per call or per line basis. Some phone companies have decided not to offer the service in areas that make the blocking too easy, though. After all, who would pay for the service if all the IDs were blocked? But Caller ID block rejection would allow the called party to reject calls from those who do not reveal their Caller IDs. The name of the calling party may be transmitted as well. In fact, the data channel that carries caller identification information could eventually be used to exchange brief messages before picking up the phone. ("Answer this call and win a trip to Florida." "Make it a trip to Hawaii, and maybe I will.") Only time will tell whether the consumer or the telemarketers will get the upper hand in the battle over Caller ID.

objections from consumer advocates and civil libertarians. In many areas where Caller ID is available, there is also a Caller ID blocking feature, which lets you prevent the display of your number on a call-by-call basis.

Unlisted telephone numbers are another privacy protection option. An unlisted number is not an absolute guarantee of privacy. In one case, a gangster obtained an unlisted number by browbeating a telephone operator and located a family whom he kidnapped and tortured, but the telephone company was not legally liable. Most consumers are trying to avoid telemarketers and survey researchers rather than gangsters, but an unlisted number is still poor protection, since random digit dialing is now used routinely. No one is safe from a random call, especially since many phone banks use dialing machines that place random digit calls with superhuman speed. Other telemarketing operations use phone numbers obtained from magazine subscription forms, personal checks, credit card charge slips, credit applications, and appliance warranties.

Electronic telephone directory systems pose a new privacy threat, since they will make it even easier for telemarketers and pollsters to track you down. Pacific Telesis was prevented from releasing computer-readable directory information after an outcry from consumer groups in California, but electronic directory services are probably inevitable in the long run.

Are you wasting your money by having an unlisted number? If your primary concern is avoiding telemarketers and pollsters, an unlisted number has little value. You can ask telemarketers to remove your name from their lists, and you can contact the Direct Marketing Association in New York, which acts as a clearinghouse for consumers who wish to be dropped from all lists. If unwanted or crank calls are your problem, you may find the new Caller ID or call trace services more effective, although also more costly. If you wish the world would stop bothering you and just go away, you might buy a phone with a ringer switch—or just unplug your phone.

CONSUMER SCAMS TO WATCH OUT FOR

Communications media are involved in a wide variety of fraudulent schemes that all consumers should be wary of. These schemes fall into two general classes: telemarketing scams in which you are the victim, and theft of service scams that make you an accomplice in a felony.

Telemarketing Scams

It is important to recognize that not all telemarketers are fraudulent. The industry has received a bad reputation because of a few bad apples. Here are some common fraudulent schemes to watch out for:

> *You just won a contest* . . . Congratulations! All you have to do is pay a small fee for a coupon book that will entitle you to discounts on travel, entertainment, and dining worth thousands of dollars." What the callers are after is that "small fee,"

and everybody they call is a "winner." Those coupons come loaded with fine print and could *cost* you thousands to use.

"Our truck just broke down . . . and my load of (lobsters, photocopier supplies, roses) will perish before they can fix it, so my boss told me to call around and sell the stuff at a special low, low price." Callers like to pull this one during lunch, when student interns tend to be watching the phones. Those "discounts" are substantially above the retail price.

"Want to buy a ticket for the policeman's ball?" Who doesn't like to help out the local police force, especially when the caller seems to know who we are and calls us at home? Anybody can throw a dance and call it a "policeman's ball," even if no policemen are invited. Check with your police department before you buy.

We have already discussed ways to keep your name off telemarketers' lists. Unfortunately, anyone crooked enough to hit you with one of these scams is also unlikely to be a member in good standing with the Direct Marketing Association. To curb telemarketing abuse, other proposals have been aimed at the technologies that make unwanted calls, such as automatic dialers, Caller ID, and machines that seize the line while delivering a tape-recorded message. To date, only the last have been banned under federal law. Some prohibitions have been enacted at the state level, but unscrupulous telemarketers evade these rules by moving to states where the practice in question is still legal. Politicians are also reluctant to pass legislation that might "throw the baby out with the bathwater"—measures that prevent telemarketing might also prohibit calls from public opinion pollsters.

HOW TO AVOID COMMUNICATIONS FRAUD

• Never give out your phone calling card number, and "cover up" when dialing it in a public place.

• Review your long-distance bills immediately and report unauthorized calls to your carrier.

• Disconnect your phone service before you move.

• Never buy anything over the phone until you check with your local consumer affairs office.

Theft of Service

Other consumer communications frauds offer you "free" service, but in reality you are stealing service and opening yourself to a possible felony indictment:

"Free" long-distance calls. What the caller is really offering is telephone credit card numbers or access numbers to corporate long-distance networks that are stolen from their rightful users. Use them and you can go to prison.

"Free" cable. "Blue boxes" for illegal cable reception are still sold from the trunks of old cars, but you can also construct your own from readily available electronics components. Cable operators have electronic devices that can detect the pirate converters without entering your home, and many conduct periodic system audits, so beware. Under the Cable Act of 1984, you could be fined $10,000 for the theft of cable service.

"Free" cellular radio. What you are being sold is a cellular telephone with a stolen user identification code programmed into it. As with the stolen long-distance number, the free calls last only until the rightful user gets their next bill.

"Discount" software. Audio- and videotapes and computer software that you buy out of the trunk of an old Oldsmobile are also illicit, the product of unauthorized duplication.

REFERENCES

DeMaria, R., & Fontaine, G. R. (1988). *Public-domain software and shareware.* Redwood City, CA: M&T Publishing.

Michigan Public Service Commission. (1994). *Consumer Alerts.* Lansing, MI: Michigan Public Service Commission.

Paul, F. (1993, March 1). NetWare users to get help with software licensing. *Network World,* pp. 1, 42.

Stang, D. (1993, March 8). Eliminating software piracy can help avoid "a heap of trouble." *Network World,* pp. L4, L16.

Glossary

A

Account executives supervise advertising campaigns for clients inside the advertising agency.

Accuracy of information refers to making sure that media or information content is truthful, correct, and not deceptive.

Acoustic is music that is not electronically amplified.

Active audiences are selective in use of media, interpret media messages in their own way, and are not necessarily affected by media contents.

Addressable converters turn themselves off and on in response to numerical computer codes that authorize reception of specific channels or programs.

Advertisers are the organizations that commission advertising campaigns to help sell their products.

Advertising is media selling audience access to those who wish to pay to put their sales message before the audience.

Advertising agencies are organizations that create and place commercial messages for advertisers.

Advertising managers coordinate the advertiser's efforts across all of its products.

Advertising media are the communications media used to deliver the advertising message.

Affiliate fees are monthly per-subscriber fees that cable networks charge to local cable operators for the right to carry their programs.

Affiliates in broadcasting are stations that contract to use the programming of and share advertising/financing with a network.

Agenda setting is the ability of the media to decide what is important.

AM or **amplitude modification** refers to the fact that the sound information is carried in the height, or amplitude, of the radio wave.

Analog transmission uses continuously varying signals corresponding to the light or sounds originated by the source.

Anticompetitive practices are those that unfairly use market power or statements to damage potential competitors.

Antisocial behavior is behavior contrary to prevailing norms for social conduct, such as racism, sexism, or violence.

Appalachian music developed from English, Scottish, and Irish roots with similar instrumentation and ballad forms.

Aristotle's golden mean holds that "moral virtue is appropriate location between two extremes."

Art directors coordinate the graphic artists and video and film producers who make the visual elements of an ad.

Artificial intelligence is the ability to mimic human thinking processes with a computer.

Assembly language uses mnemonic symbols to simplify programming for humans.

Asynchronous means "not all at the same time."

Asynchronous transfer mode (ATM) is a standard for high-speed digital transmission of voice, text, and video.

Audience segment is a subgroup of consumers with specialized tastes and media habits.

Audimeters are automatic devices for measuring household television viewing.

Audiographic teleconferencing involves voice and still graphics.

Audiotext means audio information services provided over 900, 976, 576, or 800 numbers.

Automatic call directors (ACDs) are systems that manage and distribute calls to work groups, as in telemarketing centers.

Automatic number identification (ANI) is an intelligent network service that identifies the number of the party who is placing a call.

Automatic switching automatically connects calls without operator intervention.

B

Baby Bells are the local telephone companies created by the breakup of AT&T in 1984.

Bandwidth is a measure of the capacity of communications systems.

Barriers to entry include the expenses of setting up a new media business that may make it difficult for all but a few to enter.

Basic cable includes the local channels, distant stations, and satellite signals that cable operators offer for a basic monthly fee.

Bits, short for binary digits, are the basic 1's and 0's of computer data.

Blues is an African American musical tradition based primarily on guitar and distinctive plaintive lyrics.

Brand awareness is the consumer's ability to recall the name of a specific brand of product.

Brand imagery is an advertising approach that seeks to give a product a personality of its own.

Brand loyalty is the consumer's propensity to make repeat purchases of a specific brand of product.

Brand managers are in charge of one specific product.

Bridges are devices used to connect the different locations involved in a teleconference.

Broadband media have the capacity to carry video.

Bullet or **hypodermic** model posits powerful, direct effects from the mass media.

Bulletin board systems (BBSs) are small-scale, user-supported videotex services.

Business videos are programs created by organizations for their employees and customers.

Bypass networks bypass the local telephone exchange to connect organizations directly to long-distance carriers or to private networks.

C

Caller ID displays the number of the party who is trying to call on a small screen.

Camera tube transforms light into electrical impulses.

Capture theory suggests that regulators are often effectively captured by the interests of the industry they regulate.

Carrier systems act like wireline radios, transmitting multiple channels simultaneously on different frequencies.

Catalogs are compilations of advertisements mailed to the consumer in booklet form.

Catharsis hypothesis states that antisocial urges can be satisfied by watching others act them out in the media.

Cathode ray tubes (CRTs) are the TV-like display devices on computers.

CD-ROM is a compact disc computer storage medium with read-only memory.

Cellular data are wireless networks that connect mobile computers.

Cellular radio is a mobile telephone service that subdivides service areas into many small cells to maximize the number of users.

Cellular television combines cellular radio and broadcast television technologies into a two-way multichannel TV system.

Censorship is control over media content by those in higher authority in a society.

Centrex is a portion of a telephone company's switch dedicated to a particular group of users.

Chain broadcasting refers to radio networks and their control over talent and affiliated stations.

Chapbooks were cheaply bound books or pamphlets of poetry or prose aimed at a broader audience, much like early paperbacks.

Chat lines are audiotext services in which callers join together in group discussions.

Chief information officers (CIOs) are the top-level specialists who direct the use of communications media in an organization.

Chilling effect is the idea that rules about fairness or right of reply inhibits stations from airing controversial programs.

Classified ads are brief newspaper advertisements, usually a single column wide.

Client review is the process of obtaining approval from the advertiser for the advertising campaign.

Coaxial cable is the high-capacity wire used for cable TV transmission.

Codecs digitize video for use in video teleconferences.

Commission is a percentage fee paid to an agent as a reward for completing a transaction.

Common carriers are transportation or telecommunications companies that carry others' goods or messages.

Communication is the process of exchanging information.

Communications media include all forms of communication mediated through mechanical or electronic channels.

Competition refers to the existence of several companies competing for dominance in an industry.

Competitive access providers can offer local telephone service in competition with local telephone companies, like the RBOCs.

Computer addiction is the compulsive use of the computer.

Computer anxiety is a debilitating fear of computers.

Computer-assisted design/computer-assisted manufacturing (CAD/CAM) systems apply communications media to manufacturing.

Computer conferences are written communications via computer networks in which a group discussion takes place.

Computer-integrated manufacturing (CIM) is putting the entire manufacturing process under the control of computer and telecommunications systems.

Computer literacy is the basic understanding of computers.

Computer-mediated conferences are discussions on a computer network.

Computer services refer to the processing of computer applications and the delivery of computerized information for end users.

Computerization movements are social movements promoting the adoption of information technologies within organizations.

Concentration of ownership occurs when media are owned by a small number of individuals, government agencies, or corporations.

Confidentiality usually refers to protecting the identity of news sources.

Consent decree of 1956 opened up competition for IBM in the computer market.

Consolidation refers to a reduction in the number of media outlets and a concentration of the ownership of media among fewer owners.

Consumption refers to a social ethic that values the purchase and possession of goods above most other competing values.

Content analyses are quantitative descriptions of the content of media systems.

Contested reading occurs when the audience rejects the producer's preferred reading.

Contingent employees are temporary employees who can be hired or fired at will.

Convergence means integration into a common technological base.

Converters descramble and retune cable channels so they can be received by an ordinary TV set.

Coproduction indicates cooperation between film or television producers in two or more countries.

Copy platform describes the creative issues to be addressed in advertising from the perspective of the consumer.

Copy testing evaluates the effectiveness of advertisements.

Copyright is a legal privilege to use, sell, or license intellectual property, such as a book or film.

Copyright or **royalty fee** is a payment legally required for use of another person's intellectual property.

Copywriters write the text of advertisements.

Corantos, the ancestors of newspapers, were irregular news sheets that appeared around 1600 in Holland and England and covered foreign affairs.

Core and ring is a structure in which a small group of permanent professional employees manages a fluctuating temporary work force.

Corporate underwriting on PBS television stations is financial support of programs in return for a mention of the underwriter on the air.

Cost per thousand (CPM) is a way of comparing advertising costs in terms of how much it costs to reach 1,000 members of the target audience for an ad.

Creative approach refers to the type of appeal that a copywriter incorporates into an ad.

Creative departments produce the copy and artwork that go into advertisements.

Creative directors coordinate the activities of the creative department on behalf of a specific product.

Critical mass is the minimum number of users required for a collectively used technology to be useful and to take off.

Cross-ownership is owning various kinds of media, usually in the same geographic locale.

Cross-subsidy applies revenues from a profitable area to a less profitable one.

Cultivation theory argues that mass media exposure cultivates a view of the world that is consistent with the mediated "reality."

Cultural autonomy refers to the goal of being mostly self-sufficient in media and cultural productions.

Cultural capital is based on a person's education, family background, and other sorts of learning.

Cultural determinism implies that media messages can impose new meanings and be read by audiences in new ways, different from what economic interests would prefer.

Cultural fragmentation occurs when different groups and individuals customize their own information and cultural experience so that people share less of a common culture.

Cultural imperialism occurs when countries dominate others through media exports, advertising, and media institution models.

Cultural proximity is the desire of audiences to see or hear media products from their own or similar cultures.

Culture is a system of images and symbols shared by a group.

Culture as a process of refinement puts a normative or value judgment on culture, suggesting it should be used to improve people.

Custom calling includes call waiting, call forwarding, speed dialing, and three-way calling.

Custom local area signaling services (CLASS) are intelligent network options such as Caller ID, distinctive ring, call block, redial, call trace, and selective call forwarding.

Custom publishing refers to creating customized versions of print newspapers, magazines, or books for particular audiences.

Customer premise equipment (CPE) is equipment that the end user connects to the telephone network.

D

Database marketing is used when advertisers maintain computerized lists of consumers so they can contact them directly.

Database service providers package multiple information services.

DBS (direct broadcast satellite) is a satellite service that is marketed directly to home receivers.

DBS radio or **RDBS** would bring signals directly from satellites to home receivers.

Decoding is the reading of the text by the audience or reader.

Demographic channels are designed to appeal to audiences with shared demographic characteristics.

Demographic segmentation is based on social or personal characteristics such as age, sex, education, or income.

Dependent variables are the consequences studied in an experiment.

Deregulation refers to decreasing government oversight in the anticipation that competition will minimize abuses of power.

Deskilling is reduction of the skill requirements of a job through mechanization or automation.

Desktop publishing is the composition, layout, and sometimes printing of materials using a personal computer.

Desktop video is using personal computers to "play" video presentations or display video teleconferences.

Developing countries are those in Asia, Latin America, the Middle East, and Africa that are struggling to grow economically and develop socially.

Difference engine was an early precursor of the computer invented by Charles Babbage in England in 1822.

Diffusion is the process whereby innovations spread in a social system.

Digital means computer readable.

Digital compression reduces the number of computer bits that have to be transmitted.

Digital computers store and manipulate information in the form of binary code (1's and 0's).

Digital data services (DDS) are dedicated, all-digital lines.

Digital television cameras sample pictures by cutting them up into thousands of elements (pixels) and assigning a binary number to each point.

Dime novels were inexpensive paperback novels that aimed at a mass or at least a broad readership.

Direct mail refers to direct targeting of customers with mailed catalogs, advertising, or other materials.

Direct marketing is a form of advertising in which an immediate response is requested of the receiver.

Direct sales of media hardware, software, and services are straight from producers or retailers to audiences or users.

Direct satellite broadcasting is a television or radio satellite service that is marketed directly to home receivers.

Disc jockey is a radio station announcer who often emphasizes delivery and personality.

Distance learning refers to formal education programs delivered through communications media.

Distant signals are cable channels imported from major television markets.

Diurnos, later ancestors of newspapers, gave daily reports and tended to be more focused on domestic events.

Diversity of content implies a variety of ideas, cultural traditions, and values in media.

Diversity of ownership implies that media owners are of diverse ethnic backgrounds and gender.

Downsizing is replacing mainframe computers with networked personal computers.

E

Ecological validity is the extent to which conditions under which studies are conducted adequately reflect real-world situations.

Economic capital is a person's personal or family wealth.

Economies of scale refer to reduced per-unit costs when large numbers of copies are manufactured.

Electromagnetic recording rearranges metallic particles in the tape according to modulated current produced by a microphone.

Electronic blackboards are audiographic conferencing devices that let participants at a remote location see what is written on a blackboard.

Electronic data interchange (EDI) is an electronic system for placing and tracking transactions between firms.

Electronic mail is a written message sent over a computer network.

Electronic switches replace electro-mechanical components with solid-state components.

Encoding is the creation of a text containing certain signs and meanings.

Encryption means to write a message in a secret code.

ENIAC was the first general-purpose electronic digital computer.

Entry costs are the costs of starting up a media company: technology, distribution, personnel, and raw material.

Ethics are moral rules or rules of conduct that guide one's actions in specific situations.

Ethnography is a naturalistic research method in which the observer obtains detailed information about human behavior from personal observation or interviews over extended periods of time.

Experimental research studies the effects of media under carefully controlled situations.

F

Facsimile (fax) is a way of sending images of documents electronically over phone lines.

Fairness refers to responsibility in selecting and treating topics and sources.

Feature films are longer story films, usually over one and a half hours or more.

Fiber optic systems use light instead of electricity to communicate.

Fifth-generation computers employ parallel processing.

First Amendment to the U.S. Constitution guarantees freedom of speech and press in the United States.

First-copy costs are the initial costs involved in producing a mass media work regardless of how many copies are actually produced.

First-generation computers used vacuum tubes in their data processing units.

First-run or **original syndication** is licensing programs directly for nonnetwork time, independent stations, and cable networks.

Flattened pyramid is an organizational structure in which the layers of middle management have been stripped away.

Floppy disk drives store computer data on a flexible ("floppy") plastic disk coated with a magnetized film.

FM or **frequency modulation** means that the sound information is carried in variations in the frequency of the radio wave.

Focus groups are small-group interviews intended to explore consumer reactions in depth.

Fordism is the application of the assembly-line process, reducing work to the endless repetition of a single task.

Fourth-generation computers use very large scale integration.

Frame refers to what a writer chooses to include within the view or frame of a story, documentary, or drama and what conceptual framework to use.

Free and balanced flow refers to achieving more equal flows of media between countries via the freedom to produce and receive media.

Free press is the extension of freedom of speech to media.

Freedom of speech is the right to speak what one wishes free of government or other restraints.

Freeware and **shareware** are programs that may be used free of charge.

Freeze-frame video teleconferences use a sequence of still images that do not convey a sense of continuous motion.

Frequency is the number of cycles that waves complete in a set amount of time.

Frequency allocations are parts or bands of the radio frequency spectrum authorized for a particular purpose.

Full-service networks are cable television systems that provide telephone, data transmission, and interactive television as well as conventional (one-way) cable television.

G

Gatekeepers decide what will appear in the media.

General audience means that the audience is made up of a large group of people from all walks of life.

Generalizability is the degree to which social science studies can be applied to the real world.

Genre channels feature programs of a certain type, such as movies or sports events.

Genres are types or formats of media content.

Geodemographic clustering categorizes consumers based on the demographic characteristics common to the area in which they live.

Gospel originated as southern Protestant religious music, with distinctive but related African American and white forms.

Government access channels feature meetings of local government bodies.

Graphical user interfaces (GUIs) use icons and symbols to issue commands to computers.

Group communication involves three or more people.

Group owners own a number of broadcast stations but do not always provide them with common programming, as a network would.

H

Hacking is the use of information technology for unlawful purposes.

Handbills are printed advertisements distributed by hand.

Hard disk drives are long-term memory devices that store data inside a computer on a rigid magnetic disk.

Hardware manufacturers make computers or other media.

HDTV (high-definition television) uses more scanning lines or more pixels to provide a clearer and more detailed television picture.

Head ends are the origination points for local cable television systems.

Hegemony is a society's underlying consensus of ideological assumptions.

Helical scanning stores video frames at a slant, like cutting up tape and stacking it slantwise.

Hidden curriculum is the notion that by learning information technologies, students adopt the dominant culture.

Hierarchy of needs is a way to categorize the "pecking order" among human needs.

High-level languages use words to further simplify programming.

Home shopping channels are cable or broadcast television channels that carry nothing but direct response advertisements.

Homogenize means to treat all audience members alike.

Horizontal integration is concentrating ownership by acquiring companies that are all in the same business, such as radio stations or local cable distribution.

Households using television (HUTs) are homes that have their TVs turned on at a given time.

I

Ideology is an uncritically held set of beliefs about fundamental values.

Incidental learning refers to the positive educational side effects of mass media consumption.

Indecency is usually defined as depiction or description of sex or excretion in the media or arts.

Independence in media usually refers to freedom from governmental control, not from owners or advertisers.

Independent filmmakers ("indies") usually produce fewer films and for much less than the majors, often a few million dollars.

Independent stations are those not affiliated with a network.

Independent telephone companies are LECs that are not part of the RBOCs.

Independent variables are the causes of any changes that occur in dependent variables.

Industrial policy is a comprehensive national plan for developing certain sectors of the economy.

Industrialization of culture is changing both high (classical) culture and folk culture into a mass culture.

Infomercials are program-length direct response commercials.

Informal education is entertaining educational programming consumed outside of a school setting.

Information is the content of communication.

Information as a commodity refers to the idea of buying and selling information rather than seeing it as a free resource.

Information campaigns use the techniques of advertising in an attempt to convince people to adopt prosocial behaviors.

Information economy has the manipulation of information, rather than manufacturing or agriculture, as its base.

Information gap hypothesis posits that the "information rich" benefit more from new information technologies than the "information poor."

Information infrastructure is the computer, telecommunications, and media network that people use to accomplish other tasks.

Information jobs include all those involved primarily in producing, processing, or distributing information.

Information service providers create or package the content for an information service.

Information services reproduce media content for multiple receivers and are produced by information service providers.

Information society refers to a society in which exchange of information is the predominant economic and social activity.

Information society as an ideology refers to using the idea as a slogan to get people to accept economic changes.

Information superhighway is a universal, high-speed network that will carry all forms of text, audio, computer data, and video.

Information technologies store, process, or transmit computer-readable information.

Information workers produce, process, or distribute information as their primary work activity.

Infrastructure refers to the services and facilities that enable people to do work or other kinds of activities.

Innovation is a new idea, technology, or way of doing things.

Integrated circuits are computer "chips" with thousands of circuit elements etched onto tiny wafers of silicon.

Integrated services digital network (ISDN) is an end-to-end digital telephone network.

Integrated systems are computer programs for public relations professionals that combine a wide range of management functions in one package.

Integration is the process of combining voice, data, and video on a single network.

Intelligent networks can sense and respond to the content of the information they carry.

Interactive cable lets cable subscribers carry on two-way interactions with programs and complete transactions from their homes.

Interactive communication uses feedback to modify a message as it is presented.

Interexchange carriers carry long-distance traffic inside the United States.

International law includes treaties between countries, multicountry agreements, and rules established by international organizations.

International record carriers (IRCs) carry international long-distance calls.

Internet is a network of computer networks used by millions for electronic mail and database access.

Interpersonal communication involves two or more people.

Intrapersonal communication is with ourselves.

Inventory is the stock of unsold advertising space that is still available.

J

Job displacement occurs when a job is eliminated by automation.

Joint operation agreements occur when competing newspapers share facilities, costs, administrative structure, and advertising, while maintaining editorial independence.

Just-in-time systems use computerized inventory management systems to reduce the inventory by coordinating deliveries from suppliers.

K

Kant's categorical imperative says we should act according to rules that we would like to see universally applied.

Key sector of economy is the main sector driving overall economic growth.

Key systems are privately owned telephone switches for small organizations.

L

Labels of record companies are particular names for a group of recordings that usually follows a consistent line of music.

Lasers produce intense beams of pure light for fiber optic systems.

Leaks refer to the release of confidential information by officials, often policy ideas or facts they do not wish to be quoted about.

Leased lines are dedicated to a particular user for a flat monthly rate.

Libel is harmful or untruthful criticism by media which damages someone.

Liberalization in telecommunications policy refers to opening up monopoly services to competition.

License is a permission to operate a service on a specific radio frequency.

License fees are annual fees or fees on the sales of radio or television receivers to pay for public broadcasting.

Licensing is an agreement granting permission to use a copyrighted or trademarked work, usually in return for an agreed-on fee.

Lifeline service subsidizes telephone service for low-income households.

Lifestyle channels are targeted to audiences with certain common interests.

Lifestyle segmentation categorizes people on the basis of their attitudes, interests, and opinions.

Light pens are used to write on specially designed computer screens.

Literacy usually refers to the number of people in a society who are able to read.

Lobbies are interest or business groups that try to influence policymaking, lawmaking, or enforcement.

Local access and transport areas (LATAs) mark the boundaries between local and long-distance calls and are smaller than area codes.

Local area networks (LANs) are high-speed computer networks that link computers within a department, a building, or a campus of buildings.

Local exchange carriers (LECs) provide local telephone service.

Local market monopolies are those with only one daily newspaper.

Local origination is cable programming created within the community by the cable operator.

Localism refers to giving broadcast stations to all possible local areas and encouraging them to serve local interests.

Long-term memory stores data and programs after a computer is turned off.

M

Machine language is the fundamental "language" used by computers to complete their calculations.

Magazine was a colonial-era term for a warehouse; print magazines were storehouses of various materials from books, pamphlets, and newspapers.

Magnetic recording stores information in magnetic fields, much like cassette tapes do.

Mainframe computers are large computers capable of high-speed processing for multiple simultaneous users.

Major film producers are the larger studios that each produce fifteen to twenty-five movies per year.

Mall intercepts are consumer interviews conducted in shopping centers.

Management information systems (MIS) departments operate and maintain companies' computer services.

Manuscript originally meant written or copied by hand.

Marketing managers are in charge of a family of products for an advertiser.

Marketing research compiles data about sales and consumer attitudes, usually for the advertiser.

Marketplace of ideas is the concept that, with free speech, the best ideas will win in competition with others.

Mass audiences are those that include a large proportion of the public.

Mass communication is one-to-many, with limited means for audience feedback.

Mass distribution uses industrial technologies like railroads to distribute media to a broader mass audience.

Mass market is a large group of consumers brought together by media, urbanization, and industrialization.

Mass production of culture uses the techniques of industry to create media products cheaply enough for most people to afford.

Mass society reflects industrial mass production in which people consume the same industrialized products and culture.

Matching is the cross-correlation of consumer databases.

MDS (multipoint distribution systems) are wireless cable systems that use high frequencies in the microwave band to transmit programs.

Media buyers negotiate on behalf of the advertiser and the agency to buy advertising space from the mass media.

Media department selects the media that will be used to carry an ad.

Media flows are sales or exchange of media products between countries or direct cross-border broadcasting to other countries.

Media representatives are intermediaries between advertising agencies and media outlets.

Media research compiles data about media consumption for the advertising industry.

Microwave is a high-capacity system that transmits information between relay towers on highly focused beams of high-frequency radio waves.

Mill's principle of utility holds that we should "seek the greatest happiness for the greatest number."

Minicomputers, or personal computers, are small computers for individual users.

Mobile communication carriers provide paging and radio telephone services.

Mode of production refers to the ways that work is done, money is made, and people are employed.

Modems convert digital data to analog tones that can be transmitted over the telephone network.

Modernity is a way of seeing the world as rational and controllable and seeing change as positive.

Monitoring is the practice of tracking employees' performance through their interactions with communications media.

Monopoly is ownership or domination of an entire industry by one firm.

Motion pictures are the technical means for taking a series of photographs at a constant speed to portray motion.

Motivational research examines the reasons that people consume the products and media they do, rather than how much they consume.

Mouse is a device used to locate objects on a computer screen and to activate program features.

MPAA (Motion Picture Association of America) is a sales and lobby organization that represents the major film studios.

MPAA ratings are a movie rating system, instituted in 1968.

MPEAA (Motion Picture Export Association of America) is a sales and lobby organization that represents film studios overseas.

Muckraking is journalism that invesigates scandal, "raking up the muck" of dirty details.

Multichannel MDS (MMDS) systems are MDS systems with more than one channel.

Multilateral trade negotiations are between a number of countries at the same time, usually within an international organization.

Multimedia systems integrate text, audio, and video and let the user select the presentation mode.

Multiple system operators (MSOs) are cable companies that operate systems in two or more communities.

Multiplexing places multiple telephone calls on a single pair of wires.

Multistep flow model assumes that media effects are indirect and are mediated by opinion leaders.

N

Narrowcasting directs media channels to specific segments of the audience.

National sovereignty is keeping domestic forces in control over the economy, politics, culture, and so on.

National spot advertising can be placed by national advertisers on local media, such as radio stations.

Natural language programs allow untrained humans to converse with computers in their own tongue.

Natural monopoly is a business or service area that inherently lends itself to domination by a single firm.

Negotiated reading occurs when the audience makes their own interpretation of media content, accepting some of the producer's ideas but not others.

Network service providers transmit information over telecommunications networks.

Networks are groups of stations that centralize the production and distribution of programming and carry most of the same programming and ads.

Neurocomputers replicate the structure of the human brain.

Nickelodeon is a phonograph or player piano operated by inserting a coin, originally a nickel.

Nonwireline carriers are cellular radio companies that provide service in competition with the local exchange (wireline) carrier.

NTSC is the U.S. television standard, developed in 1941 by the National Television Systems Committee.

O

O&O's are stations owned and operated by corporations that also own networks.

Observational learning occurs when the rewards and punishments encountered by the characters in media influence viewers's own behavior.

Office automation is the application of communications media to office tasks such as typing and filing.

Oligopoly occurs when only a few companies dominate an industry.

On-demand systems let users obtain whatever they want, when they want it.

Open contract plus commission is a business arrangement between advertiser and advertising agency that allows the agency to collect a commission on the advertising it places.

Operating systems are computer programs that provide basic computer functions.

Opinion leaders are people in our daily lives who influence our opinions on certain topics.

Oral cultures are those that communicate primarily on the basis of spoken language.

Organizational communication is within a formally structured organization.

Outsourcing is the practice of subcontracting tasks to outside firms instead of performing them "in-house."

Ownership structures are patterns of who owns media industries and how concentrated and integrated that ownership is.

P

Packet switching breaks up long streams of computer data into packets and mixes packets from multiple users in a single communication channel.

Paging services alert miniature radio receivers with specially coded messages.

Partisan refers to media with clear support for various political parties, leaders, and ideas.

Passive audiences are not selective, readily accept media messages, and are easily, almost automatically affected by them.

Patent is a written document that secures to an inventor for a number of years the exclusive right to make, use, or sell an invention.

Patent pool was several companies sharing technologies that had been awarded government protection via a formal patent.

Pay-per society is one in which people pay to use information resources that are currently available free at libraries or from other sources.

Pay-per usage is a direct charge to customers for each use of various kinds of information, entertainment, and games.

Pay-per-view cable is a subscription to a specific program with a separate fee just to receive that one show.

Pay TV is the practice of charging cable customers an additional monthly fee to receive a specific channel, usually a movie or sports channel.

Payola occurred when record companies gave gifts or even bribes to key DJs to get their records played.

PBS is the Public Broadcasting Service, which offers news and other programming to a national noncommercial radio network.

Penny arcades were commercial entertainment areas with coin-operated sound and film nickelodeons and other amusements.

Penny press were daily newspapers after 1830 that sold at low costs, were aimed at a mass audience, and depended on advertising.

People meters are electronic devices that register individual television viewing.

Peripherals are computer accessories, such as printers and modems.

Personal communication networks (PCNs) combine the low cost of cordless phones with the mobility of cellular radio.

Personal computers are computers for individual users.

Personal data assistants (PDAs) are pocket-sized computers.

Personal telephone numbers give phone subscribers a single number through which they can be reached at all times.

Persuasion is the use of convincing arguments to change people's beliefs, attitudes, or behaviors.

Picture tube fires an electron gun at dots on the inside of the TV screen, which glow with varying intensity to create an image.

Plain old telephone service (POTS) is basic local telephone service without any extra-cost options.

Playlists are the categories and titles of songs picked to fit the radio station's format and target audience.

Policy is government or public consideration of how to structure and regulate media so that they contribute to the public good.

Political action committees (PACs) are organizations that collect donations for political candidates on behalf of an organization or cause.

Political economy is the overlap or fit between economic and political power and control structures.

Political press refers to media that are clearly engaged in political comment or struggle.

Popular culture is a culture with books, songs, movies, and so on familiar to and accessible to the general public.

Positioning is the process of comparing a brand with competing products.

Post-Fordism deskills jobs to the point where workers no longer need to be paid a decent living wage.

Preferred reading is the interpretation that the producer of some media content or text intends the audience to get.

Press release is the means by which public relations professionals distribute information to the mass media.

Price averaging mixes the costs for areas expensive to serve, such as remote or rural areas, with costs for service to denser, cheaper urban areas.

Price caps index telephone rates against the cost of living and replace rate of return regulation.

Primary information sector produces, processes, and sells information goods and services as its main business.

Privacy is the right to keep certain information or activities out of the scrutiny of media, government, or private observers.

Private branch exchanges (PBXs) are privately owned telephone switches.

Private networks are privately owned telecommunications networks.

Productivity is the amount of output relative to input, often expressed in terms of the number of units produced per hour of work.

Propaganda is media content aimed at persuading people to accept an idea or ideology.

Prosocial behaviors are those that a society values and encourages, such as tolerance, sharing, and cooperation.

PTT is a national government-owned post, telephone, and telegraph monopoly, which usually runs telecommunications.

Public access is cable programming created by community residents and organizations without the involvement of the cable operator.

Public corporations in broadcasting are nonprofit companies financed by government or license fees.

Public diplomacy is using media or other channels to reach and influence public opinion in other countries.

Public interest is usually defined for broadcasting in terms of the variety or diversity of programming and the amount of news and public affairs programs carried.

Public opinion is the view held by large numbers of people on specific political issues.

Public ownership refers to ownership by nonprofit groups or by government bodies.

Public relations is any organized effort to gain favorable action.

Public relations counsel is a person or organization who advises others about public relations matters.

Public service campaigns are advertising campaigns intended to promote desirable social behavior or ideas rather than to sell specific products.

Public utilities are closely regulated government or private companies, usually monopolies, that provide public services.

Publics are the audiences for public relations.

Q

Quotas are limits on imports placed by national governments, designed to keep out foreign films and programs.

R

Radio Act of 1912 was the initial government regulation for licensing of transmitters.

Radio Act of 1927 created a Federal Radio Commission, defined the broadcast band, standardized frequency designations, and limited the number of stations operating at night, when AM signals carry farther.

Radio format is a programming approach, often linked to music genres, news, or talk, focused on a particular audience.

Radio waves are composed of electromagnetic energy and rise and fall in regular cycles.

Ragtime is an early form of jazz most frequently played on the piano.

Random access memory (RAM) is a type of short-term memory that allows rapid access to data and programs.

Rate of return regulation allows telecommunications companies to earn only a specified fixed rate of profit based on the value of their capital investments.

Ratings are the percentages of TV households watching particular programs.

Read-only memory (ROM) stores the computer's permanent instructions in solid-state memory.

Reading is the overall process by which audiences receive, interpret, and make sense of media content and events.

Record format in audio playback equipment refers to record standards.

Regional Bell Operating Companies (RBOCs) are the local telephone operating companies that were divested by AT&T in 1984.

Regional TV markets are based on language, culture, religious values, and geography.

Regulated monopoly is a company without competitors regulated by government to prevent abuse of its position.

Reinvention is the process in which users of a technology or idea create new ways to use it beyond those initially anticipated.

Relational databases are computer programs in which data may be cross-referenced by key words and categories.

Remote sensing usually refers to satellite observation using photography, infrared photography, and radar to "see" objects, vegetation, weather patterns, and so on.

Repeater amplifiers strengthen faint electrical signals so long-distance calls can be made.

Repetitive stress injury is a debilitating pain caused by excessive use of computer keyboards.

Research organizations compile statistics about consumers and their media habits and evaluate advertising presentations.

Resellers are long-distance companies that lease their networks from other carriers and then resell telephone service to their customers.

Reskilling is redesigning jobs so that they entail a wide range of skills.

Restraint of trade refers to practices by a company that limit other companies' ability to enter or compete in trade.

Right of reply gives opportunities for the expression of opposing views on broadcast stations when only one side had been aired.

Royalty is a fee required to use another person's intellectual property.

S

Sales refers to media products themselves being sold as goods.

Satellite carriers transmit telephone calls via satellite.

Satellite footprint is the surface area covered by the satellite's signal.

Satellite media tour is held when a public relations spokesperson is interviewed by media outlets via satellite.

Satellites are microwave systems in which the relays are in earth orbit instead of on towers.

Scanning samples a certain number of lines per frame by the electron beam.

Scarcity argument is that careful government regulation was required to allocate and oversee use of a limited number of frequencies.

Scrambling disrupts cable channels electronically so only authorized customers with descramblers can receive them.

Second-generation computers used transistors for processing data.

Secondary information sector produces, processes, and distributes information for internal use in noninformation companies, such as automobile manufacturers.

Segmentation occurs when media focus on more specific, smaller audiences with more specialized programs and formats.

Selective binding allows publishers to create multiple versions of the same publication.

Selective exposure is the tendency to avoid media content inconsistent with one's preexisting beliefs.

Selective perception is the tendency to misinterpret media inconsistent with one's own views.

Selective retention is a process by which people forget media that diverge from their previously held positions.

Self-regulation refers to industry codes and practices of monitoring the industry's own performance.

Semiotics is the science of signs, of how meaning is generated in media "texts."

Shares are the percentages of households using TV watching particular programs.

Sheet music is print reproduction of song lyrics and musical notation for people to perform.

Sherman Antitrust Act of 1890 is the main U.S. law against monopolies or agreements to restrain or limit trade.

Short-term memory stores data and programs for immediate use in the computer.

Signage refers to signs and billboards used for advertising purposes.

Signs are the carriers of meaning in media "texts."

Simulcasts refer to broadcasting the same signal on several stations, such as networks, or on both AM and FM stations.

Site licenses are group discounts on computer software.

Situation comedies feature a group of characters in a comic situation dealing with new tensions or issues each episode.

Situation ethics holds that moral ideas and judgments must be made relative to the situation at hand.

SMATV (satellite master antenna television) is a TVRO system serving an entire apartment building or housing complex from a central satellite antenna.

Social class refers to social groups divided by occupation, economic status, education, and family status.

Social influence model recognizes that social dynamics within an organization are involved in the decision to adopt communications media.

Social learning theory describes how viewers of mass media imitate the media through a process of observational learning.

Social presence is the degree to which sensory cues are present that convey hidden meanings.

Social stratification is the division of society into unequal groups or classes of people by wealth, education, and occupation.

Software consists of the programs and codes that instruct computers what to do.

Software publishers make the standard programs that run computers.

Source attribution refers to methods used to cite sources without revealing their identity.

Spiral of silence describes how unpopular beliefs are extinguished through the joint action of the media and interpersonal influence.

Stages of development reflect changes in society that link technology, economics, politics, culture, and media together.

Standards rules, developed in 1952 by the FCC, created new UHF channels and clarified channel separation to avoid interference for the VHF channels.

Star system was the film studios' use of stars' popularity to promote their movies.

Stereotyping is the formulation of generalizations about groups of people based on limited information.

Storage devices include hard and floppy disk drives.

Story films or "movies" introduced the idea of telling a story, usually fictional, with a plot and characters.

STV (subscription television) is a wireless cable system that uses conventional television channels.

Subscription libraries lent books to the public for a fee or a regular subscription.

Subscriptions permit media to be sold on a regular basis over time for a standard fee.

Subsidization implies transfer of funds from one source to support another activity.

Supercomputers are advanced high-speed mainframe computers.

Superstation is a distant signal that is distributed widely via satellite.

Survey studies make generalizations about a population of people by addressing questions to a random sample of that population.

Syndication is rental or licensing of media products by their producers to other media companies for broadcast, distribution, or exhibition.

T

T1 carriers transmit telephone calls and text in digital form at the rate of 1.5 million bits per second.

Talent in media refers to the newspeople, actors, and singers in front of the microphones and cameras.

Talkies were films with synchronized soundtracks, which emphasized dialogue, singing, and music.

Target audience is a narrow, specifically defined audience that an advertiser or communications medium wants to reach.

Tariffs are taxes imposed by governments on goods imported from other countries; also the published rates that common carriers charge for their services.

Taylorism refers to the process of scientific management, which seeks to improve the efficiency of work by routinizing it.

Technocracy is application of the scientific method to all aspects of life.

Technological determinism is the idea that technological change tends to determine all other economic and social changes.

Technopoly is a culture in which technology controls all aspects of life.

Telecommuting occurs when work is performed in the home and workers are linked together by telecommunications networks.

Teleconferencing is an electronic meeting involving three or more people.

Telemarketing is using the telephone in direct marketing to solicit or receive sales responses.

Telematics describes the combination of telecommunications and computers.

Teletext is an information service that is broadcast as part of a television signal.

Television households are homes with working TV sets.

Texts are media contents and events, such as films, television programs, magazine articles, or performances.

Theater chains are movie houses owned and operated by a single company to coordinate and control movie distribution.

Theatrical films are those released for distribution in movie theaters.

Third-generation computers used integrated circuits.

Third World or developing countries include those in Africa, Latin America, and Asia that are less developed economically.

Time-sharing systems share computers between multiple simultaneous users.

Toll broadcasting was charging someone to carry a radio program or advertisement, parallel to long-distance or "toll" telephone calls.

Top 40 is a radio format that plays only top single records, the top 40 on record sales charts.

Touch-tone phones have push buttons and dial with musical tones.

Town criers announced the news of the day before the advent of the newspaper.

Traditions in music are genres passed along from one generation to another.

Traffic department is the part of an advertising agency that coordinates the delivery of the finished advertising message to the media.

Transborder data flow is the communication of computer data across borders.

Transistors are semiconductor devices that act like tiny electronic switches.

TVRO (television receive only) is a backyard satellite receiver that lets individual homes receive the same channels that are intended for cable systems.

U

UHF stands for ultra high frequency, most widely known for use with television in channels 14 to 69.

Unbalanced flow refers to an unequal flow of media or news between countries.

Unintended effects are effects counter to those that the designers of a prosocial program hope for.

Unique selling proposition is a unique attribute that a product has that its competitors do not.

Universal service is the provision of telephony or other services to all or almost all households.

Unlisted numbers are not published and also may not be given out by directory assistance operators.

Unpublished numbers do not appear in the phone book but may be given out by directory assistance.

Upskilling means raising the educational requirements of a job through the application of automation.

Usage-based segmentation divides consumers according to their amount of consumption.

Usage charges are direct charges to customers for the amount of media time, access, or content used.

V

Vacuum tubes can amplify and precisely modulate a weak signal by controlling the flow of electrical charges inside the tube.

Value added networks (VANs) provide enhanced services on data networks, such as videotex and transactional services.

Variable resistance transmitters create an electrical current that varies in response to the human voice.

Vaudeville was a stage show of mixed specialty acts, such as songs, dances, skits, comedy, and acrobatics.

VCRs (videocassette recorders) are home videotape machines.

Vehicles are the specific media programs or publications in which advertisements are carried.

Vertical integration is concentrating ownership by acquiring companies that are in related businesses.

Very large scale integration (VLSI) squeezes entire computers onto a single silicon chip.

Very small aperture terminals (VSATs) are small satellite antennas that connect organizations to private satellite networks.

VHF stands for very high frequency, most widely known for use with television in channels 2 to 13.

Victrola was an early phonograph and also a specific trademark.

Video dial tone means providing the basic ability to receive and originate video calls on a telephone network.

Video news releases are press releases distributed in video form.

Videoconferencing is a teleconference with moving images.

Videotex services deliver text and graphics through computer networks.

Virtual private networks are private networks defined by software in the intelligent network instead of by full-time physical connections.

Virtual reality gives users the sense that they are "inside" a computer-generated reality.

Voice mail is a service in which the phone company performs the function of an answering machine.

Voice recognition refers to the ability of computers to understand verbal commands.

W

WANs are wide area computer networks that are national or international in scope.

Wide area networks extend data communications beyond individual buildings or campuses.

Wide area telecommunications service (WATS) lines, also known as 800 numbers, bill the cost of a long-distance call to the party called instead of the caller.

Windows are times in the film release sequence for showing films in theaters, on pay per view, and so on.

Wire services were news services that supplied a variety of newspapers, named for their use of the telegraph and its wires.

Wireless communication takes place through radio or light beams.

Wireless cable delivers cable channels to homes via earth-based broadcasting systems.

Wireless LANs are local area networks that send computer data via radio waves or infrared radiation instead of over wires.

Workstations place the power of a mainframe at the disposal of an individual user.

Z

Zapping or **channel surfing** uses remote controls to browse briefly through a number of channels, viewing short bits of each.

Index

Photo Credits

Chapter 1

10: (top left) © Jeff Greenberg/The Picture Cube, (top right) © Michael Newman/Photo Edit, (bottom) © Grafton Smith/Gamma Liaison Network; 13: Official White House Photo; 21: © Eric Neurath/Stock•Boston, (inset) Courtesy of Greystone Technology, Inc., San Diego.

Chapter 2

26: © Mireille Vautier/Woodfin Camp & Associates; 28: © Jim Anderson/Woodfin Camp & Associates; 30: © Lee Corkran/Sygma; 31: © Forrest McMullin/Black Star.

Chapter 3

48: Edward Hicks, *Residence of David Twining, 1787*. Courtesy of Abbey Aldrich Rockefeller Folk Art Center, Williamsburg, VA; 49, 52: The Granger Collection; 54: The Bettmann Archive; 57: The Granger Collection; 59: © Joe Sohm/Stock•Boston; 64: © Mike Yamashita/Woodfin Camp & Associates.

Chapter 4

72: Craig McClain; 76: Photo of Reuters, Courtesy of Prodigy Services Company; 79: Craig McClain; 80: Courtesy of General Motors; 82: © Dale C. Spartas/Gamma-Liaison Network; 85: Courtesy of General Motors; 86: © Dale C. Spartas/Gamma-Liaison Network.

Chapter 5

92: © George Hunter/Tony Stone Images; 94: Photo by Ankers Photographers, Inc., Washington, DC; 101: The Granger Collection; 104: Used with permission and courtesy of University of California, Irvine, Bookstore; 106: © Robert Wallis/Sipa Press; 108: PhotoDisc.

Chapter 6

118: (top) © Eastcott Momatiuk/Woodfin Camp & Associates, (bottom): Reuters-Bettmann; 121: Robert Harbison/Christian Science Monitor; 125: © 1994 CNN. All rights reserved; 130: © Peter Magubane/Liaison Network; 136: © Chuck O'Rear/Woodfin Camp & Associates; 142: (top) © Peter Magubane/Liaison Network.

Chapter 7

144: The Granger Collection; 146: Archivio de Stato Siena, Italy, Scala/Art Resource, NY; 147, 148: The Granger Collection; 149: Collection of the New York Historical Society; 150–152: The Granger Collection; 153: Courtesy of the Reader's Digest Association, Inc., 1994; 156: Courtesy of MediaFAX; 161: Craig McClain; 164: © Charles Gupton/Stock•Boston; 167: The Granger Collection.

Chapter 8

174: The Granger Collection; 175: The Bettmann Archive; 176: David Sarnoff Library; 177: The Bettmann Archive; 179, 189: UPI/Bettmann.

Chapter 9

205: The Bettmann Archive; 206: Springer/Bettmann Film Archive; 207: Courtesy of Broadcast Pioneer's Library at University of Maryland, College Park; 208: By permission of Hallmark Hall of Fame, photo courtesy of the University of Maryland, College Park; 209: The Bettmann Archive; 210: UPI/Bettmann; 216: (top left) AP/Wide World Photos, (top right) The Bettmann Archive, (bottom left) UPI/Bettmann, (bottom right) John Springer Collection/Bettmann Archive; 229: Broadcast Pioneers Library at University of Maryland, College Park.

Chapter 10

237: © Bohdan Hrynewych/Stock•Boston; 238: Courtesy of Black Entertainment Television; 248: Courtesy of CNBC/Cable Station.

Chapter 11

261, 266: Permission of AT&T Archives; 273: © Mike Yamashita/Woodfin Camp & Associates; 276: Permission of AT&T Archives.

Chapter 12

288, 290, 291: Courtesy of IBM Corporation; 293: Courtesy of Apple Computer; 296: (top) AP/Wide World Photos, (bottom) Courtesy of IBM Corporation; 300, 305: Courtesy of IBM Corporation; 309, 314: © Laima Druskis/Stock•Boston.

Chapter 13

321: Courtesy of America Online; 325: Multiple displays from *QuickClips,* © Apple Computer, Inc., 1992, dog from Digital Stock; 329: Digital Stock; 331: Courtesy of IBM Corporation; 332: Courtesy of Mead Data Central; 335: Courtesy of The WELL; 340: Multiple displays from *QuickClips,* © Apple Computer, Inc., 1992.

Chapter 14

344: Library of Congress; 349: AT&T Archives; 351: Courtesy of Apple Computer; 355: © Mike Yamashita/Woodfin Camp & Associates; 356: Courtesy of IBM Corporation; 361: AT&T Archives.

Chapter 15

366, 368: The Granger Collection; 370, 376: Copyright © 1994 Mazda Motor of America, Inc. Used by permission; 379: Craig McClain; 382: Courtesy of Pepsi Cola Company; 385: Copyright © 1994 Mazda Motor of America, Inc. Used by permission; 386: Courtesy of Pepsi Cola Company.

Chapter 16

388, 391, 393: The Granger Collection; 400: Craig McClain.

Chapter 17

414: Courtesy of Albert Bandura; 421: Craig McClain; 423: © Jacques Chenet/Woodfin Camp & Associates; 424: Courtesy of the Advertising Council of America; 428: © Erich Hartmann/Magnum Photos; 432: Craig McClain.

Chapter 18

441: © David Young-Wolff/Photo Edit; 444: © Seth Resnick/Stock•Boston; 451: Courtesy of IBM Corporation; 453: © Seth Resnick/Stock•Boston.